PATIENT POWER

Solving
America's
Health
Care
Crisis

PATIENT POWER

Solving
America's
Health
Care
Crisis

**John C. Goodman and
Gerald L. Musgrave**

CATO
INSTITUTE
Washington, D.C.

To Jan and Jeanette

Library of Congress Cataloging-in-Publication Data

Goodman, John C.
  Patient power : solving America's health care crisis / John C. Goodman
  and Gerald L. Musgrave.
      p.   cm.
  ISBN 0-932790-92-5 : $29.95.—ISBN 0-932790-91-7 (pbk.) : $16.95
  1. Medical policy—United States.
  2. Insurance, Health—Government policy—United States.
  3. Medical care—United States—Cost control.
  4. Medical care, Cost of—United States.
  I. Musgrave, Gerald L.   II. Title.
  RA395.A3G655   1992
  362.1'0973—dc20   92-32984
                                                                          CIP

Cover Design by Colin Moore.

Printed in the United States of America.

CATO INSTITUTE
1000 Massachusetts Ave., N.W.
Washington, D.C. 20001

Contents

Preface

The thesis of this book is simple: If we want to solve the nation's health care crisis, we must apply the same common-sense principles to medical care that we apply to other goods and services.

In a 1991 *New York Times*/CBS News poll, almost 80 percent of the respondents agreed that the American "health care system is headed toward a crisis because of rising costs."[1] The irony is that health care costs are rising because, for individual patients, medical care is cheap, not expensive.

On the average, patients pay only 5 cents out-of-pocket for every dollar they spend in hospitals. The remainder is paid by private and public health insurance. Patients pay less than 19 cents out-of-pocket for every dollar they spend on physicians' services, and they pay less than 24 cents out of every dollar they spend on health care of all types. Patients therefore have an incentive to purchase hospital services until, at the margin, they're worth only 5 cents on the dollar and to purchase physicians' services until they are worth only 19 cents on the dollar. The wonder is that we don't spend even more than we do.

Health care is often said to be a necessity. However, there are other necessities such as food, clothing, housing, and transportation. If we paid for any of these items the way we pay for health care, we would face a similar crisis. If we paid only 5 cents on the dollar for food, clothing, or housing, for example, costs would explode in each of those markets.

If we are to control health care costs, we must be prepared to make tough decisions about how much to spend on medical care versus other goods and services. So far, we have avoided such choices, confident that health care spending can be determined by "needs," rather than by choices among competing alternatives. In this respect, the U.S. health care system is unique. The United

---

[1]Erick Eckholm, "Health Benefits Found to Deter Job Switching," *New York Times*, September 26, 1991.

States is the only country in the world where people can consume medical care almost without limit, unconstrained by market prices or by government rationing.

Consider the case of an 80-year-old man who suffered from the condition of "slowing down." Despite the physician's counsel that the condition was perfectly normal at age 80, the patient and his wife went on a literal shopping spree in the medical marketplace. As the physician explained to the *New York Times:*

> A few days ago the couple came in for a follow-up visit. They were upset. At their daughter's insistence they had gone to an out-of-town neurologist. She had wanted the "best" for her father and would spare no (Medicare) expense to get it. The patient had undergone a CAT scan, a magnetic resonance imaging, a spinal tap, a brain-stem evoke potential and a carotid duplex ultrasound.
>
> No remediable problems were discovered. The Medicare billing was more than $4,000 so far . . . but they were emotionally exhausted by the experience and anxious over what portion of the expenses might not be covered by insurance.
>
> I have seen this Medicare madness happen too often. It is caused by many factors, but contrary to public opinion, physician greed is not high on the list. I tried to stop the crime, but found I was just a pawn in a ruthless game, whose rules are excess and waste. Who will stop the madness?[2]

The potential demand for health care is virtually unlimited. Even if there were a limit to what medical science can do (which, over time, there isn't), there is an almost endless list of ailments that can motivate our desire to spend. About 83 million people suffer from insomnia, 70 million have severe headaches, 32 million have arthritis, 23 million have allergies, and 16 million have bad backs. Even when the illnesses are not real, our minds have incredible power to convince us that they are.

If the only way to control health care costs is to have someone choose between health care and money (that is, other goods and services), who should that someone be? There are only two fundamental alternatives: The choices must be made either by the patients themselves or by a health care bureaucracy that is ultimately

---

[2]Elliot Rosenberg, letter to the editor, *New York Times,* September 18, 1991.

answerable to government. This book makes the case for the patients.

Almost all arguments against empowering patients are variations on the notion that individuals are not smart enough or knowledge- able enough to make wise decisions. But if that argument is persua- sive in health care, why isn't it equally persuasive in every other walk of life? With respect to almost any decision we make, someone else is always smarter or more knowledgeable than we are. If the case for freedom rested on the assumption that free individuals always make the best decisions, we would have discarded liberty and democracy long ago.

The case for empowering patients rests on a different assump- tion. No one cares more about us than we do. Thus, while prudent people seek and get advice from specialists before making many decisions, it does not follow that we should turn over control of our lives to the experts. In the long run, more good than bad decisions are made when self-interested individuals are free to accept or reject advice from many quarters.

A corollary to the goal of empowering patients is the goal of creating competitive markets in the health care sector, for physi- cians' services, hospital services, health insurance, and other ser- vices. Individuals pursuing their own interests in a market are best served by suppliers who compete vigorously to meet consumer needs with high-quality services produced at the lowest possible cost.

This book represents a radical departure from what is considered normal and acceptable in the field of health policy. Whereas the vast majority of health policy commentators take a bureaucratic approach to health care, our approach is individualistic, focusing on the decisions that individuals make and the incentives they face when they make them. Whereas the vast majority of health policy proposals call for more regulation and more government spending, we find that government is the problem, not the solution—that solving America's health care crisis requires undoing the harmful distortions introduced into the system by government and that only a market-based system will work.

The dominant view of health policy is regularly reported in the national news media and parroted by syndicated columnists, edito- rial writers, and politicians. What is needed in health care, they tell us, is not competition, but monopoly. Instead of empowering individuals, they assert, we should empower the bureaucracy. Rather than look to the private sector for solutions, we should look to government. When speaking to the general public, the socialism-works-in-health-care crowd points to national health insurance in other countries, arguing that the quality is high, the cost is low, and the vast majority of people like it. Behind closed doors, though, they tell politicians that other countries control health care costs by refusing to spend money and by forcing doctors to ration health care.

It is no surprise that most people who live under national health insurance like it. For minor aches and pains, they have no difficulty seeing general practitioners and they perceive such services to be "free." But that's not a useful test of a health care system. In any given year, only about 4 percent of the population require access to the remarkable advances made possible by modern medical science. The better test is: When people need such services, can they get them? And if they do get them, how long do they have to wait? It is in answering these questions that we uncover the worst tragedies of socialized medicine.

Two recent news items underscore the potential horror of combining medicine and politics. One story comes from South Africa, the other from newly liberated Romania.

When South African anti-apartheid activist Stephen Biko was imprisoned in 1977, he died after sustaining multiple head injuries. The physician who examined and failed to hospitalize Biko was subsequently disciplined for "disgraceful" conduct. Much later, in explaining his actions, the physician wrote:

> In reflection on the cause of this failure, I came to realize that, over the period of the 30 years I had been employed by the state as a district surgeon, I had gradually lost the fearless independence that is required of a medical practitioner when the interests of his patient are threatened. I had become too closely identified with the interest of the organs of the state.[3]

Medicine controlled by the state ultimately serves only the state.

[3]Reprinted in Benjamin Tucker, "An Apology on Biko," *New York Times*, October 24, 1991.

After Romania's communist regime fell in 1989, Americans saw photographs of Romanian hospitals. On the one hand, a modern hospital with the latest technology and luxury conveniences was reserved for Communist party officials and key bureaucrats. On the other hand, hospitals for ordinary people were operated out of World War II army barracks. Bureaucratic medicine ultimately serves only the bureaucrats.

Most people in the health policy community recoiled in horror at these two revelations. Yet they failed to grasp the underlying lesson. The difference between the Romanian health care system and the systems of most other countries is one of degree, not of kind. The difference between Stephen Biko's treatment and that of victims of government-sanctioned health care rationing in other countries is also one of degree, not of kind. These tragedies represent the ultimate, logical consequences of a goal that is almost universally accepted by health policy analysts: the complete elimination of markets, prices, competition, and choice from the health care sector.

The medical marketplace today is far from normal. In a normal market, producers search for ways to satisfy consumer needs for a price consumers are willing to pay. Demand is a given. The problem for producers is to reduce the costs of meeting that demand. In health care, the opposite is true. All too often, consumer preferences are regarded as irrelevant. Producers decide what their costs are going to be and then wrestle with getting consumers to pay those costs—through out-of-pocket payments, through employers and insurance companies, or through the government.

In a normal market, increases in sales are universally regarded as good. The more consumers buy, the more their needs are being met. If domestic automobile sales increased each year as a percent of our gross national product, most people would cheer. In health care the opposite is true. The annual increase in health care services is viewed not as a benefit, but as a burden.

In the topsy-turvy world of health care, what would normally be viewed as "good" is considered "bad," and vice versa. Thus, in order to truly understand the medical marketplace, we have to discover all of the ways in which normal market forces have been undermined.

In this book we use the term "cost-plus finance" to describe the predominant way in which we are paying for medical services. Our goals are (1) to describe the cost-plus system of health care finance—how it works, how it evolved, and how we are living with it today; (2) to show how the cost-plus system is creating America's current health policy crisis; and (3) to show how we can move from cost-plus to a system that will solve the majority of America's health policy problems.

In Part I, we describe how recent changes in our health care system threaten the quality of care patients receive and why this is a natural and inevitable consequence of the way we pay for medical care. We show that most of the major problems in health care are the consequence of unwise government policies, and how those problems could be solved by adopting better policies. These policy changes, however, require a clear vision and a commitment to replacing cost-plus medicine with a competitive medical market-place in which patients, rather than bureaucracies, are given the freedom to make all of the important decisions.

In Part II, we consider how the cost-plus system evolved, with special attention to the enabling role of public policy. We examine its operation prior to the 1980s and the changes that are undermining it today.

In Part III, we examine the role of government policies in the 1980s—the cost containment stage of cost-plus medicine—with special attention to the role of special interests that have shaped and molded cost-control strategies. Part III also examines how millions of Americans have been closed out of the health insurance market, and examines some misguided proposals for addressing those problems through even more regulation.

Part IV examines the one sector of the medical marketplace that is completely dominated by government: health care for the elderly, a sector with almost unlimited potential for future spending.

In Part V, we examine how other countries have responded to the crisis of cost-plus medicine through rationing and the political allocation of health care resources. Special attention is given to what those systems mean for patients and what Americans could expect if this country adopted a system of national health insurance. Even though the cost-plus system is quasi-governmental, we argue that the effects of explicit government allocation of health care resources are much more harmful to patients and much more wasteful. We also discuss why many of the political pressures that guide decision-making in other countries are already apparent in Medicare and other government health care programs.

In Part VI, we conclude by summarizing the international trend away from socialism in health care and by proposing some innovative solutions to the special needs of underserved groups in our society.

In writing this book, we have benefited from the insights of a very small group of health policy researchers—scholars who have courageously resisted the collectivist assault on our health care system. We extend special thanks to Jesse Hixson (American Medical Association Center for Health Policy Research) for helping us to develop the concept of the Medical Savings Account; to Peter Ferrara (Cato Institute) and Richard Rahn (Novecon Corporation) for helping us to develop the concept of the Medical IRA; to Aldona and Gary Robbins (Fiscal Associates, Inc.) for their analysis of Senator Kennedy's proposal to mandate employer-provided health insurance and of the cost to private industry of national health insurance; to Dale A. Rublee and his associates (American Medical Association Center for Health Policy Research) for their analysis of foreign health care systems; to Patricia Danzon (Wharton School of Business, University of Pennsylvania) for her analysis of administrative costs; and to William J. Dennis, Jr. (The NFIB Foundation) for his analysis of the health care plan proposed by the Democrats in the U.S. Senate.

We also have benefited from the advice and information we received from J. Patrick Rooney, John Whelan, Therese Rooney, and others at Golden Rule Insurance Co., one of the few health insurance companies that have consistently advocated private-enterprise solutions to the nation's health care problems. Golden Rule is a welcome maverick in an industry that seems all too ready to cooperate with government in managing a national health insurance system.

In formulating private-sector solutions to our nation's health care problems, we received valuable input from an informal health care task force.[4] In addition to the health policy analysts listed above, we

[4]The informal task force ultimately led to a formal publication which was not necessarily endorsed by all of the individuals listed here. Task Force Report, *An Agenda for Solving America's Health Care Crisis*, NCPA Policy Report no. 151 (Dallas: National Center for Policy Analysis, May 1990). Institutional affiliations were current as of the time of the task force.

PREFACE

would like to thank Lee Benham (Center for the Study of American Business), Cotton M. Lindsay (Clemson University), William H. Mellor III (Pacific Research Institute), Tom Miller (Competitive Enterprise Institute), John Andrews (Independence Institute), Charles D. Baker (Pioneer Institute), Sam Brunelli (American Legislative Exchange Council), John Carlson (Washington Institute for Policy Studies), James W. Carr (American Studies Institute, Harding University), A. Lawrence Chickering (Institute for Contemporary Studies), Robert Cooke (Institute for Business Ethics), John W. Cooper (James Madison Institute for Public Policy Studies), Lloyd C. Daugherty (South Foundation), Porter Davis (Southwest Policy Institute), Richard Sweetser (Yankee Institute for Public Policy Studies), David J. Theroux (Independent Institute), Thomas Gale Moore (Hoover Institution, Stanford University), Robert M. Sade (Medical University of South Carolina), Norman Ture (Institute for Research on the Economics of Taxation), Michael Walker (Fraser Institute), Carolyn Weaver (American Enterprise Institute), Harold Eberle (South Carolina Policy Council), Don Eberly (Commonwealth Foundation for Public Policy Alternatives), Mark J. Greenfield (Heartland Institute, Wisconsin), Jacques Krasny (Bogart, Delafield, Ferrier), Andre V. Murchison (New England Center for Political Studies and Research, Inc.), Lawrence W. Reed (Mackinac Center), Simon Rottenberg (University of Massachusetts at Amherst), Michael Sanera (Barry Goldwater Institute for Public Policy Research), Richard Sherlock (Institute of Political Economy), Fritz S. Steiger (Texas Public Policy Foundation), Michael Warder (Rockford Institute), Bob Williams (Evergreen Freedom Foundation), Walter Williams (George Mason University), Ronald Utt (U.S. Chamber of Commerce), and Robert Moffit (Heritage Foundation).

Several physicians gave generously of their time to provide information, ideas, and encouragement, including Barry D. Brookes, W. Daniel Jordan, Frank A. Rogers, Francis A. Davis, Jerald R. Schenken, John Magrann, Steven F. Reeder, Allan N. Shulkin, Robert M. Sade, Jane Orient, and Robert J. Cihak.

Several in the pharmaceutical industry provided us with data and advice. Among them were Mitchell E. Daniels and Douglas L. Cocks (Eli Lilly and Company); Robert A. Wilson, Paul R. Meyer, and Fred W. Telling (Pfizer Inc); and Peter E. Carlin (Ciba-Geigy Corporation).

The production of this manuscript would not have been possible without invaluable support from members of our staffs who provided research, typing, and editing assistance. Present and former members of the staff of the National Center for Policy Analysis who helped in the preparation of this book include Dorman Cordell, David Williams, Phyllis Guest, Clair Schniederjan, Rena Brand, Staci Yaeger, Sonja Nelson, Robert Porter, Merrill Matthews, Jr., and Sanyal Sabyasachi. Among present and former members of the staff of Economics America who helped in the preparation of the book, we would like to thank Jan Musgrave, Samie Rehman, Robert Juneja, Tracey Kennedy, and Penelope Naas.

At the University of Michigan, we thank Jack Tobias in the School of Public Health for his masterful assistance in locating library reference material, and Professor Jan Kmenta for helpful and expert advice on econometric matters. Over several years we benefited from discussions with Rita Ricardo-Campbell (Hoover Institution), Paul J. Feldstein (University of California, Irvine), and Thomas R. Saving (Texas A&M) concerning some of the issues discussed in this book.

We would like to thank current and former members of the staff of the Cato Institute for reading the manuscript and making valuable suggestions, and for their time and patience in working with us on this project. Among these are Edward Crane, David Boaz, William Niskanen, Sheldon Richman, and Peter Ferrara.

We also wish to thank Dr. Phil L. Gausewitz of Pathology Medical Laboratories in San Diego, whose enthusiasm, careful reading, suggestions, and support helped to make this book possible.

Although we acknowledge help from many quarters, we alone take responsibility for the final manuscript.

A final note to the reader: Some of the material presented in this book is discussed in more than one chapter. Our goal was to make each chapter reasonably self-contained, so that readers interested in some particular aspect of health policy could read our chapter on it without the necessity of reading all of the other chapters. This added convenience for some readers creates a small, but necessary, burden for others due to a certain amount of repetitiveness. Readers will also find in chapters 3 and 4 a summary of all of the major policy recommendations made in this book and an explanation of how those policy changes would solve our most pressing problems.

PART I

INTRODUCTION

1. America's Health Care Crisis

America's health care system is in crisis. That's the conclusion of virtually every commentator on American medicine, regardless of political persuasion. Ask any doctor, any patient, any business executive or politician. Indeed, virtually everyone who has even remote contact with health care agrees that the system is in serious need of reform.

The crisis is not new. It has been emerging for at least two decades. Over that period, an almost unlimited number of recommendations for reform have been made. Yet we are no closer to solving the crisis today than we were 20 years ago.

One reason there is no consensus on the solution is that there is no agreement on the problem. What each of us believes the nature of the crisis to be depends on where we stand in relation to the health care system.

Why We Can't Agree on the Nature of the Crisis

For employers and many public officials, the crisis is one of costs. America, they remind us, is spending more than $800 billion a year on health care—about $3,200 per year for every man, woman, and child. Health care spending is approaching 13 percent of our gross national product, more than in any other country in the world.

Yet for every cry of alarm over rising health care spending, there are at least two or three cries over our failure to spend more. Some 34 million Americans, we are told, lack health insurance. The policies of many who do have health insurance exclude mental health care or treatment for alcohol and drug abuse. Then there is a seemingly endless list of unmet health care needs: prenatal care for the young, nursing home care for the old, organ transplants, and underfunded medical research. The most popular measures before Congress and the state legislatures are proposals not to lower health care spending but to extend health insurance to more people and more services.

3

The conflict of perspectives does not end there. For example, to most doctors the main problem is bureaucratic interference from government, insurers, employers, and even hospital administrators—interference that raises costs and sometimes lowers the quality of patient care. But to almost all third-party (insurance) payers and many hospital administrators, the problem is that doctors have too much freedom—especially to increase prices. Almost every patient who sees a hospital bill believes the hospital overcharges. Almost all employers and insurance companies share that view. But almost all hospital administrators believe their hospitals are undercompensated and worry about what services they will cut if they do not somehow increase revenues. Many physicians have a similar view. Before examining this list of conflicting perspectives, it is worthwhile to consider how they develop.

A Trip through the Health Care System with the Adams Family

The people in the following vignettes are fictitious. The kinds of events described are real, however, and occur all too frequently.

Jeff Adams (Patient)

Jeff Adams was furious. He had been out of the hospital for more than a month, but "$3,296.24" was indelibly stamped in his mind. That was the bill for minor surgery and a few days' stay in a hospital run by his own brother! He tried to see the other side of things. That was what his wife, June, kept telling him to do. Sure, hospital costs were up—hospitals could do a lot more things these days. And his share of the bill was less than $800. Blue Cross would pay the rest, or at least that was what he initially thought. Still, it was the principle of the thing.

He had gone to see his brother about the bill. "Bob," he had said, "there's got to be some mistake here. Fifteen dollars for one Tylenol tablet? You've got to be kidding. Had I known that, I would have gotten out of my sickbed, walked across the street, and bought my own Tylenol." It was Bob's attitude that bothered him more than anything else. Bob wouldn't even back down on the price of the hospital admission kit, which had contained personal items such as a toothbrush, comb, and small razor. "Twenty-five dollars for a little kit, just like the ones airlines give you for free on international flights? C'mon, Bob, that's ridiculous," he had said.

4

"Maybe it would have ended there, with me blowing off some steam," Jeff thought. "But hell, I'm a businessman. I see these damn insurance premiums going up year after year, and no wonder—$15 for a Tylenol tablet?" That's why he'd gone to Blue Cross. He'd felt a little guilty, pointing a big insurance company toward his brother. Still, Blue Cross was paying 80 percent of the bill. And somebody has to do something about these health care costs, don't they?

Things hadn't worked out in quite the way he'd expected. Oh, they had been pleasant enough at Blue Cross. The woman had listened carefully. She'd promised to look into the matter. But somehow Jeff had known at the time that nothing was going to change.

He'd almost gotten over the whole thing. Until last night when June had invited Bob over for dinner. It was supposed to be the time for reconciliation. "And I certainly tried to be nice," Jeff thought. The trouble had started when Bob made that comment about the hospital's charges.

"Look at it this way, Jeff," Bob had said. "You paid less than $800 for three days in the hospital. That's about what you'd pay to stay in a nice hotel without any medical care at all. That's cheap."

"Sure, that made me angry," Jeff thought. "But I controlled it. Without even raising my voice, I patiently explained to Bob how health insurance premiums work. June was probably right. I probably was patronizing. Maybe that's why Bob got personal."

"Jeff, you and I both know that you took advantage of your health insurance, just like everybody else does," Bob had said. "Your doctor told you that the surgery could be done as an outpatient. But you both agreed you'd check into the hospital and rest for a couple of days because your health insurance would pick up most of the tab. You and June thought that was a great idea."

That had made him even angrier, Jeff remembered. But he'd controlled himself. In fact, he'd controlled his emotions all evening—until Bob brought up that stuff about Blue Cross.

Bob Adams (Jeff's Brother, Hospital Administrator)

Bob Adams was feeling unsettled. He never should have told Jeff about the deal with Blue Cross. He'd known it was a mistake the minute he'd said it. "Jeff," he'd said, "we have a special deal with Blue Cross. They paid a flat rate of $640 for each day you were in the hospital. They couldn't care less what was on your hospital bill." That was when Jeff hit the roof.

"No question. That was a mistake. But the biggest mistake is what the hospital's computers keep putting on patients' statements," Bob thought. Jeff's hospital statement stretched halfway across Bob's office. Jeff could probably read only four words on the whole thing—"Tylenol tablet" and "admission kit." But Jeff had found them. That's the way Jeff was.

What had they said at the hospital convention last year? "Take the line items that patients can recognize and can buy on their own. Next to those items put 'no charge' and make up the difference by raising some other price that they don't understand. Make the patients think they're getting a good deal. That way, they're happy. You're happy. Everybody's happy." "Brilliant," Bob had thought at the time. He just hadn't gotten around to it. There were so many problems. Like Mr. Hansen.

Hansen had come to the emergency room the previous Saturday. Seventy years old. Dying of prostate cancer. Unable to take oral medication. Family did not know how to give injectables. "So what do you do? You admit him to the hospital," Bob thought. "At least that's what we would have done 10 years ago. But not today. Medicare won't pay."[1] "Acute care not justified" is the official bureaucratese for the whole thing.

"Not justified," Bob thought. The next day, Hansen was dead. Bob felt irritated without understanding why. Hansen wasn't the first case like that. Why did it bother him so much? Maybe it was that scene with the emergency room physician on Monday morning. "Your hospital rules are killing people, and I'm resigning as of now," the physician had said. Bob could identify with that. He'd probably have done the same thing 30 years ago.

"But what can you do?" Bob said out loud. "Medicaid pays 50 cents on the dollar,[2] Medicare won't pay to save a patient's life, and Jeff complains because he's been charged a few extra dollars for a stupid pill!"

"Only a few more years until retirement," Bob thought, as he became more reflective. Too many tragedies . . . like June's mother.

---

[1]Medicare is the federal government's health insurance program for the elderly.

[2]Medicaid is a federal program designed to pay medical bills for low-income people. The program is administered by the states, which also pay about one-half of its cost.

He could never tell Jeff and June about what really happened there. No . . . he'd take that one to his grave.

Kay Pierce (June Adams's Physician)

Kay Pierce was unhappy. Why had she ever gone into medicine in the first place, she wondered? "You get to help people and you get paid a lot of money for doing it." That's what they'd told her when she'd entered medical school. But they hadn't told her the rest of the story.

June Adams had just been to see Kay about her tension headaches. That's what Kay thought they were. Still, there was always some chance. . . . When Kay had talked about expensive tests, June wasn't interested. But when Kay told her that she could fill out the forms so that Blue Cross would pay for most of it, June's attitude changed.

"So here we are," Kay thought, "about $3,000 later—including the magnetic resonance imaging (MRI) scan, hospital admission (so Blue Cross would pay), physician visits, and prescription drugs—lots of drugs. People want to know why health care is so expensive? I think I'll write an article and explain it," she thought. "Let's see . . . if half the people in the country have tension headaches and if we spend $3,000 on each of them. . . . " Kay was confident that was going to be a very large number. But as she reached for her calculator, another thought struck her. There were also cases like June's mother.

June's mother, Irene, had been Kay's patient, too. Formerly a heavy smoker, Irene should have gotten a chest x-ray each year. But there was the problem with Medicare. Irene didn't show any symptoms of cancer (no coughing, for example), and Medicare won't pay for screening tests if there are no symptoms. On the other hand, if Irene had paid for the x-ray with her own money, there would have been other problems. Kay would have had to complete a complicated form and spend at least 20 minutes explaining to Irene why Medicare wouldn't pay. That's time for which she couldn't bill Irene.

Kay could have lied to Medicare by writing a symptom such as "coughing" on the Medicare reimbursement form. She'd done that before. But it was risky. She could have given Irene a free x-ray. But if she provided free screening tests for all of her Medicare patients, she'd go broke. Besides, Irene had seemed so healthy.

7

Irene did have lung cancer, and by the time Kay discovered it, it was too late—six months later she was dead. "It was the most traumatic thing I've ever been through," Kay thought. Talking to her friend Jack, an oncologist, helped a lot. "Kay, it's not your fault," Jack had said. "In my field, Medicare kills people all the time. The government won't pay for the best drugs, so we treat cancer patients with inferior drugs. If I took personal responsibility for every preventable death, I'd have to check into a mental institution."

"People need to know about these things," Kay had told Jack.

"Yeah, but unless you want a malpractice suit, you're not the one to tell them," Jack had said.

Kay thought about that. Then she remembered another problem she'd heard about at the hospital that day—the problem involving Jeff Adams's father.

Mark Adams (Jeff's Cousin, Pacemaker Manufacturer)

Mark Adams was angry. What had he spent his whole adult life doing? Nothing less than making the best pacemakers in the whole world. And what did his cousin, Jeff, do when his own father needed a pacemaker? Totally ignored every damn thing he told him!

The incident began over a year ago, when Jeff's father George was diagnosed as having a heart problem. But Mark found out just this morning what had ultimately happened. He vividly remembered his conversation with Jeff when the issue first came up. "Jeff," he had said, "I make pacemakers. Now I can sell you an old-fashioned one, or I can sell you a really good one. The government won't pay for the good ones. But your father's still employed. That means he's covered by private insurance, not by Medicare. I'll tell you what kind of pacemaker to get, and you make sure George gets it."

Mark had assumed it had all been taken care of. Until this morning, that is. Mark was talking to George on the phone when he casually asked what kind of pacemaker George had. It was the wrong kind. Not wanting to alarm George, he controlled his anger and got off the phone as quickly as possible. He showed no such restraint when he got George's doctor on the phone. Before the doctor could hang up on him, Mark learned that George's private insurance carrier had adopted the same policy as Medicare. They refused to pay for higher quality pacemakers.

Mark had always thought that government was the greatest single threat to Western civilization. But it was increasingly clear to him that insurance companies were in second place and closing fast. The only thought that comforted him was his decision to end his company's employee health insurance plan. "What more evidence," he thought, "does anyone need to see the correctness of that decision?"

About three months earlier, Mark had met with his accountant. "We're a small company competing with Williams, Inc., a giant multinational," Mark had said. "The only way we can compete is to keep our costs down. So let's make sure our health insurance costs are below theirs."

"Can't be done, Mark," his accountant had said. "Why not?" Mark had asked. "Because Williams has a no-frills, bare-bones policy. Your policy covers acupuncture, in vitro fertilization, alcohol and drug abuse treatment, chiropractic services, and lots of other extras."

"Then get rid of the frills," said Mark, without thinking twice about it. "Can't," said the accountant. "Why not?" asked Mark. "State law," the accountant said. "Well, how the hell does Williams get around all that?" asked Mark. "Williams is a large company," he was told. "Federal law allows large companies to escape state regulation. Small companies can't escape."

That's when Mark decided he'd had it with health insurance. For the past two years his company had faced premium increases of 30 percent per year. "At that rate, we'll be bankrupt in five years," Mark had told his employees. To compensate, Mark gave every employee a $750 bonus to buy their own health insurance if they wanted it.

"But Mark," his accountant had said, "you've got to take taxes out of that $750. And lots of employees will just spend the remainder on other things. You're going to have a lot of people around here without any health insurance."

Privately, that thought bothered Mark. But it bothered him even more that Williams, Inc., had a way out of this problem, and he didn't. "There's government again," he thought, "sticking it to the little guy. And what am I supposed to do about it? It's better for the employees to be without health insurance than without jobs."

Then Mark remembered that his sister worked for a U.S. senator who was very involved in health care issues. He decided to give her a call.

Nancy Adams (Mark's Sister, Aide to a U.S. Senator)

Nancy Adams was troubled. She had just talked by phone with her brother Mark. What Mark had said bothered her. But what bothered her even more was the conversation she'd had with Senator Blake the day before.

She'd worked for the senator for two years. Since Blake was the most important person in Congress on health care issues, she'd received many telephone calls in those two years from people all over the country—people just like Mark, but with far more serious problems. In most cases, the senator gave her brief instructions on how to handle the problem (send a letter to this person, place a call to that person, etc.). But yesterday the senator had really talked with her.

He had just come back from an important meeting. She'd never seen him so depressed. He'd sat down and started talking. "Nancy," he'd said, "let me tell you how health care works in this country. If we did everything doctors know how to do to help people, we would spend our entire gross national product on health care. Nobody but a lunatic would suggest that. So what we do is say to the medical community, 'This is all the money you get; you figure out how to spend it.'"

"We don't put any restrictions on how they spend it?" Nancy had asked.

"Restrictions?" Blake had responded. "Of course we've got restrictions. Thousands of them. Medical care in this country is an $800 billion-a-year industry and every interest group is here in Washington trying to get a slice of it. We've got so many special-interest rules that I don't know how the hospitals keep track of them."

Blake had leaned back in his chair, becoming more reflective. "Nancy, we can pass laws all day and all night, and it's not going to matter whether the hospitals obey them or break them." Blake had paused for a moment. Then he'd said, "The bottom line is this. If you don't have money, you can't give care. The squeeze is on. And if the hospitals think they're being squeezed now, they have no idea how bad it's going to get."

"But why can't you just explain to people what the problems are?" Nancy had asked.

"Because nobody dares," Blake had retorted. "You can't talk authoritatively about something unless you know about it. You can't know about it unless you've participated in the decisions. And if you've been involved in the decisions, then you're personally responsible for causing people a lot of harm. If I admitted what I do here in Washington, I'd never get reelected. If hospital administrators or physicians admitted what they are doing, they'd be sued for malpractice."

"But what do people in other countries do?" Nancy had asked.

"It's worse. In Britain, doctors probably spend more time denying people care than giving it."

Nancy had been baffled. The longer she worked for the senator, the more convinced she was that the health care system had problems. Now she had heard from the horse's mouth that the problems were worse than she had ever imagined.

"So what can we do?" she had blurted.

"What I'm going to do is stay here a few more years, collect a nice pension and leave Washington for good," Blake had said. "As for the health care system, I don't know what you can do. I don't know what anybody can do."

Senator Blake had gotten up slowly and left the room. He never discussed health care with Nancy again.

How This Book Differs from Other Books on Health Policy

In the brief account of the Adams family, we met people who had interacted with the health care system—from patient to physician, hospital administrator to equipment manufacturer, employer to politician. In each vignette there were also unseen actors whose behavior was vitally important. Even though we examined only a few episodes, the problems we encountered were wide-ranging—from how government should spend its health care dollars to how hospitals, insurance companies, employers, and even patients make important decisions. In some cases, it was clear that too much was being spent and resources were being wasted. In other cases, too little was being spent, sometimes at the cost of human life.

11

Yet one common denominator united each of the Adams family's experiences and distinguished those experiences from what happens in other sectors of our economy: when individuals pursued their own interests, bad consequences resulted for other people.

In the current health care system, when individuals make socially bad decisions, the cost of those decisions often is borne by others, not by the decisionmaker. Conversely, when people make socially good decisions, most of the benefits of those decisions go to others. On the whole, people neither bear the full costs nor reap the full benefits of their decisions. As a consequence, the health care sector is replete with perverse incentives. Most of the time, what's good for the individual decisionmaker is bad for everyone else, and vice versa.

In most other sectors of our economy, individuals who make decisions realize most of the benefit from good ones and bear most of the cost of bad ones. To be sure, almost everything individuals do affects others, so the link between personal and social benefits is rarely perfect. Nonetheless, in most markets perverse incentives have been eliminated. The market for health care could be organized in a similar way.

In this book we depart substantially from previous works on public policy toward health care. The principal point of departure is the construction of two visions of the medical marketplace and the central role we assign to the individual pursuit of self-interest in each vision. The first is a vision of the medical marketplace as it operates now. The second is a vision of the medical marketplace as it can and should operate.

Aside from economists who produce purely technical works, most writers view the medical marketplace as primarily altruistic and charitable. The role of self-interest is rarely discussed. The word "market" is commonly avoided, as is the word "business." In most cases, these writers have been impressed by the fact that the health care sector is dominated by nonprofit institutions, which people mistakenly assume are characterized by selfless goals.

The few writers who have introduced the notion of self-interest have done so in the context of creating villains (for example, politicians, the American Medical Association, insurance companies, and hospital administrators). In their approach, greed has been assumed to intrude on a sector that is otherwise charitable and altruistic.

12

In this book, we accept self-interest as a normal characteristic of human behavior. Pursuit of self-interest is no more or less common in health care than in any other sector. The fact that some of our most important health care institutions are nonprofit (for example, medical schools, hospitals, insurance companies, and nursing homes) does not change human nature. That people actively pursue their own interests is not a bad thing. It is simply a fact. What matters most in the health care sector are the institutional arrangements under which self-interest is pursued.

Clearly, all of the principals in our Adams family vignettes were self-interested. They made decisions that benefited them personally, even when their decisions subsequently hurt others. At the same time, none of the principals were greedy, mean-spirited, or indifferent to the suffering of others. *There were no villains in this drama.*

Not only did the characters pursue their own interests, but in most cases they believed they had little choice about doing so— and they were right. If Bob Adams had known that Mr. Hansen was going to die the next day, undoubtedly he would have made an exception to the rules and admitted Hansen to the hospital. But he didn't know, and changing the rules for all patients would have increased hospital costs without increasing revenue. Too many decisions like that, and the hospital's board of directors would be looking for a new administrator. If Kay Pierce, the physician, had known that Irene Adams had cancer, she would have behaved differently. But she didn't know, and giving free tests to all Medicare patients would probably have bankrupted her practice. Senator Blake might have been able to make minor changes in the system. But if he had tried to make radical changes, he wouldn't have been reelected. Mark Adams might have been able to continue his employees' health insurance a bit longer. But ultimately, his uncompetitive costs would have forced him out of business.

Pursuit of self-interest, then, is much more than a natural characteristic of human behavior. In most institutional settings, it is a survival requirement. The institutional setting, however, determines whether our pursuit of self-interest is primarily beneficial or harmful to others. In regulated markets dominated by bureaucratic institutions, the self-interests of individuals frequently conflict. One person's gain is another's loss. More for me means less for you, and vice versa. In such an environment, when others pursue their interests, you and I are often made worse off.

Quite a different result emerges in competitive markets with clearly defined private property rights and individual freedom of choice. In this environment, you and I cannot pursue our own interests (for the most part) without creating benefits for others. Conversely, others rarely can pursue their interests without creating benefits for us.

Health Care Delivery as It Can and Should Be

Consider how differently the Adams family would have fared in a world in which the medical marketplace works at least as well as the market for other complex services, and the market for health insurance works at least as well as the market for other kinds of insurance.

Jeff Adams's Surgery

If the medical marketplace worked the way other markets do, Jeff Adams would pay for his surgery with his own money. It might be money he had saved or money he had received from his health insurer once his condition had been diagnosed. But the money would belong to Jeff Adams and he—not some remote bureaucracy—would be the principal buyer. In all probability, Jeff would choose outpatient surgery, the less expensive option. But if he chose inpatient surgery, the hospital would behave quite differently from the way hospitals operate today.

Before admitting Jeff, the hospital probably would give him a single package price covering all services. He could then compare it to the prices of competing hospitals. Few hospitals would refuse to state their prices in advance or present unreadable statements at the time of discharge. Hospitals that did those things would have mostly empty beds.[3]

June Adams's Headaches

If the health insurance market worked the way other insurance markets work, it is highly unlikely that June Adams would receive any insurance money for headaches.

---

[3]Some hospitals might quote an estimate or a range, or give an average with a not-to-exceed maximum. We would also expect some variety in pricing schemes.

Health insurance would be restricted to rare, unusual events that have very costly consequences.[4] Because using health insurance to pay small medical bills for routine services is costly and wasteful, June Adams would use her own money to pay for most physicians' visits and diagnostic tests. If June's insurer did pay her some money for headaches, it would be hers to spend as she chose. Given her initial reaction to her doctor's questions, it is unlikely that she would pay for an MRI scan. If she did, she certainly would not check into a hospital.

George Adams's Pacemaker

As in the cases of Jeff and June Adams, George Adams would be purchasing a pacemaker with his own money. A large part of what he spent would come from the insurance check he received once his heart problem was diagnosed. But he might also have to use some of his savings.

Because George, not an insurance company, would be the customer, pacemaker manufacturers would seek him out. Higher quality pacemakers would still cost more, so George would have to evaluate the risks and the costs. Certainly he would consult his physician. But because the insurance company would no longer be the principal client, his doctor's advice would be far more informative and complete.

Irene Adams's X-ray

If Medicare insurance worked the way most other insurance works, Medicare would be irrelevant in Irene's life unless she were diagnosed with a major illness. At that point she would receive a check. In the meantime, Medicare would not care whether Irene coughed or didn't cough, and her doctor would have no forms on which to report such trivia.

Her doctor would be in the business of selling services, and if Irene chose to purchase chest x-rays, she would be spending her own money. Because Irene, not Medicare, would be the customer, her doctor would have an incentive to encourage her to have an annual chest x-ray, especially in view of her smoking history. Irene

[4]Reimbursement would probably be limited to severe cases in which the individual is diagnosed as needing treatment by a specialized professional.

15

could also solicit advice from other physicians. In all probability, x-ray machine manufacturers would advertise directly to people such as Irene—since Medicare would no longer be their client either.

Odds are that Irene would receive encouragement from many sources to get the annual x-ray. The choice would be hers.

Mr. Hansen's Hospital Admission

If the medical marketplace functioned as other markets do, when Mr. Hansen got to the emergency room he, not Medicare, would be the hospital's potential customer. If he entered the hospital, he would be spending his own money, although Medicare might already have paid a claim to him for his condition.

The Hansen family may not have much money. But Hansen was not on Medicaid, so he probably was not living in poverty. Hansen and his family might have been a hard sell. But a hospital in a competitive medical marketplace would be in the business of selling services to people, not insurers, and in the Hansen case the argument for immediate hospitalization would be very persuasive. At the very minimum, the Hansen family would make an informed choice.

Group Insurance for Mark Adams's Employees

If the health insurance market were freely competitive (or at least as free of regulatory obstacles as the market for life, fire, and casualty insurance), state legislators would not tell Mark Adams's company what to include in the company's group health insurance plan. Mark and his employees would simply agree on an affordable package of benefits. The employees might have to forgo some frills, but they would still have catastrophic insurance.

The problems that Mark and his employees had with government under the present system did not end with the state legislature. Federal tax law also interfered. If Mark's company purchased the insurance, it could pay with pretax dollars. But if employees purchased insurance on their own, they had to pay with aftertax dollars. If federal tax law had been designed for individuals rather than for companies, it would have permitted a full range of options for each employee. In that case, not all employees would be forced to accept the same package of health insurance benefits. Each could choose among competing health insurance plans and purchase the policy with nontaxed dollars (the same way their employers do now).

Making Senator Blake's Life Easier

Senator Blake's principal problem stemmed from the federal government's attempts to do something of which it is incapable: operate a giant insurance company. Moreover, as in the case of private health insurance, Medicare insurance has long since ceased to be genuine insurance—it is instead prepayment for the consumption of medical care. Thus, Senator Blake and his colleagues must decide who gets to consume what and how much—an unpleasant task.

To make matters worse, decisionmakers such as Blake are continually pressured by special interests. Not surprisingly, by the time all of the pressures have sorted themselves out, Medicare has violated every principle of sound insurance. That is not unusual. In every field in which the government operates an insurance program, sound insurance principles are sacrificed to political pressures.

Is there a way of replacing Medicare with a program that takes advantage of private-sector strengths in providing the elderly with health care? Yes—and at least one country, Singapore, has made substantial progress toward implementing a totally private system. We will examine emerging market-based systems in later chapters.

The market for medical care will never be exactly like the market for corn or wheat, but there is no reason why we cannot create a similar institutional framework. We can transfer the power to make important decisions from large institutions such as government, corporate employers, insurance companies, and hospitals to individuals. We can allow supply, demand, and competition to allocate resources. Consumer preference and individual choice can determine the ultimate form of our health care system.

2. Two Competing Visions of the Health Care System

Within the last several years, dozens of proposals to reform the U.S. health care system have been produced by task forces, government agencies, and private groups. Almost all have had one thing in common: They have adopted the same vision of the medical care marketplace that has dominated the U.S. health care system since the end of World War II.

An exception was a task force report issued in May 1990.[1] The task force was composed of representatives from 40 universities and research organizations, including the American Enterprise Institute, the Hoover Institution, and the Cato Institute. The report was published by the National Center for Policy Analysis (NCPA) in Dallas. What made the NCPA report radically different was its endorsement of a different vision of how the medical marketplace could function. Whereas other proposals called for enlargement of the role of third-party insurers, the NCPA report called for less reliance on third-party insurance and more reliance on individual self-insurance. Whereas other proposals called for larger bureaucracies and greater centralization, the NCPA report called for decentralization and competitive markets. Whereas other proposals implicitly accepted the idea that the medical marketplace cannot function like other markets, the NCPA report sought ways to reap the benefits of competition and consumer choice for the health care delivery system.

In this chapter, we develop more fully the distinction between the vision proposed in the NCPA report and the vision accepted by most other health policy commentators. In the following two chapters, we present the task force's specific recommendations and show how they can be used to solve major health policy problems.

---

[1]Task Force Report, *An Agenda for Solving America's Health Care Crisis*, NCPA Policy Report no. 151 (Dallas: National Center for Policy Analysis, May 1990).

How the Medical Marketplace Differs from Other Markets

In a normal market, major problems are solved by individual initiative on the part of consumers and producers pursuing their own self-interests. Consumers circumvent waste, inefficiency, and resulting high prices by searching for good products at attractive prices offered by efficient suppliers. Producers search for less costly ways of meeting consumer needs. Pursuit of self-interest by consumers rewards the most efficient producers, and pursuit of self-interest by producers rewards consumers.

In the health care sector, however, normal market processes have been replaced by bureaucratic institutions and normal market incentives by bureaucratic rule making. As a result, the scope for individual initiative is greatly restricted, and often people can pursue their own interests only by creating costs for others. For example:

- Whereas consumers in a normal market spend their own money, in the medical marketplace consumers are usually spending someone else's money. Only 5 cents out of every dollar of hospital income and only 19 cents out of each dollar of physicians' fees is paid by patients using their own funds.
- Whereas producers in a normal market continuously search for ways to reduce costs, when physicians and hospitals increase costs, they often also increase their incomes. Their success depends less on service to patients than on meeting the requirements of third-party (government and private insurance) reimbursement formulas.
- Whereas individuals in other insurance markets may choose from diverse products, the vast majority of people who have health insurance are covered under an employer or government plan. Despite so-called cafeteria options, an individual usually cannot purchase a less expensive plan with a different type of coverage without making considerable personal sacrifice.
- Whereas innovation and technological change in a normal market are viewed as good for consumers, third-party payers in the medical marketplace are increasingly hostile to new technology and discourage its development.
- Whereas producers in a normal market advertise price discounts and quality differences, most patients in the hospital

marketplace cannot find out what the cost will be prior to admission and cannot read the hospital bill upon discharge. Patients rarely can obtain information about the quality of physicians or hospitals, even when quality problems are well-known within the medical community.

The result is a marketplace in which the pursuit of self-interest often does not solve problems, but creates them instead. When consumers consume, they drive up insurance premium costs for other consumers. The primary ways in which physicians and hospitals increase their incomes also lead to increasing insurance premiums. Rarely can individuals act to change things without operating through large bureaucracies, and when bureaucracies attempt solutions, their "success" usually creates new problems and new costs for other bureaucracies.

How America's Health Care Crisis Evolved

In most Western industrial democracies, health care systems shaped by government policies have evolved through three stages.

The Cost-Plus System of Health Care Finance (Stage I)

From the end of World War II through the mid-1980s, Americans paid for hospital care principally through a cost-plus system of health care finance. Cost-plus reimbursement worked like this: If Blue Cross patients accounted for 25 percent of a hospital's patient days, Blue Cross reimbursed the hospital for 25 percent of its total costs. If Medicare patients accounted for 30 percent of the hospital's patient days, Medicare paid the hospital 30 percent. Other insurers reimbursed in much the same way.[2] Health insurance literally ensured that hospitals had enough income to cover their costs and health insurers acted as agents not for their policyholders, but for the suppliers of medical services. Because the only way the suppliers could increase their incomes was to increase costs, the cost-plus system invariably led to rising health care costs.

---

[2]See John C. Goodman and Gerald L. Musgrave, *The Changing Market for Health Insurance: Opting Out of the Cost-Plus System*, NCPA Policy Report no. 118 (Dallas: National Center for Policy Analysis, September 1985). The cost-plus system is described in detail in chapters 5, 6, and 7 of this book.

A cost-plus system could never exist if patients were spending their own money in a competitive marketplace. Therefore, the prerequisite for cost-plus medicine was a market in which the supply side was dominated by nonprofit institutions that competed in only limited ways. The demand side was dominated by large, third-party bureaucracies that were more responsive to the needs of sellers of medical services than to the needs of the insured. By the 1970s, those institutions were well in place.[3]

In a cost-plus system, the pressures to increase spending on health care were inexorable. Patients had no reason to show restraint, since the funds they spent belonged not to them but to third-party institutions. When they entered the medical marketplace, they were spending someone else's money, not their own.

Physicians often believed that the "pure" practice of medicine could and should be free from the constraints of money. In prescribing tests and other medical treatments, physicians not only did not think about costs, they had no idea what those costs were. Guided by the sole consideration of patient health, physicians were inclined to do anything and everything that might help the patient—restrained only by the ethical injunction to do no harm.

The system in its pure cost-plus phase rewarded scientists, inventors, and research and development personnel. The message of the medical marketplace was, "Invent it, show us it will improve health, and we will buy it, regardless of the cost."

The role of the hospital was to provide an environment in which cost-plus medicine could be practiced, in which all of the latest technology was available, within easy reach and on demand. In such a world, hospital administrators did not manage doctors. To the contrary, they served the physicians' interest in practicing medicine by interfering as little as possible in the physicians' activities.

Such a hospital environment would be inconceivable were it not for a system that reimbursed hospitals on the basis of their costs. The role of third-party payers in the system, therefore, was to pay whatever bills were submitted, with few questions asked. Cost

---

[3]For an analysis of how these institutions evolved, see John C. Goodman, *The Regulation of Medical Care: Is the Price Too High?* (Washington: Cato Institute, 1980). A different perspective, one more sympathetic to the suppression of market incentives, is presented in Paul Starr, *The Social Transformation of American Medicine* (New York: Basic Books, 1982).

increases were passed along to policyholders in the form of higher health insurance premiums.

The Cost-Plus System in Its Cost-Control Phase (Stage II)

Because there is a limit to how much any society will pay for health care, the cost-plus system was ultimately forced to limit the decisions of the suppliers of medical care in arbitrary ways. The limitations took the form of rules and restrictions written by impersonal bureaucracies, far removed from the doctor/patient relationships they sought to regulate.

During the 1980s, the U.S. health care system evolved from a pure cost-plus system (Stage I) into a cost-plus system in its cost-control phase (Stage II). In this second stage, there are many different third-party paying institutions, some public and some private. Each is engaged in a bureaucratic struggle—not merely to resist the cost-plus push of the medical care providers, but also to reduce its share of the total cost. Each separate third-party institution is free to initiate its own cost-control strategy in random and uncoordinated ways. But since the basic structure of cost-plus finance has not changed (that is, no real market has been created), Stage II only secondarily is about holding down total spending. Primarily, it is about bureaucratic warfare over shifting costs.

The central focus of third-party paying institutions is to eliminate "waste." Yet bureaucratic institutions (operating principally through reimbursement strategies chosen by people remote from actual patients and doctors) usually cannot eliminate waste without harming patients. Third-party payers may seek to eliminate waste by controlling price, or quantity, or both. In the very act of trying to control prices, however, they invariably focus on a normal price for a normal service, ignoring patients and institutional settings that are not normal. In the very act of trying to control quantity (for example, by eliminating "unnecessary" surgery or "unnecessary" hospital admissions), they again invariably set standards for what is normal—ignoring the unanticipated, abnormal circumstances in which medical care is often delivered.

On the supply side of the medical marketplace, institutions have great resources and considerable experience at resisting change. So, in the face of a cost-control measure initiated by one institutional buyer, the suppliers attempt to shift costs to another, without changing their fundamental behavior. The suppliers are sufficiently adept at this so that, over the long haul, costs are not really controlled in Stage II. At best, each new wave of buyer restrictions slows the rate of increase. But after suppliers adjust to the new restrictions, costs rise again. Precisely for this reason, a system in Stage II evolves into Stage III. It is in this final stage that institutional buyers acquire the ultimate weapon in the cost-control battle—the power of government.

Evolution to National Health Insurance (Stage III)

In the final phase of the cost-plus system's evolution, third-party payers directly or indirectly control the entire system. They begin to determine what technology can be used, what constitutes ethical behavior in the practice of medicine, even what illnesses can be treated and how. Ultimately, they determine who lives and who dies.

In most countries with national health insurance, many of the perverse incentives that were present in Stage I are still in place. The appetite to spend is held in check, or misdirected, by rules and regulations enforced either directly by government or by insurance company proxies for government. In this third stage, government not only controls the total amount of spending on health care but also actively intervenes in the allocation of health care dollars. Stage III is pure special-interest warfare, fought out in the political arena. It takes all of the struggles present in Stage II and elevates them to the realm of politics.[4]

How the Cost-Plus System Affects Patients

In Stage I of the evolution of a cost-plus system, the quality of medical care delivered may be very high. That is because medical care is administered in an environment in which cost is no object, and physicians are trained to do everything possible to alleviate any and all illnesses, real or imagined. Once the system enters its cost-control phase, however, the quality of care can deteriorate rapidly. That is because competing institutions begin a monumental struggle over resources. In this environment, the patient is no longer seen as a consumer or buyer of medical care. Indeed, individual patients are largely unimportant except insofar as their formal

---

[4]See "The Politics of Medicine" in John C. Goodman, *National Health Care in Great Britain: Lessons for the USA* (Dallas: Fisher Institute, 1980), ch. 10.

consent is needed to legitimize the bureaucratic warfare over vast sums of money.

The Role of Insurance

Outside of the health care sector, there are well-developed markets for insurance for a wide variety of unforeseen, risky events: life insurance (for an unforeseen death), automobile liability insurance (for an unforeseen automobile accident), fire and casualty insurance (for unforeseen damage to property), and disability insurance (for unforeseen physical injuries). Indeed, there is hardly any risk that is not, in principle, insurable. Lloyd's of London will even insure against the failure of a communications satellite to achieve orbit, and it wrote coverage for ships in the Persian Gulf and off the coast of Israel from the day Operation Desert Storm began.

All of these markets have certain common characteristics.[5] The amount to be reimbursed is based on a risky event. Once the event has occurred and the damage has been assessed, the insurer writes a check to the policyholder for the agreed-upon amount. Policyholders are free to do whatever they prefer with the money they receive.

In the market for health insurance, however, things are very different. Often, there need not be any risky event to trigger insurance payments. (June Adams, for example, had had tension headaches for years.) Once it is determined that a health insurer owes something, the amount to be paid is not a predetermined sum but is instead determined by the consumption decisions of the policyholder. (Jeff Adams, for example, chose to have surgery in a hospital rather than as an outpatient, and June Adams elected to undergo a battery of tests.) Finally, payment is made not to the insured but to medical providers, based on the consumption decisions that are made.[6] These differences shape the way the health insurance market functions. In fact, in many respects health insurance is not insurance at all. It is instead prepayment for the consumption of medical care.

---

[5]An exception is insurance for tort liabilities, which has many of the defects of health insurance and leads to many of the same problems.

[6]There are a few exceptions, such as policies that indemnify patients in the form of a fixed sum of money per day spent in the hospital for a procedure or a diagnosis (for example, cancer).

Because health insurance is the primary method of payment for the medical services Americans consume, in a very real sense it is the insurer rather than the patient who is the customer of medical providers. Thus, June Adams and Jeff Adams were not the principal buyers of the medical care they received. Blue Cross was. Similarly, Irene Adams and Mr. Hansen were not the principal buyers of their medical care. Medicare was.

The Relationship between Buyer and Seller

In a normal marketplace, buyers and sellers negotiate over price, quantity, quality, and other terms for big-ticket items or important transactions. For smaller, frequent, and less critical transactions, buyers search for the most favorable terms or conditions. Sellers adjust terms and conditions to meet customers' needs and to react to the offers of their rivals. An exchange is not consummated unless it benefits both parties. The preferences of other people, not parties to the exchange, are rarely considered. In the medical marketplace, however, things are very different.

In reflecting on the experiences of the hypothetical Adams family, it is interesting to note that there was never a real exchange. That is, there was no case in which a buyer and seller reached a mutually beneficial agreement, independent of the wishes of others. To the contrary, in every case an entity (for example, government or an insurance company) not a party to the exchange was far more important in determining what ultimately happened than the parties who interacted.

In the cases of Jeff, June, and George Adams, the medical procedures performed were far more influenced by the reimbursement policies of private insurers than by any mutually beneficial exchange between patients and their doctors. In the cases of Irene Adams and Mr. Hansen, what was done or not done was virtually unaffected by the preferences of the patients and their families. Instead, the decisions of the medical providers were determined exclusively by the Medicare bureaucracy.

When the legislators in some distant city decided what elements had to be contained in a group health insurance policy, none of them asked Mark Adams or his employees what their preferences were. So, unlike their counterparts at Williams, Inc., Mark Adams and his employees never had the opportunity to find a scaled-down policy that the company could afford. The decision to end group health insurance at Mark Adams's company was not a mutually beneficial agreement between employer and employees. It was an outcome dictated by politicians who didn't even know Mark Adams and the people who worked for him.

In the medical marketplace, rules imposed by third-party institutions increasingly shape medical practice. When Medicare patients interact with the health care system, *what* procedures are performed—and *whether* a procedure is performed—is determined more by reimbursement rules than by patient preferences or the physician's experience and judgment. Although this phenomenon is more evident in government health care programs (Medicare and Medicaid), private insurers and large companies are increasingly copying the methods of government.

The Role of Information

One of the most striking things about the Adams family's experiences is how little information the people had. Those making decisions lacked not only information about the monetary cost of those decisions, but often the information that could have saved their lives.

Consider the differences between the experiences of the Adams family and our everyday experiences in nonhealth care markets. Jeff Adams agreed to hospital surgery with no idea what it would cost him. When he was discharged, he was presented with a statement that he could not read or understand. He assumed Blue Cross would look out for his interests, but he had no idea how Blue Cross handled claims. Unquestionably, there is no other market in which Jeff Adams could be a buyer (including the market for any other type of insurance) in which anything even remotely similar takes place.

In almost every other market, the biggest problem that sellers have is getting information to prospective buyers. Those who have a better product or a better way to meet consumer needs often go to great expense to convey the information to potential customers. But in the experiences of the Adams family, precisely the reverse was true. In fact, in example after example, essential information was intentionally concealed and withheld.

George Adams, for example, had no idea that his pacemaker was not of the highest quality or that better products existed. The person in the best position to tell him about the options (his physician) didn't do so. Irene Adams, who died of lung cancer, did not understand how Medicare works. She didn't know that there were services that she could and should have been purchasing with her own money. Again, the person in the best position to tell her (her physician) failed to do so. In all probability, when Mr. Hansen came to the emergency room, no one explained to the Hansen family the options, and the probable costs and risks associated with each.

Why is vitally important information persistently withheld and concealed in the medical marketplace? Because in the health care sector, people discover that it is in their self-interest to withhold information. In general, medical equipment manufacturers, pharmaceutical companies, and other suppliers with information about quality do not communicate the information to patients because they do not view patients as the principal buyers.[7] Their principal customers are hospitals, physicians, and third-party institutions. Patients frequently do not have information about quality for yet another reason. In an effort to suppress competition among providers, associations of physicians and hospitals have made it difficult, if not impossible, for patients to get information about quality. Avoiding quality comparisons has become a matter of professional ethics. In the past, adherence to such ethical codes was backed by the force of state law. As a result, in most communities patients cannot even discover the mortality rate for surgery and for specific surgeons at public hospitals funded by the patients' own tax dollars.

An Exception: Cosmetic Surgery

In one area of the medical marketplace, cosmetic surgery, most of the generalizations made above are no longer true. In general, cosmetic surgery is not covered by any private or public health insurance policy. Yet, in every major city, it is thriving. Patients pay with their own money and, despite the fact that many separate fees are involved (payments to the physician, nurse, anesthetist or anesthesiologist, hospital, etc.), patients are almost always given a fixed price in advance—covering all medical services and all hospital charges.[8] Patients also have choices about the level of service

---

[7] In some cases they are prohibited by law from communicating the information.

[8] To our knowledge, no one has studied the market for cosmetic surgery. That is unfortunate because most of what employers and insurers have unsuccessfully tried to accomplish for other types of surgery over the past decade has occurred naturally with few problems and little fanfare in the market for cosmetic surgery.

(for example, surgery can be performed in a physician's office or, for a higher price, on an outpatient basis in a hospital). Many readers will be aware of the recent controversy over the potential risk to patients of (silicon) breast implants. They may not be aware that there are dozens of medical procedures—far more risky for patients and about which there is considerable disagreement in the medical community—that are not investigated by the federal Food and Drug Administration (FDA) and routinely reported on by the national news media. Overall, patients probably have more information about quality in cosmetic surgery than in any other area of surgical practice.

The characteristics of the market for cosmetic surgery also are evident in other medical markets in which patients are paying with their own funds. For example, private-sector hospitals in Britain frequently quote package prices for routine surgical procedures. And U.S. hospitals often quote package prices to Canadians who are willing to come to this country to get care that is being rationed in Canada.

Vision of an Ideal Health Care System

Before we recommend solutions to America's health care problems, we need a clear idea of where we want to go. That is, we need a vision of an ideal medical marketplace in order to plan the steps that will take us there. By "ideal," we do not mean a visionary world in which there are no problems. The ideal medical marketplace is simply one that works at least as well as most other markets in which we buy and sell.

Goals of an Ideal Health Care System

We can identify five goals of an ideal health care system. In the very act of reaching these goals, we would be simultaneously solving America's health care problems. Specifically, an ideal system would seek to:

- Transfer power from large institutions and impersonal bureaucracies to individuals.
- Restore the buyer/seller relationship to patients and medical suppliers, so that patients (rather than third-party insurers) become the principal buyers of health care.

29

- Create institutions in which patients (as much as possible) spend their own money, rather than someone else's, when they purchase health care.
- Remove health care (as much as possible) from the political arena, in which well-organized special interests can cause great harm to the rest of us.
- Subject the health care sector to the rigors of competition and create market-based institutions in which individuals reap the full benefits of their good decisions and bear the full cost of their bad ones.

How an Ideal Health Care System Would Function

In a health care system designed to pursue the goals listed above, the roles of patients, physicians, hospitals, insurance companies, employers, and even government would be radically different. The principal differences would be that:

- Patients rather than third-party payers would become the principal buyers of health care, with opportunities to compare options, compare prices, and make decisions.
- Physicians would no longer serve as the principal agents of third-party payers, but would serve as the principal agents of patients and help them to make informed choices.
- Hospitals would no longer serve as the principal agents of either physicians or third-party payers, but would become competitors in the business of health care delivery and would compete for patients by improving quality and lowering prices.
- Health insurance companies would no longer be buyers of health care, but would specialize in the business of insurance and reimburse policyholders in the case of unforeseen and risky adverse health events.
- Employers would not be buyers of health care and would not make decisions for employees concerning their health insurance, but would be agents for individual employees and help them to make informed choices and to monitor the performance of competing insurers.
- Government—in its role as an insurer of last resort—would no longer serve as a buyer of health care but would pay health insurance premiums for indigent policyholders.

- Government—in its policymaking role—would facilitate the goals of the system on the demand side by encouraging private savings for small medical bills, private health insurance for large medical bills, and lifelong savings for medical needs during retirement; on the supply side, government would encourage free and open competition in the markets for physicians' services, hospital services, and private health insurance.

If the ideal is so obvious, why hasn't the private sector implemented it? The answer is that virtually every private-sector action that would move us in the direction of the ideal health care system is discouraged by government policy. In the next chapter we examine these government-created obstacles in detail and consider the policy changes needed to remove them.

Implementing the Ideal: The Health Care System of Singapore

Singapore's health care system is part of a much wider system based on an explicit goal: no government subsidies. The government of Singapore has attempted to identify all of the major needs that other governments approach with welfare and entitlement programs and to meet those needs by requiring people to save. In Singapore, personal savings accounts are replacing the welfare state.

For example, instead of a government-run social security system, Singapore's residents are required to save for their own retirement. Instead of a government-run health care system, people are required to place 6 percent of their annual income in medical savings accounts. Funds build up in these accounts tax free and can be spent only on medical care. The program of forced savings also covers other needs. Required (retirement) savings can be used to buy life insurance and disability insurance, make a down payment on a home, or finance a child's college education.

The philosophy of Singapore is: Each individual should pay his or her own way; each family should pay its own way; and each generation should pay its own way. Government transfers should be minimal. Progress toward that goal has been remarkable. Over the last decade, savings account balances have soared and government spending on traditional welfare programs has decreased dramatically.

With respect to health care, the Singapore system makes sure that money spent on medical services is in the hands of the consumers of those services. In general, 6 percent of a person's income over an entire working life will pay for hospitalization for the vast majority of medical episodes that can occur, and only recently has Singapore introduced catastrophic health insurance to pay for large medical bills.

Singapore is far from perfect. Readers of the *Wall Street Journal* are well aware that Singapore practices censorship, and the government violates other civil rights as well. Health economists will have no difficulty in spotting defects and recommending improvements in the country's health care system. Nonetheless, there is great value in studying carefully Singapore's system, and we shall examine it more closely in chapter 18.

Can Patients Function as Informed Consumers in the Medical Marketplace?

The most common objection to using markets to solve health care problems relates to the complexity of medical decisions and the inability of patients to make wise choices. Medical science is complicated and becoming more so. Moreover, most medical episodes (such as gall bladder malfunction) occur only once in a person's lifetime. Given that, for any one person, such episodes occur infrequently, individual patients cannot be expected to learn from experience or to invest much time, energy, and money in learning about a medical procedure on the slight chance that they may need it some day. How then, even under the best of circumstances, can patients make wise decisions about whether to have gall bladder surgery, what physician to use, and what hospital to enter?

The answer is that they must rely on the advice of others. Short of going to medical school themselves, there is no alternative. However, just because we must depend on others for advice does not mean that we should surrender power to them.

The primary difference between markets and nonmarket bureaucracies is consumer sovereignty. In general, the more complicated a market, the stronger the case for consumers' not surrendering the power to make ultimate decisions. If choosing a physician is complex, choosing a politician who will appoint a bureaucrat to choose a physician is even *more* complex. Elevating choices to the realm of politics only makes the choices harder. In selecting a politician, we consumers would not simply be selecting a doctor-chooser; we would be selecting a person who would make many other decisions affecting our lives. If choosing the wrong doctor can cause harm, then choosing the wrong politician to choose the doctor for us can cause even more harm. What is true of politicians is also true of employers, insurance companies, and any other bureaucracy.

Imagine you live in a country with national health insurance, in which health care is routinely and arbitrarily rationed by the medical bureaucracy. Knowing the institutional setting, you are predisposed to distrust the advice you receive from a physician. If told that you do not need an expensive diagnostic test or surgical procedure, you have no way of knowing whether the advice represents state-of-the-art medicine or potentially lethal rationing. Discovering whether you really need an expensive procedure is only half the problem. Once you know you need it, you still have to cope with the complexities of bureaucratic rationing. Getting to the head of the line is, in itself, a skill and an art. Unless you are willing to totally give up control and do whatever physicians tell you, your problems in a bureaucratic system are even more complex than in a market system.

An important principle to remember is: No one cares more about you and your family than you do. And the further removed decisionmakers are from you and your family—geographically, economically, and politically—the less likely they are to make the same decision you would have made with respect to your health care. Another important principle is: We can often take advantage of the wisdom and experience of others without transferring power to them. If politicians have wise advice to give, we can take their advice while retaining the ultimate authority to make our own decisions.

Precisely because the medical marketplace is complex, employers, insurance companies, governments, health organizations, and nonprofit entities collect and assimilate information that no single patient (or physician) would ever collect individually. The concept behind "managed care," for example, is that organizations can collect information and use it to raise the quality and reduce the cost of medical care—especially with respect to complicated and expensive procedures. Whether the goal is reached depends on the institutional environment. In a market-based system, organizations that specialize in collecting information can be valuable to both patients and physicians. In a bureaucratic system, such organizations are used to control the behavior of patients and physicians. One system uses information to help people reach their own goals, the other to prevent them from doing so.

In market-based systems, people find it in their self-interest to communicate information to consumers. In bureaucracies, the reverse is true. The more information consumers have, the harder life is for bureaucrats. Dissemination of knowledge is good for the life of markets—it makes them work better—but it is bad for the life of bureaucracies.

The U.S. health care system is far more bureaucratic than most people know. Perhaps, for this reason, too much information is communicated by cranks and quacks, too little by responsible parties. Yet there are welcome signs of change. The cover story of a 1990 issue of *U.S. News & World Report* was entitled "America's Best Hospitals: A National Guide That Helps You Choose."[9] The fact that the article was a cover story shows how rare and unusual it is for such information to be communicated to the general public. A recent book published by Consumers Union (also the publisher of *Consumer Reports*) is entitled *The Savvy Patient: How to Be an Active Participant in Your Medical Care.*[10] What is astonishing is that the book is new. Consumers Union has been in existence since 1936.

Information about the quality of medical practice has been available to the intellectual and economic elite for some time, through various formal and informal sources. For example, *Town and Country* subscribers, who have a median annual income of $98,200 and a median net worth of $875,400, could consult "Town and Country's Exclusive Directory of Outstanding Medical Specialists in the U.S."[11] Now readers of such publications as *Good Housekeeping* can

[9]*U.S. News & World Report,* April 30, 1990.

[10]David R. Stutz, Bernard Feder, and the editors of Consumer Reports Books, *The Savvy Patient: How to Be an Active Participant in Your Medical Care* (Mount Vernon, NY: Consumer Reports Books, 1990).

[11]Stephanie Bernards Johns, "Town and Country's Exclusive Directory of Outstanding Medical Specialists in the U.S.," *Town and Country,* October/November 1989.

refer to surveys of academic department chairs and section chiefs of major medical centers.[12] Publishing these lists is consistent with the growing realization that individuals not only can influence their own health care status by lifestyle choices but also can influence the outcome of their own treatment by judicious selection of hospital, mode of treatment, and physician.

The most important conclusion that follows from the observation that the medical marketplace is complex is the necessity of creating an institutional environment in which "experts" will find it in their self-interest to give us accurate information and wise advice. And the best way to create that environment is to empower patients by giving them greater control over health care dollars. Let us now turn to ways in which public policies can be changed to help achieve that goal.

[12]Maxine Abrams, "The 400 Best Doctors in America," *Good Housekeeping*, March 1991.

3. Moving toward the Ideal: An Agenda for Change

The message coming to our shores from virtually every corner of the globe is: Free markets work and socialism, collectivism, and bureaucracies do not. For the most part, Americans find that message a welcome one. But in the area of health care, the message is falling on deaf ears.

It is worth repeating, therefore, why the message is true. In a market system, the pursuit of self-interest is usually consistent with social goals. When one individual pursues his own interest, his actions usually benefit others as well. Precisely the reverse is true in bureaucratic, nonmarket systems. The social goal may be clearly articulated, but each individual in the bureaucratic system finds it in his self-interest to take actions that defeat that goal.

The hallmark of bureaucratic thinking is the belief that individuals don't matter. All that matters is the social plan and the intelligence and ability of the people administering it. The hallmark of the economic way of thinking is the realization that neither the plan nor the people who administer it matter very much. What really matters is what is in the self-interest of the individuals who actively participate in the system.

Viewed in this way, it is obvious that we cannot solve America's health care crisis if 250 million Americans find it in their self-interest to act in ways that make the crisis worse. By contrast, the crisis will be solved if 250 million Americans find it in their self-interest to take actions that promote solutions. Accordingly, this chapter explores ways of changing the institutional environment in which health care is delivered, with the goal of making problem-solving a matter of individual self-interest.

We cannot dismantle the current health care system overnight. We can move in the right direction, however, by adopting policies that promote the development of an ideal system and by eliminating policies that make such a system unattainable. The policy agenda described in this chapter is designed to remove harmful, government-created obstacles and to create new incentives under which people will be encouraged to solve problems through individual initiative and choice. Specifically, this agenda would

- Give individuals greater opportunity to purchase no-frills catastrophic insurance for a reasonable price.
- Give individuals greater opportunity to choose among competing health insurance plans and to select the type of coverage best suited to their individual and family needs.
- Give individuals the opportunity to choose between employer-provided group health insurance and individual or family policies—without income tax penalties.
- Give individuals the opportunity to choose between self-insurance and third-party insurance for small medical bills—without income tax penalties.
- Give individuals the opportunity to choose health insurance plans with effective cost-control techniques and to realize the financial benefits from making such choices—without income tax penalties.
- Give individuals the opportunity to build a reserve of savings for future medical expenses, so that they can rely less on third-party insurance and reduce their annual health insurance premiums.
- Give individuals greater opportunity to compare prices in the hospital marketplace and realize the financial benefits of prudent buying practices.
- Give people covered by Medicare and Medicaid opportunities to avoid the harmful effects of health care rationing.
- Give suppliers of medical services new opportunities to search for cost-reducing ways of delivering medical care.
- Give all participants in the medical marketplace an opportunity to avoid the costly effects of the tort system through voluntary contract and exchange.
- Give local communities new options to meet the needs of underserved populations and to create a genuine safety net—unburdened by restrictive, cost-increasing regulations.

- Give rural residents and the urban poor new opportunities to meet their health care needs—unburdened by unnecessary, cost-increasing regulations.
- Give physicians and hospitals providing charity care a fairer way to receive compensation for their services.
- Give all Americans the opportunity to gain from a more rational expenditure of public health care dollars.

Fifteen Policy Proposals

In what follows, we briefly describe 15 changes that are needed and the reasons for these changes.[1] Many of these issues will be discussed at greater length in other chapters in this book.

1. Establishing Equity in Taxation

Under current law, health insurance provided by an employer is excluded from the taxable wages of the employees, but insurance premiums paid by individuals are not tax deductible. Consequently, some people realize generous tax advantages from the purchase of health insurance, while others do not. A reasonable solution is to grant the same tax treatment with respect to health insurance to all Americans, regardless of employment and regardless of who purchases the health insurance policy—an individual, employer or self-employed person.

As Figure 3.1 shows, workers in the 28 percent federal income tax bracket face a marginal tax rate of 43.3 percent, leaving them with less than 57 cents in take-home pay out of each additional dollar of earnings. If state and local income taxes also apply,[2] the situation is much worse. Indeed, millions of American workers take home less than 50 cents of each dollar of earnings. Such high tax rates give employers and employees strong incentives to replace wages with nontaxable health insurance benefits, even if health insurance would not otherwise have been purchased. The total tax deduction for employer-provided health insurance is about $60 billion per year, or roughly $600 for every American family. Yet

---

[1]The policy agenda described in this chapter is based on solutions proposed in Task Force Report, *An Agenda for Solving America's Health Care Crisis*, NCPA Policy Report no. 151 (Dallas: National Center for Policy Analysis, May 1990). The first 10 points included here are taken from the task force report; the final 5 have been added.

[2]Tax rate equals 6 percent.

Figure 3.1
TAKE-HOME PAY FROM AN ADDITIONAL DOLLAR OF WAGES*

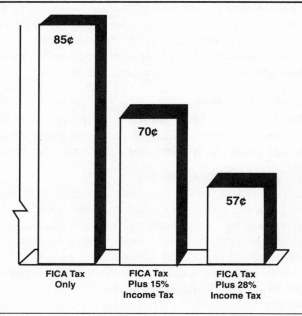

| FICA Tax Only | FICA Tax Plus 15% Income Tax | FICA Tax Plus 28% Income Tax |

*Includes employer's share of FICA taxes.

most of the 34.4 million individuals who do not have health insurance (including about 18.8 million with a family member in the workforce[3]) and about 12 percent of insured individuals who purchase health insurance on their own receive no tax subsidy. As a result, some employees of large companies have lavish health insurance, totally tax deductible, while other Americans have none.

In general, the value of the right to exclude health insurance coverage from taxable wages ranges from about $1,200 per year in reduced taxes for an auto worker to about $300 for a worker in the

[3]Jill D. Foley, *Uninsured in the United States: The Nonelderly Population without Health Insurance* (Washington: Employee Benefit Research Institute, April 1991), Table 1, p. 21.

retail trade.[4] Yet, self-employed individuals,[5] the unemployed, and employees of firms that do not provide health insurance receive little or no tax deduction for the health insurance they purchase. Not surprisingly, people respond to such incentives. About 92 percent of Americans who have private health insurance acquired it through an employer.[6] The more generous the tax subsidy, the more likely people are to have health insurance. Those most likely to be uninsured are people who receive no tax subsidy.

If it is desirable for people to have health insurance, and if we care about equity, then all Americans should receive the same tax encouragement to purchase health insurance, regardless of employment. Accordingly, the self-employed, the unemployed, and employees who purchase health insurance on their own should be entitled to a tax deduction or tax credit that is just as generous as the tax treatment they would have received if their policies had been provided by an employer. (This issue is considered in greater detail in chapter 9.)

2. Equalizing Tax Advantages for Families with Unequal Incomes

Under the current system, the ability to exclude employer-provided health insurance from taxable income is more valuable to people in higher tax brackets. However, if it is socially desirable to use the income tax system to encourage families to purchase health insurance for large medical bills, then all families should receive the same encouragement.

For a low-income worker who is paying no income tax, federal tax law makes a dollar of health insurance benefits equivalent to $1.18 in wages. For a worker who is in the 28 percent bracket and paying the Social Security (FICA) tax, a dollar of health insurance benefits is equivalent to $1.76 in wages.[7] Because the value of the

---

[4]Aldona Robbins and Gary Robbins, *What a Canadian-Style Health Care Scheme Would Cost U.S. Employers and Their Employees*, NCPA Policy Report no. 145 (Dallas: National Center for Policy Analysis, February 1990).

[5]Currently, the self-employed are allowed to deduct 25 percent of health insurance premiums, a deduction that must be periodically reaffirmed by Congress and is threatened in every congressional budget negotiation.

[6]Foley, Table 17 (pp. 46–47).

[7]The value of the benefit equals $1/(1-t)$, where t is the marginal federal income tax rate plus the combined employer-employee Social Security payroll tax rate. For a worker in the 15 percent bracket, $t = 0.15 + 0.153$. For a worker in the 28 percent bracket, $t = 0.28 + 0.153$.

Figure 3.2
PERCENT OF NONELDERLY POPULATION COVERED BY EMPLOYER-PROVIDED HEALTH INSURANCE, 1989

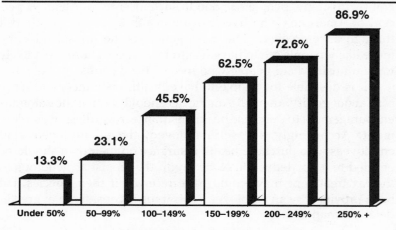

Income as a Percentage of Poverty Level

SOURCE: C. Eugene Steuerle, "Finance-Based Reform: The Search for an Adaptable Health Policy," paper presented at an American Enterprise Institute conference, "American Health Policy" (Washington, October 3–4, 1991).

tax subsidy rises with income, it is hardly surprising that the lower a family's income, the less likely the family is to have health insurance. About 61 percent of all people who lack health insurance have annual incomes of less than $20,000.[8] As Figure 3.2 shows, among people with incomes at least 2.5 times the poverty level, about 87 percent have employer-provided health insurance. Only a small fraction of those at or below the poverty level have it, however. As a result, the current system is highly regressive, conferring the largest subsidies on those families with the highest incomes. As Figure 3.3 shows, families in the top fifth of the income distribution receive an annual subsidy of about $1,560 per year. By contrast, families in the bottom fifth receive an annual subsidy of only $270, on the average.

[8]Foley. Not all people who lack health insurance have low incomes. About one-fifth have family incomes in excess of $30,000.

Figure 3.3
AVERAGE VALUE OF ANNUAL FEDERAL TAX SUBSIDIES FOR EMPLOYER-PROVIDED HEALTH INSURANCE, 1992*

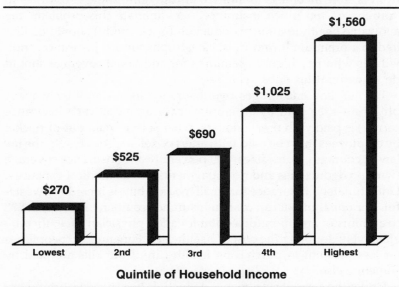

Quintile of Household Income

SOURCE: C. Eugene Steuerle, "Finance-Based Reform: The Search for an Adaptable Health Policy," paper presented at an American Enterprise Institute conference, "American Health Policy" (Washington, October 3–4, 1991).

*Revenue loss includes both Social Security (FICA) and income taxes.

To give all people the same economic incentives to purchase health insurance, premiums paid by employers should be included in the gross wages of their employees, and all taxpayers should receive a tax credit equal to, say, 30 percent of the premium.[9] That would make the tax subsidy for health insurance the same for all taxpayers, regardless of income and regardless of whether the policies are purchased individually or by employers. For individuals who pay no federal income tax, the tax credit could be made refundable. (This proposal would also have other advantages, as discussed below.)

[9]See the discussion in Stuart Butler and Edmund Haislmaier, eds., *A National Health System for America*, rev. ed. (Washington: Heritage Foundation, 1989).

43

3. Ending Tax Subsidies for Wasteful Health Insurance

Under the current system, the ability to exclude health insurance from taxable income is unlimited, encouraging some employees to "purchase" too much insurance. To eliminate this problem, the allowable health insurance deduction (or tax credit) should be limited to a premium for no-frills, catastrophic health insurance. Individuals who pay higher premiums for additional coverage should do so without tax subsidy.

The tax law encourages overinsurance in yet another way. A physician's fee paid by an employer (or an employer's insurance carrier) is paid with pretax dollars, whereas fees paid out-of-pocket by employees must be paid with aftertax dollars. As a result, the tax law encourages (subsidizes) 100 percent health insurance coverage (with no deductibles and no copayments) for all medical expenses. Unfortunately, insurance for small medical bills is incredibly wasteful. For one thing, it can cost an insurance company more than $25 to administer and monitor a claim for a $25 physician's fee, thereby effectively doubling the cost of health care. For another, people are far less prudent in purchasing health care if the bills are paid by someone else.

Under the current system, tax-deductible health insurance expenditures range from a high of $3,055 a year under the generous health care plans provided by the automobile manufacturers to as little as $793 a year, which is the average for workers in retail trade. Although this system may appear to benefit large companies with highly paid employees, in the short run many companies are trapped by benefit plans that eat into company profits and raise production costs. In the long run, lavish health plans mean lower aftertax wages. The current system not only encourages and subsidizes rising health care costs but also harms the very industries and companies that are subsidized the most.

To correct this abuse, national policy should encourage individuals to purchase health insurance for catastrophic medical expenses and to save to pay small medical expenses with their own funds.

4. Creating Individual Self-Insurance for Small Medical Bills

The easiest way to hold down health insurance premium increases is to choose policies with high deductibles. On a representative individual health insurance policy for a middle-aged male,

Table 3.1

COST OF EACH ADDITIONAL DOLLAR OF HEALTH INSURANCE
COVERAGE IN CALIFORNIA*

Age of Head of Family	Lowering Deductible from $1,000 to $500	Lowering Deductible from $500 to $250
Under 30	$2.52	$2.22
30–39	2.16	3.60
40–49	2.82	4.68
50–59	3.90	5.04
60–64	2.04	10.14

SOURCE: Blue Cross of Southern California, 1991.
*Based on Blue Cross plans sold in Orange, Santa Barbara, and Ventura counties in early 1991.

lowering the annual deductible from $1,000 to $500 costs 64 cents in additional premiums for each additional dollar of insurance coverage.[10] Lowering the deductible from $500 to $250 costs 74 cents in additional premiums for each additional dollar of insurance coverage. Although lower-deductible policies may occasionally be a good buy for a particular individual, they cannot possibly be a good buy for policyholders as a group, who will pay far more in premiums than they will collect in medical benefits.

For people who live in high-cost areas, low-deductible health insurance is even more wasteful. Consider, for example, the costs of lowering the deductible on a Blue Cross family policy in California. As Table 3.1 shows, any deductible lower than $1,000 is a terrible buy unless federal tax law offsets the waste in the manner described above. Suppose a 40-year-old living in Orange County, California, has a Blue Cross family policy with a $250 deductible. If the family chose a $1,000 deductible instead, it would give up $600 of health insurance coverage (since Blue Cross pays only 80 percent of the additional $750 of expenses). But in return, the family would cut its health insurance premiums by $2,064! Savings of this magnitude are not typical. However, this example illustrates dramatically that opportunities for saving do exist in the health insurance market.

[10]These calculations are based on policies sold by Golden Rule Insurance Company, the largest seller of individual and family health insurance policies in the country. Other insurance companies sell similar policies at similar prices.

Despite the fact that low-deductible insurance policies are often wasteful, the tax law encourages such policies and discourages high-deductible policies. On a $1,000-deductible policy, for example, the first $1,000 must be paid out-of-pocket with aftertax dollars. If that $1,000 were paid by employer-provided insurance, the premium could be paid with pretax dollars.

To eliminate the perverse incentives in the current system, individuals should be allowed to choose higher deductibles and deposit the premium savings in individual medical savings (Medisave) accounts. Such accounts would serve as self-insurance for small medical bills. Medisave accounts would be the private property of the account holder and become part of an individual's estate at the time of death. Contributions to Medisave accounts would receive the same tax encouragement as payments for conventional health insurance.[11]

Creating individual and family Medisave accounts (discussed in greater detail in chapter 8) would represent a major departure from the current system of paying for health care. These accounts would have immediate advantages that would become even more important over time. Because Medisave accounts would last over an individual's entire life, they would allow people to engage in lifetime planning—recognizing that health and medical expenses are related to choices that people make throughout their lives. Moreover, Medisave accounts would eventually become an important source of funds from which to purchase health insurance or make direct payments for medical expenses not covered by Medicare during retirement.

5. Creating Freedom of Choice in Health Insurance

The number of Americans without health insurance now totals as many as 34.4 million people.[12] One reason so many lack health

---

[11]See John C. Goodman and Gerald L. Musgrave, *Controlling Health Care Costs with Medical Savings Accounts*, NCPA Policy Report no. 168 (Dallas: National Center for Policy Analysis, January 1992).

[12]This is the estimate of the Employee Benefit Research Institute; see Foley. Other estimates place the number closer to 30 million. See the review of the literature in Michael A. Morrisey, "Health Care Reform: A Review of Five Generic Proposals," paper presented at a policy forum, "Winners and Losers in Reforming the U.S. Health Care System," sponsored by the Employee Benefit Research Institute Education and Research Fund (Washington: October 4, 1990).

insurance is the existence of state regulations. State-mandated benefits, along with other state regulations, are increasing the cost of health insurance and pricing as many as one out of every four uninsured people out of the market.[13] A reasonable solution is to allow individuals to buy no-frills health insurance tailored to individual and family needs.

In recent years, there has been an explosion of state laws requiring health insurance policies to cover specific diseases and specific health care services. These laws are called mandated health insurance benefit laws. In 1970, there were only 48 such laws in the United States. Today there are more than 1,000, with legislation enacted by every state in the union.

Mandated benefits (examined in greater detail in chapter 11) cover ailments ranging from AIDS to alcoholism and drug abuse, and services ranging from acupuncture to in vitro fertilization. They cover everything from life-prolonging procedures to purely cosmetic devices: heart transplants in Georgia, liver transplants in Illinois, hairpieces in Minnesota, marriage counseling in California, pastoral counseling in Vermont, and deposits to sperm banks in Massachusetts. These laws reflect the influence of special-interest groups that now represent virtually every disease, disability, and health care service.[14]

Currently, 45 states require health insurance coverage for the services of chiropractors, four states mandate coverage for acupuncture, and two states require coverage for naturopaths (who specialize in prescribing herbs). At least 13 states limit the ability of insurers to avoid covering people who have AIDS or a high risk of getting AIDS. Forty states mandate coverage for alcoholism, 27 states mandate coverage for drug addiction, and 29 states mandate coverage for mental illness. Seven states even mandate coverage for in vitro fertilization.[15]

Collectively, state mandates add considerably to the cost of health insurance, and they prevent people from buying no-frills insurance

---

[13]See John C. Goodman and Gerald L. Musgrave, *Freedom of Choice in Health Insurance*, NCPA Policy Report no. 134 (Dallas: National Center for Policy Analysis, November 1988).

[14]Ibid.

[15]*Health Benefits Letter* 1, no. 15 (August 29, 1991).

Figure 3.4
INCREASES IN INSURANCE PREMIUMS CAUSED BY SPECIFIC HEALTH INSURANCE BENEFITS

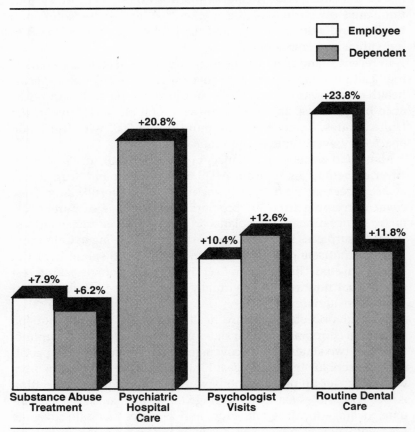

SOURCE: Gail A. Jensen (Wayne State University) and Michael A. Morrisey (University of Alabama at Birmingham), "The Premium Consequences of Group Health Insurance Provisions" (September 1988), mimeograph.

at a reasonable price. As Figure 3.4 shows, mandated coverage can increase premiums by 6 to 8 percent for substance abuse, by 10 to 13 percent for outpatient mental health care, and by as much as 21 percent for psychiatric hospital care for employee dependents.

Employees of the federal government, Medicare enrollees, and employees of self-insured companies are exempt from these costly regulations under federal law. Often, state governments exempt Medicaid patients and state employees. The full burden, therefore, falls on the employees of small businesses, the self-employed, and the unemployed—the groups that are increasingly uninsured.

Freedom of choice in health insurance means being able to buy a health insurance policy tailored to individual and family needs. That freedom is rapidly vanishing. To restore it, insurers should be permitted to sell federally qualified health insurance both to individuals and to groups. This insurance should be free from state-mandated benefits, state premium taxes, and mandatory contributions to state risk pools.

6. *Giving Employers and Employees New Options for Cost Containment and Individual Freedom of Choice*

Under current employee benefits law, employers have few opportunities to institute sound cost-containment practices without substantial income tax penalties, and employees have few opportunities to purchase less costly or more appropriate health insurance. To eliminate these problems, health insurance benefits should be personal and portable, with each employee free to choose an individual policy that would remain with the employee in case of a job change. Health insurance benefits should be included in the gross wages of employees who would be entitled to tax credits for premiums on their personal tax returns, so that employees reap the direct benefits of prudent choices and bear the direct costs of wasteful ones.

Suppose a small firm considers purchasing an individual policy for each employee to take advantage of the favorable tax treatment of health insurance. As Table 3.2 shows, the firm immediately is faced with four problems. First, the cost of the policy varies with the employee's age (a 60-year-old male, for example, is about four times more expensive to insure than a 20-year-old male). The obvious solution is to pay the premiums for the policies and reduce each worker's salary by the premium amount. Second, not all employees want health insurance (for example, some may be covered by a spouse's policy). The obvious solution is to give health insurance only to those who want it, reducing the salary of each by the amount of the premium. Third, some employees may have preexisting illnesses for which the insurer wants exclusions and riders. The

49

Table 3.2
SOLVING HEALTH INSURANCE PROBLEMS FOR SMALL EMPLOYERS AND THEIR EMPLOYEES*

Problem	Solution
Costs differ by age, sex, type of job, and other employee characteristics	Reduce each employee's gross salary by the amount of that employee's premium
Not all employees want or need employer-provided coverage	Give health insurance only to employees who want it
Some employees have preexisting illnesses	Negotiate the best coverage possible for each individual employee
Employees have different preferences about health insurance coverage (deductibles, services covered, etc.)	Allow each employee to choose a policy best suited to individual and family needs

*Each of these solutions requires changes in the tax law and employee benefits law to avoid costly tax penalties.

obvious solution is to negotiate the best possible deal for each employee. Fourth, employees may have different preferences about the content of their policies. Some may want to trade off a higher deductible for a lower premium. Others may want coverage for different types of illnesses and medical services (for example, infertility coverage). The obvious solution is to let each employee choose a policy suited to his or her needs and preferences.

Despite the obviousness of these solutions and the fact that each employee may gain from them, they are generally forbidden under federal law. In general, the tax law prevents employees from choosing between wages and health insurance and insists that all be offered the same coverage on the same terms. The result is that the employer must turn to a more expensive group policy with a package of benefits that no single employee may want. To make matters worse, the employer is forced to adopt a health care plan in which benefits are individualized but costs are collectivized.

Although large employers have a few more options, they too are forced into a system that has two devastating defects. First, because there is no direct relationship between health insurance premium costs and individual employee wages, employees see no relationship between the cost of employer-provided health insurance and personal take-home pay. Second, because there is no relationship between imprudent health care purchases and salary under conventional employer health plans, employees have no personal incentives to be prudent buyers of health care.

In the face of constraints imposed by federal policy, employers are trying to hold down health care costs by taking actions that have very negative social consequences. Unable to adopt a sensible approach to employee health insurance, many large firms are asking employees to pay (with aftertax dollars) a larger share of the premium.[16] Often, employers pay most of the premium for each employee, but ask the employees to pay a much larger share for their dependents.[17] Such practices result in some employees' opting not to buy into an employer's group health insurance plan. More frequently, they choose coverage for themselves but drop coverage for their dependents. Indeed, three million people who lack health insurance are dependents of employees who are themselves insured.[18]

Because employee benefits law prevents smaller firms from adopting a sensible approach to employee health insurance, many firms are responding to rising health insurance premiums by canceling their group policies altogether. Often, they then give bonuses or raises to their employees and encourage them to purchase individual health insurance policies (with aftertax dollars) on their own. Many employees, of course, do not do so. One of the great ironies of employee benefits law is that, although it was designed to

[16]In most large companies, employees can pay their share of the premium with pretax dollars under salary-reduction agreements with employers or through "flexible spending accounts." These options exist under section 125 of the Internal Revenue Code. However, the costs of setting up section 125 plans are often prohibitive for small employers. On the options for large employers, see Alain Enthoven, "Health Tax Policy Mismatch," *Health Affairs* (Winter 1985), pp. 5–13.

[17]Kenneth H. Bacon, "Business and Labor Reach a Consensus on Need to Reduce Health Care Costs," *Wall Street Journal*, November 1, 1989.

[18]Employee Benefit Research Institute, *A Profile of the Nonelderly Population without Health Insurance*, EBRI Issue Brief no. 66 (May 1987), p. 7.

encourage the purchase of health insurance, its more perverse provisions are increasing the number of people without health insurance. Because employers cannot individualize health insurance benefits, many are turning to other practices that are increasing the number of uninsured people.

To remedy these problems we recommend that: (1) health insurance benefits be made personal and portable; (2) health insurance premiums be included in the gross wages of employees with tax credits for those premiums allowed on individual tax returns; (3) individual employees be given an opportunity to choose between lower wages and more health insurance coverage (or vice versa); and (4) individual employees be given freedom of choice among all health insurance policies sold in the marketplace.

If implemented, these recommendations would have five major advantages:

1. Rising health care costs would no longer be a problem for employers, since health insurance premiums would be a direct substitute for wages.
2. Employees would have opportunities to choose lower cost policies and higher take-home pay.
3. Employees would have the opportunity to select policies tailored to their individual and family needs.
4. Employees would be able to retain the tax advantages of the current system but avoid the waste inherent in collectivized benefits.
5. Employees would be able to continue coverage at actuarially fair prices if they quit work or switched jobs.

When there is a direct link between salary and health insurance premiums, employees will be more prudent about the policy they choose. For example, those who want policies with no deductibles and all the bells and whistles will pay the full premium cost in the form of a salary reduction. Faced with this choice, employees are more likely to choose high-deductible, no-frills catastrophic coverage.[19]

7. Introducing Freedom of Information in the Hospital Marketplace

Because they lack access to the necessary information, individual patients often are unable to play an effective role in containing

[19]See Butler and Haislmaier, *A National Health System for America*, rev. ed., ch. 3.

52

hospital costs. In most American cities, patients cannot find out a hospital's total charge for a procedure prior to treatment. At the time of discharge, they learn there is not one price but hundreds of line item prices for everything from a single Tylenol capsule to the hospital's admission kit. After a patient has been in the hospital for only a few days, a typical bill can stretch many feet in length. If restaurants priced their services the way hospitals do, at the end of an evening meal customers would be charged for each time they had used the salt shaker, taken a pat of butter, and had their water glass refilled. There would, however, be this difference: at least they could read the restaurant's bill.

About 90 percent of the items listed on a hospital bill are unreadable. In only a handful of cases can patients both recognize what service was rendered and judge whether the charge is reasonable. For example, $15 for a Tylenol capsule is common but clearly outrageous, as is $25 for an admission kit. In other cases, patients may recognize the service but have no idea whether they are being overcharged. What's a "reasonable" price for an x-ray, a complete blood count, or a urinalysis? The patient who tries to find out is in for another surprise. Prices for items such as these can vary as much as five to one among hospitals within walking distance of each other, and in most cases the prices charged bear no relationship to the real cost of providing the service.

Patients who try to find out about prices prior to admission face another surprise. A single hospital can have as many as 12,000 different line item prices. For example, for patients doing comparison shopping among the 50 hospitals in the Chicago area, there are as many as 600,000 prices to compare. To make matters worse, different hospitals frequently use different accounting systems. As a result, the definition of a service may differ from hospital to hospital.

Although hospital administrators do not have to give patients advance notice of their total bill, hospitals in Illinois are required to tell the state government. The following are some examples of total charges for outpatient services reported by Chicago hospitals in 1988: The charge for a mammogram varied from $13 to $127 (a difference of almost 10 to 1), the charge for a CAT scan varied from $59 to $635 (a difference of more than 10 to 1), tonsillectomy charges ranged from $125 to $3,365 (a difference of 27 to 1), and cataract removal charges varied from $125 to $4,279 (a difference of 34 to 1).[20] If patients knew about these differences, they could significantly reduce their medical bills. Unfortunately, most do not.

Hospital prices today are an unfortunate remnant of the system of cost-plus hospital finance. Because 90 percent of hospital revenue came from insurers who reimbursed on the basis of costs, a hospital's line item prices were relevant only for a small fraction of the hospital's income—the 10 percent paid out-of-pocket by patients. Hospital line item prices were used in some of the more complicated cost-plus reimbursement formulas, however. This gave hospitals an incentive to manipulate third-party reimbursements through artificial pricing. Hospital prices quickly became artifacts rather than real prices determined by supply and demand.

We cannot possibly control spiraling health care costs unless patients can make prudent buying decisions. That cannot happen unless patients are given package prices prior to hospital admission. Accordingly, any hospital that receives Medicare money should be required to quote preadmission prices—either per procedure or per diem—to all patients.[21] This is a requirement to quote prices, not an attempt to create price controls. Hospitals would remain free to charge any price to any patient.

What do hospital managers say about quoting preadmission, package prices for surgery? That depends. Publicly, they say that such a system would not work because physicians cannot predict in advance what complications will arise (and therefore what costs will be) with respect to any particular patient's surgery. Privately, they are already quoting package prices to major third-party buyers of health care. In late 1990, for example, the St. Louis Area Business Coalition on Health formally and publicly requested the area's 40 hospitals to voluntarily submit their retail prices for 205 different patient services. There was apparently considerable controversy about the proposal and what it might portend for the future. In a follow-up survey of the heads of state hospital associations, 73

---

[20]Illinois Health Care Cost Containment Council, *A Report of Selected Prices at Illinois Hospitals: Outpatient Services* (August 1989).

[21]In some cases, for example exploratory surgery, a hospital might quote "not to exceed" prices.

percent of the respondents said they would oppose public disclosure of their retail prices.[22]

On the other hand, the practice of quoting preadmission prices is far more common than many people believe. In 1983, the federal government began paying fixed prices to hospitals for surgical procedures classified in one of 467 diagnosis-related groups (DRGs). Many states reimburse hospitals in a similar way through their Medicaid programs. Although hospital managers complain (justifiably, in many cases) that the DRG payments are too low, many hospitals voluntarily charge (higher) DRG prices or fixed per diem prices to large third-party payers. In Nebraska, for example, Blue Cross reimburses almost all hospitals based on prospective DRG rates.

A more radical move would be to combine the hospital charges with surgeons' fees and other charges into a single package price, covering all costs of surgery. A step in this direction was recently taken as part of a demonstration project undertaken by the Health Care Financing Administration, the organization that administers Medicare.[23] Medicare has contracted with four major hospitals to provide heart bypass surgery at fixed prices. When Medicare announced its intention to conduct this three-year project, more than 200 hospitals applied to participate. Although Medicare did not select hospitals on the basis of price, the agreed-upon prices are between 5 percent and 20 percent below the amount Medicare was paying when all of the components of the surgery were reimbursed separately.

The Medicare demonstration project is not unique. Individual hospitals and hospital groups are forming "centers of excellence" and bidding in a national market for the right to perform as many as 25 types of high-cost surgery. A Houston hospital, for example, has approached Blue Cross of Indiana with an offer to perform all of its bypass surgery for half of what Blue Cross would normally pay.[24] With some of the best heart surgeons in the country, the Houston hospital offers high-quality surgery at a price that often

[22]David Burda, "Many State Hospital Association Presidents Would Resist Efforts to Establish Price Lists," *Modern Healthcare*, January 28, 1991, p. 34.

[23]Hilary Stout, "Medicare Starts Experimental Program to Curb Costs of Heart Bypass Surgery," *Wall Street Journal*, January 31, 1991, p. B5.

[24]Authors' communication.

includes the patient's airfare, as well as airfare and room and board (at the hospital) for the patient's spouse.

The concept of a package price covering all services has been common for years in the field of cosmetic surgery. Similarly, some physicians or optometrists quote fixed prices for performing refractions and fitting contact lenses, and dentists often quote fixed prices for new dentures. Of course, the underlying variation in costs for these procedures is small, so the provider is not at great risk when charging a package price. But in at least a third of the DRG categories, the variation in costs is also quite small. For high-ticket items such as heart surgery, costs can vary a great deal. But the market is showing us that, when the volume for these types of surgery is high, many hospitals are willing to charge a package price and accept the risk.

8. Encouraging Savings for Postretirement Medical Expenses

One of the greatest social challenges we face as we move toward the next century is paying retirement pensions and medical expenses for the elderly. Because both Social Security and Medicare are pay-as-you-go programs in which there is no current saving to meet future obligations, tomorrow's obligations will have to be met mainly by taxes on tomorrow's workers. The bill will be high. According to reasonable projections (see chapter 13), by the year 2000, total health care expenses for the elderly will equal 14 percent of workers' payroll, and health care plus Social Security will equal 26 percent. By the year 2050, total health care spending for the elderly will equal 55 percent of payroll, and health care plus Social Security will equal 78 percent.[25]

Currently, the elderly pay about one-third of their own health care expenses. Even if we can continue that practice, the future burden on workers will be enormous. The combined burden of elderly health care and Social Security will be 21.5 percent of payroll by the year 2000, and could reach 60 percent of payroll by the year 2050.[26]

---

[25]These projections are based on assumptions used in the Social Security Administration's pessimistic projections. See John C. Goodman and Gerald L. Musgrave, *Health Care after Retirement*, NCPA Policy Report no. 139 (Dallas: National Center for Policy Analysis, June 1989), Table III (p. 6).

[26]Ibid.

Although the federal government subsidizes spending on current medical needs to the tune of $60 billion a year, individuals receive no tax subsidy when they save for postretirement medical needs.[27] Corporations also are greatly constrained by current tax law in their ability to set aside funds today for the postretirement health care expenses of their employees. As a result, the federal government is encouraging employers and employees to adopt the same pay-as-you-go approach that characterizes Medicare and other government health care programs for the elderly. Currently, unfunded liabilities for U.S. employers for postretirement health care exceed $300 billion. If these liabilities had been accounted for in 1989, they would have reduced corporate earnings of companies with postretirement health care liabilities by 33 percent—and their net worth by 30 percent.[28]

To address this problem, individuals and employers must be encouraged to save and invest today for future health care expenses. One method would be to use deposits to Medisave accounts, which would grow tax-free and provide funds for medical expenses (including nursing home care and long-term care insurance) not now covered by Medicare. More is needed, however.

Individuals and their employers should be given tax incentives to contribute to Medical IRA (MIRA) accounts. Funds deposited to MIRAs would substitute for future claims against Medicare. By making annual contributions over time, people would rely more on private savings to support their postretirement medical needs, and less on Medicare. Eventually, we would move to a postretirement health care system in which each generation pays its own way and in which postretirement health care dollars become the private property of the elderly, out of reach of politicians and special-interest bureaucracies (see chapter 15).[29]

[27]Jonathan C. Dopkeen, *Postretirement Health Benefits,* Pew Memorial Trust Policy Synthesis 2, Health Services Research 21, no. 6 (February 1987): 810.

[28]Mark J. Warshawsky, "Retiree Health Benefits: Promises Uncertain?" *The American Enterprise* (July/August 1991), p. 63. Corporations will be required to estimate their liabilities and account for them beginning in 1993. See discussion in chapter 13 of this book.

[29]In principle, there could be three types of deductible deposits to the same account: one for savings for current medical expenses, a second for funds to supplement Medicare during retirement, and a third to replace Medicare. Institutions that manage these accounts would keep separate balances for each of the three purposes.

9. Creating Catastrophic Health Insurance Coverage for the Elderly

The Medicare program pays too many small medical bills that the elderly could easily afford to pay out-of-pocket, but it leaves Medicare beneficiaries exposed to the risk of a catastrophic medical event, such as Alzheimer's disease, requiring an expensive nursing home stay. To address this problem, private insurers should be given the opportunity to repackage Medicare benefits and compete for customers based on the package of benefits they offer.

A major reason why Congress was unable in 1989 to solve the problem of catastrophic coverage for the elderly was the fact (as discussed in chapter 15) that Medicare is a one-size-fits-all insurance policy designed for a very diverse group. Because the elderly who have few assets would be on Medicaid anyway, they are less interested in a catastrophic health care bill than in coverage for small medical bills. The elderly who have substantial assets are capable of paying several thousand dollars of small medical bills each year, but do need catastrophic coverage.

Private health insurers should have the opportunity to repackage Medicare benefits by offering private policies as an alternative to Medicare. The only required benefit would be catastrophic hospital insurance. If an elderly person chose a private insurer, the insurer would receive 95 percent of the actuarially fair value of Medicare insurance. For example, a private insurer might offer Medicare beneficiaries a policy with a $2,000 hospital deductible, a $2,000 physician deductible, and a combined deductible of $3,000. In return for these higher deductibles, the insurer might offer immediate nursing home coverage for Alzheimer's disease and an expanding nursing home benefit for other illnesses, depending on the number of years of coverage.[30]

Currently Medicare offers the 95 percent option to health maintenance organizations (HMOs), provided that they cover all of the benefits prescribed by Medicare. The same offer should be open to other insurers, who would compete for patients, and HMOs and other insurers should be free to repackage the benefits in ways attractive to Medicare beneficiaries. No one should be forced to

[30]Under this proposal, private insurers could reimburse hospitals at Medicare's fixed DRG rates. They could also seek less expensive ways to deliver medical care. For a similar proposal, see Peter Ferrara, "Health Care and the Elderly," in Butler and Haislmaier, pp. 85–87.

participate, but these alternative plans could provide needed services, equity, and efficiency for the beneficiaries.

10. *Empowering Medicaid and Medicare Patients*

Medicare and Medicaid are price-fixing schemes in which the level of reimbursement is often too low to ensure high-quality health care. The result increasingly is implicit and sometimes explicit health care rationing. To deal with this problem, Medicare and Medicaid patients should have the right to circumvent the normal reimbursement rules in ways that empower them and make them full participants in the medical marketplace.

In virtually every state, the people who matter least in the construction of health care programs for the poor are poor people. Far from empowering the indigent, the health care poverty industry consists of relationships between large bureaucracies in which poor patients are an excuse for the transfers of large sums of money.

The Medicaid program in many states pays about half as much as other insurers for comparable services. In itself, such a practice is not bad. Medicaid patients may have to wait for a hospital bed in order to obtain elective surgery, but in return for waiting they receive free medical care. What is bad is that they have no input into the terms of the discount or the conditions of the surgery, and they have increasingly fewer options in the market for any medical service. The reason is that Medicaid patients are not the principal clients of the medical community; the Medicaid bureaucracy is. The type of medical service the patients receive is often dictated by the amount the bureaucracy will pay. Patients cannot add to this amount to purchase higher quality service.

Nationwide, "good" doctors increasingly will not see Medicaid patients, especially for prenatal care. Some who do see them often practice revolving door medicine in which the objective is to service patients—and submit Medicaid reimbursement forms—as quickly as possible. To make matters worse, state laws generally prohibit nurse practitioners and physicians' assistants (including people who gave medical care to our troops in Vietnam and the Persian Gulf) from providing low-income patients with primary care services. The result is a continuing deterioration in the quality of care that Medicaid patients receive. In some places, outright rationing schemes have been installed—schemes constructed by the health care bureaucracy, not by the patients themselves.

As an initial step toward empowering patients and dismantling the Medicaid bureaucracy, we should identify areas in which to suspend the normal reimbursement rules. Pregnant women on Medicaid, for example, should have an account to draw on for prenatal care. They should be able to add personal funds to this account, negotiate prices, and pay any amount they choose for prenatal care from any physician. They should also be allowed to share in any cost savings they achieve.

Similar reforms are needed under Medicare. Medicare's DRG system for reimbursing hospitals is not structured so that government is simply one more buyer in a competitive market. Instead, the system is a price-fixing scheme in which the government attempts to create an artificial market. Medicare literally fixes the price of services rendered, independent of supply and demand, forbidding hospitals to charge more than the DRG price even to patients willing to pay more. Medicare also prohibits hospitals from giving rebates to patients who use their services. Moreover, a single, national rate of reimbursement that ignores local differences is under consideration, and plans are also under way to include physicians' services in fixed DRG payments.[31]

Attempting to establish an artificial market creates perverse incentives for providers, which may adversely affect patients' health and may even increase health care costs. At the most basic level, in any price-fixing scheme the price can be set either too high or too low. If it's too high, the system encourages too many medical procedures, as was the case under pure cost-plus reimbursement. If it's too low, the system encourages too few.

In principle, the DRG price covers the average cost of treatment for hospitals that treat a wide variety of patients. But it is unlikely that any particular hospital will have an "average" case load. Clearly, survival in the hospital marketplace in this system means attracting below-average-cost patients and avoiding above-average-cost patients. Who are the high-cost patients? They are the sickest

[31]See Robert Pear, "Government Seeks New Cost Control on Medicare Plan," *New York Times*, June 9, 1991. Under a Health Care Financing Administration (HCFA) contract, 3M Health Information Systems developed 297 ambulatory patient groups similar to DRGs for inpatient services. The new regulations will probably become law in 1993. Current law requires the DRG system to be designed for the HCFA by October 1, 1991. See *Modern Healthcare*, June 24, 1991, p. 48.

Figure 3.5
HOSPITAL COST PER ADMISSION BY RACE*

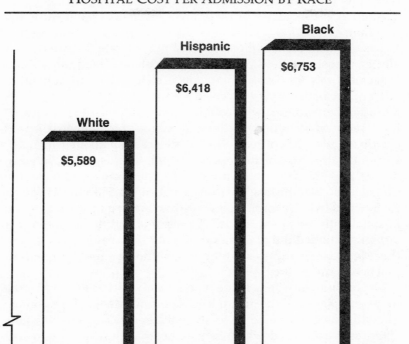

SOURCE: Eric Muñoz et al., "Race, DRGs, and the Consumption of Hospital Resources," *Health Affairs* (Spring 1989), p. 187.

*Based on admissions to Long Island Jewish Medical Center during 1985–87. Adjusted for DRG weight index.

patients, and more often than not they are low-income and non-white. For example, blacks and Hispanics have more severe illnesses, longer hospital stays, and (as Figure 3.5 shows) higher hospital costs than white patients, on the average.[32]

There is increasing evidence that hospitals are responding to the financial initiatives created by the DRG system. Thus, they give care readily and quickly to the "profitable" Medicare patients, but

[32]Eric Muñoz et al., "Race, DRGs, and the Consumption of Hospital Resources," *Health Affairs* (Spring 1989), p. 187.

slowly, reluctantly, and often of a lesser quality to the "unprofit-able" Medicare patients.

Another consequence of Medicare's method of payment is the rationing of medical technology. For example, although hearing loss is the most prevalent chronic disability among the elderly and affects almost one-third of all Medicare patients, Medicare's reim-bursement rate for cochlear implants is so low that only a handful of Medicare patients have received the treatment.[33] Of about 68,000 Medicare beneficiaries who could benefit from the device, only 69 have received it under Medicare reimbursement—which makes each patient's odds of receiving the device only about 1 in 1,000. Currently, the cost of the operation plus the device is between $25,000 and $35,000. But, on the average, Medicare reimburses only $10,500,[34] so that the hospital loses between $14,500 and $24,500 on each case. Medicare forbids patients from making up the loss to the hospital with their own funds. The result is that the technology is virtually rationed out of existence. Rather than being an anomaly, this Medicare financing strategy is likely to become the standard practice in the future.

The recommendations made here are only partial steps toward a more complete reform of the Medicaid and Medicare programs. The ultimate goal should be to allow the beneficiaries to negotiate all prices in a market in which they, rather than third-party bureauc-racies, are the principal buyers of health care. We should continue to limit the amount that taxpayers pay. But we should allow the market to determine the price and quality of health care.

11. Avoiding the Costs of the Tort System

No one knows how much the tort liability system adds to an average medical bill. Most people think the number is quite large. Apart from measurable items (such as attorneys' fees, court costs, damage awards, and settlement checks), there are thousands of unseen ways in which the tort system affects costs. Out of fear that adverse medical events will trigger a lawsuit, for example,

[33]Nancy M. Kane and Paul D. Manoukian, "The Effect of the Medicare Prospective Payment System on the Adoption of New Technology," *New England Journal of Medicine* 321, no. 21 (November 16, 1989): 1380.

[34]"Proposed Rate for Prospective Payment of Cochlear Implantation," *Government Affairs Review* (September/October 1990), p. 7.

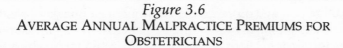

Figure 3.6
AVERAGE ANNUAL MALPRACTICE PREMIUMS FOR
OBSTETRICIANS

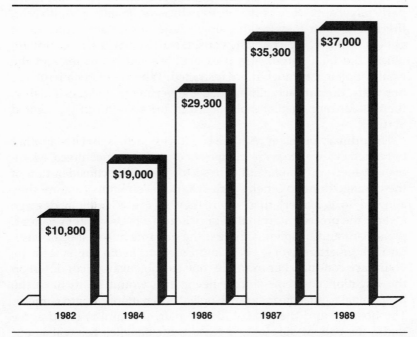

| $10,800 | $19,000 | $29,300 | $35,300 | $37,000 |
| 1982 | 1984 | 1986 | 1987 | 1989 |

SOURCE: Martin L. Gonzales, ed., *Socioeconomic Characteristics of Medical Practice* (Chicago: American Medical Association, 1991), Table 55, p. 147.

physicians order extra tests, perform extra procedures, and otherwise practice defensive medicine. The American Medical Association's Center for Health Policy Research estimates that physicians spent $4.2 billion on malpractice insurance premiums in 1989 and $12.8 billion more on defensive medicine, for a total of $17 billion. Other estimates place the number even higher.[35] As Figure 3.6 shows, insurance premiums for obstetricians soared during the 1980s and are much higher in areas where lawsuits are more likely. Obstetricians in New York's Nassau and Suffolk counties pay about

[35]See Peter W. Huber, *Liability: The Legal Revolution and Its Consequences* (New York: Basic Books, 1988).

$100,000 a year and obstetricians in southern Florida pay $200,000.[36] These costs ultimately are borne by patients and their insurers.

The tort system is not all bad. In an environment in which third-party payers pressure providers to reduce the quality of health care, the tort system may be the single most important protector of patient welfare. By contrast, consider a country such as Britain, where the quality-reducing pressures are much greater and the rights of plaintiffs much more restricted. When British patients sue hospitals, they are actually suing the government. Unquestionably, there is far more actual malpractice in Britain than in the United States.[37]

The primary problem with the U.S. tort system is that it is another bureaucracy, replete with its own set of perverse incentives. Moreover, it feeds off the health care sector with little consideration of the damage done to others. Juries do not even know (nor are they allowed to consider) that when they give a $5 million damage award, the precedent from that decision affects every other patient, physician, and hospital—not just the litigants in the specific case. To make matters worse, it is impossible to avoid the system by voluntary contract. For example, one sensible way to cut down on the litigation costs for simple negligence would be to have the hospital take out a life insurance policy on a patient prior to surgery. The hospital and the patient (or the patient's family) could agree that if the patient dies for any reason, the beneficiaries will accept the policy's payment as full compensation, even if there was negligence. The same principle could apply to other injuries, such as a disability leading to a loss of income. Litigation costs would be avoided, and life insurance companies would have incentives to monitor the quality of hospital care. But the current tort system does not permit such arrangements.[38]

Not only can patients and medical providers not get around the inefficiencies of the tort system by voluntary agreement, but the

[36]Milt Freudenheim, "Costs of Medical Malpractice Drop after an 11-Year Climb," *New York Times*, June 11, 1989.

[37]See John C. Goodman, *National Health Care in Great Britain: Lessons for the USA* (Dallas: Fisher Institute, 1980): 121–2.

[38]More precisely, the current system ignores contractual waivers of tort liability claims. What is needed is a legal change requiring the courts to honor certain types of contracts under which tort claims are waived in return for compensation.

tort system introduces a new set of perverse incentives that can be harmful to patients. Fear of tort liability is a strong incentive for medical providers to withhold and conceal information that is vitally important to patients. Most proposals to solve this problem would place arbitrary limits on the rights of plaintiffs in malpractice suits. Such proposals, while not all bad, attempt to solve problems by bureaucratic fiat rather than by voluntary exchanges that are mutually beneficial to both patients and providers. A more direct solution would be to give patients the right to make contractual agreements in their own interests. Patients should have the same rights as buyers in other markets, including the right to waive certain tort claims in return for reductions in the cost of services or for other monetary compensation.

12. Creating Medical Enterprise Zones

There are 111 rural counties in the United States that have no physician. About half a million rural people live in counties with no physician trained to provide obstetric care, and 49 million live in counties with no psychiatrist. Although hospitals are closing in most parts of the country, rural hospitals have been closing at twice the rate of urban hospitals.[39]

Many people assume that the only way to meet the health care needs of rural citizens is to spend more government money on rural health care programs. In fact, current government programs and policies are probably a far greater obstacle to good quality care at a reasonable price than is lack of funds.

As noted above, in most states, medics who treated soldiers in the field in the Vietnam War or the Persian Gulf War are not allowed to treat ordinary citizens, even if no doctor lives in the area. The same restrictions apply to nurses and physicians' assistants, despite studies showing that paramedical personnel can deliver certain kinds of primary care as well as—and sometimes better than—licensed physicians (see chapter 5).[40]

Many state and federal regulations discriminate against rural areas in other ways. For example, Medicare rules require rural hospitals to maintain a staff of numerous professionals (whether

---

[39]For a survey of health care problems in rural areas, see U.S. Office of Technology Assessment, *Health Care in Rural America* (Washington: September 1990).

[40]See the discussion in chapter 5.

needed or not), including a full-time director of food and dietary services. State licensing laws often require rural hospitals to have fully equipped operating rooms and a surgical staff—even if the hospital performs no surgery.[41] These cost-increasing regulations may make sense in large urban areas, but in rural areas they often cause existing facilities to close and prevent new facilities from opening.

The concept behind Medical Enterprise Zones (MEZs) is that underserved areas should have the freedom and flexibility to make their own decisions about the best way to meet health care needs with scarce resources. Accordingly, within MEZs, many of the normal restrictive rules and regulations would be suspended, thereby creating new options and opportunities for people who live there. (The concept of the MEZ and its applicability to rural health care are examined more fully in chapter 20.)

Closely related to the MEZ is the concept of a Medical Enterprise Program (MEP). Whereas an MEZ is defined in terms of a geographical area, an MEP is defined in terms of a market being served. The urban poor often face many of the same problems as residents of rural areas—not because of a lack of physicians and facilities, but because they have been priced out of the market by government regulations that are often the result of special-interest pressures. Accordingly, people who are primarily providing medical services to low-income families should be allowed to participate in MEPs. MEP providers and MEP facilities would be permitted to avoid many government regulations in much the same way those in MEZs do.

13. Restoring the Safety Net by Empowering Local Communities

One of the most critical sources of waste in our health care system is the set of rules and regulations governing the spending of public health care dollars. Politicians in Washington and in state capitals—far removed from the day-to-day, problem-solving activities of local communities—dictate who is eligible for aid and the terms and conditions under which medical care can be delivered. In doing so,

[41]For a more comprehensive list of cost-increasing regulations that discriminate against rural health care facilities, see U.S. Office of Technology Assessment, pp. 181–93.

they tie the hands of local citizens and prevent them from efficiently using limited resources to meet health care needs.

We have already seen how the Medicaid program serves poorly (and inefficiently) the needs of poor, pregnant women. Almost anyone involved in indigent health care in the United States can point to hundreds of other examples. For example, largely because of regulations and special-interest political pressures, about one-third of all Medicaid dollars are spent on the elderly, even though only one in eight beneficiaries is elderly and even though the elderly have about the lowest poverty rate of any population age group. Furthermore, it is federal law—not the preferences of local communities—that dictates that an elderly chronic patient must be treated in an expensive nursing facility (at a cost as high as $60,000 per year) rather than in a home (at a cost of $15,000). A better solution would be simply to give Medicaid funds to local communities, unrestricted except for the requirement that the money be spent on indigent health care. The decisions about how much aid to give, and to whom, would then be made by people best able to judge the needs, resources, and alternatives, which vary considerably from area to area.

A more radical solution would be to turn all means-tested welfare dollars (including food stamps, housing, etc.) over to local communities. The argument for doing so is compelling. Considering that the nation is spending $500 million in hospital costs to treat cocaine babies,[42] should some of the money now being spent on treatment be used to prevent the problem from arising in the first place? Local people dealing directly with the problem are likely to arrive at better answers to that question than politicians in Washington. If local communities, rather than the federal or state governments, controlled the $200 billion plus that we now spend each year on means-tested welfare programs, there would be considerable experimentation and innovation. Local communities would learn much through trial and error and from each other. In some communities (the District of Columbia comes to mind), the results might be worse than what we have now. But in the vast majority of cases we could

---

[42]Ciaran S. Phibbs, David A. Bateman, et al., "The Neonatal Costs of Maternal Cocaine Use," *Journal of the American Medical Association* 266, no. 11 (September 18, 1991): 1521–6.

expect a considerable improvement over the current welfare state. (These and similar ideas are developed more fully in chapter 20.)

14. Creating the Right Kind of Play-or-Pay Plan

In what way does government have a legitimate interest in whether people with the means to do so buy health insurance? The standard argument is that, if people are free to choose as individuals, some (perhaps many) will choose not to be insured. If they have a catastrophic illness, however, many of those uninsured people will be unable to pay the full costs—thus creating a financial burden for the rest of us. It follows that it is a matter of financial self-protection for the majority of people who have health insurance to insist that everyone else purchase it as well.

This argument has persuaded "conservative" organizations, such as the Heritage Foundation[43] and the American Enterprise Institute,[44] to propose laws requiring everyone to purchase health insurance whether they want to or not. Many "liberal" groups pursue the same goal but with more deception—they would force employers to purchase health insurance for their employees. Because virtually all economists agree that fringe benefits such as health insurance are a substitute for wages, employer mandates are nothing more than disguised employee mandates, and the cost would come out of the pockets of workers. As an alternative to direct employer mandates, some propose a play-or-pay option: People would either have to purchase health insurance or pay a tax in return for government-provided health insurance.

Almost all plans for mandating health insurance would impose a tax on labor, leading to less work, fewer jobs, and an expensive burden for those who work in the small-business sector, which is the job-creating sector of the economy (see chapter 12). In addition, once health insurance is mandated, an immediate constituency is created to pressure government to control the costs. Mandating

[43]The Heritage Foundation plan is presented in Butler and Haislmaier, *A National Health System for America*.

[44]The American Enterprise Institute proposal is presented in Mark Pauly et al., "A Plan for 'Responsible National Health Insurance'," *Health Affairs* (Spring 1991), pp. 5–25.

health insurance is an open invitation to government to step in and regulate the entire health care system (see chapter 6).[45]

Fortunately, there is a better way. If the proposals made above were adopted, every American would face a choice: buy subsidized health insurance or pay higher taxes. The extra taxes paid by those who choose to be uninsured should go into a special fund and be returned to local hospitals that provide free care to indigent patients. Of course, free care is not likely to be as desirable as purchased care and may involve considerable health care rationing. Moreover, those who receive free care will still be personally liable for their health care costs and may be forced into bankruptcy. Thus, while providing a mechanism for paying for health care for the uninsured, this proposal retains financial and other incentives for people to purchase health insurance.

If people who chose not to purchase health insurance paid higher taxes, would those extra taxes be enough to pay the unpaid health bills they generate? That's not clear. But there are reasons to think that they might be. People who do not have health insurance today are not really getting a free ride (see chapter 20). Because they do not receive employer-subsidized health insurance, they pay higher taxes. And based on the average tax subsidy received by those who have employer-provided health insurance, the higher taxes paid by the uninsured are about equal to the amount of unpaid hospital bills they generate.

What is unfair about the current system is not that uninsured people are not paying their own way; it is that, unlike most people with health insurance, most people without it never get an opportunity to purchase it at a tax-subsidized price.

15. Employing a Cost-Benefit Standard for Health and Safety Regulatory Agencies

There is probably no single source of waste in our health care system that can compare to the routine amount of waste generated by federal regulatory agencies, including the Occupational Safety

---

[45]A play-or-pay plan endorsed by leading Senate Democrats (discussed in chapter 12) hints that sweeping federal regulation may be necessary. A plan proposed by House Ways and Means Committee chairman, Dan Rostenkowski (D-IL), accepts regulation as inevitable and proposes a mechanism for instituting it.

and Health Administration (OSHA) and the Environmental Protection Agency (EPA). In most calculations, the amounts spent and the costs imposed on the private sector by OSHA and the EPA are not included in the nation's annual health care bill. But a significant amount of the activities of both agencies is just as much a health care expenditure as is a physician's fee.

For example, the air toxics section of the recently amended Clean Air Act has only one real goal: to reduce cancer. Accordingly, it is fully comparable to any other expense designed to prevent or cure cancer. How well does the EPA perform as a cancer-preventing agency? Despite the fact that industrial products and food additives cause less than 3 percent of all cancers,[46] the federal government is imposing billions of dollars of costs on the American public in its efforts to prevent exposure to trace amounts of chemicals in our environment.[47] The most common government standard is that a chemical should be outlawed if one person out of one million exposed over a lifetime could theoretically get cancer from it. Even though 300,000 people out of one million will get cancer anyway, regulations cost the public billions of dollars to prevent the theoretical death of one more.

Typical EPA methods for evaluating the public health risks from air pollution greatly overstate those risks. For example, the EPA calculates potential risks from exposure to an air pollutant by testing the chemical for toxicity in laboratory animals. The chemical is administered to rats and mice in massive daily doses just below the amount that would kill them immediately. At such high levels of exposure, one out of every two chemicals ever tested (both natural

---

[46]A study by Oxford University professors Richard Doll and Richard Peto, commissioned by the U.S. Office of Technology Assessment, examined U.S. national cancer mortality records from 1933 to 1978 and found that only approximately 2 percent of all cancers are caused by environmental contamination or pollution. See Doll and Peto, "The Causes of Cancer: Quantitative Estimates of Avoidable Risks of Cancer in the United States Today," *Journal of the National Cancer Institute* 66, no. 6 (1981): 1191–308. The EPA's own findings, based on the use of toxicological risk assessment, corroborate Doll and Peto's analysis. According to the EPA, only between 1 and 3 percent of all cancers are caused by "pollution." See EPA, *Unfinished Business*. The EPA figures were extrapolated in Michael Gough, "Estimating Cancer Mortality," *Environmental Science & Technology* (August 1989), p. 925.

[47]See Frederick Rueter and Wilbur Steger, "Air Toxics and Public Health," *Regulation* (Winter 1990).

and man-made) eventually causes cancer in at least one species of rodent. The EPA then extrapolates from rodents to humans and estimates the human risk of cancer from exposure to the same chemical.

Scientists are increasingly skeptical about the value of extrapolating from these rodent experiments the risk to humans from ordinary exposure. Many are also skeptical about what the EPA does next. To calculate the risk to human populations, the EPA postulates an imaginary "Most Exposed Individual" (MEI), who lives on the property line of the emissions source and breathes the highest level of emissions from that source for 70 years, 24 hours each day. The EPA then assumes that everyone is an MEI.[48] Even with these pessimistic assumptions, the EPA estimates that only 1,700 to 2,700 cancers are caused each year by exposure to approximately 90 potentially hazardous air pollutants. Although that hypothetical number may seem large, it is a small fraction of the almost one million cancer cases that occur each year in America.[49] By some estimates, the air toxics section of the amended Clean Air Act will cost from $20 billion to $30 billion—about 10 to 15 times the entire annual budget of the National Cancer Institute. But because the regulations target only the largest polluters, the maximum reduction in cancer cases is likely to be 350 to 500 per year. That represents a cost of between $40 million and $86 million per cancer avoided.[50]

The EPA's extreme-risk models are notoriously faulty, however. A study of the largest concentration of industrial coke ovens in the country (Allegheny County, Pennsylvania) concludes that the EPA's estimate of cancer caused by coke emissions is exaggerated by a multiple of 100.[51] By the EPA's own calculations, its regulations on coke emissions cost $6.8 million per cancer prevented. Based on

[48]The EPA's high estimates of risk are generally hidden behind the large probability that any given individual will develop some type of cancer. However, its method of calculation so exaggerates risk that in at least one case (a Texaco plant at Port Neches, Texas) the EPA estimated that the added risk of cancer from living near the plant was one in ten. This is such a high figure that it should show up in public health figures. The EPA tries to avoid direct contradiction by arguing that these risk estimates should be used only for purposes of comparing relative risks.

[49]Rueter and Steger.

[50]"Air Toxic Madness," *Executive Alert* 4, no. 3 (May/June 1990): 5.

[51]Rueter and Steger.

more realistic calculations, the cost is $682 million to prevent a single instance of cancer.

The EPA's cost-is-no-object approach is also reflected in its new benzene regulations, which impose a cost of $200 million a year to prevent an EPA-estimated 3.4 cases of cancer.[52] By the EPA's own calculations, its new benzene regulations will cost $59 million to prevent a single instance of cancer. By more realistic calculations, the cost of each cancer prevented will be $5.8 billion.

Applying a more realistic method to all air toxics, it appears that the Clean Air Act's new air toxic regulations may prevent three to five cancers per year rather than 350 to 500. The cost per cancer prevented will be between $4 billion and $9 billion per year. (See Figure 3.7.)

The examples given above are by no means the most wasteful ones. Researchers at the Office of Management and Budget have calculated that some EPA regulations cost as much as $5.7 trillion per (expected, hypothetical) life saved.[53] This implies that the EPA is willing to spend the entire gross national product to save a single life. Clearly, scarce dollars designed to promote health are much better spent in areas in which the return promises to be much higher. Indeed, it is time to rethink the federal government's approach to preventing a great many diseases, including cancer.

About one in every three Americans will get cancer. About one in five will die from it. What should be done? An executive of the EPA says that the most effective way to combat cancer would be to give the entire EPA budget to the American Cancer Society. The National Cancer Institute's goal is to reduce the nation's 470,000 annual cancer deaths by one-half by the year 2000. Yet the institute does not even mention reducing carcinogenic chemicals in the environment as one of its objectives.

Consequences of Change

Adoption of the proposals made in this chapter would not immediately solve America's health care problems. But they would empower individuals, and create market institutions through which problems eventually would be solved by people pursuing their own

---

[52]Ibid.

[53]Private communication with the authors.

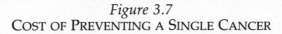

Figure 3.7
COST OF PREVENTING A SINGLE CANCER

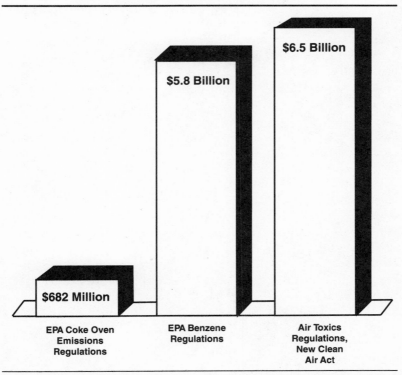

$6.5 Billion

$5.8 Billion

$682 Million

EPA Coke Oven
Emissions
Regulations

EPA Benzene
Regulations

Air Toxics
Regulations,
New Clean
Air Act

SOURCE: Task Force Report, *Progressive Environmentalism*, NCPA Policy
Report no. 162 (Dallas: National Center for Policy Analysis, April 1991).

self-interest. They would give individuals the incentive to solve
problems that can never be solved through bureaucracies, regulations, or the power of government. The implementation of these
proposals would constitute a national commitment to follow a path
that is distinctly American in character—one that relies on individual choice and the efficiency of free markets.

4. Using the Agenda to Solve Problems

In chapter 2, we presented two conflicting visions of the health care system. This chapter will show how the two visions influence the health care debate. In general, the vision of the health care system that we accept determines what we think is possible and desirable, what we consider to be problems, how we analyze those problems, and how we propose to solve them. In the cost-plus vision, which has dominated thinking about health care in the United States since the end of World War II, the primary relationships are between bureaucracies rather than between individual patients and physicians. People who accept this vision inevitably attempt to solve health care problems through bureaucratic rule making or by changing the ways in which bureaucracies relate to each other. The other vision is of what we have called the ideal health care system, a system under which problems would be solved by relying on the power of competitive markets and the self-interested behavior of individuals.

Twenty Major Social Problems and Their Solutions

We now turn to 20 major social problems that are said to exist in the U.S. health care system. Our goal is neither to provide a complete elaboration of the problems, nor to construct detailed solutions for them (many are discussed at length in later chapters). Rather, our goal is to sketch the nature of the problems and to show how the approach to solving them is critically dependent on one's vision of how the health care system should operate.

1. Rising Health Care Costs

The rate of increase in America's health care spending is a serious social problem. Over the past two decades, this rate has been twice the rate of increase of the gross national product (GNP). If this trend

Figure 4.1
TRENDS IN HEALTH CARE SPENDING AND GNP

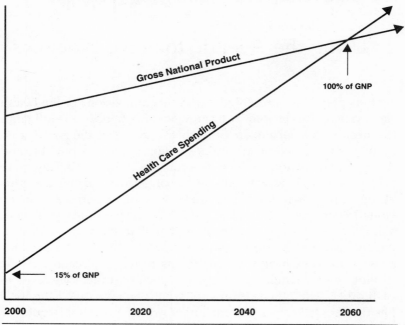

2000   2020   2040   2060

continues, we could be spending our entire GNP on health care by the year 2062.[1] (See Figure 4.1.)

The major reason costs are rising is that when patients and physicians get together, they are spending someone else's money rather than their own. In the hospital sector today, 95 percent of expenses are paid for by someone other than the patient, and as Figure 4.2 shows, since 1965 there has been a dramatic increase in the share of medical bills paid by third parties for every category of medical services. The share of physicians' fees paid by third parties, for example, has more than doubled, rising from 38.4 percent in 1965 to 81.3 percent in 1990. Moreover, the numbers in Figure 4.2 are averages; for many people, the extent of health insurance coverage is much greater.

[1]Projection based on data from the Health Care Financing Administration, Office of the Actuary.

76

Figure 4.2
PERCENT OF PERSONAL HEALTH EXPENSES PAID BY THIRD PARTIES, 1965 AND 1990

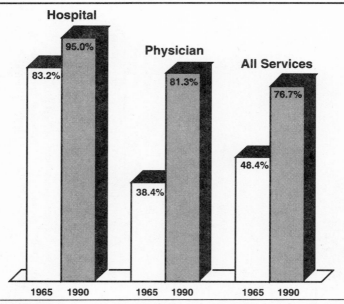

SOURCE: Health Care Financing Administration, Office of the Actuary.

One consequence of the rise in third-party payment of medical bills is that most people have no idea how much they are personally contributing to cover the nation's health care costs. As Table 4.1 shows, in 1992 we will spend about 12.9 percent of our GNP on health care, an amount equal to $8,000 for every U.S. household. This $8,000 burden is largely disguised, however. For a working-age family, the visible outlays are $1,580 for out-of-pocket expenses and $590 for payment for employer-provided health insurance.[2] For the nation as a whole, such visible expenses amount to only 3.6 percent of GNP. Because the remainder of the $8,000 burden is hidden in taxes and reduced wages, there is a universal illusion that health care costs are being paid by someone else.

A related illusion is that most people cannot afford to pay for health care. In fact, they are already affording it. As Table 4.1

[2]These amounts are net of government tax subsidies.

Table 4.1

HOW WE PAY FOR HEALTH CARE[1]

Method of Payment	Average per Household[2]	Percent of GNP	Percent of Personal Income	Percent of Money Income
Paid indirectly				
Medicare payroll taxes	$ 860	1.4%	1.6%	2.1%
Other federal, state, and local taxes[3]	3,070	4.9	5.8	7.4
Reduced wages—(employer-provided insurance)[4]	1,580	2.5	3.0	3.8
Other[5]	190	0.3	0.4	0.5
Paid directly				
Private health insurance premiums[6]	590	0.9	1.1	1.4
Out-of-pocket payments	1,580	2.5	3.0	3.8
Medicare premiums	130	0.2	0.2	0.3
Total	$8,000	12.9%	15.1%	19.4%

SOURCE: C. Eugene Steuerle, "Finance-Based Reform: The Search for an Adaptable Health Policy," paper presented at an American Enterprise Institute conference, "American Health Policy," Washington, October 3–4, 1991.

NOTE: Columns may not add to totals due to rounding.

[1]Based on estimated total health care spending for fiscal year 1992. Estimates are based on mean GNP per household of $62,160; mean personal income per household of $53,130; and mean money income per household of $41,320.

[2]Average household size in the United States was 2.63 persons in 1990. Amounts rounded to nearest $10.

[3]Includes taxes needed to finance direct government health spending out of general revenues, plus the amount that general taxes must be raised to compensate for revenue lost owing to special tax treatment of certain health-related income (about 26% of total).

[4]Employer contributions for health insurance, less government tax subsidies.

[5]Nonpatient revenue for the health care industry, including charitable donations, interest income, hospital parking, and gift shops.

[6]Includes employee contributions to private group health insurance plans, as well as individual policy premiums.

shows, 12.9 percent of GNP is equal to almost 20 percent of the average household's money income. Most families probably would claim that they could not possibly spend 20 percent of their income on health care. They would be shocked to learn that they are already spending that much.

How much should we as a nation spend on health care? Many people believe that health care spending should be determined by medical needs. Yet, if we followed the practice of spending health care dollars whenever a need was being met (or a medical benefit created), we could easily spend our entire GNP on health care. In fact, we could probably spend half of the entire GNP on diagnostic tests alone. Medical science has identified, for example, at least 900 tests that can be done on blood.[3] But for the inconvenience, why not make all 900 part of our annual checkup? Similarly, an annual checkup could include a brain scan, a full body scan, and numerous other tests.

As an example of how the demand for the services of primary care physicians could soar, consider the trade-off between the self-administration of nonprescription drugs and the use of physicians' services. In any given year, there are about 472 million office visits to primary care physicians. But economist Simon Rottenberg estimates that, if only 2 percent of nonprescription drug consumers chose professional care rather than self-medication, the number of patient visits would climb to 721 million, thereby requiring a 50 percent increase in the number of primary care physicians. If every user of nonprescription drugs sought professional care instead, we would need 25 times the current number of primary care physicians.[4]

More diagnostic tests and increased physicians' visits are just the beginning. Once we discover something really wrong, there is almost no limit to what medical science will eventually be able to do. We are reaching a point where we can replace virtually every joint and organ, including hips, elbows, heart, and lungs, and even eyes and ears. And, like those of the bionic man, the replacements

---

[3]Glenn Ruffenbach, "Medical Tests Go under the Microscope," *Wall Street Journal*, February 7, 1989. The University of Michigan Medical Laboratories perform, in house, approximately 900 different tests on blood. Other tests can be performed, but they are so rare that they are sent to private reference laboratories.

[4]Simon Rottenberg, "Unintended Consequences: The Probable Effects of Mandated Medical Insurance," *Regulation* 13, no. 2 (Summer 1990): 27–28.

are often better than the originals. If someone else pays the bill, our potential demand for medical care could consume many times the nation's GNP, even today.

Proposals in the Cost-Plus Health Care System. From the bureaucratic perspective, some of the most commonly proposed solutions are to pass laws regulating hospital prices; pass laws limiting the number of hospital beds and the amount of hospital equipment; implement full-scale health care rationing; and nationalize the entire health care system and turn the problems over to the government. Each of these solutions would widen the gap between institutional rule making and the day-to-day practice of medicine. Far from eliminating perverse incentives, they would create even more. Individuals in the medical marketplace would still find it in their self-interest to spend other people's money while bureaucracies would attempt to block the pursuit of self-interest with more rules and regulations. The government-run health care systems of other countries are not more efficient than our own (as explained in chapter 17), and the governments in most of those countries are attempting to keep spending down by limiting hospital budgets. That usually means doing so by denying people medical care.

Solutions in the Ideal Health Care System. Health care costs cannot be controlled unless we empower individuals and make it in their self-interest to become prudent buyers of health care. When individuals have control of their own health care dollars through medical savings accounts, Medical IRAs (MIRAs), and health insurance reimbursements, they won't buy unless the services are worth the price. Most of us have no idea what percent of GNP is spent on orange juice or shoes. Because the people buying those products are spending their own money, not ours, we have no reason to care. In general, there is no right amount of money to spend on health care. The right amount is whatever people choose to spend, providing they are spending their own money and are facing prices that reflect the real social costs of medical services.

Controlling health care costs also means creating new incentives for the suppliers of services. In a competitive medical marketplace, suppliers would find it in their self-interest to lower price and improve quality and to communicate with potential buyers about price and quality.

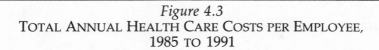

Figure 4.3
TOTAL ANNUAL HEALTH CARE COSTS PER EMPLOYEE,
1985 TO 1991

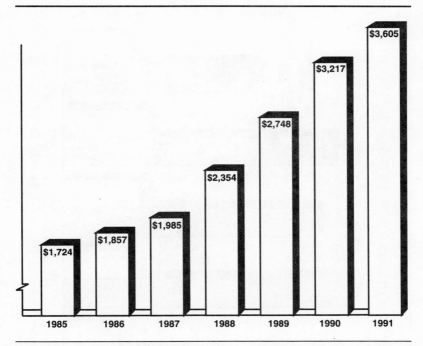

SOURCE: A. Foster Higgins & Co., *Health Care Benefits Survey, 1991: Indemnity Plans: Cost, Design and Funding.*

2. Controlling Costs in Employer-Provided Health Insurance Plans

As Figure 4.3 shows, between 1985 and 1991, the amount that employers spent annually on health care for each employee (and dependents) climbed from $1,724 to $3,605, an increase of 100 per-cent.[5] As Figure 4.4 shows, health care costs for employers have been increasing at about three times the rate of inflation and, in recent years, we have witnessed double-digit increases. Even the most profitable corporations cannot sustain increases in that range for long. It would be a mistake, however, to conclude that these

[5]A. Foster Higgins & Co., *Health Care Benefits Survey, 1990: Indemnity Plans: Cost, Design and Funding.*

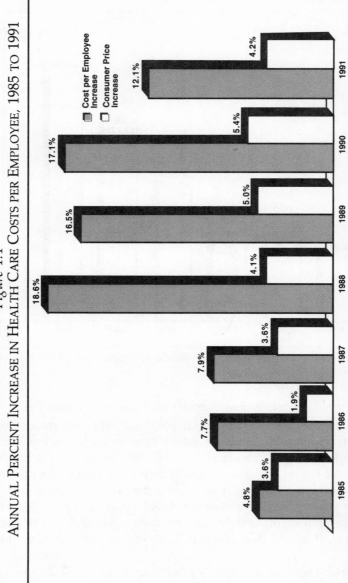

Figure 4.4

ANNUAL PERCENT INCREASE IN HEALTH CARE COSTS PER EMPLOYEE, 1985 TO 1991

- Cost per Employee Increase
- Consumer Price Increase

	1985	1986	1987	1988	1989	1990	1991
Cost per Employee Increase	4.8%	7.7%	7.9%	18.6%	16.5%	17.1%	12.1%
Consumer Price Increase	3.6%	1.9%	3.6%	4.1%	5.0%	5.4%	4.2%

SOURCES: A. Foster Higgins & Co., *Health Care Benefits Survey, 1991: Indemnity Plans: Cost, Design and Funding*; and U.S. Bureau of Labor Statistics.

costs are ultimately borne by firms. Health insurance is a fringe benefit that substitutes for wages. Ultimately, therefore, the cost of wasteful health insurance comes out of the pockets of workers, not their employers.[6]

Proposals in the Cost-Plus Health Care System. For those who seek bureaucratic solutions, the proposals run the gamut: for example, make special deals with certain hospitals and require all employees to use only those hospitals, negotiate similar contracts with selected physicians, eliminate benefits from the company's health insurance policy, require corporate approval prior to major surgery, etc. Each of these proposals, however, further intrudes on the doctor/patient relationship. And each new set of rules expands the system's perverse incentives. These solutions operate within a framework in which the self-interest of employees and their physicians is diametrically opposed to the goals of the employer and/or the health insurance carrier. To appreciate the impact of this dichotomy, consider that two-thirds of the physicians in a 1989 poll indicated a willingness to help patients get health insurance benefits by misrepresenting a test as being "diagnostic" rather than for "general screening."[7]

Solutions in the Ideal Health Care System. If health insurance were individualized, and if employee patients controlled their own health care dollars, there would no longer be a corporate problem. The role of the employer would be to help negotiate good deals for employees or to help them choose a policy wisely. Each employee would choose a package of benefits tailored to individual and family needs. Cost-control devices, if needed, would be chosen voluntarily, not imposed from above. Moreover, for each individual employee, health insurance premiums would become a dollar-for-dollar substitute for wages. In the ideal health care system, employers would not attempt to force employees to do what was not in

[6]Automobile industry executives have often said that health insurance for auto workers adds $700 to $800 to the price of every new car. For example, see Lynn Wagner, "Business Agitates for Health System Revamp," *Modern Healthcare,* November 24, 1989, pp. 16–19. In fact, health insurance premiums add nothing to the price of cars. The $700 to $800 in premiums comes at the expense of higher wages for auto workers.

[7]John C. Pezullo et al., "Physicians' Attitudes towards Using Deception to Resolve Difficult Ethical Problems," *Journal of the American Medical Association* 261, no. 20 (May 26, 1989): 2980–85.

their self-interest in the medical marketplace. The only relevant goals would be employee goals, and the role of the employer would be to help employees reach those goals.

3. Prenatal Care and Infant Mortality

Using the latest medical techniques, physicians are able to keep alive low-weight babies whose lungs would have collapsed and caused death only a few years ago. These techniques are used to rescue crack babies and other premature infants.[8] Then the real expenses begin. These babies usually have severe medical problems that require lengthy treatment that can ultimately cost more than $1 million per baby. The tragic irony is that the hospitals delivering the medical care are often in inner-city neighborhoods where as many as one-third of expectant mothers do not receive basic prenatal care and a few hundred dollars of medical services might have prevented the problem in the first place.

With each passing year, doctors get better at the lifesaving techniques, breaking all previous records in their ability to rescue babies at lower weights and after fewer months of pregnancy. There seems to be no limit to the money they can spend. But who decides that it's appropriate to spend so much on low-weight babies and so little on prenatal care for their mothers? Certainly not the people in the neighborhoods that the medical facilities are designed to serve. Most of those being helped know little about the latest advances in medical science and not much more about prenatal care. The decisions are made by politicians and the health care bureaucracy.

The problem is especially acute in the black community. Nationally, a black woman with a family income of less than $10,000 a year is almost twice as likely as a white woman with similar income to give birth to a low-weight baby and about four times as likely to do so as a white woman with an annual family income of more than $40,000.[9] Overall, black babies die before their first birthday at twice the rate of white babies, which may partly explain why life

---

[8]Low-weight babies are usually premature babies.

[9]James W. Collins, Jr., and Richard J. Davis, "The Differential Effect of Traditional Risk Factors on Infant Birthweight among Blacks and Whites in Chicago," *American Journal of Public Health* 80, no. 6 (June 1990): 679–81.

Table 4.2
INFANT HEALTH IN NEW YORK CITY

Category	Low-Income Area (East Harlem)	High-Income Area (Kips Bay–Yorkville)
Infant deaths per 1,000 live births, 1989	23.4	7.3
Live births per 100 with late or no prenatal care, 1986–88	35.8	6.1
Low birth-weight babies (less than 5.5 pounds) per 100 live births, 1989	18.5	6.0
Low birth-weight babies (less than 3.3 pounds) per 100 live births, 1989	3.8	0.9

SOURCE: New York City, Department of Health; reported in *New York Times*, December 29, 1990.

expectancy at birth has been falling for blacks, although rising for whites.[10]

Table 4.2 compares infant health statistics between the low-income, minority area of East Harlem and the high-income area from Kips Bay to Yorkville in New York City. As the table shows, expectant mothers in East Harlem are six times less likely to receive prenatal care and three to four times more likely to have a low-weight baby.

Before turning to possible solutions, it is important to correct four common misconceptions. First, the high rate of infant mortality in

[10]According to the National Center for Health Statistics, life expectancy for blacks at birth fell continuously from 69.7 years in 1984 to 69.2 years in 1988, the last year for which statistics are available. Over the same period, life expectancy for whites at birth increased from 75.3 years to 75.6 years. In addition to infant deaths, other reasons for the decline in black life expectancy include deaths from homicide, motor vehicle accidents, and AIDS.

inner-city areas is unquestionably affected by lifestyle decisions (drinking, smoking, taking drugs, etc.) and it is not clear that any amount of spending on prenatal care will appreciably change the lifestyles of expectant mothers.[11] Second, even when all income and educational differences between blacks and whites are removed, a substantial difference in birth outcomes remains. For example, middle-class, college-educated black women are twice as likely to give birth to low-weight babies as white women with the same levels of income and education.[12] Third, not all minorities face the same problem. The infant mortality rate for Hispanic mothers is about the same as for white mothers, and in New Mexico it is lower. The difference between Hispanics and blacks may be partly attributable to values and culture.[13] Finally (as discussed in chapter 17), although the United States has one of the highest rates of infant mortality among developed countries, once mothers and their babies enter the health care system, American doctors outperform those in any other country. Mothers are also in better hands. A woman in Japan is twice as likely to die during childbirth as a woman in the United States.[14]

Proposals in the Cost-Plus Health Care System. Most proposals from those who hold a bureaucratic view would expand the current bureaucracy and increase the number of dollars under its control, either by increasing the number of expectant mothers covered by Medicaid or by making prenatal care free to all women under a limited program of national health insurance. What these proposals overlook is that prenatal care is already free for low-income women in most inner-city areas, through Medicaid or other government programs. Yet (as made clear in chapter 3), free prenatal care is not necessarily easy to obtain.

Solutions in the Ideal Health Care System. If low-income women could draw on a special Medicaid account (and purchase care the

---

[11]One study found that nearly 30 percent of babies born in New York hospitals were addicted to crack. See Harmeet K. D. Singh, "Stork Reality: Why America's Infants Are Dying," *Policy Review* (Spring 1990), pp. 56–63.

[12]Collins and Davis.

[13]Robert Pear, "The Hard Thing about Cutting Infant Mortality Is Educating Mothers," *New York Times*, August 12, 1990.

[14]Joseph Schnelman, "Japan's Healthy Babies—An American Doctor's View," *World Health Forum* 10, no. 4 (1989): 69.

way other pregnant women do), or if they had their own medical savings accounts, they could become real consumers exercising real buying power in the market for prenatal care. That would not solve the problem of lifestyle choices, but it would create new opportunities for people to meet their health care needs.

4. *Preventive Medicine*

Many medical procedures can potentially save lives and, possibly, money. They include chest x-rays, mammograms, pap smears, and cholesterol tests. Between 1980 and 1986, according to a study in the *International Journal of Epidemiology*, there were 121,560 deaths from disorders that are not usually lethal if discovered and treated early. They included deaths from appendicitis, pneumonia, gallbladder infection, hypertensive heart disease, asthma, and cervical cancer.[15] About 80 percent of the premature deaths reported in the study were among blacks, even though blacks make up only 13 percent of the U.S. population.

If we knew in advance which patients had serious problems, solutions would be relatively easy. But often we don't know. As a result, there is considerable debate over how many people should be tested and how frequently. One thing we do know, however, is that some people who should realize they have a problem fail either to see a physician or to receive the necessary preventive care.

The problem is especially acute in low-income areas, where there are sometimes epidemics of diseases many people thought had been eradicated only a few years ago. Some inner cities now report skyrocketing rates of tuberculosis, hepatitis A, syphilis, gonorrhea, measles, mumps, whooping cough, etc. All too often, those who are infected see physicians too late. For example, at Harlem Hospital in New York City, only 30 percent of the women diagnosed with breast cancer live as long as five years, compared with 70 percent of white women and 60 percent of black women in the country as a whole.[16]

---

[15]Eugene Schwartz, Vincent Y. Kofie, et al., "Black/White Comparisons of Deaths Preventable by Medical Intervention: United States and the District of Columbia 1980–1986," *International Journal of Epidemiology* 19, no. 3 (September 1990): 592.

[16]Elizabeth Rosenthal, "Health Problems of Inner City Poor Reach Crisis Point," *New York Times*, December 24, 1990.

Such statistics have led many to conclude that America's private health care system is not serving low-income people and that a public system is needed. This view overlooks the fact that many of the people who are apparently not receiving needed preventive care are already part of a free public system, partly supported by funds collected from low-income, minority taxpayers. New York City, for example, is experiencing an epidemic of congenital syphilis (with about half the cases in the country), a surprising increase in cases of measles, and increasing instances of other preventable diseases.[17] Yet, the city has perhaps the most extensive system of free health care and free public hospitals in the country.

In addition to low-income families (that presumably face financial constraints), many nonpoor families that can afford to purchase preventive care choose not to do so. One reason may be that diagnostic tests themselves expose patients to risks. According to one study, from 5,000 to 10,000 cases of breast cancer each year may be caused by x-rays.[18] Health insurance companies, which clearly have a direct financial interest in such questions, generally do not require or encourage preventive medical tests. But the perspective of insurers may not be the best guide. Since people frequently switch carriers, insurers have less financial interest in the long-run consequences of a failure to detect a medical problem. And paying for diagnostic tests through insurers often doubles the cost of the tests.

Moreover, carefully conducted economic studies do not confirm that preventive medicine pays for itself. With the exception of targeted high-risk groups, preventive medicine generally adds to the cost of health. It is an investment in future good health, not a cost-control device.[19] Further, attitudes toward risk vary. Risk-averse people place a higher value on preventive medicine than do those who are less risk-averse. Yet, in the current health care system, the delivery of preventive medical services tends to be determined by bureaucratic reimbursement policies rather than patients' preferences.

---

[17]Ibid.

[18]Michael Swift, Daphne Morrell, et al., "Incidence of Cancer in 161 Families Affected by Ataxia-Telangiectasia," *New England Journal of Medicine* 325, no. 26 (December 26, 1991): 1831–36.

[19]See Louise B. Russell, *Is Prevention Better than Cure?* (Washington: Brookings Institution, 1986).

Proposals in the Cost-Plus Health Care System. Commonly proposed solutions are to force private insurers to cover diagnostic tests (with no out-of-pocket cost to the patient), change Medicare rules to achieve the same objective for elderly patients, and make diagnostic tests free to targeted groups through a limited national health insurance program. Each of these proposals would use health insurance as a vehicle for the prepayment of the consumption of medical services. They would probably double the cost of the services. And they would give all decisionmaking power to third-party payers. As we shall see in chapter 17, countries that make all health care free to patients at the point of consumption do not necessarily expand the scope of preventive medicine. In the United States, we already perform more diagnostic tests than are performed in most countries with national health insurance.

Solutions in the Ideal Health Care System. An ideal health care system would recognize that the answer to the question of whether a test is worth its cost depends as much on patient preferences and attitudes toward risk as on cost-benefit calculations. In the ideal system, patients would be the principal buyers of health care, and test manufacturers would market directly to them, as well as to health care providers. Health insurance would not be used as wasteful prepayment for the consumption of medical care. Instead, public policy would encourage private savings for diagnostic tests.

5. *Child Care*

In recent years, rates of preventable childhood diseases have soared, especially in low-income areas of large cities. For example, the number of whooping cough cases has tripled since 1981, there were 17,000 measles cases in 1989, up from only 1,500 in 1983, and measles is at epidemic levels in many major cities.[20]

Former Colorado governor Richard Lamm complains that this is evidence that our national priorities are wrong. At the same time we are expanding Medicare to cover heart transplants for the elderly, 20 percent of America's children do not get all of their vaccinations.[21] But is a 100 percent vaccination rate ideal? Consider that every vaccine has risks of its own, including a small risk of death. In the

---

[20]U.S. Public Health Service data.

[21]Richard D. Lamm, "Again, Age Beats Youth," *New York Times*, December 2, 1990, p. A16.

case of the pertussis vaccine, used to prevent whooping cough, the risk of disease of the brain (encephalopathy) is 1 in 110,000, and the risk of permanent brain damage (and possibly death) is 1 in 310,000. Although the risks are low, they are considerably higher than the risk levels allowed by most federal health and safety regulatory agencies. On the other hand, if a child gets whooping cough, the risk of brain damage is 1 in 240, and for babies less than six months old the risk of death is 1 in 100.[22] Given such odds, we would expect parental attitudes to vary considerably. We would also expect fewer vaccinations at those times and in those areas where the risk of whooping cough is lower. As whooping cough neared eradication in 1981, vaccination rates dropped, and that was certainly a rational response. Since then, the incidence of the disease has risen, making vaccination more desirable.

The problem of preventive treatment for children is not solely, or even mainly, a problem of private-sector medicine. Some people estimate that about half of unvaccinated children who get measles are covered by Medicaid or some other government program, even though the cost of a complete set of vaccinations is only about $91.[23] Britain, where free health care is available to everyone through the National Health Service, has had worse problems than the United States. When parent fears over the whooping cough vaccine in that country led to sharply lower immunization rates, a six-year epidemic followed, with 104,000 whooping cough cases leading to almost 400 deaths.[24]

In addition to the issue of children's vaccinations, there is the more general issue of how often children should see physicians and what preventive medical procedures should be performed on apparently healthy children. The American Academy of Pediatrics (with an obvious financial interest in the issue) recommends 12 well-child care visits to physicians for children from birth through age six. Studies by the Rand Corporation and the U.S. Office of

[22]Data are from the U.S. Centers for Disease Control and the American Academy of Pediatrics. Reported in Sonia L. Nazario, "A Parental Rights Battle Is Heating Up over Fears of Whooping Cough Vaccine," *Wall Street Journal*, June 20, 1990.

[23]Robert Pear, "Proposal Links Welfare Funds to Inoculations," *New York Times*, November 29, 1990.

[24]See Aaron Wildovsky, *Searching for Safety* (New Brunswick, NJ: Transaction Publishers, 1988).

Technology Assessment fail to support that recommendation. In fact, aside from inoculations, it's not clear that a case can be made for any well-child care visits to a physician.[25] From an economic point of view, the exercise appears to be wasteful.

Arguably, there are social reasons (the control of communicable diseases) to care about inoculations. But the argument does not extend to physician visits for apparently healthy children. The justification for well-child care appears to be relief of anxiety or reassurance for parents. But those are private benefits, not social ones. Despite this fact, politicians around the country are making well-child care an issue under the slogan "You can't say 'no' to children." Florida was the first state to mandate that private insurers cover a specific number of physician visits for children at different ages, with no deductible or copayment for the insured family.[26] Even though such laws double the cost of routine care, encourage spending in excess of any expected social benefit, and raise the cost of real insurance, they are being actively considered in virtually every state.

Proposals in the Cost-Plus Health Care System. Those who take a bureaucratic view of health care tend to endorse a technocratic view as well. Whether a preventive medical procedure should be performed on a particular patient is a matter for the experts to decide, they maintain. Patient preferences and attitudes are irrelevant.

The technocratic view lies behind state laws that require vaccinations for school-age children and the Bush administration's proposal to make childhood vaccinations a precondition for receipt of welfare or Medicaid benefits.[27] This view is almost always endorsed by medical associations. For example, although 19 states allow parents to forgo the whooping cough vaccine for "philosophical or religious" reasons, the American Medical Association would like to rescind that right.[28] The American Academy of Pediatrics actively

[25]See Judith Wagner, Roger Herdman, and David Alpers, "Well-Child Care: How Much Is Enough?" *Health Affairs* (Fall 1989).

[26]John C. Goodman and Gerald L. Musgrave, *Freedom of Choice in Health Insurance*, NCPA Policy Report no. 134 (Dallas: National Center for Policy Analysis, November 1988).

[27]Pear, "Proposal Links Welfare Funds to Inoculations."

[28]Nazario, "A Parental Battle Is Heating Up over Fears of Whooping Cough Vaccine."

91

lobbies state governments to require private insurers to cover well-child care, with no copayment or deductible.

The experts, of course, are often wrong. For example, the swine flu vaccine, heavily promoted by the federal government, led to numerous unnecessary deaths among elderly patients.[29] But a more basic objection to the technocratic view is that the experts are rarely disinterested. Take cholesterol tests for children. Researchers whose medical journal articles encourage such tests often have a personal research interest in seeing the tests promoted. Companies that make cholesterol-testing devices have a financial interest in their use, as do the physicians who charge for the test.[30] Thus, under prodding from the experts we have seen a rise in cholesterol testing in children in recent years, even though the best evidence indicates that routine testing is a waste of money.[31]

Solutions in the Ideal Health Care System. The alternative to the technocratic view is the recognition that experts often disagree and acceptance of the fact that the preferences and levels of risk aversion of parents are important. The agenda presented in chapter 3 seeks to ensure that families have resources set aside to pay for child care, including child vaccinations. But parents, not the medical bureaucracy, should decide what care to obtain and how much to spend obtaining it.

6. Lifestyle and Health

Medical researchers are increasingly convinced that health is determined in important ways by lifestyle—what we eat, what we drink, whether we smoke, whether we exercise regularly. Table 4.3, for example, shows that researchers believe that the major causes of cancer are lifestyle-related and have very little to do with

[29]Robert Formaini, *The Myth of Scientific Public Policy* (New Brunswick, NJ: Transaction Books, 1990).

[30]Gina Kolata, "Routine Child Cholesterol Tests: Doubts," *New York Times*, December 19, 1990.

[31]Ronald M. Lauer and William R. Clarke, "Use of Cholesterol Measurements in Childhood for the Prediction of Adult Hypercholesterolemia," *Journal of the American Medical Association* 264, no. 3 (December 19, 1990): 3034–38; and Warren Browner et al., "The Case against Childhood Cholesterol Screening," *Journal of the American Medical Association* 264, no. 3 (December 19, 1990): 3039–43.

Table 4.3
CAUSES OF CANCER DEATHS

Cause of Cancer	Percent of All Cancer Deaths[1]
Diet	35%
Tobacco	30
Infection	10
Reproductive and sexual behavior	7
Occupation	4
Alcohol	3
Geophysical factors (for example, sunlight)	3
Pollution	2
Medicines and medical procedures	1
Industrial products	1[2]
Food additives	1[3]

SOURCE: Richard Doll and Richard Peto, "The Causes of Cancer," *Journal of the National Cancer Institute* 66 (June 1981): 1256 (Table 20).
[1]These numbers represent the midrange of estimates from various studies. The numbers do not add up to 100 because the estimates from different studies are not consistent.
[2]Less than 1 percent.
[3]Less than 1 percent and possibly negative because some food additives prevent other causes of cancer.

pollution, pesticides, and other risks over which individuals have little control.[32]

It is important to emphasize that much of what we think we know about the relationship between lifestyle and health is conjecture, not scientific fact. For example, researchers have observed that the Japanese have lower rates of certain types of cancer than Americans. Yet when the Japanese immigrate to the United States (and presumably adopt American eating habits), after one or more generations their cancer rates are very similar to those of other Americans. This evidence is highly suggestive, but not conclusive.

It is also important to note that lifestyle changes may not increase life expectancy. Some evidence indicates that a normal human life

[32]See also the discussion in Richard Stroup and John C. Goodman, *Making the World Less Safe: The Unhealthy Trend in Health, Safety and Environmental Regulation*, NCPA Policy Report no. 137 (Dallas: National Center for Policy Analysis, April 1989).

span is about 85 years, regardless of what we do. Lifestyle may have a lot to do with how much we spend on health care during those 85 years, however.[33]

Proposals in the Cost-Plus Health Care System. In a collectivist, bureaucratic environment, the lifestyle choices of any one person impose costs on others. Thus, the economic incentives to make good choices are greatly reduced, and individual choices become social problems. Almost all solutions to such problems within the context of the cost-plus system involve putting group pressure on individuals to change their behavior.[34] Thus, corporations institute programs to encourage lifestyle changes.[35] Governments institute programs that either persuade or coerce, such as laws requiring the use of motorcycle helmets and auto seat belts, and excise taxes for alcohol and tobacco products.

Solutions in the Ideal Health Care System. Recognizing that "a man convinced against his will, is unconvinced still," the ideal health care system would internalize as much as possible the costs and benefits of lifestyle choices. If it is true that health is the consequence of a lifetime of decisionmaking, then decisionmakers should have financial incentives to plan for health care spending over a lifetime. Both Medisave accounts and MIRAs would enable individuals to profit from the financial and the physical/medical aspects of good lifestyle choices. In the health insurance marketplace, we would also expect people with riskier lifestyles to be charged higher premiums. Evel Knievel should not pay the same health insurance premiums as you and I. In the ideal health care system, we may have altruistic reasons to encourage others to adopt good lifestyles. But, for the most part, we are not forced to pay for their bad choices. Group pressure and cultural influences may help, but self-interest and financial incentives are the keys to changing behavior.

---

[33]See James F. Fries, "Aging, National Death, and the Compression of Morbidity," *New England Journal of Medicine* 303 (July 17, 1980): 130–35; and James F. Fries, Lawrence W. Green, and Sol Levine, "Health Promotion and the Compression of Morbidity, " *The Lancet* (March 4, 1989): 481–83.

[34]See the articles on "promoting health" in *Health Affairs* (Summer 1990).

[35]Many corporations have adopted physical fitness programs out of a desire to reduce health care costs, even though the evidence of success is fragmentary and weak. Others are refusing to hire people with risky lifestyles or are charging them higher health insurance premiums. See the discussion below.

7. *People Who Are Uninsurable because They Have Preexisting Health Care Problems*

A small, but not inconsequential, number of people are unable to purchase private health insurance because they have a known—usually expensive-to-treat—health problem. As Table 4.4 shows, health insurers either refuse to cover such people or exclude them from coverage for the preexisting illness. Of course, the primary reason that people with a serious preexisting condition want health insurance is to get an insurer to pay for medical expenses they are virtually certain to incur.

A related problem occurs when people become sick while covered by one insurance carrier, but then are forced to leave that carrier and search for another, either because they change jobs or because the original insurer cancels the policy. The original insurer covers the first phase of the illness, but any new insurer tries to avoid paying for its subsequent treatment. These problems also affect other people. Large companies with health insurance plans that pay for any and all conditions, preexisting or otherwise, attract employees with medical problems, thus contributing to the companies' health insurance costs. In addition, uninsured people with such problems may generate unpaid hospital bills, which then must be paid by everyone else.

It is not surprising that private insurers refuse the obligation to pay for clearly foreseeable medical expenses. If they charged a fair premium, it would be roughly equal to the future medical expenses plus the cost of administering the policy. People with preexisting medical problems would have nothing to gain by purchasing such insurance. Still, many people face severe financial problems because they have high medical bills and no health insurance.

Before turning to solutions, it is worth asking why we do not have a similar problem in a related field: life insurance. The answer is that most people have the opportunity to buy life insurance that is "guaranteed renewable" long before they develop a serious illness. As a result, they can continue paying premiums and can expect a large payment to their beneficiaries even if they are diagnosed with a terminal illness.

Interestingly, most individual and family health insurance policies sold in the 1950s were also guaranteed renewable. If a person became sick while covered by a health insurance policy, that person

Table 4.4

SOME HEALTH CONDITIONS THAT FREQUENTLY CAUSE HIGHER PREMIUMS,
AN EXCLUSION WAIVER, OR DENIAL OF INSURANCE

Higher Premium	Exclusion Waiver	Denial
Allergies	Cataract	AIDS
Asthma	Gallstones	Ulcerative colitis
Back strain	Fibroid tumor (uterus)	Cirrhosis of liver
Hypertension (controlled)	Hernia (hiatal/inguinal)	Diabetes mellitus
Arthritis	Migraine headaches	Leukemia
Gout	Pelvic inflammatory disease	Schizophrenia
Glaucoma	Chronic otitis media (recent)	Hypertension (uncontrolled)
Obesity	Spine/back disorders	Emphysema (severe)
Psychoneurosis (mild)	Hemorrhoids	Stroke
Kidney stones	Knee impairment	Obesity (severe)
Emphysema (mild-moderate)	Asthma	Angina (severe)
Alcoholism/drug use	Allergies	Coronary artery disease
Heart murmur	Varicose veins	Epilepsy
Peptic ulcer	Sinusitis (chronic or severe)	Lupus
Colitis	Fractures	Alcoholism/drug abuse

SOURCE: U.S. Office of Technology Assessment, 1988.

could count on coverage for medical bills indefinitely into the future. Today, it's almost impossible to find a health insurance policy that is guaranteed renewable. Why? There are apparently three reasons. First, because state regulations impose onerous burdens on any insurance company that sells such policies, they have been regulated almost out of existence. Second, the tax law has encouraged the development of a health insurance system that is almost entirely employer-based, despite the increasing mobility in U.S. labor markets; when people switch jobs, they almost always have to switch health insurance policies, and the new carrier typically tries to avoid paying for preexisting illnesses. Third, government policy has encouraged health insurance to evolve into prepayment for the consumption of medical care. To a large extent, real health insurance no longer exists.[36]

Proposals in the Cost-Plus Health Care System. The most common proposals would force insurers to cover preexisting illnesses, often with no additional premium. Many state-mandated health insurance benefit laws already attempt to do that with respect to certain health conditions. Under proposals being considered in many states, insurers would not be able to deny anyone a health insurance policy, or charge a higher premium, because of a preexisting condition. The losses that insurers incur would be subsidized by a tax imposed on all health insurance sold in the state. Another proposal would create state risk pools that would allow patients with preexisting conditions to purchase health insurance at subsidized rates. In most states that already have risk pools, the losses are covered by taxing the health insurance premiums of everyone outside the pool.[37]

Each of these proposals would use health insurance to prepay for the consumption of medical care. People who are already sick would pay premiums well below the actuarially fair value. The losses would be subsidized by forcing others to pay more than the actuarially fair value. In other words, these proposals would force some people to pay for the medical expenses of others. Although the objective may seem humane, the proposals are highly regressive, imposing special burdens on low-income families in order to

---

[36]The problems with health insurance and the reasons for the changing nature of health insurance are discussed in greater detail in the next section of this book.

[37]The exception is Illinois, which subsidizes the losses from general tax revenues.

benefit middle- and upper-income families. As is the case with existing state-mandated benefits laws (which also primarily benefit the middle class), the proposals would raise the price of insurance, thereby imposing a tax on low-income consumers or causing more of them to forgo health insurance altogether.

Solutions in the Ideal Health Care System. If there is a social reason to bail out uninsured people with high medical bills, the efficient way would be through direct monetary payments to those people. An income-related system of disability payments would accomplish that goal. If there is a social reason to subsidize health insurance for some, the efficient and fair way to do it would be to make the subsidy income related, giving the most help to those with the greatest need. Our recent experiences with risk pools suggest that the size of the subsidy would not have to be that large. Currently, about 13 states have mature risk pools, which have been in operation for some period of time. In general, people with preexisting conditions are able to buy into the pool for premiums that average about 50 percent higher than comparable policies for other people (see chapter 11). Even with the high premiums, these risk pools lose about $53 million a year. By one estimate, if this system were extended to all the states, the nationwide deficit would be about $300 million,[38] less than one-twentieth of 1 percent of the nation's annual health care bill. Under a system of public subsidies, with the subsidy falling as income rises, the taxpayer's burden would be even smaller.

In the ideal health care system real insurance, with actuarially fair premiums, would be encouraged and promoted. Government programs to help those in need would work within the context of a competitive health insurance market, rather than undermine the market. Moreover, many of the problems discussed here would never arise in an individualized health insurance marketplace. If health insurance were tailored to individual needs, not employer needs, it would anticipate job changes, the long-term consequences of recurring illness, and other problems. If health insurance were sold in a competitive marketplace, it would probably resemble life

---

[38]Karl J. Knable, Morris Melloy, and C. Keith Powell, "State Health Insurance Risk Pools," *Health Section News*, no. 21, April 1991, pp. 9–12.

insurance. Because guaranteed renewable policies are valuable and desirable, a market for such policies would quite likely develop.

8. *The Rising Number of People Who Lack Health Insurance*

In addition to the uninsurable, there is a much larger number of people who could buy insurance but choose not to. The estimated 34.4 million Americans not covered by either private or public insurance represent about 16 percent of the population. Interestingly, 85 percent of the uninsured are members of a family with a working adult, and more than half of them live in families with an adult who has steady, full-time employment.[39]

There is considerable debate over the dimensions of this problem and how much difference it makes. For example, although as much as 16 percent of the population is uninsured at any point in time, only 4 percent is uninsured for two years or more.[40] Thus, being uninsured is similar to being unemployed. Although many people may experience being uninsured over the course of their work lives, only a small number experience it for a long time. Still, it is a problem that is exacerbated by unwise government policies.[41]

We have already identified three reasons for this problem. First, state legislatures keep passing regulations that increase the price of

---

[39]Jill D. Foley, *Uninsured in the United States: The Nonelderly Population without Health Insurance* (Washington: Employee Benefit Research Institute, April 1991). These estimates are based on the March 1990 *Current Population Survey* and differ somewhat from other estimates. For example, the actual number of uninsured may be closer to 30 million people—about 12.4 percent of the population—and the proportion of uninsured with a workforce affiliation may be only 65 percent, rather than 85 percent. See the summary of the literature in Michael A. Morrisey, "Health Care Reform: A Review of Five Generic Proposals," paper presented at "Winners and Losers in Reforming the U.S. Health Care System," a policy forum sponsored by the Employee Benefit Research Institute Education and Research Fund, Washington, October 4, 1990.

[40]See C. Nelson and K. Short, *Health Insurance Coverage: 1986 to 1988*, U.S. Bureau of the Census Report, no. 17 (1989), p. 70. Reported in Louis P. Garrison, Jr., "Medicaid, the Uninsured, and National Health Spending: Federal Policy Implications," *Health Care Financing Review*, 1990 Annual Supplement, p. 169.

[41]Just as it is easy to minimize the problem, it is also easy to exaggerate it. The figure of 63 million uninsured Americans, widely reported by the national news media, includes people who lacked health insurance for brief periods (rather than continuously) during a 28-month sample period examined by the U.S. Bureau of the Census. See Spencer Rich, "28% in U.S. Seen Lacking Steady Health Insurance," *Washington Post*, April 12, 1990.

Table 4.5
PEOPLE WITHOUT HEALTH INSURANCE,
BY FAMILY INCOME LEVEL, 1989

Family Income	Number of People (Millions)
Under $5,000	4.7
$5,000–$9,999	5.0
$10,000–$14,999	5.6
$15,000–$19,999	4.6
$20,000–$29,999	5.9
$30,000–$39,999	3.2
$40,000–$49,999	1.9
$50,000 or more	3.3
Total	34.4

SOURCE: Jill D. Foley, *Uninsured in the United States: The Nonelderly Population without Health Insurance* (Washington: Employee Benefit Research Institute, April 1991), Table 5 (p. 25).
NOTE: Does not add to total due to rounding.

health insurance. As many as one out of four uninsured people may have chosen not to purchase health insurance because of the price-increasing effects of state regulations. Second, people not covered by employer-provided health insurance are discriminated against under tax law. Unlike employees of large companies, they must pay health insurance premiums with aftertax dollars, effectively doubling the cost for many of them. Third, tax law and employee benefits law are causing employers to act in ways that result in even more employees and their dependents going without health insurance. As Table 4.5 shows, these policies have the greatest impact on low-income families.

Even if they were not priced out of the market by bad public policies, many uninsured people conclude there is no reason to buy health insurance. If they get sick, they find ways of becoming insured through an employer's plan. Even if they cannot get insurance, they still get medical care—paid for by someone else.

Proposals in the Cost-Plus Health Care System. Some commonly discussed proposals are to force everyone to purchase health insurance, force employers to purchase insurance on behalf of all their employees,[42] expand the number of people covered by Medicaid and state risk pools, and force everyone to participate in a system of national health insurance. Each of these proposals, though, ignores the principal reason why people lack health insurance in the first place: They are denied the opportunity to buy it at actuarially fair prices with equal advantage under federal tax law. Instead of encouraging market competition and giving individuals more control over their health care dollars, the proposals would force people to buy into a defective system of third-party insurance coverage and undermine the development of a genuine health insurance market.

Solutions in the Ideal Health Care System. Under an ideal health care system, people would face fair prices for insurance, sold in a freely competitive market. Special-interest politics would not artificially inflate health insurance premiums. All people would receive the same tax advantage for the purchase of insurance, regardless of employment. And people would have stronger incentives to purchase health insurance before they develop chronic illnesses. The ideal system would not ignore the fact that health insurance premiums may be beyond the means of some families. But the solution is to empower the families, not impersonal third-party bureaucracies. Through a system of tax credits, low-income families would be encouraged to exercise free choice as buyers in a health insurance marketplace.

9. Uncompensated Hospital Care

Each year, American hospitals have about $8 billion in uncollected charges. It is not clear how much of this amount is unpaid because people cannot afford to pay and how much is unpaid simply because the hospitals make insufficient efforts to collect. Some studies suggest that half of uncollected hospital bills are generated by patients who have health insurance coverage.[43]

---

[42]Because employers will not employ people unless the value of the employee's output is roughly equal to the value of his or her compensation, forcing employers to provide health insurance is equivalent to forcing them to substitute a fringe benefit (health insurance) for wages. This issue is considered at greater length in chapter 12.

[43]See Robert M. Saywell et al., "Hospital and Patient Characteristics of Uncompensated Hospital Care: Policy Implications," *Journal of Health Politics, Policy and Law* 14, no. 2 (Summer 1989): 287; and Congressional Research Service, *Costs and Effects of Extending Health Insurance Coverage* (Washington: October 1988), pp. 101, 103.

Almost all businesses have some bad debts. But consumers seldom have reason to care. In the health care system, things are different. Third-party payers pay not only for the medical care of their policyholders, but also for the bad debts of others. In other words, the hospital rates that you and I pay are partly determined by how many other patients fail to pay. Bad debts are not distributed evenly among the nation's hospitals. For example, a special problem arises for hospitals designated to receive charity patients. In many communities, this is the county hospital. County hospitals complain that they are undercompensated from public funds for the care they provide. They also complain of patient dumping—the practice of transferring charity patients from other hospitals to county hospitals, in some cases risking the health of the patient.[44]

Proposals in the Cost-Plus Health Care System. The most common proposals are similar to those for dealing with the uninsured. They would force all people to have health insurance, either through their place of employment or through national health insurance. Those proposals could cost in excess of $100 billion, while reducing hospital bad debts by only about $8 billion.

Solutions in the Ideal Health Care System. In an ideal health care system, hospitals would be expected to cover their costs while charging competitive prices to all patients. Some provision would exist to reimburse hospitals for indigent care under carefully defined conditions. When those conditions are met, the best solution would be to reimburse hospitals from public funds rather than attempting to shift the cost of care to other patients. If hospitals are required by law to treat patients, whether or not the patient can pay, then the government (and voter/taxpayers) imposing this requirement should be willing to pay the cost. This provision should not relieve hospitals of the responsibility of collecting fees, however. Those with excessive bad debts would be allowed to fail. One reasonable method for funding indigent care (as we discussed in chapter 3) would be based on a fair system of tax subsidies for the purchase of health insurance. Those who choose not to insure would pay higher taxes, and the extra tax payments could serve as

---

[44]See L. M. Beitsch, "Economic Patient Dumping: Whose Life Is It Anyway?" *Journal of Legal Medicine* 10, no. 3 (1989): 433–87; and "'Dumping' Mandated by Law," *AAPS News* 47, no. 1 (January 1991).

a pool of funds from which to pay for free care delivered at charity hospitals.

In an ideal health care system, people would be encouraged to insure for major illnesses and save for minor ones. But no one would be forced to do so. People who failed to purchase health insurance would pay higher taxes, and people who incurred bad hospital debts would suffer financial penalties, the same as for other bad debts.

10. Health Insurance Coverage for Substance Abuse and Mental Health

In a competitive health insurance market, it is very difficult to insure for treatment of alcohol or drug abuse or mental health problems. The majority of people—those who do not have or expect to have such problems—would choose not to purchase optional coverage for them. Those choosing it almost certainly would have a problem and intend to file claims. A fair premium for such coverage, then, would be extremely high—roughly equal to the cost of medical claims that are almost certain to be incurred. Such a premium would simply be prepayment for the consumption of medical care. As a result, coverage for alcoholism, drug abuse, mental health, and similar illnesses is almost never offered as an option in individual policies unless state law requires it. Coverage for these items is almost always found in group policies (where individuals are not given choices) and in states that mandate it. Where coverage is available, its cost tends to be quite high, especially since there are few objective standards for determining when an "illness" is present, when it has been "cured," and what treatment is "necessary." Small wonder that almost unlimited amounts of money can be spent.

When patients paid for alcohol and drug abuse treatment out-of-pocket, the treatment of choice was usually Alcoholics Anonymous (AA). The program is incredibly cheap, and it's still not clear that any other program is better.[45] Once third-party insurers started paying the bills, however, programs sprang up everywhere and costs began to soar.

---

[45]Most studies find little difference in the methods of treatment, including no difference in inpatient versus outpatient care. See, however, D. C. Walsh et al., "A Randomized Trial of Treatment Options for Alcohol-Abusing Workers," *New England Journal of Medicine* 325, no. 11 (September 12, 1991): 775–82.

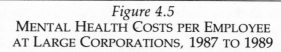

Figure 4.5
MENTAL HEALTH COSTS PER EMPLOYEE
AT LARGE CORPORATIONS, 1987 TO 1989

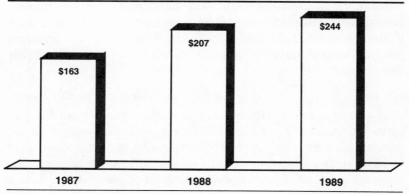

SOURCE: A. Foster Higgins & Co., *Health Care Benefits Survey, 1989: Mental Health and Substance Abuse Benefits.*

Among those paying are large corporations with generous health insurance programs. As Figure 4.5 shows, company spending for mental health benefits has increased by 50 percent in only two years.[46] Often the benefit goes to an employee dependent, rather than the employee, covering problems ranging from eating disorders and sexual abuse to "codependency." One critic contends that mental health hospitals are becoming "dumping grounds for adolescents whose parents want nothing to do with them." One-fifth of all private psychiatric hospital admissions are now patients under age 18.[47]

Proposals in the Cost-Plus Health Care System. Most people with a proposal urge us to ignore the costs and force all policyholders to have coverage for alcohol and drug abuse, mental health, and related treatments.[48] Their proposals would extend prepayment of

[46]See, however, Richard Frank, David Salkever, and Steven Sharfstein, "A New Look at Rising Mental Health Insurance Costs," *Health Affairs* (Summer 1991), pp. 116–23.

[47]Tim W. Ferguson, "Any Wonder Medical Premiums Are Anything But Shrinking," *Wall Street Journal*, May 22, 1990.

[48]See, for example, the articles on "Paying for Mental Health Care" in *Health Affairs* (Spring 1990).

medical care through third-party insurers to an area in which cost containment is extremely difficult, and the costs would be reflected in everyone's health insurance premiums.

Solutions in the Ideal Health Care System. In an ideal health care system, people would always be free to purchase policies tailored to individual and family needs; insurance would never be used as a vehicle for the prepayment of medical care; and if insurers were to reimburse policyholders for unexpected alcoholism, drug dependence, or mental illness, the policyholders and their families would become the principal buyers of medical care at the time it was administered, perhaps using insurance reimbursement funds. When people are paying out-of-pocket for alcohol and drug abuse therapy, they won't pay much unless the treatment is clearly more valuable than the free therapy offered by Alcoholics Anonymous. Furthermore, in the ideal health care system, people are encouraged to save for precisely those contingencies for which it is impossible to insure in a competitive marketplace.

11. Medical Expenses for the Terminally Ill

In America, we spend an enormous amount of money on patients who are very near death and occasionally on patients who (for all practical purposes) are already dead. In the Medicare program alone, we spend almost one out of every three dollars on elderly patients who are in the last year of their lives; as much as one out of every ten Medicare dollars is spent on elderly patients within the last 40 days of their lives.[49] In some highly publicized cases, families have been forced to sue hospitals to disconnect artificial life support systems from loved ones who had become little more than human vegetables. These facts are surprising only if we view health care dollars as primarily belonging to patients and if we view patients and their families as the primary customers of hospitals. They are not surprising once we acknowledge that most health care dollars are transferred from bureaucracy to bureaucracy, far out of reach of patients and their families.

Unlike in the United States, cancer patients in Britain are spared not only the high cost of death but also the agony of painful therapies. Terminally ill cancer patients in Britain are often sent to hospices, where they are given heroin injections to ease their pain. The

---

[49]Estimates of the U.S. Department of Health and Human Services.

British solution seems sensible, but with one caveat. In Britain, as in America, the money is controlled by bureaucracies, not by patients and families. So it's not clear whether the choice of a hospice over continued treatment reflects family preferences or bureaucratic rationing. Cancer patients with the potential to be cured are much better off in the American health care system.[50]

It is interesting, once again, to contrast health insurance with life insurance. Prudential Insurance Company has announced plans to pay life insurance benefits to terminally ill patients prior to their death. Other insurers are considering following suit, on the theory that people should be able to enjoy their death benefit in the last months of life.[51] Because the primary health insurer of terminally ill patients is the federal government (Medicare), we are not likely to see innovation on the health insurance side. But there is the opportunity to merge the British approach to terminal illness with the approach of U.S. life insurance companies. Patients could be given a choice to take some portion of the money that would be spent on high-technology care and use it to live out their remaining months in a more pleasant hospice environment—or, for that matter, to take a Caribbean cruise.

Proposals in the Cost-Plus Health Care System. Aside from the almost universally accepted concept of a living will, the most common proposals involve the creation of more bureaucracies—that is, committees of experts (even more removed from families than are hospital physicians) who will search for ethical answers to these difficult questions.

Solutions in the Ideal Health Care System. In an ideal health care system, patients and families would control the health care

[50]Cancer treatment rates in Britain are much lower than in the United States, with 10,000 to 15,000 British cancer patients failing to receive chemotherapy relative to U.S. levels. See Henry J. Aaron and William B. Schwartz, *The Painful Prescription: Rationing Hospital Care* (Washington: Brookings Institution, 1984). The British system is discussed more fully in chapter 17.

[51]Payments can be in the form of a lump sum or a monthly annuity. The principal obstacle is government. State regulators have to approve the scheme and, as of January 1990, only ten had done so. Some state insurance laws prohibit accelerated death benefits, and there is some fear that the Internal Revenue Service will try to tax them, although life insurance benefits are normally not taxable. Tamar Lewin, "Terminally Ill Can Collect Death Payout While Alive," *New York Times,* January 27, 1990.

dollars and—most of the time—hospitals would respond to family wishes. The role of the hospital would be to inform the patient and family of their choices.

12. *Long-Term Nursing Home Care for the Elderly*

Currently, Medicare does not pay for long-term nursing home care for elderly patients. Medicaid (for the poor) will pay, but only after an elderly patient has exhausted virtually all personal financial resources. One consequence is that nursing home care is the largest single health care expense likely to confront an elderly individual. As Figure 4.6 shows, among out-of-pocket expenses for the elderly in excess of $2,000, about 81 percent goes for long-term care.

Is there a need for additional nursing home care for the elderly? That's not clear. For every elderly person in a nursing home, two other—equally disabled—elderly people are not. This situation reflects the fact that, when people are forced to pay with their own money, many find cheaper options. Nursing home care costs about $25,000 a year, in part owing to government regulations that require most nursing homes to be structurally safer than the average Hilton hotel. For the most part, Medicaid patients in nursing homes cannot take the money spent on their behalf and try to find the same care for a lower price. As with other parts of the health care sector, the system is not designed to help patients find a good deal or a reasonable price. Rather, it is designed to funnel billions of dollars into nursing homes.

There is very little private insurance for nursing home care. One reason is that it is extremely difficult to construct objective definitions of the circumstance under which nursing home care is indicated. Entry into a nursing home requires a physician's statement that the treatment is necessary, but physicians often base their judgments, not on the patient's medical condition, but on family preferences. Nursing home care very often is a choice about living arrangements rather than a medical necessity. Another reason for the lack of long-term care insurance is federal tax policy, which creates tax subsidies for health insurance for current medical expenses but disallows tax deductions for premiums for future medical expenses. Savings or insurance premiums for future medical expenses must be paid with aftertax dollars.

There is no question that if nursing home care were provided free to the elderly, the demand would soar. Some estimate the

Figure 4.6
ANNUAL OUT-OF-POCKET EXPENSES FOR THE ELDERLY IN EXCESS OF $2,000

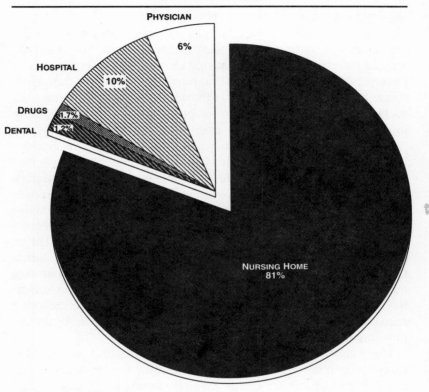

SOURCE: Health Care Financing Administration.

additional cost at $60 billion a year, but it could be much higher. If every elderly person spent one year in a nursing home, the total cost would be about $627 billion per year.

Proposals in the Cost-Plus Health Care System. Most current proposals encourage us to ignore the costs and extend free nursing home care to elderly Medicare patients. In general, such proposals would concentrate even more power over long-term care dollars in the hands of a federal bureaucracy. They would not give the elderly more choices.

Table 4.6
COST OF ORGAN TRANSPLANTS IN THE UNITED STATES

Type of Transplant	Cost	One-Year Survival Rate
Kidney (living)	$30,000	96%
Kidney (cadaver)	30,000	91
Pancreas	40,000	91
Liver	230,000	60–70
Heart	110,000	80
Heart-Lung	200,000	65
Bone marrow	95,000	13–55
Cornea	5,250	55–90
Lung	240,000	35

SOURCE: *Health Span,* June 1991; reprinted in *Medical Benefits* 8, no. 15 (August 15, 1991), Table 1 (p. 6).

Solutions in the Ideal Health Care System. Under an ideal health care system, patients would not stay in nursing homes if they could find better options at lower prices. Real long-term care insurance would make payments to people, not nursing home administrators. Individual patients would enter nursing homes only if the services offered were worth the price. Moreover, an ideal tax system would encourage savings for long-term care.

13. *Organ Transplants, Designer Drug Therapy, and Other Lifesaving but Expensive Medical Technologies*

One of the strangest features of health care politics is the inordinate effort to get coverage for items that most people can afford to pay for out-of-pocket (for example, mammograms and pap smears) and the lack of attention to coverage for inordinately expensive, lifesaving technologies that few could pay for out-of-pocket. To the degree that there has been any real discussion of organ transplants, for example, the focus has not been on the need to insure for such procedures but on how to decide, bureaucratically, who among the uninsured will get transplants.

Most people are not insured for organ transplants. Yet, as Table 4.6 shows, if the need arose most people would find it difficult to pay for one. Although we frequently hear that the constraint on

109

Table 4.7
ORGAN TRANSPLANTS IN THE UNITED STATES:
NEED VERSUS SUPPLY

Type of Transplant	Number of Transplants Performed	Number of Additional People on the Waiting List
Kidney	9,560	17,938
Pancreas	549	473
Liver	2,656	1,242
Heart	2,085	1,794
Heart-Lung	50	226

SOURCE: United Network for Organ Sharing, *Transplant Statistics* (Richmond, VA, 1991).

transplants is a lack of donors (see Table 4.7), an additional constraint is money. Kidney transplants are less expensive and usually paid for by government. Other transplants often must be paid for with private funds.[52]

In addition to organ transplants, other emerging technologies have great promise but will be very costly. One of the most intriguing is "designer drugs." These drugs are tailor-made for a specific patient, based on the patient's DNA makeup. In the future, undoubtedly there will be other technologies that promise to save lives but carry price tags far beyond the financial means of most people.

Proposals in the Cost-Plus Health Care System. Proposals usually fall into two camps: those to get government to fund expensive procedures that hospitals are already performing and want to perform more of, and those to set up rationing committees to determine which uninsured patients receive the treatment. The focus of the proposals is on institutions and the money they will have to spend, not on patients and their preferences. For example, it is almost never suggested that a patient should be able to choose between having an expensive procedure done or keeping the money to spend for some other purpose.

[52]See Robert H. Blank, *Rationing Medicine* (New York: Columbia University Press, 1988).

Solutions in the Ideal Health Care System. In an ideal health care system, insurers would have incentives to develop policies anticipating new technologies and helping people insure for them. New, lifesaving, expensive technologies are viewed as the enemy of today's health insurers, who often refuse to pay on the grounds that treatments are experimental, sometimes even after they have been proved effective. Once health insurers get out of the business of buying health care, however, they will see new technologies as a reason why policyholders should buy more insurance, so they can afford the technologies if needed.

14. *Health Care Rationing*

Because we could in principle spend many times our gross national product on health care, it must be rationed in some way. The primary way in which it is rationed in the United States is by individual choice. When the expected cost of medical care exceeds its expected benefit, people forgo it. For example, some people choose self-medication with nonprescription drugs. What deters them from going to the doctor's office every time is the physician's fee, the time cost, the travel cost, lost wages, and other inconveniences. As discussed earlier, if everyone who purchased nonprescription drugs saw a physician instead, the United States would need 25 times the current number of physicians.

For years, advocates of socialized medicine have argued that all health care (*all* health care) should be free at the point of consumption and that it is unfair (and perhaps also unwise) to ask people to compare the value of health care with the cost of getting it. But if health care were made absolutely costless, the system that provides it would collapse into chaos. Thus, even in countries such as Britain and Canada where health care is theoretically free, people are deterred by other costs (including waiting costs) and an enormous amount of self-rationing goes on.

The alternative to self-rationing is bureaucratic rationing. For example, many large companies are seeking ways to deter health care spending. Most are opting for bureaucratic solutions. But at least one company, Hewlett Packard, has announced a plan that explicitly calls for employee rationing by choice. The plan involves many of the concepts discussed in this book, including giving patients more information, encouraging choices between money

111

and medical care, and using physicians as "patient advisers rather than technicians or deliverers of care."[53] Until recently, rationing by bureaucracy in the private sector was rare, confined largely to organ transplants and occasional triage situations in hospitals. Rationing is more frequent in the public sector and is increasing in the Medicare and Medicaid programs.

Outside the United States, every country that has national health insurance rations health care through bureaucracies. It is almost never done through open, rational debate. Instead, politicians limit the budgets of hospitals or of area health authorities and leave rationing decisions to the health care bureaucracy. Indeed, politicians almost never admit that they are in any way responsible for rationing.

Among the characteristics of health care rationing as practiced in other developed countries (as discussed in chapter 17) are the following. If health care is rationed by bureaucracies, the tendency is to discriminate in favor of higher income patients, in favor of whites (especially male whites), and in favor of the young. The sophisticated, the wealthy, and the powerful almost always find their way to the head of rationing lines. Whereas markets empower individuals, bureaucracies empower special interests.

Rationing decisions in the United States appear to be no different. Studies have discovered that, when transplants are rationed, bureaucracies appear to discriminate on the basis of income, race, and sex. For example, a study by the Urban Institute found that, for black and white males, the higher their income, the more likely they are to receive an organ transplant.[54] In 1988, according to the United Network for Organ Sharing, whites received 97.6 percent of the pancreases and high percentages of livers, kidneys, and hearts; and men received 79.2 percent of hearts, 60.6 percent of

[53]Karl Palzer, "Rationing by Choice," *Business and Health* (October 1990), pp. 60–64.

[54]Phillip J. Held et al., "Access to Kidney Transplantation: Has the United States Eliminated Income and Racial Differences?" *Archives of Internal Medicine* 14 (December 1988): 2594-2600. A likely reason for the discrepancy is Medicare reimbursement policies, which place greater burdens on lower income patients. Prior to 1987, Medicare did not pay for outpatient drugs such as cyclosporine, which can cost transplant patients up to $5,000 per year. It would be irrational to spend $50,000 on a transplant and have it rejected because the patient could not afford $5,000 in medication. Currently, Medicare pays for 80 percent of immunosuppressive drugs for one year.

kidneys, and 54.4 percent of pancreases.[55] According to the American Society of Transplant Physicians, although the rate of end-stage
renal disease is four times higher among blacks than among whites,
blacks constitute 28 percent of the kidney patients and receive only
21 percent of the kidney transplants.[56] The *Pittsburgh Press* found
that if the donors were not living relatives, the average wait for a
kidney transplant in 1988 and 1989 was 14 months for black patients
and only 8.8 months for whites.[57]

In the United States, the elderly have a privileged position with
respect to health care. Medicare covers virtually all of them, plus a
small percent of people under 65 (the disabled). But in other countries, where the entire population is part of the same government-
funded health care plan, the elderly are usually pushed to the end
of the rationing lines. Thus, in Britain, it is extremely difficult for
an elderly patient to get kidney dialysis or a kidney transplant—or
any other transplant, for that matter.[58] Moreover, pressures that
have developed in other countries are developing in our own.
Former Colorado governor Richard Lamm and other prominent
individuals (including "medical ethicists") are calling for rationing
health care to the elderly and reallocating the funds to the younger
population.[59]

Proposals in the Cost-Plus Health Care System. Until a few years
ago, the practitioners and defenders of cost-plus medicine did not
believe in health care rationing. Their goal was to lower all financial
barriers through public and private insurance and to meet any
and all needs. Today, almost everyone recognizes that rationing is
necessary. Many people in the modern cost-plus bureaucracy not

[55]Associated Press, May 20, 1989.

[56]Bertram L. Kasiske, John F. Neylan III, et al., "The Effect of Race on Access and
Outcome in Transplantation," *New England Journal of Medicine* 324, no. 5 (January
31, 1991): 302–7

[57]Reported in the *Dallas Morning News,* August 19, 1990.

[58]See John C. Goodman and Gerald L. Musgrave, *Health Care for the Elderly: The
Nightmare in Our Future,* NCPA Policy Report no. 130 (Dallas: National Center for
Policy Analysis, October 1987); and Aaron and Schwartz, *The Painful Prescription.*

[59]For a summary of these views, see Norman G. Levinsky, "Age as a Criterion for
Rationing Health Care," *New England Journal of Medicine* 322, no. 25 (June 21, 1990):
1813–15.

113

...t also welcome it with open arms—pro-

...s controlled by the (health care) bureaucracy

patients.[60]

...eal Health Care System. In an ideal system,

...y patient choice wherever possible. The system

...l so that people would have the funds necessary

...n care through medical savings and reimburse-

...ers. But people would have strong incentives not

to purc... ...lth care unless the expected value of the care were greater than the monetary costs. Patients, of course, could consult their physicians. But the power of choice would be in the hands of the patients, not the bureaucrats.

15. Unnecessary Medical Care

Robert Brook of the Rand Corporation maintains that "perhaps one-fourth of hospital days, one-fourth of procedures and two-fifths of medications could be done without."[61] James Todd, executive vice president of the American Medical Association, disagrees.[62] But evidence produced by Rand researchers has become part of the national health care debate.[63]

Rand researchers first discovered wide variations in 123 medical procedures for Medicare patients in various parts of the country. The rate at which the procedures were performed varied by as much as 6, 7, or 8 to 1, with no apparent explanation. Areas that were high in performing one procedure were often low in performing another. The Rand study was consistent with other studies of non-Medicare patients, which have found widespread variations in medical practice across geographical areas for several decades. Just knowing about the variations, however, did not reveal whether some patients were being shortchanged and others overtreated.

[60]For a representative point of view, as well as a good review of the literature on rationing, see Blank.

[61]Robert H. Brook, "Practice Guidelines and Practicing Medicine: Are They Compatible?" *Journal of the American Medical Association* 262, no. 21 (December 1, 1989): 3028.

[62]Ron Winslow and Sonia L. Nazario, "AMA, Rand Go after Modern Ill: Unneeded Procedures," *Wall Street Journal*, March 22, 1990.

[63]A summary of Rand Corporation research may be found in Mark R. Chassin, ed., *The Appropriateness of Selected Medical and Surgical Procedures* (Ann Arbor, MI: Health Administration Press, 1989).

Table 4.8
RAND CORPORATION STUDY ON UNNECESSARY MEDICINE AS REPORTED BY THE NATIONAL MEDIA

	Panel's Assessment[1]		
	Appropriate	Equivocal	Inappropriate
Coronary angiography[2]	74%	9%	17%
Carotid endarterectomy[3]	35	32	32
Upper gastrointestinal endoscopy[4]	72	11	17
Overall	60	18	22

SOURCE: Rand Corporation study results, reported in the *Wall Street Journal*, March 22, 1990.
[1]Based on medical records of 5,000 Medicare patients.
[2]Use of x-rays and dye to explore obstructions of the heart.
[3]Surgical removal of obstructions in major arteries to the brain.
[4]Fiber-optic examination of the esophagus, stomach, and upper intestine.

Consequently, a follow-up Rand study collected medical records for 5,000 Medicare patients and convened a panel of experts to judge the appropriateness of three procedures. The results (as reported by the national news media) are shown in Table 4.8. As the table shows, in more than a fifth of the cases, the procedure performed was judged to be inappropriate and therefore unnecessary. For carotid endarterectomy (the removal of plaque in major arteries to the brain), the procedure was judged to be appropriate only about one-third of the time.[64]

Before we jump on the doctors, it's worth noting that in some ways the Rand study was unfair. Suppose we convened experts in your field and asked them to review decisions you have made. Would they agree with every decision? You might respond, as the doctors do, that you didn't have the opportunity to consult with a panel of experts before you made your decisions. A second problem with the Rand results is the way in which they have been reported. What Rand means by "equivocal" is that a majority of the experts

[64]"Appropriateness" is not determined by Monday morning quarterbacking. It is based on indications prior to the procedure. A procedure is judged appropriate if the expected benefit (increased life expectancy, relief of pain, etc.) exceeds the expected negative consequences (mortality, morbidity, etc.) by a margin sufficient to justify the procedure. See Chassin.

Table 4.9
ANOTHER VIEW OF THE RAND STUDY ON
UNNECESSARY MEDICINE

	Percent of Time 7 of 9 Experts Agree That Procedure Is		
	Appropriate	Inappropriate	Total
Coronary angiography	50%	12%	62%
Carotid endarterectomy	13	17	30
Upper gastrointestinal endoscopy	46	7	53
Overall	36	12	48

SOURCE: Rand Corporation, as reported in Robert H. Brook, "Practice Guidelines and Practicing Medicine: Are They Compatible?" *Journal of the American Medical Association* 262, no. 21 (December 1, 1989): 3021.

couldn't agree. But in newspaper reports, the word "equivocal" often became "questionable" (as in "40 percent of the procedures were either inappropriate or questionable"), which is not the same thing. Equivocal means that not performing the procedure is just as problematic as performing it. A third problem is that media reports of the Rand study obscured the actual extent of disagreement and uncertainty in the medical community. The reason why Rand had to convene a panel of experts was that researchers could not answer questions about appropriateness by merely consulting the medical literature. Once the experts were convened, they were far less unified than is commonly known.

Table 4.9 presents a different way of looking at the Rand study, showing the number of times that 7 of 9 experts agreed (the two opinions ignored are the two most extreme views, on either side of the middle). As the table shows, when 7 of 9 experts were asked to agree, they found only 12 percent of the procedures to be inappropriate, not 22 percent. And even this degree of consensus is misleading. In the Rand study, each expert initially expressed a personal judgment. Then they met in group discussions (where group pressure had an opportunity to forge a consensus), after which several members often changed their minds.[65] Indeed, the most

[65]"Disagreement among the panelists diminished following their discussions, but by no means disappeared." Chassin, p. 8.

remarkable fact about the Rand study was that even with all of those efforts to arrive at a definitive judgment, 7 of 9 experts could agree that the procedures were either definitely appropriate or definitely inappropriate less than half the time.

So when Rand spokesmen state that 40 percent of surgery is "unnecessary," that's a personal point of view, not the unanimous conclusion of experts. Rand researchers have adopted the viewpoint that, if physicians can't agree that surgery should be performed, it should not be. Rand research, however, shows something different. The fact that the experts couldn't agree in half the cases tells us much more about the state of medical science than about the state of medical practice.

A fourth problem is that the data from the Rand study were for 1981, more than a decade ago. Generalizing about today's health care based on what happened in 1981 is clearly wrong. The 1980s produced major changes in the way hospitals are run. For better or for worse, American physicians today are scrutinized more closely by peers and third-party payers than physicians anywhere else in the world. There are probably still cases in which experts would agree that the surgery promised more harm than good, but those cases are likely to be presented to disciplinary committees and are probably far less than the 12 percent shown in Table 4.9.

A fifth problem is that Rand researchers tried to develop a purely medical test to determine whether surgery should have been performed, when the real problem they were trying to address was an economic one.[66] Their study compared the medical benefits of procedures with the medical harm. However, as noted above, cases in which the expected medical harm exceeds the expected medical benefit are probably quite rare. The real question is whether procedures are worth their cost. And the only people who can accurately answer that question are patients who can choose to spend that same money on other goods and services.

A final problem is that the Rand research is frequently used by advocates of socialized medicine to criticize the U.S. system of private

[66]With reference to the numbers in Table 4.9, Rand's Robert Brook agrees that, from a purely medical perspective, perhaps only 12 percent of the procedures (which all the experts agree should not be done) are unnecessary. But when economic factors are considered, perhaps only 36 percent of the procedures (which all the experts agree should be done) are justified. Brook, 3027.

medical care. What the critics fail to mention is that countries with national health insurance also experience wide variations in medical practice. In Britain, for example, physicians have no direct financial interest in performing any medical procedure. But the rate at which British general practitioners refer patients to hospital physicians varies by at least 4 to 1 and, according to one study, by 25 to 1. Moreover, there is a high correlation between patient referrals and subsequent hospital admissions.[67]

What can we conclude? The most important implication from the Rand study is that medical practice is still more an art than a science, and that when physicians are faced with difficult choices, they may not be able to get firm direction either from the medical literature or from a national panel of experts. A second implication is that a small number of physicians may be systematically putting their patients at risk by using clearly inappropriate procedures—and, if that is the case, something should be done about it. A third implication is that patients who are told they need a medical procedure should ask questions before agreeing to it, especially if the procedure is expensive or risky.

Can medicine be made more scientific? Some apparently think so. The American Medical Association and the Rand Corporation are working to develop "practice guidelines" for physicians considering certain procedures, and Congress has mandated that the Department of Health and Human Services draw up similar guidelines. The goal is the development of "computerized protocols" that will let physicians know what they should do when confronted with certain patient symptoms and conditions.

Will the guidelines work? That's not clear. Many people believe they will be a waste of money. Some argue that their development is such a lengthy process that medical science will have outpaced them by the time they are available. In other words, computerized protocols will always be years behind scientific developments in medicine. Others raise the philosophical objection that computerized protocols assume correct medical procedures usually can be determined by a computer program, which obviously has never met or talked to the patient. Studies have not borne out that assumption,

[67]Office of Health Economics, *Variations between General Practitioners*, OHE Briefing no. 26 (July 1990).

however. In one test, judgments of general practitioners were matched with three different computerized protocols in the treatment of patients with abdominal pain; the GPs outperformed the protocols in every test.[68]

If workable computerized protocols were available to physicians, they might prove to be valuable tools. A physician could consult the computer, then substitute his own judgment where appropriate. Less complicated protocols might become available to patients for use on their home computers, giving advice on whether to see a physician, for example.

On the other hand, if computerized protocols and practice guidelines were used to control the behavior of physicians and patients, they could threaten the quality of medical care. And, unfortunately, that threat is real. Researcher Robert Brook has argued that the Rand Corporation's techniques can be used to ration health care under the Medicare system, if Medicare funds run short.[69]

Proposals in the Cost-Plus Health Care System. Lurking behind the public discussion of practice guidelines is a fundamental difference of philosophy that is rarely discussed in print. The bureaucratic view of health care is usually also a technocratic view. Its more extreme proponents are fundamentally antiphysician and antipatient, in the sense that they believe the attitudes and judgments of individuals are largely irrelevant. Ultimately, the technocrats do not see the computer as an aid to physicians and patients but as a substitute. They envision medical practice being literally dictated for the country as a whole from a central location in—well, Washington.

Although the discussion of practice guidelines frequently is couched in terms of helping physicians make good decisions, the technocrats also see the guidelines as a means of exerting control. In their view, physicians who substitute their own judgment for the computer's should have to prove that they are right, which would require them to use cumbersome and costly bureaucratic procedures. As a result, instances in which the guidelines were not followed would be rare and unusual events.

---

[68]Jane Orient, "An Evaluation of Abdominal Pain: Clinicians' Performance Compared with Three Protocols," *Southern Medical Journal* 79, no. 7 (July 1986): 793–9.
[69]Brook, 3029.

Solutions in the Ideal Health Care System. In an ideal system, patients would become far more involved in the decisionmaking process. They would have new opportunities to learn about the potential costs and benefits of medical procedures and to make decisions based on their evaluations of those costs and benefits. The role of the physician would be to help patients make those difficult decisions, based on their own values. To the extent that computer programs can be a real aid to patients and physicians, they would be used for that purpose. But people would not surrender their decisionmaking authority. Most important, patients would not be told there is only one correct way of treating a condition when the opinions of physicians vary. When professional opinions diverge, patients would be the first to know. Most unnecessary surgery today is unnecessary only in the sense that it's not worth the cost. In an ideal health care system, patients would be encouraged to weigh its benefits against its costs and have the option of forgoing the procedure and spending the money elsewhere.

16. Medical Ethics

It is widely believed that the Hippocratic oath embodies a code that has formed the basis for physicians' decisions from the time of ancient Greece to the present day. Recent scholarship has brought this notion into question, however. There is strong evidence that the Hippocratic oath was not written by Hippocrates. Further, the code may have represented the ethical and medical views of a small religious sect—views explicitly rejected by mainstream Greek physicians. Moreover, the Hippocratic oath contains positions both on ethics and on medical science that the vast majority of modern physicians reject.[70]

Although many physicians still honor the tradition and general sentiments of the Hippocratic oath, as a practical matter, the oath is largely ignored in modern medicine. Yet one of its legacies is the injunction that a physician, if unable to heal or cure, shall do no harm. To some physicians, the injunction implies that they should

[70]Ludwig Edelstein, *The Hippocratic Oath: Text, Translation, and Interpretation* (Baltimore: Johns Hopkins Press, 1943). See also W.H.S. Jones, *The Doctor's Oath: An Essay in the History of Medicine* (Cambridge, MA: Cambridge University Press, 1926); and Wesley D. Smith, *The Hippocratic Tradition* (Ithaca, NY: Cornell University Press, 1979).

do everything possible to ensure the physical well-being of their patients. Or, given that almost everything in medicine is probabilistic, it implies to some that they should do everything that *might* help the patient. Many patients and policymakers have the same expectations. In economic terms, that means that medical science is required by medical ethics to devote resources to the healing and care of patients until such point that the marginal effect on health of the last dollar spent approaches zero. Were we to follow this injunction rigorously, we easily could spend our entire gross national product on health care many times over.

What will replace the old medical ethics? American physicians are increasingly pressured to adopt the newer ethics of cost-benefit analysis. They are supposed to compare the health value of a procedure with its monetary cost. In effect, the new ethic says: "Perform procedures until the marginal health benefit is greater than or equal to the marginal monetary cost." The new ethic results in less medical care, but it ensures that whatever we get is worth the resources it costs.

The standard objection to cost-benefit analysis is that it is impossible to compare the value of health (or of life) with the value of money. But that objection is weak. Each of us makes choices between health (and safety) and money every day, and most of us are comfortable doing so. A larger automobile is safer, but it costs more money. Walking is safer than driving, but it takes more time, and, for most of us, time is money. Indeed, we are constantly balancing health and safety against money, and we don't always come down on the side of health and safety. A stronger objection is that although we may feel comfortable making our own choices between health and money, most of us are uncomfortable making choices for others. The obvious solution is to let each individual choose. If a reasonably well-informed patient makes a choice between health care and money, then we presume the patient will choose the option that has the higher value for him or her. But for individuals to make such choices, they have to have the option of keeping the money. In today's system, each of us makes choices between our own health care and somebody else's money. Real cost-benefit analysis demands that we choose between health care and our own money.

If we deny individual choice and insist on collective decisionmaking about health care resources, then we are forced to use a different technique. Health economists must judge (or guess) the trade-offs that an average individual would make. Such cost-benefit analysis then forces everybody else to make the same decision, even though individual preferences differ radically. The technique is justified on the grounds that we are comparing social cost with social benefit.

Because cost-benefit analysis is complicated, physicians are not trained in it, and the health care bureaucracy doesn't trust physicians anyway, no advocates of the collectivist approach suggest that physicians should implement it. Instead, they envision that technocrats will decide what procedures physicians will use under various circumstances—perhaps with the aid of the computerized protocols described above. Physicians will make far fewer ethical decisions because they will make far fewer medical decisions.

Although cost-benefit studies are routinely done by economists in and out of government in every policy field, there appear to be very few programs that are actually run on the basis of such analyses. The reason is that politics always interferes. An apparent exception was the federal government's program to administer swine flu shots to the elderly—a program that resulted in unnecessary deaths.[71]

Proposals in the Cost-Plus Health Care System. Physicians and health administrators for most of the post–World War II period were encouraged to believe that money should not even be considered in making medical decisions. Today, they are being told that money should always be considered. Moreover, because bureaucrats are usually technocrats, it is only natural that they will gravitate toward a cost-benefit standard—a collectivist standard not always in the best interest of individual patients.

Solutions in the Ideal Health Care System. At the individual level, cost-benefit analysis is simply a fancy name for routine decisionmaking. The old medical ethic led physicians to encourage patients to ignore monetary costs and focus only on health care benefits. What physicians should do is encourage patients to consider both. In an ideal system, the physician would act as adviser to patients and help them to understand the probabilities, the medical consequences of various outcomes, and the costs of various procedures. Ideally, physicians would help patients choose between

[71]Formaini.

122

money and health care and thus increase the odds that patients would choose the option they value most highly.

17. *Administrative Costs*

In 1987, according to one study, each doctor in the United States spent an average of more than 134 hours filling out insurance forms. Overall, the cost of administering the U.S. health care system was estimated to be between $96.8 billion and $120.4 billion, or almost one-fourth of total health care spending that year. By contrast, the administrative costs of the Canadian system of national health insurance were estimated to be less than one-half that high.[72] Such comparisons of the administrative costs in the United States and Canada are seriously flawed (see chapter 17). They overestimate U.S. administrative costs and underestimate Canada's. Moreover, those who assume that the United States could substantially lower its health care costs by adopting the Canadian system are engaged in wishful thinking. Countries with national health insurance try to control health care costs by limiting the amount of money that physicians and hospitals have to spend and by forcing them to ration health care. They often do so with very little oversight.

The United States, by contrast, is moving in the opposite direction. Physicians and hospital administrators spend an enormous amount of time on paperwork, not just to facilitate the exchange of money but because third-party payers also want to ensure that the medical care is appropriate and necessary. Were the United States to adopt a program of national health insurance, there is every reason to suppose that administrative costs would go up, not down. There is little chance that we would follow the Canadian practice of giving providers a fixed budget from which to ration health care with few questions asked. Nevertheless, almost everyone familiar with the administrative burdens faced by providers has concluded that the burdens are way too heavy, causing inefficiency and waste.

Proposals in the Cost-Plus Health Care System. Because the cost-plus mentality sees no value in, and no role for, a market in health

[72]Steffie Woolhandler and David U. Himmelstein, "The Deteriorating Administrative Efficiency of the U.S. Health Care System," *New England Journal of Medicine* 324, no. 18 (May 2, 1991): 1253–58. Woolhandler and Himmelstein estimated that administrative costs as a percent of total costs are between 8.4 percent and 11.1 percent in Canada and between 19.3 percent and 24.1 percent in the United States. See, however, the problems with these estimates discussed in chapters 8 and 17.

care, monopoly and central planning are almost always preferred to competition and decentralization. The concept of patients shopping in the medical marketplace and negotiating and bargaining with providers is foreign to the cost-plus way of thinking. Thus, they reason that if a single payer (read: government) wrote all of the checks, costs would be lower than they are when the checks are written by Medicare, Medicaid, and thousands of employers and private insurers.

Solutions in the Ideal Health Care System. One of the reasons why administrative costs are high is precisely because the U.S health care system is bureaucratic, rather than market-based. By contrast, one of the most important functions of competitive markets is to eliminate waste and inefficiency. More than half of the money now spent by third-party payers could instead be spent by patients out of individual Medisave accounts (see chapter 8). If those expenditures were made with health care debit cards, the administrative costs would be a little over 1 percent. Not only would there be huge savings in administrative costs, there would also be a substantial reduction in spending on unnecessary care, or care of marginal value. Overall, we estimate that if every family in America had a Medisave account covering the first $2,500 of annual medical bills, the nation's total health care spending would be reduced by as much as one-fourth, with no detrimental effect on the health of patients.

18. Health Insurance for Small Business

Health insurance has increasingly become prepayment for the consumption of medical care rather than genuine insurance, and the consequences have been especially detrimental for small business (as discussed in chapters 6 and 7).

For large companies, the evolution of the prepayment concept means that each year's premiums are determined by last year's costs. Employers pay in health insurance premiums an amount equal to the cost of whatever their employees consume. That is one of the reasons why so many large employers self-insure, sometimes using insurance companies to administer their plan. In a sense, self-insurance merely formalizes a relationship that was previously implicit between the employer and the health insurance company. Moreover, because large employers have many employees, they have a self-contained insurance pool, and their total costs are reasonably predictable.

Insurance as prepayment for the consumption of medical care has wreaked havoc among small employers, however. The principal reason why small businesses purchase health insurance is to avoid the risk of having to pay unexpectedly large medical bills. However, because the policies they purchase are not real insurance, when a small company generates a large claim, the insurer may triple or quadruple the company's premiums and may even cancel the policy. Thus, employers who thought they were buying insurance are surprised to find out that there is very little risk sharing and, instead, they are mainly expected to pay their own way.

Before turning to solutions, it is worth contrasting small group insurance with the market for individual and family policies—about the only market where real insurance is still sold. In most states, insurers cannot raise an individual's premium without raising all other premiums (for the same type of policy) by an equal amount. Thus, insurers can't single out those who get sick and charge them more than others. Moreover, the more they raise the premiums for all policyholders, the greater the risk that healthy ones will leave the pool and buy a low-priced policy from some other insurer. Problems in the market for small groups are now stimulating reform movements in almost every state, but (as discussed in chapter 12) some reforms will only make the problem worse.

Proposals in the Cost-Plus Health Care System. One of the reasons why the cost-plus system evolved was to prevent the development of a competitive health insurance market. In the 1950s, advocates of cost-plus medical care favored "community rating," a system under which everyone paid the same premium, regardless of age, sex, occupation, or any other indicator of health care risk. Such a system was bound to fail. If everyone is charged the same premium, it will be too high for healthy (low-risk) people and too low for less healthy (high-risk) people. As fewer healthy people buy health insurance, the premium needed to cover the health care costs of those who do buy will rise in a continuous upward spiral.

Today, the intellectual heirs of the architects of the cost-plus system favor a return to community rating, either in a pure or modified form. Central to all their reform proposals is the notion that insurers should be forced to sell to anyone who wants to buy ("guaranteed issue") at prices that do not reflect real risks. Of course, the modern versions of community rating face the same problems as the older version. That is why the modern advocates also often favor employer or individual mandates, which would force people to buy health insurance whether they want to or not. The ultimate reform along these lines is national health insurance, a system under which everyone is forced to pay a tax (price) that is also unrelated to real insurance risks.

Solutions in the Ideal Health Care System. To the cost-plus mentality, the purpose of health insurance is to pay medical bills. By contrast, under an ideal health care system, the purpose of health insurance would be similar to the purpose of any other type of insurance—to allow people to protect their assets by transferring risk to others. Accordingly, an ideal system would place a high value on pricing risk accurately and encouraging a competitive market that will accomplish that task. As in the case of life insurance, however, once people have purchased a policy, insurers should not be able to change the rules of the game simply because an individual's probability of filing a claim suddenly increases.

Many of the problems in the market for small groups would disappear if small group insurance functioned in the same way as individual insurance does. One way of moving in that direction is to individualize employer-provided health insurance. Many of the problems in the market for individual insurance would disappear if health insurance more closely resembled life insurance. However (as discussed in chapters 6 and 7), achieving the ideal requires a commitment to it by policymakers.

19. The Right to Work

An efficient, productive economy requires a mobile labor market—one in which people are free to switch employers and move to new jobs where they can earn more and produce more. Yet, that goal is increasingly unattainable because health insurance is employer-based.

One problem is that workers are afraid to switch jobs because of fear that they will lose health insurance coverage or that their new employer will not cover preexisting illnesses. A *New York Times/ CBS* poll found that 30 percent of Americans said that they or someone in their household have at some time stayed in a job they wanted to leave in order to keep the health benefits, and 26 percent said that "a household member took one job rather than another mainly for health benefits."[73] A second problem is that choosing a job or staying in a job for health benefits is no guarantee of coverage since an employer can change health benefits and deny coverage even after a person has become sick. In one case, an employee with AIDS saw his maximum health benefits slashed from $1 million to $5,000 because the employer changed health insurance policies.[74]

A third problem is that employers, increasingly, will not hire people who engage in activities that increase the probability of high health costs. For example, Turner Broadcasting System, Inc. (parent of Cable News Network) is one of about 6,000 companies that refuses to hire smokers. Multi-Developers won't hire anyone who engages in high-risk activities such as skydiving, mountain climbing, motorcycling, or piloting a private aircraft. Other companies refuse to hire people who drink or who have high cholesterol levels.[75]

A fourth problem is the increase in strikes and walkouts over health insurance issues. Because employees do not see health insurance benefits as a dollar-for-dollar trade-off against wages, it is not surprising that they resist reductions in those benefits. According to the most recent survey, nearly two-thirds of the major walkouts and 30 percent of the major strikes in 1989 were over medical benefits. They included the largest, most prolonged, and most bitter labor-management confrontations, including a 17-week walkout at the Nynex Corporation and a nine-month walkout by miners at the Pittston Coal Company in Virginia, West Virginia, and Kentucky.[76]

Proposals in the Cost-Plus Health Care System. Most proposals fall into two categories: They would either impose new restrictions on employers (and employees), or they would force everyone into

[73]Erick Eckholm, "Health Benefits Found to Deter Job Switching," *New York Times*, September 26, 1991.

[74]Robert Pear, "Court Approves Cuts in Benefits in Costly Illness," *New York Times*, November 27, 1991.

[75]See Zachary Schiller, Walecia Konrad, and Stephanie Anderson, *Business Week*, August 26, 1991, reported in *Medical Benefits* 8, no. 18 (September 30, 1991): 3; and "None of an Employer's Business," *New York Times*, July 7, 1991.

[76]Alan Finder, "The New Crux of Contract Negotiations: Who Will Pay Health Care Costs?" *New York Times*, October 27, 1991.

Table 4.10
LIFESTYLE POLICIES OF EMPLOYERS

Company	Policy	Started
Baker Hughes	$10 monthly surcharge on health insurance for smokers	1990
ICH	$15 a month off medical contributions for employees who haven't smoked for 90 days and meet a weight guideline	1991
Texas Instruments	$10 monthly surcharge on health insurance for employees and dependents who smoke	1991
U-Haul International	Biweekly $5 charge for health insurance for employees who smoke or chew tobacco, or whose weight exceeds guidelines	1990

SOURCE: *Business Week*, August 26, 1991, pp. 68–72; reprinted in *Medical Benefits* 8, no. 18 (September 30, 1991): 3.

a general system of national health insurance. In the former category are proposals to mandate a basic benefit package and require the benefits to be portable, as employees move from employer to employer. Note that this proposal ignores an important source of the problem—the ability of some people to impose costs on others as a result of their behavior. Under national health insurance, the connection between individual behavior and individual costs would be severed completely.

Solutions in the Ideal Health Care System. If health insurance were individualized, policies would automatically be personal and portable. An employee would not have to fear a loss of benefits either because of a change of job or the arbitrary decision of an employer. If people engaged in more risky lifestyles, they would probably face higher premiums to reflect the greater risks. Many private insurers already charge higher premiums for certain lifestyle choices, and, as Table 4.10 shows, many employers are currently employing this practice. But as long as individual employees pay their own way, their employability in the labor market should be unaffected. Moreover, if health insurance were individualized, there would be no reason for workers to strike over health care benefits. Employees could choose to spend as much of their compensation on health care as they individually preferred.

20. *The Profit Motive in Medicine*

One reason why our health care system has evolved to its current condition is a series of legislative steps designed to remove the profit motive from virtually every aspect of medicine (as discussed in chapter 5). Doctors are trained in nonprofit medical schools. Most hospitals are nonprofit, and—until recently—the health insurance industry was dominated by nonprofit entities.

One consequence of the lack of a profit motive is an industry with too few entrepreneurs and too little innovation, at least with respect to cutting costs and meeting patient needs. In those areas in which the profit motive is still the major driving force (for example, the manufacture of medical equipment and pharmaceuticals) innovation and change are rampant. But in the area of solving patient problems, cost-reducing innovations have been few and far between. Consider, for example, patients with chronic ailments. An estimated 32 million people have arthritis, 16 million have bad backs, 9 million have migraine headaches, and 23 million have allergies.[77] According to Gallup polls, one-third of Americans report they have insomnia,[78] and 70 million Americans claim they have severe headaches.[79] How innovative has the health care system been in treating these problems? Harvard University professor Regina Herzlinger has reported the statement of a patient with a bad back: "I couldn't find a multidisciplinary team that could treat my problem. So instead I went from one doctor to the next. They all offered different prescriptions. Neurologists wanted to medicate, radiologists to take pictures, orthopedic surgeons to operate, and

[77]Regina E. Herzlinger, "Healthy Competition," *Atlantic Monthly*, August 1991, p. 70.

[78]Reported in Mike Snider, "Sleepy Days Caused by Restless Nights," *USA Today*, June 20, 1991.

[79]Reported on Cable Network News.

sports-medicine types to exercise my abdominal muscles. My back still hurts!"[80]

Indications are that things are beginning to change, however. Physician entrepreneurs were largely responsible for the 1980s boom in such cost-reducing innovations as emergency care clinics and outpatient surgery units. Some physicians and pharmacists are now using 900 numbers to give telephone advice for a fee.[81] At least one for-profit company maintains a patient hotline to help people avoid purchasing more health care than they need and avoid seeing the wrong kind of physician.[82] And some physicians are now advertising package prices (including the physician fee and facility charges) for routine types of surgery.

On the other hand, physician entrepreneurs are coming under attack by those who charge that the profit motive simply contributes to escalating health care costs.[83] For example, a study conducted by the Florida Health Care Cost Containment Board found that 40 percent of Florida physicians involved in direct patient care had a financial interest in joint ventures to which they could refer patients. Patients treated at physician-owned therapy centers averaged 43 percent more visits. Although the prices per treatment or visit were lower, total costs to patients (or their third-party payers) were 31 percent higher. Clinical laboratories owned by referring physicians performed twice as many diagnostic tests per patient.[84]

It is not obvious that more tests and more physician visits are bad. However, when physicians have a direct financial interest in the therapy they prescribe, their judgment may be influenced by that fact. What should be the role of the profit motive in medical practice?

Proposals in the Cost-Plus Health Care System. One of the original goals of those who promoted the cost-plus vision of health care

[80]Herzlinger, p. 70.

[81]Leonard Stone, "For Round-the-Clock Diagnoses, Just Pick Up Your Telephone," *New York Times*, July 13, 1991.

[82]The company is Informed Access of Boulder, Colorado. See Udayan Gupta, "Enterprise," *Wall Street Journal*, January 9, 1991.

[83]Robert Pear, "When Healers Are Entrepreneurs: A Debate over Costs and Ethics," *New York Times*, June 2, 1991.

[84]*Modern Healthcare* (August 19, 1991) reported in *Medical Benefits* 8, no. 17 (September 15, 1991): 5.

was to eliminate the profit motive from the medical marketplace. That goal is still cherished by most of those in the cost-plus tradition. Hostile to the pursuit of self-interest in general, especially financial self-interest, the cost-plus mentality sees the search for profit as a source of problems, not a solution. Accordingly, the bureaucratic approach to medical care frequently favors laws barring physicians from having any financial interest in facilities to which they refer patients. Under this view, it is permissible for physicians to invest in the market for corn futures (about which they may know nothing), but impermissible for them to invest in a medical laboratory (about which they may know a great deal).

Solutions in the Ideal Health Care System. In an ideal system, self-interest would be seen as a normal and natural characteristic of human behavior. The trick is to harness this drive, so that it is directed toward solving problems rather than creating them. Historically, physicians have been the primary innovators and entrepreneurs in the medical marketplace, and that is a tradition that should be encouraged. There are plenty of ways to prevent abuse—for example, by requiring physicians to disclose their financial interest to patients. But our concern over potential abuses should not lead us to prohibit entrepreneurship in the one market where it is most needed.

Some Unresolved Problems Involving Individual Rights

Although not a subject of this book, some key issues involving the rights of individuals to make choices will become increasingly important in the remainder of this decade and in the next century. These include the right of terminally ill patients to take experimental drugs, the right of people to sell their organs to patients who need transplants, and the right to die.

A strong case can be made for allowing individuals full freedom of choice in these areas. The objection is that the choices may be irreversible and often occur under circumstances in which real patient preferences may be hard to discern and opportunities for abuse may be rife. Although that objection may justify careful procedural safeguards, the possibility of abuse cannot possibly justify a blanket, sweeping prohibition against individual choice.

Experimental Drugs for Terminally Ill Patients

The federal Food and Drug Administration (FDA) has a power that is unique in the health care system, and which in some respects is hard to justify. Although physicians may legally engage in almost any kind of experimental surgery, they cannot administer a drug unless it has first been approved by the FDA. This is a puzzling division of power, considering that on the whole surgery is much more life threatening than drugs. Moreover, since 1976, the FDA has extended its reach, and it now controls all implanted devices, ranging from pacemakers and artificial joints to breast implants. Whereas cosmetic surgeons have virtually unlimited freedom to perform experimental breast surgery, their right to use a conventional breast implant is regulated by the FDA. In addition (as discussed in chapter 18), Medicare is citing FDA policies in refusing to pay for the latest cancer-fighting drugs.[85]

In recent years, the wisdom of investing the FDA with so much power has been called into question. AIDS patients, unable to get access to experimental drugs, have invaded the FDA's Washington headquarters in protest. Alzheimer's disease patients, unable to obtain the drug THA, have filed a class action suit. Breast cancer patients have formed an anti-FDA lobbying group, and even the National Cancer Institute has complained about FDA tardiness in approving new drugs.[86]

Such complaints are not new. In the professional literature in the 1970s, the FDA was accused of responsibility for 10,000 heart-related deaths a year because it kept beta-blockers off the U.S. market long after they had proved successful in Europe.[87] The current policy of denying people on death's doorstep an opportunity to take risks would seem unwarranted and in need of change.

The Market for Organs

Why is it legal for people to sell their "soft tissues" such as blood or semen, but illegal for them to sell their bone marrow, corneas, or solid organs for transplant? That's not clear. Under the federal

---

[85]These are drugs that have been approved for one use, but not for other uses—even when the practice is considered normal therapy.

[86]See, for example, "Opening Up the FDA," *Wall Street Journal*, November 15, 1991.

[87]See the discussion and the references in John C. Goodman, *The Regulation of Medical Care: Is the Price Too High?* (Washington: Cato Institute, 1980), pp. 129–32. See also Dale Gieringer, *Compassion vs. Control: FDA Investigational Drug Regulations*, Cato Institute Policy Analysis no. 72 (May 20, 1986); and Joanna E. Siegel and Marc J. Roberts, "Reforming FDA Policy," *Regulation* (Fall 1991).

National Organ Transplant Act, passed in 1984, people can give their organs to any transplant patient they wish to designate. But if they accept money in return, they are subject to a fine of $50,000, or five years in prison, or both.

The ban on the sale of organs has the effect of imposing a price of zero. And as is the case with all price controls, shortages are the natural consequence. A few other countries have taken a different course. In India, where payments for organs are legal, the going price for a kidney is $1,800, about six times the average annual wage.[88] As a result, the supply of kidneys in India is much higher than it otherwise would be. In the United States, it is evident both that there is a shortage of organ donors and that potential donors would respond to financial incentives. Accordingly, H. Tristram Engelhardt, Jr., a bioethicist and physician at Baylor College of Medicine in Houston, thinks organ sales should be legalized, but carefully regulated to prevent abuse. A growing number of his medical colleagues are coming to the same conclusion.[89]

The Right to Die

In the fall of 1991, voters in Washington state narrowly defeated a right-to-die proposition. Although most polls show that a majority of people favor the right to die, the Washington defeat occurred because of a concern about the potential for abuse. Although that concern is legitimate, the real ethical question is whether people have the right to choose how to spend their final days. Terminally ill British cancer patients often retire to hospices and spend their final days there receiving pain-relieving injections of heroin, but no heroic medical intervention. These and other options will become heated topics of debate in the United States, as increasing numbers of people assert that they, rather than health care bureaucracies, should make the final decisions.

[88]Ronald Bailey, "Should I Be Allowed to Buy Your Kidney?" *Forbes* (May 28, 1990): 367.
[89]Ibid., pp. 368–70.

PART II

FROM COMPETITION TO COST-PLUS HEALTH CARE

5. How the Cost-Plus System Evolved

The cost-plus system of health care finance is incompatible with competitive markets in which prices are determined by supply and demand. Cost-plus finance requires a regulated, institutionalized market in which normal competitive pressures are either outlawed or suppressed. This chapter briefly describes how the U.S. market for medical services evolved from a competitive to a regulated market, first for physicians' services, then for hospital services, and finally for health insurance.

The first building blocks of the cost-plus system were put into place by the political activities of physicians more than 100 years ago. Those activities, coordinated through the American Medical Association (AMA) and county medical societies, are called the actions of organized medicine, to distinguish them from the uncoordinated actions of individual physicians competing against one another in the marketplace. By the 1950s, organized medicine had achieved virtually all of its political goals: the creation of nonprofit institutions designed to control entry into the medical profession and to suppress competition for physicians' services; the creation of a nonprofit hospital sector, chiefly responsive to physicians; and the creation of a nonprofit health insurance sector that paid most medical bills with little scrutiny and few questions asked. That was Stage I in the evolution of the cost-plus system, and it survived for at least three decades.[1]

During the 1980s, however, we entered Stage II, the cost-control stage. Physicians now are encountering harassment from third-party institutions and are increasingly torn between their obligations to patients and the demands of third-party payers. The irony

---

[1]Similar developments also took place in other countries. For the early history of the politics of medicine in Canada, see Ronald Hamowy, *Canadian Medicine: A Study in Restricted Entry* (Vancouver: Fraser Institute, 1984). For the British experience, see David Green, *Working Class Patients and the Medical Establishment: Self-help in Britain from the Mid-nineteenth Century to 1948* (Hampshire, Eng.: Gower/Maurice Temple Smith, 1985).

is that the problems of today's physicians are attributable in part to the political actions of their counterparts more than a century ago. Today's health care system frustrates many people, who often search for someone or some group to blame. Physicians are all too often their targets. Throughout the past 150 years, though, most physicians have not been involved in politics. To the extent that they have had political preferences, most have favored free enterprise. The vast majority have been far more altruistic than the practitioners of other professions.

The historical facts recounted in this chapter will surprise most physicians as much as they surprise others. Those facts include the ways in which doctors' representatives pursued legislative goals and changed the institutional environment in which medicine is practiced.[2] In doing so, the representatives of physicians had the same motives and many of the same objectives as the representatives of other professions and trades. If there is a difference, it is only that special-interest politics proved more successful in medicine than in other fields. Today's doctors are not responsible for the political activities of doctors in the past. Indeed, physicians today are among the most tragic victims of cost-plus medicine. If they could, the majority would surely undo the harm done through the medical politics of the past.

Early History of Government Controls[3]

In medical care, as in many other sectors of the American economy, a genuinely free market emerged not in 1776 but during the middle of the 19th century. Between 1830 and 1850, many of the medical licensing laws left over from the colonial period were repealed.[4] Historian Ronald Hamowy has described the condition

---

[2]For a lengthier historical treatment, see John C. Goodman, *The Regulation of Medical Care: Is the Price Too High?* (Washington: Cato Institute, 1980).

[3]This section is based largely on Ronald Hamowy, "The Early Development of Medical Licensing Laws in the United States, 1875–1900," *Journal of Libertarian Studies* 3, no. 1 (1979): 73–119.

[4]Although 20 states and the District of Columbia had some form of licensing prior to 1850, these laws were commonly short-lived and poorly enforced. Five states provided no penalty for practicing without a license, and in six more the worst penalty was that unlicensed practitioners could not sue for recovery of fees. Only in New York, South Carolina, Georgia, and Louisiana did unlicensed practitioners face the possibility of imprisonment. See Joseph F. Kett, *The Formation of the American Medical Association: The Role of Institutions, 1780–1860* (New Haven: Yale University Press, 1968), pp. 181–84; and William G. Rothstein, *American Physicians in the Nine-*

138

of the American medical profession at the close of the Civil War as follows:

> The profession was, throughout the country, unlicensed and anyone who had the inclination to set himself up as a physician could do so, the exigencies of the market alone determining who would prove successful in the field and who would not. Medical schools abounded, the great bulk of which were privately owned and operated, and the prospective student could gain admission to even the best of them without great difficulty. With free entry into the profession possible and education in medicine cheap and readily available, large numbers of men entered practice.[5]

This experiment in free-market medical care was short-lived, however. The AMA was established in 1847 and quickly became the spokesman for the practitioners of orthodox medicine in the United States. Although the AMA often stressed the importance of raising the quality of care for patients and protecting uninformed consumers from "quacks" and "charlatans," its principal goal—like that of other trade associations—was to advance the financial well-being of its members. It pursued its objective by promoting the establishment of state medical licensing laws and the legal requirement that, to be licensed to practice, a physician must be a graduate of an AMA-approved medical school. Clearly, it sought to raise the incomes of existing practitioners. A report submitted by the committee on educational standards to the first AMA convention in 1847 was unusually candid:

> The very large number of physicians in the United States . . . has frequently been the subject of remark. To relieve the diseases of something more than twenty millions of people, we have an army of doctors amounting by a recent computation to forty thousand, which allows one to about every five hundred inhabitants. And if we add to the 40,000 the long list of irregular practitioners who swarm like locusts in every part of the country, the proportion of patients will be still further reduced. No wonder, then, that the profession of medicine has measurably ceased to occupy the

---

teenth Century: From Sect to Science (Baltimore: Johns Hopkins University Press, 1972), pp. 332–39.

[5]Hamowy, "The Early Development of Medical Licensing Laws," 73.

elevated position which once it did; *no wonder that the merest pittance in the way of remuneration is scantily doled out even to the most industrious in our ranks*—and no wonder that the intention, at one time correct and honest, will occasionally succumb to the cravings of hard necessity.[6]

It is ironic that most unorthodox ("irregular") practitioners at the time probably did more good—or less harm—to their patients than did the orthodox ones.[7] A second irony is that the committee recommended standards so high that few of the convention's delegates could have met them. Indeed, one historian has concluded that "rigid enforcement of the AMA's preliminary standards would have closed down practically every medical school in the country and would have depleted the ranks of formally educated physicians in a few years."[8]

Early Licensing Laws

Virtually every law designed to restrict the practice of medicine was enacted not on the crest of widespread public demand but because of intense pressure from the political representatives of physicians. Moreover, AMA-sponsored legislation invariably contained grandfather clauses that exempted existing practitioners. These laws did nothing to protect the public from quacks and charlatans already active. What they did was protect practitioners from the competitive pressures posed by potential new entrants into the medical profession.

---

[6]"Proceedings of the National Medical Convention held in the City of Philadelphia, in May 1847," *New York Journal of Medicine* 9 (July 1847): 115. Emphasis added.

[7]Rothstein, p. 120.

[8]According to Hamowy, regular medicine in the 19th century relied heavily on "bloodletting, blistering, and the administration of massive doses of compounds of mercury, antimony, and other mineral poisons as purgatives and emetics, followed by arsenical compounds thought to act as tonics." The two major schools of nonorthodox medicine were electicism and homeopathy. Electicism relied exclusively on botanical remedies, steam baths, and rest. Homeopathy advocated small doses of drugs that, when tested in a healthy person, produced symptoms most closely approximating the symptomology of the disease. Homeopathic doctors were also strong proponents of fresh air, sunshine, bed rest, proper diet, and personal hygiene—therapeutic remedies that the practitioners of regular medicine regarded as being of little or no value. See Hamowy, "The Early Development of Medical Licensing Laws," 73–74.

At the first meeting of the AMA in 1847, the delegates not only endorsed collective fee-setting but unanimously endorsed a code that made adherence to established fee schedules a matter of medical ethics. Chapter II, article 7, section 1, of the organization's original Code of Medical Ethics, read as follows: "Some general rules should be adopted by the faculty, in every town or district, relative to the *pecuniary acknowledgments* from their patients; and it should be deemed a point of honor to adhere to this rule with as much steadiness as varying circumstances will permit."[9] In other words, the AMA endorsed the ideal of a medical cartel and made participation in it ethically mandatory. Over time, the AMA expanded the range of activities considered "unethical" to include (1) "solicitation of patients, either directly or indirectly," (2) "competition and underbidding," (3) "compensation . . . inadequate to secure good medical service," (4) "interference with reasonable competition in a community," and (5) "impairment of 'free choice' of physicians."[10]

AMA goals were also promoted by threats of license revocation. The most common causes for revocation, "dishonorable" or "unprofessional" conduct, were mainly euphemisms for what the AMA considered unfair competition. "Incompetence" was grounds for revocation in only 2 of the 42 states that had revocation provisions in their medical practice acts in 1907.[11]

In 1888, the *Journal of the American Medical Association* editorialized that "*wholesome* competition is the life of trade; unrestricted competition may be the death of it."[12] In 1898, the New York state medical fraternity proposed to prevent free vaccination and the administration of free diphtheria antitoxin on the grounds that it was "inimic to the best [financial] welfare of young medical men."[13] The AMA's

[9]"Code of Medical Ethics," *New York Journal of Medicine* 9 (September 1847).

[10]These conditions were contained in a minority report to the report of the Committee on the Costs of Medical Care in 1932, and subsequently were endorsed by the AMA. See Elton Rayack, *Professional Power and American Medicine: The Economics of the American Medical Association* (Cleveland: World Publishing Co., 1967), p. 152.

[11]Hamowy, "The Early Development of Medical Licensing Laws," 106–7.

[12]"Competition, Supply and Demand, and Medical Education," *Journal of the American Medical Association* (September 15, 1888): 382–3.

[13]See "Proposed 'Practical' Medical Legislation for New York State," *Journal of the American Medical Association* 30 (March 12, 1898): 625.

code of medical ethics condemned the practice of giving free care to affluent patients without compensation as "dishonorable" and "unprofessional" because it tended to injure other physicians financially.[14]

In addition, organized medicine vigorously sought to eliminate competition from any unlicensed person who would treat the sick for compensation, regardless of the form of treatment and its effect on the patient. In most states, physicians were successful in broadening the definition of medical practice to include drugless and spiritual healers (for example, Christian Scientists, osteopaths, and chiropractors).[15] At the urging of organized medicine, courts ruled that it was not a defense that patients knowingly accepted the mode of treatment offered, nor that patients may have benefited from the treatment.[16]

In one case, the Nebraska Supreme Court ruled in 1894 that a Christian Science practitioner had violated the state's medical practice act by accepting compensation in return for treating solely by prayer those who called on him.[17] A similar decision was reached by the Ohio Supreme Court in 1905. In that case, the court ruled that Christian Science treatment in return for a fee constituted the practice of medicine, even though the cure was to come from God and not from the defendant.[18]

By 1901, all states and territories except Alaska and Oklahoma had medical examining boards. Of the 51 jurisdictions, 30 required candidates for a license to undergo an examination and to present

[14]Hamowy, "The Early Development of Medical Licensing Laws," 96.

[15]Ibid., p. 98. For an account of the rise of medical licensing laws in terms of their reception by the courts, see Lawrence M. Friedman, "Freedom of Contract and Occupational Licensing, 1890–1910: A Legal and Social Study," *California Law Review* 53 (1965): 487–534.

[16]Chapter II, article 5, section 9 of the code of medical ethics, adopted at the first AMA convention, read: "A wealthy physician should not give advice *gratis* to the affluent because it is an injury to his professional brethren. The office of physician can never be supported as an exclusively beneficent one; and it is defrauding in some degree, the common funds for its support, when fees are dispensed with, which might justly be claimed." See "Code of Medical Ethics." The injunction apparently does not apply to ministering gratis to another physician—a practice that is quite widespread. See the analysis of the practice in Reuben A. Kessel, "Price Discrimination in Medicine," *Journal of Law and Economics* 1 (October 1958): 20–53.

[17]*State* v. *Buswell*, 40 Nebraska 158, 58 N.W. 728 (1894).

[18]*State* v. *Marble*, 72 Ohio State 21, 73 N.E. 1063 (1905).

a diploma in medicine; seven required either an examination or a diploma; and two made the M.D. degree a prerequisite for the practice of medicine. Although the number of physicians continued to increase, the number per 100,000 people fell from 163 in 1880 to 157 by the turn of the century.[19]

Nonetheless, in 1901 the *Journal of the American Medical Association* continued to complain about overcrowded conditions in the medical profession.[20] Hamowy explains why: Licensing laws mandating an examination were clearly not sufficiently restrictive to severely limit the numbers of new physicians entering the profession, even when these laws also required a diploma in medicine. The answer was to lie in statutes which both required a diploma and, in addition, empowered the state examining boards to exclude graduates of "substandard" colleges from consideration for licensure.[21]

The Flexner Report

In 1906, the AMA's Council on Medical Education inspected the existing medical schools and found the training acceptable in less than half of them. These findings were never published, however. Arthur Bevan, head of the Council on Medical Education, explained why: "If we could obtain the publication and approval of our work by the Carnegie Foundation for the Advancement of Teaching, it would assist materially in securing the results we are attempting to bring about."[22]

The AMA's efforts were successful. In 1910, the foundation commissioned Abraham Flexner to perform what amounted to a repeat of the AMA's inspection and grading of medical schools. Flexner had absolutely no qualifications for the task. He was not a physician, scientist, or medical educator. He had an undergraduate degree in the arts and was the owner and operator of a for-profit preparatory school in Louisville, Kentucky.

Flexner evaluated existing medical schools by conducting a grand inspection tour. Sometimes he evaluated an entire school in one

[19]Hamowy, "The Early Development of Medical Licensing Laws," 102.

[20]"Oversupply of Medical Graduates," *Journal of the American Medical Association* 37 (July 27, 1901): 270.

[21]Hamowy, "The Early Development of Medical Licensing Laws," 103.

[22]Arthur Bevan, "Cooperation in Medical Education and Medical Service," *Journal of the American Medical Association* 90 (1928): 1178.

afternoon. He measured the schools by comparing each to the medical school at Johns Hopkins. He was accompanied on the tour by the secretary of the AMA's Council on Medical Education, N. P. Colwell, who provided him with the results of the AMA's previous labors. Flexner apparently accepted a good bit of assistance from the AMA and spent many hours at its Chicago headquarters preparing his report.

Control of Medical Schools

The Flexner report[23] had an enormous impact on the future of medical education in the United States. Indeed, as Reuben Kessel has written, "If impact on public policy is the criterion of importance, the Flexner report must be regarded as one of the most important reports ever written."[24] It convinced legislators that only graduates of first class (Class A) medical schools ought to be licensed, and they delegated the classification of institutions— explicitly or implicitly—to the AMA. In time, every state established standards of acceptability for obtaining a license to practice medicine. These standards, set either by statute or by state medical examining boards, provided that the boards consider only the graduates of schools approved by the AMA and/or the American Association of Medical Colleges, whose lists were identical.

Ultimately, the Flexner report led to the large-scale closing of medical schools that failed to meet AMA standards. By exercising its power to certify, the AMA caused an almost continuous reduction in the number of medical schools in the United States over the next four decades.[25] (See Figure 5.1.) As a consequence, the number of medical students dropped dramatically.[26] As Figure 5.2 shows, following the release of the Flexner report the ratio of doctors to population fell steadily for two decades. To see how effective the AMA's policies were, consider that doctors in 1963 had far more to offer patients than at the turn of the century and were in far greater

[23]Abraham Flexner, *Medical Education in the United States and Canada*, Bulletin no. 4 (Carnegie Foundation for the Advancement of Teaching, 1910).

[24]Kessel, "Price Discrimination in Medicine," 28.

[25]Ibid., 29.

[26]See U.S. Department of Health, Education and Welfare, U.S. Public Health Service, *Health Manpower Source Book*, Section 9, "Physicians, Dentists and Professional Nurses" (1958).

144

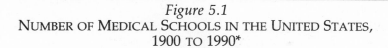

Figure 5.1
NUMBER OF MEDICAL SCHOOLS IN THE UNITED STATES,
1900 TO 1990*

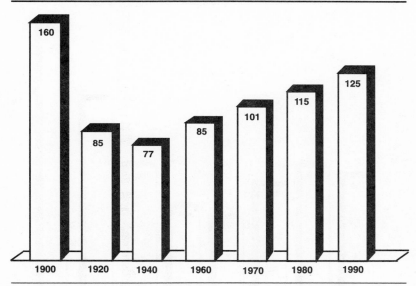

SOURCES: For 1900–50, U.S. Bureau of the Census, *Historical Statistics of the United States, Colonial Times to 1970*, Bicentennial Edition, Part 2 (Washington, 1975), Series B 275–90, pp. 75–76; for 1960, U.S. Department of Health and Human Services, *Health, United States, 1989* (Washington, 1990); and for 1970–90, Undergraduate Medical Education: Annual Issue on Medical Education, *Journal of the American Medical Association*, various years.

*The numbers given are for academic sessions ending in specified years. Beginning in 1954, the totals include Puerto Rico; beginning in 1960, the totals include osteopathic medical schools.

demand. But the number of doctors per 100,000 people in 1963—146—was precisely what it had been in the year that Flexner had written his report.[27]

The impact of the Flexner report may be unique in U.S. regulatory history. Kessel explains why:

[27]See Cotton M. Lindsay and James M. Buchanan, "The Organization and Financing of Medical Care in the United States," in *Health Services Financing* (London: British Medical Association, 1974), Table 2 (p. 540).

Figure 5.2
NUMBER OF PHYSICIANS IN THE UNITED STATES PER 100,000 PEOPLE, 1870 TO 1990[1]

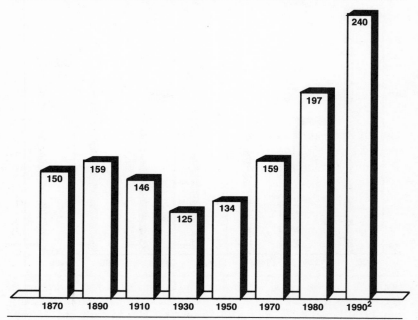

SOURCE: For 1870–1970, U.S. Bureau of the Census, *Historical Statistics of the United States, Colonial Times to 1970,* Bicentennial Edition, Part 2 (Washington, 1975), Series B 275-90, pp. 75–76; and for 1980–90, U.S. Department of Health and Human Services, *Health, United States, 1989* (Washington, 1990), Table 85.

[1]Figures may include physicians not in active medical practice. Beginning in 1960, totals include osteopaths.
[2]Projected total.

The delegation by the state legislature to the AMA of the power to regulate the medical industry in the public interest is on a par with giving the American Iron and Steel Institute the power to determine the output of steel. This delegation of power by the states to the AMA, which was actively sought and solicited, placed this organization in a position of having to serve two masters who in part have conflicting interests. On the one hand, the AMA was given the task of providing an adequate supply of properly qualified doctors. On the other, the decision with respect to what is adequate training and an adequate number of doctors affects the pocketbooks of those who do the regulating as well as their closest business and personal associates. It is this power that has been given to the AMA that is the cornerstone of the monopoly power that has been imputed by economists to organized medicine.[28]

Effects on Medical Practice

The most important consequence of the control of medical education by organized medicine, then, was that physicians acquired the power to reduce the supply of medical services and increase their incomes. But there were other effects. One was a shortage of minority physicians. Of the 375,000 physicians in the United States in 1977, only 1.7 percent were black.[29] Moreover, 83 percent of the black physicians were trained at two predominantly black medical schools, Howard and Meharry.[30] Prior to 1910, there had been more black medical schools, and blacks and other minorities had found it relatively easy to enter the profession. Following the Flexner report, most black medical schools were closed, and black would-be physicians confronted rationing schemes at those medical schools that did remain open.[31] Discrimination against other minorities, such as Jews, and against women, became rampant.[32]

Because the decisionmakers on medical school admissions boards could not, or would not, discriminate on the basis of price, they discriminated on other grounds. As Lee Benham has explained, "It

[28]Kessel, "Price Discrimination in Medicine," 29.

[29]Ibid.

[30]R. M. Henig and D. Rafalik in *New Physician, Minority Education Issue*, April 1977, p. 24.

[31]See Reuben A. Kessel, "The AMA and the Supply of Physicians," *Law and Contemporary Problems* (Spring 1970): 270 ff.

[32]See Richard H. Shryock, "Women in American Medicine," *Journal of the American Medical Women's Association* 5 (1950): 371–79; Jacob A. Goldberg, "Jews in the Medical Profession—A National Survey," *Jewish Social Studies* 1 (1939): 327–36; Kessel, "Price Discrimination in Medicine," 46–51; and Kessel, "The AMA and the Supply of Physicians," p. 270 ff.

should not surprise us that the successful members of the subsequent queue looked remarkably similar to those making the admissions decisions."[33] No doubt many of those decisionmakers reflected the views of Flexner himself. Flexner wrote that "a well-taught negro sanitarian will be immensely useful; an essentially untrained negro wearing an M.D. degree is dangerous," and "the practice of the negro doctor will be limited to his own race."[34]

Other effects of the Flexner report were that medical education became increasingly lengthy and costly, and its subject matter became increasingly unrelated to the conditions of medical practice.[35] The fact that only nonprofit medical schools could become "approved" probably contributed to the nonmarket-oriented attitude of many medical schools and their willingness to cooperate with the goals of organized medicine.

Several writers have observed that the AMA's changing positions on the proper standards for medical education correlated far more closely with the financial pressures faced by practicing physicians than with any clearly defined goals of medical training. For example, Philip Kissam has written:

> The AMA's Council on Medical Education has been able to reduce the number of new physicians entering the profession by increasing the standards for accreditation of medical schools, thereby driving some schools out of business, discouraging new schools from opening, and reducing the size of others [yet the] quality standards imposed for physician licensure have never been carefully correlated with definitions of acceptable medical performance. Most significantly, major "improvements" in standards for accredited medical schools generally have been imposed at times when physicians' incomes were relatively depressed and have been accompanied by open expressions of concern by leaders

[33]Lee Benham, "Guilds and the Form of Competition in the Health Care Sector," in Warren Greenberg, ed., *Competition in the Health Care Sector: Past, Present and Future* (Germantown, MD: Aspen Systems Corp., 1978), pp. 455–56.

[34]Flexner, p. 180.

[35]Kessel, "The AMA and the Supply of Physicians," p. 270 ff. See also Lee Benham, "Guilds and the Form of Competition in the Health Care Sector," pp. 363–74; and Lee Benham, *Aspects of Occupational Licensure* (St. Louis: Center for the Study of American Business, 1979), p. 42.

of organized medicine about the "over-crowded" medical profession.[36]

Economic Effects of the Licensing of Physicians

After surveying the development of licensing laws in various professions, economist Thomas Moore concluded that "licensing raises the cost of entry which, in turn, benefits practitioners already in the occupation at the time of licensing."[37] Because that is the principal effect of licensing, Moore concluded that it is also the principal purpose.

Traditionally, a medical license was an unlimited license to perform medical services. A physician, once licensed, could theoretically perform any kind of surgery—including open-heart and brain surgery—without any special training as a surgeon. Further, most state licensing laws granted a lifetime tenure to the licensee. Although most states required periodic license renewal, renewal was generally a clerical procedure requiring little more than the signature of the physician and the payment of a nominal fee. Until recently, few states required physicians to show evidence of having updated their knowledge as a condition for maintaining a license.

Not only were physicians not required to keep abreast of the state of medical science in their specialty but, in some states, a physician could continue to practice even if mentally ill. A 1967 survey found that only one state, Arizona, required that a candidate for a medical license be "physically and mentally able safely to engage in the practice of medicine."[38] Some statutes did establish mental illness or mental incompetence as grounds for suspension or revocation of a license, if the extent of the illness rendered the physician "unsafe or unreliable as a practitioner." But other states provided

[36]Philip Kissam, "Physician's Assistant and Nurse Practitioner Laws: A Study of Health Law Reform," *Kansas Law Review* 24 (1975): 15. See also Rosemary Stevens, *American Medicine and the Public Interest* (New Haven: Yale University Press, 1971), pp. 66–69; and Kessel, "The AMA and the Supply of Physicians," p. 282.

[37]Thomas G. Moore, "The Purpose of Licensing," *Journal of Law and Economics* 4 (October 1961): 110.

[38]Edward Forgotson, Ruth Roemer, and Roger Newman, "Licensure of Physicians," *Washington University Law Quarterly* 332 (1967): 266.

for license revocation or suspension only if the physician entered a mental hospital.[39]

In the 15 states that listed malpractice among the specific grounds for licensing discipline, the standard was usually "gross malpractice," "gross neglect," "gross carelessness," or "gross incompetence." The practical effect of these provisions, as one study concluded, was that the "disciplinary criteria are . . . analogous to less stringent criminal standards of gross malpractice, which are usually included in state penal statutes."[40] It would appear that Kessel's 1970 observation that "once a doctor wins a license to practice, it is almost never revoked unless he is convicted of law-breaking" was not an exaggeration.[41]

Restrictions on Nurses and Other Paramedical Personnel

Although medical practice statutes did little to protect the public from incompetent doctors, they did a great deal to discourage competent nonphysicians, such as nurses, paramedics, and physicians' assistants. Numerous studies in the 1970s established that nonphysicians can safely perform many routine medical acts.[42] They include physical examinations, diagnosis and treatment of common illnesses, minor surgery, and decisions to continue or modify prescribed treatment for convalescing or chronically ill patients. Studies also showed that when trained nonphysicians were used innovatively under the direction of physicians, the costs of medical treatment could be substantially reduced.[43]

[39]Ibid., 286.

[40]Ibid., 284.

[41]Kessel, "The AMA and the Supply of Physicians," p. 275.

[42]See Goodman, ch. 3; for a more recent assessment see U.S. Congress, Office of Technology Assessment, "Nurse Practitioners, Physician Assistants, and Certified Nurse-Midwives: A Policy Analysis," case study 37, *Health Technology* (Springfield, VA: National Technical Information Service, December 1986).

[43]See I. R. Pondy, "Physician Assistants' Productivity: An Interim Report" (Duke University School of Business Administration, January 1971); Kenneth Smith, Marianne Miller, and Fredrick Golladay, "An Analysis of the Optimal Use of Inputs in the Production of Medical Services," *Journal of Human Resources* 7 (1972): 218–23; Frederick Golladay, Marilyn Manser, and Kenneth Smith, "Scale Economies in the Delivery of Medical Care: A Mixed Integer Programming Analysis of Efficient Manpower Utilization," *Journal of Human Resources* 9 (1974): 50–62; and Office of Technology Assessment, "Nurse Practitioners, Physician Assistants, and Certified Nurse-Midwives: A Policy Analysis."

But standing between the patients and safely administered, lower cost medical treatment were numerous state laws. A 1975 survey found that, in the country as a whole, many—or perhaps most— routine medical procedures could be carried out only by licensed physicians. Moreover, in those states that allowed delegation of medical acts, the nonphysicians usually had licensing laws of their own and lobbied to keep other qualified nonphysicians from legally performing those same acts.[44] Although many states liberalized their medical practice statutes during the 1970s, many of their unjustifiable restrictions exist even today.

Restrictions on Advertising

Professional licensing of physicians was also used to protect physicians from competition with each other.[45] The AMA not only made adherence to a fee schedule an issue of professional ethics, but also pronounced advertising to be unethical and unprofessional. In 1961, the licensing laws of 40 states defined advertising as unprofessional conduct, and thus grounds for license suspension or revocation.[46] However, only advertising that benefited an individual physician was "unprofessional." Advertising that benefited the medical community as a whole was a different matter. Kessel has explained the distinction:

> The advertisement of medical services is approved by the medical profession if and only if such advertisements redound to the interest of the medical profession as a whole. Advertisements in this class are, for example, announcements of the availability for sale of Blue Cross–type medical plans. These plans allow their subscribers the choice of any licensed practitioner. . . . On the other hand, advertisements that primarily redound to the interest of a particular group, for example, advertisements by a closed panel medical group, are . . . . resorted to only by "unethical" doctors. . . . [A]dvertising in this class constitutes competitive behavior and leads to price cutting. It tends to pit one doctor

---

[44]Kissam, "Physician's Assistant and Nurse Practitioner Laws," 1–65.

[45]See Kessel, "The AMA and the Supply of Physicians"; Rayack, pp. 267–83; and David R. Hyde et al., "The American Medical Association: Power, Purpose and Politics in Organized Medicine," *Yale Law Journal* 65 (May 1954): 938–1022.

[46]See Forgotson, Roemer, and Newman, "Licensure of Physicians," 281.

or one group of doctors against the profession as a whole
with respect to shares of the medical care market.[47]

Organized medicine used its state-created powers to punish devi-
ant advertising behavior on numerous occasions. Here are some
examples from the 1970s: In Minnesota, a gynecologist was warned
against making radio and newspaper announcements of his one-
week drive to encourage women to obtain pap smears by offering
discount prices; in Santa Clara, California, the county medical society prohibited clinic doctors who specialized in preventive industrial medicine from seeking new corporate clients; and in St. Louis,
the local medical association forced the director of Washington
University's sterilization and pregnancy termination clinic to apolo-
gize for mailing a brochure describing the center's facilities, even
though the brochure was mailed to local physicians.[48]

The attitude of the AMA toward advertising and price competition was paralleled by that of the associations of related health
practitioners. The code of ethics of the American Dental Association, for example, stated:

> It is unethical for a dentist to give lectures or demonstra-
> tions before lay groups on a particular technique (such as
> hypnosis) that he employs in his office.
> It is unethical for specialists to furnish so-called patient
> education pamphlets to general practitioners for distribution
> to patients where pamphlets, in effect, stress unduly the
> superiority of the procedures used by specialists. Publica-
> tion of such so-called patient education material has the
> effect of soliciting patients.[49]

As another illustration, consider the rules and regulations of the
Michigan Optometric Association in 1969. Eligibility for membership in the association was based on a point system and initial
membership required 65 points. Constraints on advertising or dis-
seminating information accounted for 70 out of the 100 possible
points.

[47]Kessel, "Price Discrimination in Medicine," 43–4.

[48]"The AMA's Bad Case," *New York Times*, December 6, 1978.

[49]Reprinted in Benham, "Guilds and the Form of Competition in the Health Care
Sector," p. 459.

Virtually all of the restrictive practices described above either have been declared illegal by the federal courts or are almost certainly destined to become illegal. Yet the attitudes shaped and molded by the restrictive practices remain pervasive.

Effects on Health Insurance

Until recently, there were only three basic types of medical insurance.[50] Under indemnity medical insurance, doctors and patients determined medical fees jointly at the time the medical services were sold. All or part of the medical bill was then paid by the insurance plan, depending on the specifics of the policy. Examples of medical indemnity insurance were policies sold by Aetna, Travelers, and other "commercial" insurance companies. Nonindemnity medical insurance plans, on the other hand, provided medical care itself, rather than funds to buy those services. Such plans were often called prepaid plans because the patients' insurance premiums generally covered all of the medical services they subsequently consumed. Examples were Blue Cross and Blue Shield plans. Under the original Blue Cross and Blue Shield plans, there was no deductible and no copayment. Coverage allowed patients to see almost any doctor or receive services in almost any hospital. Physicians and hospitals were compensated directly by the insurers.

The AMA clearly favored Blue Cross "service benefit" insurance and went to great lengths to encourage it. Although both tend to increase the overall demand for physicians' services, prepaid plans removed visible prices as a factor in patient choices and thus helped eliminate price competition.

The AMA was even more hostile to the third type of insurance: prepaid plans with restricted choice of provider. Under those plans, insurers not only offered a service benefit, but specified which physicians could supply the service and often employed those physicians and/or regulated the way in which they practiced medicine. These plans tended to benefit only the providers associated with the plan, often at the expense of other providers. Examples are health maintenance organizations (HMOs).

[50]For a detailed analysis of a wide variety of insurance plans and their economic effects, see H. E. Frech III and Paul B. Ginsburg, *Public Insurance in Private Medical Markets: Some Problems of National Health Insurance* (Washington: American Enterprise Institute for Public Policy Research, 1978).

The AMA did not merely condemn HMOs and HMO-type health insurance; it denounced them as unethical. According to an AMA House of Delegates resolution adopted in 1932, such plans are "unethical":

1. Where there is solicitation of patients, either directly or indirectly;
2. Where there is competition and underbidding to secure the contract;
3. When the compensation is inadequate to secure good medical service;
4. When there is interference with reasonable competition in a community;
5. When free choice of physicians is prevented;
6. When the contract because of any of its provisions is contrary to sound public policy.[51]

Five of the six conditions for deeming a prepaid plan unethical were obviously intended to protect the economic position of other physicians. The sixth was open-ended, making it possible to condemn any form of prepaid practice. As Elton Rayack wrote, "Clearly what was involved [in the list of conditions] was a question of medical economics rather than medical ethics, though the two are often synonymous in the jargon of organized medicine."[52]

Physicians who participated in prepaid health plans sometimes had their licenses and hospital privileges revoked,[53] and states were encouraged to pass laws outlawing or restricting the availability of HMOs. A 1972 survey found that 9 states prohibited HMOs altogether, and 20 states either prohibited them or restricted them so severely that they could not operate. Among the restrictions were acts that required medical society approval of the articles of

[51]Listed in Rayack, p. 152. These conditions were contained in a minority report to the report of the Committee on the Costs of Medical Care. See *Medical Care for the American People*, Report of the Committee on the Costs of Medical Care (Chicago: University of Chicago Press, 1932). The minority report was subsequently endorsed by the AMA House of Delegates in 1932. See American Medical Association, *Digest of Official Actions*, 1846–1958 (Chicago: American Medical Association, 1959), p. 314.

[52]Rayack, p. 153.

[53]Descriptions of some notorious cases can be found in Kessel, "Price Discrimination in Medicine," 153; Rayack, pp. 180–95; and Goodman, pp. 74–78.

incorporation, medical society sponsorship or control of the directors or trustees of the plan, or actual medical society control of the plan itself.[54] These restrictions, however, were overridden by federal law in the 1970s.

Effects on the Quality of Medical Care

The primary goal of laws regulating the right to practice medicine was to raise the incomes of physicians. Did those laws also raise the quality of medical care? That is doubtful. In fact, medical practice laws may have lowered the quality of patient care.[55] One reason was that organized medicine used its powers to discourage quality comparisons among physicians. The "no criticism" of fellow physicians rule and the "conspiracy of silence" in malpractice and disciplinary records of practicing physicians were examples.

In addition, the AMA-backed education standards substantially reduced the proportion of practicing physicians who were trained in U.S. medical schools. In 1979, for example, about 5,000 students were enrolled in medical schools in the Caribbean.[56] Although the quality of training in many of those schools was suspect, they successfully prepared students to pass medical licensing exams administered in the United States. It is ironic, in view of the AMA's emphasis on a high quality of medical education, that 46 percent of all newly licensed physicians in 1972 were graduates of foreign medical schools![57] Even today, more than 130,000 U.S. doctors (including 20,000 U.S. citizens) are graduates of foreign medical schools. This is equal to one out of every five practicing physicians in the United States.[58]

---

[54]Robert T. Holley and Rick J. Carlson, "The Legal Context for the Development of Health Maintenance Organizations," *Stanford Law Review* 24 (April 1972): 657.

[55]See Milton Friedman, *Capitalism and Freedom* (Chicago: University of Chicago Press, 1962), chapter 9.

[56]Gail Bronson, "New Medical Schools in the Caribbean Provoke Controversy in the U.S.," *Wall Street Journal*, June 19, 1979.

[57]Henry R. Mason, "Foreign Medical Graduates: Profiles of Those Qualifying for Practice in the United States, 1957 to 1971," *Journal of the American Medical Association* 229, no. 4 (July 22, 1974): 428.

[58]For a brief survey of the role of foreign-trained physicians in the U.S. health care system, see Kenneth H. Bacon, "Foreign Medical Graduates Claim Licensing Bias," *Wall Street Journal*, September 18, 1990.

Figure 5.3
PROPRIETARY HOSPITALS AS A PERCENT OF TOTAL HOSPITALS

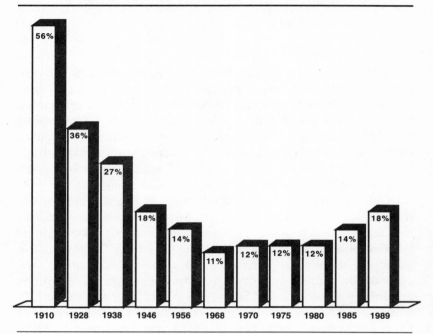

SOURCES: For 1910–68, Bruce Steinwald and Duncan Neuhauser, "The Role of the Proprietary Hospital," *Law and Contemporary Problems* (Autumn 1970): Table 1, p. 819; for 1970–85, U.S. Department of Health and Human Services, *Health, United States, 1989* (Washington, 1990), Tables 93–94; American Hospital Association, *Hospital Statistics 1989–90* (Chicago, 1990), Table 9-A.

Controls on the Form of Delivery: The Hospital

In 1910, approximately 56 percent of all hospitals in the United States were proprietary, or for-profit, hospitals. By the 1960s, less than 11 percent were proprietary, and they accounted for only 8 percent of admissions and only 4 percent of outpatient visits. (See Figure 5.3.) The decline in the role of proprietary hospitals is puzzling, in that both theoretical and empirical evidence suggests that they are more efficient.

The answer to the puzzle lies in explicit government policies. Some states outlawed proprietary hospitals altogether. In states that permitted them, they suffered from several government-imposed competitive disadvantages. First, proprietary hospitals paid property taxes and corporate income taxes, whereas nonprofit hospitals did not. Second, nonprofit hospitals received enormous subsidies under the Hill-Burton Hospital Construction Act of 1946, whereas proprietary hospitals did not. Third, only charitable contributions made to nonprofits were (and are) deductible under federal income tax laws. Note that the first and third disadvantages still exist today.

Several states subjected proprietors to regulatory restrictions that did not apply to nonprofit hospitals. In addition, regulatory agencies often discriminated against proprietary hospitals.[59] In fact, under certificate-of-need regulations still in effect in some cities, opening a new hospital, expanding an existing one, or even purchasing major equipment required the permission of a local planning agency. Yet, such agencies were often influenced by powerful nonprofits, which felt threatened by innovative entrepreneurs.[60] In the late 1970s, for example, Hospital Corporation of America (HCA) spent as much as $500,000 on a Dallas certificate-of-need fight and still failed to get approval.[61]

It is not known what role organized medicine played in the demise of proprietary hospitals. What is known is that proprietary hospitals, like proprietary medical schools, were subjects of the AMA's general hostility toward the "corporate practice of medicine."[62] Organized medicine had a financial reason to oppose proprietary institutions in both fields. Proprietary institutions are typically dominated by owners interested in maximizing profit. Nonprofits, on the other hand, frequently pursue other goals, many of

[59]See Bruce Steinwald and Duncan Neuhauser, "The Role of the Proprietary Hospital," *Law and Contemporary Problems* (Autumn 1970): 817–38; Ralph Berry, "Cost and Efficiency in the Production of Hospital Services," *Health and Society—Milbank Memorial Fund Quarterly* (Summer 1974); David Salkever, "Competition among Hospitals," in Greenberg; Alonzo Yerby, "Regulation of Health Manpower," in National Academy of Sciences, *Controls on Health Care: Papers of the Conference on Regulation in the Health Industry* (January 7–9, 1974), p. 96.

[60]Lewin and Associates, Inc., *Evaluation of the Efficiency and Effectiveness of the Section 1122 Review Process* (Springfield, VA: National Technical Information Service, 1975), pp. 5–19; and Clark C. Havighurst, "Regulation of Health Facilities and Services by 'Certificate-of-Need,' " *Virginia Law Review* 59, no. 7 (October 1973): 1143–1232.

[61]Based on authors' interviews with HCA officials.

[62]See Paul Starr, *The Social Transformation of American Medicine* (New York: Basic Books, 1982).

157

which are consistent with the aims of organized medicine, and such institutions can be more easily dominated by the medical profession. Nonprofit medical schools, for example, tend to prefer longer and more costly physician training, which is consistent with the traditional AMA desire to make entry into the profession more difficult. In the case of the hospital sector, nonprofit institutions are more likely to cooperate with the AMA in restricting price competition among practicing physicians. For example, they frequently restrict their medical staff to members of local medical societies. Expulsion from the medical society for purportedly unethical conduct, then, also would mean loss of hospital privileges and impair the physician's ability to practice and earn income.

Are proprietary hospitals better than nonprofits at lowering costs? Earlier studies found that they were, but more recent studies have found that the nonprofits have lower costs.[63] What the later studies overlook, however, is that hospitals operating under the cost-plus system do not necessarily have incentives to lower their costs.

A better question is, what type of hospital is most efficient? And the answer is not in doubt. During the 1980s, proprietary hospital chains revolutionized the way in which hospitals were run and managed. Prior to that, most nonprofit hospitals were managed by people with little training or experience in modern business management techniques. The hospital chains found they could take over nonprofit institutions suffering annual losses and make substantial profits in a short period of time, while serving the same patient population.

Controls on the Method of Payment: Health Insurance

Much of the blame for escalating health care costs is centered on our system of health insurance. Insurers traditionally have paid whatever bills doctors and hospitals have submitted. This arrangement has encouraged too many tests and too many procedures. It also has encouraged the purchase and use of every new piece of medical technology that has appeared on the market. However,

[63]For a summary of these studies, see J. Rodgers Hollingsworth and Ellen Jane Hollingsworth, *Controversy about American Hospitals* (Washington: American Enterprise Institute, 1987).

nothing inherent in the market for insurance produces such distortions. Insurers in many other fields use techniques that prevent abuse and keep down costs. Moreover, competition encourages those insurers to search for new and effective ways to reduce costs. That is also the way in which the health insurance market once worked, when it was free to do so.

In the early part of the 20th century, a large number of prepaid medical insurance plans developed in Oregon and Washington, largely as a result of the hazardous working conditions in the lumber, railroad, and mining industries. Many of the plans were proprietary, and the insurers looked hard at each claim they received. Physicians' fees were scrutinized closely. Physicians were often warned about unnecessary surgery, and were frequently asked to justify procedures. They were also often asked to explain or justify hospital stays that were out of line with the average stays for particular procedures.

Enter organized medicine. Oregon's local medical societies created their own medical insurance plan. Using state-derived powers to discipline individual physicians, predatory pricing, and similar techniques, organized medicine captured the lion's share of the market for its own plan. Moreover, once the scheme came to dominate the market, health insurance in Oregon resembled the type of insurance that later expanded in other states. The physicians' insurance scheme is today called Blue Shield.[64]

There are numerous examples in other states of organized medicine's using its powers to combat the growth of insurance plans designed to hold down costs and create more price competition. Physicians who started or cooperated with unauthorized plans sometimes lost hospital privileges and even their licenses.[65] Moreover, the plans viewed most favorably by organized medicine, Blue Cross and Blue Shield, were often given competitive advantages by state insurance regulations.

---

[64]See Lawrence Goldberg and Warren Greenberg, "The Effect of Physician-Controlled Health Insurance: *U.S. v. Oregon State Medical Society*," *Journal of Health Politics, Policy and Law* 2 (Spring 1977): 48–78; and Lawrence Goldberg and Warren Greenberg, "The Emergence of Physician-Sponsored Health Insurance: A Historical Perspective," in Greenberg, pp. 288–321.

[65]For a summary of some of the most notorious cases, see Goodman, chapter 5; Kessel, "Price Discrimination in Medicine," 34–41; and Rayack, pp. 180–85.

In most states, for example, taxes are assessed on insurance premiums, and the revenue is used to finance the regulatory apparatus. In a majority of states, however, commercial insurers paid taxes on the order of 2 to 3 percent of premiums while the Blues paid lower taxes or no taxes at all.[66] Considering the fact that net revenues (premiums minus benefit payments) on group policies are usually less than 5 percent of the total premiums, a 2 to 3 percent premium tax is equal to about 50 to 60 percent of net revenues.

The Blues were also often exempted from other taxes, such as real estate taxes. In some states, commercial insurance policies sold to individuals were required to meet minimum benefit/premium ratios, whereas Blue Cross–Blue Shield policies were not. Other states regulated the rates charged by the Blues, but in terms of overall premium rather than the benefit/premium ratio. In most states, required reserves were also lower or nonexistent for the Blues.[67] Moreover, in the early years, physicians and hospitals gave discounts to Blue Cross–Blue Shield plans that were not available to other insurers, and hospitals and physicians were encouraged to place Blue Cross–Blue Shield advertisements (AMA-approved) in their admitting offices and waiting rooms.

As a consequence, Blue Cross and Blue Shield plans soon monopolized the marketplace and began shaping the market for health insurance.[68] By 1950, Blue Shield was selling 52 percent of all regular medical insurance and Blue Cross was selling 49 percent of all hospital insurance. For the next three decades, the share of total insurance sold by the two plans never dipped below 40 percent.[69]

Two things are important about this development. First, unlike the early health insurance companies, Blue Cross and Blue Shield

[66]David Robbins, "Comment," in Greenberg, p. 263.

[67]Ibid.

[68]It is important to note that, although there is a national Blue Cross organization and members typically have similar views, there are also 67 separate, autonomous plans in the United States, each of which sets its own policies. For most Blue Cross plans, there is a companion Blue Shield plan. Often the two work together and share services and billings. In some cases, the two have merged into a single corporate entity. See Howard J. Bermand and Lewis B. Weeks, *The Financial Management of Hospitals*, 5th ed. (Washington: Health Administration Press, 1982), pp. 110–21, 145–73.

[69]Health Insurance Association of America, *Source Book of Health Insurance Data*, 1975–76.

never saw themselves as adversaries of the medical community. To the contrary, their plans were largely created and governed by the institutions whose bills they were paying. Not only was there no question of an adversarial relationship, but it was generally thought from the beginning that the Blues were created to represent the medical community, not patients. Two experts in hospital finance have flatly said, "Blue Cross was founded to save hospitals from financial ruin!"[70]

The second important point about the Blues is that they dominated the market, while any single rival had only a very small market share. That made it difficult for a commercial insurance company to adopt reimbursement procedures that differed fundamentally from those of Blue Cross and Blue Shield. If a commercial company attempted radical deviation, the medical community could threaten a boycott. Even Aetna Life and Casualty, with nearly 12 million policyholders, discovered that it could not fundamentally alter its reimbursement procedures in a way that threatened conventional methods.[71]

What were the reimbursement procedures adopted by the Blues? In general, they involved very little interference with the clinical judgment of the physicians or with the medical decisions of hospitals. More important, under Blue Cross leadership, hospitals came to be reimbursed in a way that hospitals almost unanimously approved of—cost-plus.

[70]Bermand and Weeks, p. 147.

[71]See Charlotte L. Rosenberg, "He Challenged Aetna's Hard-Line Fee Policy—and Won," *Medical Economics* (September 1982.)

6. How the Cost-Plus System Works

The cost-plus system of public and private health insurance, effective from the end of World War II until the mid-1980s, virtually assured hospitals that their costs would be covered. Very rarely did hospitals go bankrupt. The system insulated them from the potentially fatal risks that competition naturally creates in other markets.

What is good for hospitals, though, is not necessarily good for patients and policyholders. An insurance system designed to cover hospital costs is inherently adverse to the interests of the insured. The cost-plus system virtually guarantees that health insurance premiums will continue rising, because the people responsible for controlling hospital costs find that they can increase their revenues only by increasing their costs.

In this respect, health insurance contrasts markedly with most other forms of insurance. The automobile insurance industry is not organized to ensure that auto repair shops remain in business. The fire and casualty insurance industry is not organized to ensure that builders and home repair firms stay in business. Insurers are supposed to act on behalf of their clients (the policyholders), not on behalf of those who provide services. However, in the market for health insurance, the situation has been very different.

How Hospitals Get Paid under the Cost-Plus System

Suppose a male patient enters a hospital for a medical procedure. He has a Blue Cross health insurance policy with a $200 deductible and a required copayment of 20 percent. When he is released from the hospital, he receives a bill detailing all of the services that the hospital performed and indicating a charge for each. The amount owed by the man is $200 (the deductible), plus 20 percent of the remaining charges. As our hypothetical patient leaves the hospital, folding his copy of the bill, placing it in his coat pocket, and feeling sadness over the reduction in his bank account, he takes some consolation from the thought that Blue Cross will pay the remaining 80 percent of the charges. But the man is quite wrong. What Blue Cross pays may be more than 80 percent, or it may be less. More to the point, what Blue Cross pays is only tangentially related to the bill of our hypothetical patient.

The amount paid to the hospital by the patient is based on the hospital's "charges." The patient might have compared these prices with those of other hospitals. If he chose a lower priced hospital, he might have felt that he was helping to keep health care costs down and, at the same time, to keep insurance premiums down for his employer and fellow workers. But again, he could be quite wrong.

Under cost-plus reimbursement, what Blue Cross pays is not based on the prices that hospitals charge patients, but on hospital costs, which may or may not be reflected in the prices. In choosing a lower priced hospital, our hypothetical patient inadvertently might have chosen a higher cost one, thus contributing to escalating health care costs and higher insurance premiums—and doing precisely the opposite of what he had intended.

Reimbursement Formulas

Table 6.1 lists three formulas traditionally used by Blue Cross to reimburse hospitals. The most common is the per diem method. If, on the average, 30 percent of the patient-days of a particular hospital are accounted for by Blue Cross patients, Blue Cross will pay 30 percent of the hospital's total costs. Cost is determined by various accounting techniques, about which there can be much bickering. Usually, a "plus" factor is thrown in to cover the value of working capital and equity capital. Hence the term "cost-plus."[1]

One does not have to study the per diem reimbursement formula for long to realize that the one sure way for a hospital to increase its revenues is to increase its costs. If a hospital adds more beds (even if they go unfilled), buys expensive equipment (even if it goes unused), or cares for more patients or more seriously ill patients, it increases its costs and therefore its revenues from Blue Cross. Conversely, anything a hospital does to decrease its costs also decreases its revenues. Under cost-plus reimbursement, then, Blue

[1]For a discussion of this and other reimbursement formulas, see Sylvia A. Law, *Blue Cross: What Went Wrong?* (New Haven: Yale University Press, 1974), pp. 59–114.

Table 6.1
How Blue Cross Reimbursed Hospitals under Cost-Plus Finance

Per Diem Method

$$\left(\frac{\text{Total hospital costs}}{\text{Total patient days}}\right) \times \begin{array}{c}\text{Percent of patient}\\ \text{days accounted for}\\ \text{by BC patients}\end{array} = \begin{array}{c}\text{Amount}\\ \text{BC pays}\end{array}$$

Department Method

$$\left(\frac{\text{BC patient charges}}{\text{Total patient charges}}\right) \times \begin{array}{c}\text{Total cost of the}\\ \text{department}\end{array} = \begin{array}{c}\text{Amount}\\ \text{BC pays}\end{array}$$

Combination Method

$$\left(\frac{\text{Total cost of routine services}}{\text{Total patient days}}\right) \times \begin{array}{c}\text{Percent of patient}\\ \text{days accounted for}\\ \text{by BC patients}\end{array} +$$

$$\left(\frac{\text{BC patient charges for ancillary services}}{\text{Total patient charges for ancillary services}}\right) \times \begin{array}{c}\text{Total cost of}\\ \text{ancillary services}\end{array} = \begin{array}{c}\text{Amount}\\ \text{BC pays}\end{array}$$

SOURCE: Herman Miles Somers and Anne Ramsey Somers, *Medicare and the Hospitals: Issues and Prospects* (Washington: Brookings Institution, 1967), pp. 166–68.

Cross pays for hospital care in much the same way the Department of Defense pays for some weapons systems, but without the same rationale.[2]

Two other reimbursement formulas (also depicted in Table 6.1) are the "department" and "combination" methods, which, like the per diem method, essentially reimburse hospitals on the basis of the costs they incur. A 1976 survey showed that of Blue Cross plans using cost-based reimbursement formulas, 61 percent used the per diem method, 25 percent the department method, and 14 percent the combination method.[3]

Blue Cross plans have been moving away from these formulas over the past two decades. In 1973, 69 percent of Blue Cross plans reimbursed hospitals on the basis of costs and 31 percent reimbursed on the basis of charges (prices). In 1976, 50 percent reimbursed on the basis of costs and 50 percent on charges.[4] In 1983, 28 percent of Blue Cross contracts were cost-based, 59 percent were charge-based, and the remainder were mixed.[5]

In the cost-plus system, prices do not have the same function they have in the normal market, however. In the cost-plus system (as explained below), prices are chosen to manipulate reimbursement formulas rather than produced by natural market forces. Consequently, it is probably fair to say that all traditional Blue Cross reimbursement methods are ultimately cost-plus.

The cost-plus method of reimbursement was not confined to the private sector. Under the original Medicare and Medicaid programs, the federal government adopted the same payment methods used by Blue Cross.[6] Thus, the two fastest growing health insurance

---

[2]The rationale for the Department of Defense is that new weapons systems are one-of-a-kind items that are being built for the first time. Exact costs are harder to estimate than for off-the-shelf items. In that case, cost-based procurement with competitive bidding may be a reasonable policy.

[3]Howard J. Bermand and Lewis B. Weeks, *The Financial Management of Hospitals*, 5th ed. (Washington: Health Administration Press, 1982), p. 153.

[4]Ibid., pp. 152–3.

[5]Susan W. Melczer, *Hospital—Blue Cross Contract Provisions* (Chicago: American Hospital Association, July 1, 1983), p. 1.

[6]Specifically the department method and the combination method. See Herman Miles Somers and Anne Ramsey Somers, *Medicare and the Hospitals: Issues and Prospects* (Washington: Brookings Institution, 1967), p. 168.

programs in the medical marketplace were firmly entrenched in the cost-plus system.

Hospital Prices

One of the most interesting developments in hospital finance over the last several decades has been the decreasing proportion of hospital bills paid by patients out-of-pocket. In 1950, roughly half of all hospital bills were paid out-of-pocket by patients and half by third parties (employers, insurance companies, or government). In the 1970s, about 90 percent of hospital income came from third-party payers, with about half coming from employers and insurance companies and half from government. Less than 10 percent was paid out-of-pocket by patients. What that means is that only 10 percent of hospital revenue was directly connected with the hospital charges. As Figure 6.1 shows, the other 90 percent was cost-plus reimbursement. Such reimbursement was so pervasive that some health economists concluded that the prices charged by hospitals were little more than numerical artifacts. Writing in the late 1960s, Somers and Somers stated that because hospital "charges now have meaning for only a minority of patients and hospital finances, they have become largely a set of arbitrary statistical factors, instead of a set of prices."[7]

Not only did hospital prices fail to allocate resources the way prices do in other markets, but under the original Medicare and Medicaid reimbursement formulas, hospitals had an incentive to manipulate their prices to maximize their reimbursement from government. Under the department method of reimbursement, for example, the amount paid by Medicare is equal to the total charges to Medicare patients divided by total charges to all patients times total cost. One health economist has shown how a hospital can double its income from Medicare under this method of reimbursement by artificially raising its charges for services typically used by Medicare patients and by lowering its charges for other services.[8] Moreover, this practice is not considered illegal or even unethical. Hospitals can buy computer programs that show them how to maximize their revenues under various reimbursement rules.

[7]Ibid.
[8]Law, pp. 78–81.

Figure 6.1
HOW HOSPITALS GET THEIR MONEY IN THE COST-PLUS SYSTEM

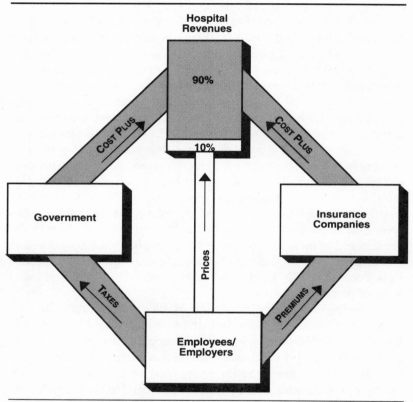

SOURCE: National Center for Policy Analysis.

Perverse Incentives

The cost-plus system is antithetical to the market system, in which prices and competition allocate resources. Frequently, the cost-plus system creates incentives that are the precise opposite of market system incentives. One cannot be certain what the market for hospital services would look like if it were truly competitive. But it is easy to speculate. When a grocery store discovers that it has ordered too many apples, it tries to sell those apples by lowering the price. When a manufacturing company has excess capacity, it seeks new business and new products and offers attractive prices. Presumably, similar things would happen in a competitive hospital marketplace.

But no matter how many beds go empty, hospitals rarely advertise cut-rate prices on surgery or sales on elective procedures. If prices and competition were allocating resources in the hospital marketplace, a surplus of hospital beds would be great news for consumers. It would mean that prices and therefore health care costs soon would tumble. By contrast, in a cost-plus hospital marketplace, surplus beds and other unused capacity frequently mean just the opposite—that costs will rise. The reason for this anomaly is that what really drives the system is unseen. The prices and competition are apparent, giving the impression of a genuine market at work, but the force that really drives the system is cost-plus.

Hospital Services

Consider the results of a comparison of hospital costs (not prices) prevailing in the 1970s. The study found that the daily cost of maternity care was more than seven times higher at some hospitals than at others, and that the daily cost of medical/surgical care was more than two and one-half times greater.[9] The daily cost of short-term alcoholism treatment was almost five times higher at some hospitals than at others. The reasons for these cost differences varied. According to the authors of the study, 130 out of 138 hospitals invested too much in capacity and equipment. Most had too many admitting physicians. But the most important reason appears to be volume. A great many hospitals were delivering services at such a low volume that they could not take full advantage of economies of scale. As Table 6.2 shows, the differences in costs varied by as much as seven-to-one between high-volume and low-volume hospitals.

How can a hospital stay in business while providing a service that is seven times more costly than that of a rival? In a genuinely competitive market, it couldn't. But the cost-plus system ensures that reimbursement matches costs. One result is a system in which hospitals have very weak incentives to be efficient—to get rid of

[9]Thomas G. Cowing and Alphonse G. Holtman, "Multiproduct Short-Run Hospital Cost Functions: Empirical Evidence and Policy Implications from Cross-Section Data," *Southern Economic Journal* 49, no. 3 (January 1983): 648.

Table 6.2
HOSPITAL COSTS AND HOSPITAL VOLUME, 1975*

Type of Service	High Volume	Low Volume
Emergency room visits		
Cost per patient per day	$20	$32
Number of visits per day	275	148
Medical/surgical care		
Cost per patient per day	$100	$255
Number of visits per day	824	17
Maternity		
Cost per patient per day	$75	$540
Number of visits per day	55	4
Short-term alcoholism		
Cost per patient per day	$50	$240
Number of visits per day	247	NA

SOURCE: Thomas G. Cowing and Alphonse G. Holtman, "Multiproduct Short-Run Hospital Cost Functions: Empirical Evidence and Policy Implications from Cross-Section Data," *Southern Economic Journal* 49, no. 3 (January 1983): 648.

*Based on data from 138 short-term and general care hospitals in New York State.

high-cost services, take advantage of economies of scale, specialize in procedures in which they are the low-cost producer, etc. Another result is a hospital system in which the nation's annual health care bill is much higher than it needs to be. Indeed, it is a system that rewards and even encourages waste and inefficiency. As Somers and Somers observed, "In no other realm of economic life today are payments guaranteed for costs that are neither controlled by competition nor regulated by public authority, and in which no incentive for economy can be discerned."[10]

Risks to Patient Health

What is bad economics also frequently is bad for patient health. Studies have shown that when various types of surgery are performed infrequently, not only are surgery costs higher but the mortality rates are higher as well. For example, the U.S. Department

[10]Somers and Somers, *Medicare and the Hospitals*, p. 192.

of Health and Human Services has judged that, for satisfactory results, a hospital should perform at least 200 open-heart surgeries per year. However, in the 1980s, 55 percent of U.S. hospitals that performed open-heart surgeries performed fewer than 200 per year.[11]

This problem was not confined to rural areas, where the incidence of surgery was necessarily small. It also was seen in large cities where consumers had many choices and information was more readily available. American Hospital Association (AHA) data for 1981 showed that annual open-heart surgeries performed in New York City hospitals ranged from a high of 1,337 (at St. Luke's–Roosevelt Hospital Center) to a low of 75 (at the VA Medical Center in Brooklyn).[12] In 14 Chicago hospitals, the range was from a high of 926 to a low of 6; in 10 Los Angeles hospitals, it was from 1,071 to 35; and in 5 Detroit hospitals, it was from 674 to 2.[13]

Why don't hospitals with a high volume of surgery and lower mortality rates advertise that fact to attract customers? Because that would be inconsistent with the traditional philosophy of the cost-plus system. Competition and competitive advertising were actively discouraged in the market for physicians' services. A similar historical development occurred in the hospital sector, where advertising is still largely confined to statements about amenities, quality of food, and convenience of location. Almost never is there any mention of comparative mortality rates or patient safety. Moreover, the AHA has left no doubt about its desire to discourage such advertising. The AHA's guidelines state:

> Self-aggrandizement of one hospital at the expense of another may be counterproductive, and, if inaccurate, could lead to charges of libel and claims for damages. . . . Quality comparisons, either direct or by implication, between one hospital's services, facilities, or employees and those of another hospital may be counterproductive, libelous, or difficult to present in a firm and objective manner.[14]

[11]Warren Greenberg, "Demand, Supply and Information in Health Care and Other Industries," in Jack A. Meyer, ed., *Incentives vs. Controls in Health Policy* (Washington: American Enterprise Institute, 1985), p. 100.

[12]Ibid., pp. 101–3.

[13]Ibid.

[14]American Hospital Association, *Guidelines—Advertising by Hospitals* (Chicago, 1977), p. 2, cited in Greenberg, p. 100.

Cost Shifting

In competitive markets, people tend to be charged prices that reflect actual costs. In virtually every regulated market, some consumers end up subsidizing others. For example, in a regulated telephone industry, long-distance calls subsidize local calls. In a regulated airline industry, heavily traveled routes subsidize lightly traveled routes. In this respect, the cost-plus system resembles a regulated market. It is replete with cross-subsidies.

Cross-subsidies are sometimes overt and direct. For example, a 1976 survey found that 30 Blue Cross plans reimbursed hospitals for the bad debts of non–Blue Cross patients. The cost of charity care for non–Blue Cross patients was reimbursed by 27 Blue Cross plans.[15] Cross-subsidies are at other times informal and indirect. For example, it is commonly believed that, within hospitals, the surgery department subsidizes the obstetrics ward; within emergency rooms, patients with minor ailments subsidize patients with serious injuries; and among all patients, paying patients subsidize charity care patients.

What is not generally realized, however, is that cross-subsidies are a natural and inevitable by-product of the cost-plus system of hospital finance. Once it is accepted that the de facto purpose of health insurance is to make sure that hospitals cover their costs and that hospitals are free to determine what costs they will incur, cross-subsidies are unavoidable. Indeed, once those premises are accepted, the only thing left to argue about is how the hospital bill is to be divided among third-party payers.

That is what gives rise to the debate over "cost shifting." In the early years, Medicare and Medicaid officials argued that their payments were forced up so that payments by private health insurance companies could be kept down. Today, the situation is reversed. Private insurance companies complain that the government's reduction of Medicaid and Medicare payments has increased their payments. Likewise, many commercial insurers argue that Blue Cross's efforts to keep its payments down will force their own payments up. Given their premises, that is true. In the cost-plus system, if any third-party payer reduces its payments, the payments of all others will rise to cover the shortfall.

[15]Bermand and Weeks, *The Financial Management of Hospitals*, p. 153.

Consider the pronouncements of the Health Insurance Association of America (HIAA), a group of private health insurance companies other than Blue Cross. The HIAA estimated that $5.8 billion in costs were shifted from Medicaid and Medicare patients to private patients in 1982. In response, private insurance companies trimmed benefits and raised premiums by 20 to 40 percent.[16] In other words, when government's share of hospital costs goes down, the share borne by private insurance companies goes up.

Rethinking the Role of Blue Cross

Although we have discussed the cost-plus system in terms of the dominant role of Blue Cross, it would be a mistake to believe that Blue Cross administrators bear personal responsibility for the system. The national Blue Cross organization is merely a trade group that represents 67 Blue Cross plans, each administered separately by its own governing board. There is every reason to believe that each Blue Cross plan's administrators respond to economic incentives in much the same way as managers of any other firm do. The incentives in the health insurance marketplace have largely been created by government policies. Recent policy changes have caused the various participants in the cost-plus system to change their behavior in ways that undermine that system and move toward a competitive market. Blue Cross administrators are responding to these new incentives, along with everyone else in the health insurance marketplace.

Hospital Prices in the 1980s

Although the cost-plus system is dissolving and is being replaced by a more competitive market for medical care today, that change is occurring slowly. Meanwhile, the system is far from being a relic. It continues to dominate the medical marketplace—especially in the hospital sector.

Table 6.3 presents recent prices charged by seven Dallas-area hospitals for a complete blood count and a routine urinalysis. They are two of the most common procedures performed in a hospital, and all of the hospitals cited are within easy driving distance of each other. Moreover, since the prices primarily apply to nonelderly

[16]Stanley Wohl, *The Medical Industrial Complex* (New York: Harmon Books, 1984), p. 188.

Table 6.3
LINE ITEM PRICES IN DALLAS AREA HOSPITALS, 1988*

Hospital	Cost of Complete Blood Count	Cost of Routine Urinalysis
Hospital A	$11.00	$28.00
Hospital B	20.00	15.00
Hospital C	21.00	16.25
Hospital D	21.60	16.00
Hospital E	27.75	20.00
Hospital F	28.00	19.50
Hospital G	33.25	11.75

SOURCE: Medical Control, Inc.
*Based on actual hospital invoices.

patients, most of whom have employer-provided health insurance, the buyers of the tests are usually private companies. Considering these facts, one would expect that the prices charged by the seven hospitals would be fairly similar. However, as Table 6.3 shows, the charge for a complete blood count at the highest priced hospital is more than three times that at the lowest priced. For urinalysis, the highest price is almost two and one-half times the lowest one. Even more surprising is the fact that the hospital that charges the most for the complete blood count charges the least for urinalysis. The converse is also true. Thus, to minimize health care costs, a patient should purchase the complete blood count at Hospital A and the urinalysis at Hospital G. Moreover, because there is as much or more variation in other prices that Dallas hospitals charge, patients could minimize total health care costs only if they travel among the seven hospitals in much the same way that one might shop for bargains at seven supermarkets.

Unlike supermarket prices, these hospital prices do not represent attempts to attract buyers. That is, Hospital A does not advertise that it has the lowest priced complete blood count in Dallas. To the contrary, a patient in need of a blood test would probably have to go to considerable lengths to find out what the seven hospitals charge for the service. Odds are also high that the patient's physician would not know the seven prices or whom to contact in the hospital bureaucracies to get the information.

Table 6.4
AVERAGE CHARGE FOR WELL-BABY DELIVERY
IN DALLAS AREA HOSPITALS, 1986*

Hospital	Cost
Humana–Medical City	$2,024
Baylor Medical Center	1,698
St. Paul Medical Center	1,486
Irving Hospital	1,449
Presbyterian Hospital	1,423
Lewisville Memorial Hospital	1,400
HCA Medical Center–Plano	1,337
Memorial Hospital of Garland	1,069

SOURCE: Dallas Business Group on Health.
*Based on actual hospital invoices.

Such differences in charges cannot possibly represent differences in actual costs. The tests are performed with standard equipment, purchased in a competitive market. The human skill involved is standard. Although there may be some differences in other costs (for example, a hospital within Dallas may have higher operating costs than one in the suburbs), the costs do not vary by a factor of three to one. The differences in charges are consistent with cost-plus accounting procedures, however. Under cost-plus finance, if a hospital undercharges on one item, it will tend to overcharge on another.

Table 6.4 shows charges for a complete procedure or package of services for eight Dallas-area hospitals. In this case, the procedure is well-baby delivery, a fairly common, well-defined hospital service. As the table shows, the highest priced hospital has an average delivery charge almost twice that of the lowest priced, a surprising difference considering that prospective patients have plenty of time to investigate differences in hospital charges in advance. It is probable, however, that an expectant mother would find it impossible to ascertain the average delivery charge in any Dallas hospital. Indeed, it is not clear that most hospitals would know.[17]

[17]Note that the total charge for the procedure is the sum of all of the line item prices for each separate service (hospital admission kit, blood test, etc.).

Table 6.5
HOSPITAL PRICES NATIONWIDE, 1986 TO 1988[1]

Item or Test	Low Price[2]	High Price[3]
Electrocardiogram	$8.00	$78.35
Complete blood count	1.00	42.00
Urinalysis (routine)	3.20	28.00
Admission kit	2.25	33.00
Baby diapers	0.30	20.75

SOURCE: Medical Control, Inc.
[1]Based on actual hospital invoices.
[2]Price at the 10th percentile of the distribution.
[3]Price at the 90th percentile of the distribution.

Table 6.5 shows that Dallas is not unique. Line item prices for common items and tests show remarkable variation among the nation's hospitals. For an electrocardiogram, the variation in price is more than 9 to 1. For the complete blood count, the variation is 42 to 1. For baby diapers, the variation is more than 69 to 1. Similar price differences exist for most other items and tests.

One might suppose that this extreme variance in hospital prices would allow smart buyers to exploit the differences through comparison shopping. For example, consider a large company with employees in many localities around the country. Could the company collect hospital prices and tell its employees where to go for the lowest priced tests, procedures, and services? In the cost-plus system, things are not that simple. Each hospital has as many as 12,000 line item prices. Further, each can use a different accounting and coding system. So prices charged by different hospitals cannot be compared until their accounting is converted to a common system. For the 50 hospitals in the Chicago area alone, there are as many as 600,000 prices to compare. For a company operating nationwide, with employees who have access to approximately 7,000 hospitals, a comparison shopper could possibly be confronted with as many as 84 million different line item prices. Such comparison shopping is a formidable task for any corporate buyer, no matter how sophisticated the computers that assist in making buying decisions.[18]

[18]However, some firms such as Medical Control Inc. in Texas, Medstat Inc. in Michigan, and Mediqual Systems in Massachusetts attempt to do it for large, third-party payers.

176

What the Cost-Plus System Means for Patients

One of the worst things about being sick in America is having to confront the hospital's bill. In most cities in the United States, patients cannot find out a hospital's total charge for a procedure prior to treatment. At the time of discharge, they learn that there is not one price, but hundreds of line item prices. About 90 percent of the items listed on a hospital bill are in principle unreadable. In only a handful of cases can the patient both recognize the service rendered and judge the reasonableness of the charge. Moreover, things are getting worse. To avoid patient outrage, many hospitals are taking recognizable items, such as Tylenol capsules, off their line item statements and hiding the cost in other charges. The end result is that hospital bills are totally incomprehensible.[19]

As in the case of hotels, the one price that patients can learn about prior to admission is the hospital's basic room rate. If these rates signaled differences in other prices, patients would at least be able to pick out the lowest priced hospital prior to admission. Unfortunately, other hospital prices are not tied to room rates. In most cities, hospital room charges differ by no more than a factor of two to one. Total hospital bills, on the other hand, can differ as much as ten to one for similar procedures. Moreover, the hospital with the highest room rate does not necessarily charge the highest prices for any or all other services. A 1988 report showed that the Chicago hospital with the highest room rate had some of the lowest charges in the city for laboratory tests, a phenomenon that is consistent with cost-plus accounting.[20]

Although hospital administrators do not have to give patients advance notice of their total bill, hospitals in Illinois are required to tell the state government. Among the total charges for outpatient services reported by Chicago hospitals to the state of Illinois in 1988, the charge for a mammogram varied by almost 10 to 1, for a CAT scan more than 10 to 1, for a tonsillectomy 27 to 1, and for cataract removal 34 to 1.[21] If patients knew about these differences, they

[19]Elizabeth Gardner, "Trying to Make Sense of Hospital Charges," *Modern Healthcare* (December 17, 1990), p. 24.

[20]Illinois Health Care Cost Containment Council, *A Report of Selected Prices at Illinois Hospitals* (July 1988).

[21]Illinois Health Care Cost Containment Council, *A Report of Selected Prices at Illinois Hospitals: Outpatient Services* (August 1989).

177

could reduce their medical bills dramatically. Unfortunately, most do not.

Health Insurance as Prepayment for the Consumption of Medical Care

A major argument developed in this book is that health insurance today is often not real insurance; it is instead prepayment for the consumption of medical care. That is especially true of group health insurance plans sold to, or administered by, employers. But in many ways, it is also true of individual and family policies purchased outside of the workplace.

The cost-plus mentality does not view health insurance as a vehicle for protecting the financial assets of people against adverse medical contingencies. Instead, it sees health insurance as a vehicle for paying for medical services. In the cost-plus vision, health insurance (whether public or private) is simply a way of transferring resources from people to providers. Real insurance would interfere with this objective. Thus, real insurance is an anathema to the cost-plus bureaucracy.

One way to appreciate the unusual nature of health insurance is to consider how it differs from other types of insurance including life insurance and fire and casualty insurance. At the risk of over-simplification, we have presented some of these differences in Tables 6.6 and 6.7. Let's consider some of them in more detail.

Prepayment for Consumption Decisions

The essence of conventional insurance is the pooling of risk. Insurable risks are largely risks outside of the policyholder's control. Premiums are set based on the probability that those risky events will occur, and if they do occur, the insurer pays policyholders (or their heirs) a predetermined amount, or an amount established by a predetermined method of assessing damages.

In the market for health insurance, things are very different. Often, benefits are paid even if no risky event has occurred. Thus, insurers often pay for general checkups, diagnostic tests, and exploratory surgery. The insurer agrees to pay for these services even when doctors subsequently discover that there was no illness and, thus, no risky adverse condition. Insurers in these cases are paying for the consumption decisions of policyholders. Even if a risky event does occur, the amount paid is again often determined

Table 6.6

COMMON DIFFERENCES BETWEEN HEALTH INSURANCE AND LIFE INSURANCE

Category	Life Insurance Purchased by an Individual	Health Insurance Provided by an Employer
Payee	Policyholder	Providers
Amount paid	Amount fixed in advance	Amount depends on consumption decisions of the employee
Events that cause a benefit	A risky event	Consumption decisions of the employee; no risky event required
Insurer's obligation to pay benefits	Once a risky event has occurred, insurer is fully liable; no further premium payments required	Insurer pays providers only as long as continued premiums are paid; insurer can cancel policy and cease paying benefits even after a risky event has occurred
Employment conditions	Coverage continues after switch of jobs	Coverage eventually ends after switch of jobs
Right to future coverage	Guaranteed renewable	No future coverage guaranteed
Use of premium dollars	Most are kept in reserve for benefits in future years	Most are paid out in benefits the year they are collected
Premium costs of benefits	Premiums are actuarially fair	Premiums often are not actuarially fair

Table 6.7
HOW BENEFITS ARE DETERMINED UNDER HEALTH INSURANCE AND CASUALTY INSURANCE

Category	Casualty Insurance	Health Insurance
Amount of benefit	Replacement cost or value of the lost asset	Determined by the consumption decisions of the policyholder (sometimes managed by the insurer)
Method of settling claims	Claims adjuster and policyholder agree on extent of damage	No claims adjuster, but may be managed by the insurer
Insurer's liability	Insurer is liable for damages from the time of the risky event, even if it takes years to assess damage	Insurer is liable only as long as the policyholder continues to pay premiums; insurer can cancel the policy and cease paying benefits even after the risky event has occurred
Method of payment	Policyholder receives cash and is not obliged to repair or replace the asset	Policyholder can only receive benefits in the form of medical services

by the consumption decisions of the patient. Suppose, for example, that a patient is diagnosed as having a heart condition. The patient, after consultation with a physician, may opt for less expensive drug therapy, a $25,000 bypass operation, or some intermediate therapy. The amount the insurer pays is totally determined by the treatment chosen. If auto collision insurance worked the same way, a policyholder whose car had been destroyed would be able to choose from a wide array of replacements: from economy car to Cadillac to Rolls Royce. Insurers would pay, depending on which replacement the policyholder preferred. Auto insurance that worked like that would be very expensive.

Insurer's Obligation to Pay for Damages

Because conventional insurance payments are tied to the incidence of risky events, once the event has occurred, insurers are completely liable for the damages covered. Health insurance, once again, is different. Under a typical policy, the insurer is liable only as long as the insured continues to be covered and to pay premiums.

Suppose that a couple has a low-weight baby with predictable medical expenses lasting for several years. During that period, the couple's health insurance policy may be segregated in a special way with other policies and the premiums charged may skyrocket (even though the same insurer offers similar coverage to other couples for very low premiums). If the couple drops the policy, the insurer will no longer be obligated to pay. If the policy is acquired through an employer and the employee changes jobs, the insurer is relieved of the obligation to pay after a certain period of time. Moreover, the insurer can cancel the policy, as long as it cancels all similar policies, and cease paying benefits after a period determined by state law.

If life insurance worked the same way, following the death of a spouse, an elderly widow would receive a monthly annuity from the life insurance company. But to receive the annuity, she would have to continue paying monthly premiums, which in time could increase and even exceed the value of her monthly annuity check. Furthermore, the widow would live in fear that her policy would be canceled, leaving her without future income.

Payments to Providers

Conventional insurance is based on the idea that the policyholder is the beneficiary. Thus, payments from insurers are ultimately disposed of according to the policyholder's preferences. Under automobile liability insurance, a person who loses a car in an accident is not required to buy a new car. Under home owners' insurance, a family whose house is destroyed in a fire is not required to build a new house. But, under almost all health insurance policies, the only way a policyholder can realize benefits is to consume medical services. Suppose a terminally ill man is confronted with the choice of expensive, end-of-life medical care or forgoing medical care and opting for a more peaceful end. Health insurers will pay hundreds of thousands of dollars for the medical care, but not one cent to the policyholder if he forgoes the treatment. If life insurance worked the same way, an elderly widow would be required to spend her entire life insurance benefit on her husband's funeral, with nothing left over to meet other financial needs.

Reserves for Future Expenses

Conventional life insurance is based on the idea that more policyholders will file claims in future years than in the current year. For example, consider a group of life insurance policyholders. In the current year, very few of them (perhaps none) will die. But eventually, they all will die. As a result, a large part of a life insurance premium goes into a reserve fund to pay for risky events that will happen in the future.

Health insurance, particularly group health insurance, is different. Most health insurance premium dollars are paid out in the very year they are collected. Rather than creating reserves for future years, health insurance tends to be organized on a pay-as-you-go basis. That helps explain one of the most perplexing problems faced by small business. Suppose that an employee has a premature baby and generates large and continuing medical expenses. Suppose also that there is no possibility of any other employee ever having another baby. The company manager will reason that next year's insurance premium should not rise any more than the industry average. After all, the company paid for this year's risk with this year's premium. Next year, the company will have less risk. So if anything, next year's premium should go down. Under cost-plus health insurance, however, that's not the way premiums are determined. In all probability, the health insurer will try to raise the employer's premium to three or four times its current level. "Who's going to pay for the expenses of last year's premature baby?" they will argue. "We can't ask other companies to pay for it." If life insurance worked the same way, you would not only be asked to pay a premium that reflected your probability of dying; you would also be asked to help pay the insurer's expenses for all of the policyholders who died last year—deaths that are totally unrelated to your risk of dying this year.

Critics of the use of the market in health care often make three arguments: (1) there is a great deal of discretion in how doctors and hospitals treat illness and injury, and much of what is done is unnecessary; (2) patients often are too sick and too frightened at the time of treatment to make reasoned decisions; and (3) even if they are rational, patients do not have the knowledge and sophistication to bargain effectively with providers.[22]

It is worth considering, therefore, how the market deals with similar problems in automobile collision insurance and home owners' insurance. Unquestionably, there is a great deal of discretion in how much people spend on car repair or home repair, and objective studies would undoubtedly find many expenditures unnecessary. Who can doubt that after an auto accident or home fire, the average policyholder would be distraught? And, because people deal with such problems infrequently, few are sophisticated buyers in either the car repair or home repair market, especially in the aftermath of major casualties. These experiences are not identical to medical episodes, but there is great similarity.

In the market for casualty insurance, problems are dealt with in the following way. A claims adjuster (a representative of the insurer) assesses the damage and negotiates a cash settlement with the policyholder. Often the policyholder will be asked to solicit bids from one or more firms that specialize in repair, and the settlement is often based on those bids. Although the policyholder may not be sophisticated in such matters, the claims adjuster is experienced, and it is not uncommon for the adjuster to negotiate directly with a repair firm to ensure that the price is reasonable.

To use the language of the medical marketplace, people with casualty insurance have free choice of providers, they have the

[22]See Uwe E. Reinhardt, respondent's comments in "Symposium: International Comparisons of Health Care Systems," *Health Care Financing Review*, 1989 Annual Supplement.

assistance of an experienced person in making buying decisions, and they negotiate a preadmission package price before the service is rendered. Moreover, because payment can be made directly to the policyholder, they can forgo the repairs altogether and use the cash settlement for other purposes.

Table 6.7 shows other important differences between health insurance and casualty insurance. As in the case of life insurance, once a risky event has occurred, the casualty insurer is fully liable for the damages related to that event and cannot cancel the policy and refuse to pay benefits or require that the insurer continue to pay premiums while repair services are being rendered. Moreover, once the risky event has occurred, insurers are liable for damages even if it takes years to determine the extent of those damages, as would be the case in the event of a major hurricane or tornado.

Actuarially Fair Prices and the Politics of Insurance

In an ideal insurance system, people face premium prices that are actuarially fair.[23] Roughly speaking, that means that each person pays a premium that reflects the expected cost and risk that person adds to a large insurance pool. There are advantages to pooling risks across a large number of people in different industries and circumstances, either directly or through reinsurance arrangements. After insurers take full advantage of those opportunities, an actuarially fair premium for an individual reflects the real marginal costs of adding that person to the pool.

Actuarially fair prices are produced naturally in a competitive insurance marketplace. They are comparable to competitive prices for food, clothing, housing, and any other good or service. Moreover, like other competitive prices, they are unavoidable. If one person pays less than an actuarially fair premium, someone else must pay more—either in higher premiums or (in the case of public insurance) in higher taxes. Because some people will have difficulty paying actuarially fair prices, there may be social reasons why we might choose to help them buy insurance—through income tax

[23]For an analysis of the beneficial effects of a competitive equilibrium in an insurance market and ways in which government can interfere with its attainment, see Roger Feldman and Bryan David, "Biased Selection: Fairness and Efficiency in Health Insurance Markets," paper presented at an American Enterprise Institute conference, "American Health Policy" (Washington, October 3–4, 1991).

credits, private charity, or other means. But the fact that we subsidize some people's health insurance is no reason to abolish the price system altogether. However, that is precisely what the cost-plus mentality wants to do.

Prices for Health Insurance

The antipathy of the cost-plus bureaucracy toward actuarially fair insurance prices is not confined to private insurance. They are equally vehement in their opposition to actuarially fair "tax prices" in a system of national health insurance. But the literature on health economics contains few discussions of their reasoning on this issue. In an unusually frank discussion, however, Princeton University health economist Uwe Reinhardt has written as follows: "Europeans tend to view actuarially fair health insurance premiums as manifestly unfair and believe that contributions to health insurance should be based on ability to pay. *Most Americans probably abhor actuarially fair health insurance premiums as well.* Indeed, the bulk of Americans are covered either by tax-financed government programs or by private group policies that socialize health insurance, at least within the community of a single business firm."[24] Although it is clear that Reinhardt abhors actuarially fair insurance premiums (or tax prices), it is not at all clear that most Americans or Europeans share that view. Because most people on both continents overpay under the current system, it seems likely that a majority would opt for an actuarially fair system if given a clear choice.

Under the current system, lower income (healthier) young workers subsidize the health insurance of higher income (less healthy) older workers in both Europe and the United States. Moreover, on both continents, lower income workers subsidize the health insurance of higher income retirees.[25] Despite the pervasiveness of these subsidies, we have never seen a coherent argument explaining why lower income families should subsidize the health insurance of people who are financially better off. Why, then, are these subsidies permitted? Because of politics.

[24]Reinhardt, p. 97. Emphasis added.

[25]In Europe, higher income workers do tend to pay higher taxes. But there is no reason to believe that the higher tax payments offset the heavier use of the health care system. In the United States, the per capita aftertax income of the elderly (covered by Medicare) is considerably higher than that of the nonelderly (who pay Medicare taxes). The same is probably also true in many European countries.

Setting Insurance Premiums through the Political System

Recent breakthroughs in understanding the behavior of political systems have shown that when governments have the power to set prices, they almost never choose efficient prices.[26] In insurance terminology, when governments set premiums (or tax prices), they never choose actuarially fair premiums. The reason is that various interest groups exert unequal pressures on the political system and government decisionmaking reflects those pressures.

Government-sponsored insurance schemes at the federal and state level in the United States bear out the theory. Every attempt to establish deposit insurance for banks and savings and loan associations, for example, has failed to charge actuarially fair premiums, and that has led to debacles of which the recent S&L crisis is only one example.[27] Similarly, the failure of the federal government to establish actuarially fair prices through its private pension insurance scheme has undermined the stability of the private pension system.[28]

Case Study: Automobile Liability Insurance

Massachusetts has the highest automobile insurance premiums in the nation. It also has the highest rate of auto insurance claims. One reason is that Massachusetts subsidizes bad driving through artificially low insurance rates. Under Massachusetts law, insurers are forbidden to base their premiums on age, sex, or marital status. Insurers are required to sell policies to almost any driver, and they cannot charge higher premiums for policies transferred to the state's risk pool. As a result, about 94 percent of young male drivers and 82 percent of young female drivers are in the risk pool. As a proportion of all premiums, policies assigned to the risk pool soared from 23 percent of the market in 1977 to 65 percent in 1989.[29]

[26]John C. Goodman and Phil Porter, "A Theory of Competitive Political Equilibrium," *Public Choice* 59 (1988): 51–66.

[27]There have been many failed attempts to manage deposit insurance at the state level, dating back to the 19th century. See A. James Meigs and John Goodman, *Federal Deposit Insurance: The Case for Radical Reform*, NCPA Policy Report no. 155 (Dallas: National Center for Policy Analysis, December 1990).

[28]The scheme is administered by the Pension Benefit Guarantee Corporation (PBGC). See Edward J. Harpham, *Private Pensions in Crisis: The Case for Radical Reform*, NCPA Policy Report no. 115 (Dallas: National Center for Policy Analysis, January 1985).

[29]Ibid.

Whereas nationally only about 8.3 percent of auto insurance premiums represent risk pool insurance, the Massachusetts risk pool now accounts for one-fifth of all the auto risk pool insurance in the United States. The risk pool invariably loses money, and the deficits are financed by higher premiums charged to other drivers. For all Massachusetts drivers, there is little relationship between driving behavior and insurance premiums.[30]

Proposals to Treat Health Insurance like Auto Insurance

In almost every state, people are required to buy auto liability insurance as a condition for the right to drive. Many—including some who otherwise advocate free-market solutions to health care problems—have argued that health insurance should be mandatory, in an analogous way.[31] The above discussion should give pause to proponents of such views. If individual health insurance were mandatory, health insurance prices—like auto liability insurance prices—would be determined in the political arena. Moreover, because health insurance is a far more emotional issue than auto liability insurance, the experience of Massachusetts and other states is only a small indication of the political crisis that would be created.

Realistically, governments cannot require the purchase of health insurance and leave insurers, providers, and state legislators free to increase the price without limit. Mandating health insurance is an open invitation to government regulation of the entire health care system.[32]

Why Health Insurance Is Different

During the early years of its development, health insurance had many of the characteristics of other forms of insurance. During the 1950s, for example, premiums charged by commercial insurers

---

[30]Simon Rottenberg, *The Cost of Regulated Pricing: A Critical Analysis of Auto Insurance Premium Rate-Setting in Massachusetts* (Boston: Pioneer Institute, 1989).

[31]See Stuart Butler and Edmund Haislmaier, *A National Health Care System for America*, rev. ed. (Washington: Heritage Foundation, 1989); and Mark Pauly et al., "A Plan for 'Responsible National Health Insurance'," *Health Affairs* (Spring 1991), pp. 5–25.

[32]The Heritage Foundation plan would require everyone to purchase health insurance under federal law, but under the doctrine of states' rights, it would leave state governments free to impose an unlimited number of mandated health insurance benefits.

reflected real actuarial risks. Policies were often guaranteed renewable, so that once people became sick, they could continue to get insurance coverage. Insurance benefits were usually paid to the patient. Under prepaid schemes, insurers reimbursed hospitals and doctors on the basis of charges, not costs. And the history of health insurance in the logging and mining industries in Washington and Oregon indicates that insurers made real efforts to prevent overuse of medical services and overcharging.

Nevertheless, these characteristics of health insurance slowly vanished as Blue Cross and Blue Shield began to monopolize the health insurance marketplace and as state governments increasingly regulated the market. The philosophy of the Blues was that everyone should pay the same premium, regardless of risk. Thus, the Blues practiced community rating, charging the same premium to everyone in the same community, and explicitly rejected risk rating or experience rating. The group health insurance plans of large employers reflected a similar view, charging employees an artificial premium that was the same for all, regardless of age, location, or job task. Eventually, Blue Cross policies began to have deductibles and copayments. But the Blue Cross philosophy was that people covered by such policies were underinsured. The ideal plan, in the Blue Cross vision, was one that provided first-dollar coverage for all medical expenses, and those were the plans that Blue Cross encouraged employers to buy.

Because of community rating, sick people could buy Blue Cross policies for the same premium price as healthy people. Because of the policy of reimbursing hospitals on the basis of costs, Blue Cross often overpaid for hospital services. How, then, could Blue Cross compete against commercial insurers for healthy customers? The answer was that the Blues were given special regulatory treatment by state governments and, in the early years, special discounts by hospitals and physicians. Physicians also frequently told patients that Blue Cross–Blue Shield plans were "good," while other plans were "bad." Once the Blues dominated the market, all other insurers were forced to reimburse hospitals on the basis of costs and to offer similar plans.

In the cost-plus vision, all payments for health care should come from insurers rather than patients. Even today, hospital administrators often complain about patient deductibles and copayments, preferring instead to have no financial relationship with patients. And there are still Blue Cross spokesmen who view people as underinsured if their health insurance contains any deductible or copayment.

In the cost-plus vision, everyone should pay the same premium for health insurance, regardless of risk or health status. Insurers should pay health providers based on the costs of needed care—costs wholly determined by physicians' judgments and patients' consumption decisions, with no consideration of monetary costs. Why are actuarially fair insurance premiums incompatible with the cost-plus system? Because they are competitive prices—and in the cost-plus system, no one faces competitive prices for any service.

The cost-plus answer to every financial problem in the medical marketplace is a system of price discrimination in which some buyers are overcharged while others are undercharged. How should we finance the free or below-cost care that physicians provide to low-income patients? The physicians' answer is to overcharge all other patients. How should we finance the hospitals' expenses for people who cannot or will not pay their bills? The hospitals' answer is to overcharge all other buyers. How do we subsidize health insurance premiums, so that sicker and riskier people can afford to pay for them? The insurers' answer is to overcharge everyone else.

The cost-plus vision is not a malevolent one. The goal, after all, is to make medical care and health insurance available to people who might otherwise have none. But the practical consequences are malevolent. Without competitive prices, ordinary people cannot make rational choices between medical care and other goods and services, and between self-insurance and third-party insurance. Without competitive prices, suppliers of medical services cannot be guided to find efficient ways of delivering medical care. Without competitive prices that allow individuals to make rational decisions, there is no alternative to health care rationing administered by large, impersonal bureaucracies.

Perhaps the worst consequence of the cost-plus vision has been the destruction of real insurance and its replacement by a system of prepayment for the consumption of medical care. One way to appreciate what a difference that makes is to consider our discussion about the origins of health insurance (see chapter 5). Health insurance developed in the riskiest industries—principally mining and logging—where the demand was greatest. But a 1990 report in the *New York Times* found that today's health insurers are blacklisting the industries with the greatest health risks, and heading the blacklist are mining and logging.[33]

The Inevitability of Change

The cost-plus system may either evolve into a system of national health insurance or be replaced by a system of competitive markets. Even the vested interests who publicly support it privately search for ways to opt out of it. In the next chapter we examine ways in which individual employers, insurers, hospitals, and physicians have attempted to partially opt out of the cost-plus system.

[33]Milt Freudenheim, "Health Insurers, to Reduce Losses, Blacklist Dozens of Occupations," *New York Times*, February 5, 1990.

7. Opting Out of the Cost-Plus System

From its inception some 50 years ago, the cost-plus system contained a fatal flaw that ultimately would have to be dealt with. The day of reckoning came less than a decade after the enactment of the Medicare and Medicaid programs. Once the federal government began funneling billions of dollars into the cost-plus system, health care costs exploded. Everyone agreed that something had to be done.

From Regulation to Competition

The initial response was to take a regulatory meat-ax to the system. Laws were passed to effectively keep hospitals from spending money. Certificate-of-need legislation required that hospital management get government permission before it built new hospitals, added new capacity, or purchased expensive equipment. Legislation creating physicians' standards review organizations (PSROs) sought to eliminate "unnecessary" surgery and "unnecessary" lengths of stay.

If the history of government regulation teaches us anything, it is the extreme difficulty of keeping people from doing what is manifestly in their self-interest. That is true even in areas in which the product or service is fairly uncomplicated, such as airline travel or telephone calls. It is much more difficult in a market such as hospital care, in which the service being rendered is not easy to define.

The attempt to keep hospitals from spending money by regulation failed. In the late 1970s and early 1980s, the federal government took a different tack. That consisted of a series of steps designed to partially opt out of the cost-plus system, or to at least limit government's exposure. States were allowed and even encouraged to experiment with alternative methods of Medicaid reimbursement. Medicare abandoned its cost-plus reimbursement formulas and instituted a prospective reimbursement system under which

Figure 7.1
NUMBER OF SURGERIES PERFORMED IN SURGI-CENTERS, 1986 TO 1990

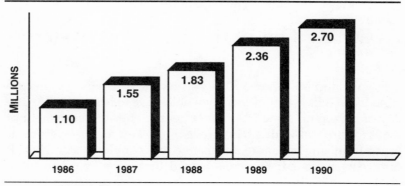

SOURCE: SMG Marketing Group.

hospitals were paid fixed prices for treating specific conditions.[1] In addition, competition began to make headway.

The medical marketplace today is schizophrenic. On the one hand, it is still dominated by the remnants of cost-plus finance. On the other hand, there is a swirl of competitive, entrepreneurial activity, as health care providers and employers who fund group plans search for alternatives. Such activities threaten the foundations of the cost-plus system, which cannot coexist with a genuine market system. The cost-plus system, which required government help to come into existence, will require more government help to survive. That is why its defenders invariably favor government regulation and abhor competition.

As in other regulated markets, the existence of cross-subsidies in the hospital sector creates opportunities for entrepreneurs. Surgi-centers (for outpatient surgery) came into existence to serve patients that hospitals overcharged for minor surgery (see Figure 7.1). For-profit emergency care clinics began to cater to patients that hospital

---

[1]Under this system, the diagnosis of a patient is supposed to be categorized by physicians into one of 492 diagnosis-related groups (DRGs). Medicare pays hospitals a fixed price for each DRG. In principle, if the hospital can perform the service for less than Medicare's price, it makes a profit; if the cost is higher than Medicare's price, it incurs a loss.

emergency rooms overcharged for minor injuries. Proprietary hospitals expanded to cater to patients who paid their own way and had no desire to subsidize the bad debts or charity care of others. In these ways, entrepreneurship, innovation, and the search for profit tended to eliminate the cross-subsidies.

To the individual consumer in the medical marketplace, such developments are quite welcome because they lead to lower prices. Consumers with minor injuries may see their medical expenses cut in half by choosing an emergency care clinic over a hospital emergency room. A candidate for surgery may be able to achieve similar savings by choosing an outpatient surgical clinic over hospital surgery. In either clinic, the patient is not charged for empty hospital beds, bad debts, charity care, the education of medical students, and dozens of other items unrelated to the person's own treatment.

But those who are firmly entrenched in the cost-plus system view each of these developments with alarm. Why? Because although such developments may lower prices charged to patients, they are not perceived to lower hospital costs. After all, the cost-plus mentality reasons, all of the hospital's emergency room expenses still have to be paid. So do the expenses for the bad debts, charity cases, teaching activities, empty hospital beds, etc.

Every time a paying patient with an uncomplicated medical problem is drawn out of the conventional hospital system, it is seen as a loss of revenue—revenue that otherwise would have been used to cover fixed costs. Once lost, the revenue must be made up, and who is left to make it up but the third-party payers who fund the cost-plus system? To the cost-plus mentality, anyone who opts out of the conventional hospital system leaves behind a greater burden to be shared by those who remain. That gives those who remain an even greater financial incentive to join those trying to opt out.

The Changing Market for Health Insurance in the 1980s

Competition and pursuit of self-interest, then, are causing the cost-plus system to unravel. And during the early 1980s, the most important forces for change were the activities of large employers who were paying ever-increasing amounts for the health insurance of their employees.[2]

[2]See John C. Goodman and Gerald L. Musgrave, *The Changing Market for Health Insurance: Opting Out of the Cost-Plus System*, NCPA Policy Report no. 118 (Dallas: National Center for Policy Analysis, September 1985).

Figure 7.2
NUMBER OF HMO MEMBERS, 1976 TO 1990

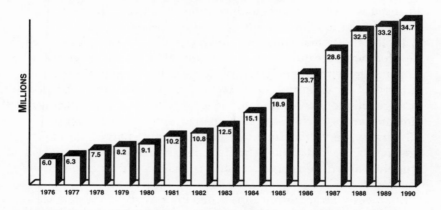

SOURCE: For 1976–87, *The Trauma of Transformation in the 1990s: An Environmental Assessment of U.S. Health Care* (Minneapolis: Health One, 1989); for 1988–89, Jerry Geisel, "Open-Ended HMOs Grow More Popular: Interstudy," *Business Insurance,* January 1, 1990, pp. 34–35; for 1990, "Managed Care Update," *Modern Healthcare* (April 23, 1990), p. 33.

Health Maintenance Organizations

One of the best-known attempts to opt out of the cost-plus system involved opting out of fee-for-service medicine altogether and relying on prepaid health care, usually through a health maintenance organization (HMO).[3] During the Nixon administration, the use of HMOs in the private sector was encouraged by federal legislation, which overrode state laws that discouraged or outlawed them and required employers to offer an HMO alternative to conventional health insurance. In 1962, 2 percent of all health insurance was accounted for by HMO premiums. As Figure 7.2 shows, membership in HMOs grew from 6.0 million in 1976 to 28.6 million in 1987, almost a fivefold increase. In some localities, HMOs have more than one-third of the market today.

[3]The term "health maintenance organization" was either coined or popularized by Dr. Paul M. Ellwood, Jr., the man generally credited with being the architect of the Nixon administration's pro-HMO health care strategy.

194

Self-Insurance

The truly spectacular change in the 1980s, though, was the move by employers from conventional health insurance to self-insurance. In many instances, companies opted for complete self-insurance. Others self-insured up to a very large amount and paid a "minimum premium" for third-party insurance that became effective only if a high-dollar limit was exceeded. In either case, the companies had the option of operating their own insurance program or contracting with an independent firm or a conventional health insurance company (such as Blue Cross) to administer the program.[4]

Consider the "administrative services only" plan run for an employer by Blue Cross. Under the plan, employees are given Blue Cross cards that are presented to hospitals at the time of treatment. But when Blue Cross gets the bills, it sends them to the employer. All Blue Cross does is process claims. All bills are paid by the employer, who assumes all of the financial risk under the plan.

As a variation on this idea, consider the "minimum premium plan," also administered by Blue Cross. Under this plan, the employer agrees to pay all bills up to an amount sufficient to cover employees' normal and expected health care expenses. The money needed to cover these expenses is often deposited in a trust fund, which can earn tax-free interest. If the employer's total health care bills exceed the maximum the employer has agreed to pay, Blue Cross makes up the difference. The insurance premium that the employer pays Blue Cross to assume this top-end risk, the "minimum premium," is much smaller than the premium would be for all the insurance risk.

In 1976, employer self-insurance accounted for only 5 percent of all health insurance. By 1983, 32 percent of all health insurance was accounted for by plans that were either wholly or largely self-insured.[5] Between 1965 and 1983, the Blue Cross–Blue Shield market share dropped from 45 to 35 percent, and the market share of other conventional health insurance companies dropped from 48 to

[4]For a description of these techniques and an explanation of some of the benefits, see *Employee Benefit Plan Review* (June 1980), p. 12 ff.

[5]Ross H. Arnett III and Gordon Trapnell, "Private Health Insurance: New Measures of a Complex and Changing Industry," *Health Care Financing Review* 2 (Winter 1984): 31.

27 percent.[6] Another way to view this change is to consider the extent to which American business turned to alternative health insurance of all types. In 1976, unconventional insurance (prepaid plans or self-insurance) accounted for only 7 percent of all health insurance; by 1983, it accounted for 38 percent.[7]

The trend toward alternative forms of health insurance was initiated by the nation's largest firms. A survey by the Health Research Institute discovered that, of the 1,500 largest employers, 83 percent were relying on some form of self-insurance by 1984.[8] But the trend was by no means confined to large companies.[9] The growth in self-funding also was evident among medium-sized and even relatively small firms.[10] For example, a 1988 survey found that of firms with 1,000 or more employees, 70 percent were self-insured; of firms with 100 to 999 employees, 29.7 percent were self-insured; and of firms with 100 or fewer employees, 26.7 percent were self-insured.[11] In 1981, 21 percent of employees of medium- and large-sized firms were covered by self-insurance. By 1985, that number had doubled, to 42 percent.[12] Today, 56 percent of employees with health insurance work for an employer who is fully or partially self-insured.[13]

When companies self-insure, they are usually entering a field in which they have no prior experience. Thus it is not surprising that studies show that the act of self-insuring raises health care costs by about 12.3 percent.[14] For self-insurance to be a cost-effective

[6]Ibid.

[7]Ibid.

[8]Cited in Meg Fletcher, "More Small Firms Self-Funding Health Plans," *Business Insurance* (December 10, 1984): 12.

[9]Coopers & Lybrand, *Employee Medical Plan Costs: A Comparative Study* (Dallas, 1984), p. 41.

[10]It is difficult for small firms to self-insure because of the administrative costs and the risk. For large firms, the risk is spread over a larger number of employees and the administrative costs per employee are smaller.

[11]Health Insurance Association of America—Johns Hopkins survey of 1,457 firms, 1988. Reported in Jon Gabel and Gail Jensen, "The Price of State-Mandated Benefits," *HIAA Research Bulletin* (July 1989).

[12]Gail Jensen and Jon Gabel, "The Erosion of Purchased Insurance," *Inquiry* 25 (Fall 1988): 329.

[13]Cynthia B. Sullivan and Thomas Rice, "The Health Insurance Picture in 1990," *Health Affairs* (Summer 1991), p. 111.

[14]Jensen and Gabel.

alternative, there must be offsetting advantages that reduce health care costs. Such advantages are twofold. First, employers who self-insure avoid costly state government regulation of health insurance and take advantage of provisions of the federal income tax code that encourage self-insurance. Second, employers who turn to self-insurance put in place important cost-management techniques that traditional insurers were unwilling to implement. Let us consider briefly these two incentives.

Self-Insurance: Escape from Regulation

Health economists Gail Jensen and Jon Gabel have identified five advantages of self-insurance that directly relate to government policies.[15] They are (1) avoiding the state premium taxes, (2) avoiding state-mandated benefits, (3) avoiding capital and financial reserve requirements, (4) avoiding payments to risk pools, and (5) enjoying tax advantages.

Avoiding State Premium Taxes

All 50 states levy taxes on the premiums of commercial insurance companies, and 26 states now levy premium taxes on Blue Cross and Blue Shield. Such taxes are typically 2 to 3 percent of annual premiums. For a company such as General Motors, annual premium taxes could easily exceed $50 million.[16] Companies that self-insure avoid these taxes.

Avoiding State-Mandated Benefits

The market for health insurance has been hit by a tidal wave of state-mandated benefit regulations in recent years (see chapter 11). These are laws requiring insurers to cover specific services and diseases. For insurers, the mandates can be enormously expensive. Take psychiatric care, for example. In 1973, Chrysler Corporation, which offered only limited employee mental health benefits, experienced 30,000 psychiatric visits at a cost of $800,000. In 1978, under a new agreement negotiated with the United Auto Workers, Chrysler greatly liberalized its mental health benefits. Total visits jumped to

---

[15]Jensen and Gabel, p. 329.
[16]Ibid.

200,000 at an annual cost of more than $5 million.[17] Nationwide, outpatient psychiatric benefits add about 11.8 percent to the cost of a family insurance policy.[18] But 36 states require insurers to cover the services of psychiatrists, whether or not the policyholders want this benefit.[19] Because companies that self-insure are not subject to these regulations, mandated health insurance benefit laws give companies a powerful incentive to choose self-insurance. According to one study, the mandate for mental health care alone increases the probability that a large firm will self-insure by 93.2 percent.[20]

Avoiding Capital and Financial Reserve Requirements

Partly to ensure the financial solvency of insurers, state governments require that insurers have large capital reserves. Setting aside large reserves can be costly and raises the cost of insurance. Companies that self-insure are exempt from such requirements.

Avoiding Payments to Risk Pools

Some states have established pools to subsidize health insurance for high-risk individuals. In most cases, the subsidies are financed by taxing all insurers operating within a state. Currently, 15 states have risk pools and many more are considering them. Companies that self-insure are exempt from such taxes, and one study has estimated that the existence of a risk pool increases the probability that a large firm will self-insure by almost 56 percent.[21]

Enjoying Tax Advantages

Yet another advantage of self-insurance has been created by a change in the federal income tax law. Employers who establish their own health insurance funds can deduct contributions to those funds and earn tax-free interest on the amount accumulated. A 1984

[17]Speech by former Secretary of Health, Education, and Welfare Joseph Califano, (January 1984). See "Cost Crisis and Perspectives—Health Care 1985," *Insurance Sales* (July 1985), p. 40.

[18]Gail Jensen and Michael Morrisey, "Group Health Insurance: A Hedonic Price Approach," *Review of Economics and Statistics* 72, no. 1 (February 1990): 38–44.

[19]A. Ralston, M. Power, and S. McGinnis, *State Legislatively Mandated Life and Health Insurance Coverages* (The Legislatively Extended Assistance Group, University of Iowa, 1988). Cited in Jensen and Gabel, p. 3.

[20]Gail Jensen and Michael Morrisey, "State Insurance Regulation and the Decision to Self-Fund," Working Paper (University of Illinois at Chicago, 1989).

[21]Ibid.

survey by The Wyatt Company found that 21 percent of surveyed employers self-insured for that reason, up from 9 percent in 1980.[22]

In the Employee Retirement Income Security Act (ERISA) of 1974, the federal government exempted companies that self-insure from state laws regulating health insurance, such as those listed above. Numerous court decisions have upheld this exemption in the face of attempts by state governments to undermine it. This development has proved to be important. For example, a study of firms that chose to self-insure over the period from 1981 to 1984 concluded that 51 percent would not have opted for self-insurance had it not been for state government regulations that increase the cost of health insurance.[23]

Self-Insurance: Escape from Traditional Insurance Methods

The cost-plus system is at its very worst when health insurance companies do not aggressively monitor the behavior of health care providers. At the risk of unfair characterization, the system can be described in the following way. Under the cost-plus system, hospitals submit bills and insurance companies pay them. At the end of each year, the insurance company compares the employer's total premiums with the reimbursements that the insurance company actually made. If reimbursements are greater than premiums, the employer's premiums are raised in the following year. Insurance companies that act in this way are doing little more than processing claims. Thus, one way to look at self-insurance is to view companies as simply formalizing an arrangement that has already existed de facto. Under one form of self-insurance, a conventional insurance company is retained formally to do nothing more than process claims. Under complete self-insurance, the company does its own claims processing. In both versions, however, the role of aggressively monitoring health care expenses and influencing how the funds are spent is left to the employer.

---

[22]Jerry Geisel, "Surveys Find Most Employers Self-Funding Health Benefits," *Business Insurance* (January 28, 1985), p. 10. The funds to which these contributions are made are called voluntary employee beneficiary associations (VEBAs), or 501(c)(9) trusts.

[23]Ibid.

But the change to self-insurance was important. For even if the change in responsibility was a mere formality, it laid the groundwork for more change. In the early 1980s, companies that controlled their own health insurance plans were in a better position to institute and experiment with other cost-control techniques that traditional insurers refused to implement. By the end of the 1980s, all health insurance companies (including Blue Cross) were actively implementing similar cost-control techniques. To survive in the health insurance market today, management of health care costs is essential.

Case Study: U.S. Administrators, Inc.[24]

One example of how unconventional health insurance can help employers opt out of the cost-plus system is the case of U.S. Administrators, Inc., an innovator in cost-management techniques used in the 1980s. When a company self-insures, it immediately saves about 2 to 3 percent on its health insurance bill by avoiding the payment of state taxes on insurance premiums. According to Samuel Kaplan, president of U.S. Administrators, though, the potential total savings are 10 to 15 times that amount.

How can these savings be realized? For one thing, Kaplan says, a typical company can save 6 to 12 percent simply by engaging in better auditing and claims review techniques than those used by traditional insurance companies. In addition, companies can save 10 to 15 percent more by employing cost-management techniques. One of the most important of those is comprehensive utilization review—keeping meticulous records to identify doctors and hospitals that overcharge, are too quick to admit patients, or keep patients in the hospital too long.

Kaplan's company also engages in other cost-containment practices. For example, it maintains a hotline so that patients and physicians can call for prior approval before elective surgery. Physicians describe the diagnosis, state why they recommend surgery, and what they intend to charge. U.S. Administrators keeps records of what other physicians in each geographical area charge and frequently negotiates with the physician over the price.

[24]This discussion is based on authors' interviews with Samuel X. Kaplan, president of U.S. Administrators, Inc.

U.S. Administrators also employs another cost-management technique. Say a gall bladder operation normally costs about $3,000, and about $1,000 of that amount is the physician's fee. U.S. Administrators reasons that the physician has a great deal of control over the other $2,000. So U.S. Administrators might strike the following deal: If the total procedure is under $3,000, the physician gets 125 percent of the agreed fee; if it is over $3,000, the physician gets only 75 percent of the fee. This arrangement gives physicians an incentive to care about all of the costs they can influence.

Kaplan is convinced that such techniques work. And he is willing to bet money on it. U.S. Administrators often puts part of its fee at risk, contingent on how well it performs for its clients. Suppose that an employer has been experiencing average health care costs of $1,000 per employee. U.S. Administrators might strike the following deal: If the company manages to reduce the employer's cost to $900 per employee, U.S. Administrators gets its contractual fee plus a percentage of the amount saved; if costs go up above $1,000, the employer pays only 75 percent of the contractual fee.

Do these cost-cutting techniques threaten to reduce the quality of health care patients receive? Kaplan is adamant on this point. "Good cost-management leads to better health care," he says. If patients can avoid unnecessary surgery and unnecessary tests, they also avoid the risks associated with those procedures. Many medical procedures are indeed risky and should be avoided unless doing so poses even greater risks to the patient's health.

Cost-Management Techniques Developed in the 1980s

U.S. Administrators, Inc., is not alone. In just a few years in the 1980s, these and other cost-control techniques were implemented, first by large companies and then by smaller ones. Soon, traditional insurers climbed on the cost containment bandwagon. Figure 7.3 shows how radically employer-provided health insurance changed in just five years. In 1984, 96 percent of insured workers were enrolled in a traditional fee-for-service plan. By 1988, the figure had dropped to 28 percent. Today, there are very few traditional insurers. As a representative of a large insurance company explained, "If you're not involved in cost-management, you can't be in the market for health insurance."

Various cost-control techniques implemented in the early 1980s by Fortune 500 companies are commonplace today (see Table 7.1).

Figure 7.3
EMPLOYER-PROVIDED HEALTH INSURANCE, 1984 AND 1988

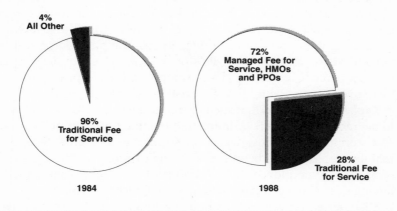

SOURCE: Health Insurance Association of America.

At the time of their implementation, however, they were considered radical. A brief description of some of the techniques follows.

Contracting Directly with Health Care Providers

One way of opting out of the cost-plus system is to negotiate directly with hospitals, doctors, and other health care providers. When employers engage in the negotiations, they are bargaining over price, not merely reimbursement for costs. The use of HMOs is an example of this behavior. Another is the use of a preferred-provider organization (PPO) (see Figure 7.4). Under this arrangement, employers negotiate discounts with doctors and hospitals. Frequently, employees share in the savings if they use designated providers. One survey of U.S. companies found that one-half of all workers who are employed by companies with 1,000 or more employees are covered by an HMO or PPO.[25]

Increasing Employees' Deductibles and Copayments

During the 1960s and 1970s, the trend in employer-sponsored health insurance was toward greater and greater coverage of employees' health care expenses. To employees, a good health

[25]A. Foster Higgins & Co., *Health Care Benefits Survey, 1988*, p. 4.

Table 7.1
COST-CONTAINMENT STRATEGIES OF EMPLOYERS*

Strategy	Percent of Employers Who Use the Strategy	Percent Using the Strategy Who Find It Effective
Precertification of admissions	64%	33%
Require second opinion	61	14
Improve employee awareness	49	14
Coordination of benefits	41	26
Conduct utilization reviews	39	30
Individual case management	33	35
Increased deductible	32	32
Special pretax spending accounts	30	36
Employee assistance programs	30	24
Review of claims checking	28	25
Special coverage of generic drugs	27	30
Improved data analysis	25	19
Wellness/fitness programs	25	19
Preemployment medical exams	24	28
Improved monitoring	23	26
Reduce benefits	22	34
Require outpatient care	18	24
Choices/cafeteria-type plans	17	44
Increase copayment	13	35
Coverage for special facilities	8	25
In-house medical service	5	22

SOURCE: Society for Human Resource Management, reported in *Business and Health* (September 1990), p. 9.
*Based on a survey of 1,277 firms.

Figure 7.4
NUMBER OF PPOs, 1980 TO 1990

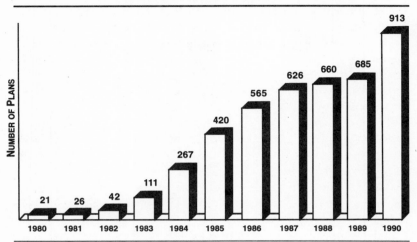

SOURCE: For 1980–88, *The Trauma of Transformation in the 1990s: An Environmental Assessment of U.S. Health Care* (Minneapolis: Health One, 1989); for 1989–90, authors' interview with Linda Robinson, American Association of Preferred Provider Organizations, April 23, 1991.

insurance policy was one that paid for almost everything. Today, that view is vanishing and is certainly not held by most employers. During the 1980s, there was a rapid movement in the opposite direction. A 1985 Business Roundtable survey of large companies found that most had increased the share of costs borne directly by employees by raising deductibles and copayments. Of the companies surveyed, 57 percent had an annual deductible, more than half had raised the deductible since 1982, and 98 percent required a copayment of some type.[26] That trend has continued. Between 1985 and 1988, about 79 percent of all employers increased their deductibles.[27]

[26]The survey covered the health plans of 122 Business Roundtable members (mostly Fortune 500 companies) for 7.5 million employees and dependents. See *Highlights: The 1984 Business Roundtable Task Force on Health Survey* (1985), p. 2 (hereinafter referred to as *Business Roundtable Survey*).

[27]A. Foster Higgins & Co., p. 17.

204

Offering Flexible Benefits

Closely related to the concept of greater employee cost sharing is the practice of giving the employee a choice between a high-cost health insurance policy (with low deductibles and low copayments) and a low-cost plan (with high deductibles and high copayments). Employees who choose the low-cost plan are allowed to pocket the savings or apply it to some other fringe benefit. The ideal way to structure the option is to allow employees to reap the full financial benefits of choosing the lower cost plan or, conversely, to pay the full cost of choosing the higher cost plan.

Take Pepsico Inc. for example. In 1980, the company offered this option to its employees. However, because it underpriced the high-cost plan, 65 to 75 percent of Pepsico employees chose a plan with no copayment. After Pepsico raised the price of its high-cost plan to reflect actual costs, more than 50 percent of Pepsico employees chose the lower cost plan.[28]

A natural extension of this idea is to offer employees a full range of fringe benefit choices, a practice sometimes known as the cafeteria plan. Under this arrangement, employees who save money by choosing lower cost health insurance can divert the savings to some other tax-favored employee benefit (such as a pension plan or day care benefits), and avoid realizing additional taxable income.

According to Harvard Business School professor Regina Herzlinger, Quaker Oats successfully used employee options (including cash dividends to employees) to hold its health care cost increases to only 6 percent per year from 1983 to 1990.[29] When Quaker Oats employees became involved in choosing their own health care plans, they reduced their hospital usage by 46 percent. Overall, the company kept its health care cost increases from 27 percent to 67 percent below the national average.

Encouraging Employees to Make Low-Cost Choices

In the traditional market for hospital care, more than 90 percent of the cost is paid by someone other than the patient. That means

[28]Regina E. Herzlinger and Jeffrey Schwartz, "How Companies Tackle Health Care Costs: Part I," *Harvard Business Review* (July-August, 1985), p. 75. See also Jack Meyer, Sean Sullivan, and Sharon Silow-Carroll, *Private Sector Initiatives: Controlling Health Care Costs* (Washington: Healthcare Leadership Council, 1991), p. 36.

[29]Regina E. Herzlinger, "Health Competition," *Atlantic Monthly* (August 1991), p. 77.

205

that when patients make wasteful choices, 90 percent of the waste is shifted to someone else, and when they make prudent choices, 90 percent of the savings is realized by someone else. Many companies are changing their health benefit plans to give employees incentives for cost-reducing choices, especially when there are great opportunities to reduce costs. An example of a PPO arrangement with employee incentives is the plan adopted by AT&T, which spends more than $1 billion a year on employee health care. Doctors and hospitals who are part of AT&T's PPO have agreed to limit charges and get company approval prior to expensive procedures. AT&T employees may choose their physicians, but those who choose PPO doctors pay a $150 deductible, a 5 to 10 percent copayment for most charges, and nothing for hospitalization. Those who go outside of the network pay a $200 deductible and a 20 percent copayment for all services.[30]

Another method of encouraging low-cost consumption is through direct cash payments to employees who are patients. Among Milwaukee HMOs, for example, Samaritan Health Plan offers a $100 gift certificate at a local toy store for mothers who are discharged within 24 hours of giving birth (the average hospital stay in Milwaukee is 48 hours), Compcare offers mothers a choice of two days of home health services by a registered nurse or a $100 U.S. savings bond, and Managed Health Services offers 12 hours of free nanny services and four weeks of diaper service (also valued at about $100). Given that the average daily cost at a Milwaukee hospital is $700, the HMOs make about a $600 profit on the exchange.[31]

Another technique is an extension of the practice of negotiating over the phone, described above. Health Benefits Research Corporation (HBRC) has a toll-free telephone number for employees of client firms to call prior to surgery. HBRC contacts the physician, determines the fee, and then tells patients what their out-of-pocket costs will be. HBRC negotiates price discounts with physicians and, if a physician refuses to negotiate, refers the patient to a board-certified surgeon who agrees to accept "reasonable and customary"

[30]Milt Freudenheim, "AT&T's Plan to Slow Costs," *New York Times*, February 27, 1990.

[31]Neil Rosenberg, *Medical Tribune*, November 1, 1990, reported in *Medical Benefits* 7, no. 23 (December 15, 1990): 2.

reimbursement. The company reports that 63 percent of physicians are willing to negotiate fees and that the savings average 38 percent of the original charges.[32]

Companies have also created incentives in other ways. For example, the Business Roundtable found that almost all companies surveyed covered outpatient surgery and that more than 40 percent paid a higher percentage of the bill for outpatient than for inpatient surgery. In addition, 98 percent paid for second opinions and 55 percent offered employees a financial incentive to obtain a second opinion.[33]

Auditing Claims and Reviewing Utilization

Most large companies today have a formal procedure for auditing health insurance claims to determine the accuracy of the claim, the eligibility of the claimant, or whether the service is actually covered by the policy. Most large companies also conduct utilization reviews to identify unnecessary procedures or inappropriately long hospital stays. With increasing frequency, companies are employing utilization review techniques before the service is rendered. Many companies require prior approval for surgery. The 1988 Foster Higgins & Co. survey found that almost 75 percent of all large employers (1,000 or more employees) had mandatory utilization review procedures for hospitalization and surgery.[34] Moreover, 68 percent of large employers and 37 percent of smaller ones had catastrophic case-management programs to ensure appropriate, cost-effective treatment in the most severe cases.[35]

Promoting Wellness

Yet another cost-control technique is to promote preventive measures. In the Business Roundtable survey, one-third of the companies gave new employees screening physicals, one-fourth offered periodic physicals to all employees, and one-half provided physical fitness programs. In addition, 49 percent offered employee counseling for alcohol and drug abuse, 30 percent did so for family problems, and 29 percent did so for job-related stress.[36] Moreover (as

---

[32]Reported in *Health Benefits* 7, no. 3 (February 15, 1990): 6.

[33]Ibid., p. 3.

[34]A. Foster Higgins & Co., p. 5.

[35]Ibid., p. 28.

[36]*Business Roundtable Survey*, p. 5.

noted in chapter 4), by the end of the decade many employers had become more aggressive. An estimated 6,000 companies refused to hire smokers. Others refused to hire people who drink or engage in risky activities (such as motorcycling). Some companies instituted differential premiums for employees, charging more to those employees who smoked or were overweight.

The Changing Nature of the Medical Marketplace

The medical marketplace cannot be changed by the actions of a single company. But when many engage in the cost-cutting techniques described above, each act is a nibble at the foundations of the cost-plus system. The cumulative effect is to set in motion a process of change.

It is interesting how this change is occurring. A company alters its health benefits policy because to do so is in its self-interest. The self-interested actions of one causes others to change. As companies change their behavior, so do hospitals and insurers. At Blue Cross, for example, administrators have not been sitting idly by, watching their market share disappear. According to a Blue Cross and Blue Shield Association publication released in the mid-1980s, the Blues' plans had 66 HMOs with more than two million members and as many as 40 PPOs. Blue Cross plans across the country are adopting procedures to encourage outpatient surgery, require prior approval of hospital admissions, mandate second opinions before surgery, establish utilization review programs, and encourage reductions in length of stay.[37]

Most of the changes taking place in the medical marketplace are in the direction of a more competitive market. Why are these changes occurring? One reason is that health care has become more expensive. That gives consumers of medical resources a greater incentive to find ways to economize. A second reason is that the supply of medical resources has outstripped demand—more doctors, more hospitals—largely as a result of government subsidies. That puts greater pressure on the providers of medical services to find new ways of attracting patients. A third reason is that many government impediments to competitive activity have been removed, and there

---

[37]Blue Cross and Blue Shield Association, *Questions and Answers on the New Health Care* (May 1985).

Figure 7.5
LENGTH OF STAY IN COMMUNITY HOSPITALS, BY AGE GROUP,
1977 TO 1989

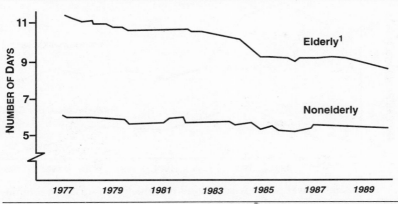

SOURCE: American Hospital Association's monthly panel survey of community hospitals. Graph reproduced from *The Trauma of Transformation in the 1990s: An Environmental Assessment of U.S. Health Care* (Minneapolis: Health One, 1989).

[1]The elderly are those aged 65 and older.

is now more freedom to compete. A fourth reason is the change in Medicare reimbursement rules. By adopting a policy of paying fixed prices for hospital procedures, the federal government has shown itself less willing to pay for the inefficiencies that raise the costs of hospital services.

How Well Are Cost-Management Techniques Working?

The number of hospital admissions steadily declined throughout the 1980s. Perhaps partly as a result of the change in Medicare's reimbursement policies, there has also been a steady decline in average length of stay for elderly patients (see Figure 7.5). Annual increases in hospital revenues also have been falling (see Figure 7.6).

Now for the bad news. Medical inflation continued to outpace consumer prices in the 1980s. Between 1981 and 1986, hospital expenditures grew by 60 percent. Moreover, after about five years of moderate increases in insurance premiums paid by employers in

209

Figure 7.6
HOSPITAL REVENUES PER CASE, 1980 TO 1988

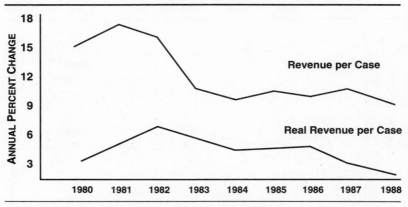

SOURCE: American Hospital Association's monthly panel survey of community hospitals, compiled by ProPAC, 1988. Graph reproduced from *The Trauma of Transformation in the 1990s: An Environmental Assessment of U.S. Health Care* (Minneapolis: Health One, 1989).

the mid-1980s, premium prices began to soar. Over the three-year period from 1985 through 1987, health care costs per employee grew at 6.5 percent per year, or at about twice the rate of inflation (3 percent); over the three-year period from 1988 through 1990, they grew at 17.4 percent, or more than three times the rate of inflation (see Figure 4.4 in chapter 4).

Many of the cost-management techniques that worked well in the early 1980s are not working as well today, and some are not working at all. For example, employers who offered HMOs are now discovering that those who choose the HMO option tend to be healthier. That leaves sicker, more-expensive-to-cover employees in the company's primary health plan. Employers who negotiated PPO arrangements with hospitals are discovering that the initial savings are slowly vanishing. Discounts on hospital prices accomplish little when everyone has the same discount and nominal prices (which few are paying) continue to rise. Employers who encouraged their employees to choose outpatient surgery are finding that increases in the cost of outpatient care are more than offsetting decreases in inpatient costs.

Table 7.2
CATARACT SURGERY: MEDICARE PAYMENT AMOUNTS

Category	Hospital Inpatient	Certified Hospital Outpatient	Ambulatory Surgical Center
Facility fee	$1,200–$1,500	$1,000–$2,000	$485–$553
Lens	Included in DRG	$250–$790	$280–$400
Total	$1,200–$1,500	$1,250–$2,790	$765–$953
Average	$1,350	$2,020	$860

SOURCE: National Center for Policy Analysis.

What went wrong? One explanation is that corporate purchasers of health care underestimated the resilience and determination of the cost-plus bureaucracy. With each change in reimbursement policies, the providers found ways of maximizing revenues under the new set of rules. Take outpatient surgery, for example. When performed at a surgi-center, it can cut the cost of inpatient cataract surgery by 37 percent (see Table 7.2). That provides strong incentives to encourage outpatient treatment. But hospitals have responded by setting up their own outpatient services, and hospital outpatient surgery costs can be 50 percent more. Corporate buyers of health care who encourage outpatient procedures and do not carefully monitor them can end up paying more, not less.

Another way in which providers have responded to new reimbursement procedures is by unbundling their services and charging separate prices for items that were previously lumped in a single package. In principle, virtually every physician-provided service—from an office visit to a heart transplant—is described by a standard five-digit code. The codes are used by Medicare, Medicaid, Blue Cross, and other insurance organizations to determine the amount of payment. However, as Table 7.3 shows, doctors in Chicago and elsewhere have discovered that unbundling can often increase their income even though there has been no change in the amount of services.[38] By charging for each separate component of the procedure, physicians were able to bill $5,339, whereas the usual charge

[38]See Robert Pear, "Federal Auditors Report Rise in Abuses in Medical Billings," *New York Times*, December 20, 1991.

Table 7.3
UNBUNDLING IN CHICAGO

Procedure	Price
Hysterectomy	
Usual, customary charge	$3,304
Separate charges	
Remove fallopian tubes and ovaries	2,135
Pelvic examination under anesthesia	340
Dilation and curettage	848
Abdominal exploration	2,016
Total	$5,339
Gall bladder operation	
Usual, customary charge	
Removal of gallbladder through	
illuminated tube or laparoscope	$2,576
Separate charges	
Remove gallbladder	2,225
Look into belly through fiber-optic tube	1,202
Total	$3,427
Total knee replacement	
Usual, customary charge	$5,889
Separate charges	
Replace upper part of knee joint	3,012
Replace lower part of knee joint	2,844
Reline kneecap	2,677
Total	$8,553

SOURCE: Medicode Inc., *Physicians' Current Procedural Terminology*, reprinted in the *New York Times*, December 20, 1991.

for a hysterectomy in Chicago is $3,304. Similarly, through unbundling, a $2,576 gall bladder fee became $3,427 and a $5,889 fee for a knee replacement grew to $8,553.

Another reason that employers have not been more successful is that, even with more cost sharing on the part of employees, the vast bulk of medical expenses is still paid by third parties. Large corporations and large insurance companies have not made the employees and policyholders full participants in the attempt to opt out of cost-plus medicine.

How Employers Are Overlooking the Role of the Consumer

Despite the dramatic changes of the 1980s, most employers still make no real effort to empower their employees as consumers in the medical marketplace. Employees still perceive that they are spending someone else's money rather than their own. Thus, it is still in the self-interest of employees and their physicians to overspend and overuse health care services.

Patients and Doctors

Through innovative utilization review techniques, employers have had some success in negotiating lower physicians' fees and avoiding some unnecessary surgery. But the self-interest of patients and doctors is still antithetical to the employer's. And further intrusions into the doctor-patient relationship will not alter that fact.

The American Medical Association is correct in its complaint that interference in the clinical decisions of physicians threatens to lower the quality of medical care. All too often, physicians must get telephone approval for a procedure from a nurse who bases her judgment on a computerized manual of "acceptable practices."[39] So-called cookbook medical guidelines can harm patients to the extent that such guidelines become barriers to medical care. And once physicians learn what's in the cookbook, they find ways of getting around the system. In one survey, most of the physicians said they would help patients get insurance coverage for a test by representing it as necessary for a diagnosis rather than as part of a general screening.[40] It is simply a matter of time before physicians become equally skilled at obtaining telephone approvals.

Hospital Prices

Although employers have made some progress in informing employees about out-of-pocket costs for surgery, most have done little to help their employees become intelligent shoppers in the hospital marketplace. In most major cities, patients still cannot find out what their total hospital charges will be prior to admission and cannot read the line item bills they receive after discharge.

---

[39]Reported in *Medical Benefits* 7, no. 3 (February 15, 1990): 6.

[40]Dennis Novak et al., "Physicians' Attitudes toward Using Deception to Resolve Difficult Ethical Problems," *Journal of the American Medical Association* 261, no. 20 (May 26, 1989): 2980.

In the early 1980s, the federal government attempted to get out of the cost-plus system altogether. Under the Medicare program, the federal government began paying fixed prices (determined in advance) for hospital procedures for Medicare patients. As we move along in the 1990s, private-sector, third-party payers increasingly are doing the same thing. It is not uncommon for insurance companies and large employers to cut their own deals with hospitals. That takes the form of a predetermined price per procedure (similar to Medicare) or a predetermined price per patient-day. Such arrangements usually apply only to the employer's share of the bill, however. Employees are left to fend for themselves.

Thus, we have now come full circle. Prior to 1980, private paying patients were the only people who had to struggle with hospital bills they could not understand. In the 1990s, we are again evolving toward a system in which those least capable of coping with hospital line item prices are the only people asked to pay them.

Shifting Premium Costs to Employees

One of the most common cost-containment techniques is to ask employees to pay more of the premium in aftertax wages. It is not unusual for employees to pay from 30 to 50 percent of premiums out-of-pocket with aftertax dollars.[41] This procedure does not really lower costs, however. Instead, it is an inefficient way of replacing wages with fringe benefits. Total health care costs (employer plus employee) remain the same.[42] But every dollar paid aftertax is a dollar that loses out on the potential tax subsidy for health insurance. Employees would be better off (would have more take-home pay) if gross wages were lowered and the employer paid the full premium.

Consider a company with annual employee health costs averaging $2,700 per employee. If employees pay one-third of the premium in aftertax wages, they will receive no tax subsidy on $900 of premium payments. That means employers and employees are

---

[41]Many larger companies can take advantage of provisions in the tax law that allow employees to pay their share of premiums with pretax dollars, however. See the discussion in chapter 9.

[42]To the extent that total health care costs really are lowered, they are lowered only because employees forgo health insurance for themselves or for their dependents. But that leads to a larger number of people without health insurance.

paying an additional $300 to $450 in taxes. If employees pay one-half of the premium in aftertax wages, employers and employees together are paying from $390 to $650 in additional taxes. The fact that such a practice is common indicates that there is even greater waste in the employee benefits laws that regulate employer-provided health care.[43]

Levels versus Trends

A common mistake made by employee benefits managers is to confuse a one-time shift in costs with a change in the rate of increase in costs. Instituting a procedure to audit claims or negotiate discounts reduces health care costs in the year in which the change is made. But if utilization continues to increase, costs will continue to increase as before. Suppose a company's health insurance costs are increasing at 15 percent per year. In the year in which it adopts cost-containment strategies, its costs drop from the trend line as shown in Figure 7.7. But unless employees have incentives to purchase less health care, costs will continue to climb 15 percent per year from the lower base.

The Leverage Effect of Deductibles

Another mistake made by employee benefits managers is to fail to consider the leverage effect of deductibles that are not increased in line with total health care costs. Table 7.4 provides a simple illustration. In this case, total health care costs rise by 10 percent. But if the employee deductible remains fixed, the employer's cost will rise by 20 percent, or twice the rate of increase in health care spending. On the other hand, if the deductible is also increased by 10 percent, the employer's cost will match the general increase in health care spending.

Casualty of Change: Health Insurance as Prepayment for Consumption of Medical Care

Health insurance in the cost-plus system tends to be prepayment for the consumption of medical care. For large companies it works

---

[43]Increasing deductibles and copayments (thus requiring more expenditures with aftertax dollars at the time of consumption of medical care) also eliminates the tax subsidy. In this case, however, there is a more socially useful benefit, in that employees are less wasteful in consuming health care.

Figure 7.7
HEALTH CARE COSTS—LEVELS AND TRENDS

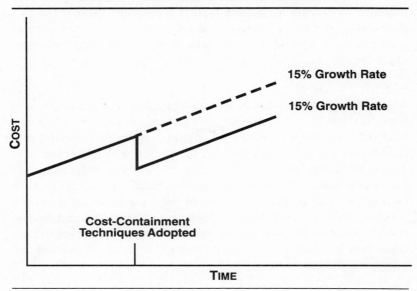

Table 7.4
LEVERAGE EFFECTS OF DEDUCTIBLES

	Initial Year, 1990	No Increase in Deductible in 1991	10 Percent Increase in Deductible in 1991
Total cost	$1,000	$1,110	$1,100
Employee deductible	$500	$500	$550
Employer's cost	$500	$600	$550
Increase in total cost		10%	10%
Increase in employer's cost		20%	10%

like this: Employees (through their employer) pay premiums for the right to receive medical care virtually for free at the point of consumption; if the cost of last year's consumption exceeds the total premium payment, this year's premium is increased to make up for the loss; and premium payments from the employees finance the consumption decisions of those same employees.

In such a system, health insurance companies are not performing any real insurance function. Instead, they are processing claims and doing the accounting. Thus, when large companies self-insure, they are not really entering the insurance business; they are simply taking over the paperwork. Self-insured companies now have entered the cost-containment business in an effort to control the consumption decisions of their employees. To the extent that the companies contract with traditional insurers to manage health care costs, the health insurers are also in the business of cost-management, not insurance.

The employees of a large company form a self-contained pool. The health risks present are kept within the company pool and not combined with health risks elsewhere. Thus, when the company substitutes prepayment for the consumption of medical care for real health insurance, the most visible problem it faces is the problem of rising costs. Not surprisingly, then, the modern corporation faces a vigorous, competitive market for cost-containment services. For all practical purposes, though, it is not part of a market for health insurance.

Things are very different for small companies and individuals. Consider the case of a single individual who wants to buy health insurance as protection against catastrophic medical expenses. Such a person has no interest in prepayment for the consumption of medical care. That would mean that his premiums would always have to match his medical expenses, which would defeat the purpose of having health insurance in the first place.

The original Blue Cross solution to this problem was to monopolize the market and charge everyone the same premium regardless of risk (as discussed in chapter 6). If medical consumption expenses went up, Blue Cross would raise the premiums for everyone. But because Blue Cross could not keep commercial insurers out of the market, the plan was destined to fail. Other insurers sought out the healthier policyholders who were being overcharged by Blue Cross and undercut the price. To the extent that the tactic was successful, Blue Cross was left with riskier policyholders for whom it had to charge even higher premiums.

Plans that offer prepayment for the consumption of medical care cannot compete in a free market with real health insurance. Such

217

an environment creates profitable opportunities for the latter and large losses for the former. Perhaps for this reason, most of the large commercial health insurers suffered large losses and left the market for individual health insurance during the 1980s. Many also left the market for small group insurance.

The consequences of this exodus were not all good. The more accurate pricing of risk was a benefit for healthier people and for small companies with healthier employees. But for those people and those groups of employees with higher risks, health insurance became increasingly difficult to purchase. Health insurance originally came into being to meet insurance needs in those industries and occupations in which the health risks were greatest. But by the end of the 1980s, we had come full circle. Those insurers who remained in the market sought only the healthiest policyholders, while avoiding and even blacklisting those industries and occupations in which health risks were the highest.[44]

What should be done about this problem? To those steeped in the cost-plus tradition there is only one answer: government must intervene and prevent the accurate pricing of risk. There is "fierce competition for the small group insurance market [based] mainly on risk selection," Congress has been told by representatives of the Health Insurance Association of America and Blue Cross and Blue Shield. "The major risk in insuring small groups is biased selection, and this risk is so large relative to other risks that it drives the market," according to Gordon Trapnell, chief economist for the American Association of Actuaries. Competition based on risk selection "should be replaced by competition based on efficiency, service and ability to control costs," they all agree.[45] Those views are echoed by Jack Meyer, a health economist who formerly headed the Center for Health Policy Research of the "conservative" American Enterprise Institute in Washington, DC. "Providers and insurers are competing on the basis of good health risks in the United States because they are not yet being forced to compete on the basis of good performance," he says.[46]

[44]Milt Freudenheim, "Health Insurers, to Reduce Losses, Blacklist Dozens of Occupations," *New York Times*, February 5, 1990.

[45]Cited in Mary Jane Fisher, "Officials: Fierce Competition on 'Risk Selection' Must End," *National Underwriter* (April 30, 1990).

[46]Jack A. Meyer, respondent's comments in, "Symposium: International Comparison of Health Care Systems," *Health Care Financing Review*, 1989 Annual Supplement, p. 110.

If such comments do not immediately seem strange, imagine their application to life, automobile liability, fire, and casualty insurance. We do not normally criticize insurers in those fields because they are not actively involved in cost management. Cost-containment activities, to the extent they exist, are considered incidental to the real task of insurance, which is the pricing and managing of risk.

The social function of a competitive market for insurance is to move as close as possible to the accurate pricing of risk. Just as in other fields of insurance, there is enormous value in having health insurance risks priced accurately. Only in such an environment can individuals rationally choose between self-insurance and third-party insurance. Only in such an environment can individuals and companies minimize the costs of achieving any particular degree of financial security. In the complex world of modern medicine, cost-management techniques can be quite valuable, at least for expensive medical services. But, as we learned in the 1980s, insurance and cost management are two different services that do not have to be delivered by the same supplier.

The Threat of a Counterrevolution: Price Controls for Health Insurance

As the building blocks of the cost-plus system begin to slowly crumble, those with a vested interest in its continuation are not idle. Increasingly, they are turning to politicians to protect them from the pressures of the emerging competitive market. For example, many major insurers and other special interests are pressuring state governments to impose new regulations on the market for health insurance. Although various proposals differ in detail, the goal is to move toward the original Blue Cross ideal—a single premium for everyone, independent of risk. These regulations would institutionalize health insurance as prepayment for the consumption of medical care and would force insurers into the permanent business of managing health care costs. Under such regulations, it would be impossible for a competitive market for real insurance to emerge.

The Effects of Price Controls

Figures 7.8 and 7.9 illustrate what can happen when government regulations prevent risk from being priced accurately. In this example, 20 people who are known to have expensive-to-treat illnesses

219

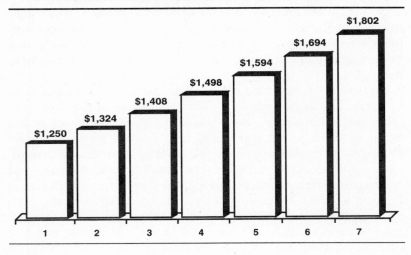

Figure 7.8
PREMIUMS INCREASE AS HEALTHY PEOPLE DROP OUT

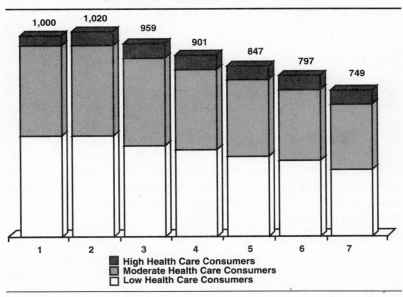

Figure 7.9
NUMBER OF INSURED PEOPLE FALLS

High Health Care Consumers
Moderate Health Care Consumers
Low Health Care Consumers

are allowed to enter an insurance pool for the same premium charged to 1,000 people already in the pool.

Because health care costs for each of the 20 newly insured, high-risk individuals are $5,850 greater than the premiums they pay,[47] the premium must be immediately increased by 6 percent for all policyholders. Because of this increase, some of the healthiest people begin to drop their coverage. (One percent are assumed to drop coverage for every 1 percent increase in premiums.)

As healthy people drop their coverage, they reduce income to the pool but have little effect on the pool's health care costs. As a result, each time a healthy person drops out, premiums must be increased again. In this case, after seven adjustment periods, health insurance premiums have increased by more than 60 percent and more than one-fourth of all policyholders have dropped their coverage. Although this is only a hypothetical example, it illustrates some consequences of the vast majority of "reform" proposals. In almost every case they would exacerbate the nation's two most pressing health policy problems: rising health insurance costs and a rising number of uninsured.

Imposing a Regressive, Hidden Tax

By forcing insurance companies to pay the medical bills of people who are already sick, politicians would be indirectly shifting the cost (through premium increases) to healthy people who buy health insurance. In so doing, they would be imposing a hidden tax on unsuspecting families. It is a tax which is highly regressive. Whereas the income tax system is designed so that higher income families pay higher tax rates, many health insurance reform proposals would impose the highest hidden tax rates on the lowest income families.

For example, if health insurance reform causes the premiums to rise by $1,000 for family coverage, that's a 10 percent tax on a family with a $10,000 annual income but only a 1 percent tax on a family with $100,000 in annual income. Thus, the tax rate on a family with a $10,000 annual income would be ten times as high as the rate for a $100,000-a-year family.

---

[47]These statistics are based on the Bush administration estimate that the least healthy uninsured Americans incur per capita health care costs of $7,100 per year.

Increasing the Number of People without Health Insurance

Contrary to widespread impressions, most of the 33 to 34 million people who are currently uninsured are healthy, not sick. Sixty percent of the uninsured are under 30 years of age and in the healthiest population age groups.[48] They have below-average incomes and few assets. As a result, they tend to be very sensitive to premium prices.

Moreover, the primary reason why most of the uninsured lack health coverage is that they have judged the price too high relative to the benefits. Very few have been denied coverage. According to one estimate, only 1 percent of Americans under the age of 65 are "uninsurable."[49] And according to an HIAA survey among employers who do not provide insurance to their employees, 86 percent cite high costs as the reason.[50] The artificial premium increases that would result from many health insurance reform proposals would substantially increase the number of employers who fail to provide coverage for their employees and the number of individuals who are uninsured by choice.

Case Study: President Bush's Health Care Plan

As part of his new health care plan, President Bush has made two major proposals—one good and one bad. On the positive side, the president's proposal would give tax deductions and tax credits to families who purchase their own health insurance.[51] Since the tax law currently subsidizes employer-provided health insurance, this is a reform that is long overdue on grounds of fairness alone. On the negative side, the president's health insurance reforms

[48]Jill D. Foley, *Uninsured in the United States: The Nonelderly Population without Health Insurance* (Washington, DC: Employee Benefits Research Institute, April 1991), p. 16.

[49]Employee Benefit Research Institute (EBRI) *Issue Brief*, no. 110, January 1991.

[50]Congressional Budget Office, "Rising Health Care Costs: Causes, Implications, and Strategies," *CBO Papers*, April 1991, p. 97.

[51]"President's Comprehensive Health Reform Program," February 6, 1992. People with income below the tax filing threshold (approximately the poverty line) would receive tax credits of $1,250 (for an individual) and $3,750 (for a family of three or more). The amount of the credit would decline as income rises, and taxpayers would have the option of taking the credit or a tax deduction. No health insurance credit or deduction would be available to individuals or families with incomes above $50,000 or $80,000, respectively. [p. 2.]

would more than wipe out any advantage the tax incentives create for moderate-income families.

According to the president's proposal, no employer or insurance company should be able to deny coverage or charge a higher premium to people who have expensive-to-treat illnesses.[52] Thus, a person with AIDS should be able to purchase health insurance for the same price as someone who does not have AIDS. People in hospital cancer wards should be able to buy health insurance for the same price as people who do not have cancer. The Bush proposal would require insurers to subsidize the cost of health insurance for the ill by charging higher premiums to the well. Thus people who do not have AIDS would be forced to pay higher premiums so that people who already have AIDS could pay lower premiums.

Particulars of the Bush Plan

George Bush is not the first person to propose charging the healthy and the sick the same premium for health insurance. Community rating is about to be implemented in Vermont and variations on that idea are under consideration in a dozen states. The only important difference among the proposals is the ease with which sick people can enter a pool and healthy people can leave.

Most proposals give healthy people at least some incentives to buy health insurance. For example, a typical provision is that preexisting conditions are not covered until after a 12-month waiting period. Thus someone who purchases insurance after an illness occurs risks 12 months of medical bills before the insurer starts paying the tab. The Bush proposal, by contrast, has no waiting period. Page 22 of the president's "white paper" on health policy proposes that hospitals be able to get patients insured the moment they enter the emergency room. Uninsured people would face no financial risk. They could get insurance coverage as they enter a hospital and drop it as they leave.[53]

---

[52]"President's Comprehensive Health Reform Program," February 6, 1992. During an initial transition period, premium "bands" would allow some variation in premiums for individuals of the same age and sex. Ultimately, however, through a reinsurance mechanism, "insurers would be able to provide coverage at a near uniform premium for the sick and the healthy" (p. 23).

[53]"In cases where a hospital emergency room is an individual's first point of contact with the system, rotating assignment would be used to enroll an uninsured credit-eligible individual to a specific health plan if the individual were unable to make a choice. So, for example, a homeless person entering the hospital and having no

Applying the Concept to Life Insurance

One way to appreciate how radical this reform would be is to imagine applying the same concept to life insurance. Suppose people could buy life insurance for a family member who was terminally ill. Clearly, there would be a huge demand for life insurance among the families of people on death's doorstep. If people could buy life insurance for the same price regardless of how sick they are, there would be no reason for the healthy to buy it. Life insurance premiums would soar. And since the premium for a $1 million death benefit for someone about to die would be $1 million, real life insurance as we know it would cease to exist. Similarly, if you knew you could buy health insurance after you became sick for the same price charged to the healthy, there would be no reason to purchase it while you were healthy. Only sick people would buy it and premiums would be exorbitant.

Subsidies vs. Price Controls

The worst feature of the Bush plan and other price control solutions is that they would cause enormous harm in order to accomplish a small amount of good. A much better approach would be to tackle the problems of sick people directly and allow healthy people to buy real health insurance. In the example illustrated by Figure 7.8, the attempt to subsidize the medical bills of 20 people led to a 60 percent price increase for 1,000 people and caused 271 people to become uninsured. Those negative consequences could be completely avoided by directly subsidizing the medical bills of the 20 sick people through a government program.

President Bush's health care plan is not a solution to the problems of private health insurance in the United States. It would cause health insurance premiums to soar, lead to an increasing number of uninsured people, and impose its greatest burdens on moderate-income families. The nation's health care crisis will not be solved by regulating private health insurance out of existence. To the

---

preference for any carrier would be assigned to an insurer by rotation and the credit would automatically flow to the insurer" (p. 22). Technically, a "credit-eligible" person is defined as a person whose annual income does not exceed $50,000 (for an individual) or $80,000 (for a family). However, since the hospital will almost certainly not know the emergency-room patient's income until several days after treatment, and since there is no waiting period, the proposal apparently envisions a mechanism that will ensure any uninsured patient entering the hospital.

Table 7.5
THE LANGUAGE OF MISGUIDED REFORM

Reformers' Assertions	Reality
"In order for insurance to work, people need to be combined into large pools."	Almost all insured people are already combined into large pools.
"Some insurers try to take all the good risks, leaving others with the bad ones."	If insurance is priced accurately, "good" risks are no more profitable than "bad" ones.
"Medical underwriting (basing premiums on the health condition of potential policyholders) is destabilizing the market."	There is no evidence that the accurate pricing of risk causes instability. There is a lot of evidence that the failure to price risk accurately causes instability.
"Competition among insurers should be based on skills at managed care, not on skills at guessing who will become sick."	Predicting the likelihood of claims and pricing based on those predictions is what the business of insurance is all about. Managing expenses is a different business—one that does not necessarily require insurance companies.

contrary, we need a competitive insurance market in which premiums reflect real risks.

The Health Insurance Reform Debate

The goal of President Bush's health insurance reform proposal is to force healthy people to pay higher premiums in order to subsidize the medical expenses of less healthy people. Since most people would not voluntarily pay higher premiums, the president's proposal would create an elaborate price-fixing scheme—designed to prevent insurers from charging healthy people fair prices.

This goal is not clearly stated in the White House health policy position paper, however. Nor is it clearly stated in similar reform proposals. Instead, the advocates of price control talk of "pools," "medical underwriting," and the like. But, as Table 7.5 shows, such industry jargon bears little relationship to real problems and real solutions.

Do We Need Larger Insurance Pools?

An argument often made by price control advocates is that insurance cannot work unless people are placed in large pools. What they often neglect to say is that everyone who has health insurance is already in a large pool. Large insurance companies automatically group policyholders with other policyholders around the country. Most small companies reinsure in a larger, national market.

President Bush's proposal would not lead to larger pools. In fact, it might lead to smaller ones (e.g., as states are encouraged to create self-contained pools). The Bush reform proposal would regulate the *price of entry* into the pool and the *price of remaining* in the pool. The proposal is not really about pools, it's about prices.

What's Wrong with Medical Underwriting?

As in the case of life insurance and property and casualty insurance, most health insurers try to base the premiums they charge on the likelihood of future claims. Thus, less-healthy people can expect to pay higher premiums or face exclusions and riders.[54] In this respect, the health insurance market is no different from any other insurance market. To the extent that underwriting is successful, it leads to the more accurate pricing of risk; which leads to lower and more stable prices; which leads to more insured people; which leads to less uncompensated care; which leads to still lower prices, etc.

Many advocates of reform, however, view the accurate pricing of risk as a problem rather than a solution. In their view, the social purpose of health insurance is to pay medical bills rather than to price and manage risk. One frequent argument is that underwriting is destabilizing because some companies try to take all of the "good" risks, leaving other companies with all of the "bad" ones. If risk is priced accurately, however, a good risk is no more profitable than a bad one. Lloyds of London has prospered for more than 100 years insuring risks that other insurers avoided. Moreover, there is nothing in economic theory and no historical evidence to support

---

[54]Exclusions and riders are additions that become part of an insurance policy, excluding or limiting benefits otherwise payable.

the contention that markets in which risk is priced accurately are unstable. To the contrary, both theory and evidence demonstrate that instability is created when risk is not priced accurately.

How Should Health Insurance Be Priced to New Buyers?

If the health insurance marketplace is competitive, there will be a natural tendency to price risk accurately. Different people will pay different premiums depending upon the likelihood that they will incur claims. Policies sold to individuals will be combined with other policies in a larger market. The price charged to a specific buyer will reflect the risk that individual adds to the large pool. Currently, the cost of insuring a 60-year-old male is about four times that for a 25-year-old male. The likely cost of insuring someone living in Los Angeles is about four times that of someone living in Vermont. In competitive markets, premium prices would reflect these expected costs. Buyers would each pay for what they get.

How Should Health Insurance Be Priced to People Already Insured?

Some of the most troublesome problems in the health insurance industry relate to the experience of policyholders who become sick. As we saw in chapter 6, most life insurance contracts are guaranteed renewable. This means that the insurer cannot cancel the policy after a person has a life-threatening illness. Terminally ill people, for example, have the right to continue paying premiums, often at guaranteed rates. In addition, there are usually limits on how much the premiums can rise in future years, and the insurers cannot increase the premium for one policyholder without increasing the premium by the same amount for everyone else who holds that same type of policy.

Not long ago, the health insurance marketplace functioned in a similar manner. Policies that were guaranteed renewable were common. Insurers could not cancel coverage simply because a policyholder became sick, and a premium increase for one had to be matched by increases for all others. There is some evidence that state regulation is responsible for the virtual disappearance of guaranteed renewable policies in the market for individual and family policies.

Real Problems, Real Solutions

There are real problems in the health insurance industry. These problems arise because the traditional insurance philosophy has been abandoned. To solve the problems, legislation is probably needed. But a workable solution must be one which encourages a competitive market for real insurance—one in which risk is accurately priced.

Solutions must be found for the problems of four separate groups of people: (1) healthy people who choose not to buy health insurance, (2) unhealthy people who are uninsurable, (3) sick people whose policies are canceled or whose premiums are unfairly increased by insurance companies, and (4) employees who experience "job lock."

Problem: Healthy People Who Are Uninsured

As noted above, most uninsured Americans are healthy, not sick. They lack health insurance because they have been priced out of the market. Part of the answer is to encourage insurers to charge these people low premiums that reflect their low level of risk. Moreover, the tax law should grant every bit as much encouragement (about a 30 percent subsidy) for individually purchased insurance as it now grants for employer-provided health insurance.

Problem: People Who Are Uninsurable

A small but important group of people cannot buy health insurance because they are sick or at high risk. Government can help by creating risk pools or subsidizing the purchase of conventional health insurance with tax dollars, rather than by artificially raising the premiums charged to healthy people. And the amount of subsidy should depend on family income. Low-income families need government help. Ross Perot does not.

Problem: Unfair Cancellations and Premium Increases

Sensible reform is needed for people who already have insurance. Insurers should not be able to change the rules of the game after a risky illness has occurred. They should not be able to cancel a policy or unreasonably raise premiums. As noted above, terminally ill people who have life insurance can continue their coverage at pre-agreed premiums. There is no reason why health insurers can't follow the same practice.

Problem: Job Lock

Thirty percent of Americans say they or someone in their household has stayed on a job they wanted to leave because they did not want to lose employer-provided insurance coverage.[55] Even though economists are almost unanimous in the belief that health insurance costs are fully paid for by workers (as a fringe benefit which substitutes for wages), our outmoded employee benefits system treats the policy as belonging to the employer, not the employee. This might be acceptable if employees worked for the same employer for the whole of their work life. In fact, most do not.

A reasonable solution is to insist that health insurance benefits be personal and portable if they are to receive favorable treatment under the tax law. Thus, employers who want the tax advantages of employer-provided coverage would have to purchase (or provide) a conversion option that would allow employees (or a new employer) to continue coverage after the employee leaves the firm.

The Threat of a Counterrevolution: Outlawing Cost-Control Techniques

Other special interests in the health care industry have also been active. In 1991, for example, there were 195 pieces of legislation introduced at the state level to stop, or cripple, many of the cost-control techniques described here.[56] For example, an Indiana law requires that PPOs must accept any physician willing to join. Thus, Indiana Bell has a PPO that includes every physician in the state. Montana and Oklahoma have adopted similar measures.

In some states, hospital and physicians' groups are supporting legislation that would require all utilization review to be done by local providers, mandate that utilization review firms remain open 24 hours a day, and require state-specific statistical reporting. Such legislation would raise the cost of utilization review and inhibit its aggressive application. In addition, some states (including Texas) restrict the amount of discount that insurers can give to patients who choose PPO doctors.[57]

---

[55]Erik Eckholm, "Health Benefits Found to Deter Job Switching," *New York Times*, September 26, 1991.

[56]The Wyatt Co., "Cost Analysis of State Legislative Mandates on Six Managed Care Practices," produced by the Health Insurance Association of America, July 1991, and reported in *Medical Benefits* 8, no. 17 (September 15, 1991): 9–10.

[57]Ron Winslow, "Effort to Curb Health Costs Is Hitting Snags," *Wall Street Journal*, August 8, 1991.

The Threat of a Counterrevolution: Total Government Control

Other proposals would have even more devastating effects on the market for private health insurance. Proposals for pay-or-play plans that have been introduced at the federal and state level, for example, would force employers to provide health insurance to employees or pay a tax that is largely unrelated to the real cost of health insurance. These proposals are designed to force people into a regulated, institutionalized health care system—protected from the pressures of competition (see chapter 12). As in the case of mandated automobile liability insurance in California, New Jersey, and Massachusetts (see chapter 6), these proposals would necessarily politicize all health insurance in the United States. They would constitute an open invitation for government to impose controls on the entire health care system. The ultimate threat, however, is growing support for national health insurance, which also would completely prevent competitive market pressures from solving problems (see chapter 16).

The events of the 1980s created an opportunity for a competitive market for real health insurance to develop in the 1990s. But that will not happen unless public policies encourage its development.

8. Cost-Plus Finance and Low-Deductible Health Insurance

The vehicle by which we spend other people's money in the medical marketplace is third-party health insurance (provided by an employer, an insurance company, or government). Prior to 1965, increases in health care costs were relatively modest because a large part of the payment was made out-of-pocket by patients. Since then, Medicare and Medicaid have expanded government third-party insurance to more and more services for the elderly and the poor, and private health insurance has expanded for the working population. As Table 8.1 shows, 95 percent of the money Americans now spend in hospitals is someone else's money at the time they spend it. Four-fifths of all physicians' payments are now made with other people's money, as are more than three-quarters of all medical payments for all purposes.

The expansion of third-party insurance coverage since 1965 has had a predictable consequence: Health care spending has soared from 6 percent to 12 percent of our gross national product, and the rate of increase shows no sign of abating.

Numerous economic studies have shown that the amount of medical care that people consume varies with the out-of-pocket price they have to pay, often with no effect on health. For example, a Rand Corporation study found that people who had access to free care spent about 50 percent more than those who had to pay 95 percent of their bills out-of-pocket (up to a maximum of $1,000). People who had free care were about 25 percent more likely to see a physician and 33 percent more likely to enter a hospital.[1] Despite

---

[1]See Robert Brook et al., *The Effect of Coinsurance on the Health of Adults* (Santa Monica, CA: Rand Corporation, 1984); and Willard Manning et al., "Health Insurance and the Demand for Health Care: Evidence from a Randomized Experiment," *American Economic Review* 77, no. 3 (June 1987). For a survey of economic studies of the demand for medical care, see Paul Feldstein, *Healthcare Economics* (New York: John Wiley & Sons, 1988).

231

Table 8.1
SHARE OF PERSONAL HEALTH EXPENDITURES PAID BY THIRD
PARTIES, 1965 AND 1990

Type of Service	1965	1990
Hospital	83.2%	95.0%
Physician	38.4	81.3
Drugs	6.4	26.4
Nursing home	35.5	55.2
All other professional services	NA	72.2
All personal health care expenditures	48.4	76.7

SOURCE: Health Care Financing Administration, Office of the Actuary. Data from the Office of National Cost Estimates.

differences in consumption, there were no apparent differences between the two groups in terms of health outcomes.[2] The Rand study was conducted between 1974 and 1982. A $1,000 deductible over that period would be equivalent to a deductible of between $1,380 and $2,482 today.

The Self-Insurance Alternative

People familiar with insurance have long known that it creates perverse incentives for the insured. To take advantage of the benefits under their policies, the beneficiaries do things they would not otherwise do. In recognition of this fact, insurance in most fields is restricted to risks beyond the control of the insured. (For example, automobile casualty insurance does not pay for oil changes, tire rotation, brake adjustment, or other routine maintenance, even though these activities are important for the health of a car and safety of its driver.) Financial advisers almost always recommend

[2]The one exception was vision care, which is not surprising in that eyeglasses are often viewed as a marginal health care expenditure. High blood pressure was close to statistical significance. Researchers could find no other significant differences in health outcomes. See Joseph Newhouse et al., "Some Interim Results from a Controlled Trial of Cost Sharing in Health Insurance," *New England Journal of Medicine* 305, no. 25 (December 17, 1981): 1501–7; and Robert Brook et al., "Does Free Care Improve Adults' Health?" *New England Journal of Medicine* 309, no. 23 (December 8, 1983): 1426–34.

high-deductible policies, because low-dollar claims are the ones in which the most abuse is likely to occur and the premiums needed to cover such claims are often much too high relative to the extra coverage. The same principles apply to health insurance.

The alternative to third-party insurance is self-insurance. Rather than relying on insurers to pay every medical bill, we could put money aside in personal savings for the small expenses involved and use insurance only for rare, high-dollar medical episodes. Such a practice would result in much lower premiums and curtail a great deal of wasteful spending. But instead of exploiting opportunities for self-insurance and taking advantage of its benefits in the health care field, we have moved in the opposite direction, with insurers paying for all manner of routine expenses, including checkups and diagnostic tests, even when there is no illness and no risky event has occurred.

Why Low-Deductible Health Insurance Is Wasteful

Because employees, through their employers, are able to purchase health insurance with pretax dollars but individuals are not permitted to self-insure (personal savings) for small medical expenses with pretax dollars, people often buy low-deductible health insurance and use insurers to pay small medical bills that would be much less expensive if paid out-of-pocket. The following examples show how wasteful this practice can be.

The Cost of a Low-Deductible Policy in Cities with Average Health Care Costs

The cost of catastrophic health insurance is usually quite low. Consider a standard individual health insurance policy for a middle-aged male in a city with average health care costs, such as Indianapolis. (See Table 8.2.) If the policy has a $2,500 deductible, the policyholder is at risk for $2,500. The insurance company, on the other hand, is at risk for $1 million. Given an average premium, this health insurance costs the policyholder about 6/100th of one penny in premiums for each dollar of coverage.

Now contrast this policy with a $1,000-deductible policy that has a 20 percent copayment for the next $5,000 of expenses. In theory,

Table 8.2
COST OF LOWER DEDUCTIBLES FOR A 40-YEAR-OLD MAN IN A CITY WITH AVERAGE HEALTH CARE COSTS[1]

Lowering the Deductible[2]	Additional Annual Premium	Cost of Each $1 of Additional Coverage[3]
From $2,500 to $1,000	$168.84	14¢
From $1,000 to $500	255.12	64
From $500 to $250	153.24	77

SOURCE: Golden Rule Insurance Co.
[1]Data are for 1991.
[2]For deductibles of $1,000 or less, the policy has a 20 percent copayment up to a maximum of $1,000.
[3]Because the policy has a 20 percent copayment, additional coverage is 80 percent of the difference between the two deductibles.

the $1,000 deductible gives the policyholder $1,500 of extra insurance coverage. But because of the 20 percent copayment, the additional coverage actually is only $1,200.[3] People who choose the $1,000 deductible will pay about $169 in additional premiums in return for $1,200 of additional insurance coverage. As a result each additional dollar of insurance coverage costs the policyholder 14 cents.[4] Table 8.2 also shows the marginal cost (premium increase per additional dollar of coverage) of buying down the deductible even further. As the table shows, lowering the deductible from $1,000 to $500 costs 64 cents in additional premiums for each additional dollar of insurance coverage. Lowering the deductible from $500 to $250 costs 77 cents in additional premiums for each additional dollar of insurance coverage.

[3]Unless the policyholders have reached the cap on their copayment ($1,000), they must pay 20 percent of medical expenses above the deductible. Thus, if policyholders with a $1,000 deductible have medical expenses of $2,500, they must pay the first $1,000 plus 20 percent of the next $1,500 (or $300). The insurance company, in this instance, will pay $1,200.

[4]These calculations are based on policies sold by Golden Rule Insurance Co., the largest seller of individual and family policies in the country. Other insurance companies sell similar policies at similar prices. See John C. Goodman and Gerald L. Musgrave, *Controlling Health Care Costs with Medical Savings Accounts*, NCPA Policy Report no. 168 (Dallas: National Center for Policy Analysis, January 1992).

Table 8.3
COST OF LOWER DEDUCTIBLES FOR A 40-YEAR-OLD MAN IN A CITY WITH HIGH HEALTH CARE COSTS[1]

Lowering the Deductible[2]	Additional Annual Premium	Cost of Each $1 of Additional Coverage[3]
From $2,500 to $1,000	$389.64	$0.33
From $1,000 to $500	715.44	1.79
From $500 to $250	440.28	2.20

SOURCE: Golden Rule Insurance Co.
[1]Data are for 1991.
[2]For deductibles of $1,000 or less, the policy has a 20 percent copayment up to a maximum of $1,000.
[3]Because the policy has a 20 percent copayment, additional coverage is 80 percent of the difference between the two deductibles.

In general, buying a $250 deductible policy rather than a $500 deductible is a good deal only if the policyholder is confident he will have at least $500 in medical expenses. Even in that case, the gain is a small one—a dollar's worth of medical expenses for each 77 cents in premiums. For the vast majority of people, however, a low-deductible policy is quite wasteful. Considering the administrative expenses, insurers on the average will pay out only 54 cents in claims for each 77 cents in premiums. Policyholders as a group, therefore, will pay far more in premiums than they will receive in benefits.

The Cost of a Low-Deductible Policy in Cities with High Health Care Costs

In general, the higher the health care costs in an area, the more expensive low-deductible health insurance becomes. Table 8.3, for example, shows the costs of a lower deductible for a middle-aged male in a city such as Miami. As the table shows, lowering the deductible from $2,500 to $1,000 is quite expensive, being 33 cents for each additional dollar of coverage. Lowering the deductible from $1,000 to $500 is inherently wasteful, costing $1.79 for each additional dollar of coverage. Lowering the deductible from $500 to $250 costs $2.20 for each additional dollar of coverage, or $1.20 more than any possible benefits the policyholder could derive.

235

The Cost of a Low-Deductible Policy under Blue Cross Plans in California

Southern California has health care costs that are among the highest in the nation. As a result, Californians who buy lower deductible policies are being especially wasteful. Table 8.4 shows what policyholders would pay to reduce the deductible under Blue Cross plans currently sold for individuals and families in different age groups. Even lowering the deductible from $2,000 to $1,000 is a bad buy in many cases. A deductible of less than $1,000 is always a bad buy.

A California couple with no children will pay from $1 to $2.63 (depending on their age) for each dollar of additional insurance if they choose a $500 rather than a $1,000 deductible. If they further lower the deductible to $250, they will pay from $1.92 to $9.54 for each additional dollar of coverage.

Opportunities for Premium Savings

Because low-deductible health insurance is so wasteful, in most places people would realize substantial premium savings if they increased the deductible. For example, the average employee in the U.S. economy has a deductible of about $250.[5] If it were increased to $1,000, the employee would lose $600 worth of coverage (80% x $750).

Figure 8.1 shows the potential annual savings on individual policies sold in Indianapolis (an average health care cost city), Dallas (an above-average cost city), and Miami (a high-cost city). As the figure shows, in return for giving up $600 of coverage, policyholders would realize immediate savings of 68 percent of that amount in Indianapolis and 90 percent in Dallas through lower premiums. In Miami, policyholders would save $1,156 in reduced premium payments, or $556 more than the coverage they would forgo.

In most places, the savings for families that choose higher deductibles are even greater. In a city with average health care costs, families can save about $1,315 a year by choosing a $1,000 deductible rather than a $250 deductible—savings that are more than twice as much as the value of the coverage forgone. By choosing a $2,500

[5]See John C. Goodman, Aldona Robbins, and Gary Robbins, *Mandating Health Insurance*, NCPA Policy Report no. 136 (Dallas: National Center for Policy Analysis, February 1988).

Table 8.4
BLUE CROSS PLANS IN SOUTHERN CALIFORNIA: COST OF LOWER DEDUCTIBLES*

Status and Age	Cost per Dollar of Additional Insurance Coverage for			
	Lowering Deductible from $2,000 to $1,000	Lowering Deductible from $1,000 to $500	Lowering Deductible from $500 to $250	
Single person				
Under 30	$0.14	$0.72	$1.80	
30–39	0.20	1.05	1.02	
40–49	0.27	1.20	1.80	
50–59	0.42	0.99	2.82	
60–64	0.51	1.08	3.84	
Subscriber and spouse				
Under 30	$0.29	$1.44	$2.28	
30–39	0.24	2.52	1.92	
40–49	0.51	2.07	4.62	
50–59	0.77	2.64	5.64	
60–64	1.02	1.71	9.54	
Subscriber and child				
Under 30	$0.15	$0.96	$1.62	
30–39	0.23	1.14	1.74	
40–49	0.24	1.86	2.58	
50–59	0.38	2.55	3.18	
60–64	0.53	1.05	5.34	

(Continued on next page)

237

Table 8.4—Continued
BLUE CROSS PLANS IN SOUTHERN CALIFORNIA: COST OF LOWER DEDUCTIBLES*

Status and Age	Cost per Dollar of Additional Insurance Coverage for		
	Lowering Deductible from $2,000 to $1,000	Lowering Deductible from $1,000 to $500	Lowering Deductible from $500 to $250
Family			
Under 30	$0.42	$2.52	$2.22
30–39	0.56	2.16	3.60
40–49	0.62	2.82	4.68
50–59	0.87	3.90	5.04
60–64	1.16	2.04	10.14
Subscriber and children			
Under 30	$0.27	$1.38	$2.52
30–39	0.29	0.96	3.90
40–49	0.30	1.44	4.62
50–59	0.44	1.44	6.96
60–64	0.62	1.23	6.18

SOURCE: Blue Cross.

*For Orange, Santa Barbara, and Ventura counties in California in 1991.

Figure 8.1
ANNUAL PREMIUM SAVINGS FOR A 40-YEAR-OLD MAN IF THE
DEDUCTIBLE IS INCREASED FROM $250 TO $1,000*

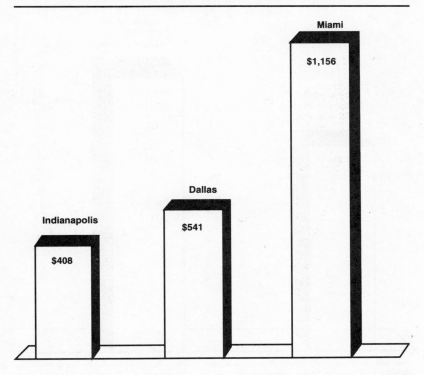

SOURCE: Golden Rule Insurance Co.

*Data are for an individual male aged 40 in 1991. Because the policy has a 20 percent copayment, the increase in the deductible eliminates only $600 of health insurance coverage unless the policyholder has medical expenses in excess of $5,000.

deductible rather than a $1,000 deductible, they can save $1,749, or $51 less than the value of the coverage they forgo.[6] (See Figure 8.2.)

However, under current federal tax law, if such policies are purchased by employers who attempt to pass the savings on to their

---

[6]The forgone coverage is 80% x ($2,500 − $250) = $1,800.

Figure 8.2
Annual Premium Savings if the Deductible Is Increased for Families in Cities with Average Health Care Costs*

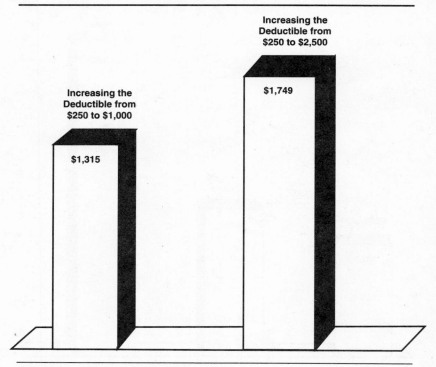

Increasing the
Deductible from
$250 to $2,500

$1,749

Increasing the
Deductible from
$250 to $1,000

$1,315

Source: Golden Rule Insurance Co.

*Data are for two adults and two children in a city with average health care costs. For deductibles less than $2,500, policyholders face a 20 percent copayment up to $1,000. Unless policyholders have medical expenses of $5,000, they forgo $600 of coverage by moving up from a $250 deductible to a $1,000 deductible and $1,800 of coverage by moving up from a $250 deductible to a $2,500 deductible.

employees in the form of higher wages, up to half the premium savings will go to the government in the form of taxes.

Opportunities for Premium Savings in Large Groups

Considerable savings are possible for individuals and families who choose higher deductible policies, for two reasons. First, when

240

policyholders spend more of their own money on small medical bills, they are more prudent consumers; they hold down medical costs and, therefore, health insurance premiums. Second, when people have the choice between higher and lower deductibles, healthy people tend to choose high-deductible policies whereas those who are not as healthy tend to choose low deductibles. Thus, people who choose high deductibles are less of an insurance risk.

Suppose, however, that an employer with a large group of employees increases the deductible for every member of the group—the healthy as well as the sick. In that case, any reduction in total medical expenses would be attributable solely to changes in the employees' consumption behavior. But even if there were no behavior changes, health insurance premiums could be cut substantially.

The Experience of Large Groups

Many people, including representatives of major employers and large insurance companies, question whether there are substantial savings in raising the deductible. Yet the claims experiences of large groups show that substantial savings do occur. The reason for the confusion is that apparently contradictory statements can be made about the distribution of claims. For example:

- About 4 percent of the people account for 50 percent of health care spending and 20 percent of the people account for 80 percent of the spending.
- About two-thirds of all health care spending is on medical bills of $5,000 or less.

The first statement, popularized in a widely distributed Blue Cross–Blue Shield publication,[7] implies to many people that most of the money is spent on people who are very sick. By contrast, the second statement implies that most medical bills are small. As Figure 8.3 shows, both statements are correct. The distribution of medical expenses in Figure 8.3 is a reasonable representation of what happens in most large groups. In this case, 50 people spend $60,000, or $1,200 per person on the average. A small percentage of people spend most of the money and at the same time two-thirds of spending is on medical bills below $5,000. If the example were

[7]Blue Cross and Blue Shield System, *Reforming the Small Group Health Insurance Market* (March 1991), p. 6.

241

Figure 8.3
DISTRIBUTION OF MEDICAL EXPENSES AMONG 50 PEOPLE*

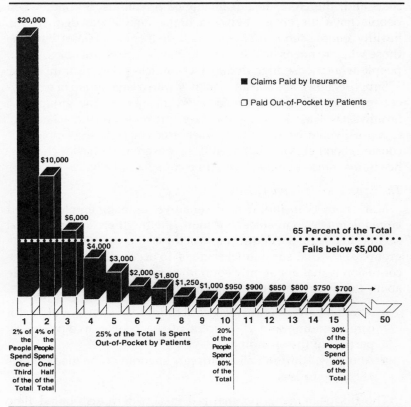

*Assumes a $250 deductible and a 20% copayment on the next $5,000 of expenses. Period of coverage is one year.

broadened to include a much larger group, the extremes of the distribution would become more evident. A few people would have medical expenses of several hundred thousand dollars, and many others would have no medical claims. The characteristics of the distribution, however, would be about the same as those shown in Figure 8.3.

When individuals are given a choice, those who choose a $1,000 deductible rather than a $250 deductible can expect a one-third reduction in health insurance premiums. A one-third reduction in claims costs (and therefore in premiums)[8] is possible for a large group if the deductible is increased from $250 to about $2,500. Considering that higher deductibles cause people to change their behavior, however, a one-third reduction in premiums for a large group would probably occur at a deductible of between $1,000 and $2,500.

Winners and Losers with Higher Deductibles

Except in those instances in which people pay more in premiums than the value of coverage they receive, higher deductibles represent a gamble. On the one hand, a higher deductible results in premium savings. On the other hand, it puts policyholders at greater risk. Thus, some people will gain from a higher deductible and others will lose. A priori, most people won't know which group they are in.

As Figure 8.3 shows, the vast majority of people would gain from a higher deductible. In any one year, about 70 percent would have very few medical expenses, accounting for only 2.5 percent of all health insurance claims. Those who have large medical bills, on the other hand, would be worse off. Nevertheless (as discussed below), even people who have high medical expenses in any one year would be better off with a high deductible, provided they do not have recurring large medical bills over many years. Take a leukemia patient, for example, who faces large medical expenses indefinitely into the future. With a high annual deductible, the out-of-pocket costs for this patient will simply rise over time.

However, there are ways of structuring health insurance so that even potential leukemia patients are better off with a high deductible. Instead of the annual deductible that is common these days, health insurance could have a "per condition deductible" as was common some years ago. With a per condition deductible, a person diagnosed with cancer would pay the deductible only once, and insurance would pay all of the remaining costs of the cancer treatments, even if those costs were incurred over many years.

---

[8] Assumes that administrative costs are proportional to claims, an assumption that is consistent with industry experience.

Allowing People to Self-Insure
through Medical Savings Accounts

To help eliminate the perverse incentives in the current system, we should allow individuals to make tax-free deposits each year to individual Medisave accounts. These accounts would serve as self-insurance and as an alternative to the wasteful use of third-party insurers for small medical bills. Funds in the accounts would grow tax free, and withdrawals would be permitted only for legitimate medical expenses. Funds not spent during a person's working years could be spent on postretirement health care or rolled over into a pension fund.

Medisave accounts would be the private property of the account holder and become part of an individual's estate at the time of death. If created by an employer, they would be personal and portable for the employee. Medisave contributions should receive at least as much tax encouragement as payments for conventional health insurance.[9]

Medisave Accounts with a $1,000 Deductible

Most people have no medical expenses in any given year, and it is not uncommon for people to go for several years without incurring medical costs. Figure 8.4 shows how Medisave balances would grow if not spent in the case of an individual who switches from a $250 deductible to a $1,000 deductible, with $400 in premium savings each year. Consider the benefits of the two alternatives. With a $250 deductible and a 20 percent copayment, the policyholder would pay $400 out of the first $1,000 of medical expenses, and health insurance would pay 80 percent of the remainder.[10] With a $1,000 deductible, the policyholder would be at risk for $600 more each year. With a $1,000 deductible and a Medisave account, however, the policyholder could have at least $400 in additional cash each year—and at worst would pay an additional $200 in medical expenses out of personal funds. On the other hand, if the policyholder makes it through the first 18 months without any medical expenses, the person is clearly better off with a Medisave account

---

[9]The concept of medical savings accounts was originated by Jesse Hixson, currently a health policy economist with the American Medical Association.

[10]The employee's expenses would be the $250 deductible plus a coinsurance payment of $150 (20% x $750).

Figure 8.4
GROWTH OF MEDISAVE ACCOUNTS WITH $400
ANNUAL DEPOSITS*

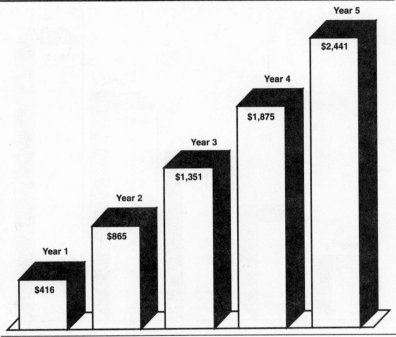

*End-of-year balance. Assumes 8 percent interest.

even with $1,000 of medical expenses in year two.[11] If the policy-holder has no medical expenses for five years, $2,441 will accumulate in the Medisave account, which would be enough to make the Medisave option profitable even with medical expenses of $1,000 for each of the next 48 years.

Medisave Accounts with a $2,500 Family Deductible

As noted above, a family in a city with average health care costs can expect to save about $1,749 in insurance premiums if it chooses

---

[11]Under a conventional policy, the insured would have to pay $400 out of personal funds. When insurance is combined with Medisave funds, however, the insured would have to pay less than $400 out of other personal funds.

Figure 8.5
GROWTH OF FAMILY MEDISAVE ACCOUNTS WITH $1,750
ANNUAL DEPOSITS*

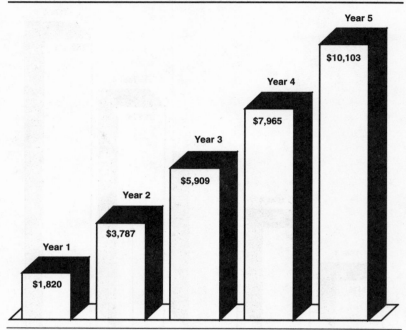

*End-of-year balance. Assumes 8 percent interest.

a $2,500 rather than a $250 deductible. Figure 8.5 shows how Medisave account balances would grow over time if none of the money were spent. Compare this Medisave option with a conventional health insurance policy. A family with a $250 deductible and a 20 percent copayment (up to $1,000) is at risk for $700 on the first $2,500 of medical expenses in any given year.[12] With the Medisave option, the family will have $1,750 in its account the first year, leaving it at risk for $750 more, or only $50 more than under a conventional policy. Allowing for interest accumulation, this family will be better off with a Medisave account even if it has $2,500 of

[12]The family's expenses would be the $250 deductible plus a copayment amount of $450 (20% × [$2,500−$250]).

246

medical expenses at the end of each year, every year, indefinitely into the future.

Encouraging Self-Insurance: A Revenue-Neutral Proposal

One way to encourage Medisave accounts without any loss of revenue to the federal government is to permit employers and employees to choose higher deductible policies and place the untaxed premium savings in Medisave accounts.[13] For employees, there would be no change in the amount reserved for health care benefits or in the total tax subsidy for employee benefits. And the change would encourage prudence, eliminate waste, and give employees greater control over their health care dollars.

Currently, many large employers maintain flexible spending accounts (FSAs) for their employees under Section 125 of the Internal Revenue Code. Under this arrangement, employees can reduce their salaries and make contributions to an individual FSA with pretax dollars. The funds are then used to purchase medical expenses at the employee's discretion. The only difference between an FSA and a Medisave account is that FSA funds are governed by a "use it or lose it" requirement. If employees fail to spend the entire amount in their FSAs in one year, they forfeit the balance.[14] Thus, FSAs create the opposite incentives of Medisave accounts; employees are penalized for not spending FSA funds. A small change in the tax law could change this perverse incentive into a positive incentive: "Use it or keep it."

Extending Medisave Accounts to Others: A Nonrevenue-Neutral Proposal

Although the federal government grants generous tax subsidies to employer-provided health insurance, a deduction of only 25 percent is given to self-employed people who purchase their own health insurance. No deduction is given for the purchase of health

[13]Under the current budget rules, any change in policy proposed in Congress must not cause a net loss of federal revenue. The forecasting techniques used to estimate revenue effects are "static" rather than "dynamic," however. Thus, forecasters tend to ignore any behavioral economic responses that would result from a change in the composition of the total amount of nontaxed employee benefits.

[14]See Alain Enthoven, "Health Policy Mismatch," *Health Affairs* (Winter 1985), pp. 5–13.

insurance by the unemployed, employees of firms that do not provide health insurance, or employees who must pay for health insurance coverage for their dependents with aftertax dollars.

Most of the 34 million Americans who lack health insurance have no tax encouragement to obtain it. One of the most effective ways to increase the number of people with health insurance would be to grant a tax deduction (or tax credit) to individuals who purchase health insurance with aftertax dollars. Because the choice to purchase health insurance would remain voluntary, this would create far fewer distortions in the labor market than would mandating employer-provided insurance.[15] At the same time we extend tax encouragement for third-party insurance to all Americans, we should also establish tax incentives to self-insure for small medical bills.[16]

Creating Medisave Accounts in Public Programs

Under the current system, the political pressures governing Medicare (for the elderly) and Medicaid (for the poor) are to expand benefits and refuse to pay for them. One consequence is increasing evidence of health care rationing. Medisave accounts could solve problems in both programs. For example, pregnant Medicaid women might have an account to draw on that they could freely spend in the medical marketplace. That would empower patients and expand the number of providers to whom they have access. Similarly, the elderly could choose higher Medicare deductibles and make deposits to their own Medisave accounts.

Medisave Accounts in Singapore

Medisave accounts have been in existence in Singapore since 1984. Unlike the proposals made here, contributions to Singapore's Medisave accounts are mandatory, being part of the government's program of insisting that people save to meet needs that might otherwise be unmet or met by the state. (A more extensive discussion of the Singapore system is given in chapter 19.)

[15]See Goodman, Robbins, and Robbins.

[16]For example, individuals might be given a tax deduction for the amount of money that would be necessary to purchase a standard $250 deductible policy. For the purchase of higher deductible policies, taxpayers could be granted the right to deposit the premium savings in Medisave accounts.

Advantages of Medical Savings Accounts

Creating individual and family Medisave accounts would represent a major departure from the current system of paying for health care. These accounts would have immediate advantages, which would become even more important over time. The 12 principal advantages are:

1. **Lowering the Cost of Health Insurance.** Medisave accounts would allow people to substitute less costly self-insurance for more costly third-party insurance for small medical bills. To the degree they are self-insured, people would no longer face premium increases caused by the wasteful consumption decisions of others. And to the extent that third-party insurance is reserved for truly risky, catastrophic events, the cost per dollar of coverage would be much lower than it is today.

2. **Lowering the Administrative Costs of Health Care.** Because we rely on third parties to pay a large part of almost every medical bill, unnecessary and burdensome paperwork is created for doctors, hospital administrators, and insurers. By one estimate, as much as $33 billion a year in administrative costs could be saved by the general use of Medisave accounts.

3. **Lowering the Cost of Health Care.** Medisave accounts would institute the only cost-control program that has ever worked—patients avoiding waste because they have a financial self-interest to do so. When people spent money from their Medisave accounts, they would be spending their own money, not someone else's—an excellent incentive to buy prudently. By one estimate, the general use of Medisave accounts would reduce total health care spending by almost one-fourth.

4. **Removing Financial Barriers to the Purchase of Health Care.** Under the current system, employers are responding to rising health insurance costs by increasing employee deductibles and copayments. Market prices are encouraging people who buy their own health insurance also to opt for high deductibles and copayments. One downside of this trend is that low-income single mothers and others who live from paycheck to paycheck may forgo medical care because they can't pay their share of the bill. Medisave accounts ensure that funds are available when the family needs them.

249

5. **Removing Financial Barriers to the Purchase of Health Insurance during Periods of Unemployment.** Under current law, people who leave an employer who had provided their health insurance are entitled to pay the premiums and extend their coverage for 18 months. Yet, the unemployed are the people least likely to be able to afford those premiums. Medisave accounts solve this problem by providing funds that are separate from those available for ordinary living expenses. Medisave funds may also be used to purchase between-school-and-work policies or between-job policies of the types already marketed.

6. **Restoring the Doctor-Patient Relationship.** Medisave accounts would give individuals direct control over their health care dollars, thereby freeing them from the arbitrary, bureaucratic constraints often imposed by third-party insurers. Physicians would see patients rather than third-party payers as the principal buyers of health care services and would be more likely to act as agents for their patients rather than for an institutional bureaucracy.

7. **Giving Patients More Control over Insured Services.** Every group health insurance plan includes some services and providers and excludes others. But the preferences of the group may not necessarily be those of the individual. In addition, state legislators are increasingly imposing their views on private group policies through mandated health insurance benefit laws. To the extent that individuals are self-insured, they could make such decisions for themselves.

8. **Enjoying the Advantages of a Competitive Medical Marketplace.** Patients who enter hospitals can neither obtain a price in advance nor understand the charges afterward. The evidence suggests that these problems have been created by our system of third-party payment and are not natural phenomena of the marketplace. When patients pay with their own money (as for cosmetic surgery in the United States and most routine surgery at private hospitals in Britain), they usually get a package price in advance and can engage in comparison shopping.

9. **Enjoying the Advantages of Real Health Insurance.** Because health insurance today is largely prepayment for consumption of medical care, people with preexisting health problems

often cannot buy insurance to cover other health risks. Medisave accounts would encourage a market for genuine catastrophic health insurance and would make such insurance available to more people.

10. **Expanding the Benefits of Self-Insurance over Time.** The funds in most Medisave accounts would grow over time, thereby enabling people to choose higher deductible policies and thus rely less on third-party insurers and increase their control over their health care dollars.

11. **Creating Incentives for Better Lifestyle Choices.** Because Medisave accounts would last over an individual's entire life, they would allow people to engage in lifetime planning and act on the knowledge that health and medical expenses are related to their lifestyle choices. People would bear more of the costs of their bad decisions and reap more of the benefits of their good ones. Those who don't smoke, eat and drink in moderation, refrain from drug use, and otherwise engage in safe conduct would realize financial rewards for their behavior.

12. **Expanding Health Insurance Options during Retirement.** Medisave accounts would eventually become an important source of funds from which to purchase health insurance or make direct payments for medical expenses not covered by Medicare during retirement. Such funds would help America solve the growing problem of long-term care for the elderly.

Using Medisave Accounts to Lower the Administrative Costs of Health Insurance

Health insurance not only creates perverse incentives, but its overuse also leads to high and unnecessary administrative costs. For example, the cost of marketing and administering private health insurance averages between 11 and 12 percent of premiums.[17] A study by the American Medical Association has estimated that a physician spends six minutes on each claim and the physician's staff spends one hour on it, and also that physicians who contract

---

[17]According to estimates by Hay/Huggins Company, the "load factor" for private health insurance ranges from 5.5 percent for groups of 10,000 or more to 40 percent for groups of fewer than five people. See Uwe E. Reinhardt, "Breaking American Health Policy Gridlock," *Health Affairs* (Summer 1991), exhibit 1, p. 100.

with outside billing services pay about $8 per claim.[18] Medisave accounts offer a way of cutting these costs dramatically while at the same time maintaining—and even improving—the quality of care.

Lowering Costs with Health Care Debit Cards

A general system of Medisave accounts would lead naturally to the use of health care debit cards. Patients could pay for physician visits by using their cards, just as people now pay for merchandise at retail stores. Several health care debit card companies already exist, including Pulse Card, headquartered in Kansas City, Kansas, and Security Plus, headquartered in Newport Beach, California.[19]

With an increase in volume and with increased competition, the administrative costs of using health care debit cards would be quite low, relative to the cost of using third-party payers. Currently, the overhead cost for credit card companies is as low as 1.29 percent. Moreover, for most transactions between patients and physicians, that would be the only administrative cost other than paperwork deemed necessary for purely medical reasons. Private and public insurers would not need additional paperwork unless total costs exceeded high patient deductibles.

Health Care Debit Cards and Medical Records

Health care debit cards could be combined with another technological innovation to reduce other costs and improve the quality of care. Several companies are experimenting with technology that would put a patient's entire medical record on a credit card.[20] That would give physicians immediate access to each patient's complete medical history. Putting medical records on a credit card could be costly. But it might be less costly than the current system under which physicians often treat patients about one-third of the time without access to their records.[21]

---

[18]American Medical Association Center for Health Policy Research, "The Administrative Burden of Health Insurance on Physicians," *SMS Report* 3, no. 2 (1989).

[19]See Burt Sims, "Cutting Health Care Costs: A Major Breakthrough," *US Business to Business* (Winter 1991).

[20]Currently, there are three competing technologies: magnetic stripe cards, smart cards (with integrated circuits), and optical memory (laser) cards. See C. Peter Waegemann, "Patient Cards—The Promise of the Future?" *Medical Practice Management* (Spring 1990), pp. 264–68.

[21]Ibid., p. 264.

The Benefits of the Canadian System without the Costs

Advocates of the Canadian system of national health insurance cite two principal benefits: (1) to receive care, patients entering the health care system need produce only a national health insurance card and (2) the administrative costs of the system are lower because paperwork is reduced and other costs, such as marketing, are eliminated.

Against these advantages, there are severe disadvantages. Because patients are actually spending other people's money when they consume free health care, the potential demand is unlimited and Canadian provincial governments control costs by limiting technology and forcing physicians and hospitals to ration health care. As Canadian waiting lists grow longer, there are increasing reports of unnecessary patient deaths and increasing numbers of Canadians crossing the border for U.S. medical care. In addition, because of the perverse incentives the system creates for providers, physicians often overprovide some services and hospital managers try to avoid the costs of acute care by housing chronic patients who use the hospitals as nursing homes (see discussion in chapter 17).

A system of Medisave accounts plus health care debit cards could produce the benefits of the Canadian system without the adverse side effects. A valid health care debit card would be proof that a patient could pay small medical bills and had third-party insurance to pay large ones. Unlike Canadians, however, U.S. patients using debit cards would have strong incentives to purchase care prudently because they would be spending their own money.

A Ballpark Estimate of the Economic Effects of Medisave Accounts

Various studies have compared administrative costs of health insurance in the United States with those of Canada's national health insurance program.[22] For example, Table 8.5 shows three

[22]For example, one study claimed that administrative costs in the United States were between 19.3 percent and 24.1 percent of total health care spending and accounted for more than half the difference in cost between the U.S. and Canadian systems. See Steffie Woolhandler and David Himmelstein, "The Deteriorating Administrative Efficiency of the U.S. Health Care System," *New England Journal of Medicine* 324, no. 18 (May 2, 1991): 1253–58. See also a critique of the study's methodology by the Health Insurance Association of America in *Medical Benefits* 8, no. 10 (May 30, 1991): 5. In another study, a national health insurance advocacy group, Citizen Fund, claimed that 33.5 cents of every dollar spent by private health insurance was for overhead expenses. See Richard Koenig, "Insurers' Overhead

estimates of the annual administrative savings that could be realized by adopting the Canadian system, as well as an estimate of the costs of eliminating out-of-pocket charges. The potential savings in administrative costs range from a Lewin/ICF estimate of $34 billion to a General Accounting Office (GAO) estimate of $67 billion.[23] However, the effect of eliminating all deductibles and copayments swamps these savings and leads to a net increase in costs.

We believe the estimates of potential savings from reduced administrative costs are much too high for three reasons. First, government accounting practices always lead to underestimates of the real cost of government provision of goods and services.[24] Second, the estimates completely ignore all indirect costs (for example, the costs of rationing and of physician and hospital responses to perverse incentives) caused by Canada's method of paying for health care. Third, many of the administrative activities in the U.S. health care system are not designed merely to control spending; they also are designed to prevent inappropriate medical care and maintain high quality. The United States is not likely to follow the Canadian practice of giving hospitals global budgets and forcing physicians to ration health care with few questions asked. (These issues are considered more fully in chapter 17.)

Nonetheless, Table 8.5 is interesting. What the GAO calculates as the rock-bottom cost of administering a health care system is probably high when compared with a system of Medisave accounts and health care debit cards. We have used the GAO method to estimate the potential reduction in administrative costs under a

Dwarfs Medicare's," *Wall Street Journal*, November 15, 1990. The results of other studies are reviewed below. For critiques of these estimates, see "GAO Report on Canadian Health Care Tainted by Charges of Partisanship," *Health Benefits Letter* 1, no. 16 (September 18, 1991); and the letters to the editor in *New England Journal of Medicine* 325, no. 18 (October 31, 1991): 1316–19. For a comprehensive comparison of administrative costs in the United States and Canada—one that concludes there is very little difference between the two countries—see Patricia M. Danzon, "The Hidden Costs of Budget Constrained Insurance," paper presented at an American Enterprise Institute conference on "American Health Policy," Washington, October 3–4, 1991.

[23]See General Accounting Office, *Canadian Health Insurance: Lessons for the United States* (June 1991).

[24]See E. S. Savas, "How Much Do Government Services Really Cost?" *Urban Affairs Quarterly* (September 1979), p. 24.

Table 8.5
Estimates of the Economic Effects of Adopting the Canadian System in the United States

	Lewin/ICF	Physicians for a National Health Program	General Accounting Office
Savings in administrative costs			
Insurance overhead	−$22	−$27	−$34
Physician administrative expenses	−1	−9	−15
Hospital administrative expenses	−11	−31	−18
Total decrease in administrative costs	−$34	−$57	−$67
Expansion of coverage			
For the currently insured (based on Rand estimate)[1]	+$54	+$54	+$54
For the currently uninsured (based on Rand estimate)[1]	+19	+19	+19
Total increase resulting from coverage expansion	+73	+73	+73
Total net effect	+$39	+$16	+$6

SOURCE: General Accounting Office, *Canadian Health Insurance: Lessons for the United States*, June 1991, pp. 62–67; L. S. Lewin and J. Sheils, *National Health Spending under Alternative Universal Access Proposals* (Washington: Lewin/ICF, October 26, 1990); prepared for the AFL–CIO; and K. Grumbach et al., "Liberal Benefits, Conservative Spending: The Physicians for a National Health Program Proposal," *Journal of the American Medical Association* 265, no. 19 (May 15, 1991): 2549–54.

[1]Based on GAO estimates for increased hospital spending and GAO estimates increased to reflect the Rand Corporation results for physician spending.

Table 8.6
ECONOMIC EFFECTS OF COMBINING UNIVERSAL HEALTH
INSURANCE WITH MEDISAVE ACCOUNTS AND HEALTH CARE
DEBIT CARDS

	Change in Costs ($ Billion)	
	---	---
Adjustment	Low Estimate	High Estimate
Savings in administrative costs[1]		
Insurance overhead	− $8	− $17
Physician administrative expenses	− 5	− 10
Hospital administrative expenses	− 3	− 6
Total	− 16	− 33
Coverage for the currently uninsured[2]	+ 12	+ 12
Behavioral response[3]	− 90	− 147
Total net effect	− $94	− $168

[1]Based on GAO estimates of the potential savings in administrative costs with the following adjustments: For high estimate, one-half of GAO savings attained in reduced insurance overhead, two-thirds of savings attained in reduced physician administrative costs, and one-third of savings attained in reduced hospital administrative costs; for low estimate, one-half of those amounts. See General Accounting Office, *Canadian Health Insurance: Lessons for the United States* (June 1991), Table 5.1 (p. 63).
[2]Based on GAO and Lewin/ICF estimates. See J. Needleman et al., *The Health Care Financing System and the Uninsured* (Washington: Lewin/ICF, April 4, 1990), prepared for the Health Care Financing Administration.
[3]Based on Rand Corporation estimates. For high estimate, 23 percent reduction in total health care costs, excluding insurance overhead, research, and public health expenditures; for low estimate, spending is reduced by 45 percent for physicians and 10 percent for hospitals.

system of Medisave accounts and debit cards, and the Rand Corporation's method to estimate the likely reduction in health care spending if people had high-deductible health insurance. Table 8.6 shows the probable effects of a generalized system under which everyone (including Medicaid and Medicare patients) has third-party catastrophic insurance and uses health care debit cards, drawing on individual Medisave accounts to pay small medical bills. As the table shows, a system that combines catastrophic third-party insurance with Medisave accounts should reduce administrative

costs by as much as $33 billion. Because the presence of high deduct-
ibles would make patients more prudent purchasers of health care,
total spending should go down by as much as $147 billion. After
extending catastrophic health insurance to the currently uninsured,
the net total savings are $168 billion, or almost one-fourth of what
the United States now spends on health care.

Twenty Questions and Answers about Medisave Accounts

1. How would Medisave accounts be administered? Medisave
accounts would be administered by qualified financial institutions
in much the same way as individual retirement accounts (IRAs) are.
Individuals could exercise choice over the investment of account
balances, with the same restrictions on the types of instruments the
accounts could own as now apply to IRAs.

2. How would funds from Medisave accounts be spent? The
simplest method would be by debit card. Patients would use their
debit cards to satisfy payment at the time medical services were
rendered. At the end of each month, the account holders' statements would show recent expenses and account balances. No more
paperwork would be needed than with any other credit card.

3. What would prevent fraud and abuse? To receive Medisave
funds, a provider of medical services would have to be qualified
under IRS rules. Qualifying should be a simple procedure, involving little more than the filing of a one-page form. But if IRS auditors
discovered fraudulent behavior, the provider would lose the right to
receive Medisave funds and would be subject to criminal penalties.

**4. What types of services could be purchased with Medisave
funds?** Any type of expense considered a medical expense under
current IRS rules would qualify. In general, the IRS has been fairly
broad in its interpretation of what constitutes a medical expense.
An unhealthy step in the wrong direction, however, was the IRS
decision to disallow cosmetic surgery. There is no apparent reason
why the removal of a disfiguring scar or a change in facial appearance that improves employability and self-esteem is any less important than an orthopedic operation that allows an individual to play
a better game of tennis or polo.

5. What tax advantages would be created for Medisave deposits?
Medisave deposits would receive the same tax treatment as health
insurance premiums. Thus, under employer-provided health insurance plans, Medisave deposits would escape federal income taxes,

FICA taxes, and state and local income taxes. If the opportunity to receive a tax deduction or a tax credit for the purchase of health insurance were extended to individuals, their deposits to Medisave accounts would receive the same tax treatment. Medisave balances would grow tax free and would never be taxed if the funds were used to pay for medical care or purchase long-term care or long-term care insurance.

6. What about low-income families who cannot afford to make Medisave deposits? If low-income families can afford to buy health insurance, they can afford to make Medisave deposits, since the primary purpose of the Medisave option is to enable individuals to divide their normal health insurance costs into two parts: self-insurance and third-party insurance. Currently, no tax subsidy is available for people who purchase health insurance on their own. Health insurance would become more affordable for the currently uninsured if they could deduct some or all of the premiums from their taxable income. It would become even more affordable through a system of refundable tax credits, which would grant greater tax relief to low-income people.

7. How could individuals build up funds in their Medisave accounts? One way would be to choose a higher deductible insurance policy and deposit the premium savings in the Medisave account. For most people, a year or two of such deposits would exceed the amount of their insurance deductible. Young people and people in low-cost areas might be allowed to make even larger deposits. An alternative (which tends to be revenue-neutral for the federal government) would be to permit people to reduce the amount of their annual, tax-deductible contributions to IRAs, 401(k) plans, and other pensions and deposit the difference in a Medisave account.

8. What if medical expenses not covered by health insurance exceeded the balance in an individual's Medisave account? One solution would be to establish a line of credit so that individuals could effectively borrow to pay medical expenses. Repayment would be made with future Medisave deposits or other personal funds. Another solution would be to adopt Singapore's practice of permitting family members to share their Medisave funds. This concern would vanish as Medisave balances grew over time.

9. How would members of the same family manage their Medisave accounts? Because family members often are covered under the same health insurance policy, it seems desirable to permit couples to own joint Medisave accounts and for parents to own family Medisave accounts. In those cases, more than one person could spend from a single account. But even if family members maintained separate accounts, that should not preclude the pooling of family resources to pay medical bills.

10. What about people who are already sick and have large medical obligations at the time the plan is started? Such people might be harmed by a sudden increase in the health insurance deductible unless transitional arrangements were made. Most would benefit from a high deductible in the long run but they might suffer financially at the outset. One solution is for employers to extend credit to employees who are especially disadvantaged, with the loan to be repaid from future Medisave contributions. Another solution is for employers to bear part of the burden of those expenses (in the case of special hardship) during the transition period.

11. What about people who have a catastrophic illness with large annual medical bills likely to last indefinitely into the future? Most of these people would be disadvantaged if they have an annual deductible. A better form of health insurance would be one with a per condition deductible, in which the deductible would be paid only once for an extended illness.

12. Are there circumstances under which individuals could withdraw Medisave funds for nonmedical expenses prior to retirement? A reasonable policy is to apply the same rules that now apply to tax-deferred savings plans (for example, IRAs and 401(k) plans). Thus, nonmedical withdrawals would be fully taxed and would face an additional 10 percent tax penalty.

13. How do we know people would not forgo needed medical care (including preventive care) in order to conserve their Medisave funds? We don't. The theory behind Medisave accounts is that people should have a store of personal funds with which to purchase medical care. And because the money they spend would be their own, they would have strong incentives to make prudent decisions. Undoubtedly, some of their decisions would be wrong. But many decisions made under the current system also are wrong. Unlike the current system, people would at least have funds on hand with which to pay their share of medical bills. And, since people would have an incentive to protect future account balances against future medical costs, some would certainly spend more on preventive health care. Because we cannot spend our entire GNP on health, health care has to be rationed in some way. The only alternative to national health insurance, with rationing decisions made by a health care bureaucracy, is self-rationing, with individuals making their own choices between money and medical services.

14. Given the increasing complexity of medical science, how can individuals possibly make wise decisions when spending their Medisave funds? One thing people can do is solicit advice from others who claim to have superior knowledge. For example, most large employers and practically all insurance companies have cost-management programs in which teams of experts make judgments about whether, when, and where medical procedures will be performed. These experienced professionals could play an important role in helping patients make decisions about complicated and expensive procedures. But the professionals' role will be as advice givers only. We should let the experts advise and the patient decide. Moreover, the fact that individuals would maintain Medisave accounts would not preclude their taking advantage of employer-negotiated price discounts from providers or managed care programs.

15. Given the problems that major employers and insurance companies have in negotiating with hospitals, how can individual patients possibly do better? The reason large institutions have so much difficulty negotiating with hospitals is that the institution is not the patient. And the reason patients spending their own money would wield effective power is the same reason consumers wield power in every market—they can take their money and go elsewhere. Physicians, hospitals, and other health care providers would have considerable incentive to win their business. Moreover, Medisave accounts would not preclude individuals from using employers as bargaining agents.

16. What would happen to Medisave account balances at retirement? People should be able to roll over their Medisave funds into an IRA or some other pension fund. Thus, money not spent on medical care could be used, after taxes, to purchase other goods and services. Alternatively, Medisave balances could be maintained to purchase postretirement health care or long-term care or long-term care insurance.

17. What would prevent wealthy individuals from misusing Medisave accounts to shelter large amounts of tax-deferred income? An individual's total tax-advantaged expense for health insurance plus Medisave deposits could not exceed a reasonable amount. One definition of "reasonable" would be an annual Medisave deposit that would equal the deductible for a standard catastrophic health insurance policy.

18. What about people who join HMOs? They would have the same opportunities as those who join conventional, fee-for-service health insurance plans. Note that because many HMOs are now instituting deductibles, HMO members would have incentives to acquire Medisave accounts. Their HMO premiums plus their deposits to Medisave accounts could not exceed a reasonable amount, however.

19. Under employer-provided plans, would employees have a choice of deductibles? Permitting employees to make individual choices makes sense. Over time, different people would have different accumulations in their Medisave accounts and, quite likely, different preferences about health insurance deductibles. However, under current law, employers have the option of fashioning employee benefit plans, even though it is in their self-interest to create a plan that is most pleasing to employees, given the overall cost. As a practical political matter, it seems wise to continue that feature of the current system.

20. What would happen to flexible spending accounts now available to some employees? Medisave accounts would replace FSAs under employee benefits law. Currently, employees who make deposits to FSAs must use the money or lose it, typically within 12 months. Similar deposits made to Medisave accounts would have no such restrictions.

9. Cost-Plus Medicine and the Tax Law

Principally operating through the tax law, federal policy has shaped and molded employer-provided health insurance plans. In general, federal policy encourages and rewards first-dollar health insurance coverage and other wasteful, inefficient practices. At the same time, federal policy discourages reasonable attempts by employers to eliminate perverse incentives and reduce spiraling health care costs. To make matters worse, federal policy toward employer-provided health insurance is inextricably intertwined with federal policy toward other employee benefits, especially for large corporations. As a result, it is probably not possible to reform the health insurance system without reforming the entire employee benefits system.

Tax deductions for employee benefits totaled about $105 billion in 1990 and are expected to climb to $131 billion in 1992.[1] That is the amount of money not collected in taxes because employee benefits are excluded from taxable wages. On the average, for every dollar the government collects in personal income taxes, about 25 cents goes uncollected because of employee benefits. But for the exclusion for employee benefits, the marginal income tax rate faced by American workers could be 4 percentage points lower.[2] As a result, the "tax expenditure" for all employee benefits amounts to about $450 per year for every man, woman, and child in the country, or about $1,035 for every American family.

Ostensibly, these large tax subsidies for employee benefits exist because the federal government wants to promote general social goals. Yet, under the current system, those goals are not being met

[1]Estimate based on *Special Analyses, Budget of the United States* (1990), Table G-2, and "Estimates for Tax Expenditure in the Income Tax," *Budget of the United States for Fiscal Year 1992*, Table XI-1.

[2]For example, people in the 15 percent income tax bracket could otherwise be in the 11 percent tax bracket; people in the 28 percent tax bracket could otherwise be in the 24 percent bracket, etc.

in a reasonable way. The system is inequitable, affecting different families in radically different ways. It creates a false sense of security by misleading workers about the size of their expected retirement benefits. It encourages waste and inefficiency in the medical marketplace, thereby contributing to spiraling health care costs.

Tax subsidies for employee benefits are distributed in a highly arbitrary way. For example, the tax expenditure for employer-provided health insurance alone is about $60 billion a year, or roughly $600 for every American family. But the current system subsidizes lavish health care plans for some workers, whereas others have no opportunity to receive the tax subsidy. Tax-deductible health insurance expenditures range from a high of $3,055 per worker in the automobile industry[3] to as little as $793 for workers in retail trade.[4] Although the auto workers' plans are fully deductible, self-employed individuals are allowed to deduct only 25 percent of their health insurance premiums, and even that deduction has an uncertain future. Unemployed workers and employees of firms that do not provide health insurance receive no tax subsidy for the health insurance they purchase.

In general, the problem of a large population of uninsured people is a creation of the tax law. Most of the 34 million Americans who lack health insurance have no opportunity to purchase it with pretax dollars. At the same time, current law encourages waste and imprudence among those who do have health insurance.

Federal Tax Law and Employee Benefits

Federal tax law has an enormous impact on the employee benefits plans of employers precisely because marginal tax rates are so high. Even a moderate wage earner in the U.S. economy gets to keep less than 70 cents out of each additional dollar earned. The federal income tax rate for this worker is 15 percent and the combined (employer plus employee) Social Security tax rate is 15.3 percent. Thus, federal taxes take 30.3 cents out of each additional dollar of

[3]Aldona Robbins and Gary Robbins, *What a Canadian-Style Health Care System Would Cost U.S. Employers and Employees,* NCPA Policy Report no. 145 (Dallas: National Center for Policy Analysis, February 1990).

[4]Aldona Robbins, Gary Robbins, and John C. Goodman, *Employee Benefits: The Case for Radical Reform,* NCPA Policy Report no. 147 (Dallas: National Center for Policy Analysis, March 1990).

Table 9.1
AFTERTAX VALUE OF A DOLLAR OF MONEY WAGES

Federal Tax Category[1]	Value with No State and Local Income Tax	Value with State and Local Income Tax
FICA tax only	85¢	81¢[2]
FICA tax plus 15 percent income tax	70	64[3]
FICA tax plus 28 percent income tax	57	51[3]

[1]Includes employer's share of FICA taxes.
[2]State and local income tax rates equal 4 percent.
[3]State and local income tax rates equal 6 percent.

wages. If this employee faces a 6 percent state and local income tax, the marginal tax rate is 36.3 percent, leaving the employee with less than two-thirds of a dollar of wages in the form of take-home pay. As Table 9.1 shows, workers in the 28 percent federal income tax bracket face a marginal tax rate of 43.3 percent, leaving them with less than 57 cents in take-home pay out of each additional dollar of earnings. If state and local income taxes apply, the situation is much worse. Indeed, millions of American workers take home just about 50 cents of each additional dollar of earnings.

Such high tax rates give employers and employees strong incentives to replace wages with nontaxable benefits in employees' compensation packages. Those incentives are irresistible if employees would have purchased the benefits anyway. But even if they would not have, federal tax law makes certain benefits very attractive. For example, Table 9.2 shows the value of health insurance benefits relative to the payment of a dollar of wages. For a worker in the 15 percent tax bracket, federal tax law makes a dollar of wages equivalent to $1.43 in health care benefits. For a worker in the 28 percent bracket, a dollar of wages is equivalent to $1.76 in health care benefits.[5]

[5]The value of the benefit equals $1/(1-t)$, where t is the marginal federal income tax rate plus the combined employer-employee Social Security payroll tax rate. For a worker in the 15 percent bracket, $t = 0.15 + 0.153$. For a worker in the 28 percent bracket, $t = 0.28 + 0.153$.

Table 9.2
RELATIVE VALUE OF A DOLLAR OF EMPLOYER-PROVIDED
HEALTH INSURANCE BENEFITS

Federal Tax Category[1]	Value with No State and Local Income Tax	Value with State and Local Income Tax
FICA tax only	$1.18	$1.24[2]
FICA tax plus 15 percent income tax	1.43	1.57[3]
FICA tax plus 28 percent income tax	1.76	1.97[3]

[1]Includes employer's share of FICA taxes.
[2]State and local income tax rate equals 4 percent.
[3]State and local income tax rate equals 6 percent.

If an employer were to pay a worker in the 28 percent federal income tax bracket $1.76 in wages, the worker's take-home pay would be only $1.00 after taxes. On the other hand, if the $1.76 is spent on nontaxed health care benefits, the worker gets $1.76 of benefits.

Nontaxed employee benefits become even more lucrative if workers face state and local taxes. Consider workers facing a 6 percent state and local income tax rate, for example. For a worker in the 15 percent federal income tax bracket, the combined effect of all taxes is to make a dollar of wages equivalent to $1.57 of employee benefits. For a worker in the 28 percent bracket, the combined effect of all taxes is to make a dollar of wages equivalent to $1.97 of benefits.

Table 9.2 also shows how much waste can be present in the purchase of health insurance and still allow health insurance to be preferable to wages. (See Figure 9.1.) For example, if an employer attempted to give a higher paid employee $1.97 in wages, the employee's take-home pay would be only $1.00 after taxes. As a result, $1.97 spent on health insurance need only be worth $1.01 to be preferable to $1.97 of gross wages. Thus, 96 cents (or 49 percent of the premium) can represent pure waste and still leave health insurance more attractive than wages.

Given these incentives, it is small wonder that employers and employees respond. For example, on the average, workers in durable goods manufacturing receive employee benefits equal to 19

Figure 9.1
How Much Waste Can Be Present in Health Insurance and Still Leave Health Insurance As Valuable As the Payment of Wages?

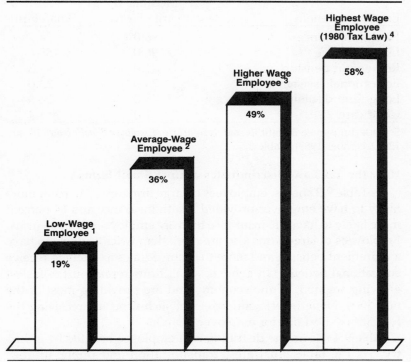

[1]Low-wage employee faces a 15 percent FICA tax and a 4 percent state and local income tax.
[2]Average-wage employee faces a 15 percent FICA tax, a 15 percent federal income tax, and a 6 percent state and local income tax.
[3]Higher wage employee faces a 15 percent FICA tax, a 28 percent federal income tax, and a 6 percent state and local income tax.
[4]Highest wage employee faced a 50 percent federal income tax and an 8 percent state and local income tax in 1980.

percent of earnings. For a manufacturing worker in the 28 percent tax bracket, that means that employee benefits are equal to about 25 percent of take-home pay.

Table 9.3
PERCENT OF EMPLOYEES WITH BENEFITS, 1988

| | Employees with Benefits | |
Employee Benefit	Medium & Large Firms	Small Firms
Health insurance	96.0%	74.7%
Life insurance	96.0	58.6
Retirement pension	91.0	43.3
Educational assistance	76.0	23.0
Long-term disability insurance	48.0	25.6
Child care	1.0	4.3

SOURCE: Employee Benefit Research Institute, *Employee Benefit Notes* 10, no. 12 (December 1989), Table 3.

How the Tax Law Discriminates against Small Firms

As Table 9.3 shows, employees of large firms are 29 percent more likely to have employer-provided health insurance and 64 percent more likely to have life insurance than are employees of small firms. Employees of large firms also are more than twice as likely to have a retirement pension and more than three times as likely to receive educational benefits. In general, small firms represent the fastest growing segment of the economy and are providing most of the new jobs. Nonetheless, employees of such firms are receiving the fewest tax subsidies for employee benefits.

Table 9.4 shows the distribution of employee benefits by industry. As the table illustrates, transportation and public utilities employees on the average receive $4,802 per year in nontaxed benefits, while retail employees receive only $1,161. That means that the tax subsidy for transportation and public utilities employees is more than four times greater. Why do small firms (and industries dominated by small firms) provide fewer employee benefits? One reason is that federal tax law governing employee benefits discriminates against small firms.

Interference with Labor Market Contracts

In general, the more competitive a market, the more essential it is that workers receive a compensation package equal to the value of what they produce. The smaller the firm, the more important is this principle. Workers with different skills must receive a different

Table 9.4
EMPLOYEE BENEFITS BY INDUSTRY

Industry	Average Annual Earnings	Average Annual Benefits
Transportation and public utilities	$25,678	$4,802
Mining	29,022	4,527
Durable goods manufacturing	23,809	4,519
Construction	26,142	4,078
Nondurable goods manufacturing	20,307	2,692
Wholesale trade	20,406	2,408
Finance, insurance, and real estate	17,630	2,080
Services[1]	15,746	1,968
Retail trade	9,839	1,161

SOURCES: Employer-provided benefits as a percentage of earnings are from the U.S. Chamber of Commerce, *Employee Benefits, 1988 Edition, Survey Data from Benefit Year 1987* (Washington, March 1989). Earnings are derived from average weekly earnings for July 1989, published by the U.S. Bureau of Labor Statistics.
[1]Estimate based on the average employee benefit as a percentage of earnings (12.5 percent) for all other industries.

total compensation, and the form of the compensation package must be the one most preferred by the worker. The easiest way to achieve this objective is for the employer and each employee to agree on the total amount of compensation and for the employee to choose the specifics (that is, how much in wages, how much in health insurance, etc.). Employee benefits law, however, is designed to prevent benefit packages from being tailored to individual needs. The philosophy implicit in employee benefits law is that all employees should receive the same benefit, and that employees should not be able to choose between taxable wages and nontaxed benefits. This approach to employee benefits is harmful for small firms in competitive markets.

Burdensome Administrative Costs and Unreasonable Compliance Rules

Because complying with the rules and regulations that govern employee benefits is so costly, many employee benefits programs allowed under the tax code can be administered only by large firms, which can spread the costs over very large numbers of employees. Giving employees choices in a cafeteria of benefits, allowing them to pay their share of health insurance premiums with pretax dollars, and allowing them to pay their deductibles and copayments with pretax dollars through flexible spending accounts are just a few of the opportunities that high administrative costs keep out of reach of small firms.

The Two-Tier System

As a result of the discrimination against small businesses, America is developing a two-tier system with respect to health insurance, retirement pensions, and other benefits. On the one hand, some large companies provide cradle-to-grave benefits for each stage in a worker's life: marriage, pregnancy, child rearing, divorce, retirement, and death. Many large companies now offer day care and elder care for dependents, medical coverage for step-children in remarriages, and job search assistance for a spouse when a two-career couple relocates.[6] On the other hand, about 18.5 million employees lack health insurance[7] and 52 million lack a private pension.[8]

Moreover, those who have the greatest benefits tend to have above-average incomes, and vice versa. As Table 9.4 shows, industries in which employees have the highest incomes are the industries that offer the highest benefits (both in absolute terms and as a percentage of income).

How the Tax Law Distorts Health Insurance Pricing in Large Firms

The original Blue Cross vision was of a system in which everyone is charged the same premium regardless of risk. In such a system, healthy people are overcharged, sicker people are undercharged, and individual health insurance premiums bear no relationship to the underlying cost of providing that insurance. In the 1990s, the

---

[6]"More Benefits Bend with Workers' Needs," *Wall Street Journal*, January 9, 1990.

[7]Employee Benefit Research Institute, *Update: Americans without Health Insurance*, EBRI Issue Brief no. 104 (July 1990), Table 5 (p. 12).

[8]Employee Benefit Research Institute, *Pension Coverage and Benefit Entitlement: New Findings from 1988*, EBRI Issue Brief no. 94 (September 1989), Table 1 (p. 7).

original Blue Cross vision of health insurance has largely vanished. Only a handful of Blue Cross plans still practice community rating, and even those usually vary their premiums by age. The philosophy still reigns, however, within large corporations.

Most large companies not only provide health insurance, they also adopt an artificial, internal pricing system under which all employees face the same premium, regardless of age, job task, or other indicators of health risk. For example, take the Foster Higgins estimate that employee health costs averaged $3,200 in 1990[9] and assume that a 60-year-old employee has four times the expected health care costs of a 20-year-old. As Table 9.5 shows, assigning the same premium to both results in a premium that—when compared with expected real costs—is $1,920 too high for the younger worker and $1,920 too low for the older worker.

If the employer pays the full premium, then it makes no real difference how individual premiums are assigned for accounting purposes. But most employers ask employees to pay part of the premium out of their gross wages, and the trend is to increase the employees' share.[10] For example, Table 9.5 also shows what the employee's share of the premium would be if employees are asked to pay half the total premium ($1,600) out of wages. In this case, even though the 20-year-old employee pays only one-half the premium, the charge is still $320 higher than the real cost of the insurance.

A younger employee who must pay the employee's share of the premium with aftertax dollars has an incentive to forgo the coverage and keep the money, or search for a cheaper (more accurately priced) policy elsewhere. Even if employees can pay their share of the premium with pretax dollars,[11] younger employees may still decide to forgo the employer's offer and buy a no-frills policy (for a cheaper price) with aftertax dollars. Thus, artificially charging all employees the same price encourages younger employees to forgo

[9]A. Foster Higgins & Co., *Health Care Benefits Survey 1990,* Report no. 1, p. 5.

[10]In 1990, 57 percent of employers required their employees to contribute an average of 22 percent of the costs of their health insurance coverage, and 80 percent required an average contribution of 29 percent for family coverage. See A. Foster Higgins & Co., pp. 11–12.

[11]For a discussion of the provisions in the tax law, see Alain Enthoven, "Health Tax Policy Mismatch," *Health Affairs* (Winter 1985), pp. 5–13.

Table 9.5
EFFECTS OF ARTIFICIAL PRICING OF HEALTH INSURANCE IN LARGE COMPANIES
(Annual Gross Premiums)

Category	Cost for Employee Age 20	Cost for Employee Age 60	Total
	Same Premium		
Artificial premium	$3,200	$3,200	$6,400
Real cost	−1,280	−5,120	−6,400
Difference	+$1,920	−$1,920	0
	Employee Cost Sharing		
Real cost of total premium	$1,280	$5,120	$6,400
Employee's share of artificial premium (50%)	−1,600	−1,600	−3,200
Net loss/gain to employee	−$320	+$3,520	+$3,200

coverage under their employers' plans. A similar argument applies to the purchase of employer-provided health insurance for employees' dependents.[12]

One way to think about the U.S. economy in relation to that of other developed countries is to recognize that corporate employee benefits plans in the United States pursue many of the same ends that are pursued through political systems elsewhere. Whereas European countries charge tax prices unrelated to the real cost of the health insurance that government provides for any particular person, the U.S. corporation also charges a common premium unrelated to expected benefits. Our answer to the European welfare state is the corporate welfare state.

Because corporations are free to act differently, why don't they? One reason may be historical accident and inertia. Unquestionably, employers were encouraged to adopt internal community rating by Blue Cross and other insurers in the early days. Moreover, at the time when many large companies started their health benefits programs, the cost of insurance was so low that it was not cost-effective to spend much time, effort, and money trying to fit differential premiums to differences in employee risks. But now that health insurance costs are so high, why not change?

In a perfectly competitive market, each employee receives wages plus fringe benefits exactly equal to what the employee produces. But in imperfect labor markets, especially those regulated by tax law and employee benefits law, employers may find it in their self-interest to continue the current practice. For one thing, charging every employee the same premium helps create the appearance of equity. For another, employers may benefit when younger, lower paid employees (for whom wages are likely to be more important than fringe benefits) voluntarily forgo coverage. The fewer the number of participants in the company health plan, the lower the total cost. Employers may also gain because of the tax law.

Table 9.6 continues the example of Table 9.5, by comparing two different ways of charging health insurance premiums to employees: (1) premiums based on real actuarial costs and (2) an artificial, same-for-all premium. In both cases, we assume that the aftertax

---

[12]This fact may help explain why one of the fast-growing segments of the market for individual and family policies is for dependents of employees.

Table 9.6
TAX CONSEQUENCES OF ARTIFICIAL PRICING OF HEALTH INSURANCE IN LARGE COMPANIES

Category	Employee Age 20	Employee Age 60	Total
Actuarially Fair Pricing			
Real cost	$1,280	$5,120	$6,400
Employee's share (50%)	640	2,560	3,200
Gross wage needed to pay employee's share aftertax	918[1]	4,515[2]	5,433
Taxes on gross wage	278[1]	1,955[2]	2,233
Artificial Pricing			
Artificial price	$3,200	$3,200	$6,400
Employee's share (50%)	1,600	1,600	3,200
Gross wage needed to pay employee's share aftertax	2,296[1]	2,822[2]	5,118
Taxes	696[1]	1,222[2]	1,918

[1] Assumes 15 percent income tax and 15.3 percent FICA tax.
[2] Assumes 28 percent income tax and 15.3 percent FICA tax.

274

wage plus health insurance coverage is the same for the employees. Given that assumption, employees should be indifferent about the two options. However, less total tax will be paid if the company adopts artificial premiums. In this example, employees are assumed to pay one-half the premium with aftertax dollars. With actuarially fair pricing, employers will pay gross wages of $5,433, out of which $2,233 will be paid in taxes—leaving $3,200 to pay the employees' share of premiums for the two workers. The older employee is assumed to be in a higher income tax bracket, however (28 percent as opposed to 15 percent). Accordingly, less total tax will be paid if the older employee is charged an artificially low premium (requiring a lower gross wage) and the younger employee an artificially high premium (requiring a higher gross wage). In this case, same-for-all premiums result in a tax savings of $315.

Although $315 may seem like a small sum, for a company with 1,000 employees that figure amounts to $315,000 a year. With 10,000 employees, the figure becomes $3.15 million. Of course, companies will not typically have only young and old workers, so the total savings will be smaller than indicated in these examples. Nonetheless, it seems clear that switching to a system of actuarially fair premiums would increase the tax burden for almost any large company and its employees in cases in which employees must pay their share of premiums with aftertax dollars. That is one way the tax law encourages the current system.

If employees are able to pay their share of premiums with pretax dollars, as an increasing number are, there are no tax advantages from artificial pricing for active employees. But if a company has retirees on the same plan, the tax law encourages artificial pricing in another way. If the 60-year-old in the previous example is retired, the retiree's share of the premium must be paid with aftertax dollars even though active workers can pay their share of the premium with pretax dollars. In this case, actuarially fair premiums would cost the retiree an additional $960 (50% × $5,120 − $1,600). To pay this additional premium, a retiree in the 28 percent income tax bracket would need $1,333 in additional pretax pension income. Thus, artificial pricing enables the employer to give retirees a $1,333 benefit for a cost of only $960, saving $373 per retiree.

How the Tax Law Contributes to Escalating Health Care Costs

Almost nine out of ten Americans who have health insurance acquire it through an employer, and the type of health insurance that employers provide responds to the incentives and obeys the regulations of the tax code. The following is a list of just four of the ways in which the tax law encourages waste and discourages prudence in the purchase of health care.

First, the tax law subsidizes overinsurance. In general, federal tax subsidies for employer-provided health insurance are unlimited. The more lavish the benefit, the greater the subsidy. Firms that choose scaled-down, no-frills health insurance are penalized with reduced tax subsidies.

Second, the tax law encourages first-dollar health insurance coverage. Under the current system, any medical bill paid by employer-provided health insurance is subsidized through the tax system. At the same time, no subsidy is available for those who save to pay small medical bills out-of-pocket.[13]

Third, the tax law severs the relationship between health insurance benefits and employee wages. The easiest way for employers to escape the burden of rising health care costs is to let their employees choose whatever health insurance plan they prefer and to deduct the premium for each employee's health insurance from that employee's pretax salary. Health insurance would then become a dollar-for-dollar substitute for wages, and employees would enjoy maximum choice and still get the advantages of a tax subsidy for health insurance. Such an arrangement would also have other advantages. With a direct link between salary and health insurance premiums, employees would be more prudent about their policy choices. Those who want policies with no deductibles and all the bells and whistles, for example, would pay the full premium cost in the form of a salary reduction. Faced with this choice, employees are more likely to choose high-deductible, no-frills catastrophic insurance. In general, however, employee health insurance cannot be individualized in this way, even for large companies. Employee benefits law encourages (and in many cases requires) employers to adopt the same policy for all employees. Often, employees have no idea what the premiums are. In those cases where they are made

---

[13]One exception is the ability to pay medical bills through flexible spending accounts (FSAs). This option is governed by a use-it-or-lose-it policy, however. In addition, medical expenses are tax deductible to the extent that they exceed 7.5 percent of income.

aware (for example, when they are asked to pay part of the premium), each is charged the same premium, regardless of age, sex, place of work, type of work, or any other factor that affects real premium costs. The upshot is that, for the individual employee, there is no relationship between the cost of employer-provided health insurance and personal take-home pay. Small wonder that employees of large companies demand lavish health care benefits. From the perspective of employees, there is no reason not to make such demands.

Fourth, the tax law penalizes cost-control efforts. Under the conventional health plans of most corporations, there is no direct relationship—for the individual employee—between salary and the value of health insurance benefits. Similarly, there is no relationship between salary and wasteful, imprudent health care purchases. In general, employees who act as prudent buyers of health care cannot reap any cash reward for doing so without tax penalty, thereby reflecting a use-it-or-lose-it national health policy. Employees also have no opportunity (under the tax law) to opt out of an employer plan and purchase a less expensive policy on their own.

How the Tax Law Is Contributing to the Rising Number of People Who Lack Health Insurance

One of the great ironies of employee benefits law is that, although it was designed to encourage the purchase of health insurance, some of its most perverse provisions are now causing an increasing number of people to be without health insurance. Because employers cannot individualize health insurance benefits, many are turning to other practices to control their health insurance costs, and those practices are causing an increasing number of people to be without insurance.

For example, an increasing number of smaller firms are responding to rising health insurance premiums by canceling their group policies. Often, employers give employees a bonus or a raise to compensate them for eliminating the health insurance benefit and to encourage them to purchase individual policies (with aftertax dollars) on their own. But, of course, many employees do not.

Many large firms are asking employees to pay (with aftertax dollars) a larger share of the premium. Some employers pay most of the premium for the employee, but ask employees to pay a much larger share for their dependents. As a result, some employees opt out of the employer's group health insurance plan. More frequently, they drop coverage for their dependents. More than three million people who lack health insurance are dependents of employees who are themselves insured.[14]

How the Tax Law Discourages Saving for Postretirement Medical Expenses

One of the most frightening social problems we face as we move toward the next century is how to pay for retirement pensions and medical care for the elderly. Because both Social Security and Medicare are pay-as-you-go programs, tomorrow's obligations will have to be met almost totally by taxes on tomorrow's workers. The bill will be high (see chapter 13). Clearly, the need is to arrange a system in which the elderly can pay more of their own medical expenses and relieve future workers of an almost impossible burden. But for that to happen, there must be increased saving by today's workers to meet postretirement medical needs.

Although the federal government subsidizes spending on current medical needs to the tune of $60 billion per year, individuals have no opportunity to engage in tax-subsidized savings for postretirement medical needs.[15] Corporations are also greatly constrained in their ability to put aside funds today for the postretirement health care expenses of their employees. As a result, the tax law discourages both individuals and employers from saving and investing today to pay for future health care.

Principles That Should Guide Public Policy

Given that our analysis of federal policy toward employee benefits in general and employer-provided health insurance in particular has been highly critical, we conclude this chapter by considering a good public policy toward employee benefits. The need for radical reform is urgent. That reform should be guided by the following seven principles.

[14]Employee Benefit Research Institute, *A Profile of the Nonelderly Population without Health Insurance*, EBRI Issue Brief no. 66 (May 1987): 7.

[15]Jonathan C. Dopkeen, *Postretirement Health Benefits*, Pew Memorial Trust Policy Synthesis 2, Health Services Research 21, no. 6 (February 1987): 810.

1. **The tax subsidy for any employee benefit should be made available to all Americans on equal terms, regardless of the nature of employment.** If there are valid social goals (health insurance, retirement pensions, day care, etc.) that merit special encouragement through use of the tax system, no taxpayer should receive more encouragement than any other at the same income level. All Americans should have equal access to tax subsidies, and that access should not be governed by one's employment.

2. **All employee benefits should be individualized (a specific amount of money attributed to a specific employee), and each worker's annual employee benefits should be recorded as part of the employee's gross compensation.** Few if any employees know the value or cost of the benefits they receive as individuals.[16] That has at least four adverse consequences. First, the current system perpetuates the myth that employee benefits are gifts from employers, rather than something that employees have earned. Second, the system permits older workers (who usually make the decisions about employee benefits packages) to reap subsidies from younger workers in socially undesirable ways. Third, the system perpetuates a retirement pension and retirement health care system under which individuals often have no well-defined property rights in the promised benefit, and thus have no guarantee of receiving it. Fourth, the system encourages waste and inefficiency in health care because there often is no immediate and direct relationship between the individual worker's consumption of health care and take-home pay. These adverse consequences would be eliminated if workers knew the value of the benefits they receive and perceived the benefits to be an alternative to money wages.

3. **All individuals should be allowed to make choices among tax-free benefits and should also be allowed to choose between nontaxed benefits and taxable income.** Many large corporations now have flexible benefit programs, but small companies are still effectively precluded from operating such programs. Even in large firms, employees generally cannot choose between taxable income

[16]In some cases, the value of group benefits is attributed to individual employees, but only after the benefit exceeds a certain amount. For example, for group life insurance coverage in excess of $50,000, the fair market value of the insurance benefit is treated as imputed income and the employee is taxed on that amount. No similar provision exists for group health insurance, however.

and nontaxed benefits. Such restrictions deny workers the opportunity to shape their tax-free benefit package to individual and family needs.

4. **The amount of tax subsidy available to any individual should be limited.** Under the current system, there are very few limits. For example, employers can spend an unlimited amount of money on employee health care plans and employer-provided day care with no tax penalty. The amount that can be spent on conventional pensions is—for all practical purposes—unlimited for most employees. Thus, people in some sectors of the economy have access to a blank check drawn on the U.S. Treasury, but millions of others do not.

5. **Public policy should encourage personal and portable benefits.** Employee benefits are almost always tied to place of employment. In general, employees who switch jobs are removed from the health insurance policy of the previous employer and must face the problem of getting a new insurance policy at the new job. Often, such changes cause great personal hardship for the employee. This situation arises because health insurance policies are viewed as belonging to employers and not to employees—the people the insurance is supposed to benefit. To make matters worse, employees can lose tens of thousands of dollars in pension benefits as a result of a job change, even if they are fully vested. Employees almost always lose any postretirement medical benefits when they switch jobs. A sound employee benefit is one in which the benefit belongs to the employee, not to the employer. In addition, a dynamic, growing economy requires a flexible labor force. Public policy should encourage rather than discourage labor mobility.

6. **Public policy toward health insurance should encourage all reasonable efforts to control rising health care costs.** The current system encourages the purchase of too much of the wrong kind of health insurance, which results in wasteful spending. Almost any health care plan designed to give employees incentives to be prudent buyers in the medical marketplace suffers tax penalties. These features of our tax code are in urgent need of reform.

7. **Public policy should encourage private savings to fund medical expenses during a worker's retirement years.** Although the current system provides lavish—and, in principle, unlimited—subsidies for employer spending on current health care needs, the

system offers virtually no incentive to save for health care during retirement. Individuals receive no tax subsidy for such savings and employers have very limited options. Such policies are unwise and imprudent.

PART III

REGULATING THE COST-PLUS SYSTEM

10. Increasing Government Control over the Price and Quality of Medical Care

The American health care system is a cost-plus system in its cost-control stage of evolution. In this second stage, many different third-party paying institutions are engaged in a bureaucratic struggle to resist the cost-plus push of the medical care providers and to reduce their shares of the total cost. Each third-party institution is free to initiate its own cost-control strategy. But because the basic structure of cost-plus finance has not been changed, Stage II is primarily about cost shifting.

The central focus of third-party paying institutions is to eliminate waste, but they usually cannot eliminate waste without causing harm to patients. On the supply side of the medical marketplace, institutions have great resources and considerable experience at resisting change. So, in the face of a cost-control measure initiated by one institutional buyer, the suppliers attempt to shift costs to another without changing their fundamental behavior. Thus, costs are not really controlled. Although ultimately the techniques adopted in Stage II do not hold down costs, their adoption and implementation affect the quality of care that patients receive. This chapter takes a closer look at how and why that happens.

The Legacy of Cost-Plus Medicine

In a pure cost-plus system, it is inevitable that there will be unnecessary surgery, unnecessary hospitalization, and many tests and procedures that are not cost-effective. How much waste is there in the U.S. health care system? Joseph Califano, a former secretary of the U.S. Department of Health, Education, and Welfare, estimates that one out of every four dollars spent is wasteful and unnecessary.[1] If true, that would mean that we are wasting about

---

[1] Joseph A. Califano, Jr., *America's Health Care Revolution: Who Lives? Who Dies? Who Pays?* (New York: Random House, 1986).

3 percent of our gross national product (GNP)—an amount equal to about $700 for every man, woman, and child in the country. No one knows for sure how much waste there is, but in the cost-plus system waste grows; it does not diminish.

Rising Health Care Costs

Despite the fact that a Stage I cost-plus system was in place from the late 1940s, increases in spending on health care were surprisingly moderate until government became a major buyer of health care. Although health care spending as a percent of GNP rose throughout the 1950s, it did so gradually and was never above 6 percent until the 1960s. Over the last three decades, however, there has been a continuous, almost unbroken increase in the percent of GNP devoted to health care. That figure is now approaching 13 percent—higher than for any other nation in the world—and is expected to reach 15 percent in 1995 and 17.3 percent by the year 2000.[2]

What happened? As Figure 10.1 shows, the single most important change in health care in the past 30 years has been the role of government. In 1960, most medical bills were still paid by patients out-of-pocket, and government spending on health care was only 33.8 percent of the total. Once government began to intervene in a major way, however, health care spending began to explode.

As Figure 10.2 shows, when tax subsidies for health insurance are included, government is now responsible for more than half of the nation's health care spending. By contrast, patient out-of-pocket spending now accounts for only one-fifth of the total.[3] One consequence of greater government intervention is that as public money was added to private money, more dollars were chasing limited quantities of medical goods and services. The result was medical inflation. The evidence indicates that, on the average, prior to the federal government's entry into the medical marketplace in the mid-1960s, each additional dollar of health care spending bought

---

[2]Health Care Financing Administration, Office of the Actuary: Data from the Office of National Cost Estimates; and Lynn Wagner, "Healthcare Spending Up Sharply," *Modern Healthcare*, April 29, 1991, p. 4.

[3]Note that Figures 10.1 and 10.2 employ two different measurements. Figure 10.2 is based on total health care spending, whereas Figure 10.1 is based on personal health care spending, which excludes research, hospital construction, and public health programs.

Figure 10.1
SHARE OF TOTAL HEALTH CARE SPENDING, 1960 AND 1990*

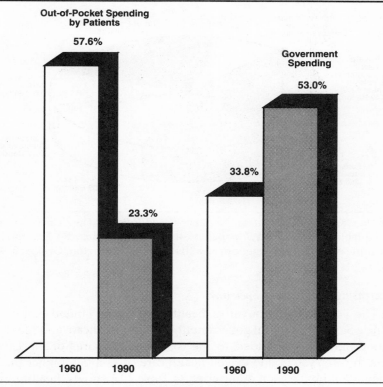

Out-of-Pocket Spending by Patients

57.6%

Government Spending

53.0%

33.8%

23.3%

| 1960 | 1990 | 1960 | 1990 |

SOURCE: Gary Robbins and Aldona Robbins, Fiscal Associates.

*Personal health care spending. Note: The totals treat tax subsidies as government spending.

50 cents of goods and services, while the remaining 50 cents was consumed by inflation. After the federal government emerged as a major buyer, things got worse. Since 1965, about 67 cents of each additional dollar of spending has been consumed by inflation.[4]

[4]Estimate of Gary Robbins and Aldona Robbins, Fiscal Associates, for the National Center for Policy Analysis. Note that this estimate is similar to others. The Health Care Financing Administration estimates that since the introduction of Medicare and Medicaid, 65 cents of each additional dollar of spending has been consumed by inflation.

Figure 10.2
SOURCES OF FINANCING FOR U.S. HEALTH CARE, 1992

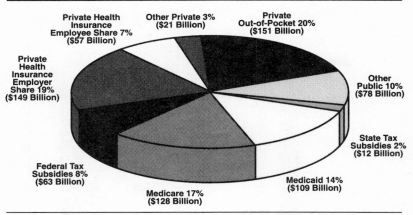

SOURCE: C. Eugene Steuerle, "Finance-Based Reform: The Search for an Adaptable Health Policy," paper presented at an American Enterprise Institute conference, "American Health Policy" (Washington, October 3–4, 1991).

Increasing Government Spending

The largest single buyer of health care in the United States is Uncle Sam. The federal government, through Medicare and Medicaid programs, has added to the cost-plus pressures of the U.S. health care system and driven health care costs much higher than they would have been otherwise. As Table 10.1 shows, health care spending by the federal government has been growing at a much faster rate than health care spending for the nation as a whole. From about 19 percent of total personal health care spending in 1970, for example, Medicare and Medicaid outlays grew to almost 30 percent in 1989.

Medicare is primarily designed to pay the acute (short-term) medical bills of the elderly. Although Medicaid is a health care program for the poor, the elderly consume a disproportionate and growing proportion of Medicaid dollars. That is partly because Medicaid pays for chronic (long-term) care, including some non-medical expenses. When the market value of in-kind benefits (such as government-provided housing, food stamps, and medical care) is included in family income, the poverty rate among the elderly is

288

Table 10.1
MEDICARE AND MEDICAID SPENDING, 1970 TO 1989

	1970	1975	1980	1985	1987	1988	1989
Percent of total spending on personal health care	18.9%	24.5%	28.1%	29.9%	29.9%	29.7%	30.0%
Percent of total spending on hospital care	26.9	30.7	35.2	38.1	37.4	37.8	36.5
Percent of total spending on physician care	16.4	21.7	24.1	26.3	27.3	27.2	27.0
Percent of total spending on nursing home care	33.0	50.4	50.7	46.3	46.8	46.3	50.6

SOURCES: Health Care Financing Administration, *Health Care Financing Review* 8, no. 1 (1986); ibid. 11, no. 4 (Summer 1990); and ibid. 12, no. 2 (Winter 1990).

289

only 2.9 percent, the lowest for any population group.[5] Despite this fact, the elderly constitute 16 percent of all Medicaid beneficiaries and account for about 36 percent of all Medicaid spending.[6]

Medicare and Medicaid combined cost about $237 billion a year. They consume more than one out of every ten dollars spent by the federal government and represent about 25 percent of all income transfer payments. Despite the tremendous growth in these two programs, though, the elderly spend a larger proportion of their budgets on health care today than ever before. In the years 1960–61 (prior to Medicare), those over age 65 spent an average of 10.9 percent of their annual income on medical care; by 1980–86, that figure had jumped to 12.05 percent.[7] Medicare has not replaced private health care spending by the elderly. Rather, it has induced elderly families to spend even more.

How Regulated Is the Medical Marketplace?

In terms of rules, restrictions, and bureaucratic reporting requirements, the health care sector is one of the most regulated industries in our economy. Consider Scripps Memorial Hospital, a medium-sized (250-bed) acute care facility in San Diego, California. As Table 10.2 shows, Scripps must answer to 39 governmental bodies and 7 nongovernmental bodies, and must periodically file 65 different reports, about one report for every four beds. In most cases, the reports required are not simple forms that can be completed by a clerk. Often, they are lengthy and complicated, requiring the daily recording of information by highly trained hospital personnel. Regulatory requirements intrude in a highly visible way on the activities of the medical staff and affect virtually every aspect of medical practice.

Another California hospital, Sequoia Hospital in the San Francisco Bay area, has attempted to calculate how many additional employees are required as a result of government regulations. As Table 10.3 shows, Sequoia's staff increased by 163.6 percent between 1966 and 1990, even though the average number of

[5]Data are for 1985. See U.S. Bureau of the Census, *Statistical Abstract of the United States: 1987* (Washington: U.S. Government Printing Office, 1986), p. 446.

[6]Health Care Financing Administration.

[7]Bureau of Labor Statistics, Office of Prices and Living Conditions.

Table 10.2

REPORTS MADE TO REGULATORY AGENCIES BY SCRIPPS
MEMORIAL HOSPITAL, SAN DIEGO, 1989

Agency	Number of Hospital Departments Reporting
Government	
Joint Commission of Accreditation of Hospitals	11
Occupational Safety and Health Administration	5
San Diego County Health Department	1
State Board of Equalization (hazardous waste tax return)	1
Internal Revenue Service	2
Franchise Tax Board	1
Secretary of State	1
Medicare	2
State Board of Equalization (sales tax return)	2
California Hospital Facilities Commission	1
State Board of Health	1
Environmental Protection Agency	1
Department of Transportation	1
Department of Health Services	1
Air Resources Board	1
Office of Emergency Services	1
Health and Welfare Agency	1
Air Pollution Control/Air Quality Management District	1
Regional Water Quality Control Board	1
Local Sewering Agencies	1
Local Fire Department	1
San Diego Department of Health Services	1
State Licensing Board	1
Board of Registered Nursing	2
Licensed Vocational Nursing Board	1
U.S. Department of Labor	1

(Continued on next page)

Table 10.2—Continued
REPORTS MADE TO REGULATORY AGENCIES BY SCRIPPS
MEMORIAL HOSPITAL, SAN DIEGO, 1989

Agency	Number of Hospital Departments Reporting
Industrial Welfare Commission	1
Fair Employment Practice Commission	1
National Labor Relations Board	1
Immigration and Naturalization Service	1
Employment Development Department	1
Social Security Administration	1
Employee Retirement Income Security requirements	1
State Board of Pharmacy	1
Drug Enforcement Agency	1
Food and Drug Administration	1
Bureau of Narcotic Enforcement	1
California Department of Health, Radiologic Health Branch	1
Nongovernment	
American Hospital Association	2
American Conference of Governmental Industrial Hygienists	1
California Medical Association	1
Radiation Safety Organization (Syncor, Inc.)	1
National Association of Social Workers	1
American College of Surgeons	1
San Diego and Imperial Counties Organization for Cancer Control	1

SOURCE: National Center for Policy Analysis.

patients per day (250) did not change. Sequoia estimates the cost of regulations is about $7.8 million per year.[8]

In 1976, in another attempt to calculate the costs of regulation, the Hospital Association of New York State studied 148 acute care

[8]*Medical Benefits* 7, no. 15 (August 15, 1990): 1.

Table 10.3
EFFECT OF GOVERNMENT REGULATION ON SEQUOIA
HOSPITAL, SAN FRANCISCO, 1966 TO 1990

Size of Staff	1966	1990
Business office and accounting	26	70
Admitting and outpatient registration	13	18
Utilization review	0	10
Social services	0	9
Medical records	17	41
Quality assurance	0	5
Data processing	0	9
Medical staff office	0	4
Administration	4	9
Nurses	374	533
Maintenance	16	28
Total	450	736

SOURCE: *Wall Street Journal.* Reprinted in *Medical Benefits* 7, no. 15 (August 15, 1990): 1.

hospitals governed by 164 different regulatory agencies. Admittedly, the method of study was not entirely objective. Hospital personnel were asked to engage in a self-evaluation of the burdens of regulation, which is a bit like asking victims to assess their suffering. Still, the study is one of the most comprehensive ever undertaken, and its results indicate the magnitude of regulatory burdens. According to the study, 25 percent of hospital costs—or $1.1 billion (in 1976 dollars)—were attributable to government regulatory requirements. About 115 million staff-hours per year were needed to meet the regulatory requirements, the equivalent to having more than 56,000 hospital employees work full-time on regulatory matters. Without such regulatory burdens, enough time would have been made available to staff 75 hospitals and thereby provide medical services for about 600,000 patients.[9]

The New York study was conducted at a time when the system of health care finance was in its pure cost-plus stage. Today, things are much worse. A new form of regulation has been added—one

[9]Hospital Association of New York State, *Cost of Regulation: Report of the Task Force on Regulation* (Albany, 1978), p. 2.

that is much more subtle, but with far more impact on the practice of medicine: government control over hospital revenues. Before looking at how those controls are established and enforced, however, it's useful to look more closely at the effect of regulatory controls on physicians.

What Increasing Regulation Means for Physicians

Most people have traditionally viewed medicine as an attractive profession, one that almost always leads to a high income and a comfortable lifestyle. But a 1989 Gallup poll revealed that 40 percent of physicians now say they would not, or probably would not, go to medical school if they had to do it all over again.[10]

Applications to medical schools reveal a similar trend. Although 35,944 students applied to medical school in 1985, that number dropped to 26,915 in 1989, reflecting a downward trend that has been under way since the mid-1970s (see Figure 10.3). There has been a 50 percent drop in the number of male applicants since the mid-1970s, and white males made up less than half of the 1989–90 freshman medical class. Medical schools are accepting a much larger percent of those who do apply and some are even recruiting applicants through advertisements in student newspapers. Although the schools won't admit it, the suspicion is that medical schools are no longer getting the same quality of student they used to get.[11]

The feeling that something is going wrong is also expressed by patients. A 1989 Gallup poll of patient attitudes revealed that less than one-third felt that doctors spend enough time with them and less than half thought that "doctors usually explain things well to their patients." The public attitude about what motivates physicians has also taken a turn for the worse. According to Gallup, 57 percent of the people think that "doctors don't care about people as much as they used to" and 67 percent think "doctors are too interested in making money."[12]

---

[10]Reported in Lisa Belkin, "Many in Medicine Are Calling Rules a Professional Malaise," *New York Times*, February 19, 1990.

[11]Lawrence K. Altman and Elizabeth Rosenthal, "Changes in Medicine Bring Pain to the Healing Profession," *New York Times*, February 18, 1990.

[12]Reported in Gina Kolata, "Wariness Is Replacing Trust between Healer and Patient," *New York Times*, February 20, 1990.

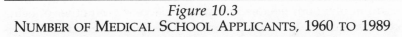

Figure 10.3
NUMBER OF MEDICAL SCHOOL APPLICANTS, 1960 TO 1989

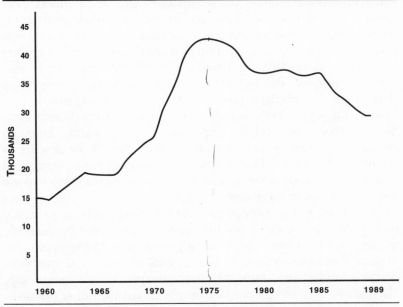

SOURCE: Association of American Medical Colleges. Graph reproduced from *The Trauma of Transformation in the 1990s: An Environmental Assessment of U.S. Health Care* (Minneapolis: Health One, 1989), p. 53.

So what's going wrong? Clearly a lot of it has to do with the way in which government and other third-party payers are changing the doctor-patient relationship. Among doctors who said they would not, or probably would not, go to medical school if they were in college today, the most commonly given reason (27 percent) was government and insurance regulations that "interfere with doing my job" and cause a "lack of autonomy." Doctors claim they are overwhelmed by paperwork and prohibited from delivering needed medical services by third-party payers. Of the physicians polled by Gallup in 1989, 63 percent—up from 54 percent in 1987— said they had less control over patient treatment decisions than a few years earlier.[13]

[13]Ibid.

Ironically, both doctors and patients accuse each other of being too commercial. Whereas patients say that physicians are too interested in making money, physicians complain that patients view medical care as just one more commodity. Buying medical care is like "going out and buying a new or used car," complained one physician. "Patients look at finding a doctor like they look at finding an automobile repair shop," said another.[14] But much less money is exchanged between patient and doctor than ever before. More than 80 percent of physicians' fees are paid by third parties.

If less money is changing hands, what is causing the deterioration in the doctor-patient relationship? The one thing that has changed radically in recent years is third-party regulation of the practice of medicine. The medical marketplace is becoming more impersonal and more bureaucratic because bureaucrats are increasingly making the decisions. Consider some examples:

In one case, a Tennessee physician performed emergency surgery on a young boy with heavy intestinal bleeding. But because the doctor did not obtain telephone approval prior to the operation, Medicaid refused to pay his fee. In another case, a Connecticut doctor admitted an elderly man to the hospital with a broken hip. The patient suffered numerous complications, including pneumonia and an instance of cardiac arrest, and his doctor visited him every day during his three-month hospital stay. But Medicare refused to pay for the daily visits, claiming that level of care and attention was unnecessary. The doctor can challenge Medicare's funding, but that would require his spending hours reviewing medical records and preparing detailed documents.[15]

Physicians also complain about HMO rules and restrictions. According to a female physician who had worked at several HMOs, administrators tried to intimidate doctors by regularly issuing lists comparing physicians in terms of time spent with patients, number of medications prescribed, number of lab tests, and number of x-rays ordered. The not-so-subtle message was that doctors who were high on the list were draining HMO resources. In other cases, the pressure to spend less time with patients was verbal and direct.

---

[14]Ibid.
[15]Belkin.

The physician left HMO practice after one administrator went so far as to schedule her restroom breaks.

Throughout the early part of this century, physician organizations struggled against the "corporate practice of medicine," under which doctors were employed by nonphysicians who could interfere with the practice of medicine.[16] The battle is being lost now, with very little protest. Although many older physicians are still self-employed, more than half of all physicians today are salaried employees, as are more than 60 percent of physicians under the age of 35.[17]

Of 200 health care careers listed by the American Hospital Association, more than one-fourth are administrative. According to the *Journal of Internal Medicine*, between 1970 and 1986, the number of health administrators increased fourfold, while the number of physicians increased by half. Increasingly, nonphysicians are telling physicians what to do.[18]

Not all of the changes are bad. Even though physicians complain about advertising, some changes seem to require it. For example, two New Jersey physicians now offer a package price for hernia operations, much as cosmetic surgeons offer a package price for cosmetic surgery. To solicit business they encourage potential patients to call 1-800-HERNIA.[19] The method may be distasteful to some, but the hospital marketplace desperately needs package prices for surgery.

Even without the growth of third-party intervention, market-based institutions surely would have evolved to solve problems. Some physicians do abuse patients and payers by overbilling. A smaller number do practice bad medicine. The federal government's solution is to publish the names of physicians who have been disciplined and of hospitals with abnormally high mortality rates.[20] This sledgehammer approach can unfairly damage reputations without even basic due process protections. Market-based

[16]Paul Starr, *The Social Transformation of American Medicine* (New York: Basic Books, 1982).

[17]Altman and Rosenthal.

[18]Belkin.

[19]Altman and Rosenthal.

[20]The federal government is compiling the National Practitioner Data Bank, more popularly known as "Docs in a Box," which will record the names of physicians who have been disciplined by hospitals, state medical boards, and professional societies. The data bank will also list physicians who have settled malpractice suits,

297

institutions might have found better ways of dealing with such problems.

If patients controlled their health care dollars and were more involved in medical decisions, there would undoubtedly be fewer instances of overbilling and unnecessary procedures. In fact, many problems arise precisely because third parties are paying the bills. When third-party payers attempt to establish price controls, physicians respond through "creative billing," often with the assistance of their patients.[21] When the cost to the patient is zero, patients frequently find ways of getting insurers to pay for extra tests and procedures, often with the help of their physicians. Under third-party payment, the self-interests of physicians and patients are automatically at odds with the self-interests of those who pay the bills.

More fundamentally, institutions that would evolve to solve problems in a market-based system would meet the needs of patients and doctors. By contrast, institutions that evolve to solve problems in a cost-plus system are responsive to third-party payers.

How the Cost-Plus Mentality Approaches the Problem of Waste

Clearly there are problems in the medical marketplace. Given the way we pay for health care and the structure of the cost-plus system, it is hard to imagine how there could not be problems. Most people who are confronted with the structure of these problems quickly identify the system of health care finance as the major culprit. If prospective bypass surgery patients were about to spend $25,000 of their own money, they would exercise far more care in making the decision than when spending Medicare's money. If physicians were primarily dealing with patients spending their own money, they would have stronger incentives to communicate the risks and

---

which is very controversial since physicians may settle suits even when they have done nothing wrong. See Philip J. Hilts, "Oversight, Phase I: Keeping Records of Doctors with Records," *New York Times*, September 9, 1990. The government's current plans are to release the information only to hospitals and official regulatory bodies. However, the left-wing Public Citizen Research Group claims to have a national list of doctors who have been disciplined and is making the list available to the public. See *Medical Benefits* 7, no. 15 (August 15, 1990): 11.

[21]Some third-party payer organizations estimate that about 40 percent of physicians now engage in creative billing practices. See *Medical Benefits* 7, no. 16 (August 30, 1990): 11.

probable benefits of the patient's treatment. Moreover, if the medical marketplace were allowed to function as other markets do, there would be no reason to suppose that all people would make the same choices. From our observation of other human activities, we know that there are radical differences in attitudes toward risk among people who are otherwise similarly situated. Given that a great many choices in the medical marketplace involve risk, we would expect to see wide differences in choices—even among fully informed consumers.

In the case of diagnostic tests performed on blood, for example we know that as many as 900 tests can now be performed. If we consult the medical literature, we find considerable advice on which tests are appropriate in which circumstances. But there is no reason to suppose that fully informed consumers would make identical choices. To the contrary, their choices with regard to blood tests likely would vary as much as consumer choices in the markets for other goods and services. Risk takers would probably forgo all blood tests. Hypochondriacs might opt for all 900. The rest of the population would be distributed between these extremes.

That is not the way the cost-plus mentality views the world, however. As the cost-plus system evolved into its cost-control phase in the 1980s, the new industry buzzwords became "cost-benefit," "cost-effective," and "medical outcomes research." The idea was to evaluate alternatives by applying the well-regarded standards developed by economists.

In the literature of economics, "cost-benefit analysis" has a fairly precise meaning. Such analysis is always based on the preferences of individuals. Once the concept made its way into the medical literature, however, it acquired a completely different meaning. In the 1980s, the terms "cost-benefit" and "cost-effective" appeared with increasing frequency on the pages of the prestigious *New England Journal of Medicine*. In the hands of the cost-plus research establishment, however, cost-benefit analysis is a technical concept, devoid of any relationship to individuals' values and preferences.

Applying Cost-Benefit Analysis to the Practice of Medicine

In the hands of the professional economists who developed it, cost-benefit analysis has sensible things to say about the medical marketplace. For example, surgery is wasteful if a fully informed consumer would rather have the money than the surgery. It is not wasteful if the patient prefers it. So, given the choice between $25,000 in cash or a $25,000 bypass operation, the operation is "cost-effective" if the patient chooses surgery instead of money. Similarly, if a fully informed consumer is given choices between having up to 900 different blood tests and taking the costs of the blood tests in the form of cash, then the cost-effective number of tests is the number the consumer chooses. This type of cost-benefit analysis makes sense unless one believes that people should be systematically denied what they want.

In the hands of the cost-plus bureaucracy, however, cost-benefit analysis has no relationship whatever to consumer choices. Applying their technocratic tools of trade, medical researchers seek to establish the "right" number of blood tests for everyone, regardless of preference. Similarly, they seek the objective conditions under which all patients should or should not have surgery, irrespective of what individual patients want.

Using Cost-Benefit Analysis to Regulate Medical Providers

In a normal marketplace, waste tends to be eliminated as people pursue their self-interest. People do not systematically spend money on things that are less valuable than other things the same money could buy. Although consumers make mistakes, they have incentives to avoid recurrent mistakes and to patronize sellers who help them to do so. The cost-plus mentality, however, does not believe that a real medical marketplace is necessary, or even desirable, and it attempts to force providers to abide by the results of technocratic cost-benefit analysis.

In its cost-control phase, then, cost-plus is a system in which medical providers face perverse incentives and third-party payers try to keep them from acting on those incentives. Third-party bureaucracies make this bad situation worse by using an approach that is totally foreign to how physicians think, what medical schools teach, and how traditional hospitals are managed. As a nation, we spent 40 years eradicating virtually every aspect of individualized cost-benefit thinking from the medical marketplace—only to reach a point at which the bureaucratized cost-benefit standard is being used to second-guess every decision medical providers make. That is why many of the cost-containment strategies of the 1980s (discussed in chapter 7) failed to work. Both private industry and government tried to use bureaucratic rule making to repress perverse incentives rather than remove them.

Cost-benefit analysis in its sensible form (the form developed by economists) is not alien to the thinking of most physicians. They understand the concept of satisfying patient preferences. The technocratic use of cost-benefit analysis is wholly different. Not only do physicians fail to understand it, but they perceive that its misuse by third-party payers frequently conflicts with patient preferences and quality care.

The problem is significantly more dangerous when it is viewed from the perspective of the medical profession as a whole. Cost-benefit analysis is currently being used in a massive federal program to reorganize the science, as well as the practice, of medicine. This program is being conducted under the guise of "outcomes research" and the development of "practice guidelines." But its true objective is to completely define, systematize, and pass judgment on all medical knowledge. Its proponents advertise that it will review alternative treatments and see what works, what does not work, and what is cost-effective. This goal may seem sensible and consistent with the fundamental responsibility of medical research and medical education. But how long will it take for a politician to ask, "Why does Medicaid pay for something that is not cost-effective?" The end result may be that physicians will have only one way to handle every problem—the government's way.

The government does not define "cost-effective" meals for the restaurant industry or "cost-effective" designs and materials for the construction industry. But the government is taking on that task for medicine. The program will either be a multibillion-dollar blunder or it will make medicine in America even more regimented than it is in countries where it is socialized.

Regulation of Hospital Prices

In the summer of 1985, 85-year-old Leon Alger spent 19 days in a Houston hospital being treated for cerebral-spinal inflammation. On leaving the hospital, Alger was handed a 32-page bill totaling $45,797.63. Because he was a Medicare patient, Alger's share of the bill was only $257. But, furious at some of the items on the bill, he wrote to Houston newspapers complaining that neither Medicare nor anyone else should be paying the prices he saw. For example,

Alger's bill listed a daily charge of $180 for oxygen. But he happened to know that a large oxygen tank, lasting a full day, could be filled for as little as $3.80.[22]

What Alger did not know was that the bill he saw is not the bill the hospital would present to Medicare. Whether under the old system of reimbursement or the new, Medicare has never paid hospitals according to the prices they charge for services. Under the old, cost-based reimbursement, Medicare paid hospitals according to their costs, as did Blue Cross and most other private insurers. As a result, until recently about 90 percent of all hospital revenues consisted of reimbursements for hospital costs.[23]

In 1983, the federal government changed the way in which hospitals are reimbursed under Medicare. Under the new system, hospitals are paid a fixed sum for each of 492 categories[24] of illness called diagnosis-related groups (DRGs). In principle, the revenues that hospitals receive under the system are unrelated to the cost of treating any particular patient. Thus, if the hospital keeps its costs below the DRG reimbursement price, it makes a profit; if not, it suffers a loss. Take the case of Leon Alger's 32-page hospital bill. Although the total was $45,797.63, Medicare's DRG price was only $8,740. Add to that the $257 paid by Alger, and the hospital faced a shortfall of about $36,800.

On the surface, the DRG system has certain attractive features. Instead of reimbursing hospitals for waste and inefficiency, the federal government has limited its exposure; it pays a fixed fee and lets hospitals sink or swim. The system leaves certain important questions unanswered, however. If Medicare does not pay the hospital's $36,800 loss, who does? And if no one pays for it, what are the implications for future health care delivery in the United States?

[22]Janet Elliott, "Fees for Care Called Exorbitant," *Houston Post,* July 7, 1985.

[23]For a general description of cost-plus reimbursement and the difference it makes, see John C. Goodman and Gerald L. Musgrave, *The Changing Market for Health Insurance: Opting Out of the Cost-Plus System,* NCPA Policy Report no. 118 (Dallas: National Center for Policy Analysis, September 25, 1985), pp. 1–26. For an analysis of the specific reimbursement formulas, see Sylvia A. Law, *Blue Cross: What Went Wrong?* (New Haven: Yale University Press, 1973), pp. 59–114.

[24]Initially, 467 categories were established. "Report and Recommendations to the Congress," Prospective Payment Assessment Commission (Washington, DC, March 1, 1992), Appendix E, pp. 115–30.

Price Fixing

The DRG system was seen by many as an attempt by the federal government to opt out of the cost-plus system of health care finance. Some even argued that the DRG system is a market-based approach to health care. Now that the system has been in operation for several years, fewer people hold those views. Although the DRG system creates financial incentives to reduce costs, it is not structured so that government is simply one more buyer in a competitive market. Instead, it is a price-fixing scheme in which the government establishes an artificial market.

Establishing an artificial market creates perverse incentives for providers, leading to adverse health effects for patients and possibly to greater health care costs. At the most basic level, two mistakes can occur in any price-fixing scheme: Either the price can be set too high or it can be set too low. If it is too high, the system encourages too many medical procedures; if it is too low, the system encourages too few.

Incentives to Overprovide Health Care Services

Under the DRG system, physicians and hospitals receive revenues only if they perform services. As long as the DRG price compensates the hospital for its costs, health care providers have a financial incentive to perform surgery, even when the decision to operate is questionable on medical grounds. The new DRG system does encourage outpatient surgery over inpatient surgery, but it still encourages surgery. It also encourages early release after surgery and other practices that can lead to medical complications, which in turn can increase medical services and the cost to taxpayers.[25]

Incentives to Reduce the Quality of Care

In 1987 testimony before the House Government Operations Subcommittee on Human Resources and Intergovernmental Relations,

---

[25]For a review of these perverse incentives see John E. Wennberg, Klim McPherson, and Phillip Caper, "Will Payment Based on Diagnosis-Related Groups Control Hospital Costs?" *New England Journal of Medicine* 311, no. 5 (August 2, 1984): 296-300; and Robert S. Stern and Arnold M. Epstein, "Institutional Responses to Prospective Payment Based on Diagnosis-Related Groups: Implications for Cost, Quality and Access," *New England Journal of Medicine* 312, no. 10 (March 7, 1985): 621–27.

William Roper, then head of the Health Care Financing Administration (which administers Medicare), testified that as many as 891,000 Medicare patients received "dangerous care" each year. Those cases included 22,000 avoidable deaths; 149,000 avoidable traumas, including medication errors and the removal or "repair" of healthy organs; and 198,000 avoidable infections.[26]

It is not known to what extent those cases were directly related to the new DRG system. What is known is that the DRG system has created a serious problem of maintaining the quality of care. Once providers have performed the minimal services necessary to receive the DRG price, further care simply increases costs without increasing revenue. There have been numerous reports of patients being denied hospital admittance because of DRG rules,[27] and many more of patients being prematurely released. In one recent poll of physicians, 78 percent of the respondents reported being "pressured to discharge Medicare patients before they were ready to leave the hospital," and 88 percent reported that "the DRG program is adversely affecting the quality of medical care for Medicare patients."[28]

Despite the complaints of the physicians, there are studies that purport to show that the quality of care has not deteriorated under the DRG system. Which side is right? To some degree, both may be. Certainly the one-size-fits-all nature of the DRG pricing system creates incentives for providers to reduce the quality of care. On the other hand, the choices of patients and physicians who act as if care were free cannot be the right standard for the appropriate length of stay or choice of quality. In the absence of any real market for hospital care for the elderly, government-mandated controls and spending reductions are likely to reduce both desirable and undesirable care.

Case Study: Elderly Patients with Hip Fractures

In 1988, five years after the DRG system was introduced, a study compared the treatment of patients with similar conditions before and after the Medicare reimbursement rules changed. Studying

[26]Associated Press Wire Service, *Dallas Morning News*, October 21, 1987.

[27]See Robert A. Berenson, "Meet Dr. Squeezed," *New York Times*, July 21, 1989.

[28]These results should be taken as indicative, since the poll was not random. See *Private Practice* (October 1985), pp. 18–19.

elderly patients with hip fractures, the researchers found that the length of time patients spent in the hospital had dropped dramatically, as had the physical condition of patients at discharge.

Even more alarming, the study found a dramatic rise in the number of discharged patients who were immediately sent to nursing homes (up from 38 percent to 60 percent) and, perhaps because they entered nursing homes in poor condition, a substantial decline in their long-term recovery. Prior to the DRG system, only 9 percent of hip fracture patients sent to nursing homes remained after one year; afterward, 33 percent were still there after one year.[29] As the editors of the *New England Journal of Medicine* commented, this "provides a clear-cut demonstration, in a controlled study, of significantly poorer clinical outcomes for patients" treated after the implementation of the DRG system.[30]

Case Study: Elderly Mortality and State Government Regulation

Various studies have attempted to determine whether government policies are leading to higher mortality rates for elderly patients. A Northwestern University study surveyed the hospital records of more than 200,000 patients in 45 states.[31] It found that states with the most stringent regulation of hospital charges had a 6 to 10 percent higher mortality rate among elderly patients than states with the least stringent rate regulation. The study also found that states with the most stringent certificate-of-need (CON) regulations—controlling the ability of hospitals to expand and purchase equipment—had mortality rates 5 to 6 percent higher than states with less stringent CON regulations. The authors concluded that severe regulatory requirements "create incentives for hospitals to contain costs and may act as barriers to the development of innovative services that might otherwise improve the quality of care."[32]

---

[29]John F. Fitzgerald, Patricia S. Moore, and Robert Dittus, "The Care of Elderly Patients with Hip Fracture," *New England Journal of Medicine* 319, no. 21 (November 24, 1988): 1392–97.

[30]"Hospital Prospective Payment and the Quality of Care," *New England Journal of Medicine* 319, no. 21 (November 24, 1988): 1411.

[31]Stephen M. Shortell and Edward F. X. Hughes, "The Effects of Regulation, Competition and Ownership on Mortality Rates among Hospital Inpatients," *New England Journal of Medicine* 318, no. 17 (April 28, 1988): 1100–07.

[32]Ibid., 1101.

Elderly Mortality and the DRG System

Various studies have found that the DRG system apparently leads to fewer deaths in hospitals but more in nursing homes. In Hennepin County, Minnesota (which includes Minneapolis), between 1982 and 1986, the average length of stay for elderly patients in hospitals was cut in half. But because of local regulations, entry into a nursing home became more difficult. By 1987, the mortality rate for the county's elderly was more than 10 percent higher than its expected level.[33]

A Rand Corporation study for the U.S. Department of Health and Human Services disputes the contention that the DRG system has been harmful to patients. Although finding that the average length of stay in hospitals has declined by 24 percent, and patients are admitted "sicker" and released "quicker and sicker," Rand researchers maintain that the system has brought mortality down and quality up. But they also found that 12 percent of the patients received "poor care," and the death rate for these patients 30 days after discharge was double the death rate of other patients. They also found that, as a result of DRGs, more patients are being released in unstable condition, which makes them one and one-half times more likely to die within 90 days.[34]

Extending the DRG System to Other Third-Party Payers

The problems of the DRG price-fixing scheme are not limited to elderly Medicare patients. In a regulated, institutionalized market, once a method of payment becomes dominant, all third-party payers discover that they must adopt it (see chapter 3). Many state governments have adopted the DRG system in their Medicaid programs for low-income patients. Medicare and Medicaid combined represent 37 percent of all hospital revenues. Moreover, an increasing number of private insurers also are adopting Medicare's method of payment.

[33]Gregory L. Lindberg et al., "Health Care Cost Containment Measures and Mortality in Hennepin County Medicaid Elderly and All Elderly," *American Journal of Public Health* 79, no. 11 (November 1989): 1482.

[34]The Rand study was released in a series of eight reports published in *Journal of the American Medical Association* 264, no. 115 (October 17, 1990).

Table 10.4
PEDIATRIC CARE AT A NEW YORK HOSPITAL, 1985–87

Race	Average Length of Stay	Average Cost
White	7.75 days	$6,744
Hispanic	9.55 days	$8,099
Black	10.18 days	$8,408

SOURCE: Eric Muñoz, "Hospitals, Minorities Taking a Beating," *New York Times*, July 28, 1989.

Rationing Care for the Poor, the Old, and the Sick

The DRG system has other side effects, although less well recognized. For example, although it pays one fixed price for treatment of a specific condition, the actual cost to hospitals of delivering medical care can vary enormously, depending on the patient. Within a single DRG category in 1984, the cost of care ranged from a low of $5,500 to a high of $200,000. In "heart failure and shock," the DRG with the highest volume of cases, about 66 percent of the patients that year cost hospitals less than $4,000 each, whereas 7 percent cost more than $100,000 each.[35]

Who are the high-cost patients? They are the sickest and more often than not low-income and nonwhite (see chapter 3). Table 10.4 shows the length of stay and cost per treatment of pediatric patients by race. As the table shows, black children have a 31 percent longer average hospital stay and incur 25 percent higher hospital costs than their white counterparts. These cost differences are also reflected among older patients. In a cross-section of patients admitted to Long Island Jewish Medical Center between 1985 and 1987, for example, the average cost was $5,589 for white patients, $6,418 for Hispanics, and $6,753 for blacks.[36]

Among elderly patients, the young elderly are usually much less expensive to treat than the old elderly. For example, a study of

[35]Nancy M. Kane and Paul D. Manoukian, "The Effect of the Medicare Prospective Payment System on the Adoption of New Technology," *New England Journal of Medicine* 321, no. 21 (November 16, 1989): 1379.

[36]Eric Muñoz et al., "Race, DRGs and the Consumption of Hospital Resources," *Health Affairs*, Spring 1989, p. 187.

orthopedic surgical patients found that the average cost of treatment rises considerably with the age of the patient, even though the DRG price is the same for all. On patients over the age of 75, for example, hospitals lose an average of between $3,000 and $5,000 per patient for orthopedic surgery.[37]

There is increasing evidence that hospitals are responding to the financial initiatives created by the DRG system. They give care readily and quickly to the profitable Medicare patients, but slowly, reluctantly, and often with less attention to quality, to those who are unprofitable. That is especially true in the area of medical technology.

Rationing Medical Technology

Once Medicare had identified the DRG categories and prices, a reimbursement system was put into place. Medical technology, however, is changing rapidly, with new inventions and innovations coming on the market every day. A technological advance that reduces costs causes no problem and enables hospitals to make bigger profits. If a new technology causes treatment costs to rise, however, the incentives are entirely different. Unless Medicare raises the DRG price to cover the increased costs, the hospital is not able to afford the technology or may restrict its use to lower cost patients. Administrative changes in Medicare's DRG prices are made slowly if at all. Thus, many technological innovations are being rationed to Medicare patients.

Even when Medicare recognizes that an expensive technological device should be used, it often categorizes patients who need the device with those who do not in the same DRG category, and it pays an average DRG price. Hospitals with an above-average number of patients who need the device will be unable to provide it for all of them. In 1984, for example, there were 21 DRGs in which patients were combined in that way. In 18 of the 21, the DRG payment was well below the average hospital cost of providing the device. In more than half the cases, Medicare patients did not receive it.[38]

[37]Kane and Manoukian, 1381.
[38]Ibid., 1379.

Case Study: Cochlear Implants[39]

Hearing loss is the most prevalent chronic disability in the United States. It affects 30 percent of people over the age of 65 and 50 percent of people over the age of 85. Fortunately, a remarkable innovation—cochlear implants with the ability to substantially improve hearing for some patients—came on the market in 1978. The innovation prompted a congratulatory letter from President Reagan to the 3M Company, the original manufacturer, and the device won fairly prompt endorsements from the American Medical Association and the American Academy of Otolaryngology—Head and Neck Surgery. Yet, more than a decade later, most Medicare patients still cannot get a cochlear implant. In 1987, for example, Medicare reimbursed hospitals for only 69 implants.

Part of the problem is normal bureaucratic delay. But a bigger problem is the unwillingness of Medicare to pay a DRG price that covers the cost of the implant, a policy undoubtedly influenced by pressures to hold down spending. On the average, hospitals where implants are performed lose between $14,500 and $24,000 per patient.[40] One other side effect of this policy is that three of the five companies that developed and marketed the implant in the United States have now dropped out of the market, and 3M has dropped its plans to develop a new, improved implant.

Case Study: Kidney Dialysis

In 1988, Medicare paid about $3.7 billion for 147,000 patients with end-stage renal disease under a program that covers patients with kidney failure regardless of age. Since 1983, however, reimbursement for kidney dialysis (covering about 110,000 patients) has become increasingly stingy, with possible adverse effects for patients. In real terms, Medicare's payment for dialysis fell 44 percent (from $138 to $77) between 1983 and 1990. In addition, the physician's payment was frozen at about $150 per patient per month during that period. In response, many dialysis centers reduced the length of treatment time for patients, even though treatment time

---

[39]Ibid., 1378–83.

[40]"Proposed Rate for Prospective Payment of Cochlear Implantation," *Government Affairs Review*, September/October 1990, p. 7.

is related to a patient's odds of success.[41] According to one study, patients whose treatment sessions are less than 3.5 hours can be twice as likely to die as patients who receive longer treatments. Yet, as the study showed, the average treatment time for all dialysis patients has been falling since 1983, and about 20,000 patients now undergo sessions that last less than 3.5 hours.[42]

According to Alan Hull of Southwestern Medical School in Dallas, the United States is falling behind other countries in treatment success. Whereas U.S. patients receive about 10 hours of dialysis per week, the figure is 12 hours in Germany and 14 hours in Japan. Possibly as a result, in France, where treatment times are about 18 hours per week, the five-year survival rate is 87 percent, compared with a 47 percent U.S. survival rate.[43]

Why Haven't the Effects of the DRG System Been Worse?

Given the structure of DRG pricing, one would predict far worse results. Why haven't they occurred yet? The main reason is that pure cost-plus finance (Stage I) has by no means vanished, and most physicians still practice traditional medicine. As a result, unprofitable Medicare patients frequently receive the same quality of care administered to profitable patients. Hospital administrators make up for these losses by overcharging others, as they have done for the past 40 years.

Recently, executives at Golden Rule Insurance Company complained to a hospital administrator that the hospital's charges were unreasonable. In a letter of response, the administrator admitted that they were unreasonable, but enclosed a lengthy document explaining why that was the case. The document carefully noted the amount of "underpayment" to the hospital by Medicare, Medicaid, and preferred-provider organizations (PPOs) and furnished a complicated formula according to which these "underpayments" were made up by extra charges to all other payers. This is cost-plus finance in its pure form.

[41]Edward E. Berger and Edmund G. Lowrie, editorial, *Journal of the American Medical Association* 265, no. 7 (February 20, 1991): 909–10.

[42]Philip J. Held, *Journal of the American Medical Association* 265, no. 7 (February 20, 1991).

[43]Reported in Ron Winslow, "Cost Control May Harm Dialysis Patients," *Wall Street Journal*, February 20, 1991.

Cost shifting is becoming increasingly difficult, however. If competitive pressures continue in the hospital marketplace, hospitals will soon discover that they cannot overcharge any patient. Once that happens, the effects of the DRG system on Medicare patients will be devastating.

DRGs and the Cost-Plus System in Its Cost-Control Stage

When they were initiated, DRG prices were seen as an attempt by the federal government to opt out of traditional cost-plus finance. That image was deceptive. Far from moving toward a competitive market, the DRG system replaced one bureaucratic reimbursement scheme with another, in which patient preferences take a back seat to reimbursement rules. Currently, the federal government is attempting to set prices and monitor quality for 28 million potential patients and 5,000 hospitals. It is an impossible job. No matter what the rules, the medical marketplace is so complex that there are literally thousands of ways for health care providers to exploit them. Moreover, there is an inevitable conflict between price and quality of care. In the early years of Medicare, quality took precedence over costs. Under the new reimbursement rules, the reverse is beginning to occur.

Although individual hospitals are paid on a prospective basis, independent of their costs, the system as a whole has not escaped the pressures of cost-plus medical care. Under current practice, national DRG rates for this year are determined by last year's average hospital costs. Thus as hospital costs go up, DRG payments also go up. We still have a cost-plus system, but now it has a time lag. The federal government can, of course, resist such cost pressures by making DRG reimbursement rates increasingly stingy. But doing so would have even more adverse affects on the quality of patient care. The DRG system is already being used as a health care rationing device, and some argue that even more extensive rationing is inevitable.[44] By simply refusing to pay hospitals enough to cover the costs of expensive surgery, DRG administrators could force hospital personnel to ration health care, whether they want to or not.

---

[44]See David Stipp, "Medical-Cost Trend after 1990 Disputed: Growth Rate May Soar Unless Care Is Rationed," *Wall Street Journal*, January 9, 1987.

Table 10.5
REPRESENTATIVE PRICES PAID BY MEDICARE TO PHYSICIANS FOR A HOSPITAL OR OFFICE VISIT*

Reimbursement Price	Nature of Visit
$25	Brief visit; approximately 5 minutes
$35	Limited visit; brief evaluation of a chronic, stable medical problem
$50	Intermediate visit; requires adjustment of a therapeutic regime or attention to a new complaint
$70	Extended visit; requires unusual effort

*These payment schedules are being replaced by a new relative value schedule being implemented by Medicare.

Regulation of Physicians' Fees

One virtue of the DRG system is that it leaves most medical decisions up to the hospital's medical staff. In a hospital, for example, physicians do not have to answer to the federal government for ordering a diagnostic test. Quite different rules govern Medicare Part B, which pays physicians' fees and outpatient procedures.

Medicare has extensive regulations governing how physicians should practice medicine. Failure to abide by these regulations means that Medicare won't pay. If the violation is severe enough, a physician can be barred from the entire program. Some physicians try to fight the system. But they soon learn that such struggles are emotionally and financially exhausting, and no matter what the outcome, no fundamental rule is ever changed. Thus, the vast majority of physicians are working within the system, and an increasing number are providing exactly the care Medicare will pay for—no more and no less.

Table 10.5 illustrates how involved Medicare is in the practice of medicine. As the table shows, physician visits are categorized and defined, and detailed information about such visits must be supplied on Medicare reimbursement forms. Medicare also has opinions on how many visits and even what types of visits are appropriate for different medical problems. According to Medicare, for example, a certain percentage of physicians' visits to a patient's hospital room should be "brief" or "limited." There is no possibility that only "intermediate" visits would be appropriate during a patient's hospital stay. As in the case of Medicare Part A, these rules were written with the average patient in mind, and they almost always discriminate against physicians who see sicker patients.

Medicare's intrusiveness does not end there. Medicare has opinions on whether a diagnostic test should or should not be performed and enforces its opinions through its reimbursement policies. Medicare also has opinions about what drugs a physician should inject— opinions that are often at variance with the medical literature. For example, Medicare will pay only for drugs used as approved by the federal Food and Drug Administration (FDA). Yet the FDA is notoriously slow about approvals.

Often, the FDA will approve a drug for one medical purpose but never get around to approving it for any other. In the meantime, medical researchers will discover that the drug is even more valuable when used in another way. More than half of the drugs prescribed for treating cancer, for example, are for non-FDA-approved purposes. But physicians who follow the medical literature may find that they are violating Medicare policies and cannot be paid.

Medicare policies have an impact well beyond treatment of the elderly, since many state-run Medicaid programs and private insurers are adopting the same rules. Medicare payment policies, therefore, are increasingly dictating the type of care that all patients receive (see the discussion in chapter 18).

Paying Physicians by Relative Value Scales

Operating under a $2 million grant from the Health Care Financing Administration, researchers at the Harvard School of Public Health have decided how much some physicians should get paid for different types of services.[45] Their findings will be used by the federal government to set physician reimbursement fees under Medicare. Many Blue Cross and Blue Shield plans and other private third-party payers will use the same scheme.[46]

---

[45]W. C. Hsiao et al., "Results, Potential Effects and Implementation Issues of the Resource-Based Relative Value Scale," *Journal of the American Medical Association* 260, no. 16 (October 28, 1988): 2429–38.

[46]See *Medical Benefits* 7, no. 16 (August 30, 1990): 10.

The Harvard group first attempted to determine how much (physical or mental) effort was required by physicians to perform various tasks. Each task was assigned a number of points, so if one task got twice as many points as another, the first task would be twice as valuable (read: cost twice as much) as the second. The official name for the point system is the resource-based relative value scale (RBRVS). To get a sense of how the RBRVS system works, let's consider a few examples. Under the system, an "office visit, limited service, established patient" is worth 62 RBRVS points. On the other hand, an "initial history and physical examination related to a healthy individual, including anticipatory guidance, adult," is worth 114 RBRVS points if done by an internist.[47] Because the medical world is very complicated and there were thousands of physician tasks to be ranked, it is not surprising that the initial rankings frequently failed the test of common sense. For example, the removal of one lobe of the parated (salivary) gland, a fairly simple procedure, had the same relative value as an extensive and difficult cancer operation. A simple diagnostic dilation and curettage (D&C) was assigned a higher value per unit of time than a hysterectomy.

In general, the approach taken by the Harvard research group is based on the labor theory of value—a theory totally discredited by economists more than 100 years ago. The theory held that one could tell the worth of something simply by looking at how much time and effort were put into it, and by forgetting supply and demand and the role of markets. Karl Marx thought this theory could be applied to an entire society to determine the value of everyone's contribution to GNP. No communist country ever succeeded in putting Marx's theory into practice. To the extent they tried, virtually every one is rejecting it and turning toward markets to allocate resources. The lessons of socialism's failure, however, have largely bypassed the Medicare bureaucracy.

How Medicare Is Attempting to Fix Prices for the Services of Physicians

Unlike the DRG program for hospitals, Medicare does not necessarily fix the total reimbursement for physicians. In principle, Medicare limits what it pays, but patients and physicians are free to

[47]These examples are taken from Jane M. Orient, "What Is a Doctor's Relative Worth?" *The Freeman* (September 1989), pp. 355–56.

314

agree on a higher total price, with the patient paying the balance. But the Medicare bureaucracy has created strong incentives for physicians to accept assignment—an arrangement under which Medicare pays physicians directly if they agree to accept Medicare's payment as the total fee. Moreover, once physicians opt into the assignment program, they can never opt out of it. As a result, a growing proportion of physicians who treat Medicare patients do so on an assignment basis.[48] Moreover, as in the case of hospitals, the power to set fees ultimately is the power to determine the quality of care.

Regulation of the Quantity of Medical Care

The Medicare bureaucracy also exerts control over the practice of medicine in more direct ways. The bureaucracy has many opinions about what does and does not constitute cost-effective medical practice. In the hands of the Medicare bureaucracy, cost-benefit analysis is a mechanical device, which totally ignores patients' preferences and physicians' insights.

Direct Controls over Medical Practice

In many places, a hospital must receive telephone approval from the bureaucracy before admitting a Medicare patient, a practice that is also common among private third-party payment schemes. The person giving or denying the approval will not have met or examined the patient. The decision will be based on a cost-benefit analysis using statistical averages, with little or no room for the nonaverage, abnormally sick patient. These decisions can have life or death consequences.[49]

At other times, third-party payers literally attempt to dictate how medical care will be practiced. In the case of prescription drugs, for example, the restrictions placed on physicians include: (1) therapeutic drug interchange (the substitution of a less expensive drug for a more expensive one); (2) prior authorization; (3) drug formularies (limiting choice to a list of approved drugs); (4) limited reimbursement from third-party payers for prescriptions deemed "experimental" or for "off-label" applications; (5) drug protocols (in which

[48]That proportion was 40.7 percent of all physicians as of November/December 1988.
[49]Berenson.

315

Table 10.6
TEN MOST FREQUENT NEGATIVE OUTCOMES RESULTING
FROM DRUG COST-CONTAINMENT MEASURES

Negative Outcomes	Percent of Total
Lessened therapeutic response	28%
Therapeutic failure	24
Allergic reaction/side effects	13
Poor/loss of blood pressure	12
Heart failure/chest pain	8
Underdosed/lack potency/too strong	8
Convulsions/seizures	7
Recurring symptoms/pain/fever	5
Patient didn't recover	5
Adverse reaction/patient almost died	4

SOURCE: Oregon Medical Association, 1990. Reported in *Medical Benefits* 7, no. 17 (September 15, 1990).

drugs are prescribed in a predetermined sequence); and (6) generic substitution.

To determine the effects of these practices, Gallup polled cardiologists, internists, and general practitioners for the Oregon Medical Society. Table 10.6 shows the most frequently mentioned negative outcomes. On the average, there were 16.2 negative outcomes per physician polled, and in nine cases physicians reported that patients died because of the restrictions.[50]

Indirect Controls over Medical Practice

Even when Medicare cannot directly tell medical providers what to do, and even if it is not paying the bill, the Medicare bureaucracy can discourage what it believes is not "cost-effective" medicine by creating mountains of red tape. Medicare can require the completion of long, complicated forms even if the patient is paying out-of-pocket. Similar obstacles are created for patients who want to stay an extra day in the hospital—beyond the time that Medicare has deemed necessary.

[50]Reported in *Medical Benefits* 7, no. 17 (September 15, 1990): 10.

Potential Tools for Enforcing "Cost-Effective" Medicine

For the near future, the situation will get worse. Computerized protocols designed to instruct physicians about how to treat injuries and diseases could become powerful control mechanisms for the Medicare bureaucracy. The principle of a computerized protocol is not bad, provided it passes the market test. Imagine that a patient with a medical problem goes to see a physician. The physician types the patient's symptoms and other pertinent information into a computer. The computer's program digests the information and then recommends the most cost-effective first step—for example, a blood test. Once the results of that test are in, the program recommends the most cost-effective second step. At each stage in the process, the program recommends action based on other physicians' experiences and the costs and probable benefits of various options.

Such a system would undoubtedly have problems. So, given feedback from buyers and users, sellers would correct the errors, improve the techniques, and put out a better product. That is the way other computer programs are developed and improved in the marketplace. Such a development might be invaluable to physicians and patients who, of course, would always be free to ignore the computer program's advice. In the hands of the Medicare bureaucracy, however, computerized protocols could force physicians into a uniform practice of cost-effective medicine. Such a development would be harmful to patients for several reasons. First, a great deal of what medical science believes to be true at any point in time is shown later to be false. The progress of medical science requires experiment and innovation, and that implies different treatments for patients with similar conditions. Second, any computer program (like all other Medicare policies) will be based on statistical averages and lack the special insights and discoveries that come about in the relationship between patient and physician. Third, unlike the market for computer programs, the federal bureaucracy moves slowly, changes reluctantly, and is largely unresponsive to feedback from users (in this case, physicians and patients).

Finally, rules, regulations, and instructions developed by the federal government—unlike products sold in the marketplace—are anything but simple and efficient. Implementing price controls during World War II for example, the federal government took 21 pages to define a head of cabbage. How much more difficult will it be to define complicated medical procedures? Few people would realistically believe that government could develop cost-effective techniques to instruct auto mechanics. The prospects for achieving the same goal in the health care sector are even more remote. If Medicare tries it, delivery of medical care could become a practical nightmare.

How Medicare Attempts to Control the Quality of Care

The Medicare bureaucracy has been aware from the beginning that its payment scheme contains incentives to reduce quality. To combat this problem, the federal government set up yet another form of bureaucracy, peer review organizations (PROs), to monitor the quality of patient care. PROs are supposed to review the decisions of physicians and hospitals to make sure, for example, that sick patients are not released too early, that care does not cease simply because Medicare won't pay for it, and that unnecessary care is not given simply because Medicare will pay for it.

PROs have the authority to monitor and to impose sanctions. However, far from representing the interests of patients, they rarely communicate with patients and their deliberations are about as far removed from patients as a bureaucracy could be. In the main, PROs monitor one bureaucracy (hospitals) to serve the interests of another (Medicare). If patients in practically any city in the country are seeking information about quality care, a PRO is one of the last places they will find it.

Clearly there are problems of quality in America's hospitals. A recent study of the quality of care in New York State's hospitals, commissioned by the state government, is the most comprehensive study of the overall quality of hospital care ever conducted. The study found that, in 1986, negligence on the part of the hospital staff may have contributed to as many as 7,000 hospital deaths and 29,000 injuries. Although this represents only 1 percent of all patients, the instances of apparent malpractice are ten times greater than the number of malpractice lawsuits.[51]

---

[51]The report of the Harvard Medical Practice Study to the State of New York, *Patients, Doctors and Lawyers: Medical Injury, Malpractice Litigation, and Patient Compensation in New York* (Cambridge, MA: Harvard Medical Study, 1990).

318

Why Cost-Control Measures Do Not Ultimately Control Costs

Just as the private sector has attempted to control health care costs by opting out of the system of pure cost-plus finance since the 1980s, so the federal government has tried to accomplish the same goal over the same period of time. But U.S. medical costs are soaring and claiming an ever-increasing share of our GNP. Why are these efforts failing? The most fundamental reason is that the underlying defects in the way we finance medical care have not been corrected. When patients enter the medical marketplace, they are still spending someone else's money. Patients, physicians, and hospital administrators still have strong incentives to manipulate reimbursement rules in pursuit of their own interests.

Much of the time, when it appears that a new reimbursement policy is working, it is only because providers of medical services have found ways to shift costs to other third-party payers. As in the case of hip fracture patients, hospitals discover ways to shift costs to nursing homes and thus to Medicaid. During the brief period when the Medicare catastrophic coverage program was in force, the reverse was true. Medicaid found ways to shift nursing home costs to Medicare. Much of the so-called savings in Medicare hospital expenditures are not savings at all, but a shifting of costs to the private sector. In many cases, savings in Medicare Part A (hospital services) are realized only because costs have been shifted to Medicare Part B (physicians' services and outpatient care). Over the 1980s, Part A costs little more than doubled, while Part B costs more than quadrupled.

Yet another reason is that while some governmental bodies are trying to adopt policies that will hold down costs, others are passing laws that cause costs to rise. That phenomenon will be the subject of the next two chapters.

Needed Policy Changes

The federal government, operating principally through its Medicare program, is attempting to set prices and control quality in a very complex, multibillion-dollar market. Medicare payments are handled institution to institution, bureaucrat to bureaucrat. Virtually every Medicare rule or policy ignores the preferences and motives of patients on the one hand and the insights of physicians on the other. Medicare is a system in which it is often in everyone's self-interest to pursue goals that are the opposite of Medicare's goals.

Because individuals can often outsmart bureaucracies, many medical providers have made a great deal of money dealing with Medicare. But because individuals are usually powerless when they confront bureaucratic obstacles, patient care has often deteriorated.

In competitive markets for most consumer products, diversity abounds in quality and in price. There is no reason to expect the medical marketplace to be any different. All doctors are not the same. All hospitals are not the same. But the current DRG system treats them as if they were and thereby attempts to enforce a single price and maintain a single standard of quality for every medical procedure, regardless of where and by whom it is performed. Other government health care programs and the many cost-management programs in the private sector are similarly structured. This approach is destined to fail. It will be replaced either by an explicit program of health care rationing or by genuine market-based institutions.

There is nothing wrong with the attempt by Medicare to limit its expenditures and thus limit taxpayer liabilities. But there is something dreadfully wrong with its attempt to control the prices of hospital services and physicians' services in the marketplace.

The only way to ensure cost-effective, high-quality medical care is to make Medicare beneficiaries active participants in the market as the primary buyers of care and the primary monitors of the services they buy. In the short run, we should redirect the DRG system toward the goal of limiting the amount that the federal government spends in the medical marketplace, rather than attempting to control price and quality. Doctors, hospitals, and patients should be free to enter into whatever financial arrangements they choose. The marketplace, not government, should determine the price and quality of health care.

Similar changes should be instituted in the Medicaid program. Where particular health care needs warrant special attention (such as prenatal care), special accounts should be created from which pregnant Medicaid women could draw funds to purchase specific types of care. The goal should be to empower poor women, enable them to escape the indigent health care system, and make them full participants in the market economy.

For the long run, our goal should be to separate medicine and politics as much as possible. Ways of reaching that goal are suggested throughout this book.

11. Regulation of Health Insurance by State Governments

Although we have described the U.S. health care system as a cost-plus system in a cost-control stage, it would be incorrect to infer that all, or even most, government policies adopted during this stage are actually holding down costs. On the whole, it is probably fair to say that they are increasing costs. This chapter examines the role of state governments, which are yielding to special-interest pressures and passing laws that relentlessly increase the price of health insurance and the amount of health care spending.

Health Insurance Benefits Mandated by State Governments[1]

Mandated health insurance benefit laws require that health insurance contracts cover specific diseases, disabilities, and services. In some cases, laws require insurers to offer a benefit as an option for an additional premium. In 1970, there were only 48 mandated health insurance benefit laws in the United States. Yet as Figure 11.1 shows, in recent years there has been an explosion in the number of such laws, and they now total close to 1,000.[2]

Mandated benefits cover diseases ranging from AIDS to alcoholism and drug abuse. They cover services ranging from acupuncture to in vitro fertilization. They cover everything from life-prolonging surgery to purely cosmetic devices. They cover heart transplants

---

[1]Many of the statistics in this chapter were obtained from various sources in the health insurance industry. The interpretations of the statistics are those of the authors and do not constitute legal opinions. In many states, lawsuits currently are under way to determine the exact meaning of various statutes and regulations.

[2]Information obtained from *Health Benefits Letter* 1, no. 15 (August 29, 1991). For a discussion of the growth of mandated benefits, see Greg Scandlen, "The Changing Environment of Mandated Benefits," in Employee Benefit Research Institute, *Government Mandating of Employee Benefits* (Washington, 1987), pp. 177–83.

Figure 11.1
NUMBER OF MANDATED HEALTH INSURANCE BENEFITS
ENACTED BY STATE GOVERNMENTS, 1965 TO 1991

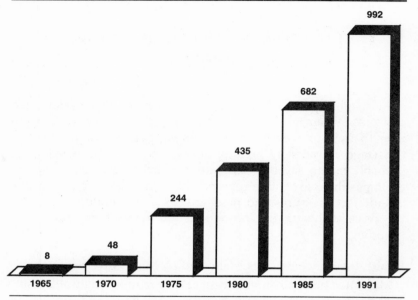

SOURCE: Greg Scandlen, *Health Benefits Letter* 1, no. 15 (August 29, 1991).

in Georgia, liver transplants in Illinois, hairpieces in Minnesota, marriage counseling in California, pastoral counseling in Vermont, and sperm bank deposits in Massachusetts. These laws reflect the politicization of health insurance. Special-interest lobbies now represent almost every major disease and disability, group of health care providers, and type of health care service. As a result, health insurance is being shaped and molded by political pressures, rather than by competition and consumer choice in a free market.

Mandated benefits legislation invariably makes health insurance more expensive. Under federal law, however, companies with self-insured health care plans are exempt from these state regulations, and virtually all large companies and many small and medium-sized ones are now self-insured. Federal employees and Medicare recipients also are exempt. State governments often exempt state employees and Medicaid recipients as well. As a result, mandated benefits regulations fall heavily on employees of small firms and on the purchasers of individual and family policies—people who typically lack economic and political power.

The Alternatives to Mandated Benefits

Before looking at specific regulations, it is useful to first consider some alternatives. In many, or perhaps most, cases, mandated benefit laws merely represent the legislative success of special interests. In other cases, however, they address issues that many people care about, such as preventive care (including mammograms), well-child care, maternity expenses, medical expenses for adopted children, and medical expenses for AIDS patients. Legislators often mandate these benefits out of a desire to remove financial barriers to obtaining health care or to relieve families of great financial burdens.

Even if the goal is humane and desirable, the method is not. In passing mandated benefit laws, state legislators are attempting to create benefits without paying for them. The cost is then imposed on other people through higher health insurance premiums. When legislators attempt to benefit one group, they raise the cost of insurance for another. The result is a redistribution of costs and benefits that is usually highly regressive. Those most likely to gain are special groups of middle-income families. Those most likely to be harmed are lower income families that are priced out of the market for health insurance as premiums rise to cover the cost of the new mandates.

A more efficient and humane way to accomplish the same objectives is through the use of direct subsidies, funded by taxes paid by all citizens. State governments, for example, could make direct payments to low-income families with particular health disabilities. The payments could be income-related so that financial help would be targeted to those who need it most. Another technique would be to subsidize purchases of particular medical services (such as prenatal care), again with the subsidies targeted to low-income families. A third strategy is to directly subsidize the health insurance premiums of people with particular disabilities (such as AIDS), based on their income.

Each of these alternatives would permit the health insurance marketplace to continue to function, and to give people options

325

among different types of coverage and premiums that reflect the real cost of the options. Each alternative also would require legislators to pay for the benefits they confer and would make it more likely that the subsidies would go to people who most need them and that the costs would be borne by those who could best afford them.

Apart from more expensive medical services, there is a trend toward state mandates for relatively inexpensive preventive services such as Pap smears, mammograms, and well-child care. The vast majority of people can pay such expenses out-of-pocket and can include planning for such expenses in a family budget. Legislators are concerned, however, that when family budgets get tight, people will skimp on medical care. Yet as noted in previous chapters, using insurers to pay small medical bills is costly and inefficient. A better solution (one advanced throughout this book) would be to encourage people to establish and use Medisave accounts for small medical bills.

Misguided Attempts to Shift Costs from the Public to the Private Sector

An important principle of insurance is that the insured event must be a risky event, one that has not already occurred. In this sense, pure insurance is a gamble. Yet some states require insurers to insure people who are already known to have an illness that will generate future medical costs in excess of the premiums they pay. The result is that all other policyholders must pay higher premiums. Another important principle of insurance is that individuals must not be able to collect as a result of their intentional behavior. Yet many states require that health insurance cover treatment for alcoholism and drug abuse for those who engage in substance abuse at the time the policy is issued.[3] The result is that social drinkers, teetotalers, and nondrug users pay higher premiums to cover the costs.

---

[3]Whether or not alcoholism and drug abuse are properly classified as diseases, they are the consequences of purposeful behavior. Thus, insurance against alcoholism or drug abuse often is not insurance against the possibility that someone accidentally will become a substance abuser but is instead a commitment to pay medical expenses for one who already is.

Such regulations are partly a result of lobbying pressures from health care providers and high-risk groups. But they also reflect a desire on the part of state legislators to force the private sector to pay costs that would otherwise be paid by government.

AIDS

The cost of treating an AIDS patient currently runs between $75,000 and $150,000.[4] Given that most AIDS patients are unable to pay that much using their own resources, the cost often is paid by government. In an effort to shift these costs to the private sector, the District of Columbia enacted a law prohibiting insurers in the District from refusing to issue a policy or charging a higher premium to individuals already diagnosed as having AIDS.[5] Some states are also moving in this same direction. (See Table 11.1.) In California, insurers may not test insurance applicants for the presence of AIDS antibodies. Three states (Florida, New Jersey, and Wisconsin) prohibit AIDS testing for group insurance, and a similar regulation has been proposed in Rhode Island. In 12 states, insurers may not ask applicants if they have ever been tested for AIDS, and similar regulations are being proposed in 5 other states.[6]

Alcoholism and Drug Abuse

Substance abuse can be even more expensive to treat than AIDS. That is partly because the treatment is prolonged, typically takes place in an expensive facility, and requires intensive use of trained personnel. In addition, the patient often must return for further treatment. As in the case of AIDS, the government might have to bear the cost of much of this treatment unless private health insurance pays for it.

Forty states now have regulations governing health insurance for alcoholism. Of these, 29 states make such coverage mandatory and 11 require that the insurer offer it as an option. Twenty-seven states

[4]In certain managed care programs, the cost may be as low as $35,000. See Roger Rickles, "Firms Turn to 'Case Management' to Bring Down Health Care Costs," *Wall Street Journal*, December 30, 1987, p. 13.

[5]In 1989, Congress passed an appropriations bill that contained language forcing the District of Columbia to repeal this law. In effect, Congress told the District that no federal funds would be available unless the law were rescinded.

[6]With the exceptions noted above, insurers may conduct their own tests, but such testing is expensive and adds to the overall cost of insurance.

327

Table 11.1
RESTRICTIONS ON HEALTH INSURANCE RELATING TO AIDS*

Regulation	Number of States with the Regulation	Number of States Where Regulation Is Proposed
HIV testing prohibited for all insurance	1	0
HIV testing prohibited for group insurance	3	1
Insurers may not discriminate on basis of sexual orientation	13	4
Insurers may not use sexual orientation, occupation, age, sex, or marital status to predict whether individual will develop AIDS	10	3
Insurers may not ask questions about sexual orientation or lifestyle	13	4
Insurers may not ask if applicant has been tested for HIV or ask about results of such tests	12	5
Insurers may not ask if applicant has had blood transfusion	2	0
Insurers may not ask if applicant has been rejected as blood donor or been advised not to donate blood	2	0

SOURCE: Information compiled by Security Life of Denver.
*As of June 1, 1988.

have regulations governing health insurance for drug addiction. Of these, 19 make benefits mandatory and 8 require coverage as an option. In some cases, the regulations are ludicrous from the point of view of genuine insurance. For example, in Louisiana, group insurers are required to offer optional coverage for treatment of alcoholism or drug abuse—an option few policyholders would choose unless they intended to file claims. In Connecticut, insurers are required to provide at least 30 days of inpatient care for the "accidental ingestion" of cocaine, marijuana, morphine, amphetamines, barbiturates, hallucinatory drugs, and other controlled substances.

Adopted Children

Twenty-five states have regulations mandating health insurance coverage for adopted children, usually requiring that adopted children be covered like other dependents. In Minnesota, however, an insurer must cover preexisting conditions. That means that if an adopted child has an expensive-to-treat condition, the insurance company (and therefore other policyholders) must bear the costs. This regulation encourages families to adopt children who might otherwise remain in state institutions at taxpayer expense. Although it saves money for some Minnesota taxpayers, the regulation raises the cost of health insurance for others.

Special-Interest Pressures from Health Care Providers

All health insurance contracts require some specification of who is authorized to diagnose and treat illness. Under traditional contracts, this authority was reserved to licensed physicians. Thus, the treatment of mental illness would include psychiatrists, but not psychologists. Diagnosis and treatment of eye diseases would include ophthalmologists, but not optometrists. In general, podiatrists and chiropractors were excluded. In recent years, however, we have witnessed a flood of regulations designed to open the market for health insurance reimbursement to scores of allied practitioners. Currently, for example, 45 states mandate coverage for the services of chiropractors. In general, chiropractors have the right to diagnose and treat diseases (including taking diagnostic x-rays) under standard insurance policies. In Nevada, insurers must reimburse chiropractors at the same rate as physicians performing similar services, even though chiropractors' fees to uninsured patients may be one-half to one-third less.

These regulations can significantly raise the cost of conventional health insurance. In general, patients of chiropractors tend to be heavy users of services. Chiropractors often will diagnose illnesses that would be dismissed by physicians and prescribe courses of treatment that would not be prescribed by physicians.

329

Table 11.2
MANDATED BENEFITS: SELECTED PROVIDERS[1]

Type of Provider	Number of States with Mandates[2]
Optometrists	46
Chiropractors	45
Dentists	40
Podiatrists (chiropodists)	37
Psychologists	36
Nurse midwives	24
Other types of nurses[3]	23
Social workers	22
Physical therapists	16
Psychiatric nurses	9
Speech/hearing therapists	8
Professional counselors[4]	7
Occupational therapists	5
Acupuncturists	4
Naturopaths	2

SOURCE: *Health Benefits Letter* 1, no. 15 (August 29, 1991).
[1]As of July 1991.
[2]Includes mandated coverage and mandated offerings.
[3]Includes nurses, nurse practitioners, and nurse anesthetists.
[4]Includes marriage, family, and child counselors.

As Table 11.2 shows, chiropractors are not an isolated example. In California, if an insurance policy covers the services of a psychiatrist, it must cover similar services by marriage counselors and child and family counselors. In Alaska and Connecticut, insurers must cover the services of naturopaths. In Nevada, New Mexico, and Oregon, insurers must cover acupuncture, and in California acupuncture coverage must be offered as an option. The potential for further mandates covering allied practitioners is almost endless. Currently, there are at least 142 health-related professions, with as many as 240 occupational job classifications (see Table 11.3).[7]

[7]John B. Welsh, Jr., "Legislative Review of Third-Party Mandated Benefits and Offerings in the State of Washington," in Employee Benefit Research Institute, *Government Mandating of Employee Benefits*, p. 194.

Table 11.3
MANDATED BENEFITS: SELECTED SERVICES[1]

Type of Service	Number of States with Mandates[2]
Alcoholism treatment	40
Mammography screening	39
Mental health care	29
Drug abuse treatment	27
Maternity	25
Home health care	20
Well-child care	12
TMJ disorders	12
Ambulatory surgery	12
Breast reconstruction	11
Pap smears	8
In vitro fertilization	7
Cleft palate	7
Hospice care	7
Diabetic education	5
Rehabilitation services	5
Second surgical opinions	5
Long-term care	3
Prescription drugs	3

SOURCE: *Health Benefits Letter* 1, no. 15 (August 29, 1991).
[1]As of July 1991.
[2]Includes mandated coverage and mandated offerings.

Building Constituencies for Specific Diseases and Disabilities

As in the case of AIDS, legislators frequently face pressure from people who are afflicted with a particular disease or disability or are at risk of affliction. In terms of the number of regulations, it would appear that the blind have the most effective special-interest lobby. Beyond blindness, constituencies extend from pregnant women exposed to cancer-causing substances to individuals concerned with virtually every form of mental illness. The following are some examples.

DES Mothers

In the 1950s and 1960s, a number of pregnant women took the drug diethylstilbestrol (DES) to control morning sickness. Subsequently, it was discovered that DES exposure could cause cervical and uterine cancer in the daughters of these women. At least six states limit the ability of insurers to act on this knowledge. In California, for example, an insurer may not charge higher premiums or refuse to cover an individual either because the person has conditions attributable to DES or has been exposed to DES.

Sickle-Cell and Other Genetic Traits

Some individuals carry a genetic trait that does not affect the health of the carrier but may produce a disease or disability in the person's offspring. Examples are the sickle-cell trait (found almost exclusively in black men) and Tay-Sachs disease (almost exclusively affecting persons of Jewish descent). When an applicant is known to have such a genetic trait, many states restrict insurers from acting on this knowledge. For example, at least six states regulate the sale of insurance to individuals who have the sickle-cell trait. In California, Florida, and North Carolina, insurers may not deny coverage or charge a higher premium based on the likelihood that the trait may affect an individual's offspring. In North Carolina, the same restriction is extended to individuals with hemoglobin-C trait. In California, the restriction applies to all genetic traits.

Physical and Mental Handicaps

Most states regulate the sale of health insurance to the handicapped or disabled. For example, at least 34 states have regulations covering all physical handicaps or all general handicaps and disabilities, at least 29 have regulations specifically covering mental disabilities, and at least 35 have regulations specifically covering blindness or partial blindness. In general, such regulations inhibit insurance companies from selling policies for actuarially fair prices. As a result, the cost of insurance is higher for all other policyholders. In many states, insurers cannot refuse to cover the handicapped, but they may charge higher rates based on actuarial experience. In North Carolina, insurers have flexibility with respect to handicapped adults but must cover handicapped minors at the same rates as other children.[8]

---

[8]In this instance, as in most other cases discussed here, the insurer is not required to pay the cost of treating a preexisting illness. However, the insurer is precluded from charging a higher premium even when a disability increases the likelihood of future claims.

When insurers are allowed to charge higher premiums for handicapped people, the insurance company usually bears the burden and expense of proving that the rate differentials are justified. In Missouri, for example, insurance regulators assume no differential risk among classes of people unless the insurers can produce statistical evidence. In Minnesota, insurers may not charge higher premiums unless they can prove significant differences in health care costs for people who have those disabilities.

On the surface, it may seem fair to ask that differential premiums be related to differential costs of insurance. But the burden of proof may be too costly or even impossible for insurers to bear. In Louisiana, for example, insurers must cover individuals with spinal cord injuries, amputations, autism, epilepsy, mental retardation, and any other neurological impairment. A higher premium may be charged only if insurers can justify it on the basis of actuarial experience. In many cases, however, the disability is so rare that no actuarial tables exist. As a result of these restrictions, the premiums charged are less fair than they would otherwise be. Handicapped policyholders often are undercharged, and all other policyholders are overcharged to make up the difference.

Misguided Attempts at Cost Control

Some mandated benefits regulations are designed to encourage substitution of outpatient for inpatient surgery and of home care for hospital care, second and even third opinions prior to surgery, and certain types of preventive medical care. Although the regulations may have been encouraged by provider groups, some also appear to have been influenced by the states' desire to reduce health care costs. In all cases, they are misguided attempts to substitute political judgment for personal choice.

Outpatient Care

Twelve states require insurers to cover outpatient care as an alternative to inpatient care, and six of these states require that the benefits be identical. Surgery performed in an independent outpatient clinic usually costs less. But hospitals are setting up their own outpatient services, and the costs of those services may be higher than inpatient care.

Home Health Care

At least 20 states have regulations governing home health care. Coverage is mandatory in 14 of them, and must be offered as an option in the other 6. New Jersey, for example, requires coverage in the home for anything that would have been covered in a hospital on the same reimbursement basis. Yet, because it often consumes more services over a longer period, home care can cost more.

Second Opinions on Surgery

Five states require insurers to cover a second opinion prior to surgery, and Rhode Island requires coverage for a third opinion if the first two physicians disagree. Yet the experience of large corporations has been that blanket policies requiring second opinions save very little money. Second opinions are costly, and for many procedures the cost may be greater than the benefit.[9]

Preventive Medical Care

Eight states require coverage for Pap smears and 39 states mandate coverage for mammograms. Florida has mandated coverage for a specific number of physician visits for children at different ages, with a requirement that the insured not be charged any deductible in connection with the visit. Similar legislation is being considered by other states. The American Academy of Pediatrics is lobbying for 12 mandated well-child physician visits for children from birth through the age of six, implying that such an investment in preventive medicine will save Americans money. The evidence says otherwise. On the basis of cost-benefit analysis, it is hard to justify any well-child physician visits.[10] This type of preventive medicine may have important benefits for parents (relief of anxiety, reassurance, etc.), but it is not necessarily a wise way to spend scarce health care dollars. Even where preventive care can be cost-justified, paying for it through third-party insurers is almost always wasteful.

---

[9]See Glenn Ruffenbach, "Health Costs: Second Thoughts on Second Opinions," *Wall Street Journal*, July 27, 1988, p. 21.

[10]See Judith Wagner, Roger Herdman, and David Alpers, "Well-Child Care: How Much Is Enough?" *Health Affairs* (Fall 1989).

Case Study: Maternity and Childbirth

No issue illustrates the pressures on state legislators better than pregnancy and childbirth—in terms of both the emotional impact and the influence of medical providers and their potential patients. All 50 states have some regulation governing health insurance for newborns, and at least 45 states require that newborn care be included both in individual and group policies.[11] It's not hard to understand why. In 1986, the Sheraton Corporation spent $1.2 million (about 10 percent of its total health care costs) on three premature babies born to company employees. In 1984, Sunbeam Appliance Co. spent $500,000 (half of its entire employee health care costs) on four premature babies. That same year, Ameritrust Corporation spent $1.4 million on one premature baby.[12]

Clearly, having a child is a risky and potentially costly event. But many state regulations force health insurers to ignore that fact. For example, Arizona requires that a policy covering an insured person's dependents must also cover newborns, including premature babies and those with congenital abnormalities, but with no increase in premium. In Montana, coverage for a newborn is mandated even if other dependent children are not covered. In Minnesota and Ohio, a policy covering a dependent's daughter must also cover a newborn child of the (unwed) daughter. Since newborns are more expensive to insure than older children, the costs of these mandated benefits must be borne by other policyholders, including single men and childless women.

At least half the states also have regulations covering the costs of maternity and complications of pregnancy. At least 15 states prohibit discrimination on the basis of marital status, despite the fact that unwed mothers have a higher incidence of complications of pregnancy. In Colorado and New Jersey, for example, single and divorced women must receive the same coverage on the same terms as married women.

---

[11]Linda L. Lanam, "Mandated Benefits—Who Is Protected?" in Employee Benefit Research Institute, *Government Mandating of Employee Benefits*, p. 186.

[12]Rickles, p. 13; and Cathy Trust, "Corporate Prenatal-Care Plans Multiply, Benefiting Both Mothers and Employers," *Wall Street Journal*, June 24, 1988, p. 15.

Nor is that all. Even if pregnancy is viewed as a risky and unplanned event, surely the same cannot be said for in vitro fertilization. Yet five states—Arkansas, Hawaii, Maryland, Massachusetts, and Rhode Island—mandate benefits for in vitro fertilization, and in Connecticut and Texas it must be offered as an option. Moreover, because the procedure can cause multiple conceptions, leading to multiple abortions or multiple births, and because unsuccessful couples may repeat the procedure an almost endless number of times, the resulting health care expenses can be quite high.[13]

Other Types of Mandated Benefits

In addition to the medical benefits described above, some states regulate the terms and conditions under which policies may be sold. For example, some mandate that a policy must be "guaranteed renewable" for a certain period of time. That means that an insurer cannot stop covering a group of people, regardless of actuarial experience. Some also mandate that Medicare supplemental policies must be "guaranteed issued." That means that the insurer cannot refuse to sell the policy, regardless of the applicant's health. Some states refuse to permit coordination of insurance claims among companies covering the same individual. That means that an individual with coverage by more than one insurer can collect full benefits under each policy and thereby profit from being sick.

As with other types of mandated benefits, little is known about how much any single type of regulation adds to the rising cost of health insurance. However, Golden Rule Insurance Company has estimated how some regulations have increased the average policy premium in some states. Because Texas mandated that major medical plans must be guaranteed renewable for the first five years, Golden Rule's premiums in the state were increased by 15 percent. Because Georgia does not allow claims to be coordinated among insurance carriers, Golden Rule policies in that state are 15 percent higher than they otherwise would be. Maryland's requirement that

---

[13]It is estimated that one in six couples experiences infertility, and the nation is currently spending $1 billion a year to address the problem. Success with in vitro fertilization usually comes after two cycles. However, unsuccessful couples may try an endless number of cycles. See "Business Bulletin," *Wall Street Journal*, October 19, 1989.

Medigap[14] policies be guaranteed renewable adds 13 percent to premium prices. Michigan's requirement that Medigap policies be guaranteed renewable and guaranteed issued adds 30 percent. Because of unisex legislation prohibiting differential premiums for men and women in Montana, Golden Rule no longer markets insurance in that state.[15]

Guaranteed renewable is not a bad feature of health insurance policies—especially if people are willing to voluntarily pay a higher price to obtain it (see chapter 6). When health insurance more closely resembled real insurance instead of being prepayment for the consumption of medical care, guaranteed renewable was a common feature of policies sold in a competitive insurance market. Guaranteed issue is not a normal or natural consequence of a competitive insurance marketplace, however.

Price Regulation, Insurance Company Profits, and High-Risk Individuals

As Lloyd's of London has shown us, almost any risky event is insurable for a price. Lloyd's not only insures communications satellites headed for upper earth orbit; it also has insured Bruce Springsteen's voice and the beards (against fire or theft) of 40 members of the Whiskers Club in Derbyshire, England. When Cutty Sark offered $2 million to anyone who could capture the Loch Ness monster alive, Lloyd's insured Cutty Sark against having to honor its promise. Prior to and during Operation Desert Storm, Lloyd's wrote coverage for vessels in or near the conflict; in fact it opened its doors on Sunday for the first time in its 303-year history to accommodate new customers as hostilities broke out. If Lloyd's of London can insure endangered ships, men's whiskers, and promotional stakes, why can't many Americans buy health insurance? One answer is that in almost every state, health insurance premium prices are regulated.

Because health costs are continually rising, such state regulation usually consists of a restriction on how much premium prices may increase to cover those costs. In most states, insurance companies may not increase premium prices unless benefits paid are at least

---

[14]Medigap policies supplement coverage provided under Medicare.
[15]Information obtained from Golden Rule Insurance Company.

equal to a certain percentage of premium income. In all cases, regulation of premium prices translates into regulation of insurance company profits. Without sufficient annual profits, the companies cannot build reserves to cover costs that are unusual enough to occur once in every five, ten, or twenty years. This type of regulation, in turn, can make it virtually impossible for individuals with a higher than average probability of illness to obtain health insurance.

Risk and Profit

A basic principle governing all financial markets is: The higher the risk, the higher the rate of return. For example, to induce investors to purchase riskier financial assets (stocks, bonds, etc.), the sellers must convince the buyers they can earn more than on less risky assets. If we made it illegal to earn more than, say, a 10 percent return in the bond market, investors would be unwilling to purchase bonds from any but the most financially sound corporations. If we made it illegal to earn more than 8 percent on bonds, investors might be willing to purchase only government securities.

A similar principle applies to the market for health insurance: When insurers sell policies to high-risk individuals, they take on more financial risk. Other things equal, the more high-risk policyholders an insurer has, the more risky the total portfolio. Insurers voluntarily accept additional risk only if they can earn a higher return. When state governments limit the rate of return, the inevitable result is that higher risk individuals are unable to obtain health insurance at any price. One way to think of many mandated benefits laws is to see them as an attempt by state governments to force insurers to sell policies to individuals who have been regulated out of the market by state insurance regulators. Such attempts are destined to fail. When state governments force insurers to take on additional risk and forbid them to earn a higher rate of return, insurers simply quit selling policies in the state. For example, it was primarily because of the regulation of premium prices that, in September 1988, Golden Rule Insurance Company ceased marketing its policies in Alabama, Georgia, Massachusetts, Mississippi, North Carolina, New Mexico, and West Virginia.[16]

---

[16]Information obtained from Golden Rule Insurance Company.

Risk Pools

One way in which state governments have attempted to provide health insurance for high-risk individuals is through the use of risk pools. These are mandated benefits in the sense that all insurers operating in the state are usually forced to participate in the pool. Currently, 15 states have risk pools, and 22 others are considering similar legislation.[17] Under this arrangement, insurance is sold to individuals who cannot obtain policies outside the pool. Premium prices are regulated and generally are set as a percentage of the prices of similar policies sold in the marketplace. For example, in most states, the premium for risk pool insurance is 50 percent higher than for comparable policies.[18] In Florida, however, risk pool premiums may be twice as high; and in Montana, they may be four times as high. In Minnesota, the most generous state, risk pool insurance is only 25 percent more expensive.

Because all states cap the price of risk pool insurance, risk pools almost always lose money.[19] In most cases, losses are covered by assessing insurers, usually in proportion to their share of the market. In Maine, however, losses are covered by a tax on hospital revenues; and in Illinois, they are covered by general tax revenues. In most states that assess insurers for risk pool losses, companies are allowed to fully or partially offset their assessment against premium taxes paid to the state government.[20]

The most serious problem with risk pools is that they raise the cost of health care and/or health insurance for everyone not in the pool. When risk pool losses are paid by a tax on hospital revenues, the burden is placed on sick people. When losses are covered by assessing insurers, the burden is placed on other policyholders. And when insurers are allowed to offset their assessments against state taxes, additional pressure to maintain (or even increase) taxes on insurance premiums is created and causes further distortion in the health insurance marketplace.

[17]For a state-by-state survey of risk pools, see Aaron K. Trippler, *Comprehensive Health Insurance for High-Risk Individuals*, 2d ed. (Minneapolis: Communicating for Agriculture, 1987).

[18]Ibid., pp. 23–24.

[19]Among operating pools, Florida is the only state that has not had losses. Ibid., p. 47.

[20]Ibid., pp. 35–37.

Some Consequences of State-Mandated Benefits

The flood of mandated benefits legislation at the state level has had two major consequences. First, all those who can opt out of regulated health insurance and purchase nonregulated insurance tend to do so. Second, among those who cannot obtain unregulated insurance, an increasing number have no insurance at all. Ironically, those without insurance tend to represent both extremes on the spectrum of the potentially ill. Those who are very healthy and have a low probability of becoming ill choose to remain uninsured because the price of regulated insurance is too high. At the other extreme, those who have a high probability of becoming ill are uninsured because insurers go to considerable lengths to avoid them.

Escape from Regulation by Large and Medium-Sized Firms

On January 1, 1988, the Circle K Corporation, the nation's second largest convenience store chain, sent an interesting letter to its 8,000 employees. The letter announced that the company would no longer provide health care coverage for certain "life style-related" illnesses, including alcohol and drug abuse, self-inflicted wounds, and AIDS (unless acquired accidentally through a blood transfusion).[21] Given that Circle K Corporation operates in 27 states, it undoubtedly operates in states where health insurance benefits for the excluded diseases are required by state law. However, because the company does not purchase insurance, federal law exempts it from state regulations mandating health insurance benefits.[22]

Circle K is not alone. Just as there has been an explosion of mandated benefits legislation over the last decade, there has been an equally dramatic increase in the number of companies that self-insure and manage their own employee health care plans.[23] Today,

---

[21]Kenneth B. Noble, "Health Insurance Tied to Life-Style," *New York Times,* August 6, 1988, p. 1.

[22]In the fall of 1988, Circle K rescinded the policy in response to pressure from special-interest groups. Failing to comply with state mandates, however, is common practice among self-insured employers.

[23]For a description of the types of employer self-insurance and the benefits of self-insurance, see John C. Goodman and Gerald L. Musgrave, *The Changing Market for Health Insurance: Opting Out of the Cost-Plus System,* NCPA Policy Report no. 118 (Dallas: National Center for Policy Analysis, September 1985).

roughly 50 percent of all employees work for employers who are self-insured.

One reason for self-insurance is that companies are better able to manage their own health care plans and hold down rising costs. Another is that self-insured companies avoid state taxes on insurance premiums and other costly and inefficient regulations. But the most important reason may be that self-insured companies bypass the regulations and costs of mandated health insurance benefits.[24] In other words, employers who self-insure are free to tailor that insurance to the wants and needs of their employees. They are doing what any sensible consumer would do, were it not for government interference.

When companies self-insure, they usually institute cost-management techniques that are at odds with the direction of state health insurance regulations. For example, although the trend in state regulation has been to increase the number and types of services required under conventional health insurance, the tendency among self-insured companies has been to restrict and limit employee choices to certain physicians, hospitals, and types of care.[25]

With few exceptions, mandated health care benefits legislation raises the cost of conventional health insurance. Moreover, as more and more companies self-insure, the burden and costs of such legislation are being imposed on a smaller and smaller proportion of insured individuals. In some states, it is believed that as much as 75 percent of the workforce is covered by self-insured plans. That means that the full burden of mandated benefits regulation falls on the remaining 25 percent.[26]

In an effort to determine how state health insurance regulations affect the decision of firms to self-insure, health economists Jon Gabel and Gail Jensen looked at a sample of 280 firms that were not self-insured in 1981. By 1984, 24 percent chose self-insurance. Using a model that correctly predicted a firm's decision to self-insure 86 percent of the time, Gabel and Jensen found that increasing the state

[24]U.S. Office of Technology Assessment, *Medical Testing and Health Insurance*, report no. OTA-H-384 (Washington: U.S. Government Printing Office, August 1988), p. 7.

[25]Rhonda L. Rundle, "Insurers Step Up Efforts to Reduce Use of Free-Choice Health Plans," *Wall Street Journal*, May 11, 1988.

[26]Scandlen, p. 182.

premium tax from 1 percent to 3 percent increased the probability of self-insuring between 20 percent and 24 percent. Imposing a risk pool and mandating continuation of coverage increased the probability by 55.8 percent and 165.6 percent, respectively.[27]

The Gabel-Jensen study found that mandates for psychologists raised the probability of self-insuring (by 93.2 percent), as did mandates for alcohol treatment (5.9 percent) and drug dependency (58.8 percent), although the latter two mandates were not statistically significant. The impact of all state regulations taken together caused half the firms that self-insured to make that decision.[28]

Escape from Health Insurance by Small Firms

All federal employees and all people covered under Medicare also are exempted from state-mandated benefits by federal law, and states commonly exempt their own employees and all Medicaid patients. The upshot is that the burdens and costs of mandated health care benefits fall on the rest of the population: people who work for small firms, the self-employed, and the unemployed. As a result, an increasing number of small firms are discontinuing their health insurance plans for employees or choosing not to offer health insurance in the first place. Gabel and Jensen found that each new mandate lowered the probability that a small firm would offer health insurance by 1.5 percent. Raising premium taxes from 1 percent to 3 percent or imposing a risk pool lowered the likelihood of a small firm offering health insurance by at least 10 percent, and continuation of coverage mandates lowered the likelihood by 13 percent. In the absence of all regulations, Gabel and Jensen determined, 16 percent of small firms that do not now offer health insurance would do so.[29]

Higher Premiums for All Insured People

Mandated benefits legislation raises the cost of regulated health insurance in a variety of ways. Some regulations force insurers to pay for the health care of people who are already sick (for example,

---

[27]Jon Gabel and Gail Jensen, "The Price of State-Mandated Benefits," *Inquiry* 26, no. 4 (Winter 1989): 419–31.

[28]Ibid.

[29]Ibid.

AIDS victims); other regulations force insurers to cover procedures related to people's choices (for example, in vitro fertilization and marriage and family counseling) rather than to well-defined, risky events; and many regulations expand the definition of illness and the cost of treatment by expanding the range of covered providers (for example, by including acupuncturists and naturopaths).

In the case of chiropractors, for example, a study by Peat Marwick Main & Co. found that, under Hawaii's current practice of not mandating coverage for chiropractic services, there was no evidence that lack of chiropractic coverage resulted in inadequate care or financial hardship for people using those services. On the other hand, were Hawaii to mandate coverage, the total cost of the mandated benefit would be as high as $8.1 million per year[30] (see Table 11.4).

In a separate study, Peat Marwick found no evidence that lack of coverage for well-baby care resulted in inadequate care or financial hardship. But mandating coverage for well-baby care in Hawaii would increase health insurance costs by as much as $1.8 million.[31] Researchers also found only anecdotal evidence that lack of coverage for alcoholism and drug dependence resulted in lack of treatment. But the cost of mandating coverage for alcoholism and drug abuse in Hawaii would be as much as $2.3 million.[32] The cost of mandating coverage for inpatient mental health care in Hawaii was estimated to be as high as $12.3 million, and for outpatient treatment of mental illness, as high as $6.8 million.[33]

Further evidence of the costs of specific mandates was gathered by Gail Jensen and Michael Morrisey.[34] The Jensen-Morrisey study attempted to estimate the effect on premiums of various insurance policy provisions, whether or not they are mandated. The results

[30]Peat Marwick Main & Co. and the Office of the Legislative Auditor, *Study of Proposed Mandated Health Insurance for Chiropractic Services: A Report to the Governor and the Legislature of the State of Hawaii* (January 1988).

[31]Peat Marwick Main & Co. and the Office of the Legislative Auditor, *Study of Proposed Mandatory Health Insurance for Well-Baby Services: A Report to the Governor and the Legislature of the State of Hawaii* (January 1988).

[32]Peat Marwick Main & Co. and the Office of the Legislative Auditor, *Study of Proposed Mandatory Health Insurance for Alcohol and Drug Dependence and Mental Illness: A Report to the Governor and the Legislature of the State of Hawaii* (January 1988).

[33] Ibid.

[34]Gail A. Jensen and Michael A. Morrisey, "The Premium Consequences of Group Health Insurance Provisions" (September 1988), mimeograph.

Table 11.4
Annual Cost of Proposed Mandated Benefits in Hawaii*

Benefit	Low Estimate	Middle Estimate	High Estimate
Chiropractic services	$2,734,000	$ 6,245,000	$ 8,089,000
Well-baby care	1,267,750	1,521,280	1,774,810
Alcohol and drug abuse treatment	284,088	414,048	2,305,308
Inpatient mental health care	948,175	2,657,315	12,325,305
Outpatient mental health care	892,164	3,556,098	6,815,627
Total	$6,126,177	$14,393,741	$31,310,050

SOURCES: For chiropractic services, Peat Marwick Main & Co. and the Office of the Legislative Auditor, *Study of Proposed Mandatory Health Insurance for Chiropractic Services: A Report to the Governor and the Legislature of the State of Hawaii* (January 1988), Table 4.2 (p. 46); for well-baby care, Peat Marwick Main & Co. and the Office of the Legislative Auditor, *Study of Proposed Mandatory Health Insurance for Well-Baby Services: A Report to the Governor and the Legislature of the State of Hawaii* (January 1988), Table 4.5 (p. 45); for alcohol and drug abuse treatment, Peat Marwick Main & Co. and the Office of the Legislative Auditor, *Study of Proposed Mandatory Health Insurance for Alcohol and Drug Dependence and Mental Illness Services: A Report to the Governor and the Legislature of the State of Hawaii* (January 1988), Appendix A (p. 108); for inpatient mental health care, ibid., Appendix B, p. 111; and for outpatient mental health care, ibid., Appendix C, p. 114.
*The estimates would be considerably higher were it not for the fact that many Hawaiian insurance policies already have full or partial coverage for the benefits.

Table 11.5

EFFECTS ON INSURANCE PREMIUMS OF SPECIFIC HEALTH
INSURANCE BENEFITS

Feature	Change in Individual Premium	Change in Dependents' Premium
Front-end cost sharing[1]	− 7.6%	−11.4%
Second surgical opinion	+ 5.0[2]	+ 7.7
Home health care	+ 0.1[2]	− 5.0[2]
Extended care	− 0.4[2]	− 5.1[2]
Substance abuse treatment	+ 7.9	+ 6.2
Psychiatric hospital care	− 1.7[2]	+20.8
Psychologist visits	+10.4	+12.6
Routine dental care	+23.8	+11.8
Self-insurance[3]	+19.0	+ 8.7
Commercial insurance[3]	+ 8.6	+ 5.0[2]
1 or 2 HMOs[4]	+ 5.2	+ 6.0
3 HMOs[4]	+18.4	+ 5.6[2]

SOURCE: Gail A. Jensen and Michael A. Morrisey, "The Premium Consequences of Group Health Insurance Provisions" (September 1988), mimeograph.
[1]Presence of a deductible.
[2]Not statistically significant.
[3]Relative to Blue Cross premiums.
[4]Employee options.

of this study are presented in Table 11.5. As the table shows, second surgical opinions and home health care costs appear to have no individual statistically significant effect on premium prices of the primary insured, but second surgical opinions, in combination with other mandates, may cause premium prices for dependents to be higher than otherwise. Coverage for substance abuse is very costly, increasing premium prices by 6 to 8 percent. Coverage for outpatient mental health care is even more expensive, increasing premium prices by 10 to 13 percent. Psychiatric hospital care apparently has little effect on premium prices for employees. But if dependents are covered, premium prices can rise by as much as 21 percent.

Another interesting finding of the Jensen-Morrisey study is that self-insurance raises insurance costs by as much as 19 percent, possibly because many companies are not skilled at operating their own health insurance programs. The additional cost may be worth it, however, if the firm saves a significant amount of money by avoiding state-mandated benefits.

Excessive Premiums for Low-Risk Individuals

A basic principle governing the health insurance marketplace is that, in any given year, a small percentage of people will generate a majority of the health care costs. For example, a survey of employers by Johnson and Higgins found that about 1 percent of all employees account for 22 percent of company health care costs, and about 5.6 percent account for 50 percent of the costs.[35]

The experience of employers undoubtedly reflects the experience of the health insurance market as a whole. Accordingly, a major objective of health insurers is to expand coverage for the vast majority who will generate few claims or small claims and avoid those likely to generate large claims. One purpose of mandated benefits legislation is to try to force insurers to cover the high-risk population. To the extent that the regulators are successful, insurers cover more and more high-risk individuals and attempt to pay for this coverage by overcharging the low-risk population. As average premiums rise, health insurance becomes less and less attractive to people who are at low risk and fewer of them buy insurance. As a result, a vicious cycle occurs: As fewer low-risk people buy insurance, the pool of the insured becomes increasingly risky—leading to higher premiums and even fewer low-risk people choosing to insure.

The Impossibility of Obtaining No-Frills Catastrophic Health Insurance Tailored to Individual and Family Needs

Another factor that encourages people (especially low-risk people) not to insure is that mandated benefits legislation prevents them from buying insurance tailored to their needs. In some states, couples who cannot have children cannot buy policies that do not provide coverage for newborn infants. Moderate drinkers and people who abstain from using drugs cannot buy policies that do not cover alcoholism and drug abuse. People who do not intend to see

[35]Reported in Rickles.

346

chiropractors, psychologists, or marriage counselors cannot buy policies that exclude such coverage. As a result, people cannot buy insurance for a price that reasonably reflects their wants and needs.

The Lack of Availability of Health Insurance for High-Risk Individuals

An unintended consequence of mandated benefits legislation is that it probably makes it more difficult for higher risk individuals to obtain insurance. When insurers are prevented from charging a premium that reflects the risk they incur, they will not insure. As low-risk individuals drop out of the market, insurers face even more pressure to avoid high-risk policyholders. At the extreme, insurers can refuse to sell any insurance within a state.

The Growing Number of Uninsured Individuals

From World War II until the mid-1970s, the percentage of the population covered by private health insurance grew steadily. For example, the proportion covered by private health insurance for hospital care grew from 69 percent in 1960 to 83 percent in 1978, while the proportion covered for physician care grew from 46 percent in 1960 to 78 percent in 1974.[36] Since the mid-1970s, however, this trend has been reversed. Specifically, the proportion of people with private hospital insurance fell from a peak of 83 percent to 79 percent by 1984, the proportion of people with private physician insurance fell from a peak of 78 percent to 73 percent over the same period.[37]

Different studies have arrived at different estimates of the number of people without any health insurance. One study, using the same methodology for different years, concluded that the number of people without health insurance rose from 24.5 million (11.1 percent of the population) in 1980 to 33.3 million (13.5 percent of the population) in 1990.[38]

---

[36]U. S. Bureau of the Census, *Statistical Abstract of the United States, 1987* (Washington: Government Printing Office), p. 89 (Table 137).

[37]Ibid.

[38]John Sheils (Lewin/ICF), testimony before the Senate Committee on Labor and Human Resources, July 24, 1991.

Why is this growth occurring? One reason may be tax reform.[39] Another may be a shift in employment from manufacturing to services and the retail trades.[40] But it's hard to escape the conclusion that an increasing number of consumers are being regulated and priced out of the market for health insurance.

To What Extent Are Mandated Benefits Causing People to Be Uninsured?

An econometric model of the health insurance marketplace has been developed by the authors.[41] To our knowledge, this is the first model that produces statistical estimates of the factors causing people to be without health insurance. Although certain information about the market for health insurance was not available to us, the model nonetheless explains 94 percent of the variation in the percent of the population without health insurance across the 50 states.

Various versions of the model were tested, and in each test the number of mandated benefits was a strong and statistically significant cause of lack of health insurance. Specifically, as many as 25.2 percent of all uninsured people lack health insurance because of mandated benefits.

The number of mandated benefits varies considerably among the states, from a low of 4 in Delaware and Idaho to a high of 32 in Maryland. Moreover, the impact of the mandates is mitigated by

[39]Under federal tax law, employer-paid premiums for health insurance are not counted in the taxable income of employees. This tax subsidy is not available to the self-employed or to people who purchase health insurance on their own, although the Tax Reform Act of 1986 does allow self-employed people to deduct 25 percent of their premium payments. The tax subsidy for employer-provided insurance becomes less important at lower marginal tax rates, however. Thus, the lowering of tax rates in the 1980s also reduced the attractiveness to employees of employer-provided health insurance. See Gary A. Robbins, "Economic Consequences of the Minimum Health Benefits for All Workers Act of 1987 (S. 1625)," testimony presented to the U.S. Senate Committee on Labor and Human Resources, November 4, 1987.

[40]More than one-half of uninsured workers in 1985 were employed in retail trade and services. See Employee Benefit Research Institute, Issue Brief no. 66, p. 15.

[41]See John C. Goodman and Gerald L. Musgrave, *Freedom of Choice in Health Insurance*, NCPA Policy Report no. 134 (Dallas: National Center for Policy Analysis, November 1988), Appendix A.

Table 11.6
EFFECTS OF MANDATED INSURANCE BENEFITS IN SELECTED
STATES, 1986

State	Percent of People Who Lack Health Insurance Because of Mandates
Connecticut	64%
Maryland	60
Minnesota	60
New York	41
New Jersey	34
California	32
Maine	32
Missouri	30
Nevada	30
Virginia	30
Washington	30
Massachusetts	28
Ohio	28
Kansas	27
Nebraska	26
Montana	21
Arizona	20
Florida	18
Texas	18
New Mexico	16
Arkansas	15

SOURCE: John C. Goodman and Gerald L. Musgrave, *Freedom of Choice in Health Insurance*, NCPA Policy Report no. 134 (Dallas: National Center for Policy Analysis, November 1988), Appendix A.

other factors, such as the prevalence of employer-provided insurance and/or the ability to escape regulation through employer self-insurance. For these reasons, the impact of mandated benefits differs substantially among the states. As Table 11.6 shows, the proportion of people who lack health insurance because of mandated benefits exceeds 60 percent of the uninsured population in Connecticut, Maryland, and Minnesota, 41 percent in New York, and 30 percent in California, Maine, and New Jersey. Massachusetts is of

PATIENT POWER

special interest. Legislation passed in Massachusetts at the urging
of Governor Michael Dukakis was a costly attempt to make health
insurance available to all Massachusetts residents (see chapter 12).
However, as Table 11.6 shows, up to 28 percent of the state's
uninsured population already lack health insurance because of regulations imposed by the state government.

Positive Signs of Change

Although the above discussion is pessimistic in its description of
the explosion of state regulations during the 1980s and the negative
impact of those regulations, there are some signs that state legislators are increasingly aware of the harmful effects of state-mandated
benefits. Following the lead of Washington, Arizona, and Oregon,
for example, more than a dozen states now require social and
financial impact statements prior to the passage of any additional
mandates.[42] In 1983, for example, because of its concern about costs,
the Washington state legislature began putting the burden of proof
on a mandate's proponents to show that the benefits of a proposed
mandate would exceed the costs. As a result, no new mandates
were adopted in Washington for several years.[43] Such requirements
have clearly slowed the passage of state-mandated benefits, if only
because the proponents of mandates need more time and money
to overcome the new legislative hurdles.

A more positive sign is that fewer mandates are being passed
and that some states have actually rolled back mandates for small
business. As Table 11.7 shows, in the three years prior to 1990, state
governments passed an average of 71 mandates per year. In 1990
and 1991, however, they passed only 29 and 37 mandates, respectively. Moreover, at least 24 states have now rolled back mandated
benefits for small business, and a dozen other states are considering
similar legislation.[44] In Washington State, for example, health insurance policies would normally be subject to 28 mandates covering

[42]"Mandated Benefits: Mixed Signals from the States," *Health Benefits Letter* 1, no.
3 (March 13, 1991).

[43]Employee Benefit Research Institute, *Employee Benefit Notes* 8, no. 9 (September
1987): 7.

[44]The discussion that follows is largely based on *Health Benefits Letter* 1, no. 8 (May
23, 1991); and ibid. 1, no. 13 (August 8, 1991).

350

Table 11.7
NUMBER OF NEW STATE-MANDATED HEALTH INSURANCE
BENEFITS, 1987 TO 1991

Year	New Mandates
1987	62
1988	51
1989	99
1990	29
1991	37[1]

SOURCE: *Health Benefits Letter* 1, no. 15 (August 29, 1991).
[1]As of July 1991.

alcohol and drug abuse, mammographies, and the services of chiro-practors, occupational therapists, physical therapists, speech therapists, podiatrists, and optometrists. Under a law passed in 1990, however, firms with fewer than 50 employees can now buy cheaper insurance with no mandated benefits.

States also have taken other actions to encourage small businesses to purchase health insurance for their employees. Several exempt small-business policies from premium taxes, and at least six states extend tax credits to companies that are first-time buyers of health insurance. Iowa, for example, exempts "bare-bones" policies from premium taxes and provides a tax credit for employers who pay at least 75 percent of the premium for a low-income employee and half of the premium for the employee's dependents. Premium taxes also have been waived for small businesses in Nevada, New Mexico, and West Virginia. Other states that give employers tax credits for the purchase of health insurance include Kansas, Kentucky, Montana, Oklahoma, and Oregon. The credit is $15 per employee per month in Oklahoma and up to $25 in Oregon.

The Threat of a Counterrevolution

Now for the bad news. In a review of the fine print of the new legislation, Greg Scandlen of *Health Benefits Letter* finds that many state reforms are less substantial than they seem.[45] Some states have

[45]Scandlen, *Health Benefits Letter* 1, no. 8 (November 1991).

repealed some mandates but not others. Missouri, for example, has repealed only 8 of its 18 mandates.

The definition of a small business is often quite restrictive. In 14 states, an employer must have no more than 25 employees. In addition, many states allow a small business to qualify only if it has been without insurance for some period of time. In seven states, the qualifying period is at least one year; in Kansas, Maryland, and Rhode Island, it's two years; and in Kentucky, it's three years. In those states, small businesses that currently provide insurance coverage are penalized for doing so. All the benefits from the new legislation go to their uninsured competitors.

In another unfortunate trend, some states have subjected bare-bones policies to new mandates while freeing them from the burdens of old ones. For example, numerous states now require coverage for mammograms and well-child care, even though the same laws allow insurers to skimp on catastrophic coverage.

Perhaps the worst development is a new set of regulations governing insurance pricing. At least five states now require insurers to sell to any small business, regardless of the health of its employees (with limits on the premiums that can be charged). Although the objective may seem humane, these laws encourage perverse behavior. If people know they can always get insurance after they are sick, they have an incentive to wait until they are sick to buy it. Yet, if only sick people buy health insurance, the premiums will be extremely high.

Another perverse development is the trend toward community rating. Virginia, for example, requires that all applicants be charged the same premium, regardless of the likelihood that they will get sick and incur medical costs. Other states have severely limited the ability of insurers to price risk accurately, causing healthier people to be overcharged and sicker people to be undercharged. States that require insurers to take all comers and prevent insurers from charging premiums that reflect real risks usually set up "reinsurance pools," under which profitable companies are forced to subsidize the losses of unprofitable ones. The net result is that all premium prices will be higher than they would have been.

Insurance industry experts estimate that the removal of all current state mandates would reduce the cost of health insurance by about 30 percent. But this gain could be totally wiped out by the cost-increasing effects of new regulations.

Furthermore, bare-bones policies often sell at a lower price, not because of reduced regulation, but because of reduced coverage for basic medical risks. Annual insurance benefits may be capped at $100,000 per employee in Arkansas and $50,000 in New Mexico and Nevada. Such policies leave people exposed for truly catastrophic medical episodes and undermine the real purpose of insurance. Because the option to reduce coverage in this way was generally permissible even before insurance reform, it's not surprising that bare-bones policies have not made much of an impact in the half-dozen states where they are now being marketed.

The Need for Real Reform

The most basic problems with insurance reform are the refusal of state governments to allow a real market to develop and the refusal of the federal government to give the currently uninsured the same tax and regulatory breaks given to employees of large companies.

Contrary to widespread impressions, most people who lack health insurance are healthy. Sixty percent are less than 30 years of age, in the healthiest segment of our population.[46] Most have below-average incomes and very few assets. As a result, they are especially sensitive to price.

Most of the uninsured have voluntarily decided not to purchase health insurance for a very good reason: The price is higher than that faced by other people for comparable benefit levels. Whereas 90 percent of insured people purchase health insurance with pretax dollars through an employer, uninsured individuals must pay with aftertax dollars. Whereas most employees of large corporations are exempt from silly state regulations, since their employers self-insure, most of the uninsured are the victims of those regulations.

What most young, healthy people need is the opportunity to buy no-frills health insurance at a fair price. Aside from giving these people the same income tax break and the same options routinely given to others, politicians could help most by repealing bad laws and getting out of the way.

[46]Jill D. Foley, *Uninsured in the United States: The Nonelderly Population without Health Insurance* (Washington: Employee Benefit Research Institute, April 1991), p. 16.

12. Mandating Employer-Provided Health Insurance

Although costly state regulations contribute to the increasing number of people who lack health insurance, lack of health insurance does not necessarily keep people from getting medical care. Nevertheless, from the perspective of the cost-plus mentality, the people who lack health insurance are a problem that demands political solutions—solutions that will put them back in the cost-plus system.

At the urging of Governor Michael Dukakis, Massachusetts passed legislation intended to provide all state residents with health insurance beginning in 1992. Other states are considering similar legislation. Several bills in Congress—including a bill introduced by Senate Democrats and one introduced by Dan Rostenkowski (D-IL), the chairman of the House Ways and Means Committee—would implement the Massachusetts plan at the national level. Other legislation to require employers to provide health insurance for all employees nationwide has been introduced in Congress by Sen. Edward Kennedy (D-MA). This chapter takes a closer look at some of the most prominent proposals to force people to have health insurance. Our general conclusion is that the principal problem addressed by these proposals is not that of unpaid hospital bills and that the proposals carry a concealed price tag many times greater than any benefits the forced insurance coverage could provide.

What Difference Does Lack of Health Insurance Make?

It is believed widely in this country, and even more prevalently in Europe, that uninsured residents of the United States are routinely denied health care. That belief is quite wrong. What is true is that the existence or nonexistence of health insurance makes a big difference in determining how care is paid for. What follows is a brief summary of how and why health insurance makes a difference.

355

Figure 12.1
UNINSURED AS PERCENTAGE OF NONELDERLY POPULATION

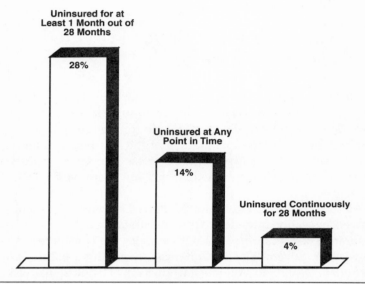

SOURCE: C. Nelson and K. Short, *Health Insurance Coverage: 1986 to 1988,* U.S. Bureau of the Census Report, p. 70, no. 17, 1989. Reported in Louis P. Garrison, Jr., "Medicaid, the Uninsured, and National Health Spending: Federal Policy Implications," *Health Care Financing Review,* 1990 Annual Supplement, p. 169.

What It Means to Lack Health Insurance

Americans have been repeatedly told that 34 million people in this country lack health insurance. But what does that mean? Most discussions of the uninsured imply that they are a well-defined class of people. But Figure 12.1 shows that is not the case. Over a 28-month period, about 28 percent of the population will be uninsured, if only for a brief period of time. On any given day, about half that number will be uninsured, however. And, over the entire 28 months, only 4 percent will be continuously uninsured. The pool of uninsured, then, is one that many people enter and leave over a period of several years. Only a small number of people remain there permanently.

In that respect, being uninsured is comparable to being unemployed. Most people will probably be unemployed at some time during their work life. At any point in time, however, only about 6 percent of the population is unemployed, and only a very small percent of people remain continuously unemployed for long periods. Like being unemployed, being uninsured is generally viewed as an undesirable state of affairs. Most people are likely to experience both, but without any serious long-term consequences.

Health Insurance and Access to Medical Care

Some apparently contradictory studies have attempted to determine how the lack of health insurance affects access to health care. Some studies claim that the uninsured get less health care. Others claim that once they see a physician or enter a hospital, the uninsured receive as much care as—or more care than—the insured. These studies are not necessarily inconsistent, but often they amount to comparing apples and oranges.

In comparing two groups of people, it is important to know much more than whether one group is insured and the other is not. For example, people with higher incomes and higher levels of education tend to place a greater value on health care and to spend more of their income on it. On the other hand, people who are sicker use more medical services than people who are healthy, and poor health tends to be correlated with low income and low levels of education.[1] Age also matters, in that younger people tend to be healthier. Interestingly, the uninsured have lower incomes and lower levels of education than the insured—and also are younger (60 percent are under the age of 30, for example).

Table 12.1 shows that if all other differences among the groups of people are ignored, there is very little difference between the insured and the uninsured in the number of physician visits (among those who see a physician) or in the number of days in a hospital (among those who enter a hospital). This generalization also applies to people known to have low health status. In fact, among people with below-average health, those without health insurance make

[1]See Attiat F. Ott and Wayne B. Gray, *The Massachusetts Health Plan: The Right Prescription?* (Boston: Pioneer Institute for Public Policy Research, 1988), pp. 26–31.

Table 12.1
USE OF HEALTH SERVICES BY NONELDERLY PEOPLE WITH AND
WITHOUT HEALTH INSURANCE

Medical Service	People with Insurance	People without Insurance
Annual physician visits[1]		
1–2 visits	52.9%	51.4%
3–5 visits	24.9	22.1
6 or more visits	22.2	26.6
Annual hospital stays[2]		
1–5 days	56.9	59.8
6–10 days	22.3	19.1
11 or more days	20.8	21.2

SOURCE: National Health Interview Survey, reported in Attiat F. Ott and Wayne B. Gray, *The Massachusetts Health Plan: The Right Prescription?* (Boston: Pioneer Institute for Public Policy Research, 1988), Table 2.15 (p. 36).
[1]Refers only to people who saw a physician.
[2]Refers only to people who entered a hospital.

more visits to physicians and spend more days in the hospital than those with insurance.[2]

However, more detailed analysis shows that there are significant differences among the two groups, once all the relevant variables are accounted for. A study by Stephen Long and Jack Rodgers, for example, weighted the probability of using health care services by health status, age, sex, marital status, family size, income, education, employment status, and residence. The results are depicted in Figure 12.2. As the figure shows, the uninsured are about 25 percent less likely to see a physician and about half as likely to enter a hospital as are people who have employer-provided health insurance. Once in the health care system, the uninsured see physicians about 16 percent less often and spend one-third as much time in the hospital. Overall, the uninsured consume about half as much health care as the insured, when adjusted for all the variables listed above.

These results are consistent with those of the Rand Corporation study discussed in chapter 8. Whereas the Rand study showed that

[2]Ibid., Table 2.15 (p. 36).

Figure 12.2
USE OF HEALTH SERVICES BY THE UNINSURED
(as Percentage of Use by People Who Have Health Insurance)*

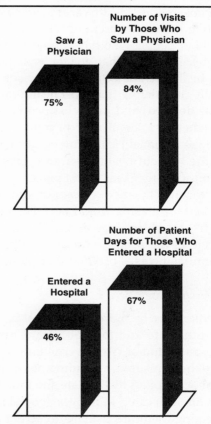

SOURCE: Stephen H. Long and Jack Rodgers (Congressional Budget Office), "The Effects of Being Uninsured on Health Services Use: Estimates from the Survey of Income and Program Participation," unpublished, Table 3, p. 11.

*Compares use of services over a 12-month period by those who were continuously uninsured/insured over the 12-month period. Probabilities of use are weighted by age, sex, income, health status, and other characteristics.

a deductible in the range of $1,000 to $2,500 reduces health care spending by one-third, the Long-Rodgers study showed that the absence of any health insurance reduces health care spending by one-half. The Rand study also found that, although the presence of a high deductible reduces health care spending considerably, the reduced spending has no apparent effect on people's health. Can the same be said of people who have no health insurance? That's not clear. But it seems likely that, for the vast majority of people, the absence of health insurance for brief periods has no effect on health, especially considering that most health care is elective (and therefore can be delayed) and that most people have a great deal of choice over whether to be insured or not.

According to the National Health Interview Survey (1984), more than half of those without health insurance gave "cannot afford" as the primary reason why.[3] Less than 1 percent gave "poor health" or "age" as a reason. The answer "cannot afford" should not be taken literally; better phrasing would be, "The price is too high." In Massachusetts, which recently enacted a universal health care plan, 58.1 percent of the people who lack health insurance live in families with annual incomes of $20,000 or higher.[4]

Legal Rights to Health Care

Access to medical care by those who cannot pay for it is guaranteed by numerous state and federal laws. Currently, 47 states require state, county, and/or city governments to provide care for the indigent and the uninsured, and numerous court decisions have upheld the right of hospitals to sue state and local governments for reimbursement for such care.[5] Moreover, federal law now requires all hospitals treating Medicare patients to accept all patients with emergency health problems and prohibits hospitals from transferring indigent patients unless the patient's condition is stabilized or

[3]Ibid., Table 2.11 (p. 30).

[4]Ibid., Table 2.2 (p. 17).

[5]Patricia Butler, "Legal Obligations of State and Local Governments for Indigent Care," in the Academy for State and Local Government, *Access to Care for the Medically Indigent*, pp. 13–44.

the transfer is requested by the patient or medically indicated because of superior facilities at another hospital.[6]

Health Care Rationing in the Public Sector

Most discussions (and most studies) of the uninsured make little distinction between people insured in the private sector and those insured by public programs. But if there is a major difference in access to health care in the United States, increasingly that difference is in whether or not patients rely on public hospitals and clinics—whether or not they have health insurance.

One survey of public hospital emergency rooms in large cities discovered that patients could wait up to 17 hours to see a physician. In the face of such waits, many patients leave in frustration, without receiving care.[7] Waits can also be lengthy at outpatient clinics. A pregnant woman in Chicago, for example, had to wait 125 days to see a public clinic physician for the free care to which she was presumably entitled.[8] Furthermore, anecdotal (newspaper) descriptions of conditions in public hospital emergency rooms in the United States are very similar to the descriptions of emergency rooms in Canada, Britain, and other countries with national health insurance (as discussed in chapter 18). In those countries, everyone is theoretically insured. The problem of access is created by public-sector health care rationing.

Health Insurance and the Protection of Financial Assets

If health insurance is not a prerequisite to health care for most people, why does anyone purchase it? For the same reason that people purchase life, automobile liability, and fire and casualty insurance: to protect assets. A major, catastrophic illness can wipe out a family's savings and investments. To protect their assets against unexpected medical bills, people purchase health insurance. It is hardly surprising that the more assets people have, the

[6]Deborah J. Chollet, "Financing Indigent Care," in Frank B. McArdle, ed., *The Changing Health Care Market* (Washington: Employee Benefit Research Institute, 1987), p. 188.

[7]Philip J. Hilts, "Many Leave Emergency Rooms Needing Care," *New York Times*, August 27, 1991.

[8]*Chicago Tribune*, November 25, 1990, cited in Emily Friedman, "The Uninsured: From Dilemma to Crisis," *Journal of the American Medical Association* 265, no. 19 (May 15, 1991): 2494.

more likely they are to have health insurance. If people with few assets choose not to purchase health insurance, their choice may be rational. It does, however, have social consequences. If society is committed to providing basic health care for all who need it, including the uninsured, some way must be found to pay the medical bills of the indigent uninsured. That is the reason usually given for the political support for universal health insurance.

Most proposals for mandatory health insurance, such as the Massachusetts health care plan and the Kennedy bill, are not primarily proposals to ensure access to health care. Instead, they are proposals designed to force people to purchase health insurance whether they want to or not. The argument generally used in favor of mandatory health insurance is that it will reduce the burden of hospital bad debts and charity care. For example, Susan Sherry, a spokesperson for Health Care for All (a coalition of consumer activist groups supporting the Massachusetts health care plan), explained to the *Washington Times* why individuals should not have the choice to buy or not buy health insurance: "That's not fair to the rest of us who have to pay when that person gets into an accident."[9]

Why Are People Uninsured?

Why do so many people lack health insurance? Part of the reason is that, for many, health insurance has little value. Because lack of health insurance is not a major barrier to receiving health care, health insurance is of value primarily to those who wish to protect their assets against catastrophic health care expenses. For those with few or no assets, the price of health insurance may far exceed its value.

Contrary to widespread impressions, most of the uninsured are healthy. Two-thirds of them are under the age of 30,[10] in age groups that have the lowest health care costs. Because they tend to be young and healthy and have few assets, they are likely to be sensitive to price and to voluntarily forgo health coverage if the price is too high. Nevertheless, there are at least three government policies that cause the uninsured to face higher prices than most other

[9]Michael Hedges, "Study Finds Massachusetts Health Law Will Cut Jobs, Help Non-Poor," *Washington Times*, October 6, 1988, p. A 4.

[10]Jill D. Foley, *Uninsured in the United States: The Nonelderly Population without Health Insurance* (Washington: Employee Benefit Research Institute, April 1991), p. 16.

people. First, because of the federal tax law, the self-employed, the unemployed, and some employees of small businesses face aftertax prices for health insurance that are as much as twice as high as the prices paid by people who have employer-provided health insurance. Second, because of state regulations, the uninsured face premiums that are 20 to 30 percent higher than those of many people who have health insurance. Third, because of employee benefits law, people working in the small-business sector find that health insurance is increasingly more expensive.

Ironically, our tax laws and employee benefits laws were originally designed to encourage greater health insurance coverage for more people. Today, the laws are having the opposite effect. Before imposing new costs on small businesses and creating yet another layer of bureaucracy, it would make sense to get rid of bad policies and give the market a chance to work. Instead, many are proposing more laws and more regulations.

Employer-Mandated Health Insurance in Hawaii[11]

Hawaii is currently the only state that can require all employers—even self-insured employers—to provide health insurance for their workers. Under the federal Employee Retirement Income Security Act (ERISA), companies that self-insure are exempt from state regulations. As a result, states such as Massachusetts that want to force all employers to provide health insurance have resorted to play-or-pay plans to get around the ERISA exemption. Under the play-or-pay approach, state governments impose a per-employee tax on employers who do not offer health insurance. Hawaii passed its employer mandate in 1974, and after the Supreme Court invalidated the law in 1981 (declaring it to be in violation of ERISA), Hawaii got an ERISA exemption from Congress. Under Hawaii state law, employers are required to provide a minimum package of health insurance benefits for employees, but not for their dependents. The contribution of employees is limited to 1.5 percent of wages.

It is not clear to what degree the state law forces employers and employees to do something they would not have done anyway. By one estimate, only 5,000 additional people—out of a population of

---

[11]This discussion is based largely on Emily Friedman, "Health Insurance in Hawaii: Paradise Lost or Found?" *Business and Health*, June 1990, pp. 52–59.

1.1 million—acquired health insurance as a result of the law. During the period from 1981 to 1983, when the law was invalidated by the Supreme Court, very few employers dropped health insurance coverage. And employer-provided benefits are commonly more liberal than the minimum benefits required by the state.

One reason why Hawaii has had fewer problems than other states could expect is that the state's population is apparently healthier and medical costs are much lower. The state has an extensive system of HMOs, and per capita hospital expenses in Hawaii in 1988 were only $506, compared to $960 in Massachusetts.

Interestingly, mandated health insurance benefits imposed by the state have been more controversial than the required minimum health care package. Over the years, the state of Hawaii has mandated in vitro fertilization, mental health, alcohol and drug abuse treatment, psychological services, and other benefits. The mandates force employees to take more of their compensation in the form of benefits they may not want or need instead of as higher wages. The state has imposed additional mandates on employers who offer optional coverage for the dependents of workers, which has undoubtedly discouraged Hawaii employers from offering dependent coverage.

Hawaii's mandates are not free. One cost is in employment growth. In the period 1980–86, Hawaii's employment grew by only 9 percent, compared with 13 percent for the nation and 20 percent for the U.S. Pacific Coast states. Another cost is reduced money wages. In 1975, when the law first went into effect, Hawaii was 25th among the states in average annual employee wages. By 1986, it had fallen to 36th.[12]

The Massachusetts Health Care Plan

On April 21, 1988, Governor Michael Dukakis signed legislation requiring employers in Massachusetts to contribute toward health insurance premiums for their employees. Perhaps because of confusion created by election year rhetoric, this plan has been widely

---

[12]Rita Ricardo-Campbell, "Business Health Care Costs and Competition," Working Papers in Economics no. E-91-6, Hoover Institution, Stanford University, February 1991, p. 34.

misunderstood. The following account is a brief attempt to clarify it.[13]

1. **Employees in Massachusetts are still not covered under the plan.** Despite 1988 election campaign statements that everyone in Massachusetts has health insurance, the law was not supposed to take full effect until 1992, and implementation has been subsequently delayed. Moreover, at the time of this writing, there is a reasonable chance that the law will be repealed before it is fully implemented. Currently, the Massachusetts state legislature wants to delay the entry of private business into the program until 1995, and the governor wants to kill the program altogether.

2. **The plan will require employers to spend money on health insurance for their employees but will not mandate a specific package of health insurance benefits.** Technically, employers will be assessed a state tax equal to 12 percent of salary up to $14,000 per year for each employee. However, employers may deduct from the tax any amount spent on health insurance for the employee. That means that employers must spend (either in taxes or on health insurance) $1,680 for employees earning $14,000 or more per year. Massachusetts would be in violation of federal law (ERISA) if it attempted to dictate specific benefits to self-insured plans.

3. **The plan is not universal health insurance; it will leave many uninsured people with the option of purchasing health insurance.** Technically, the only Massachusetts residents who will be forced to have health insurance will be college students. All employees not covered by employer-provided health insurance and all nonworking people will have the option of buying health insurance from the state. But they may choose not to buy the state's health insurance, just as many now choose not to buy private health insurance.

4. **Under the plan, Massachusetts residents may not all have access to affordable health insurance.** The clear intention of Massachusetts is to offer health insurance at subsidized prices

[13]This account is based largely on Ott and Gray; and Gail R. Wilensky, "The 'Pay or Play' Insurance Gamble: Massachusetts Plan for Universal Health Coverage," paper presented to the House Wednesday Group, Washington, September 26, 1988.

to low- and moderate-income families. However, as the specifics of the benefit package are unknown, the cost of the policies and the subsidies also is unknown. Nor is it known how many people will rely on the state for health insurance. Moreover, given Massachusetts' well-publicized financial troubles, the state may not be able to offer its residents affordable health insurance.

5. **Although Massachusetts intends to force the private sector to provide health insurance for employees, the system may evolve into a state-run version of national health insurance.** That is because the required contribution of employers is low relative to the cost of health insurance, and the benefits in the state insurance policy are likely to be quite liberal. According to one estimate, nationwide, the average employer contribution for an employee's health insurance in 1991 was $2,635—employers pay approximately 88 percent of individual coverage and 78 percent of family coverage for an indemnity plan.[14] Because health care costs are higher in Massachusetts, employer contributions to health insurance are likely to be $500 or $600 higher than the national average.[15] Moreover, the state insurance plan will include benefits such as mental health care and well-baby care not now included in many private plans. Thus, many employers may decide to pay the state health insurance tax (12 percent of wages) and turn the obligation of providing health insurance over to the state. Indeed, given the difficulties employers now have in managing health care plans, it would be surprising if they did not.[16]

6. **After the plan is implemented, the number of uninsured Massachusetts residents may actually increase.** Because employers have the option of paying the state tax and not providing employee health insurance, many may choose that option, including employers who currently have health insurance for their workers. Because uninsured individuals do not have to purchase insurance from the state, many may decline

[14]KPMG Peat Marwick, "Health Benefits in 1991," Montvale, NJ, 1991.
[15]Ott and Gray, p. 51.
[16]The plan does create tax-credit subsidies to encourage small business to provide employee health insurance during the first two years, however.

to do so. As a result, the number of uninsured people in Massachusetts may actually increase. The more perverse the incentives created by the state plan, the higher that increase will be.

Economists Attiat Ott and Wayne Gray have estimated the minimum costs of the plan. Based on requirements already written into law, they concluded that the plan will force Massachusetts businesses to increase spending on employee health insurance by at least 32 percent. The additional cost will be at least $642 million in the first year of operation. Because of the increased cost of employing workers, as many as 9,000 jobs will be lost, with low-paid employees the likely losers.[17] Although it is difficult to generalize about the rest of the nation on the basis of the Massachusetts plan, Wayne Gray estimates that if the Massachusetts health care plan were adopted nationally, the additional cost to business would be $23 billion and as many as 358,000 jobs would be lost nationwide.

Despite the considerable cost of the Massachusetts plan, Ott and Gray found little evidence of a problem that needed to be solved. For example, Massachusetts already has a health care risk pool, designed to spread the cost of uncompensated hospital care among all hospitals and thus among all patients. Moreover, there is virtually no evidence that the uninsured in Massachusetts lack access to adequate health care. Most of the state's uninsured are far from poor, more than 58 percent have annual family incomes of $20,000 or higher, and 15 percent have annual family incomes in excess of $50,000.[18]

Actions by Other State Governments

Many other states are considering forcing people to purchase health insurance by making health insurance a condition of employment. Often, the legislators in these states are trying to solve the problem they created by passing costly regulations. In almost every case, the natural legislative response is not to repeal bad laws but to pass more laws. Many of the legislatures that are considering forcing people to buy health insurance are the ones driving up

[17]Ott and Gray.
[18]Ibid., Table 2.2 (p. 17).

health insurance costs by mandating more and more health insurance benefits. As of this writing, California, Illinois, and Wisconsin are among the states in which employer-mandated health insurance is being taken most seriously. Wisconsin is considering following the Massachusetts model by forcing employers to purchase health insurance on behalf of their workers and by imposing statewide taxes to pay for health insurance for the uninsured unemployed. As in Massachusetts, such a plan would be costly for the private sector.

A study conducted by Aldona Robbins and Gary Robbins estimated the effect of the Wisconsin plan on that state's economy.[19] The study found that requiring private firms to provide health insurance for employees would cost businesses $417 million, reduce state output by $45 million to $100 million a year, and destroy 1,400 to 3,000 jobs annually. The study also found that creating a program of public health insurance for the uninsured with incomes below 155 percent of the poverty level would cost between $149 million and $327 million and destroy as many jobs as the mandated insurance plan.

The Kennedy Plan

Sen. Edward Kennedy has proposed legislation that would require employers nationwide to provide health insurance for their employees.[20] Although the bill is not currently before Congress, the purpose of most play-or-pay proposals is to force private employers to provide health insurance. Thus, it is useful to examine the effects of a proposal that would force employers to play, rather than pay.

[19]Aldona Robbins, Gary Robbins, and Richard Rue, *Mandated and Public Health Insurance* (Milwaukee: Heartland Institute, October 1989).

[20]At the time the legislation was proposed, Senator Kennedy circulated a very low estimate of its cost, prepared by Gordon Trapnell of the Actuarial Research Corporation. The Congressional Budget Office (CBO)—which did not make an independent premium estimate—promulgated even lower cost estimates, based on an apparent misreading of the Trapnell study. Both the Trapnell estimate and the CBO premium estimate are well below the market price of comparable coverage under the Blue Cross–Blue Shield "low option" policy made available to federal employees.

The most thorough analysis of the cost of the original Kennedy proposal was made by economists Aldona Robbins and Gary Robbins.[21] Subsequently, they reestimated the cost, based on a later version of the proposal.[22] Their later analysis forms the basis for many of the conclusions in the following discussion.[23]

Economic Effects of the Kennedy Plan

Far from being a solution to our current problems, the Kennedy bill would reduce the take-home pay of the vast majority of workers, increase the cost of health care for all Americans, increase unemployment by as many as one million people, increase production costs in every industry, increase the federal deficit, create billions of dollars of economic waste, and prevent the private sector from taking reasonable measures to control health care costs.

Lower Take-Home Pay

The Kennedy plan would impose on the private sector a cost of at least $108 billion, and possibly as much as $159 billion, in 1991 dollars.[24] Because the bill does nothing to increase productivity, its cost would fall on employees themselves.[25] That means that

[21]Aldona Robbins and Gary Robbins, *Mandating Health Insurance*, Economic Policy Bulletin no. 3 (Washington: Institute for Research on the Economics of Taxation, July 8, 1987).

[22]John C. Goodman, Aldona Robbins, and Gary Robbins, *Mandating Health Insurance*, NCPA Policy Report no. 136 (Dallas: National Center for Policy Analysis, February 1989).

[23]The Robbinses' estimate of the cost of the Kennedy mandate is considerably higher than other recent estimates, which place the cost of mandated health insurance at about $40 billion. That is close to the Robbinses' estimate of $37.3 billion to pay the Kennedy mandate for currently uninsured. However, as explained below, the Robbinses found that the mandate would require a substantial increase in benefits for those already insured—at an additional cost of about $68 billion. For a discussion of these other estimates, see Michael A. Morrisey, "Health Care Reform: A Review of Five Generic Proposals," paper presented at a policy forum, "Winners and Losers in Reforming the U.S. Health Care System," sponsored by the Employee Benefit Research Institute Education and Research Fund, Washington, October 4, 1990.

[24]For an explanation of these estimates, as well as others cited in this discussion, see Goodman, Robbins, and Robbins, appendix A.

[25]In competitive markets, labor compensation must be equal to the marginal product of labor. In other words, workers receive an income roughly equal to the value of what they produce. Because the Kennedy bill would not change worker productivity, health insurance benefits ultimately would substitute for wages, keeping total labor compensation the same.

Table 12.2
PERCENT OF EMPLOYERS WHOSE HEALTH INSURANCE
POLICIES ARE NOT IN COMPLIANCE WITH
THE KENNEDY PLAN

Violations of Provisions of Kennedy Plan	ICF Survey	Towers, Perrin Survey
Requires employees to pay more than 20 percent of single coverage premium	28%	28%
Requires employees to pay more than 20 percent of family premiums	54	38
Does not cover part-time workers	68	74
Waiting period of more than one month	55	46
Limitation on preexisting conditions	–	65
Does not cover seasonal or temporary workers	50	–
Does not provide full coverage for well-baby care	–	53
Does not cover physician office visits	17	–
Does not offer maternity care	16	–
Does not cover mental health care	18	–

SOURCES: ICF, Inc., *Health Care Coverage and Costs in Small and Large Businesses: Final Report*, prepared for the U.S. Small Business Administration (April 1987), Tables IV-4, IV-8, IV-9, III-10, III-12; and survey by Towers, Perrin, Forster & Crosby, reported in Jerry Geisel, "Health Plans Fail Mandate: Survey," *Business Insurance*, August 31, 1987.

employees would lose as much as $108 billion (or more) in wages and other fringe benefits.

Most discussions of the Kennedy plan focus on the problems of workers who lack employer-provided health insurance. However, about two-thirds of the cost of the bill would go to expand coverage for currently insured workers. As Table 12.2 shows, many existing employer-provided health care plans are not as generous as the Kennedy plan. The inclusion of mental health benefits is noteworthy, since mental health care is among the most expensive of all benefits. Mental health and substance abuse treatments cost over $200 per employee and account for 30 percent of the nation's health care costs.[26]

[26]*Modern Healthcare*, May 14, 1990, p. 60.

Table 12.3
COSTS OF THE KENNEDY PLAN

Cost	Amount
Direct costs for the private sector	
Cost of providing insurance for	
workers currently uninsured	$37.3 billion
Cost of expanding coverage for	
workers currently insured	$68.0 billion
Administrative costs	$3.0 billion
Total increase in insurance costs	$108.3 billion
Indirect costs for the private sector	
Number of jobs lost	1.1 million
Reduction in GNP	$27.0 billion
Increase in federal deficit	$46.5 billion
Problem the bill attempts to solve	
(unpaid hospital bills for	
uninsured workers)	$4.0 billion

SOURCE: John C. Goodman, Aldona Robbins, and Gary Robbins, *Mandating Health Insurance*, NCPA Policy Report no. 136 (Dallas: National Center for Policy Analysis, February 1989), appendix A.

Rising Health Care Costs

Passage of the Kennedy bill would result in at least $108 billion in additional spending. (See Table 12.3.) But experience shows that only about half of each additional dollar of health care spending buys additional services, while the other half is consumed by higher prices.[27] That means that as much as $54 billion of the additional spending would be consumed by medical inflation, escalating health care costs for all Americans.

Economic Waste

In the aggregate, the Kennedy bill would cost the private sector $108 billion to $159 billion per year to solve a problem estimated at $4 billion, which represents about half the total cost of uncompensated hospital care. The primary stated objective of the Kennedy bill is to cover unpaid hospital bills. But the price tag is more than 25 times the size of the problem.

[27] Robbins and Robbins, p. 21.

In 1986, uncompensated hospital care amounted to $8 billion, or about 4.4 percent of total hospital revenues.[28] That is the amount that hospitals reported as the value of care for people who would not, or could not, pay.[29] Because only two-thirds of the currently uninsured are affected by the Kennedy proposal, uncompensated hospital care would at most be reduced by two-thirds. The actual reduction would probably be much less. One of the big-ticket items contributing to hospital bad debts is the premature babies of unwed mothers, many of whom would not be covered under the Kennedy plan. Our best guess is that hospital bad debts would be reduced by $4 billion at most.[30]

Unemployment and Decreased Production

Forcing employers to pay employees with interim health benefits raises the cost of hiring unless employers can reduce wages or other fringe benefits. Often, they cannot. For example, the salaries of workers earning the minimum wage cannot legally be lowered. Yet, for part-time minimum-wage workers, the cost of mandated health insurance may be higher than the worker's salary. As many as 1.1 million fewer jobs and as much as $27 billion in reduced output for the economy as a whole would result.

Increasing the Federal Deficit

Although the Kennedy proposal purports to place the full cost of mandated health insurance on the private sector, it would affect the federal deficit in two ways. First, because the required premiums are set so high and because the bill mandates that employers pay 80 percent of them, an enormous amount of employee income would be diverted to health insurance and would not be subject to either income taxes or Social Security taxes. Second, federal tax

[28]Chollet, p. 185. When unpaid physicians' bills are included, total uncompensated care in 1986 may have been as high as $13 billion. For a discussion of the contributing factors, see Frank A. Sloan, Joseph Valvona, and Mullner Ross, "Identifying the Issues: A Statistical Profile," in Frank A. Sloan, James F. Blumstein, and James M. Perrin, eds., *Uncompensated Hospital Care: Rights and Responsibilities* (Baltimore: Johns Hopkins University Press, 1986).

[29]It is important to note that unpaid hospital bills do not necessarily mean that patients were unable to pay them. There is an important distinction between "bad debts" and "charity care," even though hospital records often do not accurately make this distinction. See Chollet, pp. 154–85.

[30]See Robbins and Robbins, pp. 11–12.

collections would be lower because employment and output would be lower. In general, federal revenues would be reduced by $17.9 billion because of lower Social Security tax collections and by $23.2 billion because of lower income tax collections. Reduced employment and reduced output would lower federal revenues by an additional $5.4 billion. The net increase in the federal deficit in 1991 would have been $46.5 billion.

Eliminating Freedom of Choice

Rather than helping the private sector forge new strategies to contain rising health care costs, the Kennedy bill would needlessly eliminate many workable programs now in place. For example, it would deny employees the right to choose high-deductible plans and keep the savings for themselves. Under the bill, the mandated employee deductible would be $250 and the cap on employee copayments would be $600. It also would force employers to pay for coverage for low-cost services such as physician office visits and well-baby care, although many employees might prefer to self-insure for such expenses. The Kennedy plan would place even greater restrictions on freedom of choice for employees of small businesses. Such firms would be grouped by region and forced to choose among plans administered by a few insurers. As a result, small firms would have even fewer options than large firms to innovate, experiment, and use new cost-control techniques.

Special Victims of the Kennedy Plan

The burden of the Kennedy bill would not be spread evenly throughout the economy. Certain groups of workers and certain types of business would be especially disadvantaged.

Low-Income Workers

The Kennedy plan would eliminate job opportunities for low-income workers. For full-time employees earning the minimum wage, the plan would increase labor costs by 21 percent for single workers and by 51 percent for workers with families. For part-time employees earning the minimum wage, the plan would increase labor costs by 48 percent for single workers and by 116 percent for workers with families.[31]

[31]Assumes 17.5 hours worked per week. About two-thirds of all workers earning the minimum wage are part-time workers.

To get a perspective on what these increases mean, consider that on April 1, 1990, federal law increased the minimum wage from $3.35 an hour to $4.25 per hour by April 1, 1991. The law increased labor costs for minimum-wage workers by 27 percent, which is much less than the economic impact of the Kennedy bill. But studies estimate that the minimum-wage increase destroyed 596,000 jobs.[32]

Minority Workers

By increasing the effective minimum wage by more than 100 percent for some workers, the Kennedy plan would be especially devastating to minorities. The impact would be greatest on minority youth, whose unemployment rate already is as high as 50 percent in many major cities.

Working Wives

As many as 48 million workers live in two-income families, and many working wives rely on the health insurance coverage provided by their husbands' employers. Under the Kennedy plan, they would be forced to carry health coverage even if they were already covered. That would raise the cost for employers of hiring such women and would make them less employable.

Workers with Families

Under the Kennedy plan, employers would be required to pay 80 percent of the cost of insuring the family members of their workers. Unless employers were able to pay employees with families a lower wage than single workers—which is highly unlikely—the cost of hiring these workers would be higher and they would become less employable.

Unemployed People with Existing Health Problems

Most existing health insurance policies exclude or limit coverage for people with preexisting health problems. The Kennedy plan would require employers to provide coverage for such conditions but would not require employers to hire such people and, indeed, would offer strong incentives not to hire them.

---

[32]*Job Opportunities Your State Could Lose as a Result of the New Minimum Wage Law* (Washington: U.S. Chamber of Commerce, March 1990).

Effects on Small Business

By design, the Kennedy plan would have a marginal effect on large employers with generous health insurance plans. Small businesses are a different matter. For example, in retail trade and construction (two industries with a high proportion of small businesses), 23 percent of employees are currently uninsured; and in the service industry (also dominated by small businesses), 16 percent of employees are currently uninsured.[33] Thus, it is precisely in the industries where small businesses predominate that the Kennedy bill would have its most adverse economic impact. Moreover, the cost per employee of meeting the Kennedy mandates would be highest in those industries. In durable goods manufacturing, the cost of mandated family coverage would be about 8.8 percent of labor compensation. That cost would be 11.8 percent in the service industry, 16.7 percent in retail trade, and 20.5 percent in agriculture. The new burdens would come at a time when the small-business sector is sustaining America's economic expansion, employing 48 percent of the workforce, and creating 50 to 80 percent of all new jobs.

Regressive Taxation and Uncompensated Hospital Care

Uncompensated hospital care is a serious problem for some of our nation's hospitals. Moreover, as the hospital marketplace becomes increasingly competitive, hospitals—especially rural and county hospitals with disproportionate numbers of charity patients—will face greater financial problems. If society is committed to providing health care for all, that commitment can be funded by paying for charity care with general taxes. The Kennedy bill, by contrast, would pay for charity care by imposing a highly regressive tax. Under the bill's terms, high-income workers with generous health insurance plans would experience negligible effects, whereas low-income workers would experience substantial real-income reductions and might lose their jobs.

An Invitation to Special Interests

The cost estimates presented here for the Kennedy proposal apply only to the initial package of benefits. Experience at the state level indicates that once the legislative door has been opened,

[33]Foley, Chart 4 (p. 9).

hordes of special-interest lobbyists will descend on Washington. Every group from acupuncturists to naturopaths will pressure Congress for inclusion in the federal mandates. Inevitably, the initial package of benefits will grow, and the costs will soar.[34] In the politics of health insurance at the state level, special interests exploit the politically weak—that is, those not represented by a disease lobby or a provider lobby. The Kennedy bill would elevate this process to national policy.

The Senate Democrats' Proposal[35]

A health care plan unveiled in 1991 by Sens. George Mitchell (D-ME), Edward Kennedy (D-MA), John Rockefeller (D-WV), and Donald Riegle (D-MI) combines many of the features of the Dukakis proposal and the original Kennedy proposal.

Under the senators' play-or-pay plan, employers would have a choice: Pay a federal tax, tentatively set at about 7 percent of payroll, or provide health insurance for their employees. If employers were to decide to pay the tax, the government would assume responsibility for providing health insurance. For example, a $2,500 family health insurance premium for a worker earning $20,000 a year costs 13 percent of payroll, not 7 percent. In this case, the obvious choice for the employer would be to pay the tax and turn the problem over to government. Indeed, considering that about 95 percent of all uninsured workers earn less than $30,000 a year, [36] most of their employers would have strong incentives to pay the tax and forget the problem.

Economist William J. Dennis of the NFIB Foundation has calculated what the incentives will look like for employers under different assumptions. The results are shown in Table 12.4. Because the Senate Democrats' proposal nominally requires employers to pay 80 percent of insurance premiums or 80 percent of the tax, the table illustrates the employer's share of health insurance premiums, expressed as a percentage of payroll. Thus, if the total payroll tax

---

[34]This process already has begun. Mental health providers successfully lobbied to get mental health benefits included in the revised committee version of the Kennedy bill.

[35]See John C. Goodman, "Wrong Prescription for the Uninsured," *Wall Street Journal*, June 11, 1991.

[36]Foley, Table 24 (p. 58).

Table 12.4

EMPLOYER'S SHARE OF HEALTH INSURANCE PREMIUMS AS PERCENT OF PAYROLL[1]

Hourly Wage ($)	$100 Premium[2]	$150 Premium[2]	$200 Premium[2]	$250 Premium[2]	$300 Premium[2]	$350 Premium[2]	$400 Premium[2]
4.00	13.3	20.0	27.6	33.3	40.0	46.7	53.3
4.50	11.9	17.8	23.7	29.6	35.6	41.5	47.4
5.00	10.7	16.0	21.3	26.7	32.0	37.3	42.7
5.50	9.7	14.5	19.4	24.2	29.1	33.9	38.8
6.00	8.9	13.3	17.8	22.2	26.7	31.1	35.6
6.50	8.2	12.3	16.4	20.5	24.6	28.7	32.8
7.00	7.6	11.4	15.2	19.0	22.9	26.7	30.5
7.50	7.1	10.7	14.2	17.8	21.3	24.9	28.4
8.00	6.7	10.0	13.3	16.7	20.0	23.3	26.7
8.50	6.3	9.4	12.5	15.7	18.8	22.0	25.1
9.00	5.9	8.9	11.9	14.8	17.8	20.7	23.7
9.50	5.6	8.4	11.2	14.0	16.8	19.6	22.5
10.00	5.3	8.0	10.7	13.3	16.0	18.7	21.3
10.50	5.1	7.6	10.2	12.7	15.2	17.8	20.3
11.00	4.8	7.3	9.7	12.1	14.5	17.0	19.4
11.50	4.6	7.0	9.3	11.6	13.9	16.2	18.6
12.00	4.4	6.7	8.9	11.1	13.3	15.6	17.8
12.50	4.3	6.4	8.5	10.7	12.8	14.9	17.1
13.00	4.1	6.2	8.2	10.3	12.3	14.4	16.4

(Continued on next page)

Table 12.4—Continued
EMPLOYER'S SHARE OF HEALTH INSURANCE PREMIUMS AS PERCENT OF PAYROLL[1]

Hourly Wage ($)	$100 Premium[2]	$150 Premium[2]	$200 Premium[2]	$250 Premium[2]	$300 Premium[2]	$350 Premium[2]	$400 Premium[2]
13.50	4.0	5.9	7.9	9.9	11.9	13.8	15.8
14.00	3.8	5.7	7.6	9.5	11.4	13.3	15.2
14.50	3.7	5.5	7.4	9.2	11.0	12.9	14.7
15.00	3.6	5.3	7.1	8.9	10.7	12.4	14.2
15.50	3.4	5.2	6.9	8.6	10.3	12.0	13.8
16.00	3.3	5.0	6.7	8.3	10.0	11.7	13.3

SOURCE: William J. Dennis, *It's Cheaper to Pay Than to Play* (National Federation of Independent Business, October 1991).
[1] Assumes full-time employees (37.5 hours worked per week, 4 weeks per month) and employer's share of premium equals 80 percent.
[2] Per employee per month.

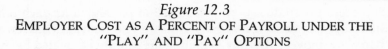

Figure 12.3
EMPLOYER COST AS A PERCENT OF PAYROLL UNDER THE
"PLAY" AND "PAY" OPTIONS

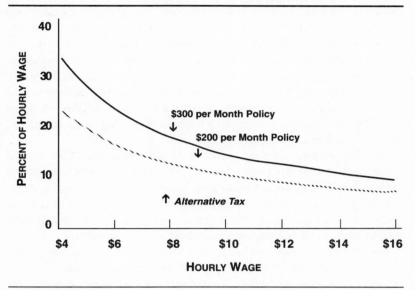

SOURCE: William J. Dennis, *It's Cheaper to Pay Than to Play* (National Federation of Independent Business, October 1991).

is set at 7 percent, as tentatively planned, the numbers in Table 12.4 should be compared with the employer's share of the tax, or 5.6 percent. However, if the total tax gets set at 8 percent, the employer's share would be a tax of 6.4 percent.

The results of the play-or-pay option are depicted in Figure 12.3. As the figure shows, under almost any realistic set of assumptions, employers would have a financial incentive to pay the tax and turn the problem over to government. For example, a small-business owner with eight employees earning $9 an hour and two part-time employees earning $6.50 an hour could cut health care costs in half by paying the tax. Overall, Dennis estimates that between one million and two million employers would find it cheaper to pay than to play.

In recognition of the special burdens that the Kennedy bill would create for small employers, the Senate Democrats have proposed a

25 percent tax credit on the first $3,000 of premiums for each full-time employee earning less than $20,000 a year for firms with fewer than 60 employees. Dennis examined the incentives created by the tax credit as well, and he concluded that only in a few special cases would they be sufficient to reverse an employer's decision to pay rather than play. Although employers would be able to pay the tax and forget the problem, employees would not have that freedom. Assuming they are already paid a wage roughly equal to the value of what they produce, a 7 percent payroll tax means that they would have to take a 7 percent wage cut or risk losing their jobs. As those earning the minimum wage can't take a wage cut, they stand the greatest risk of becoming unemployed.

Employers who already provide health insurance also would have to compare the 7 percent tax with the cost of a health insurance policy containing core benefits defined in Washington. A great many of them are likely to be tempted to pay the tax and drop existing coverage. Nor is this mere speculation. One Kennedy aide has said that the bill's sponsors expect that to happen.

Lee Iacocca would probably like the Senate Democrats' plan. For years, he's wanted to dump Chrysler's health care costs on government, and the Senate Democrats are offering him a chance. Instead of paying close to $4,000 per employee for private insurance, Iacocca could pay a tax of less than $3,000, have government provide each Chrysler worker with health insurance, and make a handsome profit. It is likely, however, that Chrysler workers would object to such an arrangement.

If the Democrats' plan is adopted, special interests press for expanded coverage, health insurance costs rise, and employers opt to pay the tax, what will happen to the workers? They will be required to join Medicaid and pay premiums that vary by income level.

Granted, under the Democrats' plan, Medicaid would be reorganized and take on a new name: AmeriCare. But Medicaid under any other name is still Medicaid. In most places, Medicaid pays doctors and hospitals fifty cents on the dollar, and sometimes less. Increasingly, the best doctors won't see Medicaid patients, and only charity hospitals will accept them.

Because Medicaid underpays, health care rationing is inevitable. And more severe rationing is right around the corner as the hospital marketplace becomes more competitive, cost shifting to other patients becomes less feasible, and government at all levels has less money to spend. So far, only Oregon has admitted publicly that rationing in its Medicaid program is routine. Medical providers know the same thing is happening in every state. The Senate Democrats acknowledge this problem. To avert it, they call for reimbursing hospitals and providers at Medicare (rather than Medicaid) rates. Because of political pressures, however, they are unlikely to succeed in achieving this goal. Even if they do, Medicare itself is becoming a rationing program.

The Democrats' plan also has other problems. One is that government is inherently incapable of administering an insurance program that prices risk accurately. Witness the deposit insurance debacle at the federal level,[37] and the auto liability insurance crises in California, New Jersey, and Massachusetts. In Massachusetts, auto insurance has become so political an issue that any possibility of rational premium prices has vanished and 65 percent of all premiums now go to the state risk pool.[38]

The Senate Democrats have already signaled their lack of interest in real insurance prices. The 7 percent payroll tax has no relationship to the actual cost of health care for any particular employee. And they are proposing a quasi-cartel in the small-group health insurance market to guarantee that private insurance premiums won't reflect real risks either. That will speed the exodus of people into AmeriCare, the risk pool of last resort.

A second problem with the Senate Democrats' plan involves small business, which employs most of the noninsured workers. The Democrats' proposal to create new taxes for small business— the primary job-creating sector of the economy—came right in the middle of a recession. To avert the obvious economic harm, the plan proposes a two-year grace period for new small businesses and a five-year phase-in period for firms with fewer than 25 employees—the firms where almost half of all uninsured workers are

[37]A. James Meigs and John C. Goodman, *Federal Deposit Insurance: The Case for Radical Reform*, NCPA Policy Report no. 155 (Dallas: National Center for Policy Analysis, 1990).

[38]Simon Rottenberg, *The Cost of Regulated Pricing: A Critical Analysis of Auto Insurance Premium Rate-Setting in Massachusetts* (Boston: Pioneer Institute for Public Policy Research, 1989).

employed.[39] Like Dukakis, the Senate Democrats propose to promise now and act after the next election. Indeed, it is worth questioning whether this is a serious proposal or merely a Democratic campaign ploy.

A third problem with the plan involves health care costs which are bound to rise as more people acquire health insurance. Initially, the Senate Democrats propose "voluntary" spending limits with targets for the total amount spent on physicians' fees and hospital services throughout the country. But given that the nation's 5,000 hospitals and 500,000 doctors could not possibly agree collectively on anything, the targets will certainly be missed, and "voluntary" will soon become "mandatory."

That is precisely the approach taken in Canada, Britain, and throughout continental Europe. Governments in those countries set arbitrary budgets for hospitals and area health authorities, then force the providers to ration health care. The consequence is a lower quality of care and less—not more—efficiency (as discussed in chapter 18).

Before taxing small business to pay for an expanded Medicaid program with health care rationing required by limits on spending, Senate Democrats might listen to Lloyd Bentsen (D-TX), author of a limited program of refundable tax credits for the purchase of health insurance that was part of the budget summit agreement in 1990. Instead of pushing more people into a government rationing program, the Bentsen approach empowers low-income families and makes them real participants in the health insurance marketplace.

Mandated Employee Benefits and Lower Take-Home Pay

Health insurance is only one of various mandated employee benefits that have been proposed in Congress. Others include family and medical leave, advance notice of plant closings and of employee layoffs, and high-risk occupational disease notification. All have two characteristics in common: (1) they remove freedom of choice from the labor market and substitute the preferences of politicians for those of workers, and (2) they threaten to lower take-home pay by reducing productivity and/or requiring the substitution of fringe benefits for wages.

[39]Foley, p. 9.

A basic principle of labor economics is that employers will not hire employees unless the value of what the employees produce is at least equal to the total compensation they receive. As a result, when employers are forced to provide certain benefits, the cost of those benefits ultimately is borne by the workers through a reduction either in wages or in other fringe benefits. To the extent that mandated benefits legislation also lowers productivity, employees bear an additional cost. Lower productivity ultimately means lower compensation.

Workers already are worse off because they often are forced to accept fringe benefits instead of receiving higher wages. In addition, total labor compensation today is lower than it needs to be because of lower productivity, in part caused by legislation that purports to protect employees.[40] Mandated benefits legislation currently being considered in Congress would cause even lower productivity and lower take-home pay.

Government Regulations and Productivity

Numerous studies have shown that the goals of health, safety, and environmental legislation could be achieved at a fraction of the cost. Meanwhile, the American worker is paying for these unnecessary and wasteful policies. Between 1959 and 1969, productivity in U.S. manufacturing increased by almost 1 percent annually. Between 1973 and 1978, it fell by more than 0.5 percent annually. Regulation by the Occupational Safety and Health Administration and the Environmental Protection Agency caused about one-third of this slowdown, resulting in a cost of about $1,000 for each manufacturing worker in 1987.[41]

Fringe Benefits and Take-Home Pay

Although the U.S. economy has grown over the last 15 years, workers' paychecks have shrunk in real terms. Since 1972, total employee compensation per hour worked has increased in real terms. Yet real wages per hour worked were lower in 1982 than in 1972. In other words, employers were paying more but employees

---

[40]The income of workers must be roughly equal to the value of what they produce. See note 26 above.

[41]Wayne B. Gray, "The Cost of Regulation: OSHA, EPA and the Productivity Slowdown," *American Economic Review* (December 1987).

were receiving less. One reason for this anomaly is that the "wedge" created by employment taxes and fringe benefits grew from 12 percent of employee compensation in 1972 to 16 percent in 1988.[42] In many cases, workers are worse off because they are forced to take fringe benefits that they do not want and may not need.

[42]Taken from the national income and product accounts data reported in U. S. Department of Commerce, Bureau of Economic Analysis, *Survey of Current Business* 68, no. 7 (July 1988), Tables 6.4B, 6.5B.

PART IV

THE CHAIN-LETTER ECONOMICS OF MEDICARE

13. Health Care after Retirement

When we move into the 21st century, the United States and other developed countries will have a growing number of elderly citizens relative to the working-age population. The cost of income maintenance and health care for the elderly, whether paid through public or private programs, will be staggering. During the latter half of the 21st century, the annual cost of Social Security plus health spending for the elderly in the United States will equal one-half to three-fourths of all workers' wages.

Projections for America's Future

Under our current system of pay-as-you-go financing, each generation depends on the government to cover its Social Security benefits and most of its health care bills by taxing the next generation. If we continue this practice, the burden we create for tomorrow's workers will be impossible for them to bear. The year 2060 seems like the distant future—so distant that it is easy to ignore. But almost everyone who will be 65 years of age or older in that year already has been born. Those not yet born are the future generations of workers who will be expected to honor promises that are being made to today's young children—about their Social Security and health care retirement benefits.

Here is the nightmare in America's future, based on official forecasts made by the Social Security Administration.

Social Security and Medicare Hospital Insurance

Projections about the future of Social Security and Medicare are made annually by the Social Security Administration.[1] These projections are often labeled "optimistic," "intermediate," and "pessimistic," and people are encouraged to believe that the intermediate

---

[1] See *The 1988 Annual Report of the Board of Trustees of the Federal Old-Age and Survivors Insurance and the Federal Disability Insurance Trust Funds,* May 9, 1988 (hereinafter referred to as *Board of Trustees Report*).

Figure 13.1
THE NIGHTMARE IN OUR FUTURE*

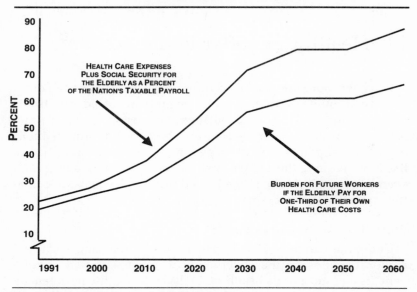

SOURCE: National Center for Policy Analysis.

*Based on the Social Security Administration's Alternative III assumptions.

forecast is the most likely. But many students of Social Security believe that the pessimistic projection more closely reflects our recent experience.[2] Currently, spending on Social Security and Medicare hospital insurance (Medicare Part A) is equal to about 14 percent of the nation's total taxable payroll. As can be seen in Figure 13.1, during the retirement years of the baby boom generation, we will either have to double the tax burden for workers or cut promised benefits in half. As Table 13.1 shows, by the year 2030 the payroll tax will have to rise to about 34 percent of taxable wages to fund benefits promised under current law. By 2050, it will rise to

[2]The "pessimistic" projection is by no means the worst that can happen. In fact, the "pessimistic" assumptions often are more favorable than our recent experience. See John C. Goodman and Peter Ferrara, "Social Security: Who Gains? Who Loses?" NCPA Policy Report no. 127 (Dallas: National Center for Policy Analysis, May 1987), pp. 6–8. The assumptions behind all three projections are discussed in greater detail below.

388

Table 13.1

PROJECTED SOCIAL SECURITY BENEFITS AND MEDICARE HOSPITAL INSURANCE AS PERCENT OF NATION'S TAXABLE PAYROLL

Year	Optimistic Projection[1]	Intermediate Projection[2]	Pessimistic Projection[3]
1991	13.6%	13.7%	13.9%
2000	12.6	14.4	16.5
2010	13.1	15.9	19.4
2020	15.6	20.2	26.6
2030	17.4	24.1	34.4
2040	17.2	25.1	38
2050	16.8	25.4	40
2060	17	26.6	43

SOURCE: *The 1991 Annual Report of the Board of Trustees of the Federal Old-Age and Survivors Insurance and the Federal Disability Insurance Trust Funds* (May 17, 1991), Appendix E, Table E-2 (pp. 138–39).

[1]Based on the Social Security Administration's Alternative I assumptions.
[2]Based on the Social Security Administration's Alternative II-B assumptions.
[3]Based on the Social Security Administration's Alternative III assumptions.

43 percent of the nation's taxable payroll.[3] This future payroll tax burden is greater than the combined burden of all federal, state, and local personal income taxes today.

Health Care Spending

By far the fastest rising component of the projections is our commitment to pay future health care costs. The burden of Medicare hospital insurance alone currently is about 2.61 percent of total taxable payroll. As Table 13.2 shows, the burden will probably more than double by 2010, more than triple by 2020, and more than quintuple by 2030.

These estimates considerably understate the magnitude of total health care spending for the elderly. Medicare hospital insurance today pays about 75 percent of their hospital costs, which represent 45 percent of their total health care spending. Thus, Medicare hospital insurance pays about 30 percent of the total health care costs for the elderly. The remaining costs are paid through Medicare Part B (funded 25 percent by premiums paid by the elderly and 75 percent by general tax revenues), Medicaid and other government programs (funded by general tax revenues), private health insurance, and out-of-pocket funds. As Table 13.2 shows, if nonhospital medical costs increase at the same rate as projected hospital costs, total health care spending for the elderly may equal 60 percent of the nation's taxable payroll by 2060.

Burden for Future Taxpayers

The Social Security Administration's practice of combining future Social Security payments with Medicare hospital insurance payments is based on a hidden assumption. The assumption is that society is contractually obligated to pay only those future medical costs that are funded by the Social Security (FICA) tax. Accordingly, anything the federal government does to shift costs from Medicare hospital insurance to Medicare Part B, the Department of Veterans Affairs, Medicaid, or private employers is viewed as reducing future obligations. That assumption is probably wrong. If the political marketplace communicates any clear message, it is that of an implicit contract with the elderly. Moreover, the political obligation

[3]The payroll tax rates cited are the rates necessary to pay Social Security retirement benefits, Medicare hospital insurance benefits, and survivors and disability benefits.

Table 13.2

PROJECTED HEALTH CARE EXPENSES FOR THE ELDERLY AS A PERCENT OF THE NATION'S TAXABLE PAYROLL, 1991 TO 2060

Year	Medicare Hospital Insurance[1]	Total Medicare[2]	Total Health Care Costs[3]
1991	2.65%	3.98%	8.79%
2000	4.16	6.24	13.77
2010	6.43	9.65	21.30
2020	10.50	15.75	34.77
2030	14.95	22.43	49.51
2040	16.93	25.40	56.07
2050	17.29	25.94	55.26
2060	18.04	27.06	59.74

SOURCE: *The 1991 Annual Report of the Board of Trustees of the Federal Old-Age and Survivors Insurance and the Federal Disability Insurance Trust Funds* (May 17, 1991), Appendix E, Table E.2 (pp. 138–39).
[1]Based on the Social Security Administration's pessimistic projection.
[2]Projection based on the assumption that Medicare hospital insurance will be equal to two-thirds of total Medicare spending.
[3]Projection based on the assumption that Medicare spending will be equal to 45.3 percent of total health care spending of the elderly.

to ensure that all elderly citizens have access to health care is probably every bit as strong as the obligation to pay Social Security
benefits.

Like Social Security, virtually all government programs that currently fund health care expenses for the elderly are financed on
a pay-as-you-go basis. With few exceptions, no funds are being
invested today to pay for health care costs that will be incurred in
the future. Thus, unless there is a fundamental change in current
policies, society will be able to pay for Social Security and health
care for the elderly in 2060 only by taking income from people who
are alive in 2060.

Table 13.3 shows the magnitude of Social Security benefits plus
total health care costs for the elderly in future years. As the table
indicates, it will reach one-third of total taxable payroll in just two
decades. It will probably be almost 70 percent of the nation's taxable
payroll by 2030 and about 85 percent by 2060.

It is not known precisely what share of their health care expenses
the elderly currently pay with their own funds. A reasonable estimate is that they pay no more than one-third.[4] As our society ages,
however, an increasing number of elders will be the "old elderly"—
with fewer assets and less income than the "young elderly." This
demographic change, in conjunction with the government's policy
of discouraging private savings for future medical costs, will probably make it impossible for the elderly to continue paying one-third
of their health care costs. Nonetheless, Table 13.4 assumes that the
future working population still will be obligated to pay only two-
thirds of the elderly's health care expenses. Even if this proves true,
the total burden on the working population of covering the elderly's
Social Security benefits and health care costs will probably exceed
one-fourth of the nation's taxable payroll in just two decades, one-
half of the nation's total taxable payroll by 2030, and about 65
percent by 2060.

The Problem of Expanding Medicare Coverage

The above projections understate the probable magnitude of the
impact of future health care spending on the elderly because they

[4]The technical issues involved in making this estimate are discussed in John C.
Goodman and Gerald L. Musgrave, "Health Care after Retirement: Who Will Pay
the Cost?" NCPA Policy Report no. 139 (Dallas: National Center for Policy Analysis,
May 1989), appendix A.

Table 13.3

PROJECTED SOCIAL SECURITY BENEFITS AND HEALTH CARE EXPENSES FOR THE ELDERLY AS A PERCENT OF THE NATION'S TAXABLE PAYROLL, 1991 TO 2060[1]

Year	Social Security[2]	Social Security Plus Total Medicare	Social Security Plus Total Health Care Expenses
1991	11.28%	15.26%	20.07%
2000	12.33	18.57	26.10
2010	12.94	22.59	34.24
2020	16.10	31.85	50.87
2030	19.51	41.94	69.02
2040	21.11	46.51	77.18
2050	22.71	48.65	77.97
2060	25.13	52.19	84.87

SOURCE: *The 1991 Annual Report of the Board of Trustees of the Federal Old-Age and Survivors Insurance and the Federal Disability Insurance Trust Funds* (May 17, 1991), Appendix E, Table E-2 (pp. 138–39); and Tables 13-1, 13-2.
[1]Based on the Social Security Administration's pessimistic projections.
[2]Includes old-age, survivors, and disability payments.

393

Table 13.4
PROJECTED BURDEN FOR FUTURE WORKERS
(Assuming the Elderly Pay for One-Third of Their Health
Care Expenditures)

Year	Burden as a Percent of Taxable Payroll
1991	17.14%
2000	21.51
2010	27.14
2020	39.28
2030	52.52
2040	58.49
2050	59.55
2060	64.96

SOURCE: Based on Table 13.3.

ignore the political pressure to expand Medicare. For example, Medicare currently pays less than 2 percent of nursing home costs for the elderly,[5] and 81 percent of the elderly's out-of-pocket medical costs in excess of $2,000 goes for nursing home care.[6] In addition, for every elderly patient in a nursing home, two equally disabled persons are not in nursing homes.[7] For these reasons, political pressure is mounting to expand Medicare to cover nursing home costs. But the costs of such coverage would be huge. If every elderly person in America spent just one year in a nursing home, the total cost would be about $627 billion, or roughly half of the entire federal budget.[8] One of the prime forces keeping the elderly out of nursing homes today is the high cost. If price were no object (that is, if Medicare coverage were extended), the number of elderly people in nursing homes would increase sharply.

[5]Task Force on Long-Term Care Policies, *Report to the Congress and the Secretary* (Washington: U.S. Department of Health and Human Services, 1987), p. 69.

[6]Thomas Rice and Jon Gabel, "Protecting the Elderly against High Health Care Costs," *Health Affairs* (Fall 1986), p. 16.

[7]Task Force on Long-Term Care Policies.

[8]John C. Goodman and Gerald L. Musgrave, "Health Care for the Elderly: The Nightmare in Our Future," NCPA Policy Report no. 130 (Dallas: National Center for Policy Analysis, October 1987), p. 5.

A Closer Look at the Assumptions behind the Projections

Because the Social Security Administration has published different projections for the next 65 years, which one should we believe? That depends on which projection is based on the most realistic expectations about the future. And the only way of evaluating the predictions is to compare them with our recent experience.

Table 13.5 summarizes the key assumptions used in each of the Social Security Administration's projections. The differences in the assumptions, which appear small, lead to huge differences in future taxpayer burdens—differences that are magnified over time. What follows is a brief analysis of some critical assumptions behind current forecasts.

Aging and the U.S. Fertility Rate

A nation's fertility rate is the average number of children that women of childbearing age will have over their lifetime. In developed countries, 2.1 is the replacement rate—the rate necessary to maintain the size of the current population. To keep the total population at its current size, each adult man and woman must be replaced by approximately two children.[9]

In 1960, virtually all developed countries had fertility rates in excess of 2.1, and most had rates substantially higher. Since then, however, as Table 13.6 shows, the rates have dropped. The United States, Canada, Iceland, and the Netherlands have experienced a drop of more than 50 percent over 25 years (see Table 13.7). In Belgium, Austria, Denmark, Australia, Germany, and New Zealand, the decrease was 40 percent or greater. Consequently, the vast majority of developed countries today have fertility rates substantially below the replacement rate. Overall, out of 22 industrial democracies, only 3—New Zealand, Ireland, and Israel—have fertility rates above the replacement level.[10]

---

[9]The 0.1 factor accounts for childhood mortality that occurs before females reach childbearing age.

[10]Ben J. Wattenberg, *The Birth Dearth* (New York: Pharos Books, 1987), chart 2A (p. 173).

Table 13.5
Key Economic and Demographic Assumptions for the Period Following the Year 2015

Assumption	Recent Experience	Optimistic Projection[1]	Intermediate Projection[2]	Pessimistic Projection[3]
Total fertility rate	1.83[4]	2.2	1.9	1.6
Annual increase in real wages (%)	0.5[5]	1.7	1.1	0.6
Annual increase in consumer price index (%)	6.6[6]	3.0	4.0	5.0
Annual decrease in mortality rate (%)	1.2[7]	0.3	0.5	1.0
Annual increase in hospital costs[8] (%)	6.3[9]	2.3	3.7	5.4

SOURCE: *The 1991 Annual Report of the Board of Trustees of the Federal Old-Age and Survivors Insurance and the Federal Disability Insurance Trust Funds* (May 17, 1991), Tables 10, 11; and *The 1991 Annual Report of the Board of Trustees of the Federal Hospital Insurance Trust Fund* (May 17, 1991), Tables A-1, A-3.

[1] Based on the Social Security Administration's Alternative I assumptions.
[2] Based on the Social Security Administration's Alternative II-B assumptions.
[3] Based on the Social Security Administration's Alternative III assumptions.
[4] Average number of children per woman of childbearing age for years 1975 to 1989.
[5] Average annual real wage rate for the years 1975 to 1989.
[6] Average annual increase for the period 1975 to 1989.
[7] Average annual decrease in the age/sex-adjusted death rate for the years 1975 to 1989.
[8] Measured as the annual rate of increase in Medicare hospital insurance expenditures minus the annual rate of increase in average hospital wages.
[9] Annual rate of growth of hospital inpatient expenditures (approximately 93 percent of hospital income spending) minus the rate of growth in wages for years 1975 to 1989.

Table 13.6
DROP IN FERTILITY RATES, 1960 TO 1985

Country	Change
Australia	−43%
Austria	−42
Belgium	−40
Canada	−55
Denmark	−44
Finland	−37
France	−33
Germany	−44
Iceland	−56
Ireland	−34
Israel[1]	−23
Italy	−39
Japan	−10
Luxembourg	−39
Netherlands	−52
New Zealand	−44
Norway	−39
Spain	−39
Sweden	−23
Switzerland	−35
United Kingdom	−33
United States	−51

SOURCE: Ben J. Wattenberg, *The Birth Dearth* (New York: Pharos Books, 1987), Chart 2A (p. 173).
[1]Jewish population only.

The fact that the fertility rate in the United States and other developed countries is well below the replacement rate has generally gone unreported.[11] Yet, as Figure 13.2 shows, even if we maintain our current fertility rate, the population of the United States

[11]For example, the Bureau of the Census "middle level" projections assumed a fertility rate of 2.1 until 1984 (when it was reduced to 1.9), despite the fact that the average fertility rate for the ten previous years was 1.796. See Wattenberg, pp. 26–27 n. 3. The intermediate projection of the Social Security Administration—the one most widely quoted in and out of government—did not use a fertility rate of less than 2.0 until 1988. See the *Board of Trustees Report*. In addition, two former administrators in the U.S. Department of Health and Human Services published a book in the mid-1980s on Medicare policy in which all of the forecasts assumed a (replacement)

Table 13.7
PROJECTED U.S. POPULATION GROWTH, 1990–2050

Population Group	Percent Increase
Total population	−6%
Ages 65–74	51
Ages 75–84	78
Age 85+	246

SOURCE: Based on U.S. Bureau of the Census lowest series projection. U.S. Bureau of the Census, *Projections of the Population of the United States by Age, Sex and Race: 1983 to 2080*, Current Population Reports, Series P-25, no. 952 (Washington: U.S. Government Printing Office, 1984), Table 6.

Figure 13.2
PROJECTED U.S. POPULATION, 1990 TO 2110*

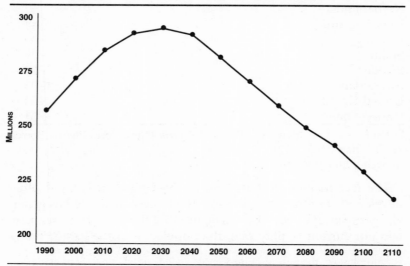

*Pessimistic projection, based on the Social Security Administration's Alternative III assumptions.

fertility rate of 2.1 without giving any justification. See Karen Davis and Diane Rowland, *Medicare Policy: New Directions for Health and Long-Term Care* (Baltimore: Johns Hopkins University Press, 1986), pp. 121–23.

398

Figure 13.3
NUMBER OF WORKERS FOR EACH SOCIAL SECURITY
BENEFICIARY, 1965 TO 2065

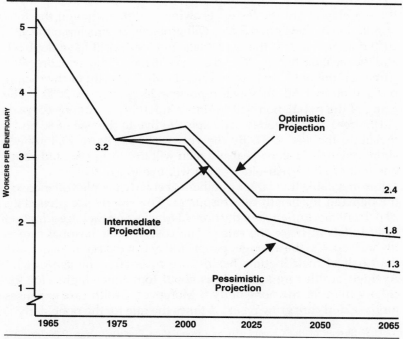

SOURCE: Social Security Administration.

will peak in the first half of the 21st century and will decline continuously thereafter.

The implications of declining fertility rates are devastating for the
social security systems of all developed countries. As Figure 13.3
shows, there will be a declining number of workers to support each
elderly beneficiary in the United States. Unless there are major
lifestyle changes, almost all developed countries will experience
indefinite population aging and growing payroll tax burdens for
social security and other retirement benefits.

Aging and Health Care Costs

As a country ages, its health care costs inevitably rise. And the
faster it ages, the faster those costs rise. At the turn of this century,

399

only 4 percent of the population was 65 or older. Today that figure is 12 percent. And it is projected is be 20 percent by 2030 and almost 25 percent by 2050 (see Table 13.7).[12] Thus, the elderly constitute the fastest growing segment of the population, and among them, the old elderly are the fastest growing group. Although the total population of the United States will probably be smaller in the year 2050 than it is today, the percentage of elderly will have doubled, and the old elderly (ages 85 and older) will have almost quadrupled. Although the old elderly represented only 9 percent of the elderly population in 1980, they will represent 20 percent by 2050.[13] The aging of the population will continue indefinitely. Among 65-year-old retirees, a male today can expect to live to the age of 80 and a female to the age of 84. By the year 2065, as Figure 13.4 shows, about one-half of all 65-year-old men will live to age 86, and about one-half of all 65-year-old women will live to age 91.[14]

It is inevitable that larger numbers of elderly people will increase the demand for health care resources. The elderly see physicians 20 percent more often than the nonelderly do, and they are admitted to hospitals at twice the rate.[15] The cost of their hospital care is higher, too. On the average, people today can expect to incur more than half of their lifetime health care costs after the age of 65.[16] Average health care spending is about four times higher for the elderly than for the nonelderly.[17] Moreover, health care expenses for the elderly are growing at 2.6 times the rate for the nonelderly.[18]

[12]U.S. Bureau of the Census, Current Population Reports, series P-25, no. 952 *Projections of the Population of the United States by Age, Sex and Race: 1983 to 2080* (Washington: U.S. Government Printing Office, 1984), lowest series projection, Tables E, F (pp. 7–8).

[13]Ibid.

[14]*Board of Trustees Report*, Table II, pp. 37–38.

[15]George W. Bush et al., "Prefunding of Postemployment Health Care: The Pension Analogy, the Insurance Need," in Robert D. Paul and Diane M. Disney, eds., *The Sourcebook on Postretirement Health Care Benefits* (Greenvale, NY: Panel, 1986), p. 296.

[16]Estimates of the Health Care Financing Administration.

[17]U.S. Department of Health and Human Services, *Catastrophic Illness Expenses: Department of Health and Human Services Report to the President* (Washington, November 1986), p. 8.

[18]Deborah J. Chollet and Robert B. Friedland, "Employer-Paid Retiree Health Insurance: History and Prospects for Growth," in Frank B. McArdle, ed., *The Changing Health Care Market* (Washington: Employee Benefit Research Institute, 1987), p. 206.

Figure 13.4
EXPECTED AGE OF DEATH FOR PEOPLE 65 YEARS OLD, 1988
TO 2065

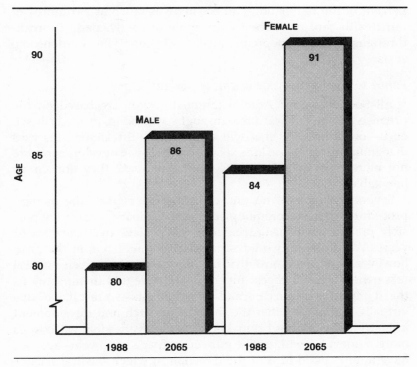

Among the old elderly, health care utilization and costs are even higher. On the average, hospital costs for people aged 85 and older are about 67 percent more than for those aged 65 to 75.[19] Long-term care for the old elderly is about ten times more costly than for the young elderly.[20] And although only 2 percent of senior citizens in their mid-60s and early 70s enter nursing homes, about 23 percent of the old elderly do so.[21]

[19]Estimates of the Health Care Financing Administration. For a recent discussion of these projections and related issues, see Peter G. Peterson, "The Morning After," *Atlantic Monthly*, October 1987, pp. 62–64.

[20]Ibid.

[21]Phillip Longman, *Born to Pay: The New Politics of Aging in America* (Boston: Houghton Mifflin Co., 1987), p. 88.

401

The elderly, who represent only 12 percent of the U.S. population today, consume almost one-third of all U.S. health care services.[22] By the middle of the next century, the elderly will represent 24 percent of the population and consume as much as two-thirds of our health care resources. Even without costly medical break-throughs, the aging population will create impossibly burdensome costs.

Future Costs and the Achievements of Medical Science

All Social Security Administration forecasts are based on the premise that no radical breakthroughs will occur in medical sci-ence—breakthroughs that will eliminate life-threatening diseases or significantly increase life expectancy. But such developments are not merely possible; over a 65-year time span, they are almost inevitable.

Seventy years ago, no one could have imagined the medical procedures that are commonplace today. Similarly, we cannot pos-sibly predict what medical science will achieve over the next 65 years. We do have two advantages over forecasters in the past, however. First, we know that modern society has given medical researchers a blank check. Invent it, we have told them; show us that it improves health care; and we will buy it. As a result, we have virtually guaranteed that the medical research and development industry will work hard at making new discoveries that will cost us more money. Second, unlike our counterparts of 65 years ago, we have a fairly good idea of the direction in which medical science will progress. For example, it is virtually inevitable that scientists will produce a complete mapping of the genetic code. The question is not if, only *when*. Given that many life-threatening diseases are related to our genetic resistance to them, a complete understanding of an individual's genetic makeup opens the door to the genetic prevention of disease by artificial intervention. In the case of cancer, for example, Americans are constantly exposed to carcinogens. They occur naturally in the food we eat, the water we drink, and the air we breathe. But some people, partly because of their genetic

[22]Frederic D. Wolinsky, Ray R. Mosely II, and Rodney M. Coe, "A Cohort Analysis of the Use of Health Services by Elderly Americans," *Journal of Health and Social Behavior* 27, no. 3 (1986): 209.

endowment, resist exposure better than others.[23] Once we understand the mechanism of susceptibility or resistance (which probably will not require a complete understanding of the genetic code), we will be able to sharply reduce and perhaps eliminate death from cancer.

The biggest uncertainty is what the achievements of modern science will do to the future financial burden of income maintenance and health care for the elderly. For example, heart disease, cancer, and strokes currently account for 75 percent of all deaths among the elderly. Moreover, these three diseases are responsible for 20 percent of all physician visits, 40 percent of all hospital days, and 50 percent of all days spent in bed.[24] If we could costlessly eliminate all three diseases, we would also eliminate three major categories of health care spending. But it is not clear that our total financial burden would go down, for the elderly would live longer and collect more Social Security checks. They would then eventually die of some other—possibly expensive-to-treat—disease.

Virtually all new government health care programs have been accompanied by a forecast of their future expenses and those forecasts invariably underestimate program costs. Assuming the past is a guide to the future, the burden of health care costs for the elderly will be much greater than even the pessimistic forecast.

Our Chain Letter Approach to Funding Retirement Needs

America is in love with chain letters. At the federal level, we have Social Security, Medicare, federal civil service retirement, and Department of Veterans Affairs retirement chain letters. Many state and local government retirement programs also are run like chain letters. In the private sector, many company pensions and virtually all health care promises have chain letter characteristics.

Under this approach, each generation avoids making the sacrifices necessary to pay its own way and expects the next generation to pay. Using this approach, there are only three sources of funds

---

[23]For example, researchers now believe that more than half of all cases of colon and rectal cancer are directly related to a genetic predisposition to such cancers. See Lisa A. Cannon-Albright et al., "Common Inheritance of Susceptibility to Colonic Adenomatus Polyps and Associated Colorectal Cancers," *New England Journal of Medicine* 319, no. 9 (September 1, 1988): 533–37.

[24]Bush et al., pp. 303–4.

Table 13.8
SOURCES OF PAYMENT FOR NONINSTITUTIONAL HEALTH CARE EXPENSES FOR THE ELDERLY[1]

Source	Share of Payment
Medicare[2]	60.4%
Out-of-pocket expenses and Medigap insurance purchased by the elderly	22.1
Employer- or union- provided health insurance[3]	7.4
Medicaid	6.0
Veterans' medical care	4.0

SOURCE: Timothy M. Smeedling and Lavonne Straub, "Health Care Financing among the Elderly: Who Really Pays the Bills?" *Journal of Health Politics, Policy and Law* 12, no. 1 (Spring 1987), Table 1 (p. 39), Table 3 (p. 43).
[1]Excludes payments for nursing home care.
[2]Includes supplemental medical insurance (SMI) premiums paid by elderly for coverage under Medicare Part B.
[3]Includes premiums paid by the elderly.

available to pay retirement benefits: (1) the income and assets of the elderly themselves, (2) the income and assets of private companies that have promised to pay, and (3) federal government taxes on the income and assets of the general public.

Table 13.8 shows the current sources of health care funding for the elderly for expenses incurred outside of nursing homes. Throughout the 1980s, attempts were made—in both the public and private sectors—to shift costs among these various sources of payment. For example, state governments paid Medicare Part B premiums for elderly Medicaid patients in an attempt to shift medical costs to the federal government. State governments also stepped up their efforts to make Medicaid the payer of last resort by collecting whenever possible from Medicare and private insurance. Although almost all employer-provided insurance is integrated with Medicare and designed to pay for expenses not paid by Medicare,[25] Congress recently made employers the payer of first resort

[25]For a description of the types of employer plans, see Jonathan C. Dopkeen, "Postretirement Health Benefits" in Paul and Disney, pp. 559–60.

for employees who continue to work after they qualify for Medicare at the age of 65.[26] Many people believe that Medicare's cost-containment efforts are partly designed to shift costs from Medicare patients to other patients, and increases in Medicare copayments and deductibles clearly are an attempt to shift costs from Medicare to the elderly themselves. However, about 23 percent of elderly males outside of nursing homes potentially can escape many of these payments by turning to the free care made available by the Department of Veterans Affairs.[27] The net result of these activities is simply to shift costs back and forth among pay-as-you-go funding sources. None of these cost-control attempts comes to grip with the reality that postretirement health care is not being prefunded by any current program.

What follows is a brief description of the pay-as-you-go nature of the three major sources of funding: the Social Security and Medicare trust funds, out-of-pocket funds of the elderly, and employer-provided postretirement health insurance.

The Myth of the Social Security Trust Funds

Partly in response to growing public concern over the program's future, one commissioner of Social Security, Dorcas Hardy, sent a letter to all Social Security recipients during the Reagan administration assuring them that the trust fund was accumulating assets and would remain in the black indefinitely into the future. Her announcement was accompanied by talk of a Social Security surplus that would grow to $12 trillion to $14 trillion.

What happens to the surplus? Contrary to popular myth, the Social Security Administration is not stashing money away in bank vaults. When revenues exceed expenditures, the Social Security Administration lends the surplus to the U.S. Treasury and the government uses the money to finance current spending. In other words, the federal government lends the money to itself, and the trust funds consist of nothing more than IOUs that the government writes to itself. To pay future benefits, the government will have to levy additional taxes at the time the payments are due.

[26]Ibid., 583.

[27]Timothy M. Smeedling and Lavonne Straub, "Health Care Financing among the Elderly: Who Really Pays the Bills?" *Journal of Health Politics, Policy and Law* 12, no. 1 (Spring 1987): 37.

As a practical matter, annual Social Security surpluses are used to finance the federal deficit. For example, when Social Security is combined with Survivors and Disability Insurance along with Medicare hospital insurance, as it should be, projected annual surpluses will never exceed 0.85 percent of the gross national product (GNP), or about $40 billion in current dollars—well below the deficit that these surpluses help finance. If current promises to pay benefits are kept, the total (accounting) surplus will vanish by the year 2013, and a continuously growing deficit will appear thereafter.[28] The surplus and deficit projected for the years 2000 through 2060 are shown in Figure 13.5. They are based on the Social Security Administration's intermediate projection; however, when the pessimistic projection is used, the future looks far bleaker. Under the pessimistic projection, the total (accounting) surplus will vanish by 1997. By the year 2035, when today's young workers retire, the Social Security (accounting) deficit will be 7 percent of GNP or about $350 billion in 1989 dollars.[29]

To repeat: The accounting surplus reported by the Social Security Administration does not represent a store of funds from which to pay future benefits. It represents nothing more than a promise to raise future taxes.

Out-of-Pocket Expenses of the Elderly

At the time Medicare and Medicaid were initiated in 1965, there was considerable pressure on Congress to relieve the elderly of the financial responsibilities of health care. But the elderly now spend a larger share of their income out-of-pocket on health care than they did before the programs existed. In 1962, for example, the elderly spent less than 8 percent of their own income for health care; today, despite the phenomenal growth in Medicare and Medicaid, they spend 15 percent.[30]

What is true of Medicare is also true of other forms of health insurance. For example, elderly individuals with Medigap insurance generate 67 percent more health care spending than those

---

[28]Peter Ferrara, *The Great Social Security Hoax*, Heritage Foundation Backgrounder no. 662 (July 1988).

[29]Ibid.

[30]Smeedling and Straub, p. 36.

Figure 13.5
PROJECTED ANNUAL SOCIAL SECURITY AND MEDICARE
SURPLUS/DEFICIT AS PERCENTAGE OF GROSS NATIONAL
PRODUCT, 2000 TO 2060*

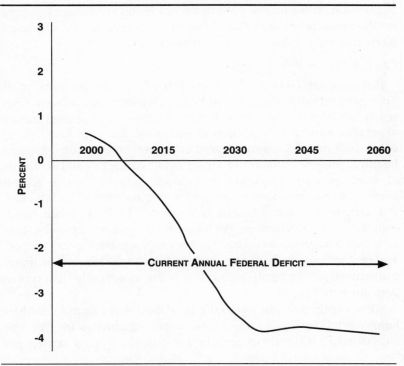

*Based on the Social Security Administration's intermediate assumptions.

without, and they spend 15 percent more out-of-pocket.[31] In general, health insurance does not replace money the elderly would otherwise have spent on health care; it adds to the total spent. Nonetheless, there clearly is a limit to the amount that the elderly can pay for health care. In addition, out-of-pocket expenditures are highest among those who can least afford it—the old elderly. For elderly families aged 65 to 69, out-of-pocket expenses for health

[31]Davis and Rowland, p. 36.

equal only 4 percent of income.[32] For those aged 85 and older, out-of-pocket expenses equal 38 percent of income.[33] But the old elderly have only two-thirds as much income as the young elderly.[34]

Because the old elderly are the fastest growing segment of our population, and because people are not being encouraged to save for their own retirement, our ability to extract greater out-of-pocket payments from retirees will surely decrease.

Commitments of Private Employers

Just as almost all large companies provide private pensions, most now pay certain postretirement health care expenses as well. Currently, about 95 percent of all large firms and a significant number of smaller ones provide postretirement health care benefits.[35] About one in four retirees is now covered by employer- or union-provided health insurance.[36] About one-third of all workers[37] and two-thirds of workers with employer-provided insurance[38] work for an employer who provides coverage for postretirement health care. The cost of this commitment is soaring.[39] In 1974, when many companies began covering postretirement medical expenses, Fortune 500 companies averaged twelve employees for every retiree. Today, there are only three workers for every retiree. For many companies, retiree health plans already are more costly than retiree pension benefits.

Some companies are especially burdened. For example, Bethlehem Steel Corp. had only 33,000 active employees in 1988 but supported 70,000 retirees and their spouses.[40] Among companies

[32]Anne M. Rappaport and Robert W. Kalman, "Financing Postretirement Medical Benefits: Assuring Economic Security for Retirees," in Paul and Disney, p. 271.

[33]Ibid.

[34]Bush et al., p. 321.

[35]Dopkeen, p. 565.

[36]Ibid., p. 583.

[37]Ibid., p. 566.

[38]Chollet and Friedman, "Employer-Paid Retiree Health Insurance," p. 210.

[39]See *America's Health Care Challenge: New Directions for Business, Government and Individuals* (Minneapolis: Northwestern Life Insurance Co., 1986); and Employee Benefit Research Institute, *Measuring and Funding Corporate Liabilities for Retiree Health Benefits* (Washington: EBRI, 1988).

[40]Amanda Bennett, "Firms Stunned by Retiree Health Costs," *Wall Street Journal*, May 24, 1988, p. 37.

reporting postretirement health care expenses, the annual expense was equal to 57 percent of net income at USX, 44 percent at Bethlehem Steel, and 23 percent at General Motors.[41] Postretirement health care expenses also are considered to have been a major factor in some corporate bankruptcies, including those of Allis-Chalmers and LTV.[42]

What is the magnitude of postretirement health care commitments for U.S. companies? Because companies have not been required to report their postretirement health care liabilities on their balance sheets, no one knows for sure. The estimates vary, ranging from a Department of Labor estimate of $98 billion to an American Enterprise Institute estimate of $332 billion. (See Table 13.9.) In general, almost all of this liability is unfunded. A study by Coopers & Lybrand and Hewitt Associates found that only 9 out of 4,000 companies surveyed were setting aside funds for retiree health benefits.[43] Other studies have placed the number of companies that prefund these obligations at less than 2 percent.[44]

Under a new accounting rule, to take affect in 1993, employers for the first time will be required to estimate and report their unfunded liabilities.[45] The results are expected to be shocking. According to one estimate, if the entire corporate sector had accrued liabilities for postretirement health care in 1989, corporate profits would have been reduced by 20 percent and net worth would have been reduced by 14 percent.[46] Among companies that have already calculated the effect of the accounting rule change, the cost will be $2.7 billion at General Electric Company, $2.26 billion at International Business Machines Corporation, and $1 billion each at Aluminum Company of America and American Airlines.[47] Chrysler Corporation's 1990

---

[41]*Business Week*, September 12, 1988, p. 94.

[42]*Institutional Investor*, May 1988, p. 106.

[43]Coopers & Lybrand and Hewitt Associates, *Non-Pension Benefits for Retired Employees—Study of Benefits and Accounting Practices* (1985).

[44]Dopkeen, p. 584.

[45]The Financial Accounting Standards Board (FASB) has issued the new rule in FASB, *Statement 106*.

[46]Mark J. Warshawsky, "Retiree Benefits: Promises Uncertain?" *The American Enterprise*, July/August, 1991, p. 63.

[47]Ibid.

Table 13.9

ESTIMATES OF ACCRUED LIABILITIES FOR RETIREE HEALTH BENEFITS:
ALL PRIVATE CORPORATIONS
($ Billions)

Estimator	Current Retirees	Active Workers	Total
Department of Labor (1983)	$40.7	$57.4	$98.1
General Accounting Office (1988)	93.0	128.0	221.0
Employee Benefit Research Institute (1988)	98.0	149.0	247.0
American Enterprise Institute (1988)	145.0	187.1	332.1

SOURCE: Mark Warshawsky, *The Uncertain Promise of Retiree Health Benefits: An Evaluation of Corporate Obligations* (Washington: American Enterprise Institute, forthcoming).

Figure 13.6
HOW ACCRUAL OF LIABILITIES FOR RETIREE HEALTH BENEFITS
WOULD HAVE AFFECTED 676 CORPORATIONS IN 1989

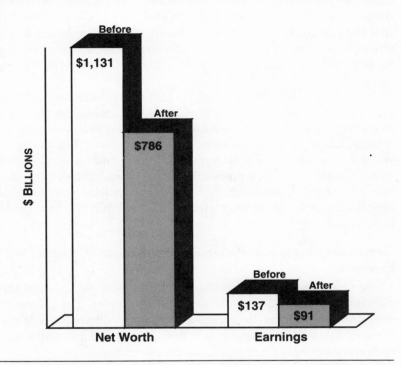

SOURCE: Mark J. Warshawsky, "Retiree Health Benefits: Promises Uncertain," *The American Enterprise* (July/August 1991), Figure 2 (p. 63).

retiree health care costs were $298 million, but the company calculates that its future liability is as much as $6 billion.

Of course not all companies will be equally affected by the accounting change. Some do not offer postretirement health care benefits. Figure 13.6 shows what the accounting change will mean for 676 companies with higher-than-average liabilities. As the figure shows, accruing the liabilities will reduce earnings by 33 percent and net worth by almost 30 percent.

At one time it was thought that an employer who faced financial problems could simply cease providing the postretirement health

411

care benefits. A series of court rulings has altered that assumption. In many cases, the courts have ruled that such promises are legally binding. That is one reason why Joseph Califano, former secretary of the Department of Health, Education, and Welfare, described the problem as "one of the world's greatest time bombs." Note also that the funding of postretirement health care by employers is not strictly a problem of paying for health care for the elderly. Among Fortune 500 companies, the average retirement occurs at 58.3 years of age.[48]

This mounting liability not only threatens the financial health of corporate America, but virtually ensures that employers will turn to the federal government—and therefore to taxpayers—to pick up a larger share of postretirement health care costs. For example, several companies (including Chrysler) and unions have announced support for a proposal to reduce the Medicare eligibility age from 65 to 60. Such a change would reduce total retiree health care liabilities by more than two-thirds and shift the burden to taxpayers.[49]

Government Barriers to Prefunding Postretirement Health Care Expenses

The fact that all major funding for health care expenses of the elderly is on a pay-as-you-go basis is no accident. The failure to save and invest today for expenses we know will arise tomorrow is exacerbated by a federal policy that discourages prudence and encourages increasing dependence on government.

Federal government policy toward health care expenses approaches the bizarre. We subsidize and encourage current health care spending while simultaneously discouraging savings for health care expenses during the retirement years. Tax subsidies for current health care expenditures are about $60 billion per year. Yet, with few exceptions, the federal government allows no tax deduction for the prefunding of future health care expenses and prohibits or penalizes the use of tax-deductible retirement savings to pay medical bills or purchase postretirement health insurance. A summary of the major elements of this perverse policy follows.

[48]Dopkeen, p. 558. Note that individuals become eligible for Medicare at age 65.
[49]Milt Freudenheim, "A Plan to Cover Early Retirees," *New York Times*, December 10, 1991.

Restrictions on Individuals

Under current tax law, individuals are not taxed on employer-paid health insurance premiums. In addition, individuals may deduct medical expenses above 7 percent of their income. But they may not deduct funds set aside to pay medical expenses during retirement. The one exception is that they may use funds in 401(k) savings plans to pay large medical bills. Because of the setup cost of these plans, however, they are often unavailable to the self-employed and to employees of small firms. Moreover, because 401(k) plans are employer-based, they are completely unavailable to the unemployed. Ironically, although Congress created tax deductions for individual retirement accounts (IRAs), Keogh plans, and 401(k) plans to encourage retirement savings, tax law forbids using the funds to obtain postretirement health insurance. Congress also has restricted the ability of individuals to save. The IRA deduction, for example, has been greatly limited despite research that concluded that 97 percent of every dollar put into an IRA account adds to total personal savings.[50]

Restrictions on Employers

Companies also are discouraged from saving for postretirement health care expenses. Prior to 1984, employers could use several vehicles to prefund employees' postretirement health care expenses. "Tax reform," however, severely limited the employers' ability to do that, despite a liability as high as $2 trillion. Employers are allowed one important option that is denied to individuals: They may take tax deductions for funds set aside to self-insure employer-provided health insurance. The amount is limited, however, and employer self-insurance appears to be prohibited from prefunding health costs to be incurred in the distant future.[51]

Employer Funding Options

The status of other common methods used by employers to fully or partially prefund postretirement medical expenses for their

[50]Steven F. Venti and David A. Wise, "Have IRAs Increased U. S. Saving? Evidence from Consumer Expenditure Surveys," Working Paper no. 2217 (National Bureau of Economic Research, April 1987).

[51]For a description of employer self-insurance and the reasons for this phenomenon, see John C. Goodman and Gerald L. Musgrave, "The Changing Market for Health Insurance: Opting Out of the Cost-Plus System," NCPA Policy Report no. 118 (Dallas: National Center for Policy Analysis, September 1985).

employees is summarized below. It should be borne in mind, though, that Congress, in its desire to remove tax deductions and increase federal revenues, has closed off virtually every option available to prefund postretirement health care expenses. To make matters worse, the few opportunities that do remain are being met with increasing congressional hostility.

401(h) Trusts

Primarily designed for pension plans, these trusts have been restricted by Congress. Contributions for medical benefits cannot exceed 25 percent of total contributions to the plan.[52]

501(c)(9) Trusts

Prior to 1984, tax-qualified trusts known as voluntary employee beneficiary associations (VEBAs) were ideal vehicles for prefunding postretirement health care. Today, contributions cannot take into account future medical inflation or increases in the use of medical services. This restriction alone limits the ability to fund future liabilities by 50 to 70 percent.[53]

Overfunded Pension Plans

It is not clear to what extent companies can put excess funds into a pension plan with the intention of using the excess to pay retirees' medical benefits.[54] Although the Reagan administration proposed such an option, Congress has not yet agreed.[55]

Company-Owned Life Insurance

Under current law, the best way for employers to prefund postretirement health insurance is by purchasing life insurance policies on their employees. Companies are increasingly turning to this option.[56] Under this procedure, the employer pays the policy premium and is the beneficiary. If an employee dies, the employer

---

[52]For a summary of the restrictions on the use of 401(h) trusts to prefund postretirement health care benefits, see Chollet and Friedland, pp. 211–14.

[53]David L. Glueck, "Congress, Auditors Pinch Retiree Plans," *Business Insurance*, June 2, 1986. For a summary of the restrictions on the use of 501(c)(9) trusts to prefund postretirement health care benefits, see Chollet and Friedland, pp. 211–14.

[54]See Dopkeen, pp. 577–78

[55]See Eduardo V. Feito and Murray S. Akresh, "Retiree Medical Benefits: Understanding the Concerns," *Journal of Compensation and Benefits* (March/April 1988): 277.

[56]See *Institutional Investor*, May 1988, pp. 108–9.

receives the death benefit tax free. While the employee lives, the cash value in the policy continues to accumulate tax free. Under either contingency, the funds can be used to pay health care benefits for retirees. If corporate-owned life insurance is placed inside a VEBA trust, the insurance premiums are deductible. If it is not, the premiums are not deductible but the company may borrow against the cash value of the policy and deduct the loan interest. However, Congress already has restricted the ability of employers to borrow against the cash value of policies, and some members would like to impose further restrictions.[57]

Building a New Approach to Funding Health Care and Retirement Needs

There is no coherent federal policy that promotes current saving to meet future needs. The few provisions that do encourage retirement savings appear randomly throughout the tax code, are largely unrelated to one another, and are totally unrelated to any clear policy objective. Congress should at the least retain the few retirement savings incentives that now exist. Much more can be done, however. To avert the financial nightmare in America's future, Congress should adopt policies with the following goals.

Saving for Postretirement Health Care Costs through Medical IRAs

The concept of medical IRAs (MIRAs), first proposed by the National Center for Policy Analysis (NCPA) in January 1984,[58] is steadily gaining public support. The concept has been endorsed by the American Medical Association; the U.S. Chamber of Commerce; former secretary of the Department of Health and Human Services, Otis Brown; numerous public policy groups; and members of Congress whose views span the ideological spectrum—from the late Sen. Claude Pepper (D-FL) to Rep. Philip Crane (R-IL). In a recent survey of employee benefits officers of large corporations, the creation of MIRAs was the most popular of all current proposals dealing with unfunded postretirement health care benefits.[59]

[57]See *Institutional Investor*, May 1988, p. 113.

[58]Peter Ferrara, John C. Goodman, Gerald L. Musgrave, and Richard Rahn, "Solving the Problem of Medicare," NCPA Policy Report no. 109 (Dallas: National Center for Policy Analysis, January 1984).

[59]"Introduction and Survey Highlights of the EQUICOR Health Survey VI: Looking to the Future of Retiree Health Benefits," in Paul and Disney, p. 108.

Several MIRA proposals have been introduced in Congress and have enjoyed both conservative and liberal support. In some versions, as in the original NCPA proposal, MIRAs would be used to privatize Medicare. In others, MIRAs would pay for medical expenses not covered by Medicare. In all versions, MIRA legislation would establish an explicit federal policy encouraging individuals to save for future health care needs. (See chapter 16.)

Integrating Lifetime Choices through Medical Savings Accounts

MIRAs would be an enormous improvement over our pay-as-you-go Medicare program. However, most MIRA proposals share with Medicare a principal defect: They would create an artificial dividing line—the age of 65, for example—beyond which individuals would pass from one method of health care finance to another. Health status, though, is partly a result of an individual's lifetime decisions, and rational health care finance requires an integrated lifetime plan. For example, it would not seem desirable to allow individuals to become financially impoverished by health care costs incurred at age 60 while hundreds of thousands of dollars sit in their MIRA accounts, untouchable until they reach the age of 65. An age limitation on the use of MIRA funds also discriminates against blacks and other minorities who have below-average life expectancies.[60] For example, according to current life expectancy tables, 40.1 percent of black males will die before the age of 65.[61] Under many MIRA proposals, these individuals would not have access to their MIRA funds to pay medical bills arising near the time of their death.[62]

A better approach—and one advocated by the authors for many years— would be to create medical savings accounts that could be used over the course of a lifetime, not merely after retirement.

Integrating Personal Choices with Employee Benefits Plans

Under current tax law, employer-paid health insurance premiums and health care expenditures are not included in employees'

[60]See John C. Goodman and Peter Ferrara, "Social Security and Race," NCPA Policy Report no. 128 (Dallas: National Center for Policy Analysis, June 1987), pp. 3–4.

[61]U.S. Bureau of the Census, *Statistical Abstract of the United States, 1987* (Washington: U. S. Government Printing Office, 1986), Table 106 (p. 70).

[62]Their MIRA accounts would become part of their estates, however, and become the property of their families or heirs.

taxable incomes—and, therefore, are effectively deductible. This tax advantage is withheld from individuals who purchase health insurance or health care services on their own. Similarly, employers are allowed tax deductions for money set aside to pay future medical costs for their employees (for brief periods of time) if they are self-insured, but no similar provision allows individuals to self-insure.

Absent the tax law, the only reason for employers to provide health insurance rather than paying higher wages would be the economies of scale that might make employer-arranged group insurance the most cost-effective choice for some employees. If such economies exist, they should be uncovered through free-market competition rather than artificial tax incentives. Additionally, employees should be free to integrate personal savings, personal health insurance, and employment fringe benefits into rational, lifelong financial plans. To achieve these objectives, however, we must make major changes in the employee benefits policies of most companies—and in the tax law.

Dismantling the Corporate Welfare State

Economic theory teaches that the value of a worker to a firm is equal to the worker's contribution to production and sales. Other things being equal, employees will tend to receive salaries and fringe benefits equal to the value of what they produce. In many corporations, though, the value of fringe benefits is related only loosely—if at all—to the workers' productivity. Because employers cannot successfully compete in the marketplace unless their total labor costs are roughly equal to the value of their employees' collective output, considerable redistribution of income takes place within the modern corporation.

Take company pensions, for example. Under the defined-contribution plans common in the academic world, employer contributions are related to workers' salaries, and the combined employer-employee contribution becomes the private property of the employee. But the most common form of pension in the for-profit sector is the defined-benefit plan. Under this arrangement, pension benefit formulas are back-end-loaded, with full benefits being paid only if employees remain with the firm for the whole of their work life. Even fully vested employees lose thousands of dollars in pension benefits if they leave employment prior to retirement. Numerous studies have shown that defined-benefit pension plans lead to

417

considerable redistribution of income.[63] Funds are redistributed from those who leave the firm to those who stay, from younger to older workers, and from those with shorter life expectancies to those with longer ones.

Like the defined-benefit pensions, postretirement health care benefits are defined benefits. They involve even more redistribution of income among employees than typical pension plans. What follows is a brief description of some of their characteristics.

1. **Postretirement health care benefits are usually the same for all retirees, regardless of final salary.** As Table 13.10 shows, in a representative postretirement health care benefit plan, there is no relationship between the benefit offered and the employees' salaries and productivity. For example, for 55-year-old retirees, the benefit is equal to about 55 percent of salary for a $100,000-a-year worker and about 336 percent of salary for a $15,000-a-year worker.

2. **Unlike defined-benefit pensions, postretirement health care benefits are indexed.** Because the benefit is a service rather than a cash benefit, its cost rises with medical inflation and increased use of health care services. For that reason, postretirement health care benefits are usually more valuable than pension benefits for low-income employees. In a representative plan, for 55-year-old retirees earning $25,000 a year, postretirement medical benefits are almost twice as valuable as pension benefits. For $15,000-a-year employees, medical benefits are more than three and one-half times more valuable than pension benefits.

3. **The value of postretirement benefits is unrelated to years of service to the firm.** Unlike pension benefits, postretirement medical benefits are an all-or-nothing arrangement. Employees receive either the full benefit or nothing. Moreover, the benefit is usually totally unrelated to the worker's lifetime service to the firm. In one survey of 250 large companies, at

[63]See Dennis G. Logue, "Pension Plans at Risk: A Potential Hazard of Deficit Reduction and Tax Reform," NCPA Policy Report no. 119 (Dallas: National Center for Policy Analysis, October 1985), pp. 6–9; and Edward J. Harpham, "Private Pensions in Crisis: The Case for Radical Reform," NCPA Policy Report no. 115 (Dallas: National Center for Policy Analysis, January 1984).

Table 13.10

RELATIONSHIP BETWEEN FINAL SALARY AND PRESENT VALUE OF POSTRETIREMENT
HEALTH CARE BENEFITS

Annual Final Salary	Present Value of Health Care Benefits	Percent of Final Salary
Retirement at age 65		
$100,000	$32,000	32%
50,000	32,000	64
25,000	32,000	128
15,000	32,000	213
Retirement at age 55		
$100,000	$55,000	55%
50,000	55,000	110
25,000	55,000	220
15,000	55,000	336

SOURCE: Martin J. Zigler, *Postretirement Health Care Benefits* (Tillinghast, Nelson and Warren, Inc., 1985), p. 25 ff., cited in Dopkeen, Table 2 (p. 569).

the normal retirement age, 40 percent of the companies provide the benefit with no years-of-service requirement. An
additional 43 percent offer the benefit to employees who have
spent five years or less with the firm.[64]

4. **Retirees usually pay little or no premium for their health
insurance coverage.** The elderly who are covered by employer-
provided health insurance pay very little in premiums. For
example, of retirees with individual coverage, 55.8 percent
make no premium payment. Of retirees with coverage that
includes their spouses, 46.5 percent make no premium payment. Only 3.5 percent of all companies require their retirees
to pay the "full premium," and even in those cases, the "full
premium" is the average premium paid by all employees, not
the actuarially fair premium.[65]

Employer-provided health insurance benefits, as currently structured, are troublesome from the point of view of public policy.
Employees today cannot possibly know whether they will be covered by such insurance during their retirement, since there is no
guarantee they will be employed by any particular employer at or
near their retirement. As a result, they cannot integrate personal
financial planning for their retirement years with employer-provided benefits.

Creating Equity in the Tax Law

The tax law creates artificial distinctions between individuals who
receive fringe benefits from employers and those who purchase
identical benefits on their own. As a practical matter, the law discriminates against employees of small firms, the self-employed, and
the unemployed. And because of the structure of most employer-
provided health insurance, individual planning for medical
expenses during retirement is almost impossible.

A much more equitable method would be to permit all individuals—regardless of employment status—to retain a certain portion
of their earned income (say, 10 or 15 percent) tax-free, provided that
it is used for certain well-defined purposes. Under this proposal, the
cash value of every qualified fringe benefit would be attributed to

[64]Dopkeen, p. 560.
[65]Ibid., pp. 561–62.

420

a specific employee. The tax law would remain neutral, however, with respect to the manner in which such benefits were acquired. For example, some workers might wish to obtain low-premium catastrophic health insurance through their employer and place the premium savings in their own MIRA to self-insure for small medical bills. Others might prefer to have their employers maintain cash balances in individual medical accounts in addition to company-provided health insurance.

The important goal would be to maximize individual and company freedom of choice in planning for income security and health care needs. That would permit individual preferences and market forces, rather than tax law, to determine retirement choices.

Integrating Choices between Medical and Nonmedical Goods and Services

One way to achieve the complete privatization of Social Security, Medicare, and Survivors and Disability Insurance is through "Super IRAs."[66] This arrangement would be similar to the Chilean system, under which workers are given generous tax incentives to opt out of Chile's social insurance programs by investing in the Chilean equivalent of IRA accounts and by purchasing private health, disability, and life insurance.

Other countries have extended this concept further. Under Singapore's totally private system of forced savings and Britain's partially privatized social security system, individuals may use their IRA-type savings to purchase a house. Of all countries, Singapore has gone the furthest in giving individuals the freedom to allocate forced savings among three alternatives: (1) the purchase of a house, (2) income maintenance during retirement, and (3) medical expenses before and after retirement.[67]

---

[66]See Peter Ferrara, *Social Security: The Inherent Contradiction* (Washington: Cato Institute, 1980); Peter Ferrara, ed., *Social Security: Prospects for Real Reform* (Washington: Cato Institute, 1985); Peter Ferrara, "The Social Security System," in Stuart Butler, Michael Sanera, and W. Bruce Weinrod, eds., *Mandate for Leadership II: Continuing the Conservative Revolution* (Washington: Heritage Foundation, 1984); and Peter Ferrara, *Rebuilding Social Security, Part 2*, Heritage Foundation Backgrounder no. 346 (April 1984).

[67]For a description of the social security systems of Chile, Britain, and Singapore, see chapter 20.

Singapore's system implicitly recognizes the fact that individual preferences and circumstances differ. It also recognizes that health care is only one of many goods and services that people want, and it gives them considerable freedom to match their spending decisions to their own needs and preferences.

The Need for Change

The current pay-as-you-go system of providing for the income maintenance and health care needs of elderly retirees has all of the characteristics of an officially sanctioned chain letter. Those who have retired early under the system have done well. Elderly retirees receive Social Security retirement benefits four to six times greater and Medicare benefits ten to twelve times greater than the taxes they paid.

Today's young people are at great risk because of political promises that are being made with no realistic plan for fulfillment. Genuine security for future retirees can be achieved only by phasing out the system under which each generation hopes that the next generation will pay for its retirement needs. We must move as rapidly as possible to a new system under which each generation saves to pay its own way in retirement.

14. The Uneasy Case for Medicare

Because of record deficits, our federal budget is being scrutinized to determine which programs have merit and which do not. As one looks down the list of spending programs, it is clear that various programs exist to meet fairly well-defined objectives—for example, to help the needy, to help minority groups, to provide for the national defense, and to promote the general welfare. Even within the category of federal spending on health care, most programs exist to meet clearly defined social goals. Medicaid exists to provide health care for the poor. The Department of Veterans Affairs hospital system arguably is part of our national defense effort. Medical research arguably promotes the general welfare. Medicare, however, does not fall into any such category. The more carefully one looks at Medicare, the more difficult it is to understand its rationale.

Medicare Beneficiaries Did Not Pay for the Benefits They Receive

Medicare is an insurance policy that pays the health care bills of those who qualify as beneficiaries. In any given year, only a small percentage of beneficiaries will have substantial bills paid by Medicare. On the average, about 78 percent of all Medicare spending pays for health care services used by only 11 percent of the program's beneficiaries. About 40 percent of all beneficiaries generate no Medicare payments.[1] However, even those who have no medical bills derive something of value from Medicare: protection of assets from unforeseen medical expenses and the sense of security that protection affords.

---

[1]Congressional Budget Office, *Changing the Structure of Medicare Benefits* (Washington, March 1983), p. 17. See also Karen Davis, "Medicare Reconsidered," prepared for the Duke University Medical Center 7th Private Sector Conference on the Financial Support of Health Care of the Elderly and the Indigent, Durham, N.C., March 14–16, 1982; cited in *New England Journal of Medicine* 306, no. 21 (May 27, 1982): 1310.

One way to evaluate Medicare is to ask what a beneficiary would pay for a similar insurance policy in the private marketplace. Ignoring administrative costs, private insurers would have to charge premiums roughly equal to the amount that Medicare spends per beneficiary per year. In 1989, that amount was about $2,970.[2] Thus the value of Medicare to retirees is about one-half of the value of the annual Social Security benefit of $6,802.[3]

A little known fact about Medicare is that its beneficiaries have paid into the program in taxes only a small fraction of the amount they are receiving and can expect to receive in benefits. For a retiree who earned the median wage, all Medicare tax payments can be expected to be recovered in one year and five months. Retirees who paid the maximum tax since the program began can expect to receive all of their Medicare tax payments back in four years and five months. Given that those who are now 65 can expect to live to 86, their expected benefits are going to be far in excess of their contributions.[4] For example, even without future increases in Medicare benefits, male beneficiaries who are now age 65 can expect to receive 17 times more in Medicare benefits than they paid in taxes, those who are 70 can expect 31 times more, those who are 75 can expect 63 times more, and those who are 80 can expect 137 times more. If these beneficiaries have dependent spouses who never worked and never paid Medicare payroll taxes, expected Medicare benefits will more than double.[5]

Medicare, then, is a program that takes billions of dollars from some Americans to pay the medical bills of others. For those on the receiving end, the program is a bonanza.

---

[2]Spending per beneficiary under Medicare Part A (hospital insurance) was approximately $1,787 and net spending under Medicare Part B (supplemental medical insurance) was $1,153. The difference between the sum of these two figures and $2,970 is attributable to the differences between calendar year data and fiscal year data.

[3]"National Health Expenditures," *Health Care Financing Review* (Winter 1990), Tables 7, 9 (pp. 10, 12).

[4]Ignores interest rate compounding.

[5]These estimates are based on life expectancy statistics available from the National Center for Health Statistics. They assume the worker earned the median wage each year since Medicare was enacted and that he retired at age 65. The calculations ignore the time value of money.

Medicare Beneficiaries Are Financially Better Off Than Medicare Taxpayers

When the Medicare program was enacted in 1965, it was part of the War on Poverty. Ever since, it has been viewed as a poverty program. Yet, Medicare does not take from the rich and give to the poor; if anything, it does the reverse. By virtually every estimate, the elderly as a group have more aftertax income and more wealth per capita than the nonelderly.

Since the early 1980s, for example, the Bureau of the Census has reported that the elderly have a higher per capita income than the nonelderly, both before and after paying taxes. According to former secretary of commerce Peter Peterson, Bureau of the Census statistics for 1984 showed that per capita cash income was $10,316 for the elderly, compared with $10,190 for those under the age of 65. Aftertax, the elderly had 13 percent more annual income, $8,886 compared with $7,876 for the nonelderly. If noncash medical benefits from public and private insurance are included, the elderly had 33 percent more annual income—$11,386 compared with $8,576 for the nonelderly.[6]

Tax returns filed with the Internal Revenue Service tell a similar story. In 1986, as Table 14.1 shows, elderly taxpayers had $31,865 in pretax income, compared with $26,199 for the nonelderly. Since these returns typically reflect household income, the discrepancy would be even greater if calculated on a per capita basis. Since the average adjustment to gross income is $8,425 for elderly taxpayers, compared with $2,024 for nonelderly taxpayers, the elderly pay less tax on more income.

Every method of estimating income has problems. For example, the Bureau of the Census typically underestimates income, intentionally excluding the value of employee fringe benefits and capital gains income.[7] Tax returns exclude those people who do not file (about 38 percent of the elderly and 5 percent of the nonelderly), and

---

[6]Peter Peterson and Neil Howe, *On Borrowed Time* (San Francisco: Institute for Contemporary Studies, 1988), p. 94.

[7]Including these items would support our general conclusion. For example, the value of Medicare insurance for an elderly individual is much greater than the value of employer-provided, private insurance for a nonelderly individual. In addition, elderly taxpayers have almost three times as much capital gains income as nonelderly taxpayers.

Table 14.1
AVERAGE INCOME OF TAXPAYERS[1]

Source of Income	Elderly[2]	Nonelderly
Wages and salaries	$ 4,727	$21,864
Social Security benefits[3]	4,622	122[4]
Pensions	4,694	521
Interest	6,952	861
Dividends	2,317	351
Capital gains[5]	7,266	2,459
Other capital income	1,287	21
Total[6]	$31,865	$26,199

SOURCE: Estimates based on tax return data. See Internal Revenue Service, *Statistics of Income—1986, Individual Income Tax Returns* (Washington: U.S. Government Printing Office, 1988), Table 2.5. Reprinted from John C. Goodman, Aldona Robbins, and Gary Robbins, *Elderly Taxpayers and the Capital Gains Debate*, NCPA Policy Report no. 153 (Dallas: National Center for Policy Analysis, July 1990), Table II (p. 3).

[1]Refers only to people who filed tax returns for 1986, the latest year for which statistics at this level of detail are available. Note that about 38 percent of elderly families and 5 percent of nonelderly families do not file tax returns. See U.S. Department of the Treasury, *Financing Health and Long-Term Care: Report to the President and Congress* (Washington: March 1990), Table 4.1.

[2]At least one person on the tax return is age 65 or older.

[3]All Social Security benefits reported, including untaxed benefits. The reported figure is below the actual number because most low-income taxpayers do not report this item.

[4]Includes early retirees, ages 62 to 64.

[5]Includes the portion of capital gains income excluded on 1986 tax returns.

[6]Totals show gross income prior to adjustments. The average adjustment is −$8,425 on elderly income tax returns and −$2,024 on nonelderly returns.

low-income taxpayers typically do not report their Social Security income. Nonetheless, evidence from a variety of sources points to the conclusion that, on the average, the elderly have more income than the nonelderly.

The elderly also have more assets. Using three different data sets to estimate the distribution of assets by age, economists Aldona Robbins and Gary Robbins have concluded that although the elderly constitute only 12 percent of the population, they hold about

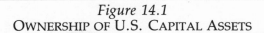

Figure 14.1
OWNERSHIP OF U.S. CAPITAL ASSETS

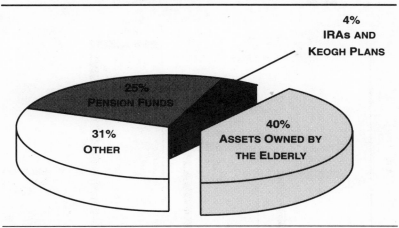

SOURCE: John C. Goodman, Aldona Robbins, and Gary Robbins, *Elderly Taxpayers and the Capital Gains Tax Debate*, NCPA Policy Report no. 153 (Dallas: National Center for Policy Analysis, July 1990).

40 percent of all the capital assets in the United States.[8] (See Figure 14.1.) On the whole, the elderly receive about 53 percent of all interest income, 52 percent of all dividend income, 30 percent of all capital gains income, and 32 percent of the income from all other sales of assets.[9]

Far from being a poverty program, Medicare takes taxes from the working poor and pays the medical bills of retired millionaires. It certainly cannot be justified on the grounds that it promotes greater equality of income and wealth.

Medicare Is Unfair to Minorities

Both Medicare and Social Security discriminate against minorities.[10] That is because black and Hispanic Americans have lower life expectancies than white Americans, and both programs pay

[8]See Aldona Robbins and Gary Robbins, *Taxing the Savings of Elderly Americans*, NCPA Policy Report no. 141 (Dallas: National Center for Policy Analysis, September 1989), appendix B.

[9]Refers to the sale of assets held for less than one year.

[10]John C. Goodman, *The Effect of the Social Security Reforms on Black Americans*,

427

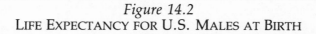

Figure 14.2
LIFE EXPECTANCY FOR U.S. MALES AT BIRTH

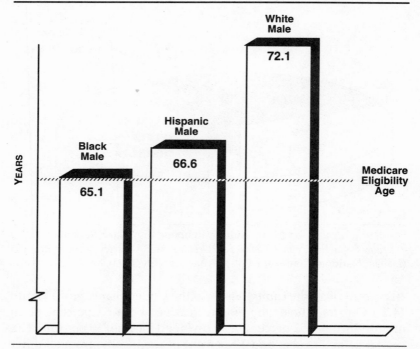

SOURCE: U.S. Bureau of the Census, *Statistical Abstract of the United States, 1990* (Washington: U.S. Government Printing Office, 1990), p. 72; and the National Center for Policy Analysis.

benefits based on age. For example, the life expectancy of a black male at birth is seven years shorter than that of a white male, and the life expectancy of a black female is about five years shorter than that of a white female. Because the eligibility age for Medicare is the same for both races, whites get much the better deal from the program.

As Figure 14.2 shows, a black male at birth has a life expectancy of 65.1 years, a Hispanic male 66.6 years, and a white male 72.1

NCPA Policy Report no. 104 (Dallas: National Center for Policy Analysis, July 1983); and John C. Goodman and Peter Ferrara, *Social Security and Race*, NCPA Policy Report no. 128 (Dallas: National Center for Policy Analysis, June 1987).

years. All three pay the same payroll tax rates. But the white male can expect to receive Medicare benefits five times greater than those received by his Hispanic counterpart, and the black male can expect to die about one month after he becomes eligible for benefits. Even at age 20, the differences between blacks and whites is striking. A 20-year-old white male can expect to receive 47 percent more in Medicare benefits than his black male counterpart. A 20-year-old white couple can expect to receive 35 percent more in Medicare benefits than a 20-year-old black couple.[11]

Black and Hispanic Americans, therefore, tend to be overrepresented among Medicare taxpayers and underrepresented among Medicare beneficiaries. More than 17.7 percent of the population of tax-paying age is nonwhite.[12] Only 13.6 percent of all Medicare beneficiaries are nonwhite.[13]

It is also instructive to look at the representation of minorities in Medicare, in which eligibility is based on age, versus their representation in Medicaid, in which eligibility is based on income. Nonwhites constitute only 13.6 percent of all Medicare beneficiaries, but about 46.8 percent of all Medicaid beneficiaries.[14] Moreover, when the federal government has felt the necessity of slowing the growth of federal spending, it has trimmed Medicaid—not Medicare—more often.

Under the Reagan administration, the Social Security Advisory Council proposed that the eligibility age for Medicare be raised from 65 to 67. If this proposal were adopted, a black male age 20 would lose 100 percent of his expected benefits under Medicare, whereas his white counterpart would lose only 25 percent. A black female age 20 would lose 19 percent of her expected benefits, whereas a white female would lose only 14 percent. Moreover, unlike the recent reforms in the Social Security retirement age, the advisory council's proposal would index the eligibility age for Medicare to gains in life expectancy. The probable effect of this change (which

---

[11]Goodman and Ferrara, *Social Security and Race*, Table VI (p. 16).

[12]U.S. Bureau of the Census, *Statistical Abstract of the United States: 1987* (Washington: 1986), p. 17.

[13]U.S. Department of Health and Human Services, *1989 HCFA Statistics* (Baltimore: 1989), p. 7.

[14]Ibid., p. 12.

was not adopted) would be that blacks, especially black males, could always expect to receive virtually nothing from Medicare.

Medicare Is Unfair to the Young

As in the case of a chain letter, those who cash in early benefit disproportionately. The latecomers pay in far more than they can expect to receive. Consider those workers who earned the median wage and retired in 1989. In just two years, they can expect to receive more in Medicare benefits than they paid throughout their working lives in Medicare taxes, and over the remainder of their lives they can expect to receive about $58,000 more than they paid. If a retiree has a dependent spouse, together they can expect to receive more than $100,000 more in benefits than they paid in taxes.[15]

A far different scenario confronts today's young workers. As Table 14.2 shows, a 20-year-old male can expect to pay considerably more in Medicare taxes than he will receive in Medicare benefits. If he is a high-income worker, he can expect to pay from four to eight times more; if he is a median-income worker, he'll pay from three to five times more. If the worker earns only 50 percent more than the minimum wage, he can expect a loss equal to as much as one-third of his current annual income. Table 14.3 shows that a 20-year-old female worker faces similarly dismal prospects under Medicare. Table 14.4 shows that virtually all workers under the age of 50 can expect substantial losses as a result of forced participation in the system.[16] (See Figure 14.3.)

Medicare, then, redistributes a vast amount of wealth from the working population to today's elderly. For current beneficiaries, it is a windfall. For current taxpayers, it is a losing proposition, even if they can convince future taxpayers to shoulder the enormous burden of their benefits.

The Criteria for Medicare Eligibility Are Arbitrary

All an individual has to do to be eligible for Medicare benefits is to reach the age of 65. For a person at 64 years and 11 months old,

[15]Based on estimates made by the U. S. Department of Health and Human Services.

[16]Note that in all these calculations the expected benefits probably are overstated. That is because, unlike Social Security retirement pensions, Medicare benefits are not paid in cash. They are benefits in kind. In many cases, the value that people place on the benefit is much less than the cost to the government of providing it.

Table 14.2
VALUE OF PARTICIPATION IN MEDICARE FOR SINGLE MALES
AGE 20 IN 1986 AT REAL RATES OF INTEREST OF 4 PERCENT
AND 6 PERCENT*

Category	At 4 Percent	At 6 Percent
Low-income workers		
Expected benefits	+$8,863	+$3,732
Expected taxes	−9,984	−6,784
Past taxes	−598	−616
Net present value	−$1,719	−$3,668
Median-income workers		
Expected benefits	+$8,342	+$3,339
Expected taxes	−24,945	−16,561
Past taxes	0	0
Net present value	−$16,603	−$13,222
High-income workers		
Expected benefits	+$8,068	+$3,134
Expected taxes	−37,003	−24,004
Past taxes	0	0
Net present value	−$28,935	−$20,870

SOURCE: Calculations made by William T. Rule III of Peat, Marwick, Main & Co. Reprinted from John C. Goodman and Peter Ferrara, *Social Security: Who Gains? Who Loses?* NCPA Policy Report no. 153 (Dallas: National Center for Policy Analysis, July 1990), Table II, p. 3.
*Assumptions: (1) Workers' lifetime average annual earnings are equal to 150 percent of the minimum wages ($10,050 per year in 1986) in the case of low-income workers, to the median income earned by adult male workers ($26,605 in 1986) in the case of median-income workers, and to the maximum taxable Social Security wage ($42,000 in 1986) for high-income workers; (2) workers enter the labor market at age 18 for low-income workers, age 22 for median-income workers, and age 24 for high-income workers; and (3) at every age, workers are assumed to have worked continuously since entering the labor market.

Medicare pays nothing. One month later, Medicare pays lavishly. Aside from age, little else matters. The following is a brief discussion of some other Medicare eligibility characteristics.

You don't have to be poor to be covered by Medicare. Medicare is not a poverty program. Several hundred thousand millionaires are either covered or can be if they so choose.

431

Table 14.3
VALUE OF PARTICIPATION IN MEDICARE FOR SINGLE FEMALES
AGE 20 IN 1986 AT REAL RATES OF INTEREST OF 4 PERCENT
AND 6 PERCENT*

Category	At 4 Percent	At 6 Percent
Low-income workers		
Expected benefits	$11,495	$4,534
Expected taxes	− 10,272	− 6,943
Past taxes	− 598	− 616
Net present value	$625	− $3,025
Median-income workers		
Expected benefits	$10,993	$4,143
Expected taxes	− 16,533	− 10,921
Past taxes	0	0
Net present value	− $5,540	− $6,778
High-income workers		
Expected benefits	$10,734	$3,941
Expected taxes	− 34,180	− 24,648
Past taxes	0	0
Net present value	− $23,446	− $20,707

SOURCE: Calculations made by William T. Rule III of Peat, Marwick, Main & Co. Reprinted from John C. Goodman and Peter Ferrara, *Social Security: Who Gains? Who Loses?* NCPA Policy Report no. 153 (Dallas: National Center for Policy Analysis, July 1990), Table II, p. 3.
NOTE: Columns may not add due to rounding.
*Assumptions same as for Table 14.2 except that median-income workers are assumed to earn the median wage paid to adult female workers ($16,472 in 1986).

You don't have to be retired to be covered by Medicare. Unlike Social Security, you do not have to quit work to receive benefits. In principle, the president of a multinational corporation can receive Medicare benefits, courtesy of the taxes paid by other employees. The corporation's private insurance plan would be the payer of first resort, however.

You don't have to pay Medicare taxes to be covered by Medicare. People who are over 89 years of age and are drawing Social Security benefits never paid a dime into Medicare. But they have received tens of thousands of dollars of benefits. Individuals reaching 65

Table 14.4
Value of Participation in Medicare for Single Workers at Different Ages in 1986 at Real Rates of Interest of 4 Percent and 6 Percent

Worker's Age	Single Male		Single Female	
	At 4 Percent	At 6 Percent	At 4 Percent	At 6 Percent
Low-income workers				
20	−$1,720	−$3,668	+$624	−$3,025
25	−2,192	−5,021	+416	−4,217
30	−2,577	−6,433	+407	−5,400
35	−2,592	−7,553	+787	−6,250
40	−1,575	−7,400	+2,244	−5,764
45	+672	−5,555	+5,003	−3,495
50	+3,251	−3,245	+8,202	−633
Median-income workers				
20	−16,603	−13,222	−5,540	−6,778
25	−16,201	−14,602	−4,614	−7,206
30	−17,034	−27,316	−4,524	−8,529
35	−17,802	−20,325	−4,348	−9,957
40	−17,337	−22,118	−3,273	−10,468
45	−14,341	−20,551	−399	−8,618
50	−10,012	−17,022	+3,551	−5,237

(Continued on next page)

Table 14.4—Continued
Value of Participation in Medicare for Single Workers at Different Ages in 1986 at Real Rates of Interest of 4 Percent and 6 Percent

Worker's Age	Single Male		Single Female	
	At 4 Percent	At 6 Percent	At 4 Percent	At 6 Percent
High-income workers				
20	−28,935	−20,870	−27,446	−20,708
25	−28,282	−22,756	−26,455	−22,407
30	−29,584	−26,633	−27,271	−26,012
35	−29,327	−29,147	−26,537	−28,228
40	−27,694	−30,280	−24,413	−29,019
45	−24,263	−29,250	−20,427	−27,560
50	−18,361	−24,624	−13,835	−22,352

SOURCE: Calculations made by William T. Rule III of Peat, Marwick, Main & Co. Reprinted from John C. Goodman and Peter Ferrara, *Social Security: Who Gains? Who Loses?* NCPA Policy Report no. 153 (Dallas: National Center for Policy Analysis, July 1990), Table II (p. 3).

NOTE: Assumptions same as for Table 14.2.

Figure 14.3
EXPECTED LOSS FROM PARTICIPATING IN
MEDICARE FOR WORKERS AT DIFFERENT AGES*
(Male Workers Earning the Median Wage)

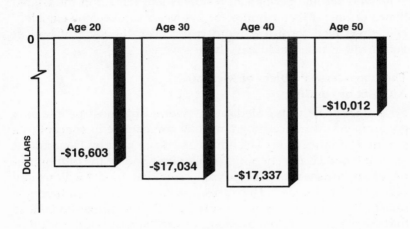

SOURCE: Table 14.3.

*Present value of Medicare benefits minus Medicare taxes. Calculations assume a 4 percent real rate of interest, and the numbers are expressed in 1986 prices. Assumptions behind the calculations are discussed in the appendix to this chapter.

today can also become eligible for benefits, even if they never paid taxes into the program. (They include employees of the federal, state, and local governments, and nonprofit institutions that have elected to get out of Social Security.) They can receive Medicare Part A (hospital insurance) by paying a monthly premium of $177 and Medicare Part B (supplemental medical insurance) benefits by paying a monthly premium of $29.90.[17] These premiums are an exceptionally good deal for elderly individuals with known illnesses who face very expensive medical procedures.

You don't have to be a good citizen to be covered by Medicare. You can break any number of laws and still be covered. According

[17]Source: U.S. Department of Health and Human Services, Health Care Financing Administration.

to federal regulations, the only crime for which an individual is tossed out is plotting an overthrow of the federal government—that is, of the people who give us Medicare.[18]

You don't have to be a citizen to be covered by Medicare. Noncitizens who become permanent residents and remain in the United States or one of its territories for five years can become eligible.[19] Had they lived for a few more years, even the shah of Iran or Ferdinand Marcos could have been covered.

The Long-Term Problem of Medicare: A Crisis in Funding

Like Social Security, Medicare is viewed by most people as a government insurance program, fully comparable in concept to a private insurance plan. This image is encouraged by Department of Health and Human Services publications and by the pronouncements of bureaucrats. The payroll taxes that fund Medicare are called "contributions." The surplus of taxes over expenditures is said to "accumulate" in a "trust fund." People are led to believe that the benefits paid out by Medicare are "in return for" contributions made during their working years. If officials of a private health insurance company made comparable claims, they would be risking imprisonment.

The Medicare "trust fund" is largely a myth. No money is being stored away for later use. Every dollar paid into Medicare is spent by the federal government the moment it arrives. Medicare, like Social Security, is strictly "pay-as-you-go."[20] And no one knows whether the next generation will support a system to which it never consented and from which it can never gain.[21]

---

[18]Treason is the only crime that disqualifies a person from Medicare coverage. However, Medicare benefits are suspended during any term of imprisonment because penal institutions are obligated to provide medical services for their inmates.

[19]Commerce Clearinghouse, Inc., *Medicare and Medicaid Guide* (Chicago: CCI, 1983), p. 1405.

[20]For a nontechnical discussion of the pay-as-you-go nature of our Social Security system, see John C. Goodman and Edwin Dolan, *Economics of Public Policy*, 2d ed. (St. Paul: West Publishing Co., 1982), ch. 7.

[21]For a more complete discussion of the nature of the Social Security crisis, see Peter Ferrara, *Social Security: The Inherent Contradiction* (Washington: Cato Institute, 1980); and A. Haeworth Robertson, *The Coming Revolution in Social Security* (McLean, Va.: Security Press, 1981).

The real long-term funding problem of Medicare is that it is putting today's children at risk. Prudence demands that we act now to relieve this risk. Chapter 15 looks at a specific way to do so.

Appendix: Assumptions behind the Calculations of the Present Value of Medicare

The statistics on the present value of Medicare benefits used in this chapter were calculated by William T. Rule III of Peat, Marwick, Main & Co. What follows is a discussion of the assumptions behind the calculations.

Labor Market Participation

Workers are assumed to enter the labor market at age 18 (low-income workers), age 22 (median-income workers), and age 24 (high-income workers). They are assumed to work continuously until they reach the age of 65, unless disabled. A computer program calculates the probability that a worker will become disabled sometime in the future, and that a worker, once disabled, will later reenter the labor market.

Expected future taxes and benefits are calculated for workers at different ages. In each calculation, it is assumed that the worker has worked continuously from the time of entry into the labor market until the time the calculation is made. However, the calculation includes the probability of future disability.

Future Wages

Workers enter the labor market at a certain wage. From that point forward, the worker's real income is expected to grow at the same rate as the rate of growth of real wages in the economy as a whole. This rate is 1.5 percent per year, according to the Social Security Administration's intermediate assumptions.

Future Benefits

Only Part A Medicare benefits are included. It is assumed that the benefit formulas currently written into law will remain in effect indefinitely. It is further assumed that the future amount spent per beneficiary will grow according to the intermediate assumptions. Note that individuals under the age of 65 may receive Medicare benefits as a result of disability, in addition to qualifying for normal coverage at the age of 65.

437

Future Taxes

All calculations are based on the assumption that promises made under Medicare will be kept and will be financed by increases in the payroll tax, whenever necessary, to pay promised benefits. For the purposes of these calculations, the portion of the total payroll tax counted as Medicare taxes is equal to the proportion of all spending from the trust funds allocated to Medicare benefits in any given year.

Expected Values

The computer program calculates the probability that an individual will live to all possible ages up to 105. For each possible lifespan, it calculates the associated costs and benefits. Expected value is the sum of all possible outcomes, each weighted by its probability of occurring. These calculations include the probability of disability and of death at each age. The expected value of participation in Medicare is included in Tables 14.2, 14.3, and 14.4.

15. Privatizing Medicare with Medical IRAs

A major difference between Medicare and Social Security is that under Social Security money is given directly to beneficiaries. As a result, when the beneficiaries spend Social Security dollars on goods and services, they treat the money as their own. By contrast, money spent under Medicare goes to entities other than the beneficiaries—doctors, hospitals, and other health care providers. Thus, when Medicare beneficiaries "spend" a dollar on medical care, it is not a dollar they could have spent on other goods and services. When they make purchases in the health care marketplace, they are spending someone else's money. Small wonder, then, that one hears little about wasteful spending of Social Security benefits but a great deal about wasteful spending of Medicare funds.

For example, an area of great potential waste is care given to patients who are near death. A remarkable fact is that 28 percent of all Medicare spending is for the treatment of patients in the last year of their lives and 11 percent is for their final 40 days.[1] If Medicare patients were spending their own dollars, it is not at all clear that they would choose to deplete their estates to prolong their lives so marginally. On the other hand, there is no economic reason not to spend someone else's money to achieve marginal benefits. Moreover, the providers of medical services often find it in their economic self-interest to increase spending under the program.

At the same time, important decisions about the elderly's access to health care are being made by the Medicare bureaucracy. They include apparently arbitrary decisions to underpay rural hospitals, to fail to cover important technological innovations, and to fail to compensate hospitals for the care of expensive-to-treat patients. The right to decide such issues should be transferred from the bureaucrats to the patients themselves.

[1]Data obtained from the U.S. Department of Health and Human Services.

Medical IRAs

The long-term problems of funding and inefficiency in Medicare and the threat of rationing caused by Medicare's reimbursement formulas necessitate radical reform. In designing a plan for such reform, we are guided by two principles. First, given appropriate government policies, most individuals can and should be responsible for paying for their own medical care (either directly or through private insurance) during their retirement years. Second, to most efficiently allocate resources and ensure freedom of choice in the medical marketplace, individuals should bear the costs and reap the benefits of their own decisions whenever possible.

One way to satisfy both principles is by creating a system under which individuals make annual contributions to qualified individual retirement accounts called Medical IRAs (MIRAs).[2] Sufficient funds would accumulate in these accounts to enable individuals to pay for their own medical expenses and/or to purchase private health insurance for their retirement years. These individuals would have partially or completely opted out of Medicare. The choice to opt out of Medicare would be voluntary. However, those doing so would be given tax credits for their MIRA contributions, and the tax credits would be structured so that individuals would find it in their financial self-interest to make MIRA contributions.

The concept behind the Medical IRA proposal is to allow workers to withdraw an amount equal to all, or almost all, of the payroll taxes they now pay into Medicare and to place those funds in a private savings account. The funds would be used to pay for medical expenses and private health insurance in retirement, in lieu

[2]Variously called medical IRAs, health care savings accounts (HCSAs), health bank IRAs, and individual medical accounts (IMAs), savings for postretirement medical care have been included in proposals to supplement, privatize, or replace Medicare. The original proposal to create such accounts was made in John C. Goodman, Peter A. Ferrara, Gerald L. Musgrave, and Richard Rahn, *Solving the Problem of Medicare*, NCPA Policy Report no. 109 (Dallas: National Center for Policy Analysis, January 1984). The proposal received considerable visibility based on the summary that appeared in John C. Goodman and Richard Rahn, "Salvaging Medicare with an IRA," *Wall Street Journal*, March 20, 1984. That same year, Singapore initiated the Medisave account. Another version of the idea was developed in Peter J. Ferrara, *Averting the Medicare Crisis: Health IRAs*, Cato Institute Policy Analysis no. 62 (Washington: Cato Institute, October 31, 1985). Ferrara's version of the proposal became the basis for a bill that has subsequently been introduced in several sessions of Congress.

440

Table 15.1
SOURCES OF FUNDS FOR POSTRETIREMENT HEALTH CARE*

MIRA Contributions	Value of Medicare Coverage	Total Resources
0	$30,000	$30,000
$10,000	25,000	35,000
20,000	20,000	40,000
30,000	15,000	45,000
40,000	10,000	50,000
50,000	5,000	55,000
60,000	0	60,000

*In 1990 dollars.

of Medicare. The federal government's role would be limited to administering a diminishing Medicare program and providing means-tested benefits through Medicaid. In what follows, we discuss two ways of designing a system that would achieve these objectives.

The National Center for Policy Analysis Proposal

In 1984, a MIRA proposal was developed for the National Center for Policy Analysis by John Goodman, Peter Ferrara, Gerald Musgrave, and Richard Rahn.[3] Under the proposal, people would receive a $1 tax credit for each $2 contributed to a medical IRA. Effectively, for each $2 of personal funds contributed to a MIRA, the federal government would contribute another $1 in the form of reduced income taxes.

Individuals would be able to trade private savings in MIRA accounts for government promises under Medicare in the following way. For each $1 contributed to a MIRA account, an individual would forgo a claim against Medicare of 50 cents. Thus, at the time of eligibility for Medicare, for each $1 in Medicare benefits that individuals do not receive, they would have $2 of private savings in their MIRA accounts or the insurance equivalent of that amount.

Table 15.1 shows how MIRAs would combine with Medicare to provide total funding for postretirement health care needs. As of 1990, lifetime coverage under Medicare is worth approximately

[3]Goodman et al., *Solving the Problem of Medicare.*

$30,000 to an individual at age 65. Medicare, moreover, can be expected to pay about half of a retiree's medical expenses. As Table 15.1 shows, people who choose the MIRA option would have enough to cover their entire expected medical expenses during retirement—about $60,000 (in 1990 dollars). The $30,000 of private savings replacing Medicare coverage would be made possible by federal dollars (income tax credits). Retirees would have the further advantage of an additional $30,000 that would accumulate with tax-free interest.

A person who reached the age of 65 with $60,000 reserved for postretirement medical expenses would have new options in the medical marketplace. For example, a small part of the money could be used to purchase catastrophic hospital insurance and a limited nursing home benefit. The remainder could be kept in the MIRA account, continuing its tax-free buildup, and used for medical expenses at the discretion of the retiree—without the hassles or encumbrances of Medicare.

Refundable Tax Credits

All people under the age of 65 would be allowed to make annual contributions to designated MIRAs and receive a 50 percent income tax credit for those contributions. The maximum annual contribution would be equal to the average Medicare (hospital insurance) payroll tax for all workers, which was $583 in 1989.[4] People could deposit more money in their MIRAs, but they would not receive a tax credit for the additional amounts. To encourage low-income individuals to exercise the MIRA option, tax credits would be refundable. A person with no taxable income would be able to make annual contributions to a MIRA, with 50 percent of the money being provided directly in the form of a tax refund granted by the federal government.

The Disposition and Tax Status of Medical IRA Funds

Because the MIRA is a private alternative to Medicare, funds deposited in this account could be used to purchase only (1) medical care for a worker who has declared retirement after age 59.5; (2) medical care for a person who has reached age 65, whether retired

[4]U.S. Department of Health and Human Services, *Social Security Bulletin Annual Statistical Supplement, 1990.*

or not; or (3) private health insurance to cover medical expenses in these two cases. MIRA funds could be used for these purposes without any tax penalty. Under certain exceptions (for example, the purchase of lifesaving medical technology not normally covered by private insurance), the funds could also be used to purchase medical services without tax penalty prior to retirement.

Until MIRA funds were used to purchase medical care or private health insurance, they would be invested, and the return on such investments would be tax-exempt in accordance with existing IRA rules. The MIRAs of individuals would be part of their estates, and funds remaining at their death would be passed on to their heirs.

The Quid pro Quo

In general, for each $1 contributed to a MIRA, an individual would forgo 50 cents of Medicare benefits, which would be reduced in the following way. At the time of eligibility for Medicare, an individual's contributions to a MIRA in different time periods would be converted to a present-value figure based on what those funds would have earned if invested in government securities. The expected value of Medicare benefits for people reaching retirement age that year would also be converted to a present-value number. An individual's claim against Medicare in the case of a Medicare-covered medical expense would be equal to the present value of MIRA contributions divided by the present value of Medicare benefits multiplied by the normal Medicare reimbursement for the medical expense.

Table 15.2 shows how these calculations would be made in 1990 dollars. As the table shows, individuals with $20,000 of MIRA contributions would have their expected Medicare benefits reduced from $30,000 of lifetime benefits to $20,000. In the case of a medical expense, they would be entitled to two-thirds of the normal Medicare reimbursement, and the retirees (or their private insurer) would be responsible for the remaining one-third. Similarly, individuals with $30,000 in a MIRA would have expected Medicare benefits reduced from $30,000 to $15,000. In the case of a medical expense, they would have a claim against Medicare equal to one-half of what Medicare ordinarily pays.

Incentives to Choose the MIRA Option

The purpose of the MIRA option is to encourage workers to save the money they will need to fund their own medical expenses

Table 15.2
CALCULATION OF A RETIREE'S CLAIM AGAINST MEDICARE FOR
MEDICAL EXPENSES*

MIRA Contributions	Value of Claim against Medicare	Claim against Medicare as a Fraction of Normal Medicare Benefits
0	$30,000	1
$10,000	25,000	5/6
20,000	20,000	2/3
30,000	15,000	1/2
40,000	10,000	1/3
50,000	5,000	1/6
60,000	0	0

*In 1990 dollars.

during retirement. Workers will be financially encouraged to exercise the MIRA option in three ways. First, of every $2 contributed to a MIRA account, $1 is contributed by the federal government in the form of a tax credit, and this $1 replaces a $1 claim against Medicare. This allows people to take $1 in cash from the government to replace a $1 promise. Second, for each $1 of personal money contributed to the MIRA account, individuals will realize a tax-free buildup of funds for postretirement medical expenses not covered by Medicare—expenses likely to be incurred if the individual reaches retirement age. Third, workers who have exercised the MIRA option at any time during their working years will have an opportunity to buy back into Medicare.

The Buy-Back Option

Every individual making contributions to a MIRA will have the opportunity to reenter Medicare at the age of 65 by making a lump sum payment to Medicare. The payment will be at least equal to the amount that the person's MIRA balance would have grown to (if invested in Treasury bonds) and perhaps will include a penalty as well.

Medicare Taxes

Because contributions to MIRAs earn income tax credits, the payroll tax (including that portion of the payroll tax designated for

Medicare) will be unaffected. That means that the payroll tax can continue to serve as the major (or even exclusive) source of funds for Medicare. As individuals exercise their MIRA options, however, the total amount of Medicare spending will gradually fall. Thus, in principle, the payroll tax can be progressively lowered through time.

The extension of tax credits for this purpose will cause the federal deficit to be larger than otherwise, unless other taxes are increased. However, studies show that about 80 percent of all deposits to IRA accounts represent new savings.[5] For every $1 of revenue lost by the government, an extra $1.60 will be added to the supply of loanable funds in the credit market through the use of MIRAs. As a consequence, the introduction of the MIRA program will not cause interest rates to rise or create additional inflationary pressures on the economy. To the contrary, it will add to the supply of credit available in private capital markets. Even if larger deficits resulted, funds would be available to finance them without crowding out private investment.

The Slaughter Proposal

Since the original NCPA proposal was made in 1984, a bill has been introduced in every session of Congress not only to privatize Medicare but also to provide for medical expenses not covered by Medicare—including long-term care. These bills have received support from both conservative and liberal members of Congress. Led by Rep. French Slaughter (R-VA), the bill was introduced in the 101st Congress as H.R. 1080.

Under the Slaughter proposal, workers and their employers would be able to make annual deposits to MIRAs up to the amount of their annual Medicare payroll tax (currently 2.9 percent of taxable income).[6] Workers would receive a tax credit equal to 60 percent of the amount contributed. At retirement, 60 percent of the funds in the account would replace Medicare coverage, and the remaining

[5]Steven F. Venti and David A. Wise, "The Determinants of IRA Contributions and the Effects of Limit Changes," in *Pensions and the U.S. Economy*, Zvi Bodie, John Shoven, and David Wise, eds. (Chicago: University of Chicago Press, 1988).

[6]These deposits are in addition to, not a replacement for, the Medicare Part A payroll tax. In the Slaughter bill, Medical IRAs are called health care savings accounts (HCSAs).

40 percent could be used for medical expenses not covered by Medicare.

One way to think of the Slaughter proposal is to see the government as paying people now to reduce their claims against it in the future. For each $1 contributed to a Medical IRA, the federal government would be providing 60 cents (through tax credits). At the time of retirement, the government would assume the contributions grew at the real rate of interest paid on long-term government securities (about 2 percent). The government would also calculate how much annual private health insurance coverage could be purchased with these funds for Medicare-covered expenses, assuming that 40 percent would be required for the administrative costs of the insurance. This annual insurance coverage would become an added deductible under Medicare. In this way, 60 cents of every $1 contributed to a MIRA would replace 60 cents of Medicare coverage.

For example, consider a middle-income couple where each spouse earns the average wage and makes the maximum contribution to a MIRA each year. As Table 15.3 shows, under the Slaughter bill, the couple would be able to make an annual private health insurance premium payment of $4,672 beginning at age 65. In today's market, such a premium would buy an elderly couple coverage equal to about $25,970 per year (assuming 40 percent of the premium were used for administrative costs). Thus, the couple would have an added Medicare deductible equal to $25,970.

Under the Slaughter bill, the government's method of calculation is very generous to individuals. The bill assumes that funds will grow at a 2 percent real rate of interest per year, whereas a conservative, diversified portfolio of stocks and bonds should be able to net 4 or 5 percent, possibly more.[7] The bill assumes that insurance administrative costs will be 40 percent of premiums, whereas most people will be able to obtain group coverage through an employer for administrative costs that are 10 percent or less. Thus, almost everyone who takes advantage of the MIRA option should be able to make a handsome profit on the part that relates to Medicare.

The rest of the Slaughter bill is even more attractive. The 40 percent of contributions designed to supplement Medicare coverage will also grow over time, tax free. Unlike the 60 percent paid

[7]See Peter A. Ferrara, *A Market for Medicare* (Washington: Cato Institute, forthcoming).

446

Table 15.3
THE SLAUGHTER PROPOSAL:
OPTIONS FOR COUPLES AT
AGE 65[1]

Category	Savings and Deductibles[2]	Net Gain[2]
Low-income couple		
Total funds in MIRA	$ 79,876	
Added annual Medicare deductible	12,924	
Hypothetical annuity that could be purchased with health care savings		$ 6,314
Annual private insurance premiums for the first $12,924 of Medicare-covered expenses		− 2,102
Annual private insurance premium for high-quality, long-term care		− 4,082
Remaining annual income		$ 130
Middle-income couple		
Total funds in MIRA	$177,504	
Added annual Medicare deductible	25,970	
Hypothetical annuity that could be purchased with health care savings		$14,030
Annual private insurance premiums for the first $25,970 of Medicare-covered expenses		− 4,672
Annual private insurance premium for high-quality long-term care		− 4,082
Remaining annual income		$ 5,276
Higher income couple		
Total funds in MIRA	$349,314	
Added annual Medicare deductible	59,800	

(Continued on next page)

447

Table 15.3—Continued
THE SLAUGHTER PROPOSAL:
• OPTIONS FOR COUPLES AT
AGE 65[1]

Category	Savings and Deductibles[2]	Net Gain[2]
Hypothetical annuity that could be purchased with health care savings		$27,608
Annual private insurance premiums for the first $59,800 of Medicare-covered expenses		−9,252
Annual private insurance premium for high-quality, long-term care		−4,082
Remaining annual income		$14,274

SOURCE: Peter Ferrara, *A Market for Medicare* (Washington: Cato Institute, forthcoming). Calculations were made by Lewin/ICF.

[1]Assumptions used in calculations: (1) workers enter the labor market at age 22; (2) low-income workers earn 45 percent of the average wage of workers covered by Social Security ($9,235 in 1989); (3) middle-income workers earn the average wage covered by Social Security ($20,522 in 1989); (4) higher income workers begin working at the average wage but then exceed the average wage by following an earnings profile over their work life; (5) couples are able to combine their health care savings, which are assumed to grow at a 4 percent real rate of interest; (6) each year, workers and their employers contribute an amount equal to the Medicare payroll tax, which grows from 2.9 percent in 1989 to 8.3 percent near the time of retirement.

[2]In 1989 dollars.

for by tax credits, the 40 percent can be withdrawn before age 65, provided that taxes and penalties are paid. After age 65, the 40 percent (plus any "profit" on the other 60 percent) could be spent on medical care without taxes or penalties. The funds also could be withdrawn and spent for other purposes, provided that ordinary income taxes were paid on the withdrawals.

Table 15.3 presents three examples of what we could expect to happen under the Slaughter proposal. In each case, people are assumed to enter the labor market at age 22 and make the maximum contribution to MIRAs throughout their working lives. In all three cases, Medicare would become a catastrophic policy only, covering expenses exceeding about $13,000 a year for a low-income couple and about $60,000 a year for a higher income couple. Moreover, in all three cases, people would be able to afford high-quality, long-term health insurance, paying up to $100 per day (in 1989 prices) of nursing home care up to four years after the first 90 days of coverage (provided under Medicare). The policy would also pay up to $50 per visit for home health care for up to two years. And both reimbursement amounts would increase by as much as 5 percent per year in future years.

After paying for these benefits (and taking into account the overly conservative assumption that 40 percent of private insurance would be needed for administrative costs), most people would still have considerable funds left over. Each year, after financing all of their own health care, a middle-income couple would have more than $5,000 to use in any way they wanted, and a higher income couple more than $14,000.

Benefits of the MIRA Proposals

The proposals discussed in this chapter eliminate for each new generation of workers the risk that succeeding generations will refuse to pay, or will underpay, for their postretirement medical care. By allowing all individuals to provide for their own retirement medical care, they would solve Medicare's long-term funding problem. Because these proposals also would lead to the phasing out of Medicare, they would reduce the size of government income transfers from the working population to the elderly. This development should do much to improve the self-esteem of seniors and to reduce the economic and political tensions between generations.

Under these proposals, individuals would be spending more of their own money for medical care to the extent that they selected high-deductible private health insurance during the years of retirement. This means that MIRA owners would have ideal incentives to weigh carefully the costs against the benefits of medical services and to avoid wasteful and inefficient spending. Moreover, when they entered the medical marketplace, elderly patients would be the principal buyers. As a result, the quality of care and the efficiency of its delivery should improve greatly.

Finally, these proposals would allow most elderly patients to escape Medicare's restrictions on access to new medical technology. With substantial private resources, the elderly would be able to avoid health care rationing imposed through the Medicare DRG (diagnosis-related group) system and other schemes. Decisions governing access to and use and continuation of lifesaving medical interventions would be made by the patients themselves.

Workers today pay an average of $583 per year into Medicare, and this money is spent on the medical care of others. There is no assurance that today's workers will have their medical expenses paid during their retirement years. Only if individuals can contribute an equivalent amount of money to their own private savings accounts can they be free from the uncertainty of doubtful promises by politicians.

Integrating Medical IRAs with Other Policy Proposals

In this book we have proposed a general program of Medical Savings Accounts to allow people to save for small medical bills. We also have proposed giving employees and employers tax incentives to save for postretirement medical expenses and allowing private insurers to repackage Medicare benefits. Now we will briefly consider how these proposals can be combined to form an integrated national approach to postretirement health care policy.

Medical IRAs and Medisave Accounts

The principal goal of Medical Savings Accounts is to enable individuals to purchase medical services with their own funds rather than through wasteful first-dollar health insurance. Over a person's work life, the amount that accumulates in a Medisave account could approach the amount that accumulates in a Medical IRA—thus effectively doubling the funds available for postretirement medical care. The strategy behind both concepts is to encourage lifetime planning for health care contingencies and to provide the resources for meeting those contingencies.

MIRA and Medisave funds could be combined, provided that the financial institution managing them kept an accounting distinction between the two balances. For the most part, MIRA funds could be used only for postretirement medical expenses. But there would be important exceptions. For example, MIRA funds might be available to pay for organ transplants or other expensive, lifesaving technology not normally covered by private insurance prior to the age of 65.

Medical IRAs and Postretirement Medical Liabilities of Employers

Just as individuals would be entitled to a $1 tax credit for each $2 contributed to a MIRA account, so employers would receive these tax credits for contributing to MIRAs on behalf of their employees. Employers exercising this option could manage MIRA and Medisave accounts and (acting as agents for the employees) purchase group health insurance for their employees' postretirement medical care. But the funds would belong to the individual employees.

Medical IRAs and Privately Repackaged Medicare Insurance Policies

The purpose of allowing private insurers to repackage Medicare benefits (discussed in chapter 3 and at greater length in the appendix to this chapter) is to extend the advantages of competition and private-sector efficiency to the Medicare program. A private market in Medicare insurance would arise with a diverse product line; each product would be tailored to the special needs of different groups of senior citizens. Medical IRAs represent a natural extension of this idea. Depending on the amount contributed to a MIRA, a retiree could purchase private insurance with the amount owed to the individual by Medicare and the amount accumulated in the individual's MIRA. Substantial private funds added to public funds would greatly expand the range of choices. Ultimately, almost all funds used to purchase postretirement health insurance would come from privately owned MIRAs.

Adopting a New Philosophy of Health Care Finance

National health insurance enjoys widespread popularity in other countries partly because it institutionalizes certain assumptions that are widely held by politicians, the medical community, and the general public. These assumptions also have heavily influenced public policy toward health care in this country. Yet each of them is false.

One false assumption is that ill health is a random event, unrelated to individual behavior. From this assumption, the conclusion is drawn that it is unfair to ask individuals to bear the cost of events over which they have no control. A second false assumption is that it is wrong to ask individuals to choose between health care and money. From this assumption, the conclusion is drawn that no one should be forced (or even be given the opportunity) to forgo health care services because of an unwillingness to pay. A third false assumption is that the profit motive is inappropriate, if not unethical, in the medical marketplace. From this assumption, the conclusion is drawn that we should forbid doctors, hospitals, and insurance companies to compete by offering services that differ in quality and price. To avert the painful choice of health care rationing caused by mounting health care costs, these false assumptions must be replaced by ones that are consistent with reality.

Mounting evidence suggests that ill health is not a random event, an "act of God," or a result of uncontrollable circumstances. Rather, individual health and life expectancy are heavily influenced by choices made over a lifetime. The central concept behind the idea of the MIRA account is that health status over an individual's lifetime is a consequence of that individual's choices. No one is in a better position than the individuals themselves to predict what choices they will make, to plan for probable adverse contingencies, and to gauge their ability to draw on personal savings and family help in case of illness. MIRAs are designed to give freedom of choice to those best suited to exercise that choice.

A free society is one in which individuals are allowed to make lifestyle, occupational, and other choices that involve varying degrees of risk. But a responsible society is one in which individuals bear the costs and reap the benefits of their choices. That means that individuals who take greater risks must be prepared to pay more—in terms of direct health care expenditures from personal savings and higher health insurance premiums.

Not only is it desirable to ask people to bear the full costs of their decisions, but failure to do so subsidizes and encourages risky behavior. When people are forced to assume the costs of their risks, they take fewer risks. Conversely, when they change their behavior and benefit from doing so, they are likely to make more behavioral changes. In both cases, health care costs are lowered.

Full freedom of choice means the freedom to choose whether or not to purchase health care services at all. That freedom is now greatly restricted. Imagine giving every candidate for surgery a choice: undergo the operation or forgo it and receive a sum equal to its cost. Such an option might reduce U.S. surgery rates by 25 or even 50 percent. Or imagine giving every Medicaid patient in a nursing home a choice: remain in the nursing home or leave with an annual income of $25,000 per year. The Medicaid population in nursing homes likely would be cut in half.[8]

The argument for freedom of choice is that health care is only one of many things that people value. We eliminate waste when we allow people to choose between health care and other goods and services. That ensures that the money spent gives people maximum satisfaction.

In only one area do we routinely offer a choice between money and health care—nursing home care for the nonpoor elderly. In principle, any elderly person may enter a nursing home and spend down his or her resources. Once the patient is impoverished, Medicaid picks up the tab. No one is denied care, but people are forced to choose between the value of government-provided care and other uses of their money. However, for every individual in a nursing home, there are two other, equally disabled individuals who are not in nursing homes (see chapter 13). Clearly, when people are asked to choose between health care services and other uses of their money, health care is not always the first choice.

By allowing individuals to build up private savings in Medical Savings Accounts and MIRAs, we enable them to make their own choices. Patients, rather than third-party institutions, become the principal buyers of medical care, and the suppliers of medical services become increasingly responsive to patients' wants and needs. The result will be not only a more economically efficient system but a more humane one as well.

Appendix: A Short-Term Privatization Solution

Using Medical IRAs to privatize Medicare is a long-term solution, one that would take years before noticeable and major changes would be observed. In the meantime, however, there are important structural problems in Medicare that could be addressed with a short-term privatization program.

Problem: Defects in Medicare Coverage

If insurance is to serve any useful social purpose, it should protect people against catastrophic losses. Most people can pay their own

---

[8]For example, four people could pool their resources and live quite well on an aftertax annual income of $100,000.

small medical bills. Even if they have difficulty making relatively small payments, purchasing insurance coverage for them is almost always uneconomical. Insurance should be reserved for very large medical bills that would deplete the insured's assets if they were paid out of pocket. As an insurance policy, however, Medicare has always been fundamentally flawed. From its inception, Medicare has always paid too many of the small bills and left elderly enrollees at risk for very large ones.[9] The following is a brief summary.

Medicare coverage for hospital expenses is bizarre. For patients who have hospital stays of only a few days, Medicare pays all expenses beyond a small deductible. For patients with lengthy stays, however, Medicare pays much less of the bill and patients pay much more. In other words, the sicker the patient, the longer the hospital stay, and the larger the health care expense—the greater the proportion of the bill the patient pays. Currently, Medicare patients are "insured" for hospital expenses in the following way:[10]

- Following an initial deductible of $628, a Medicare patient faces no additional costs for a hospital stay of up to 60 days.
- Beginning on the 61st day, the patient is charged $157 per day.
- After the 90th day, the patient's cost rises to $314 per day.
- After the 150th day, the patient is responsible for the full cost of each hospital day.

Medicare is designed so that those with the most severe health problems face the greatest financial burdens—just the opposite of private hospital insurance.

Coverage for physician expenses under Medicare also violates fundamental principles of sound insurance. After a deductible of $100, Medicare pays 80 percent of all remaining physician bills, no matter how small or large. That means that Medicare pays 80 cents of the 101st dollar spent on physician fees in any given year, an amount almost all elderly patients could easily pay out of pocket. Yet, if additional fees soar to $100,000, the patients are responsible

[9]For an analysis of the political pressures that led to this result, see John C. Goodman and Gerald L. Musgrave, *Health Care for the Elderly: The Nightmare in Our Future*, NCPA Report no. 130 (Dallas: National Center for Policy Analysis, October 1987), pp. 27–33.

[10]Health Care Financing Administration. Dollar amounts are for 1991.

454

for 20 percent, or $20,000—an amount many would have difficulty paying.

As in the case of hospital coverage, coverage for nursing home expenses is structured so that the patient's share of the bill rises as the stay becomes longer and the expense greater. A Medicare patient entering a skilled-nursing facility (following a hospital stay of at least 3 days) pays nothing for the first 20 days. On the 21st day, the patient begins paying $78.50 per day.[11] After the 100th day, the patient pays 100 percent of the cost.

In response to the gaps created under Medicare, a thriving market emerged for Medigap insurance—private insurance designed to pay for hospital and physician expenses not covered by Medicare. Yet the Baucus Amendments, passed by Congress in 1980, required Medigap policies to cover certain benefits. And the amendments directed Medigap policies, like Medicare itself, to cover a great many small medical bills while leaving the coverage of large bills discretionary. For example, a Medigap policy that meets the minimum standards of federal law must have the following features:[12]

- The policy pays the 20 percent of physician fees not covered by Medicare, subject to a $100 deductible.[13]
- The Medigap policy pays for hospital expenses not paid by Medicare up to the 150th day in the hospital.
- On the 151st day, however, the patient begins paying 10 percent of the cost of the hospital stay; after 516 days, the patient is responsible for the entire cost of hospitalization.

Genuine catastrophic health insurance is rather inexpensive to provide because very few patients stay in the hospital beyond 150

[11]A patient staying at a nursing facility that costs less than $78.50 per day pays the amount the facility charges, not $78.50.

[12]See U.S. Department of Health and Human Services, *Guide to Health Insurance for People with Medicare* (1990), pp. 10–21.

[13]Under the 1987 law, which was in effect at the time of the passage of the Medicare Catastrophic Coverage Act, insurance companies were required to cover only the first $25,000 of doctor bills. Currently, if the doctor charges more than the reimbursement allowed under Medicare, Medicare will pick up only 80 percent of the normal assessed value, with the remaining amount to be covered by the insurance company and the patient. Some insurance policies will cover the entire billing gap, but others cover only the 20 percent they normally would have covered, leaving the rest for the patient.

days, and a stay in excess of 516 days is extremely rare. However, by forcing private insurance companies to offer wasteful and inefficient first-dollar coverage, Congress caused Medigap insurance to be needlessly expensive and thereby discouraged genuine catastrophic coverage.

Failed Solution: The Medicare Catastrophic Coverage Act

In the summer of 1988, Congress passed the Medicare Catastrophic Coverage Act in order to address some of the problems described above. By the spring of 1989, however, elderly voters were looking at the fine print and protesting. To appreciate the strength of that protest consider that an April 1989 Senate amendment urging the Senate Finance Committee to hold hearings to reconsider the Medicare Catastrophic Coverage Act was passed by a vote of 97 to 2.[14] The same amendment passed by a vote of 408 to 0 in the House of Representatives. Before Congress adjourned in the fall of 1989—after a lengthy, agonizing, unsuccessful attempt to find a compromise proposal—the act was repealed.

What went wrong? The 1988 act was designed to create benefits for the elderly that were to be solely financed by the elderly. The sources of funds were higher Medicare premiums and a special Medicare surtax levied on elderly incomes. When they compared the costs with the benefits, the majority of elderly voters discovered that the program made them worse off, not better off. There were four major reasons why.

First, when economists Aldona and Gary Robbins compared the average expected benefits with the average expected costs for the first five years under the program, they discovered that the costs exceeded the benefits for elderly individuals with annual (non–Social Security) incomes in excess of $5,000 and couples in excess of $10,000.[15] One of the reasons the cost exceeded the benefits for so many people was that a large portion of revenues collected

---

[14]See Spencer Rich, "Bentsen Backs Health Care Premium Cut," *Washington Post*, April 21, 1989.

[15]Aldona Robbins and Gary Robbins, *The Insurance Value of Medicare's Catastrophic Benefits*, Economic Report no. 47 (Washington: Institute for Research on the Economics of Taxation, February 24, 1989).

from the elderly was destined to be spent on nonelderly disabled people, including AIDS patients.[16]

Second, the burden of paying for the new program was imposed in a highly regressive way. For example, the net cost (cost minus benefits) would have equaled 3 percent of the (non–Social Security) income of someone with an annual income of $30,000, but only 1.5 percent of a $60,000-a-year individual.

Third, the Medicare surtax was one of the worst possible ways of raising revenue to fund the program. Although the surtax would have raised only a small amount of money from the elderly, it was imposed in a way that had devastating effects on their marginal tax rates. The surtax would have increased the marginal income tax rate for the elderly by as much as 5.3 percentage points in the first year under the program and by 10.8 percentage points in the fifth year. According to one study, if the Medicare surtax were combined with other taxes, some elderly taxpayers would have faced marginal tax rates in excess of 100 percent.[17]

Fourth, although the program did limit hospital expenses and physician fees, it gave little help to elderly patients faced with a catastrophic nursing home expense. Since more than 80 percent of all out-of-pocket expenses in excess of $2,000 for the elderly are for long-term care, the Medicare Catastrophic Coverage Act focused on the least likely catastrophic expenses and ignored those that are most likely. Continuing Congress's predilection for creating small benefits for the many rather than real protection for the few who need it, the act created a mammography benefit but did nothing to help those who face the enormous expenses associated with Alzheimer's disease.

The Medicare Catastrophic Coverage Act was the first major piece of federal welfare legislation repealed in 100 years.[18] The repeal

---

[16]People who qualify as disabled under the Social Security program are also eligible for Medicare benefits.

[17]John C. Goodman and A. James Meigs, *The Elderly: People the Supply-Side Revolution Forgot*, NCPA Policy Report no. 139 (Dallas: National Center for Policy Analysis, February 1989). See also, Aldona Robbins and Gary Robbins, *Taxing the Savings of Elderly Americans*, NCPA Policy Report no. 141 (Dallas: National Center for Policy Analysis, September 1989).

[18]The previous case was the abolition of the Freedman's Bureau after the Civil War.

meant major embarrassment for the congressional leadership on both sides of the aisle. Given that almost everyone agrees that the Medicare insurance program is defective, that virtually all enrollees want catastrophic coverage, and that most are willing to pay for it, what was the problem? We believe it was another defect in Medicare—the fact that a one-size-fits-all program cannot meet the needs of a diverse elderly population. In a normal insurance market, one expects to find diverse products, tailored to the needs of different consumers. In Medicare, no such diversity is allowed. There is no way to change the structure of Medicare to meet the insurance needs of one group of elderly citizens without at the same time changing it for all others. This defect of Medicare needs to be addressed before a solution can be found to the problem of catastrophic coverage.

To see how their insurance needs differ, consider two groups of elderly families, an upper-middle-income group with substantial assets and a lower income group with few assets. Catastrophic coverage is most important for the first group's members, and most of them would gladly trade higher deductibles and copayments for routine medical expenses for catastrophic hospital and nursing home coverage. On the other hand, elderly families with low incomes and few or no assets do not need genuine insurance. If faced with a very large medical bill, they would quickly spend down their assets and be covered by Medicaid. For them, the effect of a medical bill of $20,000 and one of $100,000 would be much the same. Understandably, this second group is far more interested in payments for small medical bills than in catastrophic insurance designed to protect assets they do not have.

Extending an approach that is already being taken by some pilot projects, private insurers should be able to compete for Medicare enrollees by offering privatized Medicare insurance policies.[19] For each enrollee in a privatized insurance plan, the insurer would receive an amount of money from Medicare equal to about 95 percent of the actuarially fair value of Medicare coverage. Private insurers would be entitled to reimburse hospitals and physicians at the same rate that Medicare pays, although they could voluntarily pay higher rates to avoid health care rationing.

[19]We thank Dr. Phil Gausewitz for helping us develop this solution.

Competition would primarily take the form of creating different packages of benefits. The only requirement would be that the insurer provide catastrophic hospital coverage. Beyond that, insurers would have complete freedom to repackage existing Medicare benefits, and Medicare enrollees would be free to choose their packages. For example, a private insurer might offer a package with a $2,000 hospital deductible, a $2,000 physician deductible, and a combined deductible of $3,000. In return for these higher deductibles, the insurer might offer immediate nursing home coverage for certain illnesses, such as Alzheimer's disease.[20] The nursing home benefit might grow, depending on the number of years that a policyholder stayed with the policy.

Building on Current Innovations in Medicare

Medicare currently contracts with HMOs and competitive medical plans (CMPs) that serve Medicare patients who voluntarily join the plans.[21] The amount paid to the HMO or CMP is about 95 percent of the actuarial Medicare cost, based on the age, sex, and geographic location of the patient population. HMOs and CMPs are required to provide all services covered by the conventional Medicare fee-for-service program, but they can offer more services, such as no or low cost-sharing and no- or low-cost prescription drugs. HMOs attempt to control cost by managing care. Physicians and financial managers work together to provide adequate care using fewer resources. In effect, they are gatekeepers and often ration care at the point of delivery. Decisions are made by general physicians and specialists who attempt to care for and treat patients within the financial constraints of the HMO. If the HMO is to succeed, it must cut costs by reducing the volume of services. However, an HMO has an incentive not to reduce quality to a level that would cause patient dissatisfaction, although about one-third of new enrollees do opt out of the Medicare HMO within two

---

[20]To take full advantage of the strengths of private-sector competition, insurers would have to have the freedom to alter the package, depending on the age, health condition, and other attributes of the potential policyholders. That is, we could not require an insurer to provide immediate insurance coverage for Alzheimer's disease to someone who already had been diagnosed as having the disease.

[21]CMPs are capitated plans and, while not officially designated as HMOs, for all practical purpose they are HMOs.

years.[22] Another incentive to maintain quality is the threat of malpractice litigation.

If private contractors could repackage Medicare benefits, they would have incentives to reduce costs in innovative ways. Specifically, they could offer high-deductible plans under which the elderly would pay small-dollar medical expenses and get more insurance coverage for truly catastrophic expenses.

[22]"Disenrollment Experience in the Medicare Health Maintenance Organization and Competitive Medical Plan Risk Program," *Health Care Financing Review* (Winter 1990): 162.

PART V

NATIONAL HEALTH INSURANCE

16. Paying for National Health Insurance[1]

One reason why national health insurance is popular in other countries is that the taxes collected to pay for the program are often hidden or disguised. As a result, most people believe they are getting a benefit that is paid for by someone else.[2]

A similar phenomenon is occurring in the United States, where executives of some large companies have expressed interest in shifting the cost of employer-provided health insurance to "others" through government-provided health insurance. Advocates of national health insurance frequently overlook two facts. First, paying for national health insurance will require broad-based taxes, and industries with a highly paid workforce will pay proportionately more in taxes than other industries. Second, companies with generous health care plans are currently receiving large tax subsidies because of the deductibility of health insurance costs—subsidies that would vanish under a government-funded health care system.

Once they account for the loss of current tax subsidies and the probable effects of new taxes needed to pay for national health insurance, many U.S. employers and their employees will discover that national health insurance will cost them more than their current health care plans. For example, under almost any reasonable set of assumptions, the automobile industry would pay more than twice

---

[1]This chapter is based on a study by Aldona Robbins and Gary Robbins, "What a Canadian-Style Health Care System Would Cost U.S. Employers and Employees," NCPA Policy Report no. 145 (Dallas: National Center for Policy Analysis, February 1990).

[2]In Britain, for example, the national health insurance payroll tax covers only about 5 percent of the actual cost of operating the National Health Service. Polls show that a majority of Britons believe that this tax pays for the entire program. Thus, the British public underestimates what it pays for national health insurance by a factor of 20. See John C. Goodman, *National Health Care in Great Britain: Lessons for the USA* (Dallas: Fisher Institute, 1980), p. 203. See also discussion in chapter 19.

Table 16.1
ANNUAL COST OF NATIONAL HEALTH INSURANCE[1]
($ Billions)

Category	Cost
Employer health payments	$156.9
Out-of-pocket health payments plus other health insurance[2]	230.9
Total expenditures[3]	$387.8

[1]Refers to nonelderly, non-Medicaid population. Estimates are for 1989.
[2]Includes payments made under health insurance policies purchased by individuals, as well as unreimbursed care provided for the currently uninsured. About $58 billion of this amount represents cost of insuring the currently uninsured.
[3]Equal to about $3,300 per worker, including family coverage for married workers.

as much for national health insurance as it now pays for private health insurance.

The Cost of National Health Insurance

In a study undertaken for the National Center for Policy Analysis, Aldona Robbins and Gary Robbins calculated the cost of national health insurance for the nonelderly working population not on Medicaid, for the country as a whole, and for specific industries.[3] The assumptions they used were intentionally conservative, being those most favorable to the case for national health insurance. For example, they assumed that there would be no increase in health care costs under national health insurance, so that, on the average, the United States would continue to spend about $3,300 per worker per year (including current spending on deductibles and copayments and coverage for the worker's family).

Under these assumptions, the cost of national health insurance is equal to the total amount of health care costs currently incurred by employers plus all out-of-pocket costs currently incurred by individuals plus the cost of health insurance for the currently uninsured. As Table 16.1 shows, this cost would have been $387.8 billion in 1989.

[3]Robbins and Robbins.

Of the $387.8 billion, approximately $48.5 billion is assumed to be financed through an increase in income and FICA taxes, because money wages will increase to offset the abolition of a fringe benefit (employer-provided health insurance). Since private health insurance will no longer be necessary, it is reasonable to assume that employees will receive wage increases equal to the present cost of health insurance. Unlike private health insurance fringe benefits, however, money wages are subject to income and FICA taxes. If employers did not increase employee wages, but instead kept the savings to boost company profits, the government would collect more tax revenues in the form of additional corporate income tax payments.

Consider, for example, the case of General Motors. In 1989, General Motors paid about $4,100 per worker for health care under one of the most lavish health insurance plans found anywhere, and all of it was tax deductible. In the absence of any need for private health insurance, if GM increased employee wages by $4,100, the federal government would collect as much as $1,763 per worker in additional personal income and payroll taxes. If GM tried to keep the $4,100 per worker as profit, about $1,435 would go for additional corporate income taxes.

After adjusting for the increased revenues the government would receive through the abolition of private health insurance ($48.5 billion), an additional $339 billion would be needed to pay for national health insurance. This remaining $339 billion would have to be financed through new taxes.

Three General Tax Options:
Payroll, Income, or Value-Added Taxes

Because the cost of national health insurance would be so high, funding it would require a broad-based tax. Table 16.2 shows what tax rates would be necessary to fund the program under each of three possible taxes.[4]

[4]The calculations in this chapter assume that employees rather than employers will bear the full excess burden of national health insurance. Similar calculations— with similar results—were performed using the assumption that employers rather than employees would bear the full burden. Because, in the long run, employers will not continue to employ workers unless the total labor costs are equal to the value of what workers produce, the ultimate burden of national health insurance must fall on employees.

Table 16.2
ADDITIONAL TAXES NEEDED TO FINANCE NATIONAL HEALTH INSURANCE

Tax	Tax Rate Increase
Payroll tax	15.0%
Income tax	15.7
Consumption tax	9.75

SOURCE: Aldona Robbins and Gary Robbins, *What a Canadian-Style Health Care System Would Cost U.S. Employers and Their Employees*, NCPA Policy Report no. 145 (Dallas: National Center for Policy Analysis, February 1990).

If funded by a payroll tax, for example, the payroll tax rate would rise from its current level of 15 percent to at least 30 percent. If funded by an income tax, the income tax rate would increase by at least 15.7 percentage points, causing the highest rate to rise from 34 percent to 50 percent.[5] If funded by a consumption (value-added) tax, the price of almost everything we buy would increase by about 10 percent, relative to our income.

To see what these higher tax rates would mean, consider the effects of financing national health insurance with a payroll tax. For low-income employees, who currently pay no income taxes, the amount of taxes paid would double—from a current payroll tax that takes 15.3 percent of wages to a new tax that would take 30.3 percent of income. For employees who are currently in the 15 percent income tax bracket, the marginal tax rate would increase by 50 percent—rising from a combined (income and payroll tax) marginal tax rate of 30.3 percent to a rate of 45.3 percent. Employees who are currently in the 28 percent income tax bracket (and facing a 15.3 percent FICA tax) would see their combined marginal tax rate rise to 58.6 percent, with the government taking more than half of each additional dollar earned.

In general, the cost of national health insurance for any particular industry will be highest if the program is financed by a payroll tax. Under a payroll tax, for the most part, those who receive the benefits of national health insurance (the nonelderly working population)

---

[5]For taxpayers in the 15 percent income tax bracket, the income tax rate would rise to 31 percent; for taxpayers in the 28 percent tax bracket, the income tax rate would rise to 44 percent.

Table 16.3
INCREASE IN HEALTH CARE COSTS IN THE AUTO INDUSTRY
UNDER NATIONAL HEALTH INSURANCE

Tax	Increase per Production Worker	Increase as a Percent of Total Production Costs
Payroll tax	$3,491	5.9%
Income tax	2,962	13.3
Consumption tax	687	11.6

SOURCE: Aldona Robbins and Gary Robbins, *What a Canadian-Style Health Care System Would Cost U.S. Employers and Their Employees*, NCPA Policy Report no. 145 (Dallas: National Center for Policy Analysis, February 1990).

will be paying the costs of those benefits. If the program is financed with an income tax, elderly taxpayers covered by Medicare will pay part of the cost of the new program, even though they will receive no benefits from it. With a consumption tax, part of the cost of the program will also be borne by people covered by Medicaid, even though they too will receive no additional benefits.

Why National Health Insurance Will More Than Double Health Care Costs in the Automobile Industry

The cost of national health insurance will not be spread equally over all sectors of the American economy. Some industries will incur large losses, whereas others will gain. Other things being equal, the more generous an industry's current health care benefits, the more it will lose under a switch to national health insurance because of the loss of tax subsidies. Other things being equal, the more highly paid the workforce, the more an industry will lose because the taxes needed to pay for national health insurance will rise with income. Take the auto industry, for example. Table 16.3 shows the cost of national health insurance for auto production workers under each of the three types of broad-based taxes.

Effects of a Payroll Tax

As Tables 16.4 and 16.5 show, the auto industry will pay almost $6,800 per auto worker in additional taxes each year as a result of national health insurance funded by a payroll tax. But the value of national health insurance is assumed to be only $3,300. As a result,

Table 16.4
NATIONAL HEALTH INSURANCE TAXES FOR AN
AUTO WORKER[1]
(Program Funded by Payroll Tax)

Source of New Tax Burden	Additional Tax
Loss of tax subsidy for private insurance	
Increase in FICA tax	$ 428
Increase in income tax	427
NHI payroll tax[2]	5,936
Total tax burden	$6,791

SOURCE: Aldona Robbins and Gary Robbins, *What a Canadian-Style Health Care System Would Cost U.S. Employers and Their Employees*, NCPA Policy Report no. 145 (National Center for Policy Analysis, February 1990).
[1]Based on an initial annual salary of $36,760, the average salary currently paid to auto workers.
[2]New salary multiplied by the new national health insurance (NHI) payroll tax rate of 15 percent.

Table 16.5
NET COST FOR AN AUTO WORKER OF NATIONAL HEALTH
INSURANCE
(Program Funded by Payroll Tax)

Source of Cost	Net Tax Burden
Loss of tax subsidy for private insurance[1]	$ 855
Excess of NHI payroll tax over NHI benefits[2]	2,636
Total net cost	$3,491

SOURCE: Aldona Robbins and Gary Robbins, *What a Canadian-Style Health Care System Would Cost U.S. Employers and Their Employees*, NCPA Policy Report no. 145 (Dallas: National Center for Policy Analysis, February 1990).
[1]From Table 16.3.
[2]The benefit of national health insurance is assumed to be $3,300. The new payroll tax rate is 15 percent.

the auto industry will pay about $3,500 more in taxes than it will receive in benefits for each auto worker. Because the cost of employer-provided health insurance currently is about $3,055 a year,[6] the industry's costs will more than double.

Effects of an Income Tax

As noted above, an income tax has a lower cost per worker than a payroll tax, because the income tax reaches the elderly even though they do not directly benefit from the program. That does not mean that the payroll tax is more expensive in terms of total costs of production, however. An income tax reaches holders of capital and will cause the service price of capital to rise. As a result, the initial impact on the cost of production will be quite high.[7] As Table 16.3 shows, the impact of the income tax on total costs of production will be more than twice as great as the impact of a payroll tax.

Effects of a Consumption Tax

As noted above, a consumption tax reaches the broadest base of taxpayers, including people who receive no benefit from the program. Table 16.2 shows that an across-the-board value-added tax rate of 9.75 percent will be required in all industries to pay for national health insurance. Table 16.3 assumes that industries initially will try to impose the cost of this tax on consumers by raising prices. Given that auto workers (in their role as consumers) have above-average incomes, their costs will equal about 11.6 percent of production costs in the auto industry. As an economic principle, however, it is impossible for all firms to raise their prices by 10 percent, since consumers do not have 10 percent additional income to pay those prices. Ultimately, therefore, a value-added tax will be borne, not by consumers, but by the suppliers of labor and capital.

---

[6]This is the average health insurance benefit for the auto industry as a whole.

[7]In general, a tax on capital has a much more severe impact on input prices than a tax on labor. For example, a 13 percentage point increase in the income tax rate will increase the tax rate on capital by about 50 percent. If the aftertax rate of return on capital is to be held constant (as economic theory and historical experience suggest), this implies a 25 percent increase in the service price of capital to employers.

Why National Health Insurance Would Be Especially Costly to U.S. Manufacturing Industries

National health insurance involves much more than government provision of health care. Through the act of raising taxes to pay for such insurance, an enormous redistribution of income takes place. Workers in some industries will pay more in taxes than the value of their national health insurance benefits, and workers in others will pay less.

Because the manufacturing sector of our economy tends to pay above-average wages and to provide above-average (tax-subsidized) private health insurance benefits, this sector will be especially hard hit by national health insurance. As Table 16.6 shows, among those manufacturing industries hardest hit financially, the additional cost (over and above any national health insurance benefit) will range from about $1,600 to $3,500 per employee. In the industries that manufacture motor vehicles and equipment, primary metals, and chemicals, as well as in the telecommunications industry, the total additional cost to the industry in each case will be in excess of one billion dollars per year.

Why Some Industries Will Gain Financially under National Health Insurance

Some industries actually will gain as a result of national health insurance, at least in a purely financial sense. They are industries that currently provide small health insurance benefits and hence receive little tax subsidy for health insurance. Because they tend to have below-average wages, they would pay below-average payroll or income taxes. Indeed, it is ironic that, under national health insurance, the industries with the most generous health care benefits and the greatest inclination to seek government relief would be hurt the most, while those providing minimal health care benefits today would gain the most.

To see how an industry could gain, consider a national health insurance annual benefit of $3,300 per worker financed by a payroll tax or an income tax with a 15 percent tax rate. For an industry with an average annual wage of $10,000, the average national health insurance tax would be $1,500. Compared with a $3,300 benefit, this industry would gain $1,800 per worker. On the other hand, an

Table 16.6
Net Burden of National Health Insurance for Selected Manufacturing Industries*

Industry	Cost per Employee	Total Cost
Motor vehicles and car bodies	$3,524	$ 951,210,000
Tires and inner tubes	3,242	210,730,000
Petroleum and coal products	3,203	320,300,000
Motor vehicles and equipment	2,602	1,753,748,000
Photographic equipment and supplies	2,490	126,990,000
Telecommunications	2,254	1,485,386,000
Primary metals	2,007	1,216,242,000
Chemicals and allied products	1,939	1,206,058,000
Drugs	1,665	179,820,000
Pharmaceuticals	1,594	141,866,000

SOURCE: Aldona Robbins and Gary Robbins, *What a Canadian-Style Health Care System Would Cost U.S. Employers and Their Employees*, NCPA Policy Report no. 145 (Dallas: National Center for Policy Analysis, February 1990).
*National health insurance tax burden minus health insurance benefits. The calculations presented here assume that the excess burden of national health insurance is borne by employers and that national health insurance is funded by a payroll tax. Similar calculations were done assuming that the full burden falls on workers and produces similar results.

Table 16.7
NET BENEFIT OF NATIONAL HEALTH INSURANCE FOR A
WORKER IN RETAIL TRADE
(Program Funded by Payroll Tax)

Source of Net Burden or Net Benefit	Net Burden or Net Benefit
Loss of tax subsidy for private insurance	− $ 221
Excess of NHI benefits over NHI payroll tax	+ 1,714
Net benefit	+ $1,493

SOURCE: Aldona Robbins and Gary Robbins, *What a Canadian-Style Health Care System Would Cost U.S. Employers and Their Employees,* NCPA Policy Report no. 145 (Dallas: National Center for Policy Analysis, February 1990).

industry with an average annual wage of $30,000 would pay an annual tax of $4,500 per worker and lose $1,200 per worker.

Effects on Retail Trade

As an example of an industry that gains, consider retail trade. Table 16.7 shows that the average loss of health insurance tax subsidy would be about $221, and the average national health insurance tax would be about $1,714. Given that the average national health insurance benefit is $3,300, the industry would gain $1,493 per worker.

The fact that retail trade gains, incidentally, is bad for the automobile industry. Table 16.8 is constructed on the assumption that the initial burden, or gain, from the imposition of national health insurance is realized by employers—prior to being passed on to employees. As the table shows, if a foreign car dealership exhibits the characteristics of the average employer in retail trade, the dealership would experience a reduction in payroll and production costs and enjoy a competitive advantage over its domestic competitors. (See, for example, Figure 16.1.)

Why the Costs Could Be Much Higher

Our estimate that national health insurance would require $339 billion in additional taxes, increase health care costs in manufacturing by 50 percent, and double health care costs in the automobile

Table 16.8

COST OF NATIONAL HEALTH INSURANCE: U.S. AUTO INDUSTRY VERSUS
FOREIGN AUTO DEALERSHIPS*

	Domestic Auto Industry	Foreign Car Dealership
Cost per production worker		
Payroll tax	+ $3,524	– $1,488
Income tax	+ 3,019	– 2,520
Consumption tax	+ 1,018	– 2,074
Cost as percent of total production costs		
Payroll tax	+ 5.9%	– 9.3%
Income tax	+ 12.6	– 8.2
Consumption tax	+ 11.6	– 4.5

SOURCE: Aldona Robbins and Gary Robbins, *What a Canadian-Style Health Care System Would Cost U.S. Employers and Their Employees,* NCPA Policy Report no. 145 (Dallas: National Center for Policy Analysis, February 1990).
*Assumes costs or benefits are initially realized by employers prior to being passed on to employees.

473

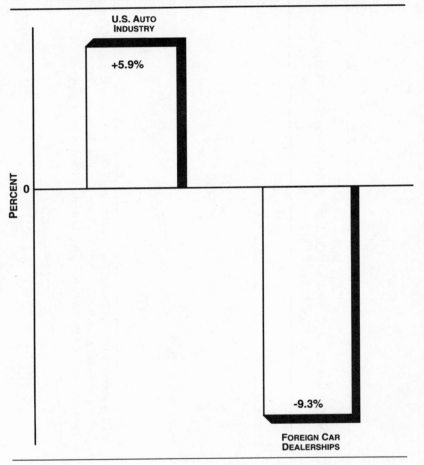

Figure 16.1
HOW NATIONAL HEALTH INSURANCE
WILL AFFECT COSTS IN THE AUTOMOBILE MARKET

industry is based on very conservative assumptions, which put national health insurance in its most favorable light. More realistic assumptions would yield even more pessimistic results.

For example, it is almost certain that Medicare beneficiaries would be included in a program of national health insurance (add $30 to $40 billion), and it is highly likely that long-term care for the elderly would be tacked on as well (add $60 to $70 billion). It is also virtually

474

certain that national health insurance would lead to a surge in demand for health care (add at least $50 billion), as has been the case in every other country. Thus, only a modest relaxation of the assumptions of this report in the direction of greater realism could easily add $150 billion to our estimate of the total costs of national health insurance—almost a 50 percent increase in the amount of new taxes that would have to be imposed.

17. National Health Insurance in Other Countries

In virtually every country with national health insurance, politicians, health ministers, and other government officials are searching for ways to reform their health care systems. Increasingly, they are adopting reforms that involve privatization, competition, and market incentives (see chapter 19). As those in other countries struggle to reform their health care systems, they often look to the United States for guidance. Yet many in this country are encouraging us to copy the health care system of some other country. Unfortunately, the advocates of national health insurance have painted a rosy picture of how it works elsewhere—often ignoring the many problems and failures.

National health insurance promises to make medical care a right and to grant all citizens equal access to it. But in those countries that have national health insurance, people are often denied access to modern medical technology, and the distribution of health care resources is far from equal. The special victims of national health insurance are the poor, the elderly, members of minority groups, and residents of rural areas.

This chapter does not focus on minor blemishes or easily correctable problems in the health care systems of other countries. Instead, it seeks an understanding of fundamental principles—by identifying common patterns that tend to emerge in all countries with national health insurance. In chapter 18 we will explain why those patterns emerge inevitably from the politics of medicine.

Twenty Myths about National Health Insurance

As the United States wrestles with the problems of its own health care system, it is tempting to look elsewhere for solutions. In general, countries with national health insurance spend less per person (and less as a percent of national income) on health care than does the United States. The assumption made by those unfamiliar with other systems is that the United States could control health care costs through national health insurance without any loss of benefits or deterioration of care. In what follows, we briefly discuss this and other common myths about national health insurance.

Myth No. 1: In Comparison with the United States, Countries with National Health Insurance Have Succeeded in Controlling Health Care Costs

The United States spends more on health care than any other country in the world, whether measured in dollars per person or as a percent of gross national product (GNP). Does that mean that the United States, with a predominately private system, is less able to control health care spending than developed countries with national health insurance schemes?

First, we should note that the United States is wealthier than other countries. Almost without exception, countries with more income spend more on health care. In fact, health economists have discovered they can explain 90 percent of the variation in health care spending among developed countries on the basis of income alone.[1] Apparently, as people obtain more income, they spend more on health care. Per capita income, therefore, is the primary force that drives health care spending, whether the spending takes place through the market, through the political system, or through quasi-public institutions. This fact should give pause to anyone who believes that the United States could significantly lower its health care spending by adopting the health care system or institutions of some other country.

Second, as we shall see below, international comparisons of health care spending are fraught with difficulties, not the least of

[1]The regression equation is:
$$\text{HEXP} = -5.99 + 1.36 \text{ GDP} \quad (R^2 = 0.89)$$
$$(-5.6) \ (11.9)$$
where HEXP is the logarithm of per capita health care spending, GDP is the logarithm of per capita gross domestic product, and the numbers in parenthesis are t values. The U.S. figure falls near the upper bound of a 95 percent confidence interval. Figures for the higher income countries such as Denmark, Luxembourg, and Norway fall closer to the lower bound, possibly because of underreporting of certain types of expenditures, such as nursing home care. See Bengt Jönsson, "What Can Americans Learn from Europeans?" paper presented at a symposium on international health care systems; published in *Health Care Financing Review*, 1989 annual supplement.

478

which are differences in the ways in which health care spending is measured. Let's look first at the problems of comparing the United States and Canada. Then we will turn to a comparison with other developed countries.

United States versus Canada: Growth in Spending[2]

In 1987, the United States spent $2,004 per person on health care, whereas Canada spent only $1,520. Some people argue that if the United States adopted Canada's health care system, it could cut health care spending by 25 percent. They buttress their argument by looking at the record over time. In 1967, the United States and Canada spent virtually identical proportions of GNP on health care (6.33 percent in the United States and 6.38 percent in Canada). After Canada's system of national health insurance was implemented between 1968 and 1971, though, the United States surged ahead. In 1987, we spent about 11.1 percent of our GNP on health care, whereas Canada spent only 9 percent.

The problem with such comparisons is that health care spending as a percent of GNP is a fraction. If the fraction grows over time, we need to know whether the growth is being caused by changes in the numerator (health care spending) or in the denominator (GNP). In this case, the differences can be almost totally explained by the behavior of the denominator. Over the 20-year period from 1967 to 1987, Canada's real GNP per capita grew 74 percent, while that of the United States grew only 38 percent.[3] If we look at health care spending alone, rather than its relationship to GNP, we discover that, before Canada implemented its system of national health insurance, the country was spending 75 percent of what the United States spent on health care per person, and in 1987, Canada continued to spend 75 percent of the U.S. level. Over the 20-year period, real increases in health care spending per capita have been virtually the same in both countries (4.38 percent in the United States versus 4.58 percent in Canada). Canada has been no more successful than

[2]The analysis that follows is based on Edward Neuschler, *Canadian Health Care: The Implications of Public Health Insurance* (Washington: Health Insurance Association of America, 1989), pp. 37–53. For a critique of this approach, see Morris L. Barer, W. Pete Welch, and Laurie Antioch, "Canadian/U.S. Health Care: Reflections on the HIAA's Analysis," *Health Affairs* (Fall 1991), pp. 229–36.

[3]Neuschler, pp. 37–53.

Figure 17.1
INCREASE IN REAL HEALTH CARE SPENDING PER CAPITA IN UNITED STATES AND CANADA, 1967 TO 1987

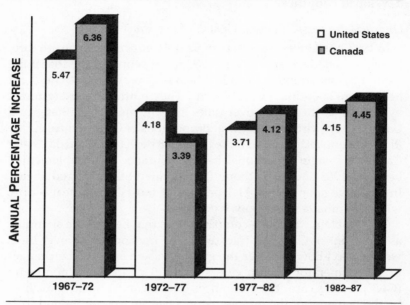

SOURCE: Edward Neuschler, *Canadian Health Care: The Implications of Public Health Insurance* (Washington: Health Insurance Association of America, 1989), Figure 4.4 (p. 41).

the United States in controlling health care spending. In fact, as Figure 17.1 shows, in recent years it has been less successful.[4]

United States versus Canada: Levels of Spending

There are other problems with this comparison. First, Canadian health care spending does not include capital spending to the same extent that the U.S. number does. Second, although both totals include research and development (R&D) costs, Canada engages in very little R&D spending, whereas U.S. R&D spending results in technological innovations that benefit Canada, as well as the rest of the world. Third, the U.S. population is slightly older, and older people inevitably consume more health care. According to one

[4]Ibid.

480

study, correcting for these differences between the two countries cuts in half the gap in the fraction of GNP spent on health care.[5]

Other adjustments also must be made. In both countries, the costs of administering government health care spending are largely hidden. For example, the cost of collecting tax dollars to pay for health care does not show up in the health care budgets of either country, whereas the cost of collecting private insurance premiums is counted as part of U.S. health care costs. Similarly, auditing expenses are usually included in the budgets of other public agencies. But because the proportion of health care spending done by government is so much larger in Canada than in the United States, much more of Canada's costs are buried in the budgets of other bureaucracies.

United States versus Canada: Differences in Health Care Needs

Because of historical and cultural differences between the two countries, the need for health care spending is often higher in the United States than in Canada. For example, the United States has a much higher violent crime rate (almost ten times the number of homicides in Canada among young males), heavier illegal drug use, and a greater incidence of AIDS, all of which generate more health care spending. According to Leroy Schwartz of Health Policy International, the U.S. male homicide rate is five times that of Canada, and for every homicide there are 100 assaults reported to hospital emergency rooms. The U.S. rate of incidence of AIDS is three times that of Canada, and the lifetime cost of treatment is about $85,000 per patient. More than 25 percent of the 10,000 to 15,000 annual spinal cord injuries in the United States are attributable to violent assaults, and treatment and rehabilitation costs are about $600,000 per patient. There are about 375,000 drug-exposed babies in the United States and the average treatment cost is $63,000 per baby— a problem that is negligible in Canada.[6]

[5]Jacques Krasny, *The Canadian Health Care System in Perspective* (Morristown, NJ: Bogart Delafield Ferrier, Inc., 1989); and Jacques Krasny and Ian R. Ferrier, "A Closer Look at Health Care in Canada," *Health Affairs* (Summer 1991), pp. 152–58. See, however, a critique of this approach in Daniel R. Waldo and Sally T. Sonnefeld, "U.S./Canadian Health Spending: Methods and Assumptions," *Health Affairs* (Summer 1991), pp. 159–64.

[6]See, for example, Leroy L. Schwartz, "The Medical Cost of America's Social Ills," *Wall Street Journal*, June 24, 1991. See also Spencer Rich, "Tracing Medical Costs to Social Problems," *Washington Post*, August 28, 1991.

Figure 17.2
TEENAGERS IN CANADA AND THE UNITED STATES:
RATE PER 1,000 WOMEN AGED 15 TO 19

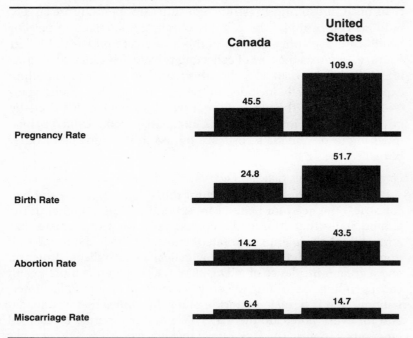

SOURCE: Alan Guttmacher Institute; reprinted in Jacques Krasny, *The Canadian Health Care System in Perspective* (Morristown, NJ: Bogart Delafield Ferrier, Inc., 1990).

The United States also has health care costs related to recent war injuries (including those of Vietnam War veterans), which Canada does not have. And Figure 17.2 illustrates another important difference: In comparison with their Canadian counterparts, U.S. teenage women have almost two and a half times the pregnancy rate, twice the birthrate, about three times the abortion rate, and more than twice the miscarriage rate. Because teenage mothers are more likely to have premature babies and complications of pregnancy, these differences cause higher health care spending in the United States.

United States versus Canada: Other Comparisons and Conclusions

No one has tried to sort out all of the differences in the two systems to arrive at a bottom line. But there is considerable anecdotal evidence that U.S. health care may actually cost less than Canada's. For example, hospitals in British Columbia contract with hospitals across the border in Seattle to perform heart surgery on Canadian patients.[7] There is a similar arrangement between hospitals in Ontario and those in Detroit. Canadian hospital managers apparently make a profit on these transactions, and at the same time reduce the public outcry over long waiting lists.

Another way of comparing health care costs in the United States and Canada is to compare Canada with some of the largest health maintenance organizations (HMOs) in the United States. The managed care programs of HMOs resemble the cost controls imposed in Canada in their commitment to control spending. Moreover, some HMOs are comparable to Canadian provinces in terms of numbers of people. About half of Canada's provinces have a population of one million or fewer people, whereas seven HMOs in the United States have more than one million subscribers. As Figure 17.3 shows, large HMOs in the United States have lower per capita costs than Canada does. The Harvard Community HMO in Massachusetts spends only 73 percent as much per capita as Canada spends, and both the Kaiser Permanente and Cigna HMOs spend about 65 percent as much.

To summarize, we can draw at least four important conclusions from the comparison of U.S. and Canadian health care spending. First, there is no evidence that Canada has done a better job than the United States of controlling health care spending over time. Second, Canada's spending on health care has equaled about 75 percent of U.S. spending, under both a private and a public system. Third, although international statistics show that the United States spends more per capita on health care than Canada does, such statistics are often misleading. Fourth, U.S. health care may be less expensive when a level playing field is used for making the comparison.

[7]See the discussion in Neuschler, p. 50.

Figure 17.3
PERSONAL HEALTH EXPENDITURE PER CAPITA,
CANADA VERSUS U.S. HMOS, 1987

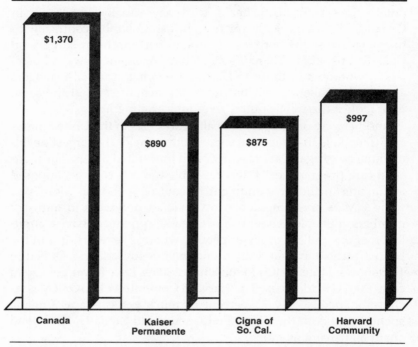

SOURCE: Alan Guttmacher Institute; reprinted in Jacques Krasny, *The Canadian Health Care System in Perspective* (Morristown, NJ: Bogart Delafield Ferrier, Inc., 1990).

The United States versus Other Developed Countries[8]

In comparing U.S. health care spending with that of other developed countries, the same kinds of difficulties are encountered. In addition, most international statistics on health care spending are produced by the Organization for Economic Cooperation and

[8]This discussion is based on Dale A. Rublee and Markus Schneider, "International Health Spending: Comparisons with the OECD," *Health Affairs* (Fall 1991), pp. 187–98. See, however, a critique of this approach in George J. Schieber and Jean-Pierre Poullier, "Advancing the Debate on International Spending Comparisons," *Health Affairs* (Fall 1991), pp. 199–201.

Development (OECD), but such statistics are not always reliable because of differences in reporting standards among countries.

Table 17.1 shows the results of an attempt to use more precise measuring techniques to develop more accurate health care spending measurements among OECD countries. As shown, the United States spends more of its income on health care than do other countries, but the difference is smaller than is commonly believed. Moreover, during the 1980s, the real growth rate for health care spending was higher in 11 of 15 countries than in the United States. In per capita terms, most countries had real growth rates that were more than double the U.S. rate.

Many believe that, in countries with national health insurance, the government can, in principle, simply limit health care dollars and tell hospital managers to ration the money they are given to spend. But this power turns out to be more apparent than real. Politicians who follow that course risk being replaced by their political competitors. In the political systems of other countries, there is unrelenting pressure to spend more on health care, just as there is pressure to spend more in the United States.

Myth No. 2: Although the United States Spends More on Health Care Than Countries with National Health Insurance, the United States Does Not Have Better Health Care

This myth is often supported by reference to the fact that life expectancy is not much different among the developed countries and that the infant mortality rate in the United States is one of the highest among developed countries. Doctors and hospitals do not control mortality in general, however. The real test of a health care system is life expectancy once under the doctors' care.

Mortality Rates and Health Care

In most developed countries, general population mortality rates tell us almost nothing about the efficacy of health care systems. That is because, throughout the developed world, there is almost no relationship between health care and general mortality, either among or within countries. General mortality rates are far more closely related to socioeconomic factors and lifestyle.

In Sweden, for example, there are striking differences in health outcomes between Stockholm and Hollard, an agricultural area in

485

Table 17.1
HEALTH CARE SPENDING IN OECD COUNTRIES, 1980 TO 1988
(Excluding Costs of Administration, Hospital Construction, and Research and Development)

Country	Spending as a Percent of GNP 1988	Annual Real Growth as a Percent of U.S. Rate 1980–1988[1]	Annual Real Growth per Capita as a Percent of U.S. Rate 1980–1988[2]
Austria	8.05%	114%	207%
Belgium	7.35	101	187
Canada	8.36	185	263
Denmark	8.35	47	86
France	8.50	225	381
Germany	8.44	158	296
Ireland	9.17	81	108
Italy	7.71	229	412
Japan	6.88	172	268
Luxembourg	6.69	155	270
Netherlands	8.31	38	25
Spain	7.11	70	84
Sweden	9.19	50	76
Switzerland	7.84	156	242
United Kingdom	6.35	102	180
United States	10.19	100	100

SOURCE: Dale A. Rublee and Markus Schneider, "International Health Spending: Comparisons with the OECD," *Health Affairs* (Fall 1991), Exhibits 3, 4 (pp. 193, 195).
[1]The U.S. rate is 2.13 percent.
[2]The U.S. rate is 1.13 percent.

the nation's south. Infant mortality in Stockholm is almost twice as high as in rural Hollard, and mortality among 40-year-olds in Stockholm is 50 percent higher. Even the middle-class suburban area outside of Stockholm city (Stockholm county) has an infant mortality rate 71 percent higher than Hollard's. Yet no one seriously claims that these differences are a result of the Swedish health care system.[9]

In Norway, people in the urban areas of Oslo and the adjoining county of Akershus have the most contacts with physicians. But infant mortality in those areas is still higher than in, say, Hordaland, a county in western Norway.[10] In virtually every country, there is a positive relationship between income and health status and between social class and health. Lifestyle also appears to matter. For example, in Norway, children born to unmarried women between 1971 to 1975 had a 55 percent higher (perinatal) mortality rate than children born to married women. Between 1976 and 1980, the rate for unmarried women was 40 percent higher.[11]

Case Study: Explaining the U.S. Infant Mortality Rate

The United States has the second highest infant mortality rate (behind Belgium) among 16 OECD countries. Is that a result of the U.S. health care system? If we were to radically change the way we deliver health care, would our infant mortality rate be substantially lower?

The answer is no, according to Nicholas Eberstadt, who has completed an exhaustive study of this question.[12] According to Eberstadt, one problem with international comparisons is that countries measure infant mortality differently. Another and larger problem is that most comparisons assume that babies in different countries are born with roughly the same health problems. That, however, turns out not to be the case.

---

[9]Finn Diderichsen, "Health and Social Inequities in Sweden," *Social Science and Medicine* 31, no. 3 (1990): Table IV (p. 363).

[10] Per Maseide, "Health and Social Inequities in Norway," *Social Science and Medicine* 31, no. 3 (1990): 331–42.

[11]Maseide, Table 1 (p. 333).

[12]Some of the results of the study are published in Nicholas Eberstadt, "Why Are So Many American Babies Dying?" *The American Enterprise*, September/October 1991, pp. 37–45.

Consider the case of Japan, which has the lowest infant mortality rate of all OECD countries. To the degree that the Japanese health care system affects the result at all, it is only through the greater utilization of (low-technology) prenatal care. But if anything goes wrong, and high-technology care is needed, the Japanese are far less able to meet the challenge than the U.S. health care system is. For example, Japan has very little fetal heart rate monitoring and fewer neonatal intensive care units.[13]

Further evidence that the health care system is not responsible for the high infant mortality rate in the United States is the fact that mortality rates among children ages one to four are about the same as in Japan. Evidence that American doctors perform better is the fact that the Japanese maternal mortality rate is twice as high as the U.S. rate. Presumably when mothers get in trouble, the high-technology care available in U.S. hospitals makes a difference.[14]

In general, American mothers have more low-weight babies than women in other developed countries, and Eberstadt argues convincingly that neither poverty nor lack of access to health care explains why that is so. Instead, the explanation lies in several factors associated with lifestyle and attitudes. Babies born to single mothers is one factor. The United States has the highest proportion of single-parent families of any major Western country.[15] Another factor is the high proportion of babies born to U.S. teenagers. By contrast, in 1983 there were only 19 women under the age of 15 who gave birth in all of Japan.[16] Yet another factor is the mother's attitude. Although there is a strong correlation between prenatal care and low infant mortality, it is not clear whether this relationship holds because of the prenatal care or because women who get more prenatal care do so because they have a more positive attitude toward the welfare of their children.

---

[13]Joseph Schulman, "Japan's Healthy Babies—An American Doctor's View," *World Health Forum* 10, no. 4 (1989): 66–69.

[14]Ibid.

[15]Sweden, with the lowest infant mortality rate in all of Europe, has one of the highest rates (50 percent) of births to unwed mothers. But cohabitation is common in Sweden, and only 16.9 percent of families are headed by a single parent. See Eberstadt, p. 43.

[16]Schulman.

What about lack of access to health care? First, there is a big gap between having the money to pay for health care and obtaining it. In the United States, the infant mortality rate among blacks is more than twice as high as among whites. But the difference cannot be explained by the inability of black women to purchase prenatal care. The gap between white and black infant mortality holds for all income and educational levels. Families with incomes above $35,000 a year, for example, can easily pay a physician's fee. But in this group, white children average 5 visits to the doctor per year, compared with 3.3 for blacks. Among families that describe their children as being in fair or poor health, white children have more than twice the number of physician visits.[17]

What about the argument that low-income families cannot afford prenatal care? That argument might be persuasive if low-income families were already spending a high proportion of their income on health care, such that any more might mean the inability to pay the rent or purchase groceries. The evidence, however, suggests that that is not the case. Families with incomes of less than $20,000 a year spend several times more on entertainment, alcohol, and tobacco than they do on health care.[18]

As Table 17.2 shows, the United States has always had a high infant mortality rate. In 1929, for example, the U.S. rate exceeded that of the Netherlands, Sweden, Switzerland, Australia, and Norway, even though the U.S. standard of living was higher. Over time, the United States has seen less improvement than have most other developed countries. We could make considerable progress if we were able to change our attitudes and lifestyles. But there is little reason to believe that we could substantially improve the results by changing our health care delivery system.

Where Health Care Makes a Difference

A population's general mortality, then, is affected by many factors over which doctors and hospitals have little control. For those diseases and injuries for which modern medicine can affect the outcome, however, it makes a big difference where a patient lives. Life expectancy is not the same among developed countries for premature babies, for children born with spina bifida, or for people

[17]Eberstadt.
[18]Ibid.

489

Table 17.2
INFANT MORTALITY AND PER CAPITA OUTPUT IN OECD COUNTRIES, 1920s AND 1986

| Country | Infant Mortality Rate[1] | | Per Capita Output | |
	1925–29	1986	1929	1986
Japan	140.8	5.2	$1,162	$9,756
Italy	122.2	9.8	2,089	9,023
Austria	120.0	10.3	2,118	8,792
Belgium	101.3	16.1	2,882	8,769
Germany	98.1	8.5	1,153	9,964
Canada	93.8	7.9	3,286	12,702
France	91.4	8.0	2,629	9,475
Finland	89.8	5.9	1,667	9,500
Denmark	82.2	8.2	2,913	9,949
Britain	73.3	9.6	3,200	9,178
United States	69.0	10.4	4,909	13,550
Netherlands	57.9	7.8	3,373	9,197
Sweden	57.7	5.9	2,242	10,328
Switzerland	55.5	6.8	3,672	11,907
Australia	53.2	8.9	3,146	9,533
Norway	50.4	8.0	2,184	11,653

SOURCE: Nicholas Eberstadt, "Why Are So Many American Babies Dying?" *The American Enterprise*, September/October 1991, Table 1 (p. 38).
[1] Per 1,000 births.

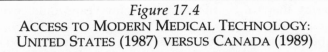

Figure 17.4
ACCESS TO MODERN MEDICAL TECHNOLOGY:
UNITED STATES (1987) VERSUS CANADA (1989)

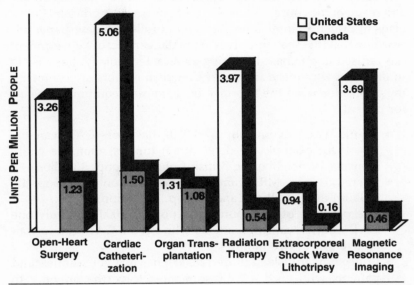

SOURCE: Dale Rublee, "Medical Technology in Canada, Germany and the United States," *Health Affairs* (Fall 1989), Table 1 (p. 180).

who have cancer, a brain tumor, heart disease, or chronic renal failure. Their chances of survival are best if they live in the United States.

Access to Modern Medical Technology in Canada

Figure 17.4 compares the availability of modern medical technology in the United States and Canada. As the figure shows, on a per capita basis, the United States has eight times more magnetic resonance imaging (MRI) units (sophisticated imaging devices that use magnetism instead of x-rays), seven times more radiation therapy units (to treat cancer), about six times more lithotripsy units (to destroy kidney stones and gallstones with sound waves), and about three times more open-heart surgery units and cardiac catheterization units (for the treatment of heart disease). Note that these figures contrast the United States in 1987 and Canada in 1989.

Comparing the two countries in the same year would reveal an even greater disparity.

Although some people claim that the United States has too much technology, all the evidence suggests that Canada has too little— as a result of the conscious decisions of government officials. Physicians in British Columbia have taken out full-page newspaper ads warning that their patients' lives are in danger because government has refused to purchase lifesaving medical technology. It is easy to understand why these and other Canadian doctors are complaining. Consider what the shortage of diagnostic equipment means for patients:[19]

- Seattle, Washington (pop. 490,000), has more CAT scanners (used, for example, to detect brain tumors) than the entire province of neighboring British Columbia (pop. 3 million).
- There are more MRI scanners in Washington state (pop. 4.6 million) than in all of Canada (pop. 26 million).
- The province of Newfoundland (pop. 570,000) has only one CAT scanner, causing patients who need a CAT scan to wait an average of two months.
- Prince Edward Island (pop. 128,000) has no CAT scanner, and patients who need a CAT scan must leave the province to obtain one.
- Because of a shortage of laboratory testing equipment in 1988, women in Newfoundland waited up to five months for a Pap smear (needed to detect cervical cancer) and two months for an "urgent" Pap smear.
- Because of a shortage of equipment, women in Newfoundland wait as long as 2.5 months for a mammogram (used to detect breast cancer).
- Women on Prince Edward Island wait for four to eight months for mammograms, and even emergency patients may have to wait as long as one month.

Access to Medical Technology in Britain

In an extensive study of Britain's National Health Service (NHS), economists at the Brookings Institution estimated the number of

[19]Michael Walker, *Why Canada's Health Care System Is No Cure for America's Ills,* Heritage Foundation Issue Briefing no. 19 (November 13, 1989), pp. 7–8.

British patients denied treatment each year, based on U.S. levels of treatment. In most cases, the patients suffered from life-threatening diseases and the denial of treatment meant certain death. Table 17.3 presents the economists' estimates, along with their estimates of what it would cost the NHS to bring British treatment up to U.S. standards. Each year, as the table shows, about 9,000 British kidney patients fail to receive renal dialysis or a kidney transplant—and presumably die as a result. As many as 15,000 cancer patients and 17,000 heart patients in Britain fail to receive the treatment that modern medicine could offer them; furthermore, as many as 1,000 British children facing the threat of death fail to receive total parenteral nutrition (TPN) therapy, and about 7,000 elderly patients living in pain are denied hip replacements.

Willingness to Adopt New Technology

Some people argue that countries with national health insurance delay the purchase of expensive technology to see if it works and is cost-effective. If true, the downside of that approach is that patients are denied access to lifesaving treatment while government bureaucracies evaluate it. During the 1970s, for example, lifesaving innovations were made in renal dialysis, CAT scanning, and pacemaker technology. Yet, as Table 17.4 shows, the rate of implants of cardiac pacemakers in the United States during the mid-1970s was more than four times that of Britain and almost 20 times that of Canada. Furthermore, CAT scanners were more than three times as available in the United States as in Canada and almost six times as available as in Britain, and the treatment rate of kidney patients was more than 60 percent greater in the United States than in Canada or Britain.[20]

There is considerable evidence that cost-effectiveness is not what drives the bias of other governments against modern medical technology. CAT scan technology was invented in Britain, and until recently Britain exported about half the CAT scanners used in the world—probably with government subsidies. Nevertheless, the British government has purchased only a handful of the devices for

[20]The treatment for patients with chronic renal failure and the use of CAT scanners continued to rise in virtually every country throughout the 1980s—an acknowledgment of the medical value of those innovations. Some people, though, have argued that the United States went too far in its use of pacemaker implants.

Table 17.3
Rationing Care in the British National Health Service

Treatment	Number of Patients Denied Treatment Each Year	Added Cost of Treating the Patients ($ Millions)[1]
Renal dialysis	9,000	$140
Cancer chemotherapy	10,000–15,000	40
Total parenteral nutrition	450–1,000	45
Coronary artery surgery	4,000–17,000	175
Hip replacement	7,000	50

SOURCE: Authors' calculations based on Henry J. Aaron and William B. Schwartz, *The Painful Prescription: Rationing Hospital Care* (Washington: Brookings Institution, 1984).
[1]In 1984 dollars.

Table 17.4
International Use of Modern Medical Technology in the 1970s

	Pacemakers per 100,000 Population—1976		CAT Scanners per Million Population—1979		Kidney Dialysis and/or Transplants per Million Population—1976[1]	
	Number	Rank	Number	Rank	Number	Rank
Australia	7.3	6	1.9	4	65.8	7
Canada	2.3	8	1.7	5	73.4[2]	5
France	22.6	3	0.6	7	111.3	2
West Germany	34.6	2	2.6	3	105.0	3
Italy	18.8	4	NA		102.0	4
Japan	2.7	7	4.6	2	NA	
United Kingdom	9.8	5	1.0	6	71.2	6
United States	44.2	1	5.7	1	120.0[3]	1

SOURCE: Pacemaker data from Eli Lilly Co.; CAT scanner data from the National Center for Policy Analysis; treatment of chronic renal failure data from British Office of Health Economics, *Renal Failure: A Priority in Health?* (London: Office of Health Economics, 1978), Table 7 (p. 30); data on Canada from Mary-Ann Rozbicki, *Rationing British Health Care: The Cost/Benefit Approach*, Executive Seminar in National and International Affairs (U.S. Department of State, April 1978), p. 22; U.S. figure estimated from data from U.S. Department of Health, Education, and Welfare (now U.S. Department of Health and Human Services).

[1] As of December 31, 1976.

[2] As of December 31, 1975.

[3] Excludes transplants. With transplants included, the number would be approximately 170.

Table 17.5
KIDNEY PATIENTS[1] TREATED BY DIALYSIS OR TRANSPLANT
(December 31, 1984)

| Country | Patients per Million Population | |
	Number	Rank
Australia	263.0	7
Belgium	393.6	2
Canada	287.3	5
Denmark	252.0	8
France	285.7	6
East Germany	117.7	13
West Germany	308.5	4
Israel	356.7	3
Italy	237.9	9
New Zealand	217.0	10
Sweden	197.6	12
United Kingdom	200.2	11
United States	413.7[2]	1

SOURCES: U.S. statistic from *End Stage Renal Disease Quarterly Statistical Summary*. All other data from *Canadian Renal Failure Register* (European data from XXII Proceedings of the European Dialysis and Transplant Association—European Renal Associations; Australian and New Zealand data from the Eighth Report of the Australia and New Zealand Combined Dialysis and Transplant Registry, 1985, Australian Kidney Foundation).
[1]Patients suffering from end-stage renal disease.
[2]As of July 31, 1984.

the NHS and has even discouraged gifts of CAT scanners to the NHS by wealthy donors. Britain also was the codeveloper of kidney dialysis, a lifesaving method of treating patients with chronic renal failure, but Britain has one of the lowest dialysis rates in Europe.[21]

One could argue that the need for technology varies from country to country. For example, the incidence of chronic renal failure may be higher in the United States than in other developed countries. Even if that were true, however, Table 17.5 shows that every country had substantially increased the number of patients being treated

[21]See John C. Goodman, *National Health Care in Great Britain* (Dallas: Fisher Institute, 1980), pp. 96–104.

by 1984—a strong indication that thousands of kidney patients had been denied lifesaving treatment in the 1970s. By 1984, even East Germany was treating more patients than Britain or Canada had been treating only eight years earlier, even though the technology remained essentially the same.

The Politics of Medical Technology

It would be a mistake to think of the U.S. health care system as a model for the world, however. Over the past several decades, the United States has not always been the first to adopt new technology (even technology that works and is cost-effective), has not always purchased the most technology, and has not always made cost-effective choices among competing technologies. In 1970, before a dialysis benefit was extended to the entire population under Medicare, the U.S. treatment rate for patients with renal failure was on a par with Britain's and less than half that of Sweden and Denmark. Only after Medicare provided a virtual blank check did the U.S. treatment rate soar ahead of all others.[22]

How we treated kidney patients was also dictated by government reimbursement policies. Studies show that home dialysis is less expensive than dialysis in a hospital or a clinic, and prior to the Medicare expansion, about 40 percent of U.S. dialysis treatment was home-based. But because Medicare gave physicians incentives to avoid home-based dialysis, the rate fell to 12 percent by 1978. There is also evidence that kidney transplants are more cost-effective over the long run than dialysis. But because Medicare reimbursement policy favored dialysis, the United States was 12th among 20 developed countries in the percent of kidney patients treated by transplant in 1985.[23]

A more recent technological innovation is extracorporeal shock wave lithotripsy (ESWL) for kidney stones and gallstones. The treatment uses shock waves to disintegrate the stones, eliminating the need for surgery. In 1989, the United States had more lithotripters per capita than most countries, but Germany (where ESWL was invented) and Belgium had still more.[24]

[22]Jönsson, Table 8 (p. 88).
[23]Ibid., pp. 88–89.
[24]Ibid., Table 10 (p. 89).

Overall, the best way to think about government policies toward technology is in terms of the politics of medicine. As the role of government in health care expands, it tends to evolve from a pro-technology phase to an antitechnology phase. In the first stage, government tends to spend on items perceived as being underprovided by the market or by conventional health insurance. Thus, practically every less-developed country has used government funds to build at least one very modern hospital, usually in the largest city, and to stock it with at least one piece of each new type of technology, even though the vast majority of its citizens lack basic medical care and public sanitation. As government's role in medicine begins to expand, however, more and more interest groups must be accommodated. In this stage, government policy tends to be antitechnology because the small number of people who need the technology are so heavily outnumbered. Along the way, these general trends may be violated with respect to any particular technology because of the varied (and even random) ways in which special-interest pressures are exerted. (See chapter 18 for a discussion of the politics of medicine.)

When the United States had a pure cost-plus health care system, technology tended to be adopted quickly because physicians—unconstrained by considerations of cost—found the technology useful. When the role of government was minimal, it was easier to acquire public funds when conventional insurance coverage was lacking (for example, kidney dialysis and organ transplants). Thus, it is not surprising that the United States made greater use of technological innovations. Our experience in the future, though, may be very different. Now that we are well into the cost-control phase of the evolution of cost-plus medicine, more and more obstacles are being created to limit access to technology.

In the United States, we pay more for health care. We also get more. And what we get may save our lives. But increasingly, our health care system is acquiring the characteristics of the health care systems of other countries, in which access to medical technology is determined by rationing and politics.

Myth No. 3: In Countries with National Health Insurance, People Have a Right to Health Care

Virtually every government that has established a system of national insurance has proclaimed health care to be a basic human

498

right. Yet, far from guaranteeing that right, most national health systems routinely deny care to patients who need it. Not only do citizens have no enforceable right to any particular medical service, they don't even have a right to a place in line when health care is rationed. The 100th person waiting for heart surgery is not entitled to the 100th operation, for example. Other patients can, and do, jump the queue for any number of reasons.

By U.S. standards, one of the cruelest aspects of government-run health care systems is the degree to which these systems engage in nonprice rationing. In Britain, New Zealand, and Canada, for example, hospital services are completely paid for by government. All three countries also have long waiting lists for hospital surgery. In Britain, with a population of about 57 million, the number of people waiting for surgery is more than 1 million.[25] In New Zealand, with a population of 3 million, the waiting list is more than 50,000.[26] And in Canada, with a population of about 25 million, the waiting list is more than 250,000.[27]

On the surface, the number of people waiting may seem small relative to the total population—ranging from 1 percent in Canada to almost 2 percent in Britain. However, considering that only 16 percent of the people enter a hospital each year in developed countries[28] and that only about 4 percent require most of the serious

---

[25]See Patricia Day and Rudolf Klein, "Britain's Health Care Experiment," *Health Affairs* (Fall 1991), p. 43. For a discussion of British hospital rationing, see Goodman, *National Health Care in Great Britain,* chapter 6. Enoch Powell, a former minister of health, has argued that waiting lines of this magnitude are inevitable under the NHS, regardless of the resources devoted to health care. See Enoch Powell, *Medicine and Politics, 1975 and After* (New York: Pitman, 1976).

[26]For an analysis of the waiting list in New Zealand, see *Choices for Health Care: Report of the Health Benefits Review* (Wellington: Health Benefits Review Committee, 1986), pp. 78–79.

[27]Estimate of the Fraser Institute, based on sampling in five Canadian provinces.

[28]Hospital admissions as a percent of the total population average 16.1 percent for all OECD countries and are 15.9 percent for the United Kingdom, 13 percent for New Zealand, and 14.5 percent for Canada. See George J. Schieber, Jean-Pierre Pouillier, and Leslie M. Greenwald, "Health Systems in Twenty-four Countries," *Health Affairs* (Fall 1991), Exhibit 4 (p. 27).

(and expensive) procedures,[29] these numbers are quite high.[30] In New Zealand, for example, there is one person waiting for surgery for every three surgeries performed each year.[31]

In Britain and New Zealand, elderly patients in need of a hip replacement can wait in pain for years, and those awaiting heart surgery often are at risk for their lives. Perhaps because Canada has had a national health care program for only half as long, the rationing problems are not as great as they are in Britain and New Zealand, although all three countries have similar cultures. But because the demand for health care has proved insatiable, and because Canadian provincial governments severely limit hospital budgets, the waiting lines for surgery and diagnostic tests are growing. As Table 17.6 and Figure 17.5 show, patients in British Columbia wait up to a year for routine procedures such as cholecystectomies, prostatectomies, hip replacements, and surgery for hemorrhoids and varicose veins. In Ontario, patients wait up to six months for a CAT scan, up to a year for eye surgery and orthopedic surgery, up to a year and four months for an MRI scan, and up to two years for lithotripsy treatment.[32] All over Canada, heart patients wait for coronary bypass surgery, while the Canadian press tells of heart patients dying on the waiting list.[33]

Moreover, one of Canada's best kept secrets is that a growing number of Canadians are completely uninsured. For example, to help fund its health plan, British Columbia charges a monthly premium—increased by 11.5 percent in 1991—that amounts to $840

---

[29]Health insurance industry officials in the United States report that about 4 percent of the population consumes about 50 percent of health care costs. See Blue Cross–Blue Shield, *Reforming the Small Group Health Insurance Market* (Chicago, 1991), p. 6.

[30]For example, the number of people in Ontario waiting for open-heart surgery in 1989 equaled more than 25 percent of the total surgeries performed. Because of special efforts to reduce the waiting lists, Ontario achieved a rate of one person waiting for every seven surgeries by January 1991. See C. David Naylor, "A Different View of Queues in Ontario," *Health Affairs* (Fall 1991), pp. 115–16.

[31]Patricia Danzon and Susan Begg, *Options for Health Care in New Zealand* (Wellington: New Zealand Business Roundtable, 1991), Table 2.3 (p. 26).

[32]General Accounting Office, *Canadian Health Insurance: Lessons for the United States* (June 1991), Table 4.1 (p. 55).

[33]See, for example, Joan Breckenridge, "Grief, Frustration Left in Wake of Man Who Died on Waiting List," *Globe and Mail* (Ontario), January 25, 1989.

Table 17.6
WAITING TIMES IN CANADA: BRITISH COLUMBIA, 1989–1990

Procedure	Average Wait	Longest Wait
Bypass	5.5 mo.	7 mo.
Other open heart	4.9 mo.	7 mo.
Hernia repair	5.7 mo.	1 yr.
Cholecystectomy	7.3 mo.	1 yr.
Hemorrhoidectomy	6.4 mo.	1 yr.
Varicose veins	8.3 mo.	1 yr.
Hysterectomy	3.7 mo.	7 mo.
Arthroplasty (hips, etc.)	3.9 mo.	1 yr.
Prostatectomy	7.1 mo.	1 yr.

SOURCE: Steven Globerman, *Waiting Your Turn: Hospital Waiting Lists in Canada* (Vancouver: Fraser Institute, May 1990).

annually for a family, $744 for a couple, and $420 for a single person. The number of persons in the province who are uninsured because of failure to pay the premium is estimated at between 2 percent and 5 percent of the population, or 50,000 to 100,000 people. This would be the equivalent of 5 million to 12.5 million Americans. Because the government gives each hospital a fixed annual ("global") budget, hospitals in effect get reimbursed for treating uninsured patients, but the patients must pay physicians for care out-of-pocket or the doctors treating them must absorb the loss. The British Columbia Medical Society estimates that its doctors provide $15 million to $50 million in uncompensated care to the uninsured each year.[34]

Myth No. 4: Countries with National Health Insurance Hold Down Costs by Operating More Efficient Health Care Systems

A widespread international myth holds that the percentage of GNP spent on health care is an indicator of the overall efficiency of a health care system. Thus, defenders of national health insurance often point to the low level of health care spending in their countries as proof of efficient management. Nothing could be further from

[34]One other province, Alberta, also charges a monthly premium to fund its health care plan but goes ahead and makes reimbursements for uninsured patients anyway. See Edmund F. Haislmaier, "Problems in Paradise: Canadians Complain about Their Health Care System," Heritage Foundation Backgrounder no. 883 (February 19, 1992), pp. 9, 14–15.

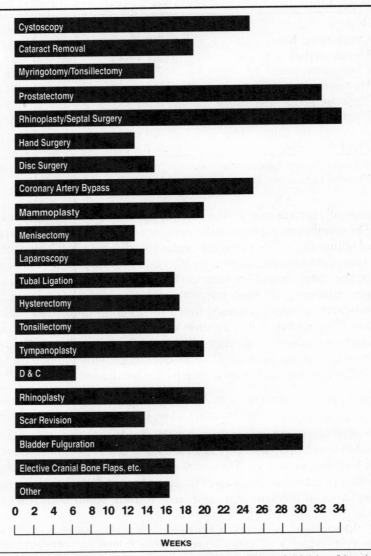

Figure 17.5
AVERAGE WAITING TIMES FOR SURGERY IN BRITISH COLUMBIA

SOURCE: Steven Globerman, *Waiting Your Turn: Hospital Waiting Lists in Canada* (Vancouver: Fraser Institute, 1990).

the truth. By and large, countries that have succeeded in slowing the growth of health care spending have done so by denying services, not by using resources efficiently.

How much does it cost a hospital to perform an appendectomy? Outside the United States, it is doubtful that any public hospitals could answer that question. Nor do government-run hospitals typically keep computerized records that would allow anyone else to answer it.[35] One reason why Margaret Thatcher called for systemic health care reform was that even Britain's best hospitals did not keep computer records, and it was not uncommon for the head of a hospital department to be unaware of how many people the department employed. In organizational skills and managerial efficiency, the public hospitals of other countries cannot begin to match hospitals run by Hospital Corporation of America, Humana, or American Medical International.

More often than not, government-run hospitals in other countries are disastrously inefficient. It is not unusual to find a modern laboratory and an antiquated radiology department in the same hospital. Nor is it unusual to find one hospital with a nursing shortage near another with a nursing surplus. Where excellence exists, it usually is distributed randomly throughout the hospital system—often being a result of the energy and enthusiasm of a few people in isolated departments rather than of any decision by hospital managers.

Moreover, even when specific inefficiencies are acknowledged, it is often impossible to eliminate them because of political pressures. For example, health economist Alain Enthoven reports that "it is more difficult to close an unneeded [British] hospital than an unneeded American military base."[36] What about bed management? Consider that, while 50,000 people wait for surgery in New Zealand and 250,000 wait in Canada, at any point in time in these

---

[35]For Britain, see the discussion in Alain C. Enthoven, "Internal Market Reform of the British Health Service," *Health Affairs* (Fall 1991). A Canadian observer reports that "Ontario hospitals lag at least a decade behind their U.S. counterparts in expenditure tracking and management information systems." See Naylor, p. 112.

[36]Enthoven, p. 62.

two countries, one in five hospital beds is empty.[37] While one million people wait for surgery in Britain, at any point in time about one in four hospital beds is empty.[38] Moreover, in Britain, New Zealand, and Canada, about 25 percent of all acute care beds are occupied by chronically ill patients who are using the hospitals as nursing homes—often at six times the cost of alternative facilities.[39]

In Canada, hospitalized chronic patients are known as bed blockers, and they are apparently blocking beds with the approval of hospital administrators. Hospital administrators apparently believe that chronic patients are less expensive to care for than acute patients because they use mostly the hotel services of the hospital and cause less of a drain on limited hospital budgets.[40]

One widely used measure of hospital efficiency is average length of stay. By this standard, U.S. hospitals are far in front of their international rivals.[41] As Figure 17.6 shows, the average hospital stay is 39 percent longer in New Zealand, 42 percent longer in Canada, and 61 percent longer in Britain. The average hospital stay in all OECD countries is 76 percent longer than in the United States.[42]

[37]For New Zealand, estimate of the New Zealand Department of Health. OECD statistics for 1983 show an occupancy rate of 74.8 percent for New Zealand and 83.3 percent for Canada. See Organization for Economic Cooperation and Development, *Financing and Delivering Health Care* (Paris, 1987), Table 29 (p. 67). The most recent OECD statistics are expected to show an occupancy rate of 80.3 percent for acute care hospitals and 82.7 percent for all hospitals in Canada for 1987. See George J. Schieber et al., Exhibits 4, 5 (pp. 27, 29).

[38]Hospital occupancy rates are 74 percent for acute beds and 82 percent for all beds. See Office of Health Economics, *Compendium of Health Statistics: 7th Edition* (London, 1989), section 3, p. 39. The most recent OECD statistics are expected to show an occupancy rate of 76.4 percent for acute care hospitals and 80.6 percent for all hospitals in 1986. See Schieber, Poullier, and Greenwald, Exhibits 4, 5 (pp. 27, 29).

[39]In Canada, the latest estimate is 23 percent. See Neuschler, p. 18.

[40]See Rosie DiManno, "Hard Choices Facing Health Care System," *Toronto Star*, January 28, 1989; "Ceiling System Needs Radical Surgery," *Toronto Star*, March 27, 1988; and Robert G. Evans et al., "Controlling Health Expenditures: The Canadian Reality," *New England Journal of Medicine* 320, no. 9 (March 2, 1989): 574.

[41]For an analysis of international length of stay statistics, see Rita Ricardo-Campbell, *The Economics and Politics of Health* (Chapel Hill: University of North Carolina Press, 1982), Table 3 (p. 85); and Cotton M. Lindsay et al., *National Health Issues: The British Experience* (Nutley, NJ: Hoffmann-LaRoche, Inc., 1980), pp. 74–78.

[42]See the discussion in Schieber et al., pp. 28–30.

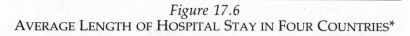

Figure 17.6
AVERAGE LENGTH OF HOSPITAL STAY IN FOUR COUNTRIES*

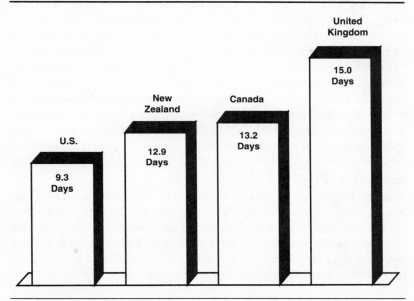

SOURCE: Based on latest statistics from the Organization for Economic Cooperation and Development. For acute care hospitals, the average length of stay is estimated at 7.2 days for the United States, 8.9 for Canada, and 7.8 for the United Kingdom. See George J. Schieber, Jean-Pierre Poullier, and Leslie M. Greenwald, "Health Care Systems in Twenty-four Countries," *Health Affairs* (Fall 1991), Exhibits 4, 5 (pp. 27, 29).

*United States, 1988; New Zealand, 1986; and Canada and Britain, 1987.

Almost all health care economists agree that widespread inefficiencies exist in the U.S. health care system. But we will not improve our efficiency by adopting the practices of other countries.

*Myth No. 5: Countries with National Health Insurance Have
Established Equality of Access to Health Care*

One of the most surprising features of national health care systems is the attention given to the notion and importance of equality. Aneurin Bevan, father of the British NHS, declared that "everyone should be treated alike in the matter of medical care."[43] The Beveridge report, a blueprint for the NHS, promised "a health service providing full preventive and curative treatment of every kind for every citizen without exceptions."[44] The *British Medical Journal* predicted that the NHS would be "a 100 percent service for 100 percent of the population."[45] To the founders of the NHS, the goal was to eliminate inequalities in health care based on age, sex, occupation, geographical location, and—most important—income and social class. As Bevan put it, "The essence of a satisfactory health service is that rich and poor are treated alike, that poverty is not a disability and wealth is not advantaged."[46] Similar statements have been made by politicians in virtually every country that has established a national health insurance program.

Inequality in Britain

Such rhetoric rarely relates to the facts. For over three decades, Britain's ministers of health have assured the British people that they were leaving no stone unturned in a relentless quest to root out and eliminate inequalities in health care. But, after an unofficial government campaign to suppress it, an official task force report (the Black report) concluded that there was little evidence of more equal access to health care in Britain in 1980 than there had been when the NHS was started in 1948.[47] Virtually every scholarly study of the issue has pointed to a similar conclusion.[48] One study of

[43]Quoted in Economic Models, Ltd., *The British Health Care System* (Chicago: American Medical Association, 1976), p. 33.

[44]Quoted in Harry Swartz, "The Infirmity of British Medicine," in Emmett Tyrrell, Jr., ed., *The Future That Doesn't Work: Social Democracy's Failures in Britain* (New York: Doubleday, 1977), p. 24.

[45]*British Medical Journal* (December 12, 1942): 700.

[46]Aneurin Bevan, *In Place of Fear* (London: Heinemann, 1952), p. 76.

[47]*Inequalities in Health* (Black report) (London: Department of Health and Social Security, 1980).

[48]See Julian LeGrande, "The Distribution of Public Expenditure: The Case of Health Care," *Economica* 45, no. 178 (1978); Anthony J. Culyer, *Need and the National Health Service* (Totowa, NJ: Rowman and Littlefield, 1976); Michael H. Cooper, *Rationing Health Care* (New York: Halstead Press, 1975); Michael H. Cooper and Anthony J. Culyer, "Equality in the N.H.S.: Intentions, Performance and Problems in Evaluation," in M. M. Houser, ed., *The Economics of Medical Care* (London: Allen and Unwin, 1972); J. Noyce, A. A. Smith, and A. J. Trickey, "Regional Variations in the Allocation of Financial Resources to the Community Health Services," *The Lancet*, March 30, 1974; and Goodman, *National Health Care in Great Britain*, chapter 9. For a recent update on government failures to make any progress in achieving

Table 17.7
GEOGRAPHICAL VARIATIONS IN HEALTH SERVICES IN NEW ZEALAND*

Service	Ratio of High to Low
Total spending per capita	190%
Surgeries per capita	630
Day patients per capita	480
Outpatients per capita	220
Number on waiting lists per capita	190
Doctors per occupied hospital bed	580

SOURCE: Patricia Danzon and Susan Begg, *Health Policy in New Zealand: Options for Reform* (Wellington: New Zealand Business Roundtable, 1991), Table 2.3 (p. 26).
*Grouped by area health boards.

health care spending across geographical areas of England found no relationship between any measure of medical need and the amount spent.[49] Another study of individual medical consumption found that people in Britain's highest social class received 40 percent more medical care (in relation to their need for it) than people in the lowest social class.[50]

Inequality in New Zealand

Other studies have documented widespread inequalities in health care in Sweden,[51] Canada,[52] New Zealand,[53] and elsewhere. For example, New Zealand's health care system is virtually identical to Britain's, and its goal of equal access to health care is just as lofty. Yet, as Table 17.7 shows, among the geographical regions of New

equality of access to health care, see "Dying of Inequality," *The Economist,* April 4, 1987, p. 52.

[49]Noyce, Smith, and Trickey, Table III (p. 556).

[50]LeGrande.

[51]See Ingemar Stahl, "Can Equity and Efficiency Be Combined: The Experience of the Planned Swedish Health Care System," in Mancur Olson, ed., *A New Approach to the Economics of Health Care* (Washington: American Enterprise Institute, 1981), pp. 187–90.

[52]Cotton M. Lindsay, *Canadian National Health Insurance: Lessons for the United States* (Nutley, NJ: Hoffmann-LaRoche , 1979).

[53]*Choices for Health Care,* pp. 19–22.

Zealand, spending on health care per person varies by a factor of almost two to one. Surgeries per capita vary by more than six to one, doctors per occupied bed by almost six to one, and the number of patients waiting for surgery by almost two to one.

Inequality in Canada

Canada also puts a high premium on equal access to medical care, if the official rhetoric is to be believed. How well have the Canadians done? Table 17.8 compares the amount of spending on the services of physician specialists for two areas in British Columbia: Vancouver, the province's largest city, with a population in excess of one million, and Peace River, a rural area of about 51,000. As the table shows, Vancouver residents receive about three times more specialist services, and this inequality holds for both males and females across all age groups. The differences are even more striking for specific specialties, with an 8-to-1 difference in the services of internists and a 35-to-1 difference in the services of psychiatrists.

One might suppose that the lower level of specialist services in Peace River would be offset by a higher level of general practitioner (GP) services. That is not the case, however. As Figure 17.7 shows, Vancouver residents also enjoy about 50 percent more GP services than do the people who live in Peace River.

Effects on Low-Income Families

There is substantial evidence that when health care is rationed, the poor are pushed to the rear of the waiting line. In general, low-income people in almost every country see physicians less often, spend less time with physicians when they see them, enter the hospital less often, and spend less time in the hospital—especially when the use of medical services is weighted by the incidence of illness. In Canada,[54] and in every other country with national health insurance, there is no national waiting list and, thus, no way of ensuring that the sickest people get care first. Even in the same hospital, there are instances in which elective patients get surgery while those in much greater need are forced to wait.[55] Moreover,

[54]General Office of Accounting, p. 53 ff.

[55]A review of the hospital records of open-heart surgery patients in Toronto found that although physicians generally assigned sensible priorities, there were "many instances of relatively short waits for elective cases while more urgent cases waited inappropriately long periods of time." See Naylor, p. 121.

Table 17.8

PER CAPITA SPENDING ON SERVICES OF SPECIALISTS FOR RESIDENTS OF TWO CANADIAN HOSPITAL DISTRICTS, 1987–1988[1]

Age/Specialty	Vancouver (Pop. 1,289,595)[2]	Peace River (Pop. 51,252)[3]
Child, age 0–4		
Male	145.7	44.0
Female	119.7	32.7
Child, age 5–9		
Male	102.1	32.7
Female	85.7	30.1
Adult, age 40–59		
Male	201.6	86.6
Female	265.2	131.3
Adult, Age 70–79		
Male	522.5	169.6
Female	404.9	204.7
All ages[4]		
All specialists	214.1	76.0
Internists	26.4	3.1
OB/GYN	11.5	6.4
Psychiatrists	14.0	0.4

SOURCE: Arminée Kazanjian et al., *Fee Practice Medical Expenditures per Capita and Full-Time Equivalent Physicians in British Columbia, 1987–88* (Vancouver: University of British Columbia, 1989), pp. 121–76.
[1]Includes all physician fees for services rendered to residents living in the areas indicated, regardless of the area in which the service was received, expressed in Canadian dollars.
[2]Greater Vancouver Regional Hospital District, British Columbia.
[3]Peace River Regional Hospital District, British Columbia.
[4]Spending statistics are age/sex standardized.

Figure 17.7
AMOUNT SPENT ON PHYSICIAN SERVICES
FOR RESIDENTS OF TWO CANADIAN HOSPITAL DISTRICTS*

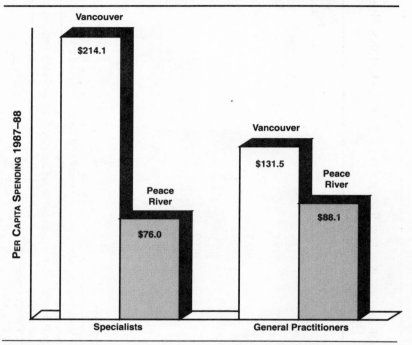

SOURCE: Arminée Kazanjian et al., *Fee Practice Medical Expenditures per Capita and Full-Time Equivalent Physicians in British Columbia, 1987–88* (Vancouver: University of British Columbia, 1989), pp. 121–76.

*Data are age/sex standardized and expressed in Canadian dollars.

anecdotal evidence from every country suggests that the wealthy and powerful do not wait as long as others. As one study of the Canadian system noted: "Critics charge that those who are rich, influential, or 'connected' often 'jump the queue,' which changes Canadian health care into a two-tier system—precisely what the government wanted to avoid."[56]

Interestingly, among the patients who jump the queue in Canada are Americans who pay out-of-pocket for care. Because U.S.

[56]House Wednesday Group, *Public Health in the Provinces* (September 22, 1989), p. 14.

510

patients pay, they add to hospital revenues and are valued by hospital administrators. Because it is illegal for Canadians to pay for care at a national health insurance hospital, the typical Canadian patient must wait in line.[57]

How does access to health care for low-income people in the United States compare with access in countries with national health insurance? Our poorest citizens—those on Medicaid—probably have more access to better health care than low-income citizens do in any other country. Being on Medicaid usually means having access to all the technology the U.S. health care system has to offer, especially because medical technology is more available in the United States and Medicaid will usually pay for it. Even though Medicaid rationing is becoming more prevalent, there is probably far less rationing in the United States than in most other countries.

International opinion surveys show that 7.5 percent of Americans say they do not receive needed health care for financial reasons compared with only 0.6 percent of Canadians and 0.1 percent of Britons. By contrast, a somewhat smaller percent of people in the United States (5.1 percent) but a much larger percent in Canada (3.1 percent) and Britain (4.6 percent) say they cannot get care for nonfinancial reasons, including inability to get an appointment, unavailability of services, and lack of transportation.[58] However, it is not clear what these responses really mean. In the United States, people are more frequently asked to choose between money and health care. In Britain and Canada, people more frequently must choose between health care and other (rationing) costs. It is not known whether people would have obtained health care if they had perceived their medical needs as being more urgent, but that often must have been the case. Two-thirds of the people in the United States who said they did not get needed care for financial reasons had health insurance.[59] A different way of comparing the United States and Canada is to look at medical care received by

[57]Walker, *Why Canada's Health Care System Is No Cure for America's Ills*, p. 9.

[58]Robert J. Blendon and Humphrey Taylor, "Views on Health Care: Public Opinion in Three Nations," *Health Affairs* (Spring 1989), p. 156.

[59]Ibid.

511

Table 17.9
ACCESS TO MEDICAL CARE IN THE UNITED STATES AND CANADA BY INCOME

Income Level	United States	Canada
Percent of Citizens Hospitalized One or More Times in the Last Year[1]		
Low income[2]	23%	22%
Middle and upper income	13	12
Average Number of Physician Visits[1]		
Low income[2]	6.7	8.7
Middle and upper income	6.6	5.5

SOURCE: Robert J. Blendon and Humphrey Taylor, "Views on Health Care: Public Opinion in Three Nations," *Health Affairs* (Spring 1989), Table 7 (p. 155).
[1]Data are age adjusted for comparison.
[2]Income less than $15,000 per year.

income group. As Table 17.9 shows, the differences are not that great among low-income citizens in both countries. Low-income Canadians see physicians more often, but low-income Americans are slightly more likely to spend time in a hospital.

In every country, some people slip through the social safety net. But for the most part, the United States has largely achieved the goal of socialized medicine: the removal of financial barriers to health care. And, considering the rationing of medical technology in countries with national health insurance, the U.S. health care system may have gone further in removing financial barriers to medical care than any other country in the world.

Myth No. 6: Countries with National Health Insurance Make Health Care Available on the Basis of Need Rather Than Ability to Pay

Most people in Britain, Canada, and in other countries with health care rationing schemes believe that the wealthy, the powerful, and the sophisticated move to the head of the rationing lines. Because government officials have little interest in verifying this fact, few formal studies exist. However, there is considerable evidence that, in the face of health care rationing, those who can pay find ways to obtain health care.

In response to severe rationing by waiting, both Britain and New Zealand have witnessed a growing market in private health insurance, whereby citizens willingly pay for coverage for private surgery, although they are theoretically entitled to free surgery in public hospitals. As a result, the privately insured pay for health care twice—through taxes and through insurance premiums. In Britain, the number of people with private health insurance policies has more than doubled and currently totals about 10 percent of the population, with about one in every five elective surgeries being performed in the private sector.[60] In New Zealand, one-third of the population is covered by private health insurance, and private hospitals now perform 25 percent of all surgical procedures.[61]

Canada does not allow private health insurance. Thus, if Canadians go to private physicians (who account for less than 1 percent of all Canadian physicians) or private hospitals (less than 5 percent of all Canadian hospitals), they must pay the full bill out-of-pocket.[62] An exception is the small number of outpatient surgery clinics operated by entrepreneurial physicians; the government will pay the surgeon's fee but not other costs. Canadians who receive cataract surgery, for example, must pay from $900 to $1,200 out-of-pocket.[63]

In addition, Canadian citizens are increasingly entering the United States to get the health care they cannot get at home. In some cases, the Canadian province pays the bill; in other cases, patients spend their own money.[64] In either event, patients must bear the costs of travel. For example, about 100 Canadian heart patients go to a Cleveland clinic each year because they cannot get timely treatment in their own country.[65] A volunteer organization, Heartbeat Windsor, arranges for Ontario heart patients to get treatment at Detroit hospitals (which accept the Ontario rate as payment in full); Alberta has indicated it will accept a similar arrangement.[66]

[60]Day and Klein, pp. 43–44.
[61]*Choices for Health Care*, p. 75.
[62]Neuschler, pp. 17–18, 20.
[63]Ibid.
[64]DiManno.
[65]Tracey Tyler, "Frustrated Heart Patients Head to Ohio for Surgery," *Toronto Star*, January 22, 1989.
[66]Neuschler, p. 50.

Because there is only one lithotripter in all of Ontario, many lithotripsy patients cross the border; at Buffalo General Hospital in New York, for example, half of the lithotripsy patients are Canadians.[67] Because of the inadequate facilities in Canada, about half of the in vitro fertilization patients at the University of Washington Medical Center are Canadians, who pay $5,000 out-of-pocket for each procedure.[68]

In general, the Ontario government will pay 75 percent of the standard U.S. hospital charges and the same physician fee it would have paid had the service been provided in Ontario. Apparently, many U.S. hospitals and physicians believe they can make a profit at those rates. U.S. drug dependency centers are actually marketing their services to Canadian citizens. Although the number of Canadian patients who cross the border is small, it is growing. In 1990, the Ontario Health Insurance Plan paid about $214 million to U.S. physicians and hospitals—up 45 percent over the previous year. Of that amount, 40 percent went to Florida, 9 percent to New York, 5 percent to Michigan and Minnesota, and 4 percent to California.[69]

Myth No. 7: Countries with National Health Insurance Maintain a High Quality of Health Care

Americans have been repeatedly told that at least the quality of care in Canada's health care system has not suffered because of the imposition of national health insurance. Yet there are increasing reports by physicians and the news media of patient deaths and near-deaths, precisely because of the government's limits on access to technology and the resulting health care rationing. Here is one physician's report of what conditions are like in Quebec:

> In my academic practice at a teaching neurologic hospital in Montreal, the wait for the treatment of a "minor" medical problem (e.g., carpal tunnel syndrome) could be half a year or longer. What I considered essential services were unavailable. I recall losing an argument with the radiologist on call over whether a patient with a new stroke should have a CT

[67]Ibid.

[68]John K. Iglehart, "Canada's Health Care System Faces Its Problems," *New England Journal of Medicine* 322, no. 8 (February 22, 1990): 566.

[69]Milan Korcak, "U.S. Cash Registers Humming As Canadian Patients Flock South," *Canadian Medical Association Journal* 144, no. 6 (February 1991): 745–47.

scan at 5:05 p.m.; he judged that the situation was not an emergency serious enough to warrant performing the procedure after regular hours.[70]

Among the victims of Canada's system of health care rationing are the following well-known cases:

- Malcolm Stevens of British Columbia died of a heart attack after two months on the waiting list. Ironically, that same day his doctor bumped another patient from the surgery schedule to make room for Stevens.[71]
- Charles Coleman, a 64-year-old man, died shortly after a heart operation in a Toronto hospital. Coleman's operation had been postponed 11 times.[72]
- Stella Lacroix's death started as a suicide. Moments after she swallowed a quart of cleaning fluid, she raced to the nearest emergency room. Because the hospital wasn't equipped to perform the surgery she needed to stop the internal bleeding, the emergency room physician spent 3.5 hours contacting 14 hospitals in an effort to secure emergency surgery and an available intensive care bed. By the time she arrived at York County Hospital, in Ontario, it was too late. She died that night.[73]
- In January 1990, two-year-old Joel Bondy needed urgent heart surgery that was repeatedly postponed. Alarmed at their son's deteriorating condition, his parents contacted Heartbeat Windsor, an underground railroad for Canadian heart patients, to arrange for the surgery in Detroit. Embarrassed by media coverage of Joel's situation, Canadian officials promised that Joel would be moved to the top of the waiting list. After a four-hour ambulance ride to a hospital that lacked an available bed,

[70]David Caplan, letter to the editor, *New England Journal of Medicine* 321, no. 2 (July 13, 1989): 115.; reprinted in the House Wednesday Group, p. 12.

[71] House Wednesday Group, p. 14.

[72]"The Crisis in Health Care: Sick to Death," *Macleans*, February 13, 1989; cited in Iglehart, pp. 565–66.

[73]"The Crisis in Health Care"; cited in Walker, *Why Canada's Health Care System Is No Cure for America's Ills*, p. 9.

the family had to spend the night in a hotel. The next day, Joel Bondy died.[74]

These examples are far from unique. Indeed, the Canadian press has produced scores of similar stories. The following are some additional examples:

- According to one report, 24 people died in 1989 while waiting for heart surgery in British Columbia.[75]
- At Winnipeg's Health Science Center, Manitoba's largest hospital, six heart patients died in 1988 before they reached the operating room.[76]
- In Toronto, where about 1,000 people are facing waits as long as a year for bypass surgery at three hospitals, two patients died in two months.[77]
- In January 1989, long waiting lists forced Toronto's highly respected Hospital for Sick Children to send home 40 children who needed heart surgery.[78]
- At Moncton Hospital in New Brunswick, some patients were kept in hallways and even in closets, and 2,300 people were on the waiting list for surgery.[79]
- Because of a four-month wait for mammograms at St. Clare's Hospital in Newfoundland in 1988, preventive screening became impossible and the hospital could only handle women who needed an immediate diagnosis.[80]
- Because of budget pressures, patients in the maternity ward of Toronto's North York General Hospital are required to bring their own pillows.[81]

---

[74]"Canadians Cross Border to Save Their Lives," *Wall Street Journal*, December 12, 1990; cited in Michael Tranner, "Canadian Health Care in America: Prescription for Disaster," American Legislative Exchange Council *State Factor* 17, no. 8 (June 1991): 1.

[75]*Ottawa Citizen*, February 4, 1989; cited in House Wednesday Group, p. 15.

[76]"The Crisis in Health Care"; cited in Walker, *Why Canada's Health Care System Is No Cure for America's Ills*, p. 9.

[77]Ibid.

[78]Ibid.

[79]"The Crisis in Health Care"; cited in Neuschler, p. 49.

[80]*Globe and Mail*, May 28, 1988; cited in Neuschler, p. 48.

[81]Ibid.

- In some Montreal hospitals, elderly patients are being kept in diapers because nurses do not have time to help them get to the bathroom.[82]

- In September 1989, Princess Margaret Hospital in Toronto announced it would not accept new cancer patients requiring radiation therapy for a six-week period so it could clear up a 300-patient backlog.[83]

- In 1990, the only hospital doing cardiovascular surgery in northern Alberta had 210 adults and children on its waiting list, with some patients already having waited for as long as a year.[84]

- In 1989, physicians at Brandon General Hospital (Manitoba) said bed closings had left 91 patients, including cancer victims, waiting for up to six weeks for urgent surgery. Most of the patients had cancer of the breast, large bowel, or lungs.[85]

- In 1989, the health minister of Newfoundland announced that lack of funds would force the closure of more than 400 beds— one-eighth of all beds in public general hospitals in the province.[86]

- In an interview with reporters on a Canadian Broadcasting Company program, ambulance drivers recounted how a patient's condition steadily deteriorated as they traveled from one emergency room to another in search of one that would take him. The patient died.[87]

Myth No. 8: Countries with National Health Insurance Eliminate Unnecessary Medical Care

A frequent criticism of the U.S. health care system is that a great deal of waste exists because a considerable number of procedures

---

[82]Ibid.

[83]*Toronto Sun*, September 14, 1989; cited in Neuschler, p. 93.

[84]*Edmonton Journal*, January 6, 1990; cited in Neuschler, p. 96.

[85]*Winnipeg Free Press*, July 5, 1989; cited in Neuschler, p. 94.

[86]*St. John's Evening Telegram*, June 28, 1989; cited in Neuschler, p. 94.

[87]Canadian Broadcasting Company radio show, "As It Appears," January 25, 1989; cited in Neuschler, p. 95.

are "unnecessary." For example, Robert Brook of the Rand Corporation maintains that "perhaps one-fourth of hospital days and two-fifths of medications could be done without."[88]

One source of evidence for unnecessary medical care is a series of studies that show wide variations in the rate of treatment among different U.S. communities. Another is a major study conducted by the Rand Corporation, which concluded that 40 percent of medical procedures were "inappropriate" or "questionable."[89]

One might suppose that in countries where health care is rationed and many medical needs are unmet, doctors would provide only "necessary" care. That turns out not to be the case. As in the United States, there is considerable variation in treatment rates in countries with socialized medicine. In Britain, for example, there are widespread differences in the referral (to specialists) rates of general practitioners and in their prescribing habits. One study found a four-to-one difference in the number of prescriptions per patient among British doctors, and the difference for prescriptions to treat specific diseases was even greater.[90] The difference in the rate at which British general practitioners refer patients to hospital specialists varies by at least four to one, and according to one study by a factor of 25 to one—and there is a high correlation between referrals and subsequent hospital admissions.[91]

Figure 17.8 shows that the practice patterns of physicians vary widely in Canada as well. For example, there is a four-to-one difference among Canadian counties in the rate of cesarean sections. In addition, there is a four-to-one difference in rates of tonsillectomy and hysterectomy, and a two-to-one difference in the rates of mastectomy, prostatectomy, and cholecystectomy. Figures 17.9 and 17.10 compare the rates in three countries for procedures for which it is believed that doctors exercise some discretion. There is no

[88]Robert H. Brook, "Practice Guidelines and Practicing Medicine: Are They Compatible?" *Journal of the American Medical Association* 262, no. 21 (December 1, 1989): 3028.

[89]A summary of Rand Corporation research may be found in Mark R. Chassin, ed., *The Approachment of Selected Medical and Surgical Procedures* (Ann Arbor, MI: Health Administration Press, 1989).

[90]George Telling Smith, *Patterns of Prescribing* (London: Office of Health Economics, 1991).

[91]Office of Health Economics, *Variations between General Practitioners*, OHE Briefing no. 26 (July 1990).

Figure 17.8
SURGERY RATES IN CANADIAN COUNTIES*

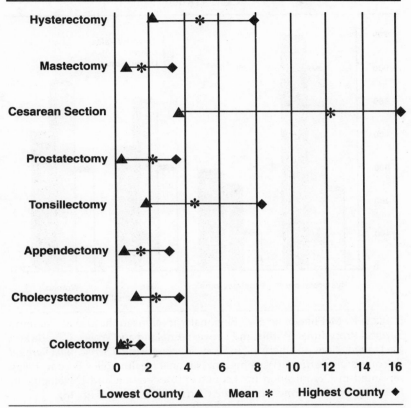

SOURCE: E. Vayda et al., "Five-Year Study of Surgical Rates in Ontario's Counties," *Canadian Medical Association Journal* 131 (1985): 111–15, reprinted in K. Lohr and R. Brook, eds., *Geographic Variations in the Use of Medical Services and Surgical Procedures: A Chartbook* (Washington: National Health Policy Forum, 1985); reprinted in Organization for Economic Cooperation and Development, *Financing and Delivering Health Care* (Paris, 1987), Chart 3 (p. 20).

*Rates of surgery per 1,000 persons in 44 counties of Ontario, Canada, in 1977.

Figure 17.9
SURGICAL PROCEDURES PER 100,000 PEOPLE IN THREE COUNTRIES*

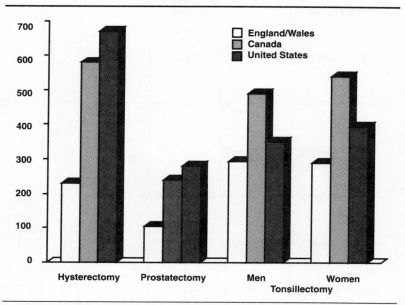

SOURCE: K. McPherson et al., "Regional Variations in the Use of Common Surgical Procedures: Within and between England and Wales, Canada and the United States of America," in *Social Science of Medical Services and Surgical Procedures: A Chartbook* (Washington: National Health Policy Forum, 1985); reprinted in Organization for Economic Cooperation and Development, *Financing and Delivering Health Care* (Paris, 1987), Chart 2 (p. 18).

common pattern, except that British surgery rates are generally lower, as they are for almost all types of surgery.

Close inspection of the Rand study in the United States reveals why there are such variations in medical practice: Physicians frequently do not agree on what should be done, and there is often no objective, or "right," answer. Indeed, when the Rand researchers went to great lengths to get consensus, a panel of experts was able to agree on a procedure's appropriateness less than half the time (see chapter 4).[92] Medicine, it seems, is often more art than

[92]Brook, p. 3021.

Figure 17.10
SURGICAL PROCEDURES PER 100,000 POPULATION IN THREE COUNTRIES*

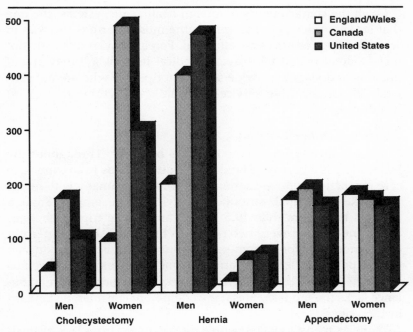

SOURCE: K. McPherson et al., "Regional Variations in the Use of Common Surgical Procedures: Within and between England and Wales, Canada and the United States of America," in *Social Science of Medical Services and Surgical Procedures: A Chartbook* (Washington: National Health Policy Forum, 1985); reprinted in Organization for Economic Cooperation and Development, *Financing and Delivering Health Care* (Paris, 1987), Chart 2a (p. 19).

science. Interestingly, the panel did agree that certain procedures were clearly inappropriate 12 percent of the time. But the cases studied were in the early 1980s, and undoubtedly less inappropriate medicine is practiced today. The reason is that the United States has devoted considerable resources to monitoring the behavior of physicians to make sure the quality of care is high. Most countries with national health insurance have done little along these lines.[93]

[93]See, for example, Adam L. Linton and David K. Peachey, "Guidelines for Medical Practice: The Reasons Why," *Canadian Medical Association Journal* 143, no. 6 (September 24, 1990): 485–90.

Myth No. 9: Under National Health Insurance, Health Care Dollars Are Allocated So That They Have the Greatest Impact on Health

Of all the characteristics of foreign health care systems, the one that strikes American observers as the most bizarre is the way in which limited resources are allocated. Foreign governments do not merely deny patients lifesaving medical technology; they spend millions of dollars to provide services for people who are not seriously ill. Often, those services have little if anything to do with health care.

Spending Priorities in Britain

Britain, once again, exemplifies this behavior. Throughout the NHS, there is a pervasive tendency to divert funds from expensive care for the few who are seriously ill toward the many with minor ills. Take the British ambulance service, for example. English patients take more than 19.5 million ambulance trips each year, about one ride for every two people in England. About 91 percent of the rides are for nonemergency purposes (such as taking an elderly person to a local pharmacy), and they amount to free taxi service.[94] Yet, for genuine emergencies, the typical British ambulance lacks the modern, lifesaving equipment considered standard in U.S. cities.

While as many as 9,000 people die each year from lack of treatment for kidney failure, the NHS provides comforts for the many chronically ill people whose kidneys are in good working order. Each year about 4.1 million people in England are treated in their homes by "health visitors" and more than 1.1 million by chiropodists, and a meals-on-wheels service delivers almost 33 million meals to people's homes. Social workers attending to the needs of the elderly and the handicapped help with the installation of more than 17,000 telephone and telephone attachments, help arrange more than 93,000 telephone rentals, help more than 49,000 people

---

[94]These and other statistics presented in this discussion are taken from Department of Health and Social Security, *Health and Personal Social Services for England, 1985 Edition* (London: Her Majesty's Stationery Office, 1985), and from the 1991 edition of the same volume. Note that throughout this book, statistics sometimes refer only to England, sometimes to Britain (England, Scotland, and Wales), and sometimes to the United Kingdom (includes Northern Ireland).

with home alterations, assist in arrangements for 63,000 vacations, and help 346,000 people with other personal appliances and aids.

While tens of thousands classified by their physicians as being in "urgent need" of surgery wait for hospital beds, the NHS spends more than $90 million each year on tranquilizers, sedatives, and sleeping pills, almost $32 million on antacids, and about $11 million on cough medicine. About 9.7 million people receive free eyesight tests every year, and about 2.3 million of these receive free or subsidized eyeglasses.[95] If the NHS did nothing more than charge patients the full costs of sleeping pills and tranquilizers, it would free enough money to treat 10,000 to 15,000 additional cancer patients each year and save an additional 3,000 kidney patients. But such options are not seriously considered.

A telephone book–sized volume would be needed to describe the many ways in which "caring" takes priority over "curing" within the British National Health Service, and readers may wish to consult other references.[96] Suffice it to say here that the tendency is pervasive.

Spending Priorities in Canada

Although not as pronounced, similar trends can be observed in Canada, where the government has expanded GP services while tightly controlling access to modern medical technology. For example, in the United States, only 13 percent of all physicians are general practitioners or family practitioners. In Canada, over half of all physicians are GPs, and the percent of physicians who are GPs has been rising over the past two decades. Ontario even requires that 55 percent of its physicians be in general practice.[97] In general, Canadians have little trouble seeing a GP. But specialist services and sophisticated equipment are increasingly rationed. Canada has actively discouraged outpatient surgery, presumably to control spending, and all over Canada, CAT scanners and other equipment are restricted to hospitals, and Ontario has even made

---

[95]New out-of-pocket charges for these services were introduced in the spring of 1989, however.

[96]See John C. Goodman, "The Envy of the World?" in Arthur Seldon, ed., *The Litmus Papers: A National Health Disservice* (London: Centre for Policy Studies, 1980), pp. 125–32; and Goodman, *National Health Care in Great Britain*, pp. 192–6.

[97]General Accounting Office, p. 38.

the restriction a law.[98] In general, the Canadian system encourages routine services for the many over special, critical services for the few. As one Canadian economist observed, "A growing number of operations are triaged because resources are used to continue first-dollar coverage for sniffles and splinters."[99]

Myth No. 10: When Health Care Is Free, Total Health Costs Are Lower because Preventive Health Services Are More Available

A common argument for national health insurance is that it saves money by encouraging use of preventive services, which enable physicians to spot problems before they develop into costly to treat diseases. The argument is wrong for two reasons. First, careful studies show that preventive medicine is economical only when it targets special at-risk groups (see chapter 4). Giving general preventive medical services to the entire population usually costs more than it saves.[100] That does not mean that preventive care is undesirable. Diagnostic tests showing that no disease is present relieve patient anxiety and reassure people of their good health. Preventive care is like a consumer good that creates benefits in return for a cost rather than an investment good that promises a positive rate of return. The second reason is that, under national health insurance, preventive care may actually become less available, precisely because it is free. A comparison of American and British GPs in the 1970s found that British patients saw a GP four times as often. Yet, when Americans did see a doctor, they spent two and a half times as much time with the physician and received far more preventive services.[101]

Because the services of GPs are free to British patients, an inordinate number of visits are for trivial complaints. To handle the case load, British doctors have reduced the amount of time spent with each patient. Moreover, because of the British government's desire

[98]Neuschler, p. 18.

[99]Michael Walker, "Neighborly Advice on Health Care," *Wall Street Journal*, June 8, 1988; cited in Neuschler, p. 51.

[100]See Louise B. Russell, *Is Prevention Better Than Cure?* (Washington: Brookings Institution, 1986).

[101]Goodman, *National Health Care in Great Britain*, pp. 55–87.

to control costs, British physicians have much less access to diagnostic equipment, and most of them send their patients to a hospital even for chest x-rays and simple blood tests. As a result, preventive medical care is precisely what is slighted in the NHS system. As one study concluded:

> Even though GPs receive an extra fee for cervical cytology tests (PAP smears), most will not provide such tests unless patients insist. The attitude is similar for breast checks. Apparently there is a great deal of deterrence going on. In 1976, only 8 percent of eligible females received PAP smears, and most of these were given to middle and upper-middle class patients. (By contrast, in 1973 almost 46 percent of American women age 17 or older had been given a PAP test within the previous 12 months.) GPs also receive extra payments for certain kinds of vaccinations. But again, it appears that the inducement is small. Over the last decade there has been a general decline in the percentage of children vaccinated against every major childhood disease.[102]

One consequence of the lack of preventive care in Britain is that many illnesses are never diagnosed. For example, screenings conducted by the British government several decades ago implied that for every case of diabetes, rheumatism, or epilepsy known to a GP, another case went undiagnosed; for every case of psychiatric illness, bronchitis, high blood pressure, glaucoma, or urinary infection, another five cases went undiagnosed; and for every known case of anemia, another eight went undiagnosed.[103]

The evidence suggests that conditions in Britain may not have improved. A fairly recent study (1989) concluded that for every diabetic being treated under the NHS, there is another case of undiagnosed diabetes, which, if untreated, could damage the retina and lead to total blindness. Another study (1988) suggests that one out of every 20 diabetics in England is first diagnosed by an optometrist (when the disease is in its late stages), who then refers the patient to a GP.[104]

---

[102]Ibid., p. 70.
[103]Cooper, p. 13.
[104]See Smith, pp. 21–22.

At one-half the age of the British system, Canadian national health insurance does a better job—but it suffers from similar problems. Although Canadians see their physicians more often than Americans do, a Canadian is not entitled to a routine cholesterol check unless some condition appears to warrant it. Once a test is given, Canadian physicians typically do not pursue further treatment unless the level is above 265, whereas most American physicians treat patients if the level is above 200.[105] Moreover, it is worth noting again that limits on technology in Canada are causing extensive waits for other types of diagnostic services, including Pap smears, mammograms, and CAT scans.

The United States does not necessarily do a better job at delivering preventive medicine. As is the case in Britain, it is believed that one out of every two U.S. diabetics is undiagnosed. And one recent study reported that, between 1980 and 1986, there were 121,560 deaths from disorders that are usually not lethal if discovered and treated early.[106] However, socializing the health care system by no means guarantees that such problems will be solved.

Myth No. 11: National Health Insurance Is the Only Way to Eliminate High Administrative Costs Inherent in a Private Health Care System

The administrative costs of any production system can be reduced by firing all of the administrators and abolishing all reporting requirements. But most systems would perform far less efficiently as a result. The real goal is not to simply slash administrative costs, but to make the system as a whole perform as efficiently as possible. A similar observation holds for marketing costs and other costs of competition. Money could be saved, for example, by abolishing all car dealerships and automobile company advertising. Money could also be saved by producing a single model car and eliminating competition among different models and different producers. We could simply pay taxes and have government provide us with a new automobile every few years. The end result would be decreased

---

[105]Elizabeth Rosenthal, "In Canada, a Government System That Provides Health Care to All," *New York Times*, April 30, 1991.

[106]Eugene Schwartz, Vincent Y. Kofie, et al., "Black/White Comparisons of Deaths Preventable by Medical Intervention: United States and the District of Columbia 1980–1986," *International Journal of Epidemiology* 19, no. 3 (September 1990): 592.

efficiency and less consumer satisfaction. After all, if socialism worked, the economies of communist countries would not have collapsed.

Some studies have claimed to show that the administrative costs of the Canadian system are well below those in the United States.[107] One problem with these studies is that government accounting techniques invariably underestimate the real cost of government provision of goods and services.[108] A more basic problem is that the studies have looked at one aspect of administration (for example, administrative salaries or the costs of paperwork) while ignoring the effects of administration (for example, how efficiently the health care system meets consumer needs).

The costs of rationing by waiting and the waste of resources caused by perverse incentives are costs of administering the Canadian system. One cannot legitimately calculate administrative savings in the system without including the adverse effects on patients in the same calculation. Moreover, many of the administrative costs in the U.S. health care system are not incurred merely to oversee the exchange of money between suppliers and third-party payers. They are also incurred to prevent inappropriate care and maintain quality. Even if the United States were to adopt national health

---

[107]For example, one study claimed that administrative costs in the United States were between 19.3 percent and 24.1 percent of total health care spending and accounted for more than half the difference in cost between the U.S. and Canadian systems. See Steffie Woolhandler and David Himmelstein, "The Deteriorating Administrative Efficiency of the U.S. Health Care System," *New England Journal of Medicine* 324, no. 18 (May 2, 1991): 1253–58. See also the critique of the study's methodology by the Health Insurance Association of America in *Medical Benefits* 8, no. 10 (May 30, 1991): 5. In another study, a national health insurance advocacy group, Citizen Fund, claimed that 33.5 cents of every dollar spent by private health insurance was for overhead expenses. See Richard Koenig, "Insurers' Overhead Dwarfs Medicare's," *Wall Street Journal*, November 15, 1990. The estimates of other studies were discussed in chapter 8. For critiques of these estimates, see "GAO Report on Canadian Health Care Tainted by Charges of Partisanship," *Health Benefits Letter* 1, no. 16 (September 18, 1991); and the letters to the editor in *New England Journal of Medicine* 325, no. 18 (October 31, 1991): 1316–19. A thorough analysis and critique of the claim that administrative costs can be reduced through national health insurance is contained in Patricia M. Danzon, "The Hidden Costs of Budget-Constrained Health Insurance," paper presented to an American Enterprise Institute conference on "Health Policy Reform," Washington, October 3–4, 1991.

[108]E. S. Savas, "How Much Do Government Services Really Cost?" *Urban Affairs Quarterly* (September 1979), p. 24.

insurance, it is unlikely that we would follow the Canadian practice of giving hospitals global budgets and forcing physicians to decide how to ration care with few questions asked.

The administrative costs and paperwork burdens of the U.S. health care system are indeed much too high, but that is not a natural consequence of private provision of health care. Rather, it is a result of federal tax policies. Most U.S. employees are overinsured—using third-party payers to pay for routine checkups, diagnostic tests, and many other small medical bills. Too much insurance not only encourages people to be wasteful consumers in the medical marketplace; it also adds to administrative costs.

If the U.S. government gave as much tax encouragement to self-insurance through Medisave accounts as it now gives to third-party insurance (see chapter 8), the administrative costs of the U.S. health care system could easily be cut in half. Whereas the administrative costs of private health insurance average about 11 to 12 percent of premiums, payment of medical bills with Medisave funds could be accomplished by use of health care debit cards, with administrative costs somewhere between 1 and 2 percent. There is no economic reason why the United States cannot move to a system in which most medical bills are paid by patients with health care debit cards, relying on third-party insurance to pay only catastrophic expenses.[109]

Myth No. 12: National Health Insurance Will Benefit the Elderly

If the experience of other countries is any guide, the elderly have the most to lose. In general, when lifesaving care is rationed, the young get preferential treatment. Consider chronic kidney failure, for example. Across Europe, 22 percent of the dialysis centers reported that they refused to treat patients over 55 years of age in the late 1970s. In Britain, as Table 17.10 shows, 35 percent of the dialysis centers refused to treat patients over the age of 55 and 45 percent refused to treat those over the age of 65. Those over 75 rarely received treatment at all for this disease.[110]

---

[109]See John C. Goodman and Gerald L. Musgrave, *Controlling Health Care Costs with Medical Savings Accounts*, NCPA Policy Report no. 109 (Dallas: National Center for Policy Analysis, January 1992).

[110]*End-Stage Renal Failure* (London: Office of Health Economics, 1980), pp. 3, 6.

Table 17.10

TREATMENT FOR KIDNEY FAILURE IN FOUR COUNTRIES
(New Patients per Million Population, 1978)

Age	Germany	France	Italy	United Kingdom
Under 15	2.3	3.9	3.5	4.0
15–24	13.1	13.9	12.5	17.7
25–34	22.8	27.6	22.0	26.9
35–44	41.7	34.2	37.2	33.1
45–54	58.8	59.8	55.7	43.5
55–64	71.3	69.5	69.5	22.7
65–74	49.9	56.6	52.2	3.5
75+	8.6	17.6	7.3	0.0
All ages	30.9	30.4	29.0	19.2

SOURCE: *Proceedings of the European Dialysis and Transplant Association*, vol. 16; reported in *End-Stage Renal Failure* (London: Office of Health Economics, 1980), pp. 3, 6.

Table 17.10, which shows treatment rates by age for four European countries, illustrates two pertinent features of nonprice rationing of medical care. First, when resources are limited, middle-aged patients get priority over older patients. In Germany, France, and Italy, the treatment rates were highest among those aged 55 to 64. In Britain, the treatment rates were highest among those aged 45 to 54. Because our kidneys do not get better with age, these treatment rates undoubtedly reflect rationing decisions rather than medical need. Second, the more limited the resources, the worse the degree of discrimination against the elderly. For the population as a whole, for example, the treatment rates in Germany, France, and Italy were 50 percent higher than in Britain. As a result, elderly patients in the first three countries had a much better chance of getting treatment.

These observations are also consistent with more recent evidence on access to heart surgery. On a per capita basis, the United States performs twice as many coronary artery bypass operations on elderly patients as Canada does. Among 75-year-olds, however, the difference between the two countries is four to one.[111]

How serious is the problem of denying the elderly access to lifesaving medical technology? Lacking hard data, one can only speculate. In general, health economists are reluctant to take population mortality rates as an indicator of health care quality because whether a person lives or dies in any given year is more likely to be determined by that person's lifestyle and environment than by anything done by hospitals or doctors. In the United States, for example, some observers believe that as many as 75 percent of all deaths are directly related to lifestyle.[112] Despite these caveats, if the life expectancy of any one population group is significantly affected by the health care system, it is likely to be that of the elderly. And international statistics on population mortality are

---

[111]See G. M. Anderson, J. P. Newhouse, and L. L. Roos, "Hospital Care for Elderly Patients with Diseases of the Circulatory System: A Comparison of Hospital Use in the United States and Canada," *New England Journal of Medicine* 321, no. 21 (November 23, 1989): 1443–48; and the discussion in Naylor, pp. 117–18.

[112]Jack A. Meyer and Marion E. Lewin, Introduction in Meyer and Lewin, eds., *Charting the Future of Health Care* (Washington: American Enterprise Institute, 1987), p. 5.

consistent with the proposition that the elderly have the most to lose by nonprice rationing of medical care.

If nonprice rationing results in discrimination against the elderly, then they ought to be better off in those countries that spend more on health care—and thus have less of a rationing problem. To test this proposition, one recent study compared life expectancy at the age of 80 among OECD countries.[113] The study found that, for life expectancy for 80-year-old males, the United States ranked second (behind Iceland), along with Canada, Japan, and Switzerland. For life expectancy for 80-year-old females, the United States was second, after Iceland and Canada. Compared with their counterparts in all other OECD countries, an 80-year-old American male can expect to live a half-year longer and an 80-year-old female can expect to live almost a year longer. Moreover, although there is very little relationship between health care spending and life expectancy at birth (which tends to correlate with per capita GDP), among 80-year-olds, there is a statistically significant correlation between life expectancy and health care spending—on a par with the influence of GDP.

Myth No. 13: National Health Insurance Will Benefit Racial Minorities

Critics of the U.S. health care system often point to the disadvantages faced by minorities. On the average, blacks and Hispanics are less likely than other Americans to have health insurance, see a physician, or enter a hospital. But is national health insurance the answer? Both economic theory and empirical studies show that minorities fare even worse under nonprice rationing.[114] What little evidence there is about health care rationing in the United States is consistent with experience in rationing in other fields.

Take the rationing of organ transplants, for example. Whites received 97.6 percent of the pancreases and high percentages of livers, kidneys, and hearts in 1988, according to the United Network for Organ Sharing (see chapter 4).[115] The *Pittsburgh Press* found that where the donors were not living relatives, the average wait for a kidney transplant in 1988 and 1989 was 14 months for black patients

[113]Schieber et al., pp. 36–37.

[114]See Walter Williams, *Legislating Black Unemployment*, NCPA Policy Report no. 112 (Dallas: National Center for Policy Analysis, July 1984).

[115]Associated Press, May 20, 1989.

and only 8.8 months for whites.[116] Note that in addition to race, income also matters. A study by the Urban Institute found that, for black and white males, the higher their income, the more likely they are to receive an organ transplant.[117]

Racial Discrimination in Canada

There have been very few studies of how racial minorities fare under national health insurance in other countries. A study of the Inuit and Cree populations of northern Quebec found that both groups had much less access to health care than did Caucasians in southern Quebec and in other areas of Canada—despite their much greater health needs.[118] For example, the age-adjusted mortality rate for the Inuit is almost twice the rate for Canadians as a whole. Infant mortality rates are three times greater than for the rest of Quebec among the Cree and four times greater among the Inuit. Life expectancy at birth in 1978 was only 58.9 years for Inuit males (compared with 72 years for all Canadian males) and 61.6 years for Inuit females (compared with 79 years for all Canadian females).[119]

About 45 percent of the aboriginal people of Ontario live in the rural, northern part of the province. And, as in Quebec, the northern counties are underserved. In 1986, there were no specialists in allergies and immunology, geriatrics, infectious diseases, or pediatric surgery in all of northern Ontario. There was only one specialist each in dermatology, endocrinology, nephrology, neurology, and rheumatology.[120] Interestingly, when national health insurance was adopted in 1969, Ontario also adopted a program to encourage physicians to move to rural areas, and that is now one of the longest running programs of its kind in the world. Yet a recent study

[116]Reported in *Dallas Morning News*, August 19, 1990.

[117]Phillip J. Held et al., "Access to Kidney Transplantation: Has the United States Eliminated Income and Racial Differences?" *Archives of Internal Medicine* 148 (December 1988): 2594–2600.

[118]Jean-Pierre Thorrez, Peter Foggin, and Andre Rannou, "Correlates of Health Care Use: Inuit and Cree of Northern Quebec," *Social Science and Medicine* 30, no. 1 (1990): 25–34. See also Clyde H. Farnsworth, "Diabetes Hits Canadian Indians Hard," *New York Times*, December 8, 1991.

[119]Averages given for all males and all females are for 1982.

[120]Malcolm Anderson and Mark W. Rosenberg, "Ontario's Underserviced Area Program Revisited: An Indirect Analysis," *Social Science and Medicine* 30, no. 1 (1990): 35–44.

concluded that "while some change has been made, northern Ontario is as underserviced compared to the rest of the province as it was in 1956."[121]

Racial Discrimination in New Zealand

There is both a significant minority population (Maoris) and a comprehensive system of socialized medicine in New Zealand. One study reported that the infant mortality rate for Maoris is 60 percent higher than for non-Maoris. Life expectancy for Maori males and females is, respectively, 7 and 8 years lower than for other New Zealanders.[122] Only 20 percent of these differences could be explained in terms of socioeconomic factors. There is also evidence that Maoris get significantly less health care—especially in relationship to the need for it—than other New Zealanders. For example, death from coronary artery diseases is significantly higher among Maoris—3.5 times as high, for example, among females age 25 to 44. But Maoris receive only a tiny fraction of the coronary artery bypass operations—well below their percentage of the population.[123]

Myth No. 14: National Health Insurance Will Be Good for Residents of Rural Areas

Little is known about who gets care and who does not under nonprice rationing schemes. Britain is one of the few countries that even publish hospital waiting lists for each region and for the country as a whole. Nevertheless, in Britain, as in other countries with national health insurance, rationing decisions are made by physicians and hospital personnel at the local level, and there is no national procedure to guarantee that those in greatest need move to the front of the waiting lines.

A study of Norway's health care system concluded that regional differences in waiting times constitute the most serious inequity in access to health care—more serious, for example, than the distribution of physicians or hospital beds.[124] What is true of Norway is probably also true of other developed countries. For example, the

[121]Ibid., p. 43.

[122]E. W. Pomare, "Groups with Special Health Care Needs," *New Zealand Medical Journal* (October 26, 1988), pp. 711–13.

[123]Ibid.

[124]Maseide, p. 331.

number of British kidney patients receiving dialysis or a transplant in 1989 averaged 305 per million population in the four metropolitan areas in and around London. However, the number was only 239 in the northern region of Yorkshire and 174 in the western region of West Midlands.[125] These differences are greater than the regional differences in health care spending per person or other measures of health inputs.

There are many reasons to believe that rural patients are at a disadvantage when health care is rationed.[126] The most serious form of rationing is rationing of access to modern medical technology. Often, such technology is available only at major hospitals in large cities. That need not be a problem if rural patients can purchase care with their own money or through public or private health insurance. Rationing by waiting, on the other hand, discriminates against rural patients.

For one thing, it often means that care is given to patients who are available when an opening appears in the surgery schedule. Urban patients who live close by thus have an advantage over rural patients who may have to travel considerable distances, requiring both time and inconvenience. For another thing, success in obtaining care often depends on the politics of bureaucracy. A patient who is represented by a physician in a rural area will tend to be at a disadvantage vis-à-vis a patient represented by a physician who lives nearby and is a colleague of the hospital staff. Urban patients also have access to political and personal relationships that may be important in dealing with bureaucratic obstacles—opportunities not generally available to rural patients.

Finally, wherever there is nonprice rationing, people will attempt to move to the head of the waiting lines by paying illegal bribes. In Hungary, the practice of "tipping" has become institutionalized, and physicians receive tips equal to about 40 percent of their official annual total income.[127] In Japan, an illegal "gift" of $1,000 to $3,000

[125]Office of Health Economics, *Compendium of Health Statistics, 7th Edition* (1989), Table 3.36(a) (p. 49).

[126]See John C. Goodman and Gerald L. Musgrave, *National Health Insurance and Rural Health Care*, NCPA Policy Report no. 107 (Dallas: National Center for Policy Analysis, October 1991).

[127]Lajos Csaszi, "Interpreting Inequalities in the Hungarian Health System," *Social Science and Medicine* 31, no. 3 (1990): 280.

can get a patient admitted sooner and ensure treatment by a senior specialist at a Tokyo University hospital.[128] In most countries, rural residents probably know less about the mechanics of currying favor with physicians.

Rural Patients in Britain

The most important philosophical principle advocated by those who established the NHS was equal access to health care. But inequalities persist across Britain and may even have grown worse since the NHS was founded in 1948. For example, the North East Thames region (near London) has 27 percent more doctors and dentists per person, 15 percent more hospital beds, and 12 percent more total health spending than the Trent region (in the more rural northern part of the country). These inequalities do not reflect differences in need. Northerners die younger and are less healthy than southerners.[129]

One way to appreciate the magnitude of these inequalities is to consider them in relation to the growing private health care sector. If the goal of the NHS is to equalize access, one would expect the service to devote more resources to those areas least well served by the private sector. In fact, though, the British government tends to spend the most in the metropolitan areas where private-sector alternatives are most abundant.

Table 17.11 lists the regions of England by the number of private beds available per capita. Although the correlation is not perfect, in general the more private beds a region has, the greater its odds of also enjoying above-average public hospital spending. For example, as Figure 17.11 shows, the North East Thames region, which had the largest number of private beds per capita, also enjoyed the greatest amount of NHS hospital spending, the second highest amount of NHS capital spending, and the third highest growth in NHS capital spending over the past decade. The Northern region, which had the lowest number of private hospital beds per capita, had only average NHS hospital spending, the second lowest amount of NHS capital spending, and the fourth lowest growth in capital spending over the past decade. The Trent region, which had

[128]Naoki Ikegami, "Japanese Health Care: Low Cost through Regulated Fees," *Health Affairs* (Fall 1991), p. 104.

[129]"Dying of Inequality," *The Economist*, April 4, 1987, p. 52.

Table 17.11
Regional Inequalities in Hospital Spending in England

Region	Private Hospital Beds per Million Population (1988)	Total Hospital Spending per Person (1988–89)	Hospital Capital Spending per Person	
			Amount (1988–89)	Percent Increase (1977–88)
N.E. Thames	433	£237	£27	8.6%
N.W. Thames	353	209	27	8.9
S.E. Thames	293	215	28	9.6
S.W. Thames	289	215	26	4.6
Wessex	190	179	24	4.8
Oxford	177	164	17	2.3
Yorkshire	159	195	19	4.3
East Anglia	158	183	15	1.0
N. Western	152	215	19	2.1
Mersey	149	209	23	1.6
S. Western	141	191	23	5.9
W. Midlands	134	193	21	8.3
Trent	96	188	16	−2.0
Northern	51	204	17	2.0

SOURCE: *Compendium of Health Statistics*, 7th ed. (London: Office of Health Economics, 1989), Table 1.3, Box 2.5, Table 3.2(a), Table 3.3(a).

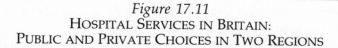

Figure 17.11
HOSPITAL SERVICES IN BRITAIN:
PUBLIC AND PRIVATE CHOICES IN TWO REGIONS

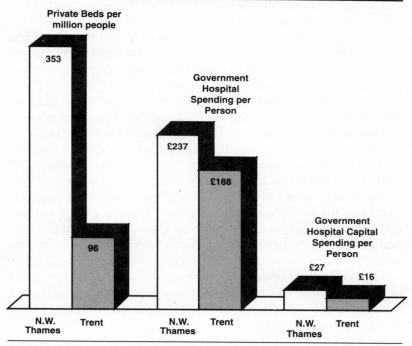

SOURCE: *Compendium of Health Statistics,* 7th ed. (London: Office of Health Economics, 1989), Table 1.3, Table 3.2(a), Table 3.3(a), Box 2.5.

the second lowest number of private beds per capita, had the second lowest amount of NHS hospital spending and the very lowest NHS capital spending, and was the only region to experience a decrease in capital spending over the past decade.

Rural Patients in Canada

Canada, too, has proclaimed equal access to health care to be a national goal. Yet there is little evidence of success in achieving it. Among the Canadian provinces, for example, the number of people per physician ranges from a low of 471 in British Columbia to a high of 1,273 in the Northwest Territories, a difference of almost three to one. Although there are 469 people per physician in Ontario on the average, there are more than four times that number in each of northern Ontario's rural counties.[130]

Health care in Canada tends to be hospital-based, with modern medical technology often being restricted to teaching hospitals and outpatient surgery discouraged. Moreover, the specialists and the major hospitals tend to be in major cities. As in other countries, residents of rural areas often travel to the larger cities to get medical care. But how often does that happen? A study from the University of British Columbia provides the answer.[131]

Since doctors are paid on a fee-for-service basis in Canada, fee-for-service income is a good measure of the volume of services actually rendered to patients. By using physician billing data, Canadian researchers determined the regional hospital district in which each patient lived, even if the service was provided in some other district. As Figure 17.12 and Table 17.12 show, people living in British Columbia's two largest cities (Vancouver and Victoria) receive about 37 percent more physician services and 55 percent more services from specialists per capita than those living in the 28 rural districts of the province. For specific specialties, the discrepancies are even greater. On the average, urban residents are 5.5 times more likely to receive services from a thoracic surgeon, 3.5 times more likely to receive the services of a psychiatrist, and about 2.5 times more likely to receive services from a dermatologist, anesthesiologist, or plastic surgeon.

These are the broad averages. The discrepancies are even greater for British Columbia's most underserved areas. Table 17.13 compares spending for selected services in two urban districts with spending in 12 other districts. As the table shows, total spending on physician services per capita among these districts varies by a factor of 6 to 1, and spending on the services of specialists by a factor of 12 to 1. Spending varies by a factor of almost 6 to 1 for OB/GYN services, 15 to 1 for the services of internists, and 140 to 1 for the services of psychiatrists. Even if we ignore the smallest districts and focus only on districts with at least 35,000 people, spending

---

[130]Anderson and Rosenberg, Table 1 (p. 37), Table 4 (p. 39). Statistics are for 1985–86.

[131]Arminée Kazanjian et al., *Fee Practice Medical Expenditures per Capita and Full-Time Equivalent Physicians in British Columbia, 1987–88* (Vancouver: University of British Columbia, 1989).

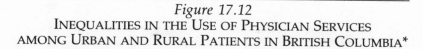

Figure 17.12
INEQUALITIES IN THE USE OF PHYSICIAN SERVICES
AMONG URBAN AND RURAL PATIENTS IN BRITISH COLUMBIA*

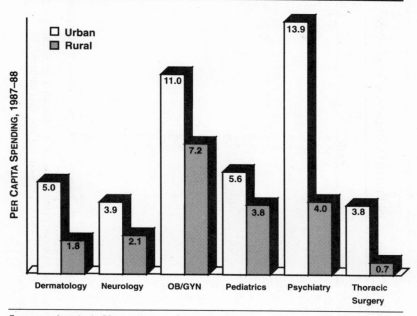

SOURCE: Arminée Kazanjian et al., *Fee Practice Medical Expenditures per Capita and Full-Time Equivalent Physicians in British Columbia, 1987–88* (Vancouver: University of British Columbia, 1989), pp. 121–76.

*Canadian dollars.

varies by a factor of almost 3 to 1 for all specialist services, almost 4 to 1 for OB/GYN services, 8 to 1 for internists, and 35 to 1 for psychiatrists.

The discrepancies among the districts are greater still if one focuses on people in specific age and sex classifications, again ignoring the areas with the smallest populations. Roughly speaking:[132]

- An 80-year-old man is 524 times more likely to receive the services of an anesthesiologist if he lives in Vancouver rather than in the Sunshine Coast district (pop. 17,049).

[132]Ibid.

Table 17.12
Per Capita Spending on Physician Services in British Columbia: 1987–1988[1]

Service	Urban[2]	Rural[3]	Ratio (%) Urban/Rural
All physician services	$347.1	$253.8	137.0%
General practice	132.1	115.7	114.0
Specialists	214.6	138.1	155.0
Anesthesia	16.6	6.9	241.0
Dermatology	5.0	1.8	278.0
General surgery	11.9	12.4	96.0
Internal medicine	26.3	15.8	167.0
Neurology	3.9	2.1	186.0
Neurosurgery	2.2	1.2	183.0
OB/GYN	11.0	7.2	153.0
Ophthalmology	16.1	8.8	183.0
Orthopedic surgery	8.5	7.1	120.0
Ontolaryngology	5.1	3.8	134.0
Pediatrics	5.6	3.8	147.0
Pathology	44.0	35.0	126.0
Plastic surgery	3.2	1.3	246.0
Psychiatry	13.9	4.0	348.0
Radiology	30.9	21.6	143.0
Thoracic surgery	3.8	0.7	543.0
Urology	5.7	4.0	143.0

SOURCE: Arminée Kazanjian et al., *Fee Practice Medical Expenditures per Capita and Full-Time Equivalent Physicians in British Columbia, 1987–88* (Vancouver: University of British Columbia, 1989), pp. 121–76.
[1]Based on fees paid to physicians for rendering services to patients living in the areas indicated, regardless of the area in which service was performed. All data are age/sex standardized and expressed in Canadian dollars.
[2]Greater Vancouver and Victoria regional hospital districts.
[3]Twenty-seven nonmetropolitan hospital districts.

Table 17.13
SPENDING ON PHYSICIAN SERVICES BY HOSPITAL DISTRICT IN BRITISH COLUMBIA*

District	Total Spending	Per Capita Spending by Category of Service			
		Specialist	OB/GYN	Psychiatrist	Internist
Urban districts					
Vancouver	$345.6	$214.0	$11.5	$14.0	$26.4
Victoria	348.4	211.8	8.5	13.2	25.6
Selected rural districts					
Bulkley-Nechako	211.0	95.9	3.5	0.7	11.2
Cariboo	203.9	96.9	5.8	1.0	9.2
Central Coast	105.4	89.3	4.9	0.5	6.7
Columbia-Shuswap	188.0	88.3	3.5	3.4	9.5
East Kootenay	224.7	99.9	3.1	0.4	7.7
Kitimat-Stikine	193.2	103.9	5.8	0.3	10.0
Mount Waddington	167.2	75.6	6.5	0.9	5.2
Peace River	164.1	76.0	6.4	0.4	3.1
Skeena–Queen Charlotte	188.5	84.8	3.9	0.4	7.8
Squamish-Lillooet	205.9	89.5	6.3	2.0	8.8
Stikine	58.2	17.5	2.0	0.1	2.5
Fort Nelson–Laird	169.3	37.1	2.1	0.3	1.7
Average for all rural districts	253.8	138.1	7.2	4.0	7.0

SOURCE: Arminée Kazanjian et al., *Fee Practice Medical Expenditures per Capita and Full-Time Equivalent Physicians in British Columbia, 1987–88* (Vancouver: University of British Columbia, 1989), pp. 121–76.
*Based on fees paid to physicians rendering services to patients living in the district indicated, regardless of the area in which service was performed. All data are age/sex standardized by regional hospital districts and expressed in Canadian dollars for 1987–88.

- A baby girl with a skin rash is 22 times more likely to see a dermatologist if she lives in Vancouver rather than in the East Kootenay district (pop. 50,660).
- A 30-year-old woman is more than 3 times more likely to see a gynecologist if she lives in Vancouver rather than in Columbia-Shuswap (pop. 39,367).
- A baby girl is 10 times more likely to see a pediatrician for any reason if she lives in Vancouver rather than in Peace River (pop. 51,252).

Rural Patients in Latin America

Although this book is focused primarily on developed countries, it is worth noting that many of the same principles apply to people living in less-developed countries. For example, people in the urban areas of Brazil are far more successful in getting government benefits than are those in rural areas. By most measures, the need for health care is greater in the northern and northeastern (rural) areas than in the southern and central (urban) areas of the country. Life expectancy at birth, for example, is about three years longer for both men and women in the cities. Yet, although most health care spending flows through government, and several government programs have been designed to create equal access to care, the spending is concentrated in the cities, and about one-third of the population lacks regular access to medical care.[133] Although more than half of Brazil's population lives in rural areas, residents of urban areas experience 9 times more medical visits, 15 times more related services, 2.7 times more dental visits, and 4.5 times more hospitalizations. Overall, the Brazilian government spends 5 times less on inpatient care and 13 times less on outpatient care in rural areas.[134]

Brazil is not unique. In neighboring Venezuela, government-provided health care is theoretically free to everyone.[135] Yet the

[133]Marlow Kivitko and Elenterio Rodriguez Neto, "Brazil," in Richard B. Saltman, ed., *The International Handbook of Health Care Systems* (New York: Greenwood Press, 1988), p. 33–55.

[134]Ibid.

[135]In Brazil, about 75 percent of hospital beds are in private institutions, although the public sector pays for most hospital care. In Venezuela, public-sector care is provided only in public hospitals.

vast majority of health care services are provided in the cities.[136] Similarly, a doctor in Bolivia is seven times more likely to practice in an urban area (where less than half the population resides) than in the countryside.[137] And in Mexico—where health care is a constitutional right—35 percent of the population (mainly in the cities) consumes 85 percent of the country's health care resources.[138]

Rural Patients in Communist Countries.

It is worth noting that many of the same principles apply to nondemocratic countries. Within communist or formerly communist countries, the variation in rural/urban characteristics is enormous. Throughout the former Soviet Union and Eastern Europe, for example, inequality between urban and rural health care is widespread. In general, the urban populations are healthier and have better access to health care. In the former Soviet Union, health care resources appear to matter a great deal. Indeed, the availability of doctors, nurses, and hospital beds explains 55 percent of the variation in infant mortality there. For Bulgaria, Czechoslovakia, Hungary, and Poland, the relationships between health care resources and health outcomes are less clear.[139]

Despite the fact that the Soviet Union was committed to the principle of equal access to health care for over 70 years, there is considerable evidence of inequality in access to medical resources and health outcomes. In the 1960s, infant mortality rates were virtually the same, on the average, among urban and rural areas. In the 1970s and 1980s, however, infant mortality rates continued to fall in the cities but began to rise in rural areas. Between 1960 and 1987, life expectancy at birth fell so much in rural areas that by

[136]Jesus E. Rodriguez and Carlos Sabino, *Social Security in Venezuela* (Caracas: Cedice), forthcoming.

[137]Joseph Bastien, "Community Health Workers in Bolivia: Adapting to Traditional Roles in the Andean Community," *Social Science and Medicine* 30, no. 3 (1990): 281–87.

[138]Kenyon Rainier Stebbins, "Curative Medicine, Preventative Medicine, and Health Status: The Influence of Politics on Health Status in a Rural Mexican Village," *Social Science and Medicine* 23, no. 2 (1986): 139–48.

[139]See Edmund Wnuk-Lipinski and Raymond Illsley, "International Comparative Analysis: Main Findings and Conclusions," *Social Science and Medicine* 31, no. 8 (1991): 879–89.

1986–87 there was a two-year difference in life expectancy between urban and rural areas.[140]

Myth No. 15: National Health Insurance Will Be Good for Organized Labor

Traditionally, the leaders of America's largest labor unions have advocated national health insurance, mistakenly believing that they can turn over the cost of employee health care to the U.S. taxpayer. What they forget is that union members also pay taxes. Under national health insurance, the employees of the nation's largest companies would pay more in national health insurance taxes than they currently pay for private health insurance. For example, in manufacturing (one of the most heavily unionized sectors of the economy), they would pay 50 percent more.[141] A national health insurance program similar to Canada's would require at least $339 billion in new taxes[142]—which would double the payroll tax rate, increase the income tax rate by 16 percentage points, or increase the prices of goods by approximately 10 percent through a consumption tax (see chapter 16). Under each of these broad-based taxes, the amount of taxes paid would rise with income. Thus, under national health insurance, the high-wage industries would pay above-average taxes, even though the workers would receive only the average national health insurance benefit.

Myth No. 16: National Health Insurance Will Improve America's International Competitiveness

Many people argue that America's health care costs make American products less competitive in the international marketplace. An example of this view is the dual assertion that health care costs add $700 to the price of every U.S. automobile and that national health insurance would solve this problem. Both assertions are wrong.[143]

---

[140]Ibid., p. 884. See also Elena Mezentseva and Natalia Rimachevskaya, "The Soviet Country Profile: Health of the U.S.S.R. Population in the 70s and 80s: An Approach to a Comprehensive Analysis," *Social Science and Medicine* 31, no. 8 (1991): 867–77.

[141]Aldona Robbins and Gary Robbins, *What a Canadian-Style Health Care System Would Cost U.S. Employers and Employees*, NCPA Policy Report no. 145 (Dallas: National Center for Policy Analysis, February 1990).

[142]Ibid.

[143]See Robbins and Robbins, pp. 20–22.

There is no evidence that private health insurance adds to the price of an automobile or of any other product. Health insurance is simply one element in the total compensation package of auto workers, a fringe benefit provided in lieu of money wages. Over the last two decades, fringe benefits for most American workers have grown steadily in real terms, while money wages have grown little, reflecting the preference of employees for nontaxed benefits over taxed money wages.

What workers are paid depends on what they produce, not what they consume. The fact that Americans spend a greater proportion of their income on health care and a smaller proportion on other goods and services does not put us at a disadvantage relative to other countries.[144] For example, the Japanese spend a greater proportion of their income on food, but food consumption does not add to the price of a Japanese car. The Canadians spend a greater proportion of their income on education, but education does not add to the price of Canadian lumber. These differences in consumption patterns merely reflect differences in consumer preferences and the relative prices of consumer products.

Although health care expenditures do not affect U.S. competitiveness, national health insurance would. That is because national health insurance involves not only the purchase of health care but also a redistribution of income among producers in different industries. On the whole, a national health insurance system would impose extra taxes on U.S. exporting industries and use the proceeds to subsidize other industries. The industries that would receive subsidies contribute mostly to domestic markets, whereas the manufacturing industries that would be penalized provide most of the nation's exports. National health insurance would raise the costs of our export goods and lower marketing costs in the United States for foreign competitors. Far from making auto producers more competitive in international markets, national health insurance would raise auto production costs relative to those of foreign rivals and would make the domestic industry less competitive.

Despite the fact that one-third of our federal budget goes to defense spending, a burden not equaled by our country's trading

[144]See Uwe Reinhardt, "Health Care Spending and American Competitiveness," *Health Affairs* (Winter 1989), pp. 5–21.

Table 17.14
TAXES IN THE UNITED STATES AND ITS MAJOR TRADING PARTNERS, 1986

Country	Taxes as Percent of GDP
Canada	33%
Japan	29
United Kingdom	39
West Germany	38
United States	29
United States with national health insurance	36

SOURCE: Organization for Economic Cooperation and Development.

partners, taxes are lower in the United States than in most other developed countries. As Table 17.14 shows, only Japan has a tax burden as low as ours. Were we to adopt a program of national health insurance, the U.S. tax burden would approach that of Britain and Germany and would be higher than that of most of our trading partners. That additional burden would have a major impact on our ability to compete.

Myth No. 17: The Defects of National Health Insurance Schemes in Other Countries Could Be Easily Remedied by a Few Reforms

The characteristics of national health insurance described above are not accidental by-products of government-run health care systems. They are the natural and inevitable consequences of the politics of medicine. Why are low-income and elderly patients so frequently discriminated against under national health insurance? Because national health insurance is always and everywhere a middle-class phenomenon. Prior to its introduction, every country had some government-funded program to meet the health care needs of the poor. The middle-class working population not only paid for its own health care but also paid taxes to fund health care for the poor. National health insurance extends the free ride to those who pay taxes to support it. Such systems are created in response to the political demands of the middle-class working population, and they are designed to serve the interests of that population.

Why do national health insurance schemes skimp on expensive services for the seriously ill while providing many inexpensive services for the marginally ill? Because those inexpensive services create benefits for millions of people (read: millions of voters), while acute, intensive care services concentrate large sums on a handful of patients (read: small number of voters). Democratic political pressures in this case dictate the redistribution of resources from the few to the many.

Why are sensitive rationing decisions and other issues of hospital management left to the hospital bureaucracies? Because the alternative is politically impossible. As a practical matter, no government can afford to make it a national policy that 9,000 people will die every year because they will be denied treatment for chronic kidney failure. Nor can any government announce that some people must wait for surgery so that elderly patients can use hospitals as surrogate nursing homes or that elderly patients must be moved so that surgery can proceed.

These decisions are so emotionally loaded that elected officials cannot afford the responsibility of making them. Decisions on who will receive care, who will not, and how that care will be delivered are left to the hospital bureaucracy because no other course is politically possible.

Myth No. 18: Public Opinion Polls Show That People in All Developed Countries, Including the United States, Prefer National Health Insurance

True enough, as far back as the presidency of Richard Nixon, polls showed up to 61 percent of the people favoring national health insurance.[145] And only 3 percent of Canadians and 12 percent of the British say they would be willing to trade their own system for the U.S. health care system.[146] But close analysis of the polls reveals that what most people prefer is a free lunch.

Polls in Britain show that most people there believe the cost to them of national health insurance is about 1/20th of what it actually is (see chapter 18). At 1/20th of its real costs, the British health care system may well look attractive to most people. Because health

[145]Jon Gabel, Howard Cohen, and Steven Fink, "Americans' Views on Health Care: Foolish Inconsistencies?" *Health Affairs* (Spring 1989), p. 111.

[146]Blendon and Taylor, p. 153.

care taxes are also disguised in Canada, Canadians probably are unaware of their individual contribution to national health insurance. Thus, most people in other countries think they get a lot more than they pay for. And given the international publicity about U.S. health care costs, it's not surprising that people prefer something for nothing to something better but more expensive.

When asked to compare benefits with costs, the people participating in polls are much more revealing in their answers. Roughly speaking, people prefer to see government spend more on health care, provided their own taxes are not increased to finance the spending. For example, by a margin of 71 to 26 percent, Americans agree that "health insurance should pay for any treatments that will save lives even if it costs one million dollars to save a life."[147] At a time when the United States was actually spending 8.2 percent of GNP on health care, most respondents thought the nation was spending 13 to 15 percent and identified 16 to 20 percent as the appropriate amount.[148] Although a majority favor covering the uninsured through employer mandates or expanded Medicare,[149] when asked about paying for expanded health insurance coverage, people were unwilling to pay higher income taxes and supported the proposal only if it were financed by "sin taxes" (for example, taxes on alcohol and tobacco) or taxes on employers.[150]

Thus, polling data give no indication that people are willing to pay 15 percent of their income to finance national health insurance. Nor do the polls indicate that Americans are willing to accept the negative aspects of national health insurance in other countries. For example, the U.S. public overwhelmingly disapproves of any cost-containment measure that translates into a lower quality of care; and by a margin of 81 to 18 percent, the public is unwilling to accept longer waits for doctor's appointments or elective surgery.[151]

Myth No. 19: Since National Health Insurance Is Very Popular in Other Countries, It Will Also Be Popular in the United States

The reason national health insurance "works" in other countries, and remains popular, is precisely because it does not function the

[147]Gabel, Cohen, and Fink.
[148]Ibid., p. 110.
[149]Ibid., pp. 109–10.
[150]Ibid., p. 112.
[151]Ibid., p. 114.

way its advocates believe it should. National health insurance works in other countries for three reasons. First, the wealthy, the powerful, and the sophisticated—those most skilled at articulating their complaints—find ways to maneuver to the front of the rationing lines. Second, those pushed to the end of the lines are generally unaware of the medical technologies they are being denied. Third, there are no contingency fees (or contingency arrangements are severely limited), no generally recognized right of due process with regard to health benefits, and no cadre of lawyers willing to represent those who are systematically discriminated against. National health insurance works in other countries because those who could change the system are the ones best served by it. If a member of the British Parliament, the chief executive officer of a large British company, or the head of a major British trade union had no greater opportunity to obtain renal dialysis than any other British citizen, the NHS would not survive for a week.

"Don't push me around" is a distinctively American phrase. In Europe, people have been pushed around for centuries. In the United States, we have widespread access to information about modern medical technology, a legal system that protects the rights of those without political power or money, and a strong devotion to due process. National health insurance, as it operates in other countries, simply would not survive in the U.S. cultural and legal system.

Myth No. 20: Adopting the Health Care Programs of Other Countries Requires Government Action

Lee Iacocca (chairman of the Chrysler Corporation), the United Auto Workers, and many others have looked longingly at the health care systems of other countries and called for a government solution to our health care problems. But do the workers at Chrysler really need government in order to adopt the health care programs of other countries? It is not at all clear that they do.

The primary way in which other developed countries control health care costs is through "global budgets." Hospitals, physicians, or area health authorities are told by government how much money they have to spend, and the rationing of funds is handled by the health care bureaucracy.[152] There is nothing mysterious about

---

[152]See the discussion in Jönsson, pp. 84–86.

this process, and there is no reason why Chrysler needs government in order to copy it. For example, Chrysler workers or any other large group could form their own HMO, called a national health insurance HMO (NHI HMO). The total amount of money given to NHI HMO each year could be 75 percent—or even 50 percent—of what Chrysler now spends on employee health care, and the NHI HMO managers could be instructed to ration care to Chrysler employees.

If Chrysler workers wanted to exert more direct control, they could elect the chief executive officer of the NHI HMO in annual balloting, and candidacy could be open to all health care bureaucrats or restricted to those possessing certain qualifications. The most obvious obstacle Chrysler would face would be U.S. tort law. If NHI HMO physicians rationed medical care the way the British do, there would be many potential malpractice suits. But if Chrysler workers owned their own HMO and if enough legal documents were signed, it is possible that even that obstacle could be overcome.

In short, Chrysler employees could realize all of the purported benefits of national health insurance through private action, provided that that is their sincere objective. On the other hand, if the rhetoric coming from Chrysler is merely a ruse to get taxpayers to pay Chrysler's annual health care bill, coercion by the federal government would be required.

Lessons

Our survey of national health insurance in countries around the world provides convincing evidence that government control of health care usually makes citizens worse off. When health care is made free at the point of consumption, rationing by waiting is inevitable. Government control of the health care system makes the rationing problem worse as governments attempt to limit access to modern medical technology. Under government management, both efficiency and quality of patient care steadily deteriorate.

The lesson from other countries is that the United States would not be well served by an expansion of government bureaucracy or by greater government control over the U.S. health care system. Instead, what is needed is to limit the role of government and allow the private sector to solve the nation's health care problems.

18. The Politics of Medicine

Public choice is the name of a relatively new discipline that attempts to integrate economics and political science.[1] Its chief goal is to explain political phenomena in terms of fundamental principles, in much the same way that economists explain purely economic phenomena. The name, however, is potentially misleading. The new discipline could just as accurately be called modern political science.

A fascinating discovery of this discipline is that economic principles, if carefully applied, explain much of what happens in politics. Consider the concept of competition. Just as producers of goods and services compete for consumer dollars, so politicians in a democracy compete for votes. Moreover, the process of competition leads to certain well-defined results. In the economic marketplace, competition inevitably forces producers to choose the most efficient method of production. Those who fail to do so either go out of business or mend their ways. The ultimate outcome—efficient production—is independent of any particular producer's wishes or desires.

In a similar way, political competition inexorably leads candidates to adopt a specific position called the winning platform. The idea of a winning platform is a fairly simple one. It is a set of political policies that can defeat any other set of policies in an election. A politician who wants to be elected or reelected has every incentive

---

[1]The two seminal works on public choice theory are Anthony Downs, *An Economic Theory of Democracy* (New York: Harper & Row, 1957); and James Buchanan and Gordon Tullock, *The Calculus of Consent* (Ann Arbor: University of Michigan Press, 1962). For a different approach to the theory, especially as it applies to government regulation, see George Stigler, *The Citizen and the State: Essays on Regulation* (Chicago: University of Chicago Press, 1975). See also John C. Goodman and Philip K. Porter, "Theory of Competitive Regulatory Equilibrium," *Public Choice* 59 (1988): 51–66; and Gary S. Becker, "A Theory of Competition among Pressure Groups for Political Influence," *Quarterly Journal of Economics* 98, no. 3 (August 1983): 371–400.

to endorse the winning platform. If he does not, he becomes vulnerable; for if his opponent adopts the winning platform, the opponent will win.

In the real world, of course, things are rarely so simple. Voters are influenced by many factors other than substantive political issues—a candidate's religion, general appearance, speaking ability, or party affiliation. Even when voters are influenced by real political issues, politicians don't always know what the winning platform is. Often they must guess at it. Nonetheless, public choice theory holds that, other things being equal, a candidate always improves his chances of winning by endorsing the winning platform. Hence, all candidates have an incentive to identify and endorse this platform. Candidates who do not do so are unlikely to survive the political competition.

This line of reasoning leads to a remarkable conclusion: In democratic systems with two major political parties, both parties tend to adopt the same policies. They do so not because the party leaders think alike or share the same ideological preferences, but because each party's top priority is to win elections and hold office.

Two corollaries follow from this conclusion. The first is that it is absurd to complain about the fact that "major candidates all sound alike," or that "it doesn't seem to make any difference who wins." The complaints are merely evidence that political competition is working precisely as the theory predicts it will work. Indeed, the more accurate the information political candidates receive through better polling techniques and computerization, the more similar they will become. The theory predicts that, in a world of perfect information, the policies of the two major parties would be identical. The second corollary is more relevant for our purposes. In its extreme form, the corollary asserts that "politicians don't matter." Over the long haul, if we want to explain why we have the political policies we have, it is futile to investigate the motives, personalities, and characters of those who hold office. Instead, we must focus on the factors that determine the nature of the winning platform.

This second corollary is critical to an understanding of national health insurance. A great many British health economists who support socialized medicine are quick to concede that the British National Health Service (NHS) has defects. But the defects, in their view, are not those of socialism; they merely represent a failure of political will, or the fact that the wrong politicians were in office. The ultimate goal, they hold, is to retain the system of socialized medicine and make it work better.

By contrast, we argue that the defects of the policies that govern national health insurance programs are the natural and inevitable consequences of placing the market for health under the control of politicians. It is not true that British health care policy just happens to be as it is. Enoch Powell, a former minister of health who once ran the NHS, seems to have appreciated this fact. Powell wrote that "whatever is entrusted to politicians becomes political even if it is not political anyhow"[2] and he went on to say that

> the phenomena of Medicine and Politics . . . result automatically and necessarily from the nationalization of medical care and its provision gratis at the point of consumption. . . . These phenomena are implicit in such an organization and are not the accidental or incidental results of blemishes which can be "reformed" away while leaving the system as such intact.[3]

Explaining the British National Health Service

An extensive analysis of the British health care system shows that all of the major features of national health insurance can be explained in terms of public choice theory.[4] That is, far from being the consequence of the preferences of politicians (who could be replaced by different politicians with different preferences in the next election), the major features of national health insurance follow inevitably from the fact that politicians have the authority to allocate health care resources and from that fact alone. The following is a brief summary.

The Total Amount of Spending on Health Services

One argument used to justify national health insurance is that, left to their own devices, individuals will not spend as much as they ought to spend on health care. That was a major reason many

---

[2]Enoch Powell, *Medicine and Politics, 1975 and After* (New York: Pitman, 1976), p. 5.
[3]Ibid., p. 67.
[4]John C. Goodman, *National Health Care in Great Britain: Lessons for the USA* (Dallas: Fisher Institute, 1980), ch. 10.

middle-class and upper middle-class British citizens supported national health insurance for the working class. It was also a major reason why they supported formation of the NHS in 1948.[5] Many expected that, under socialized medical care, more total dollars would be spent on health care than would otherwise have been the case. In fact, it is not clear that socialized medicine in Britain has increased overall spending on health care. It may have even led to the opposite result. That is the contention of Dennis Lees, a professor of economics at the University of Nottingham, who wrote that "the British people, left free to do so, would almost certainly have chosen to spend more on health services themselves than governments have chosen to spend on their behalf."[6] The same may be true in other countries with national health insurance programs.

To see why this is so, let us first imagine a situation in which a politician is trying to win over a single voter. To keep the example simple, assume that the politician has access to $10 to spend on the voter's behalf. To maximize his chance of winning, the politician should spend the $10 precisely as the voter wants it spent. If the voter's choice is to spend $5 on medical care, $3 on a retirement pension, and $2 on a rent subsidy, that should also be the choice of the vote-maximizing politician. If the politician does not choose to spend the $10 in that way, he risks losing this particular voter to a clever opponent. Now, it may seem that if the voter wants $5 spent on medical care, it is appropriate to conclude that he would have spent the $5 on medical care himself if he were spending $10 of his own money. But that is not quite true. State-provided medical care has one feature that is generally missing from private medical markets and from other government spending programs as well— nonprice rationing. Nonprice rationing imposes heavy costs on patients (the cost of waiting and other inconveniences), leads to deterioration in the quality of services rendered, and creates various forms of waste and inefficiency. Thus, other things being equal, $5 of spending on government health care will be less valuable to the average voter than $5 of spending in a private medical marketplace.

[5]Dennis Lees, "An Economist Considers Other Alternatives," in Helmut Schoeck, ed., *Financing Medical Care: An Appraisal of Foreign Programs* (Caldwell, ID: Caxton Printers, 1963), p. 80.

[6]Dennis Lees, "Economics and Non-economics of Health Services," *Three Banks Review* 110 (June 1976): 9.

It also means that, under socialized medicine, spending for health care will be less attractive to voters relative to spending programs that do not involve nonprice rationing.

Public choice theory, then, predicts that the average voter will desire less spending on health care, relative to other goods and services, when health care is rationed by nonmarket devices. Moreover, the greater the rationing problems, the less attractive health care spending will be. So one would expect even less spending on health care under a completely free service like the NHS than under a health service that charges patients more user fees.

In the real world, politicians rarely have the opportunity to tailor their spending purely to the desires of a specific voter. Generally, they must allocate spending among programs that affect thousands of voters at the same time. New spending for a hospital, for example, provides benefits for everyone in the surrounding community. No matter what level of spending is chosen, some voters will prefer more, and others less. Often, in such cases, the vote-maximizing level of spending will be the level of spending preferred by the average voter.

Inequalities in Health Care

Decisions on where to spend health dollars are also inherently political. A major argument in favor of national health insurance is that private medical care allows geographical inequalities to occur in levels of provision. Yet, those inequalities continue under socialized medicine, and many argue that the levels of provision in regions of Britain, Canada, and New Zealand are just as unequal today as they would have been in the absence of national health insurance.

In theory, creating regional equality is a relatively simple task. All governments have to do is spend more in regions that are relatively deprived and less in regions that are relatively well endowed. But most governments have not done this. Why? Public choice theory supplies a possible answer. Policymakers must make two choices about spending in a particular region. First, they must decide how many total dollars are to be spent there. Second, they must decide how to allocate those dollars. In a democracy, there is no particular reason why per capita spending will be the same in all regions. For example, per capita spending may differ across voting districts for numerous reasons. Voter turnout may be higher in some districts than in others, which suggests that those districts are willing to pay more (in terms of votes) for political largesse. Voters in some districts may be more aware of, and more sensitive to, changes in per capita spending than voters in other districts.

Given that a certain amount of money is going to be spent in a certain area or region, competition for votes dictates that the money be allocated in accordance with the preference of the voters in that area or region. To return to the hypothetical example of a politician trying to win over a voter, suppose that $10 is going to be spent in a certain city. If a majority of residents want $2 spent on health services and $8 spent on other programs, political competition will tend to produce that result. Yet, if the residents of some other city want $8 spent on health services and $2 spent on other programs, political competition will also tend to produce that result.

Prior to the establishment of national health insurance in most developed countries, geographical inequalities reflected community preferences. In general, the citizens of wealthier and more densely populated regions chose to spend a larger fraction of their income on medical care. There is no reason to suppose that their preferences were radically altered by national health insurance, and thus there is no reason to suppose that, in allocating public spending, vote-maximizing politicians are doing anything other than responding to voter preferences.

Spending Priorities: Caring versus Curing

The NHS emphasizes caring rather than curing (see chapter 17), and it is that feature of the NHS that marks a radical difference between British and American health care. There can be no doubt that the British choice is a result of conscious political decisions. American economist Mary-Ann Rozbicki once asked some British health planners the following question: "If you suddenly enjoyed a sharp increase in available resources, how would you allocate it?" The response was invariably the same. They would put the additional resources into services for the aged, the chronically ill, and the mentally handicapped.[7] Commenting on this response, Rozbicki wrote:

[7]Mary-Ann Rozbicki, *Rationing British Health Care: The Cost/Benefit Approach*, Executive Seminar in National and International Affairs, U.S. Department of State, April, 1978, p. 17.

It is difficult for an American observer to comprehend that view. He has been impressed by the support services already afforded the non-acute patient (and the well consumer)—the doctor, nurse, and social worker attendance at homes, clinics and hospitals for the purpose of improving the comfort and well-being of the recipients involved. He has also been impressed (and sometimes shocked) by the relative lack of capability to diagnose, cure, and/or treat life-threatening conditions. The U.S. patient, while having foregone the home ministrations of the family doctor and learned to endure the antiseptic quality of the hospital, also confidently expects immediate delivery of all that medical science has to offer if life or health is under immediate threat.[8]

What political pressures lead decisionmakers to prefer caring over curing? Rozbicki believes it is a matter of numbers—numbers of votes. Money spent on caring is spread out over far more people than money spent on curing. Rozbicki wrote:

In weighing the choice between a more comfortable life for the millions of aged or early detection and treatment of the far fewer victims of dread diseases, [the British health authorities] have favored the former. In choosing between a fully equipped hospital therapy and rehabilitation center or nuclear medicine technology, they have favored the former. *The sheer numbers involved on each side of the equation would tend to dictate these choices by government officials in a democratic society.*[9]

Although Rozbicki's explanation may be correct, it cannot be complete. It is true that the number of potential beneficiaries of home visiting far exceeds those of radiation therapy. But all Britons are potentially ill, so all have an interest in the spending priorities of the NHS. A complete explanation of these priorities requires an explanation of why the average citizen would approve of them.

Like the citizens of other countries, most Britons know little about medical technology. Their ignorance, moreover, is quite rational. Information is costly. Rational people have an incentive to expand their knowledge about any subject only up to the point where the

[8]Ibid.
[9]Ibid., p. 18. Emphasis added.

cost of an additional bit of information is equal to its benefit. That is the economic explanation for the commonly observed fact that the average person does not become an expert in medical science. The average Briton, however, has much less incentive to become knowledgeable about medicine than the average American does. Precisely because the medical market in the United States is largely private, a better informed person becomes a better consumer. But within the confines of the NHS, medical services are not purchased. Suppose a British citizen invests time and money to learn more about medical matters and discovers that the NHS is not offering the kinds of services it should. That knowledge is of almost no value unless the citizen can inform millions of other voters, persuade them to "throw the rascals out of office," and achieve a change of policy. Such a campaign would be enormously expensive, undoubtedly costing the citizen far more than could be recovered from any potential personal benefit.

Socialized medicine affects the level of knowledge that patients have in yet another way. In a free market for medical care, suppliers of medical services have an incentive to inform potential customers about new developments in medicine. Such information increases the demand for new services and thereby promises to enhance the income of those who supply them. Under the NHS, however, the suppliers of medical care have no such incentives. Physicians, nurses, and hospital administrators increase their income chiefly by persuading the government to pay them more. They increase their comfort, leisure time, and other forms of satisfaction by encouraging patients to demand not more but less.

Economic theory, then, would predict that in a socialized medical scheme, people will acquire less knowledge about medical care than they would have acquired in a private system. The evidence confirms this prediction. Numerous commentators have observed that British patients know far less about medical care than American patients. Rozbicki, for example, noted that "the British populace appears much less sophisticated in its medical demands than the American populace."[10]

The general ignorance about medical science that prevails among British voters has a profound impact on NHS policies. Other things

[10]Ibid., p. 17.

being equal, people will always place a higher value on those services with which they are more familiar and on benefits about which they are certain. The known is preferred to the unknown and certainty to uncertainty. The average British voter is familiar with, and fairly certain about, the personal value of the nonacute services provided by the NHS. But that voter is probably unfamiliar with, and uncertain about, the personal value of advanced services for acute ailments. Thus the voter will tend to approve of NHS spending priorities.

Another reason why voters will tend to prefer caring to curing services stems from a characteristic of nonprice rationing. All of the services of the NHS require rationing. But in some sectors, the rationing problems are far greater than in others because quality can sometimes be sacrificed for quantity. Unlike American physicians, British general practitioners (GPs) have greatly reduced the time spent with each patient and the quality of service rendered. Nonetheless, this type of adjustment allows the typical patient to actually visit his GP within two or three days of making an appointment. The quality of treatment may have deteriorated, but patients are at least certain that they will receive some treatment. Presumably, given the overall rationing problem, patients prefer this type of adjustment. Such adjustments cannot be made with most acute services. It is not as easy to sacrifice quality for quantity in, for example, CAT scans, organ transplants, and renal dialysis. Patients tend to receive full treatment or no treatment, and very few patient-pleasing adjustments can be made.

These characteristics of health care rationing have an important effect on the preferences of potential patients, even of those who are knowledgeable about medicine. The existence of nonprice rationing tends to make all health care services less valuable than those services would be in the free market. But because nonacute services can be adjusted to increase the certainty of some treatment whereas acute services generally cannot, the former tend to become more valuable relative to the latter. Thus, to a certain extent, the priority given to nonacute treatment is perfectly rational.

Spending Priorities: Current Expenditure versus Capital Expenditure

Closely related to the distinction between caring and curing in Britain is the distinction between current and capital expenditures.

559

Despite the fact that the NHS inherited a deteriorating capital stock, only one new hospital was built in the first 15 years of NHS operation. Today, more than 50 percent of the hospital beds are in 19th-century buildings. Moreover, despite one million people on the hospital waiting lists, there are fewer hospital beds today than there were when the NHS was founded in 1948.

Capital expenditure creates a flow of long-term benefits whereas current expenditure, by definition, creates short-term benefits. The distinction between the two types of expenditure is largely a distinction between benefits later and benefits now. Clearly, the political preference of the British is for benefits now. Can public choice theory help explain this preference? Indeed it can. To see how, it is necessary to first consider how decisions about capital spending are made in the free market.

Very few of us know how our consumption of, say, coffee varies over the seasons of the year. Most of us simply buy coffee when we want it and, except for the influence of general inflation or an occasional coffee tree blight in Brazil, we pay about the same price regardless of the season. The reason is that the suppliers of coffee are balancing our demand for coffee in the future against our demand for coffee right now. The free market furnishes suppliers with powerful incentives to give us precisely what we want —the ability to buy as much coffee as we like for roughly the same price at any time of the year.

The decision on the part of business firms to make capital investments is similar. Firms that make capital investments today are betting on a consumer demand for their products in the future. Once private decisionmaking is replaced by public decisionmaking, however, things are very different. In a democracy, voters are forced to decide how much capital spending there should be. And precisely because voters are rationally ignorant about such matters, these are decisions they are ill-prepared to make. Socialism in the coffee market, for example, might work something like this: Candidates competing in September might woo voters by promising lower and lower prices for coffee. Because the voters are uninformed about the future consequences of a low price of coffee today, they are naturally attracted to the candidate who promises the lowest price. For politicians to have good incentives, they must anticipate that they will be around in the spring, and that voters will make the connection between fall's policy and spring's disaster.

Yet, because voters are usually ignorant of the connection between capital spending and specific benefits, politicians cannot look forward to realizing the full costs or the full benefits of their decisions. Further, because a politician is not likely to be in office for very many years, long-term penalties and rewards are largely irrelevant. Finally, because politicians have no property rights in their decisions, the worst that can happen is that they fail to be reelected. And that may be an acceptable price to pay for the opportunity to hold office today.

John and Sylvia Jewkes, two British economists who were longtime students of the NHS, argued on numerous occasions that NHS's lack of capital spending was solely the result of the political pressures just described. Successive chancellors of the exchequer, according to the Jewkeses, skimped on "those items where the consequences in the short period would be least noticeable and least likely to arouse protest.[11] They went on to write:

> Governments followed the line of least resistance. They laid emphasis on those medical items which constituted pressing day-to-day demand, yielded their results quickly and with some certainty, made something of a public splash and conformed with the doctrine of equality. Conversely, they tended to neglect those items where spending would bring only slowly maturing results, where economy would not be quickly noticed and therefore would be less likely to arouse public opposition. . . .
>
> These were the conditions under which preventive medicine, new hospitals and medical schools, occupational health services and medical research were likely to give way to a free supply of drugs, of doctors' services and of hospital care. However anxious a government might be to take a longer view, its resolve was likely to be weakened by the pressure of immediate demands; and by the hope that easier times were coming; that perhaps next year defense expenditures would be smaller, or investment needed for other purposes would be less, or the national income would rise sharply.[12]

[11]John and Sylvia Jewkes, *Value for Money in Medicine* (Oxford: Basil Blackwell, 1963), p. 55.

[12]Ibid., pp. 59–60.

Administrative Controls

One of the most remarkable features of national health insurance is the enormous amount of decisionmaking power left in the hands of physicians. By and large, the medical communities in Britain, Canada, and New Zealand have escaped the disciplines of both the free market and government regulation. In the view of Michael Cooper,[13] Anthony Culyer,[14] and many others, this discretion is the principal reason for many of the gross inefficiencies found in Britain's NHS.

In addition to GPs and consultants, other producer interest groups also have obtained power and influence. Within the NHS, they include hospital administrators, junior doctors, and nonmedical hospital staff. The complaint made again and again is that the NHS is primarily organized and administered to benefit such special-interest groups rather than patients. As Dennis Lees observed:

> The British health industry exists for its own sake, in the interest of the producer groups that make it up. The welfare of patients is a random by-product, depending on how conflicts between the groups and between them and government happen to shake down at any particular time.[15]

Government production of goods and services always tends to be less efficient than private production. Nonetheless, the NHS could be run more efficiently than it actually is. Its administrators could adopt well-defined goals and assert more control over the various sectors to ensure that the goals are pursued. They could create incentives for NHS employees to provide better, more efficient patient care.

That these things are not done is hardly surprising. Over 200 years ago, Adam Smith observed that government regulation in the marketplace inevitably seemed to benefit producer interest groups at the expense of consumers. Things have changed very little with the passage of time. Economic studies of virtually every major regulatory commission in the United States have come to the same conclusion: The welfare of producers is regularly favored over the

[13]Michael Cooper, *Rationing Health Care* (London: Croom Helm, 1975), p. 73.

[14]Anthony Culyer, "Health: The Social Cost of Doctors' Discretion," *New Society*, February 27, 1975.

[15]Lees, "Economics and Non-economics of Health Services," p. 12.

welfare of consumers.[16] Why should we expect the NHS to be different?

Are these phenomena consistent with public choice theory? At first glance it may seem that they are not. Given that consumers outnumber producers, it might seem that, with democratic voting, consumers would always have the upper hand. If sheer voting power were the only power, that might be so. But two additional factors put consumers at a disadvantage: costs of information and costs of political organization.

To achieve any fundamental change of policy, voters must be informed about what kinds of changes they specifically seek. They must also be organized, at least to the extent that they can communicate to politicians their willingness to withhold electoral support unless their desires are satisfied. But information is costly. Organizing a political coalition is also costly. And the incentives for any single individual to bear those costs are extremely weak.

Producers are in a different position. Because they are working in the industry, they already possess a great deal of information about which policies are consistent with their self-interest and which are not. Their costs of political organizing also are much lower because they are relatively few in number and share common interests. In addition, because each producer's personal stake in regulatory issues is far greater than that of a representative consumer, each producer has a much greater personal incentive to contribute to political efforts that protect the interests of producers as a group.

Producer interest groups, then, ordinarily have enormous advantages over consumer groups in issues involving government regulation of their industry. The advantages appear to be more than sufficient to overcome their relative vulnerability in terms of sheer voting power. This insight was provided by Professor Milton Friedman 30 years ago:

> Each of us is a producer and also a consumer. However, we are much more specialized and devote a much larger fraction of our attention to our activity as a producer than as a consumer. We consume literally thousands if not millions of items. The result is that people in the same trade, like

[16]A representative sample of such studies is contained in Paul W. MacAvoy, ed., *Crisis of the Regulatory Commissions* (New York: Norton, 1970).

barbers or physicians, all have an intense interest in the specific problems of this trade and are willing to devote considerable energy to doing something about them. On the other hand, those of us who use barbers at all get barbered infrequently and spend only a minor fraction of our income in barber shops. Our interest is casual. Hardly any of us are willing to devote much time going to the legislature in order to testify against the inequity of restricting the practice of barbering. The same point holds for tariffs. The groups that think they have a special interest in particular tariffs are concentrated groups to whom the issue makes a great deal of difference. The public interest is widely dispersed. In consequence, in the absence of any general arrangements to offset the pressure of special interests, producer groups will invariably have a much stronger influence on legislative action and the powers that be than will the diverse, widely spread consumer interest.[17]

Public choice theory, then, predicts that administrative inefficiencies caused by producer interest groups within health care bureaucracies will be a permanent feature of socialized medicine. There is no reason to believe that this defect can be reformed away.

Why the NHS Continues to Exist

In 1978, an article appeared in *Medical Economics* with the heading, "If Britain's Health Care Is So Bad, Why Do Patients Like It?"[18] That British patients do like the NHS has been confirmed repeatedly by public opinion polls. The same can be said of Canadians about their health care system. The most recent surveys show that only 3 percent of Canadians and 12 percent of the Britons would trade the U.S. system for their own.[19] Why are British patients so satisfied with the NHS? There appear to be two major reasons: (1) the typical British patient has far lower expectations and much less knowledge about medicine than the typical American patient; and (2) most British patients apparently believe that they are getting something for nothing.

[17]Milton Friedman, *Capitalism and Freedom* (Chicago: University of Chicago Press, 1962), p. 143.

[18]John J. Fisher, "If Britain's Health Care Is So Bad, Why Do Patients Like It?" *Medical Economics* (August 21, 1978).

[19]See Robert J. Blendon and Humphrey Taylor, "Views on Health Care: Public Opinion in Three Nations," *Health Affairs* (Spring 1989), pp. 149–57.

Comparing British and American patients, one doctor wrote that British patients "have fewer expectations" and are "more ready to cooperate unhesitatingly with the authoritarian figure of the doctor or nurse."[20] An American economist noted with surprise that British hospital patients, "far from complaining about specialists' inattention, a lack of laboratory tests or the ineffectiveness of medical treatment, more often than not display an attitude of gratefulness for whatever is done."[21] Another doctor summarized the difference in British and American attitudes this way:

> The British people—whether as a result of different life philosophy or generally lower level of affluence—have a much lower level of expectation from medical intervention in general. In fact they verge on the stoical as compared with the American patient, and, of course, this fact makes them, purely from a physician's point of view, the most pleasant patients. The resulting service has evolved over the years into a service that would in my opinion be all but totally unacceptable to any American not depending on welfare for medical services.[22]

The expectations and the level of knowledge of British patients, however, are only part of the explanation for the popularity of the NHS. More basic is the fact that most British patients grossly underestimate the taxes they pay to finance the NHS. Public opinion polls have found that 60 percent of the British people believe that the entire cost of the NHS is met, not from general taxes, but from the weekly payroll tax (called the insurance stamp).[23] In fact, in 1972, when the opinion polls were taken, the payroll tax represented only 8.5 percent of the total cost of the NHS. Moreover, the worker's nominal share of the weekly payroll tax is only two-thirds, with the remainder being nominally paid by employers. Although most economists believe that the employers' share of the payroll tax ultimately comes out of wages that would have been paid to

[20]Derek Robinson, "Primary Medical Practice in the United Kingdom and the United States," *New England Journal of Medicine* 297, no. 4 (July 28, 1977): 189.

[21]Rozbicki, p. 18.

[22]Quoted in Harry Swartz, "The Infirmity of British Medicine," in R. Emmett Tyrrell, Jr., ed., *The Future That Doesn't Work: Social Democracy's Failures in Britain* (New York: Doubleday, 1977), p. 31.

[23]Cooper, p. 87.

workers, very few workers believe that. A loose way of interpreting these results is as follows: Most people in Britain believe that the total tax they pay to finance the NHS is about 1/20th of what it actually is. Given this perception, no wonder the British public looks upon the NHS as a good bargain.

Just how this perception affects British attitudes toward what most Americans would regard as intolerable defects in the health service was vividly illustrated by the experience of Rep. Bob Bauman on a trip to England in 1975. Traveling with a group of congressmen to examine the NHS firsthand, Bauman met a young woman with substantial facial scars received in an accident. Although the woman wanted plastic surgery for her face, she related, "I've been waiting eight years for treatment, but they tell me I'm going to be able to have surgery within a year." Yet, when Bauman asked her what she thought of the NHS, her reply was, "Oh, it's a wonderful system we have in Britain. You know, our medical care is all free."[24]

It might seem that an enterprising politician or political party could win a British election by offering the British public a better deal. Why not tell voters what the NHS really costs them, and then offer to return their tax dollars so they could purchase private health insurance and health services?

The average British voter would undoubtedly be better off as a result, but that doesn't mean that most would approve of the plan. For one thing, even if voters knew what the NHS really costs, they might not be convinced that the private marketplace could offer a better deal. For years, British politicians have told voters that the NHS is the envy of the world, and the public has been deluged with stories in the socialist press indicating that only the rich get good medical care in the United States.[25] For another thing, defenders of the NHS—including trade unions, thousands of NHS employees, and many British physicians—would play on existing fears and suspicions. Surprising as it may seem, the sagging morale and continual frustrations of NHS doctors have not produced enormous numbers of converts to free-enterprise medicine. Perhaps many prefer the protection of a government bureaucracy to the

[24]Quoted by Lew Rockwell in *World Research Inc.*, March 1979, p. 5.
[25]Ibid., p. 6.

rigors of free-market competition. Whatever the reason, most of Britain's medical profession supports the idea of socialized medicine.[26] They not only support it but they also resisted Margaret Thatcher's proposals to open it to minimal competition.

In almost every country with national health insurance, disinterested, knowledgeable observers agree on the need for substantial reform. For example, Claude Castonguay, considered the father of national health insurance in Quebec, now recommends the establishment of private health care centers to compete with public ones and a voucher system to encourage competition among suppliers.[27] Even Sweden is searching for ways to introduce the discipline of the competitive marketplace into its public system.

There have been successful attempts to privatize public health care programs (for example, in Singapore and Chile), and among less-developed countries there will probably be more (for example, in Colombia and Venezuela) (see chapter 20). But in developed countries, all serious attempts at fundamental reform have been blocked by the politics of medicine. Any public-sector retreat on health care is more likely to come about as people seek private-sector alternatives rather than through changes at the ballot box.

The Politics of Medicine in the United States

The U.S. health care system differs from the systems of other developed countries in two important respects. First, government spending on health care is largely confined to the poor and elderly. The vast majority of the middle-class working population participates in the private health care marketplace, although they shoulder the increasing tax burden of medical expenses for the poor and elderly. Second, through both public and private health insurance, the U.S. system has been a cost-plus system for almost half a century and, until recently, there has not been any significant health care rationing. If anything, Americans have experienced the reverse phenomenon; hospitals and doctors have felt free to utilize virtually every new technique offered by medical science, secure in the knowledge that someone would always pay the bill.

[26]John Walsh, "Britain's National Health Service: The Doctors' Dilemmas," *Science* 201 (July 28, 1979): 329.

[27]Edward Neuschler, *Canadian Health Care: The Implications of Public Health Insurance* (Washington: Health Insurance Association of America, 1989), p. 52.

However, now that the U.S. system has evolved into a cost-plus system in its cost-control stage, with government more involved in paying for medical care, political pressures in the United States are leading to the same kinds of decisions that have been made in many European countries. Evidence of that can be seen in virtually every government-funded health care program.

Health Care Rationing under Medicare

Under Medicare, the federal government now pays hospitals a fixed sum for each of 492 categories of illness called diagnosis-related groups (DRGs). As a result, the federal government is attempting to set prices and monitor quality for 28 million potential patients and as many as 5,000 hospitals. It is an impossible mission. No matter what reimbursement rules are adopted, the medical marketplace is so complex that health care providers will find literally thousands of ways to exploit the rules for financial gain. Moreover, there is an inevitable conflict between price and quality of care. In the early years of the Medicare program, quality took precedence. Under the new reimbursement rules, the reverse is beginning to occur.

The federal government is resisting cost pressures by making DRG reimbursement rates increasingly stingy. Yet this attempt to control costs is adversely affecting patient care. As the DRG system is now structured, it can be used (and to some extent is being used) as a health care rationing device—an eventuality that some have argued is inevitable. The following is a brief account of some of the ways in which Medicare is taking on characteristics of national health insurance.

Bias against Modern Medical Technology

One way that Medicare can avoid paying for expensive technology is by refusing to pay hospitals enough money to buy the technology in the first place. That is, Medicare's hospital reimbursement rate for a particular procedure may be high enough to reimburse the hospital for one level of care but too low to cover a higher level. In other cases (under Medicare Part B), Medicare specifically refuses to pay for a higher quality treatment. For example, Medicare reimbursement rates have denied elderly patients with hearing loss access to cochlear implants and may be endangering the lives of kidney dialysis patients (see chapter 10).

Another way in which Medicare encourages health care rationing is by refusing to pay at all. For example, despite the fact that Medicare theoretically pays for heart and liver transplants, it often will not pay for lifesaving drugs for the thousands of elderly people who die of cancer each year. In general, Medicare will not pay for physician-injected drugs unless the purpose for which the drug is being used has been approved by the federal Food and Drug Administration (FDA). But a physician guided by the medical literature will discover that many effective uses of prescription drugs have not been approved.

Physicians who treat cancer patients, for example, will normally turn to one of three bibles of drug prescribing—the *American Medical Association Drug Evaluations,* the *Hospital Formulary Service Drug Information Book,* or the *United States Pharmacopoeia.* The consensus is that once a drug's effectiveness in treating a disease is listed in one of these publications, it is no longer experimental, but instead is accepted therapy.[28] Nevertheless, about 60 percent of all chemotherapy listed in these publications is currently for "off-label" indications; that is, for uses not yet approved by the FDA. Medicare insists that pharmaceutical companies go through the expensive and laborious process of having each use "added to the label" by the FDA before they will pay for it. Effectively, that means that patients with life-threatening illnesses are often denied treatments that might save their lives.[29] Many private insurers, including the national Blue Cross and Blue Shield Association, have adopted the same policy—under the protective umbrella of Medicare's respectability and authority. Thus, Medicare's policies are indirectly affecting the nonelderly as well.

The excuse given for these practices is that insurers are trying to protect patients from false hopes about unproven or experimental therapies, such as Laetril. But the real issue is money. As Lee E. Mortenson, executive director of the Association of Community Cancer Centers, has explained, patients are being denied access to improvements in cancer therapy by third-party payers "hiding

[28]See Elizabeth Rosenthal, "Rules on Approved Uses of Drugs Could Bar Help for Some Patients," *New York Times,* August 11, 1991.

[29]See "Oncology Forum," *COPE* (April/May 1989): 17 ff.

behind concerns for patient safety but in fact struggling to keep costs down."[30]

For example, injections of the drug 5-Fluorouracil (5-FU) is one way to treat colon cancer patients, at a cost of about $9 per week. This drug, however, is effective only about 11 percent of the time. By contrast, a weekly injection of 5-FU plus Leucovorin is effective in about 48 percent of cases, but at a weekly cost of $250.[31] Until 1989, Medicare refused to pay for the higher priced drug.[32] Similarly, interferon is FDA-approved for hairy cell leukemia (a very rare form of cancer), and Medicare will pay the $1,000 a month it costs. However, Medicare will not pay for the drug's use in treating five other types of cancer for which the medical literature shows it is often indicated.[33]

Moreover, things are likely to get worse. Despite the continued protests of doctors and cancer patients, the FDA commissioner, David Kessler, has announced his intention to "crack down" on drug companies, and perhaps physicians, who promote drugs for uses not on the FDA label. That's bad news for the 500,000 Americans who will die of cancer this year.

Medicare also refuses to pay for certain higher quality medical devices. For example, Medicare refuses to pay for dual-chamber pacemakers, insisting instead that single-chamber pacemakers be used in the first implant. Medicare will pay for the higher quality pacemaker only if the lower quality device doesn't work. Medicare also refuses to pay for (pacemaker) defibrillators, which also are of higher quality and more expensive.

Bias in Favor of Caring over Curing

When politicians allocate health care resources, they face strong pressures to spend money on simple services for the many, rather

[30]Quoted in the *Wall Street Journal*, May 12, 1989.

[31]Nicholas Petrulli et al., "A Prospective Randomized Trial of 5-Fluorouracil versus 5-Fluorouracil and High-Dose Leucovorin versus 5-Fluorouracil and Methotrexate in Previously Untreated Patients with Advanced Colorectal Carcinoma," *Journal of Clinical Oncology* 5, no. 10 (October 1987): 1559–65.

[32]For California doctors, Medicare denied reimbursement until January 19, 1989—about three years after the treatment was known to be effective.

[33]For a review of the literature on the effectiveness of interferon in treating various types of cancer, see Jeffrey W. Clark and Dan L. Longo, "Interferons in Cancer Therapy," *Updates* to Vincent T. DeVita, Jr., Samuel Hellman, and Stephen A. Rosenberg, *Principles and Practice of Oncology* 1, no. 4 (April 1987).

than on expensive services for the few. Despite the fact that Medicare has had access to huge sums (growing from annual expenditures of $3.2 billion in 1967 to $128 billion in 1992), those political pressures have affected Medicare since its inception. Medicare has always paid a great many small medical bills while leaving the elderly exposed for large ones, and Congress has forced private Medigap insurers to follow similar practices (see chapter 15). The same pressures emerged in the battle over catastrophic care for the elderly. Congress was unable to approve any version of catastrophic coverage that did not also include more coverage for the small bills that most Medicare enrollees incur.

Moreover, the Medicare reforms of the 1980s left intact the practice of paying for physician visits for any and all complaints, and the most likely victims of the DRG system will be the sickest patients with the most complicated medical problems.

Political pressures have also affected Medicare in the area of preventive medicine. When the British NHS was founded, a common argument for socialized medicine centered around the value of prevention. If medical care were free at the point of consumption, it was argued, people would have an incentive to seek preventive care; thus, in many cases, diseases would be caught in their early stages, and that would save lives and maybe money as well. British patients do see physicians often. But because of the politics of medicine, access to preventive medical services is much lower in Britain than in the United States.[34]

Because of similar political pressures in the United States, Medicare patients can see physicians for almost any reason. But diagnostic tests are more rigorously controlled. To receive a mammogram, chest x-ray, Pap smear, or cholesterol test, a Medicare patient must have a very specific symptom. Of course, if the patient does display a symptom, it may be too late.

Bias against Rural Communities

One way in which inequalities in access to health care are perpetuated under national health insurance is through the bias against rural areas (see chapter 17). When the government's health care budget gets tight, rural communities are among the first to suffer.

---

[34]Goodman, *National Health Care in Great Britain: Lessons for the USA*, pp. 89–92.

The same is occurring under Medicare. In general, Medicare reimbursement to rural hospitals is 33 percent less than the reimbursement to urban hospitals for similar services.[35] This policy, adopted during the 1980s, is having a major impact—for example, in Texas, which has led the nation in hospital closings in recent years. Between 1984 and 1989, 66 rural hospitals serving three million people in Texas were closed. The care given in those hospitals was primarily to elderly, Medicare patients.[36]

The closing of rural hospitals is occurring because of a relationship between bureaucracies, not because of normal market forces. If the market will not support a rural hospital and the rural community does not want to subsidize one, there is nothing wrong with closing the hospital. But rural Medicare patients are effectively given less money to spend on health care, even though they (and the other members of the communities) pay the same tax rates as everyone else. Moreover, elderly patients are forbidden to add their own money to Medicare money. If patients controlled Medicare's funds and if the market were allowed to work, many rural hospitals now closed might have remained open.

Delegating Rationing Decisions to Providers

National governments usually go to great lengths to avoid being accused of denying lifesaving medical care to patients. The most common practice is to limit resources and leave the rationing decisions (along with the blame) to hospital administrators and physicians. Under Medicare, the DRG program adopts the European strategy. That is, under Medicare Part A, rationing decisions are forced on hospitals by limiting the amount of money Medicare pays, not by telling hospitals how to treat patients.

By contrast, under Medicare Part B, the Medicare bureaucracy tells physicians what drugs they can inject and how much time they can spend with patients. In this case, specific rationing decisions (choices about the level of care) are made in Washington. Given the politics of medicine, it should come as no surprise that there is

[35]U.S. Congress, Office of Technology Assessment, *Health Care in Rural America*, OTA-H-434 (Washington: U.S. Government Printing Office, September 1990), Table 5-22 (p. 193).

[36]Texas Bureau of State Data and Policy Analysis, *Special Task Force on Rural Health Care Delivery*, a report to the 71st Texas legislature (Austin, February 1989).

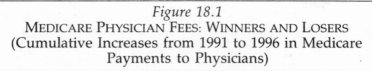

Figure 18.1
MEDICARE PHYSICIAN FEES: WINNERS AND LOSERS
(Cumulative Increases from 1991 to 1996 in Medicare
Payments to Physicians)

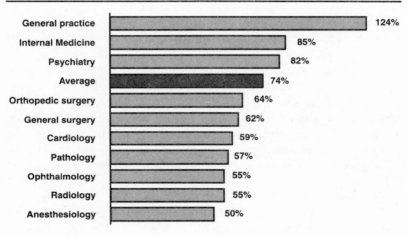

SOURCE: U.S. Department of Health and Human Services; reprinted in the *New York Times*, November 16, 1991.

considerable pressure to extend the DRG method of payment to Medicare Part B, thus fixing a total price for all services. Were this proposal adopted, Medicare could enforce all rationing decisions simply by controlling the purse strings.

Extending Price Controls to Physicians

A step in the direction of a general DRG system is a new formula for setting physician fees, adopted by the Bush administration in the fall of 1991.[37] Under the system, the physician's fee for a particular service will be determined by the following formula:

$$\text{Physician's fee} = (\text{RVUw}_s \times \text{GPCIw}_a) + (\text{RVUpe}_s \times \text{GPCIpe}_a) + (\text{RVUm}_s \times \text{GPCIm}_a) \times \text{CF}$$

We won't bother to define the variables because that would shed very little light on the bottom line, which is depicted in Figure 18.1.

[37]See Robert E. Moffit, *Comparable Worth for Doctors: A Severe Case of Government Malpractice*, Heritage Foundation Backgrounder no. 855 (September 23, 1991).

As the figure shows, the formula is designed to shift money away from physicians who perform surgical specialties to those who engage in family practice.[38] Although it may be true that GPs and internists were underpaid under the old system, the new fee schedule is consistent with political pressure to favor caring over curing. It will discourage medical students from becoming surgeons, it will discourage surgery, and it may discourage a wide range of other services. That is not mere speculation; the federal government's U.S. Physician Payment Review Commission came to the same conclusion in criticizing the proposed fee schedule when it was published in the summer of 1991.[39] The logical next step is to force physicians to accept the Medicare fee as "payment in full," which almost half of all physicians already do. Once that is done, the federal government will be able to control physician behavior in the same way it is increasingly determining the behavior of hospitals.

Health Care Rationing under Medicaid

The politics of medicine also influences public policy on health care for the poor, including patients on Medicaid. Not too long ago, a person on Medicaid had a free ticket to all that the American health care system had to offer. Today, that is less and less true.

The 33 million elderly and disabled people who participate in the Medicare program are competing for resources against beneficiaries of every other government program. Those others include the 27 million low-income families, including 13 million children that participate in Medicaid. In general, the elderly have been far more successful as a political force.

Implicit Rationing

In principle, people on Medicaid still are entitled to virtually any services. In practice, care to Medicaid patients is rationed by the terms under which Medicaid reimburses medical providers. Medicaid patients do not control the medical dollars that are spent. Nor can they add to Medicaid reimbursements with their own funds. As a consequence, the principal customer of medical providers is not the patient but the bureaucracy. Moreover, through its policy

[38]Robert Pear, "U.S. Makes a Major Change in Medicare Fees for Doctors," *New York Times,* November 16, 1991.

[39]*New York Times* News Service, August 1, 1991.

of setting reimbursement rates, Medicaid increasingly determines the type and quality of care that Medicaid patients receive.

In most states, Medicaid payments for medical services are well below the payments made by other third-party payers. For example, Table 18.1 shows the difference between Medicare and Medicaid payments to physicians for similar services. As the table shows, in only four states is the Medicaid payment as high as, or higher than, the payment made by Medicare. In New York, the Medicaid payment is only 30 percent of the Medicare payment. In West Virginia, it's only 35 percent. As a result, many physicians who used to accept Medicaid patients no longer do so.[40] By choosing to pay low prices, the Medicaid bureaucracy is ensuring that the quality of care is reduced.

A similar phenomenon is occurring in the hospital and nursing home industries. According to the American Hospital Association, Medicaid paid more than 90 percent of the cost of hospital care for Medicaid patients in 1980. But by 1988, that figure had dropped to 78 percent. One consequence is that many hospitals no longer want to accept Medicaid patients.[41]

Things would be even worse were it not for the intervention of the federal courts (which are somewhat insulated from political pressures). In response to lawsuits filed by nursing homes in 20 states and hospitals in 21 states, the courts are ruling that Medicaid payments do not meet the standards of "reasonable and adequate" compensation and are ordering higher reimbursement levels.[42] There is nothing wrong with paying lower prices in return for taking a hospital bed when it becomes available, rather than paying top dollar for immediate services. The trouble is that these decisions are not being made by patients. They are being made by the bureaucracy.

Explicit Rationing

At least two political entities have announced their intentions to explicitly ration medical care for patients using public dollars: the

[40]Robert Pear, "Low Medicaid Fees Seen as Depriving the Poor of Care," *New York Times,* April 2, 1991.

[41]Robert Pear, "Suits Force U.S. and States to Pay More for Medicaid," *New York Times,* October 29, 1991.

[42]Ibid.

Table 18.1
MEDICAID VERSUS MEDICARE—THE PAYMENT GAP

State	Medicaid to Medicare Ratio	State	Medicaid to Medicare Ratio
Alabama	.72	Montana	.74
Alaska	1.06	Nebraska	.99
Arkansas	1.20	Nevada	.79
California	.54	New Hampshire	.67
Colorado	.81	New Jersey	.40
Connecticut	.56	New Mexico	.69
Delaware	.50	New York	.30
District of Columbia	.51	North Carolina	.93
Florida	.71	North Dakota	.75
Georgia	1.12	Ohio	.60
Hawaii	.79	Oklahoma	.78
Idaho	.76	Oregon	.66

Illinois	.48	Pennsylvania	.51
Indiana	1.02	Rhode Island	.55
Iowa	.91	South Carolina	.81
Kansas	.79	South Dakota	.85
Kentucky	.63	Tennessee	.92
Louisiana	.66	Texas	.77
Maine	.62	Utah	.89
Maryland	.51	Vermont	.71
Massachusetts	.94	Virginia	.73
Michigan	.62	Washington	.69
Minnesota	.86	West Virginia	.35
Mississippi	.66	Wisconsin	.76
Missouri	.57		

SOURCE: U.S. Physician Payment Review Commission; reprinted in the *New York Times*, April 2, 1991.
NOTE: Index of Medicaid payments as compared with Medicare payments for the same physician services in 1989. Arizona and Wyoming did not respond to the survey.

state of Oregon and Alameda County in California. Oregon has announced, for example, that it will cease using Medicaid money for heart, liver, bone marrow, and pancreas transplants, and that it will spend the money instead on prenatal care and other medical services. This decision is consistent with two characteristics of rationing in other countries: discrimination against the elderly and the provision of less-expensive services for the many rather than expensive, lifesaving care for the few.[43] Although Oregon is the only state that has officially announced a policy of health care rationing, others—including Alabama, Arizona, Texas, and Virginia—have set limits on what they will pay for organ transplants.

Case Study: Prenatal Care

One of the strangest features of the modern welfare state is the contrast between the extraordinary amount of money that is spent and the failure to solve what appear to be relatively simple, not very expensive to fix problems. At the federal level, means-tested welfare spending is about $400 billion per year—enough to turn poverty families into upper-income families overnight. But the welfare state seems unable to provide inexpensive shelters for the homeless and prenatal care for poor, pregnant women; in real terms, the amount of cash given to poor people has barely changed since 1965.[44]

A pregnant woman on Medicaid has very few options (see chapter 4). Because Medicaid reimbursement rates are so low, few physicians will see her for any medical problem. Under Medicaid rules, the woman is not permitted to add her own money to Medicaid's reimbursement and purchase care in the marketplace. Because of yet another bureaucracy, the tort system, the shrinking number of physicians who give prenatal care often avoid Medicaid patients, who are the patients most likely to have medical problems that could give rise to tort claims. Moreover, a woman on Medicaid has no opportunity to waive malpractice claims or in any other way

[43]Victoria von Biel, "Rationing in Alameda: Much to Do with Nothing," *California Physician* (August 1989): 30–33. See also William Raspberry, "If We Have to Ration Medical Care . . .," *Washington Post*, October 23, 1989, p. A15.

[44]See John C. Goodman, *Welfare and Poverty*, NCPA Policy Report no. 107 (Dallas: National Center for Policy Analysis, October 1983); and John C. Goodman and Michael Stroup, *Privatizing the Welfare State*, NCPA Policy Report no. 123 (Dallas: National Center for Policy Analysis, June 1986).

Table 18.2
PERCENT OF U.S. WOMEN WHO RECEIVE PRENATAL CARE IN
THE FIRST THREE MONTHS OF PREGNANCY

Race or Ethnic Origin	Percent
White	79%
Black	62
Asian	76
American Indian	61
Puerto Rican	57

SOURCE: U.S. Department of Health and Human Services, "Health, United States" (March 15, 1989).

reach a voluntary agreement to circumvent the costly intrusion of the tort system.

When prenatal care is available, it is often rationed by waiting. The people who provide the care see Medicaid, not the patients, as their primary customer. In America, prenatal care for low-income women is rationed not by ability to pay but by bureaucracy. Table 18.2 shows the percentage of women who receive prenatal care in the first three months of pregnancy, by race or ethnic origin. As the table shows, there are considerable disparities. These disparities are reflected in the infant mortality rate, which is twice as high for blacks (17.9 percent), for example, as for whites (8.6 percent).[45] This result is not unique to the United States. In Britain, there are vast differences in infant mortality rates among regions of the country and even among parts of the same city, despite the fact that prenatal care is free.[46]

Health Care Rationing in Other Government Health Programs

In addition to Medicare and Medicaid, other government health care programs are also turning to health care rationing under the pressures of the politics of medicine. The following are a few examples.

[45]National Center for Health Statistics, *Monthly Vital Statistics Report* (September 26, 1989).

[46]Infant mortality among the regions of Britain varies by at least one-third. See Office of Health Economics, *Compendium of Health Statistics: 7th Edition,* 1989 (London, 1989), section 1, p. 17. In urban areas, the differences among population groups are even more striking.

Emergency Rooms of Public Hospitals

Just as the Canadian health care system discourages outpatient surgery and attempts to restrict all sophisticated treatment to large city hospitals, care for low-income patients in the United States is increasingly being restricted to urban hospitals. Unable to obtain treatment elsewhere, low-income patients are turning to the emergency rooms of public hospitals in inner cities, for both primary care (ear infections, sprained ankles, etc.) and other care.[47] But as the demand increases, the supply is decreasing as more hospitals close their emergency rooms.[48] "Overwhelmed and understaffed," these facilities are taking on many of the characteristics of hospital emergency rooms in countries with national health insurance.[49]

As a consequence, rationing problems are becoming acute. According to one study, the wait to see a physician in a typical emergency room ranges from 15 minutes to 17 hours. Another study—of the UCLA Harbor Medical Center—found that almost 10 percent of the patients left before seeing a physician. Of those patients who left and were later located, 45 percent were found to be in "urgent" need of medical attention, and 29 percent needed to be seen by a physician within 24 hours.[50]

Admission to a hospital through an emergency room also is increasingly rationed. According to the National Association of Public Hospitals, the average emergency room wait for a hospital bed in a public hospital is now 5.5 hours. In the worst cases, the wait can range from 3 to 10 days.[51] Public clinics outside hospitals are experiencing similar problems. For example, in the case of a Chicago clinic, a pregnant woman had to wait 125 days for an appointment with a physician.[52]

[47]Robert S. Stern, Joel S. Weissman, and Arnold M. Epstein, "The Emergency Department as a Pathway to Admission for Poor and High-Cost Patients," *Journal of the American Medical Association* 266, no. 16 (October 23/30, 1991): 2238 ff.

[48]Lisa Belkin, "Why Emergency Rooms Are on the Critical List," *New York Times*, October 6, 1991.

[49]"Do You Want to Die?" *Time*, May 28, 1990, p. 58 ff.

[50]Philip J. Hilts, "Many Leave Emergency Rooms Needing Care," *New York Times*, August 27, 1991.

[51]Philip J. Hilts, "Public Hospital Wait for Bed Can Be Days, U.S. Study Says," *New York Times*, January 30, 1991.

[52]*Chicago Tribune*, November 25, 1990; cited in Emily Friedman, "The Uninsured: From Dilemma to Crisis," *Journal of the American Medical Association* 265, no. 19 (May 15, 1991): 2494.

The Military Medical System and Veterans Hospitals

At $14 billion a year, the Pentagon's military medical system has been described as "riddled with waste" and poorly managed. Serving nine million active duty personnel, military retirees, and their dependents, special interests within the system are aggressively fighting budget cuts, whereas some project that—in a few years—the military may be spending half as much on health care as on new weapons systems.[53]

Some have suggested combining the Pentagon's health care system with that of the Department of Veterans Affairs (VA). There are reasons for the military to resist. An investigator for the General Accounting Office told Congress that VA hospitals administer shoddy care and that patient neglect has caused avoidable deaths. In one case, a man lost a leg because he had not been checked regularly. In another case, a bladder cancer victim died because he had not been treated for 45 days. The investigator, Mary Ann Curran, testified that

> I examined chart after chart where attending physicians rarely examined patients or did not examine them at all. . . . Nurses allowed patients with life-threatening illnesses to languish for hours, even days without monitoring.[54]

Community Mental Health Clinics

About 600 community mental health centers, built with federal money, were designed to provide free or low-cost services for people who have been released from mental institutions. Yet, according to an inspector general's report, nearly half are not doing so and are catering to paying patients instead. Some experts believe that this failure is contributing to the number of people who are homeless and mentally ill.[55]

---

[53]Andy Pasztor, "Military Medical System, Beset by Budgetary Ills and Riddled with Waste, Needs Some Doctoring," *Wall Street Journal*, August 26, 1991.

[54]"Investigator Cites Poor Health at Veterans Hospitals," *New York Times*, November 22, 1991.

[55]Philip J. Hilts, "Report Faults Community Mental Health Clinics," *New York Times*, October 6, 1991.

The Politics of Catastrophic Health Insurance

Most health care economists and employee benefits managers strongly encourage policies that leave patients responsible for small bills, while making the insurance company responsible for bills so large that they would financially devastate most families (see chapter 8). But Medicare pays too many of the small bills while leaving the elderly at risk for the very large ones. Medicare currently pays 80 percent of physician fees for a patient who suffers from a headache or a common cold. Yet elderly patients with acute problems requiring hospital stays face increasingly costly bills—not paid by Medicare—which rise with the duration of the illness (see chapter 15).

How can one explain a federal Medicare plan designed so that those with the most severe health problems face the greatest financial burdens? Only one explanation is possible: politics. Consider that, in 1983, about 90 percent of all Medicare beneficiaries spent less than $1,000 for medical expenses partly covered by Medicare; by contrast, only 0.4 percent of all Medicare beneficiaries had expenses of $5,000 or more.[56] Clearly, Medicare is structured for the convenience of the vast majority of patients incurring minor medical expenses, not the small minority facing catastrophic health care bills.

Private Health Insurance

In response to the gaps created under Medicare, a thriving market emerged in Medigap insurance—insurance designed to pay expenses not paid by Medicare. Yet Congress has forced Medigap policies, like Medicare itself, to cover a great many small medical bills while leaving coverage of the large bills discretionary (see chapter 15).

Reagan's First Reform Proposal

During Ronald Reagan's first term, his administration attempted to restructure Medicare to conform to generally accepted insurance principles. Under the proposal, Medicare patients would have incurred greater out-of-pocket expenses for short hospital stays,

---

[56]About 70 percent of Medicare beneficiaries had medical expenses falling in the range of $1 to $999. See U.S. Department of Health and Human Services, *Catastrophic Illness Expenses* (November 1986), Table 3.1 (p. 27).

and the savings would have been used to finance catastrophic coverage for lengthy stays. The proposal went nowhere. It is not hard to understand why. As one political scientist explained it:

> White House proposals to enhance health care benefits for catastrophic illness by reducing benefits for short-term care have fallen on deaf ears in Congress. No matter how sensible this trade-off might be on ethical and analytical grounds, *it would force Congress to disadvantage the many so that the few should gain.*[57]

Reagan's Second Reform Proposal

On February 24, 1987, President Reagan sent another proposal to Congress.[58] Unlike the administration's original approach, it involved increasing the flow of money under the direct control of politicians. Under the new proposal, Medicare coverage would have been expanded to cover catastrophic costs (in excess of $2,000) and would have been financed by an increased premium of $60 per year paid by Medicare beneficiaries.[59] The proposal was made at a time when there was considerable criticism of Medigap policies, and it was accompanied by the claim that the federal government could provide catastrophic care more cheaply than the private sector. It took Congress no time at all to think of other, more politically popular variations on the proposal.

The Medicare Catastrophic Coverage Act, 1988–89

The approach adopted by Congress became law in 1988 but was repealed one year later in one of the most remarkable legislative turnarounds in this century. Responding to the pressures of the

[57]Allen Schick, "Controlling the 'Uncontrollables': Budgeting for Health Care in an Age of Megadeficits," in Jack A. Meyer and Marion E. Lewin, eds., *Charting the Future of Health Care* (Washington: American Enterprise Institute, 1987), p. 31. Emphasis added.

[58]The details of the proposal are outlined in U.S. Department of Health and Human Services, *Catastrophic Illness Expenses.*

[59]In theory, the coverage offered was to be optional. The $60 premium would be tacked onto the current premium for Medicare Part B coverage, which is optional for Medicare patients. However, because such coverage is about 75 percent subsidized by general revenues, the option to pay for coverage would have been an offer that few elderly citizens could afford to refuse.

Table 18.3
PERCENT OF OUT-OF-POCKET MEDICAL EXPENSES PAID BY
THE ELDERLY IN EXCESS OF $2,000 PER YEAR

Type of Expense	Percent
Nursing home	81.0%
Hospital	10.0
Physician services	6.0
Dental	1.7
Drugs	1.2

SOURCE: Jon Gabel and Timothy Rice, "Protecting the Elderly against High Health Costs," *Health Affairs* 5 (Fall 1986), p. 12. Cited in the Task Force on Long-Term Care Policies, *Report to the Congress and the Secretary* (Washington: U.S. Department of Health and Human Services, 1987), p. 17.

politics of Medicare, Congress included in the Medicare Catastrophic Coverage Act many items that had nothing to do with catastrophic medical bills. Visible benefits were added, such as respite home health care benefits and coverage for mammograms.

At the same time, Congress avoided addressing the most serious catastrophic problem of Medicare enrollees—the threat of an expensive nursing home stay (see Table 18.3). The catastrophic hospital expenses covered in the bill were benefits that about 85 percent of the elderly were already entitled to under previous health insurance arrangements. Many elderly voters were deluded into thinking that the Medicare Catastrophic Coverage Act would help them with financial burdens created by a medical disaster, such as Alzheimer's disease, when, in fact, the new program barely put a dent in the cost of such care.

The political mistake behind the catastrophic coverage program was the decision to make Medicare beneficiaries pay the full cost of the new program and to make those costs highly visible. That decision enabled each Medicare enrollee to compare personal benefits with personal costs under the program. Once that was done, the program was dismantled even before most of its major provisions had become effective.

PART VI

DISMANTLING THE COST-PLUS SYSTEM

19. The International Trend toward Privatization of Health Care

Throughout the 1980s, political change around the world communicated a simple message: Free markets based on individual pursuit of self-interest work, whereas collectivism and bureaucratic decisionmaking do not. The 1980s were the decade of privatization, capped by the dramatic and continuing collapse of communist regimes. Health care proved to be no exception:

- In 1989, the British government introduced radical market-based reforms in health care and began to allow private hospitals to compete against public hospitals for National Health Service (NHS) funds.[1]
- In 1987, the Netherlands introduced a voucher system that allows consumers to choose among private and public insurance funds.[2]
- In 1987, West Germany introduced a new policy which encourages competition among hospitals.[3]
- More recently, the government of New Zealand has signaled its intent to end 40 years of socialized medicine by giving people tax incentives to purchase private health insurance and by introducing market-based reforms in the public sector.[4]
- Sweden, along with other European countries, has already introduced some "managed competition" into its national

[1]See Patricia Day and Rudolf Klein, "Britain's Health Care Experiment," *Health Affairs* (Fall 1991), pp. 39–59; and Alain C. Enthoven, "Internal Market Reform of the British Health Service," *Health Affairs* (Fall 1991), pp. 60–70.

[2]Jeremy W. Hurst, "Reforming Health Care in Seven European Nations," *Health Affairs* (Fall 1991), pp. 18–19.

[3]Ibid., p. 18.

[4]A blueprint for the reforms may be found in Patricia Danzon and Susan Begg, *Options for Health Care in New Zealand* (Wellington: New Zealand Business Roundtable, 1991).

health insurance system; and with the 1991 change of government, those reforms will undoubtedly continue.[5]

- In Canada, pressures are mounting to allow private health insurance options and to institute user fees, and Claude Castonguay, considered the father of Quebec's health care system (the oldest government health insurance scheme in Canada), has called for privatization and competition in the supply of health services.[6]
- The Soviet Union's new health care reform plan calls for decentralization, "enterprise," and the introduction of financial incentives into health care.[7]
- Chile has given its citizens financial incentives to opt out of national health insurance for the last decade, and most other Latin American countries are seeking ways to partially privatize their health care systems.[8]

Yet privatization of health care has proved far more difficult than privatization of state-owned enterprises. Among developed countries, even Britain (which pioneered the international privatization revolution) and New Zealand (which made greater strides toward economic liberalization than any other noncommunist country) have met fierce political resistance over proposals to introduce market-based health care reforms. Among less-developed,

---

[5]Commenting on the change, one news report noted that "Swedes have had to wait for years for cataract and other operations, and some have died awaiting heart bypass surgery." See Steven Prokesch, "Socialists Suffer Major Defeat in Swedish Vote," *New York Times*, September 16, 1991. For general changes in Europe, see the discussion in Bengt Jönsson, "What Can Americans Learn from Europeans?" Symposium: International Comparisons of Health Care Systems, *Health Care Financing Review*, 1989 Annual Supplement, pp. 79–93.

[6]See Clyde H. Farnsworth, "Economic Woes Force Canada to Reexamine Medical System," *New York Times*, November 24, 1991; and Edward Neuschler, *Canadian Health Care: The Implications of Public Health Insurance* (Washington: Health Insurance Association of America, 1989), p. 52.

[7]See Diane Rowland and Alexandre V. Telyrikov, "Soviet Health Care from Two Perspectives," *Health Affairs* (Fall 1991), pp. 71–86.

[8]For a description of Chile's health care reforms, see John C. Goodman and Peter A. Ferrara, "Private Alternatives to Social Security in Other Countries," NCPA Policy Report no. 132 (Dallas: National Center for Policy Analysis, April 1987); and Tarsicio Castañeda, "The Chilean Health System: Organization, Operation and Financing," in *Health Economics: Latin American Perspectives* (Washington: Pan American Health Organization, 1989), pp. 3–25.

noncommunist countries, none has made more progress toward free markets than Chile. Yet Chile's progress in privatizing health care has been painfully slow. The only country that made substantial progress toward privatization of health care in the 1980s was Singapore. And significantly, Singapore is the only country in the world that has made a genuine commitment to individual self-insurance, rather than third-party insurance for medical expenses.

Methods of Privatization

In the 1990s, most countries with government-run health care systems are searching desperately for ways to reform them; and many politicians and health economists in other developed countries are exploring partial privatization and managed competition techniques. Not surprisingly, they often look to the United States for guidance. The irony is that, as they turn to the United States for market-based health care reforms, those Americans wedded to the bureaucratic vision of health care in this country are searching the globe to find a socialist health care system they can copy. The following briefly summarizes five methods of privatization in use around the world.

Method I: Free-Market Provision in the Face of Limited Free Services Provided by Government

The most common form of privatization is not the deliberate transfer of resources from the public to the private sector. Rather, it is the growth of private supply in the face of limited government supply. When free, government-provided health care is limited in availability or poor in quality, people naturally turn to the private sector. That is especially true among less-developed countries.

Private Provision in Less-Developed Countries[9]

Private health services still play a major role in all less-developed countries. The bulk of the people in Sub-Saharan Africa prefer the traditional, indigenous systems, and they use modern facilities only as a last resort. Private provision, both traditional and modern, also is important in Asia, North Africa, and Latin America. Hank Merrill, reporting on the use of health services by the Thais (a relatively

[9]This section is based on Gabriel Roth, *Private Provision of Public Services in LDCs* (Washington: World Bank, 1987).

sophisticated and advanced people), estimated that "only 15 percent of the persons requiring or seeking medical care in Thailand go to government-sponsored facilities. An additional 20 percent seek services from pharmacists and druggists, and 15 percent seek out traditional healers, spiritual advisors or injectionists."[10]

As Table 19.1 shows, private health expenditures in less-developed countries are often more important than in the industrialized countries. Particularly striking are the figures from Asia. In India, 84 percent of health care expenditures are private; in South Korea, 87 percent are private; and in the Philippines, 75 percent are private. These high percentages reflect not only the use of traditional medicine but also the increasing availability of private, modern health facilities.

The Growth of the Private Sector in Britain and New Zealand

In both Britain and New Zealand, hospital services are completely paid for by government. Yet, both countries have long waiting lists for hospital surgery (see chapter 17). In response to rationing by waiting, both countries also have a growing market in private health insurance—used by citizens who prefer to pay for prompt private surgery, rather than wait for free surgery in public hospitals. In Britain, the number of people with private insurance has more than doubled in the last 10 years, to about 12 percent of the population. Apart from private insurance, Britons make out-of-pocket payments to obtain benefits not available from the NHS, including immediate access to a hospital for nonemergency surgery. In New Zealand, one-third of the population has private health insurance, and private hospitals now perform 25 percent of all surgical procedures.

Private Alternatives in Canada

In Canada, too, health care is theoretically provided to all, with no user fees, coinsurance payments, or extra charges. Only three of the ten provinces have premiums. The government refuses to allow private health insurance to be sold, except for incidental items not covered by the provincial plans. Unlike the British and New Zealanders, Canadians generally cannot purchase private health insurance or make out-of-pocket payments to physicians. Private

[10]Ibid.

Table 19.1
PRIVATE EXPENDITURES AS A PERCENT OF TOTAL HEALTH EXPENDITURES IN LESS-DEVELOPED COUNTRIES

Country	Percent
Afghanistan (1975–76)	88%
Argentina[1]	69
Bangladesh (1976)	87
Botswana (1978)	48
Brazil (1981)	33+
China (1981)	32
Colombia (1978)	33
Ghana (1970)	73
Haiti (1980)	65
Honduras (1970)	63
India (1970)	84
Indonesia (1982–83)	62
Jamaica (1981)	40
Jordan (1982)	41
Lebanon (1982)	50+
Lesotho (1979–80)	12
Malawi (1980–81)	23
Mali (1981)	54
Mexico (1976)	31
Pakistan (1982)	71
Philippines (1970)	75
Peru (1982)	53
Rwanda (1977)	37
Senegal (1981)	39
South Korea (1975)	87
Spain (1976)	39
Sri Lanka (1982)	45
Sudan (1970)	41
Swaziland[1]	50
Syria[1]	76
Upper Volta (1982)	19
Tanzania[1]	23
Thailand (1979)	70
Togo (1979)	31
Tunisia[1]	27
Upper Volta (1981)	24
Venezuela (1976)	58
Zambia (1981)	50
Zimbabwe (1980–81)	21

SOURCE: David de Ferranti, "Paying for Health Services in Developing Countries: An Overview," World Bank Working Paper 721 (Washington, 1985); reprinted in Gabriel Roth, *Private Provision of Public Services in LDCs* (Washington: World Bank, 1987).
[1]No date.

pay for medical or hospital care is technically not prohibited. What is prohibited is for physicians or hospitals to treat both patients whose care is financed by the provincial plans and patients who pay directly. The Canadian physician or hospital practicing private medicine must be private only, and the number of private-only doctors and hospitals is very small.

The other private option for Canadians is the health care system of the United States. Four out of five Canadians live within 200 miles of the border, thus making U.S. health care relatively accessible. Increasingly, Canadians who are not willing to suffer long delays for major operations are taking advantage of this option.

Method 2: Privatization of Supply

In many countries the supply of health care services is completely socialized. The result is almost always inefficiency and higher costs. To deal with these problems some countries are contracting with the private sector to provide services. In others, private providers are allowed to compete with public providers on a reasonably level playing field.

Public-Sector Contracting with the Private Sector

In some countries, government health authorities contract with private hospitals to provide services. In Britain, more than 40 percent of government health authorities have some contracting arrangement in place. Clinical facilities such as pathology laboratories are the most frequent recipient of these contracts. Furthermore, about one-third of health authorities contract out long-term care to the private sector. These arrangements are generally long established with religious or charitable institutions.

Contracting with private facilities is also becoming more frequent in Canada. In this case, however, the private contractors are in the United States. For example, British Columbia's hospital administrators are now contracting with hospitals in Seattle to perform heart surgery, and Ontario's administrators are doing the same with hospitals in Detroit (see chapter 17). In both cases, Canadian hospital personnel apparently believe the U.S. hospitals can perform the surgery for a lower cost or can reduce the politically embarrassing waiting times. If it were not for the proximity of the United States, many Canadians might suffer and die because of their inadequate health care system.

Competition between Public and Private Suppliers

In many countries, private suppliers compete with public suppliers for patients, even though the bill is paid by government. In the United States, Medicare (elderly) patients and Medicaid (poor) patients can choose almost any public or private hospital, even though government is the health insurer. Private clinics also compete with public clinics in France and other European countries.

Method 3: Privatization of Demand—Health Insurance

In many parts of the world individuals cannot be effective consumers of health services because the government takes their income for earmarked health programs. Under these programs, people often have very little choice. As an alternative, some countries are finding innovative ways of empowering health care consumers by privatizing the demand for health insurance.

Private Health Insurance Alternatives in Chile[11]

Chile was the first nation in the Western Hemisphere to adopt a social security system, in 1924. It also is the first nation in the world to dismantle a public social security system through sweeping privatization. In 1981, the Chilean government created a new system under which workers contribute to private pension funds instead of the public system. Under the reform, workers who had participated in the old system were allowed to switch to the private system prior to 1986. All new entrants into the labor market are required to participate in the private system.

Today, about 90 percent of all Chilean workers are in the private-sector pension system. They are required to contribute 10 percent of their earnings to the Chilean equivalent of an individual retirement account. About a dozen companies compete to manage the accounts, and workers can switch back and forth among the investment funds. The fund managers are required to follow conservative investment strategies, and the Chilean government guarantees a minimum rate of return to all workers, as well as a minimum pension benefit at the age of retirement.

Workers under the new system are required to contribute another 3.5 percent of wages for the purchase of private life and disability

[11]See Goodman and Ferrara.

insurance from the approved private insurance companies of their choice. These private insurance policies replace the survivors and disability benefits paid by the old system for preretirement disability or death. The disability policy, along with funds accumulated in the worker's retirement account, pays a monthly benefit for the rest of the worker's life equal to 70 percent of the average wage earned during the 12 months prior to disability. The life insurance policy, along with the worker's retirement fund, pays a benefit to a surviving spouse, dependent parents, or dependent children. The disability benefits under the new system amount to more than twice those under the old system, and the new system's survivors benefits are almost double. In addition, the government guarantees the same minimum benefit for disability as for retirement and guarantees minimum survivors benefits as well.

Rates of contribution for Chilean workers are shown in Table 19.2 for 1985—the last year in which workers could exercise choice. As the table shows, those who opted out of the public-sector social security system were required to contribute 13.5 percent of their income (10 percent for retirement savings and 3.5 percent for disability and life insurance) to private funds. Had they remained in Chile's social security system, they would have paid about 19–20 percent of their income in social security taxes. Thus, the choice to opt out is worth savings equal to about 6 percent of earnings each year.

Workers under the new system also are required to contribute about 6 percent of wages for health insurance coverage, and they can choose between private health insurance companies and the government health service. Private health insurance policies must provide benefits at least as good as those promised by the government's health insurance. Although this option has been in place for more than a decade and despite Chile's success in privatizing retirement pensions, only 25 to 35 percent of Chilean workers have opted for private health insurance. There are apparently three reasons for the low rate of privatization. First, although the government widely publicized the private alternative to social security, it publicized the private health insurance option very little. Even today, most Chilean workers probably do not realize they can opt out of government health insurance. Second, as Table 19.2 shows, the government created little or no financial incentive for choosing

Table 19.2
FINANCIAL INCENTIVES TO OPT OUT OF CHILEAN SOCIAL SECURITY, 1985

	Tax Rate
Total payroll tax rates for workers who opt in[1]	
Old-age, survivors, and disability insurance	18.89% – 19.94%
Health insurance	5.75% – 6.55%
Total payroll tax	24.64% – 26.49%
Required contribution for workers who opt out	
Retirement account	10.0%
Health insurance	6.0
Disability and life insurance	3.5
Total contribution rate	19.5%
Financial incentive to opt out[1]	5.13% – 6.99%

SOURCES: *Social Security Programs throughout the World 1985*, p. 52; and John C. Goodman and Peter A. Ferrara, *Private Alternatives to Social Security in Other Countries*, NCPA Policy Report no. 132 (Dallas: National Center for Policy Analysis, April 1987).
[1]The first rate given is the rate paid by workers participating in the general system for manual workers; the second rate is for workers participating in the general system for salaried workers.

private health insurance. Third, privatizing health insurance clearly has not been a high priority for the government.

If Chile continues to privatize social insurance, it will have to turn its attention to health care. More thought must be given to the mechanics of privatization. Private insurers should have no difficulty improving upon the benefits offered by the state for 6 percent of the income of workers who are young, healthy, and earn high wages. They may find it impossible to do so for workers who are old, less healthy, and/or low paid. Unlike pension benefits, use of health care services does not rise in proportion to income, and the current option could lead to large problems of adverse selection. In addition, to encourage private health insurance, the government must also encourage private health care delivery.

Even so, Chile has already made a major contribution to the privatization revolution. Chile's is the only government that has almost completely privatized social security, an accomplishment that may now be copied by other less-developed countries, including Colombia.[12] And Chile's is the first government in the world to create a private-sector alternative to participation in national health insurance.

Public Contracting for Private Health Insurance in the United States

In the United States, the contracting out of health care services is still in the infant stage. Currently, nearly 2 million Medicare (elderly) beneficiaries and 2.5 million Medicaid (poor) beneficiaries are enrolled in private prepaid health plans. These include Medicare beneficiaries who have exercised the option to enroll in a health maintenance organization (HMO) or a competitive medical plan (CMP).[13] Medicare pays the HMO or CMP a monthly lump sum equal to approximately 95 percent of Medicare's costs for the average beneficiary, adjusted for certain characteristics such as age, sex, county of residence, and whether or not the beneficiary is eligible for Medicaid or is institutionalized. Approximately 158 HMOs or CMPs in 34 states now have Medicare beneficiaries. The advantages of this alternative are significant. First, the private health option

---

[12]See "Privatizing Social Security," *Executive Alert* 5, no. 1 (January/February 1991): 6.

[13]CMPs are HMOs that do not have an official designation of "health maintenance organization." However, they are HMOs for all practical purposes.

increases choice in health care. Of the 33.7 million Medicare beneficiaries in the United States, about 10.5 million, or one-third, live in
areas where at least two competing private plans are available in
addition to traditional Medicare. Many HMOs and CMPs offer
greater benefits than those provided under Medicare. Seventy-six
percent of the plans, for instance, offer greater hospital coverage.
Deductibles and copayments are often smaller and, in some cases,
nil. Joining a private plan also reduces paperwork for the elderly,
since their claims are handled by the private plan.

Another very new innovation is Medicare insured groups (MIGs).
These groups are for elderly retirees who are covered by employer
or union postretirement plans designed to supplement Medicare
coverage. The MIGs permit employers to combine their Medicare
and private benefits in one package, to integrate cost management.
Retirees benefit because a MIG handles their paperwork and permits them to stay in the same plan they used during their working
years. Among the private companies that have participated or are
about to are Chrysler Corporation, Southern California Edison, John
Deere Company, and Amalgamated Life Insurance Company.[14]

Method 4: Privatization of Demand—Private Savings as an Alternative to Health Insurance

A popular alternative to social insurance schemes is the provident
fund. A provident fund involves forced savings: individuals (and/
or their employers) are required to contribute to savings accounts,
and the funds are reserved for contingencies such as illness and
retirement. Although governments often influence such funds, the
managing boards of the funds typically are composed of representatives of management and labor.[15] Individuals have a property right
to their share of the fund. At least 21 countries have mandated

[14]Both Chrysler and Southern California Edison have completed demonstration
projects, but have decided not to implement the program. Source: Health Care
Financing Administration (HCFA), Office of Research and Demonstration, Comprehensive Health Services Branch (Baltimore).

[15]In all cases, the workers bear the full economic burden of the programs. Some
programs are designed so that the burden appears to be on the employer, or appears
to be shared between the employee and employer. Over time, however, the forces
of supply and demand lead to reductions in real wages that redistribute the burden,
causing it ultimately to be on the employee.

participation in such plans for certain classes of workers—usually employees of large firms in urban areas.[16]

The Use of Provident Funds for Health Care Expenditures

Although the primary purpose of provident funds is to provide savings for retirement (or survivors benefits), many of these funds also permit withdrawals for other purposes, such as health care. For example:[17]

- Almost all provident funds permit their members to withdraw their share of the fund in the case of permanent disability.
- In Ghana and Montserrat, limited withdrawals are permitted in the case of sickness.
- In Kenya and Singapore, withdrawals are permitted to pay for hospitalization expenses.
- In India, withdrawals are allowed to pay for medical expenses.
- In Nepal, provident fund members are entitled to borrow from their accumulated deposits for medical expenses.
- In Zambia, withdrawals are permitted for maternity expenses.

Medisave Accounts in Singapore[18]

In 1955, Singapore introduced a compulsory savings program that now covers about three-fourths of all Singaporean workers.[19] Employer and employee contributions are made to the Central Provident Fund (CPF), which is controlled by the government and has a monopoly status. In the beginning, the CPF invested its funds entirely in government securities, and withdrawals were essentially limited to lump sum retirement benefits or survivors benefits. Over the years, the program has acquired flexibility. Workers can now direct the investment of up to 40 percent of their CPF funds[20] and

[16]See Goodman and Ferrara.

[17]Ibid.

[18]This discussion is based on Goodman and Ferrara; and Armina Tyabji, "Financing Social Security in Singapore," a presentation made to an Atlas Foundation conference, Arlington, Va., May 19, 1990. See also "The Report of the Central Provident Fund Study Group," *Singapore Economic Review* 31, no. 1 (April 1986).

[19]The program does not include people who are self-employed and people, such as university employees and pensionable civil servants, who are covered by separate plans.

[20]Investments may be made in real estate, in approved stock in Singaporean companies, and in gold. People are not allowed to purchase bonds or shares of stock in foreign countries.

can withdraw funds to purchase a home, buy life insurance, or buy home mortgage insurance; and they can borrow funds from their accounts to pay college education expenses for a family member.[21]

The required rates of contribution to CPF accounts over the past 36 years are shown in Table 19.3. Given that employer contributions on behalf of employees are undoubtedly made in lieu of the payment of wages, the table shows that the forced savings rates in Singapore have been quite high—totaling 50 percent of the first $41,000 of wages (in U.S. dollars) in 1985.[22] For the future, the government is committed to gradually moving toward a contribution rate of 40 percent—20 percent each for employees and their employers.

All employees in Singapore have a private property right to the funds that accumulate in their individual CPF accounts. The funds may be withdrawn at retirement, in the event of permanent disability, or if the individual emigrates from Singapore. At the account holder's death, the funds are payable to the individual's heirs.

Singapore's tax rates are high—probably much higher than rates that would be imposed were the United States to adopt a similar system. On the other hand, even Singapore's tax rates are low compared to the tax rates the United States will have to impose if it continues with its pay-as-you-go system of funding postretirement health care and retirement pensions (see chapter 13). Moreover, it is one thing to force individuals to sacrifice for their own and their family's future. It is another matter to force a current worker to sacrifice so that unrelated current retirees can live at a standard above that of the worker.

Prior to 1987, funds were withdrawn as a lump sum at retirement. Beginning in 1987, however, the government required retirees to use the first $18,600 (single) or $27,900 (couple) to purchase a monthly retirement annuity equal to $143 (single) or $214 (couple). Retirees can use the balance of their fund for any purpose. However, as Table 19.4 shows, the bulk of CPF withdrawals have been used to purchase a home, usually well before the time of retirement. About 86 percent of the housing in Singapore has been built by the

---

[21]These loans must be repaid.

[22]All figures expressed in U.S. dollars in this discussion are based on a conversion rate of $1.76 in Singaporean currency equals $1 in U.S. currency.

Table 19.3
FORCED SAVINGS IN SINGAPORE: FEATURES OF THE CENTRAL PROVIDENT FUND, 1955 TO 1991

	Required Contribution Rate					
Beginning	Employer	Employee	Total	Maximum Taxable Wage[1]	Size of Fund at End of Year (S$ Millions)[1]	Number of Members at End of Year (Thousands)
July 1955	5.0%	5.0%	10.0%	$6,000	$9	180
Sept 1968	6.5	6.5	13.0	27,692	540	505
Jan 1970	8.0	8.0	16.0	22,500	777	639
Jan 1971	10.0	10.0	20.0	18,000	988	715
July 1972	14.0	10.0	24.0	18,000	1,316	855
July 1973	15.0	11.0	26.0	18,000	1,771	962
July 1974	15.0	15.0	30.0	18,000	2,414	1,042
July 1975	15.0	15.0	30.0	24,000	3,235	1,104

July 1977	15.5	15.5	31.0	24,000	4,954	1,251
July 1978	16.5	16.5	33.0	36,000	5,981	1,341
July 1979	20.5	16.5	37.0	36,000	7,516	1,436
July 1980	20.5	18.0	38.5	36,000	9,551	1,519
July 1981	20.5	22.0	42.5	36,000	12,150	1,650
July 1982	22.0	23.0	45.0	36,000	15,656	1,725
July 1983	23.0	23.0	46.0	48,000	19,505	1,779
July 1984	25.0	25.0	50.0	60,000	22,670	1,847
July 1985	25.0	25.0	50.0	72,000	26,829	1,892
April 1986	10.0	25.0	35.0	72,000	29,341	1,932
July 1988	12.0	24.0	36.0	70,000	32,529	2,063
July 1989	15.0	23.0	38.0	72,000	36,052	2,126
July 1991	17.5	22.5	40.0	72,000	42,000	2,200

SOURCE: Central Provident Fund, *Annual Report* (various years).

¹S$1.76 = U.S. $1.00.

government and of these units, 70 percent have been purchased by their occupants—with CPF money.

Beginning in 1984, the government of Singapore extended its program of forced savings to require that a certain portion of CPF contributions be put into "Medisave accounts" to provide funds for hospitalization. The funds may be used only for treatment at a government hospital or an approved private hospital.[23] Strangely, Medisave funds cannot be used to purchase outpatient care, including physicians' services or expensive outpatient renal dialysis and long-term care. People also cannot borrow against future Medisave deposits to pay current bills at private hospitals, although members of the same family can pool their Medisave balances to pay another family member's hospital bill, and people who enter some government hospitals can settle their bills from future Medisave deposits.

Currently, 6 percent of an employee's salary is placed in a Medisave account until the balance reaches approximately $8,522. Once that total is reached and maintained, any additional contributions are automatically placed in an individual's ordinary pension account. In Singapore, $8,522 would be sufficient to cover hospitalization expenses except in very rare catastrophic cases. The Singapore government currently is engaged in negotiations with private health insurance companies and is apparently committed to allowing some portion of the Medisave account funds to be used for the purchase of health insurance coverage. In 1985, 145,000 members of the CPF (out of a total Singapore population of 2.6 million) made Medisave withdrawals averaging about $171 per person. As Table 19.4 shows, the use of Medisave funds quadrupled between 1985 and 1988.

A Medisave account is self-insurance for hospitalization throughout the employee's working life. At retirement, individuals must leave about $4,830 in their Medisave account to cover medical expenses after they reach the age of 55.[24] Singapore's Medisave program, therefore, combines the concepts of the Medical IRA (MIRA) and the Medical Savings Account discussed in this book.

---

[23]Hospital patients also face copayments, which they must make with out-of-pocket funds, in addition to payments from Medisave accounts.

[24]When Medisave accounts were started in 1984, the required balance was S$5,000 or the actual balance, whichever was lower. Subsequently, that amount has increased by S$500 per year, and it will continue to increase until it reaches S$10,000 in 1994.

Table 19.4
WITHDRAWALS FROM FORCED SAVINGS ACCOUNTS, BY USE, 1968 TO 1989
(S$ MILLIONS)[1]

Year	Total	Approved Housing Schemes	Reached 55 Years of Age[2]	Leaving Singapore Permanently	Medisave	Death	Other[3]
1968	$30.7	$6.3	$14.9	$5.0		$1.8	$2.7
1969	42.4	21.7	13.3	4.2		2.0	1.1
1970	45.7	22.9	15.4	4.2		2.0	1.1
1971	56.4	23.2	22.1	7.0		3.2	0.9
1972	57.9	25.1	23.8	4.1		3.8	1.2
1973	93.5	50.6	31.4	5.7		4.7	1.0
1974	154.3	92.8	46.4	8.1		5.5	1.6
1975	216.9	134.8	60.9	11.2		8.4	1.5
1976	377.7	275.2	76.2	14.1		9.3	2.9
1977	503.5	383.5	90.0	14.1		12.6	3.4
1978	657.8	488.4	123.1	15.7		13.8	16.8
1979	629.3	438.6	150.7	18.2		15.1	6.7
1980	779.1	520.9	213.9	23.2		15.6	5.4
1981	1,967.6	691.1	294.5	33.0		19.5	29.5
1982	1,241.2	796.3	322.9	56.4		27.1	38.5

(Continued on next page)

Table 19.4—Continued
Withdrawals from Forced Savings Accounts, by Use, 1968 to 1989
(S$ Millions)[1]

Year	Total	Approved Housing Schemes	Reached 55 Years of Age[2]	Leaving Singapore Permanently	Medisave	Death	Other[3]
1983	1,717.9	1,122.4	437.8	104.3		31.3	22.1
1984	3,509.3	2,692.9	606.0	96.4	$17.6	35.6	60.8
1985	3,359.7	2,566.4	506.2	146.3	43.9	40.5	56.4
1986	3,823.8	2,647.3	666.3	156.8	104.8	44.4	204.2
1987	4,297.2	2,647.5	548.0	143.9	140.5	48.6	168.7
1988	4,010.2	2,776.1	573.5	151.7	169.9	52.2	286.8
1989	3,663.3	2,415.1	619.4	161.5	178.2	54.2	234.9

SOURCES: *Economic and Social Statistics of Singapore 1960–1982* (Department of Statistics, 1988); *Singapore Yearbook of Statistics 1988*; and Central Provident Fund, *Annual Report, 1989*.

[1]S$1.76 = U.S.$1.00.

[2]Retirement age.

[3]Includes withdrawals for physicial and mental disability, for purchase of home mortgage insurance, and for investments in nonresidential real estate and approved shares of stock and gold.

Like most other provident fund systems around the world, the Singapore system forces people to save but allows them to make withdrawals for many of the purposes for which people ordinarily engage in private, voluntary savings—retirement, disability, death, education, medical expenses, and the purchase of a home. Singapore's provident fund differs from others in that there is very little insurance (and therefore no pooling of risks) for adverse contingencies such as hospitalization, disability, or death. What individuals receive in the event of these contingencies is based solely on their own contributions. An exception is compulsory mortgage insurance, for which the premium is paid from the buyer's CPF account.

The Singaporean system is far from perfect. Restrictions on the use of Medisave funds encourage people to overuse hospital care and underuse less expensive alternatives. Certain restrictions favor public over private hospitals (although Singapore now is privatizing its public hospitals) and discourage the development of a competitive market for hospital care. And some restrictions against borrowing from future Medisave deposits to pay current expenses seem unwise, since medical expenses cannot be timed to match the buildup of Medisave funds.

On the other hand, Singapore already has developed one of the most innovative ways of paying for health care found anywhere in the world—a vast system of individual self-insurance. The government of Singapore expects each individual to pay his or her own way and forces people to save for needs met by governments in most other countries. The program has been highly successful. Table 19.5 is an indication of how much progress has been made. As the table shows, the Singapore welfare state has steadily shrunk over the past two decades and is now largely devoted to helping the low-income elderly, who participated in the program for only a few years. As Table 19.6 shows, only among older workers are there many who have failed to accumulate substantial savings. On the other hand, young and middle-aged people are doing well. For example, in the 45–49 age group, 70 percent have savings of more than $17,000 (S$30,000).

Method 5: Market-Based Reforms As a Precondition for Privatization

Although some countries have introduced market-based reforms into government-run health care systems, it is clear that in Britain

Table 19.5
PUBLIC ASSISTANCE IN SINGAPORE, 1970 TO 1987

Year	Total Number of Cases Paid	Percent Elderly	Total Expenditures[1]
1970	10,982	57.6%	$3,517
1971	8,915	61.3	2,720
1972	7,881	62.6	2,341
1973	7,407	63.2	3,042
1974	7,031	63.1	2,917
1975	7,015	61.4	2,936
1976	6,640	63.9	3,618
1977	6,375	67.0	3,534
1978	6,330	67.1	3,518
1979	5,994	66.7	3,311
1980	4,580	69.2	3,165
1981	3,505	73.7	2,582
1982	3,297	75.6	3,066
1983	3,241	86.0	3,249
1984	3,278	88.7	3,600
1985	3,126	88.7	3,544
1986	3,004	NA	3,513
1987	3,082	NA	3,416

SOURCE: Ministry of Social Affairs, *Annual Report* (various years).
[1]In Singaporean dollars; S$1.76 = U.S.$1.00.

Table 19.6
CPF BALANCES OF ACTIVE MEMBERS, 1988

Age Group	Percentage of Age Group with Balances Below		
	S$30,000[1]	S$20,000[1]	S$10,000[1]
45–49	29.1%	21.6%	13.0%
50–54	27.0	19.5	10.9
55–59	58.4	41.4	24.5
60 and above	85.6	74.4	53.7

SOURCE: Computed from Central Provident Fund, *Annual Report 1989*.
[1]S$1.76 = U.S.$1.00.

and New Zealand the authors of the reforms have intended them as precursors to more far-reaching goals.

Case Study: Britain[25]

Under Margaret Thatcher, Britain became the leader of the international privatization revolution in the 1980s. Although the Thatcher government never formally proposed privatization of the NHS, a major step in that direction was taken with the health care reforms proposed in 1989 and implemented in 1991. As outlined in *Working for Patients*,[26] the government proposed to introduce competition and market incentives into the health care sector.

The single most important change is the separation of the purchase from the provision of health care. Under the new system, district health authorities (DHAs) have the responsibility to purchase health care for the residents of their districts. But they need not purchase hospital care from hospitals in their own areas. Nor are they confined to NHS hospitals. They may shop in a national hospital marketplace and purchase public or private hospital care. To encourage competition in the hospital sector, NHS hospitals are allowed (and even encouraged) to form hospital trusts—self-governing entities that can raise capital, negotiate employment contracts, and function as self-contained business entities. It is important to note that only DHAs, not patients themselves, make choices among hospitals.

In the primary care sector, a new system of paying physicians is designed to encourage competition among general practitioners (GPs) for patients, a feature that had largely been absent from the British health care system. In addition, in a move to encourage payment for performance, GPs will receive bonus payments for meeting targets for services such as vaccinating, immunizing, and screening. GPs also are allowed to become budget holders, with each establishing a sort of miniature HMO, which purchases diagnostic services and hospital services for patients. Under the system, GP budget holders have incentives to purchase lower cost hospital services and even to perform elective surgery themselves if the price of hospital surgery is too high. As of the fall of 1991, about 10

[25]See Day and Klein; and Enthoven.

[26]Secretary of State for Health, *Working for Patients* (London: Her Majesty's Stationery Office, 1989).

percent of GP practices had become budget holders, a number that was expected to double by April 1992.[27] Of 1700 NHS hospitals in existence in the fall of 1991, 56 had become self-governing, a number that was expected to triple by April 1992.[28]

The future of these reforms is uncertain, in that they have been vigorously opposed by the British Medical Association, as well as by the Labour party. Nonetheless, an important tactic of the Conservative party in all areas of the economy is that of initiating reforms that generate their own special-interest defenders over time.[29] The tactic may work in health care as it has elsewhere.

Case Study: New Zealand

In the 1980s, New Zealand underwent more economic liberalization than any other country in the world, virtually eliminating agricultural subsidies and steadily phasing out tariffs and quotas. Financial markets were totally deregulated, and almost any foreigner can now start a bank there. The country not only deregulated commercial airline travel, but it even began allowing Australian carriers to freely compete in its domestic market. It was only natural that New Zealand should launch a major program of health care reform.

In 1991, the New Zealand government announced a plan that combines several of the methods of privatization listed above—Chile's method of allowing individuals to opt out of public insurance and obtain private insurance, the U.S. method of allowing public-private competition in the supply of services, and the British plan to introduce market-based reforms into the public sector. The New Zealand plan features four major changes. First, all of New Zealand's public hospitals will be "corporatized." That means they will be turned into business entities with profit and loss statements, a common precursor of privatization in many countries. Second, public hospitals will be forced to compete with private hospitals for patients on a level playing field. Third, four regional health authorities will be created to negotiate contracts with providers, who will be forced to compete for business. Finally, individuals will

---

[27]Day and Klein, p. 54.

[28]Ibid., p. 52.

[29]See Madsen Pirie, *Dismantling the State: The Theory and Practice of Privatization* (Dallas: National Center for Policy Analysis, 1985).

be able to choose private insurance over participation in public insurance and will receive a tax rebate or a voucher in compensation.[30]

At the time of this writing, the final details of New Zealand's reforms are unknown. However, the government's commitment to the principles described above ensures that New Zealand's health care reform will be one of the most significant international health policy developments in the 1990s.

Options for Reform

A rich, multinational menu of health care privatization techniques exists today. Resistance to these techniques is inevitable. But as events in Singapore, Chile, Britain, New Zealand, and—to a lesser extent—in the United States show, privatization in health care is possible.

---

[30]One of the authors served as a consultant to a task force (chaired by Alan Gibbs) that made the initial proposals in the late 1980s. The proposals were further refined in Patricia Danzon and Susan Begg, *Options for Health Care in New Zealand: Options for Reform* (Wellington: New Zealand Business Roundtable, 1991).

20. Meeting the Needs of Underserved Populations

A widespread belief in the health policy community is that special groups of people are being underserved by the U.S. health care system. They include (1) low-income families, (2) uninsured people, and (3) people who live in rural areas.[1]

In view of the amount of political rhetoric focused on the problems of these three groups, it is surprising how little is actually known about their "unmet health care needs." Most of the available information is anecdotal, and many of the conclusions reached are based on indirect inferences (such as inferences drawn from the availability of physicians and hospitals) rather than on factual studies of actual needs (see chapter 10).

To our knowledge, no scholarly study has ever attempted to relate unmet health care needs to the institutional structures of the health care system. For example, specialists believe that about half the diabetics in the United States have not been diagnosed and treated by a physician (see chapter 17), but no one has attempted to demonstrate that a structural change in our health care system (for example, expansion of Medicaid, or employer mandates) would lead to more diagnosis and treatment. Half the diabetics in Britain are also undiagnosed and untreated, even though health care in Britain is theoretically free to all at the point of delivery.

This chapter proposes solutions to the problems of the underserved populations. It differs from almost all other commentaries in three ways. First, almost all other proposals designed to meet the needs of underserved populations begin with assertions about

---

[1] These categories are not mutually exclusive; all three characterizations could be used to describe the same family.

the nature of the needs and end with unproved assertions about how a policy change will result in more needs being met. By contrast, the solutions proposed here begin with the recognition that very little is known about how changes in health care institutions will affect those needs. Our argument for reform is quite different: The structure of the existing system arbitrarily and unfairly discriminates against certain population groups, and reform is justified on those grounds alone.

Second, almost all other policy proposals designed to meet the needs of underserved populations call for more government spending. Yet there is no known evidence that the United States is spending too little money on health care. Instead, the proposals presented below are designed to redirect the amount of money that is currently being spent to give individuals and communities greater freedom to control their own health care dollars and make their own decisions.

Third, almost all other policy proposals call (either directly or indirectly) for more government regulation and control of the medical marketplace. By contrast, the proposals made here call for government to retreat, thereby empowering individuals and communities and encouraging the development of market-based institutions.

Ten Policy Proposals

What follows is a discussion of ten proposals to meet the needs of underserved populations in ways that do not require more government spending and control. These proposals are briefly sketched, to give policymakers a general idea of concepts that need to be more fully developed. The rest of the chapter provides much greater detail on two of them—the concept of medical enterprise zones and the concept of a workable pay-or-play plan that guarantees universal health insurance.

1. Medical Enterprise Zones

In certain areas of the country, especially rural areas, the number of doctors and hospital beds per capita is well below the average for the country as a whole. These areas are often called underserved areas. The people who live in them are not necessarily deprived of medical care. They can travel to a neighboring area that is not underserved. But the cost and inconvenience of travel may create special burdens for many, especially low-income patients.

612

One of the reasons why underserved areas are underserved is that many of the laws and regulations written in Washington and in state capitals unreasonably restrict options and opportunities for rural residents. For example, regulations that may make sense for middle-income patients in large cities often make no sense for low-income families in rural areas. Medical Enterprise Zones (MEZs) are designed to solve this problem. Within specially designated areas, many of the regulations would be suspended, creating new options and opportunities for people to meet their own needs with limited resources. For example, within an MEZ, hospitals would not be required to employ a full-time dietitian or maintain 24-hour-a-day services of a registered nurse. Ordinary homes would be allowed as places in which long-term care could be delivered. And nurses, physicians' assistants, and paramedics would be allowed to deliver certain types of primary care. (See the expanded discussion below.)

2. Medical Enterprise Programs

The central idea behind the Medical Enterprise Zones is that there are distinct geographical areas within which people do not now have access to medical providers and facilities because the providers and facilities are not there. The problems faced by the urban poor are different. Providers and facilities may be nearby, but families have been priced out of the market by regulations not designed to meet their needs. Many of the regulations that govern the medical marketplace meet middle-class needs and desires. The urban poor, with less money to spend, are not given the option to choose less expensive alternatives.

Closely related to the concept of the MEZ is the concept of the Medical Enterprise Program (MEP). Unlike MEZs, MEPs are not defined by geography. Instead they are defined by the market that providers are serving. Thus, doctors, nurses, physicians' assistants, and other providers could be designated as Medical Enterprise Program providers, and hospitals, nursing homes, and other facilities could become MEP facilities if they were primarily providing services for low-income families. Under an MEP, providers and facilities would be as free of cost-increasing regulatory burdens as they would be if they operated in an MEZ. Moreover, because MEP status is defined in terms of markets being served, it is possible to conceive of a physician serving as an MEP provider while working at a clinic in a low-income neighborhood, although the same physician would be subject to normal regulations while practicing at a different location in another neighborhood.

3. Decentralized Medicaid

One of the biggest problems with the Medicaid program is that the decisionmakers who write the rules and regulations are often far removed from the problems they are attempting to solve. Politicians (pressured by special-interest groups) decide who is eligible and who is not, and in many ways dictate how health care is to be delivered. Often, their decisions result in an enormous waste of resources and prevent local communities from solving problems in a reasonable way. The regulations governing nursing homes are one of the most obvious examples.

Almost all people involved in rural health care can point to numerous ways in which health care dollars could be better spent, were it not for federal and state regulations. It's time to give them the opportunity. Medicaid funds should be turned over to local communities with only one restriction: The funds must be spent on indigent health care. The people who actually have to solve problems at the local level should be given the freedom to make decisions about who will be eligible for assistance and what type of health care is appropriate.

4. Community-Centered Welfare

As shown repeatedly in this book, decisions about health are related to many other decisions in life. Given limited resources, it is not obvious how much money should be spent on physicians and hospitals rather than on housing, food, and other goods and services. Currently, those decisions are made by politicians who govern what we loosely call the welfare state. Better decisions are likely to be made by people in local communities faced with real problems.

Accordingly, we propose that all means-tested welfare spending be turned over to local communities with only one restriction: The funds must be spent to help low-income people. Under Community-Centered Welfare (CCW), the amount given by federal and state governments would not be determined by arbitrary eligibility standards devised in the political process. Instead, the amount of CCW funds each community receives would be solely a function of the amount and degree of poverty in that community.

5. *Privatized Community-Centered Welfare*

Numerous studies have shown that private-sector charities out-perform government welfare programs. For example, in most communities, the Salvation Army does a much better job of meeting real needs than the Aid to Families with Dependent Children (AFDC) program does. Ordinary people agree with the scholars. Although billions of dollars are given to private charity each year, there are very few private gifts made to the AFDC, food stamp, or Medicaid programs.

Given the demonstrated superiority of the private sector, a strong case exists for privatizing CCW. One way to accomplish that would be to have communities specify their objectives and have private agencies compete for CCW funds. The winners would operate under contract for a limited period of time, after which the bidding process would be renewed. Note that the concept of privatized CCW advocated here is very different from the block grant program, popular in the 1970s. When the federal government made block grants, the recipient organizations began to lose their originality and adopt the federal government's view of poverty.[2] A genuinely privatized CCW program would reflect local community values, not the values of federal politicians.

Allowing local governments to award contracts to private-sector agencies still leaves room for politicians and special-interest groups to distort the purposes of the program. Thus, if there were a way to bypass politicians altogether, the results would be much better. Fortunately, a detailed proposal to achieve that end has been developed.[3]

Currently, the amount of means-tested federal welfare spending is equal to about one-third of personal income taxes. Accordingly, we should allow each individual taxpayer to allocate up to one-third of his or her tax liability to any qualified private-sector organization meeting legitimate welfare needs. Under this proposal, all private and public welfare programs would compete on a level playing field

---

[2]See John C. Goodman and Michael D. Stroup, *Privatizing the Welfare State*, NCPA Policy Report no. 123 (Dallas: National Center for Policy Analysis, June 1986).
[3]Ibid.

for taxpayer funds, and the taxpayers themselves would make the ultimate decisions about where the money goes.

6. A Play-or-Pay Plan That Works

In chapter 10, we discussed the harmful effects of employer mandates and play-or-pay proposals advanced at the state and national level. If our own proposals were adopted, however, a different kind of play-or-pay system would emerge—one which has most of the advantages and very few of the disadvantages of other plans.

The most common complaint about the existence of a large population of uninsured people is that they get a free ride, paid for by the rest of us. Since uninsured people usually get treatment if they are sick (at least in the case of medical emergencies), when they don't pay their medical bills, they get care subsidized by everyone else through the tax system or through cost shifting. But is this complaint really valid? Note that people who are uninsured are people who are not taking advantage of the generous tax subsidy for employer-provided insurance. As a result, other things being equal, the uninsured pay higher taxes than people with employer-based insurance. In fact, a back-of-the-envelope calculation suggests that the uninsured pay about $6 billion or $7 billion more in taxes each year because they do not get the average tax subsidy enjoyed by other taxpayers. Because the amount of annual unpaid hospital bills generated by the uninsured is also about $6 billion or $7 billion, it is by no means clear that the uninsured get more in free health care than they pay in additional taxes.

The difficulty with the existing system is not that the uninsured are getting a free ride at everyone else's expense. Instead, there are two other problems. First, the tax subsidy for health insurance is arbitrary and unfair. It is a regressive system under which most of the benefits go to higher income families, and it arbitrarily excludes people who purchase health insurance on their own. Second, under the current system, most of the additional taxes paid by the uninsured go to Washington rather than to local hospitals that provide the free care.

A remedy for the first problem (as discussed repeatedly in this book) would be for everyone to receive a tax subsidy for the purchase of health insurance. And the lower a family's income, the higher the subsidy should be. At the bottom end of the income scale, there should be refundable tax credits, with government directly paying a portion of the health insurance premium. A remedy for the second problem is to redirect the additional taxes paid by the uninsured to local hospitals that administer free care. Thus, individuals who choose not to be insured would pay more in taxes, and those additional taxes would help fund uncompensated care delivered to the uninsured.

Under this proposal, no one would be required to purchase health insurance. Those who chose not to would be forced to rely on charity care if they could not pay their own medical bills. Existing laws generally require hospitals to provide emergency care to patients, regardless of ability to pay. With the new source of funds proposed here, we could liberalize access to health care for indigent patients. But free care is unlikely to be perceived as being as desirable as purchased care, and it may involve health care rationing. Thus, people will have incentives to purchase health insurance— first, to protect their own assets; second, to acquire the quality of health care they want; and third, to be able to exercise choice in the medical marketplace.

7. Medical Spending Accounts

The concept of medical spending accounts is not new. Many middle-income employees of large companies use such accounts to pay expenses not covered by conventional health insurance (as noted elsewhere in this book). What is proposed here is to extend the option to low-income families as well.

Medical spending accounts are a way of empowering low-income patients and freeing them from the arbitrary shackles of the Medicaid and Medicare programs. A pregnant women on Medicaid, for example, should be given an opportunity to spend from such an account (with the right to add other funds and pay market prices) in the market for prenatal care (see chapters 3 and 4).

This concept can be expanded to other areas. For example, admission to a nursing home under government programs is supposed to be governed by specific physical disabilities. Rather than furnish nursing home care, however, we could establish a spending account—allowing patients the alternative of purchasing home care, drugs, and other services. The amount of the account might vary, depending on the degree of the disability. At a minimum, patients should have options. And granting them options makes it likely that a great deal of money could be saved. For example, it seems likely that many patients in nursing homes (at a cost of $25,000 per year) would be willing to seek alternatives in return for a $1,000-per-month medical spending account.

8. Medisave Accounts

A natural extension of the concept of medical spending accounts is the creation of full-fledged medical savings accounts. Enormous premium savings are possible for people who choose high, rather than low, deductibles under their private health insurance policies (see chapter 8). The same principle applies to public insurance, including Medicaid.

Accordingly, Medicaid patients should have the option of choosing high-deductible coverage and placing the premium savings in tax-free Medisave accounts. They should also be allowed to add other funds, up to the amount of the annual deductible, and they should be permitted to spend their Medisave funds freely in the medical marketplace—without regard to Medicaid's normal regulations and restrictions.

9. A Real Voucher Program

There have been many proposals to create health insurance vouchers for low-income people. Such proposals, however, will do little to create real empowerment unless insurers are free to offer significant diversity on the supply side. In most communities where parents have been allowed to choose among different branches of the same school system, the option to choose has proved to be of small value.

A voucher system that results in real empowerment is one that allows insurers wide discretion in the types of services they may offer. For example, providing institutions must be free to greatly reduce the amount they spend on care for premature babies in return for expanded prenatal care (or Medisave account money to purchase prenatal care). They must be free to greatly reduce the money spent on heroic medical services in return for more preventive services. They must be free to offer more home care, less institutionalized care, etc.

618

If insurance suppliers were allowed options, and Medicaid patients were given the right to exercise choice, low-income families would soon enjoy something they are now denied—the benefits of a competitive market.

10. Liability by Contract

Under traditional common-law doctrine, hospitals delivering charity care could not be sued for their torts. The theory was that because patients were receiving free care, there was no normal contract. Thus, they could not sue for negligence arising under the relationship. The doctrine of charitable immunity was eroded by a series of court decisions, and, for all practical purposes, it no longer exists today. In fact, many physicians regard Medicaid patients as the ones most likely to sue. As a result, some physicians engage in costly defensive medicine and others avoid Medicaid patients altogether.

One solution is to return to the older doctrine under which people who chose to receive free care would not be able to sue those who provide it. The disadvantage of that approach is that the tort liability system may be the only force maintaining quality under the current system in which government programs are putting relentless pressure on providers to cut costs. A different solution is possible, however, if Medicaid patients are allowed to become full participants in a competitive marketplace. Under this solution, patients would be allowed to exercise choices and negotiate liability arrangements on their own.

All patients should have the right to exercise freedom of contract in the realm of tort liability (see chapter 3). Thus, in return for patient life and disability insurance covering a medical episode, providers should be free to offer a lower price to patients who waive their right to sue for simple negligence. Because the hospitals would have to purchase the insurance policy, they would keep their premiums down by maintaining quality. Insurance companies would specialize in monitoring hospitals to know how to price their policies, thereby performing a function that individual patients would find difficult to undertake.

How could this solution be applied to Medicaid patients? Under the current Medicaid program, patients are spending taxpayer money and thus getting no direct benefit from any price reduction.

However, if patients were free to exercise choice under a real voucher system, they might have the opportunity to trade off reduced tort liability protections for expanded benefits. For example, providers might offer a greater range of services if patients agreed to waive their right to bring tort claims and accepted a guaranteed insurance settlement in the manner described above.

Solving the Needs of Underserved Populations with MEZs

The central issues presented in this book are those that are of direct and personal concern to the majority of Americans. Accordingly, we have focused primarily on the problems of middle-income families that live in urban areas, where the potential exists for a competitive market for medical services. However, there are other problems, and one is the delivery of health care in rural areas. Similar, although not identical, problems often exist in low-income areas within large cities. In this section we will take a closer look at the problems of rural health care and discuss ways of solving those problems through the creation of Medical Enterprise Zones.

The Economics of Rural Health Care

Rural areas face important policy problems because of some general economic principles that apply to rural health care in the United States and in almost all other countries. What follows is a brief summary of seven such principles.

1. Both the economics and the technical aspects of the practice of medicine create natural differences between urban and rural health care. The very fact that urban areas are characterized by higher population densities means that certain types of medical services will be found only in urban settings, whether decisions are made through the market or through the political system.

One example is the provision of highly specialized services that meet the needs of a small percentage of people distributed more or less randomly throughout the population. Because it is almost always more economical to bring the patients to the specialized service rather than the other way around, such services tend to be delivered from fixed locations. Because travel to centralized urban settings is usually cheaper and simpler, one would expect the services to be located in urban areas.

Thus, in virtually every country, we would expect to see more physician specialists in urban areas than in rural areas. That is the case in countries with national health insurance, as well as in the United States.[4] In U.S. cities, as Figure 20.1 shows, specialists constitute 62 percent of all practicing physicians. In rural areas, specialists constitute only 43 percent, and the percentage declines with the population size.

A similar principle applies to very expensive medical technology that is designed to meet special needs. One would not expect to find burn centers or organ transplant centers in remote rural villages, for example. Another difference between urban and rural health care services is that services that have large economies of scale tend to be located in urban areas. Taking advantage of economies of scale requires high volume, and high volume typically is impossible in rural areas. Thus, it is not surprising that most full-service hospitals are in larger cities, whereas hospitals in rural areas offer a limited range of services.

In the United States, hospitals with 300 or more beds make up 30 percent of all beds in metropolitan areas, but only 2 percent of the beds in nonmetropolitan areas, as shown in Figure 20.2. Hospitals with 200 to 299 beds make up 20 percent of all beds in metropolitan areas, but only 5 percent of the beds in nonmetropolitan areas. Overall, hospitals with fewer than 100 beds account for almost 75 percent of all rural hospitals, but only 23 percent of all urban hospitals.[5] These differences in hospital types between urban and rural areas persist even though the total number of hospital beds per person is about the same.[6]

A similar principle often applies to surgery. In general, if a hospital performs a high volume of a particular type of surgery, it will have a lower average cost for providing the service, and it may have

[4]U.S. Office of Technology Assessment, *Health Care in Rural America* (September 1990), Table 10.15 (p. 235). In 1988, about 23 percent of the population lived in nonmetropolitan counties as defined by the Office of Management and Budget. About 27 percent of the population lived in "rural" areas of 2,500 or fewer residents, as defined by the Bureau of the Census. A little more than 15 percent of the population is "rural" by both definitions. See U.S. Office of Technology Assessment, *Health Care in Rural America*, p. 35. In this section, U.S. statistics on rural health care refer to nonmetropolitan areas.

[5]U.S. Office of Technology Assessment, figure 1.3 (p. 12).

[6]Ibid., p. 153.

PATIENT POWER

Figure 20.1
PERCENT OF PHYSICIANS IN URBAN AND RURAL AREAS
WHO ARE SPECIALISTS, 1988*

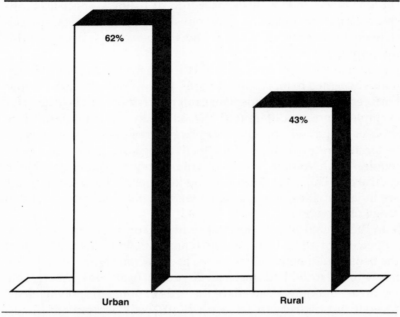

SOURCE: U.S. Office of Technology Assessment, *Health Care in Rural America* (September 1990), Table 10.15 (p. 235).

*Percentages based on total numbers of active physicians in each type of area. Nonspecialist, or primary care, physicians include physicians in general and family practice, internal medicine, pediatrics, and obstetrics and gynecology, and doctors of osteopathy.

a higher success rate as well. As a result, both cost and quality considerations favor the urban hospital setting. For example, one study of U.S. hospitals found that the cost for low-volume hospitals was 50 percent higher for emergency room visits, 150 percent higher for general surgery, and more than 600 percent higher for maternity.[7] Other studies show that mortality rates for surgeries, such as

[7]Thomas G. Cowing and Alphonse G. Holtman, "Multiproduce Short-Run Hospital Cost Functions: Empirical Evidence and Policy Implications from Cross-Section Data," *Southern Economic Journal* 49, no. 3 (January 1983): 648.

622

Figure 20.2
PERCENT OF HOSPITALS BY SIZE IN URBAN AND RURAL
AREAS*

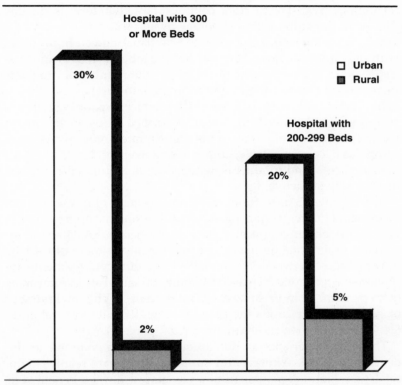

Hospital with 300
or More Beds

□ Urban
■ Rural

Hospital with
200-299 Beds

30%

20%

5%

2%

SOURCE: U.S. Office of Technology Assessment, *Health Care in Rural America* (September 1990), Figure 1.3 (p. 12).

*Percentages for each size category based on total number of hospitals in each type of area.

heart surgery, are considerably higher when performed infrequently.[8]

  2. The supply of rural health care services is directly related to the national supply of health care services. If a country has only

[8]Warren Greenberg, "Demand, Supply and Information in Health Care and Other Industries," in Jack A. Meyer, ed., *Incentives vs. Controls in Health Policy* (Washington: American Enterprise Institute, 1985), p. 100.

623

one CAT scanner, the scanner almost certainly will be located in a large city. Only as the number of scanners increases is there an opportunity for rural hospitals to obtain one. The amount of medical technology available to rural communities, therefore, is directly related to the amount of technology available in the country as a whole. A similar principle applies to health manpower. In countries with only a few doctors, both general practitioners (GPs) and specialists tend to be in large cities. Only as the number of providers increases do some of them tend to migrate to rural areas.

In market economies, the process by which expanding national supply affects the supply to rural areas is called diffusion. Resources locate first where they receive the highest rate of return. As more resources become available, competition lowers their rate of return in urban areas, and rural areas, where no competitors exist, become increasingly attractive.

In the United States, for example, the location of physicians can be explained in terms of competition and economic opportunity as well as the underlying preferences of physicians.[9] As a result, an increase in the total number of physicians means more physicians in rural areas. Between 1979 and 1988, the number of patient-care physicians per capita increased by about the same rate in rural areas (23.5 percent) as in urban areas (23.7 percent).[10] The total number of physicians per capita increased by a higher rate in rural areas (24.4 percent) than in urban areas (19.7 percent).[11]

The U.S. experience is not unique. Nor is it confined to the developed world. Wherever the supply of physicians relative to the total population expands, rural areas almost always benefit. For example, as a result of a 25 percent increase in the number of physicians in Canada, the physician-to-population ratio in the underserved provinces rose relative to that of other provinces; in

[9]See L. Jackson Brown and Jack Reid, "Equilibrium and Disequilibrium in Markets for General Practitioners: New Evidence Concerning Geographic Distribution of Physicians," *Advances in Health Economics and Health Services Research* 4 (1983): 305–33; L. Jackson Brown, Jesse S. Hixson, and Gerald L. Musgrave, "Implications of the Expanding Supply of Physicians for Geographic Distribution," unpublished manuscript (1983); and Jesse S. Hixson, "The Spatial and Specialty Distribution of the U.S. Physician Supply," American Medical Association Center for Health Policy Research, Discussion Paper no. 87–9 (October 1987).

[10]*Health Care in Rural America*, Table 10.24 (p. 246).

[11]Ibid.

rural Ontario, the ratio rose between 35 and 80 percent while increasing by 40 percent for the province as a whole.[12] Expansion of the number of physicians in Egypt led to so much saturation in the urban areas that 50 percent of all young physicians are now setting up practice in rural areas.[13] In Malaysia, there is one doctor for every 1,200 people in the capital, Kuala Lumpur, compared with one for every 9,000 people in the rural state of Kelantan. However, expansion in the number of specialists has caused GPs to open 24-hour clinics and to begin relocating in rural villages and on oil palm and rubber estates.[14] Between 1975 and 1985, the number of physicians per capita expanded by 50 percent in South Korea; as a result, the number of rural physicians expanded by 19 percent.[15]

3. As medicine becomes more complex and specialized, urban areas increase their comparative advantage in the provision of many types of care. Even as the expanding national supply of medical services leads to an expansion of services in rural areas, increasing complexity and specialization tend to reverse that flow or at least change its composition. In the field of surgery, for example, outpatient surgery is the least location-bound, and one would expect the availability of outpatient services to grow over time in rural areas. Yet, as more outpatient surgery is performed, surgery performed on an inpatient basis tends to be increasingly complex and specialized. Thus, one would expect the growth of inpatient surgery to occur in urban areas at the expense of rural areas. The U.S. experience bears out this expectation. Between 1984 and 1988, there was a general shift from inpatient to outpatient surgery in almost all areas of the country, but the shift has been more pronounced in rural areas. The number of inpatient days fell by 16.1 percent in rural hospitals, compared with a 10.4 percent drop in urban hospitals, and the number of outpatient visits grew by 33.5

---

[12]Malcolm Anderson and Mark W. Rosenberg, "Ontario's Underserviced Area Program Revisited: An Indirect Analysis," *Social Science and Medicine* 30, no. 1 (1989): 37, 39.

[13]Julius B. Richmond and Jeremiah Norris, "Egypt," in Richard B. Saltman, ed., *The International Handbook of Health Care Systems* (New York: Greenwood Press, 1988), pp. 73–91.

[14]Ho Tak Ming, "The Present Problems and Future Needs of Primary Health Care in Malaysia," *International Journal of Health Services* 18, no. 2 (1988): 285.

[15]B. M. Yang and J. Huh, "Physician Distribution and Health Manpower Policy in Korea, " *Asia-Pacific Journal of Public Health* 3, no. 1 (1989): 68–71.

percent at rural hospitals, compared with 25.5 percent at urban hospitals.[16] In general, rural communities have more general practitioners and outpatient surgery than ever before. But for specialized care and inpatient surgery, the trend is for rural patients to go to the larger cities.[17]

4. Rural health care is not necessarily less expensive. A common assumption is that because wages, rents, and other input prices tend to be lower in rural areas, the cost of providing health care is also lower. That assumption overlooks two facts. First, many health personnel perceive large cities as having advantages over rural areas and are likely to demand higher incomes to compensate for rural living. The process of diffusion that induces physicians and other personnel to locate in rural areas requires economic incentives. The minimum income needed to retain rural health staff may be higher than that needed for large cities. Second, there are economies of scale in the provision of many health services. If rural practices are unable to take full advantage of these potential economies, their average costs may be higher even when their input prices are lower.

When all factors are taken into consideration, rural health care services cost more than similar services provided in urban areas. A 1987 study by the American Medical Association found that rural family physicians had an average practice cost of $119,000, compared with $92,000 for their urban counterparts.[18]

5. The supply of rural health care services is affected by the size of the market and by competing alternatives. As in any market, potential suppliers of rural health care services can be expected to be guided by their expected rate of return. That return is partly determined by the size, density, and incomes of the patient population to be served. In general, a denser population attracts more physicians. In 1988, rural counties with 50,000 or more people averaged 14.7 physicians for every 10,000 people; by contrast, rural

---

[16]U.S. Office of Technology Assessment, *Health Care in Rural America*, Table 5.1 (p. 112), Table 5.11 (p. 123).

[17]Ibid., pp. 123–4.

[18]M. L. Gonzalez and D. W. Emmons, *Socioeconomic Characteristics of Medical Practice 1989* (Chicago: American Medical Association, 1989).

counties with fewer than 1,000 people averaged only 5.8 physicians for every 10,000 people.[19]

The amount of money that people are willing to spend on health care rises with income. That makes the wealth or poverty of a rural area an important economic determinant of the size of the market. Not all rural residents are poor, but many are. In addition, rural residents are less likely, on the average, to have private or public health insurance. In the United States, about one out of every six rural families has an income below the poverty line. About 18.2 percent of rural residents have no health insurance coverage, compared with 14.5 percent for urban residents; of people with incomes below the federal poverty level, Medicaid covers only 35.5 percent of rural, compared with 44.4 percent of urban, residents.[20]

Another important factor is the presence of competing alternatives. Although rural areas are often depicted as lacking health care alternatives, more than 84 percent of rural hospitals are actually within 30 miles of another hospital.[21]

6. There is no "right" amount of rural health care, independent of people's preferences. Many health economists who write about rural health care assume that there is a problem that is independent of the preferences of the people to be served. For example, many take the existence of counties without physicians or hospitals as self-evidently a social problem to be solved. But such a view is unfounded. No one is forced to live in "frontier" counties (containing six or fewer people per square mile). People who choose to live there give up a great many of the amenities of urban living, including immediate access to health care. Presumably they prefer the problems of the frontier to the even greater problems they associate with urban life. The right amount of health care in rural areas is the amount that the residents are willing to pay for. If people in rural areas decide to spend less on health care and more on other goods and services, that fact is not a social problem. In the United States we allow the poor and the elderly to purchase health care with public funds. But if rural patients choose to spend Medicare and

[19]U.S. Office of Technology Assessment, *Health Care in Rural America*, Table 10.24 (p. 246).
[20]Ibid., pp. 6, 7, 49.
[21]Ibid., Table 5.42 (p. 148).

627

Medicaid funds at urban rather than rural hospitals, that is an exercise of patient preference, not a social problem.

7. Survival in the rural hospital marketplace requires business-like decisions and a willingness to change. An inevitable result of the cost-plus system in the United States is that nonprofit hospitals have not been managed in a businesslike way. As the hospital marketplace undergoes radical change, a businesslike approach to hospital management is becoming evident in competitive urban areas. That is less true in rural areas. Although some hospitals have closed in recent years, there is still an abundance of rural hospital beds. Many existing rural hospitals, however, will not survive unless they adapt to a changing marketplace.[22]

How Government Policy Discriminates against Rural Areas

Between 1984 and 1988, rural hospitals closed at twice the rate of urban hospitals (a 5.5 percent closure rate versus 2.6 percent).[23] Although most people in areas where rural hospitals have closed still have reasonable access to acute care, the future looks bleak. One federal study stated bluntly that "rural . . . hospitals are going broke."[24]

Although the number of physicians in rural areas is growing, rural areas have only half as many physicians as urban areas when measured on a per capita basis.[25] In 1988, 111 counties had no physician, half a million rural residents lived in counties with no physician trained to provide obstetric care, and 49 million people lived in counties with no psychiatrist.

Government policy toward rural health care is somewhat schizophrenic. On the one hand are programs designed to subsidize rural health care through one bureaucracy or another. On the other are government efforts to discourage the development of a healthy private sector in rural health care. What follows is a brief discussion of current policies that discriminate against people who live in rural areas.

[22]Ibid., pp. 12–13; and chapters 6, 7, 8.
[23]Ibid., Table 5-1 (p. 112).
[24]Ibid., p. 8.
[25]Ibid., Table 10-15 (p. 235).

Reimbursement under Government Health Care Programs

Rural practitioners and rural hospitals complain, with some justification, that they are discriminated against under the Medicare and Medicaid programs. For example, the standard diagnosis-related group (DRG) payment that Medicare makes to hospitals was 9 percent greater for large city hospitals than it was for rural hospitals in 1989. After a "wage index" adjustment is factored in, the discrepancy is even larger.[26] Medicare's method of paying physicians relies on "customary, prevailing and reasonable charges." And because the average prevailing charge for a general checkup from a family practitioner varies from $72 in large urban areas to $53 in small rural areas (as of 1987), urban doctors tend to receive about 36 percent more for the same service.[27] Less is known about Medicaid payments, but similar discrepancies are likely to exist.

Some studies claim to justify the payment differentials on the grounds that the cost of inputs for hospitals and physicians is lower in rural areas. But focusing only on input prices may be misleading. Given that rural practices and facilities do not have the same ability to specialize or to achieve economies of scale, costs in rural areas may be higher. In addition, rural doctors and hospitals that have a disproportionately large percentage of Medicare and Medicaid patients may have few opportunities to offset lower government reimbursement by charging other patients more.[28]

More important, the entire practice of basing payments to physicians and hospitals on costs is an unfortunate remnant of the cost-plus system of finance. A better method would be to recognize that the role of government is to give patients spending power. For example, Medicare might make $60 available for a general checkup regardless of where the checkup is performed and also permit patients to add their own money to that amount if needed.[29]

[26]Ibid., p. 64.

[27]Ibid., Table 12-7 (p. 327). Note that physicians practicing in "high priority" rural health manpower shortage areas now receive a 10 percent bonus payment. Special payments are also made to certain categories of rural hospitals. See U.S. Office of Technology Assessment, *Health Care in Rural America*, pp. 61–68.

[28]For a general discussion of physician reimbursement and practice costs, see U.S. Office of Technology Assessment, *Health Care in Rural America*, pp. 325–29.

[29]Current plans are to move to a single national rate for physician payments. But these payments will be adjusted in ways that result in lower payments in rural areas. See U.S. Office of Technology Assessment, *Health Care in Rural America*, p. 68.

Government Controls on Medical Facilities

Numerous federal and state regulations effectively discriminate against rural health care facilities. They include federal Medicare regulations, federal income tax regulations, state licensing requirements, and other state regulations. For example:[30]

- Medicare rules require hospitals to provide 24-hour nursing service by a registered nurse (RN) in each department or unit of the facility, including the emergency room—an expensive requirement for a small multiservice rural hospital.
- Medicare requires hospitals to use licensed laboratory and radiology technicians and to have a full-time director of food and dietary services.
- Medicare requires hospitals to meet expensive fire and safety rules, including having emergency power, emergency water supplies, and corridors of a minimum width.
- Medicare requires extensive and burdensome paperwork (especially onerous for small hospitals without computer hardware, specialized software, or large administrative and technical staffs) and does not reimburse for the cost of meeting the requirement.
- Medicare requires a full-time RN who is responsible solely for the home health service and certified instructors to conduct classroom teaching for home health aides.
- To qualify as a rural health clinic under Medicare and Medicaid rules, a facility must meet burdensome administrative and staffing requirements.
- To qualify as a community health center (CHC), a facility must have a minimum number of patient encounters per physician and administrative costs must not exceed a certain percentage of total costs—standards that many rural CHCs cannot meet.
- Federal income tax law restricts rural facilities from participating in cooperatives and other arrangements that could provide such services as management, laundry, and housekeeping.
- Federal income tax law restricts the ability of hospitals to attract physicians by offering them loans, income guarantees, and other benefits.

[30]Ibid., pp. 181–93.

- Medicare and Medicaid have "antikickback" regulations that prevent hospital-physician joint ventures, physician ownership of hospitals, and other arrangements that might induce more physicians to practice in rural areas.
- State licensing laws often require rural hospitals to have fully equipped operating rooms and a surgical staff—even if the hospital performs no surgery.
- State licensing laws often require hospitals to employ several individuals to perform tasks that one could perform.
- State certificate-of-need laws may prevent rural hospitals from diversifying into new services or converting into a different type of facility (for example, a long-term rather than acute care facility).
- State and local property tax laws often allow exemptions for nonprofit hospitals only if no part of the hospital's property is used for a nonexempt purpose—a restriction that limits the ability of small rural hospitals to minimize costs and seize market opportunities.
- State enabling acts, many of which were passed 50 years ago, may prevent facilities from offering new services such as non-acute care, even though the market has changed radically over time.

These are only a few of the ways in which government regulations burden hospitals and increase their costs. For large hospitals in large cities, many of these burdens are easily met. But for small rural hospitals, they may mean the difference between bankruptcy and survival in a changing health care market.

Controls on Who May Practice

Numerous studies have shown that qualified nonphysician personnel can render many medical services traditionally provided by physicians—and for a lower price.[31] Collectively referred to as mid-level practitioners, they include nurse practitioners, physicians' assistants, certified nurse-midwives, and certified registered nurse anesthetists.

[31]U.S. Office of Technology Assessment, *Nurse Practitioners, Physicians' Assistants and Certified Nurse-Midwives: A Policy Analysis,* Health Technology Case Study no. 37 (December 1986). See also John C. Goodman, *Regulation of Medical Care: Is the Price Too High?* (Washington: Cato Institute, 1980).

Unfortunately, most state licensing laws are so restrictive that these potential providers of medical care are not fully utilized, even when patients would willingly pay for their services. State laws also restrict the activities of other nonphysician personnel, including pharmacists, optometrists, and the following allied health professionals: clinical laboratory technologists and technicians, physical therapists, occupational therapists, respiratory therapists, dental hygienists, dietitians, radiologic technicians, emergency medical technicians, medical records personnel, and speech-language pathology and audiology personnel.[32] In large cities, where the supply of physicians is plentiful, these restrictions may be less serious. But in underserved rural areas, nonphysician personnel may be the only option. Yet state laws continue to restrict the right of rural residents to purchase health care from nonphysicians who are apparently well qualified to provide it.

Medical Education

Since the publication of the Flexner report in the early 20th century, medical education has been tightly controlled by government. How many medical students are trained, where and how they are trained—these are decisions made by the health care bureaucracy rather than in the marketplace. One consequence is that medical education is dominated by an urban bias.

Between 1978 and 1986, the number of medical students from small towns decreased by 15 percent and the number from rural areas by 31 percent, despite the fact that students from rural areas are seven to ten times more likely to practice in rural areas. At the same time, the medical education curriculum is designed to train students to work as specialists in urban areas; residency programs prepare students to work in large teaching hospitals; and federal research grants encourage a focus on special diseases, leaving few funds available for research on family practice and primary care issues.

Creating Medical Enterprise Zones

Most policy proposals for dealing with the problems of rural health care call for more government spending and more bureaucracy. By contrast, the proposals made here call for equal treatment

[32]See the discussion in U.S. Office of Technology Assessment, *Health Care in Rural America*, ch. 10 (pp. 219–84).

for rural residents and the elimination of regulations that reduce access to care, increase its cost, or regulate it out of existence. The general principle is that some care is better than no care. These proposals are intended to apply only to situations in which care is unavailable or delivered with great difficulty. Under current conditions, many rural residents must go elsewhere for medical care. If the alternatives proposed below were available, no one would be forced to use them. Patients could continue to seek care in other areas as they do now. These proposals merely create new options and new opportunities.

Definition of an Underserved Area

Various definitions are now used, any one of which is acceptable.[33] One definition is that an area is underserved if it is 35 road miles from the nearest existing provider. Once an area has been designated as being underserved, its residents would have an opportunity to create a Medical Enterprise Zone (MEZ). Once created, the MEZ would continue in effect at the discretion of the local population, no matter how the area subsequently developed.[34]

Notification

All providers would be required to inform their patients of their qualifications. Notification could be in the form of a written notice when first-visit information is obtained from the patient, plus some visual notice to remind patients.

Professional Liability

In MEZs, patients could legally waive tort regulations. The most that any patient could recover in litigation would be actual economic damages, with no lump sum awards. States could not impose restrictions or costly insurance regulations on providers. If malpractice insurance were required, malpractice carriers could not discriminate against rural providers in rates or other conditions. Criteria for

[33]See Agency for Health Care Policy and Research, "Delivering Essential Health Care Services in Rural Areas: Analysis of Alternative Models," AHCPR Publication no. 91-0017 (Rockville, MD: U.S. Department of Health and Human Services, May 1991).

[34]In defining an underserved area, only full-time providers would be counted. That would prevent physicians or others from interfering with the process of designation by opening an office and seeing patients only one day a year.

633

malpractice would be adjusted (reduced) by the provider's ability, training, and education.

Licensing

Licensing boards and medical practice acts could not prohibit nurses and other paramedical personnel from performing services as physician substitutes in MEZs. The following describes some examples.

- Registered nurses (assuming a four-year baccalaureate degree, plus five years of experience) and nurse practitioners could prescribe any medicine or perform any operation not requiring a general anesthetic and currently performed by a physician. They could open an independent practice, not requiring the supervision of a physician. They could practice as partners with physicians. They could own any facility in any under-served area. Some RNs would acquire additional certification as physician assistants or nurse practitioners. However, that would not be a requirement.
- Emergency medical technicians (EMTs) and paramedics would be allowed to perform all of the tasks permitted to RNs except nonemergency surgery. EMTs and paramedics could perform surgery in emergency situations. Any person trained in the military as a combat medic would need no further certification to practice.
- Midwives could deliver babies at any MEZ location. An area with a hospital but no physician performing obstetrics could not restrict a nurse-midwife from admitting patients. Home deliveries or deliveries in the midwife's facility could not be restricted.
- Graduate medical students and residents could, on weekends and at other times, be used as respite providers. Residency programs could not discriminate against students who chose to be weekend providers. Such care would be fully counted as certification in their residency programs. They would serve as emergency backup for other providers.
- Foreign-trained physicians licensed to practice in any Western European nation, Israel, Australia, New Zealand, or Canada could enter America without regard to current immigration

limits and practice in an MEZ without further examination or
certification.

- Nonpharmacists could open a pharmacy and dispense prescription drugs if there were no pharmacy within the MEZ
  under the following three conditions. First, the same accounting and recordkeeping for addictive drugs would be maintained, otherwise no special regulations would apply. Second,
  the pharmacy could renew or refill any prescription not specifically marked nonrefillable. If it were marked nonrefillable,
  and the physician could not be contacted, the prescription
  could be refilled until the physician specifically informed the
  pharmacy to the contrary. Enough medicine would be dispensed to ensure the patient an adequate supply until his or her
  next appointment. Third, if there were no medical providers in
  the MEZ, a licensed pharmacist could prescribe any medication, with or without a physician's authorization.
- Any licensed health care professional, physician, nurse, etc.
  could cross state lines and practice in an MEZ without being
  reexamined or paying registration or licensing fees.

Medical Education

No state could prohibit the establishment of a nonprofit or proprietary medical school in a Medical Enterprise Zone. Graduates of
the school could not be discriminated against in terms of graduate
medical education or state licensing. Applicants to these schools
could not be discriminated against by any state or federal program.
Once opened, the school could not be closed because the area loses
its MEZ status.

Medical School Admissions

Medical students from rural areas who contracted to practice in
an MEZ for seven years would be classified as minorities for all
purposes, including admissions, scholarships, and quotas. These
students would be given preference over other minority students
who failed to sign the same contract regarding underserved areas.

Facilities

An area qualifying for the right to establish an MEZ would also
be one without a hospital within 35 road miles, plus situations in
which emergency services are more than 30 minutes away. Once

an area was qualified as an MEZ, the following conditions would prevail:

- No state could require a certificate of need for any facility in an MEZ.
- No state could require accreditation of a facility in an MEZ.
- Physical facilities used as nursing homes could not be regulated more restrictively than rental homes, motels, or hotels— whichever the physical facility most closely resembled.
- Zoning for hospitals or other health facilities would be permissive. In residential areas, great public harm would have to be demonstrated to disallow the construction of a medical facility. Medical facilities could not be restricted in any commercial or agricultural area for any reason.
- Surgery centers and emergency centers could be opened in any MEZ without regard to zoning, building code, Occupational Safety and Health Administration (OSHA), Environmental Protection Agency (EPA), or other regulations.
- Any government-owned building not on the tax rolls and not occupied for three months could be leased at fair market value to any health care provider wishing to use the buildings or space within and able to afford the first month's rent (that is, minimal capital expense). The lease would be renewable at the provider's discretion.
- Public or private insurance companies could not discriminate against a provider or a facility operating in an MEZ.
- Patients would be informed if the facility was nonconforming. They could waive their rights to litigate or could agree to have any awards limited to actual cash damages without regard to pain and suffering.

Medical Laboratories

The laws governing medical laboratories would be amended as follows:

- Medical laboratories could not be restricted in any MEZ.
- Ownership of laboratories could not be limited in MEZs.
- If unlicensed personnel were employed at such laboratories, the patient would be notified and could sign a form of written consent.

636

Medical Waste

The laws regulating medical waste would be amended as follows:

- State or federal agencies that regulate the disposal of medical waste could not discriminate against MEZs.
- As long as the facility disposed of the medical waste on its own property, no restrictions more severe than for the disposal of other hazardous waste would be allowed.

Blood and Blood Products

The laws governing the collection and distribution of blood would be amended as follows:

- Anyone could open a proprietary blood collection or distribution center.
- The center could establish any standards for donors. They could discriminate for any reason they chose in obtaining blood.
- They could produce blood with a brand name.

Health Insurance

The laws governing the sale of health insurance would be amended as follows:

- Insurance companies selling health insurance in MEZs would not be subject to mandated benefits legislation.
- Insurance policies offered in any other state could be offered in an MEZ without state restriction.
- Insurance policies could not discriminate against providers or patients who practice or live in MEZs.

Loans to Providers or Facilities

Restrictions on loans made by financial intermediaries to health facilities or providers in MEZs would be eliminated. Banks could make loans to directors who open facilities. Credit unions and other organizations would not be restricted by the percentage of their assets loaned to any one facility. State organizations could lend outside of their state or market area. Foreign investors could invest without restrictions. Interest ceilings or usury laws would not apply. Health organizations could issue commercial paper without state restrictions.

State Hospital and Nursing Home Regulations

States could not restrict the operation of a hospital or nursing home in an MEZ. That is, a state could not require that the hospital perform surgery, have a physician on staff, require an RN on duty when there are no patients, or outlaw the use of teenagers to work with patients needing long-term care. States could not restrict the ownership of facilities in MEZs.

VA Hospitals

The administrative regulations of the Department of Veterans Affairs (VA) and the Department of Health and Human Services (HHS) would be amended as follows:[35]

- Nonveterans would be allowed access to VA staff and facilities on a space-available basis.
- Nonveterans covered by Medicare, Medicaid, or Bureau of Indian Affairs programs would pay at the government-established DRG reimbursement rate (not a possibly higher or lower VA cost).
- Veterans could use their VA, Medicare, or Medicaid funds to obtain better quality care at VA facilities.
- Privately insured or private-pay patients would also have access to VA facilities on a space-available basis. Local VA administrators could negotiate prices and fees freely with insurance companies, health maintenance organizations (HMOs), preferred provider organizations (PPOs), civic groups, or employer groups.
- Local VA administrators could open outpatient surgery or direct-care satellite facilities in MEZs. Administrators could also offer extended hours at the main or satellite facility.
- All non-VA funds would remain in the local area and would not be used to lower the government's direct support for VA facilities; rather, they would be used to expand the VA's service to the community at large.
- Local VA facilities could pay bonuses to employees for overtime or duties outside their federal employee job descriptions.

[35]See Bill McAllister, "Nonveteran Health Care by VA Studied: Proposal Intended to Aid Rural Areas," *Washington Post*, August 21, 1991. As with other proposals made here, resistance from special interests is to be expected. See "Plan to Open Hospitals to Public Angers Veterans," *New York Times*, October 27, 1991.

Local VA facilities could hire full- and part-time professional and nonprofessional personnel to help serve the nonveteran clients. The new employees could be employees of the facility rather than of the VA. That would greatly reduce the administrative burden of hiring federal employees.

Pharmaceuticals

State and federal restrictions would be modified for nonnarcotic medicine in the following ways:

- In an MEZ, any pharmaceutical could be prescribed to aid the patient, without government restriction. Currently, many medicines are successfully being used to treat conditions, even though they have not been approved by the Food and Drug Administration (FDA) for that particular treatment. Some government regulators want to abolish that practice.
- Any pharmaceutical available in Western Europe, Israel, Australia, New Zealand, or Canada could be imported for the treatment of any resident of an MEZ. At present, some 1,000 medically important pharmaceuticals are approved in those countries but not yet available in the United States.[36]
- Pharmaceutical manufacturers and others could advertise any legally available pharmaceutical product to any resident of an MEZ. Commercial and medical free speech could not be limited for residents of MEZs.
- The law under which Medicaid regulations effectively discourage pharmaceutical companies from giving discounts would be amended to exempt pharmaceutical manufacturers, wholesalers, and others to sell pharmaceuticals at discount prices to rural health facilities, providers, or pharmacies for use by Medicare, Medicaid, and other patients. Firms offering discounts would not be required to provide them to nonrural organizations or to any other purchasers. Pharmaceutical firms could treat each individual rural area separately on the basis of its special needs.

---

[36]Jerry L. Schlesser, ed., *Drugs Available Abroad* (Detroit: Gale Research Inc., 1990).

- Other federal and state regulators would be prohibited from enforcing any law that would restrict any suppliers from offering discounts or reduced prices in rural areas. Nor could legislation force rural discounts provided in one area to be provided in any other area.

Medical Reimbursement

The arrangements under which Medicare, Medicaid, and VA patients are reimbursed would be revised as follows:

- Upon the diagnosis of any medical problem requiring hospitalization, the resident of a MEZ would have the option of treatment under the existing law or a one-time cash payment. The one-time cash payment would be equal to the existing DRG reimbursement for the hospital. Thus, MEZ residents would have the funds to seek treatment anywhere they chose.
- If and when DRGs for physician services are developed, the same cash indemnity payment would be allowed.
- Recurring health problems would be covered as they are covered under existing law.

Professional Referral

Given the economic conditions in rural areas, it is likely that health care professionals would develop a financial interest in local pharmacies, laboratories, hospitals, home health services, etc. That is especially true in the transition to and development of new health care services where none existed previously. For example, a physician might loan a hospital money to purchase lifesaving emergency medical equipment. Under current law, the physician could not send a heart attack victim to that same hospital. The law would be amended as follows:

- Medicare, Medicaid, and state legislation could not prohibit health care professionals in an MEZ from referring rural patients to facilities in which they have a financial interest.
- Health care professionals would be required to tell the patient that they have a financial interest in the facility or service, and inform the patient of the availability of other, competing facilities or services.

Public Health Measures

Public health dollars in an MEZ could be spent on a cost-benefit basis. Under the current system, there is a great deal of money wasted that could be spent to meet legitimate health care needs. For example, the regulation of chemicals is increasingly governed by political responses to public fear and hysteria rather than by careful, objective evaluations of the actual risks and benefits posed by the chemicals and their uses.[37]

Outline of a Play-or-Pay Plan

We conclude this chapter by briefly outlining a play-or-pay plan which (1) guarantees universal health insurance coverage, (2) gives choices and options to people who do not have private health insurance, (3) encourages competition in the delivery of health services to those without private health insurance, and (4) empowers local communities and frees them from the arbitrary rules and restrictions imposed by the federal government and state governments.

Local Health Care Agencies

This plan presupposes a change in the federal tax law such that every individual and family would have tax incentives to purchase private health insurance through a system of refundable tax credits. The lower a family's income, the more generous the tax credit would be. People who choose not to purchase health insurance would automatically pay higher taxes (the amount of the credit). These additional tax payments would be transferred to a local health care agency (LHCA) in the community in which the individual resides, and the LHCA would be responsible for providing any uncompensated health care for that individual.

Under this plan, everyone would have health insurance. Those without private health insurance (and who are not covered by a federal health insurance program) would be self-insured for the

[37]See the discussion in Bruce N. Ames, Renae Magaw, and Lois Swirsky Gold, "Ranking Possible Carcinogenic Hazards," *Science* 236 (April 17, 1987): 272; and Richard Lipkin, "Judging Limits of Safety Is a Regulator's Nightmare," *Insight*, May 23, 1988, p. 16. See also the discussion in Bruce N. Ames, testimony before the California Assembly Committee on Water, Parks and Wildlife, October 1, 1986; and Richard Lipkin, "Risky Business of Assessing Danger," *Insight*, May 23, 1988, p. 11.

amount of their personal assets. Once an individual's assets are depleted, the remaining costs would be paid by an LHCA in a manner similar to that in which Medicaid assumes financial responsibility for private-pay patients who enter nursing homes.

How Individuals Join Local Health Care Agencies

More than one LHCA may operate in the same community. When options exist, individuals may exercise choice. The LHCA selected by an individual will receive funds equal to the tax credit the individual would have received had private insurance been purchased.

Every community will have at least one government LHCA. People selecting the government LHCA will receive a government LHCA insurance card and will be entitled by law to the services the LHCA can provide with the tax credit funds. Other LHCAs will be free to operate in the community. However, people must select one. If no choice is made, individuals will be automatically assigned to a government LHCA, and an insurance card will be issued. Every individual will have an insurance card. There will be no uninsured individuals.

Individuals who have dependents may also receive health insurance coverage from LHCAs. Because the tax subsidy will increase with the number of dependents, there will be more funds for their care. Parents will select coverage or noncoverage for their children. Some adults may wish to purchase private enterprise insurance for their children and rely on the government system for their own care. This proposal allows these family-oriented choices to be made.

Nongovernment LHCAs

Any nonprofit organization could become an LHCA. Thus, the Salvation Army, Blue Cross–Blue Shield, the American Association of Retired People, labor unions, and the Red Cross are all potential candidates to operate LHCAs. The services they offer would be determined by contract and there would be an open enrollment period once a year. Every LHCA would have to cover emergency health care. Thus, people who became seriously ill could not be denied care anywhere in the country. Hospitals with emergency care facilities would be required to accept any LHCA insurance card for travelers or those moving to new areas, much as they are now required to provide emergency care, regardless of insurance status.

Nongovernment LHCAs would not be required to provide state-mandated benefits, although they could if they wished. The federal government could not mandate other than emergency and life-threatening coverage for any LHCA, either government or nongovernment.

The plan as outlined thus far, then, formalizes a procedure that is already in place, and improves on the existing system because it provides a mechanism for paying for what was formerly called "indigent health care." It also eliminates free-rider problems because people who choose not to purchase private health insurance would be contributing to their own LHCA health insurance. The amount of contribution would vary by ability to pay.

LHCAs could offer more than emergency care services, moreover. The incentive to do so would be to attract clients and therefore funds. In addition, as nonprofit organizations, LHCAs could accept charitable contributions, which would allow them to provide additional services.

LHCAs and Medicaid

Medicaid patients could be enrolled in government LHCAs, or they might be given the option to enroll in nongovernment LHCAs. LHCAs could not be forced to accept Medicaid patients, however. If they chose to cover Medicaid patients, they would not be required to provide exactly the same services for all members. An LHCA could tailor its services to meet the needs and financing levels for each group. For example, government funding might be higher for Medicaid patients than the tax credit for the voluntarily uninsured. Medicaid might choose to subsidize an LHCA to provide care for the uninsured working poor so that they did not become Medicaid patients. Similarly, all other government programs designed to provide health care to low-income families could also transfer funds under contract to LHCAs.

LHCAs and Welfare

Because of the desirability of community-centered welfare, LHCAs could provide other services in addition to health care. Thus, they might administer AFDC, food stamps, housing subsidies, and other programs. That would encourage the establishment of an integrated approach to meeting the needs of low-income families.

LHCAs and Congressional Districts

One of the dangers of transferring programs from the state and national level to the local level is that little more is accomplished than substituting one bureaucracy for another. How can we be sure that local communities will be more responsive to the needs of low-income families than the current bureaucracy? One way to accomplish that goal would be to create a government LHCA for each congressional district and appoint the member of Congress from that district as the sole trustee. Because elections are held every two years, there would be a single individual who would be answerable to voters for the LHCA's conduct.

Other than providing emergency accident and lifesaving care, the government LHCAs could provide any service, deny any service, and devise any delivery, insurance, or health care system. In their role as trustees, members of Congress could seek advice from health experts, political consultants, and public health officials. They could conduct surveys and obtain information from any source, but that would not be required. The trustees would be treated as if they were federal judges for purposes of litigation if their judgment or behavior were questioned. Upon retirement or defeat at the polls, trustees would, of course, be automatically replaced by their political successors.

Politics of LHCAs

Health care is now a political issue. In our discussion of the politics of medicine in other countries, we demonstrated that one of the worst problems is that politicians seek to distance themselves from the consequences of their decisions (see chapter 18). What is proposed here is to make explicit and open what the political process now must keep implicit and covert. There would be a single individual who would be personally in charge of each LHCA—an elected federal official with sole personal responsibility and few restrictions.

Some politicians will do an excellent job. Their creativity and capability will help their constituents. Other politicians can follow their lead. Being able to run a successful LHCA could be a credential for those who aspire to higher levels of national leadership. Others will not perform well and will probably be replaced. The competitive process will be good for the nation. Experimentation and variety in meeting public needs are reason enough to adopt this approach.

Solving Problems through Individual Choice and Competitive Markets

The proposals developed in this chapter do not require spending additional money on health care. Instead, they are designed to ensure that money is spent more intelligently and that people have maximum opportunities to use their intelligence, creativity, and innovative ability to solve problems by pursuing their own self-interest with the fewest possible obstacles created by regulatory bureaucracy.

21. Conclusion

The prevailing view in health policy is that markets cannot work in health care. This view has been used to justify the systematic suppression of prices and competition, and their replacement by regulation, bureaucracy, and nonmarket institutions.

Yet a principal finding of this book is that individuals in the medical marketplace exhibit exactly the same self-interested behavior they exhibit in every other market. When consumers face artificially low prices for health care services, they will overconsume those services. If the out-of-pocket cost is zero, they will tend to consume health services until their value at the margin is zero. On the supply side, self-interested behavior also is evident. When suppliers of medical services find that overprovision of services is profitable, they will overprovide. Moreover, they will provide more of those services for which the rewards are high, and less of those services for which the rewards are low.

Virtually every major problem in health policy stems from these elemental facts. Whereas in normal markets the pursuit of self-interest usually leads to desirable social outcomes, in health care the opposite is true. The pursuit of self-interest in health care leads to socially bad outcomes precisely because all of the checks and balances found in other markets have been eradicated or undermined.

Every proposal to solve America's health care crisis with more bureaucracy and more regulation is based on the premise that self-interested behavior can be regulated and controlled, and perhaps eliminated altogether. For example, advocates of universal, free health care are not arguing for a system in which patients are allowed to consume any health service they happen to want without paying for it. They fully realize that without constraints, free health care would bankrupt the nation. Rather, the advocates of national health insurance favor a system of health care rationing, under which patient preferences are largely ignored and medical services are delivered based on technocratic judgments about medical needs. Similarly, the advocates of national health insurance are not arguing for a world in which physicians get paid for any services they happen to deliver. Rather, these advocates favor a system in which physician preferences are tightly controlled and the supply of health care services follows a national bureaucratic plan.

The assumptions of the advocates of greater government control are false. Self-interested behavior is a normal and natural characteristic of human beings that will be with us always. Socialism does not work in health care any better than it does in any other market. Wherever we find government allocating health care resources, we also find common, persistent patterns. The pressures produced by competition for political office inevitably lead politicians to limit expensive medical technology for the few who need it in favor of marginal services for the vast majority of people who are not seriously ill. Physicians and hospital administrators are invariably rewarded for achieving political goals, not medical goals. And the patients are the losers.

Health care systems ruled by politics are always inefficient systems. They do not deliver high-quality services promptly and efficiently because there is no market mechanism to reward the providers for doing so. The special victims of health care rationing in bureaucratic health care systems tend to be the poor, the elderly, racial minorities, and residents of rural areas. Moreover, all of the characteristics of government-run health care systems in other countries are increasingly evident in our own government programs—especially Medicaid and Medicare—which are answerable to self-interested bureaucrats and politicians.

In this book we have used the term "cost-plus finance" to describe the way in which Americans have paid for health care for the past 40 years. On the surface, this system appears very different from the national health insurance schemes of other countries. On a more fundamental level, however, our health care system shares with the systems of other developed countries one fundamental feature: the lack of a genuine marketplace. Whereas other countries have formally adopted socialism in health care, our preference has been for private-sector socialism. Yet it is increasingly evident that neither public-sector nor private-sector socialism in health care can provide Americans with what they want and need.

A unique feature of this book has been the elaboration of an alternative vision of how the health care system could function. We believe that it is senseless to try to eliminate self-interested behavior from the medical marketplace. To the contrary, self-interest must be channeled and encouraged—to solve social problems in health care the way problems are solved in other markets. That requires transferring money and power from large, bureaucratic institutions to individuals and encouraging vigorous competition in the market for health care services.

The difficulty is in getting from here to there. Before normal market forces can solve our most important problems in the health care sector, the cost-plus system must be dismantled from the bottom up. The most that politicians can do is change the rules of the game. Once the rules have been changed, the tedious process of replacing cost-plus institutions with market-based institutions can begin. But the process of change must itself be market-oriented—brought about by millions of people pursuing their own interests.

Market forces are already at work, chipping away at the cornerstones of cost-plus health care finance. These forces are encountering formidable government barriers. The same public policies that enabled cost-plus health care to flourish are protecting it from collapse and replacement. The urgent need is for a reversal of policies, a removal of barriers to competition in health care. The change must be purposeful, coordinated, and designed to create a new health care system in which the preferences of individuals rather than those of impersonal bureaucracies govern the evolution of the medical marketplace.

The proposals set forth in this book—including a general agenda for solving America's health care crisis, and public policy recommendations in support of that agenda—have been designed to help the United States move to a market-based system. It is unrealistic, however, to expect major political change on the basis of a vision alone. Political change always creates hardship. Therefore, in the very act of changing rules and regulations, politicians must be seen as solving immediate problems, as well as long-range ones.

It is for that reason that the policy proposals have two distinct goals. The first is to solve well-defined, immediate social problems in the health care sector, thus making the proposals politically attractive. The second is to create a public policy framework in which an ideal health care system can flourish and prosper. The following is a summary of the general changes that are needed and the solutions we developed.

Changes in Tax Law

The U.S. system of paying for health care has, in large part, been created by federal tax law. For that reason, any fundamental change in the way that Americans pay for health care must begin at the federal level. Needed changes would affect the demand for health care and health insurance, as well as the supply.

Income Tax Treatment of Health Insurance

The current federal income tax system favors employees of large companies with benefits that are increasingly unavailable to the self-employed, the unemployed, and employees of small businesses. It is an employer-based system, originally designed to serve the needs of large companies rather than individuals.

If there is any social reason for the federal government to encourage the purchase of health insurance, then favorable tax treatment should be extended to all Americans in an equitable manner. Moreover, the proper federal goal is to benefit individuals over the whole of their work lives, not the particular firms that happen to employ them along the way.

Accordingly, all Americans should receive an income tax credit for health insurance, regardless of who purchases the policy. The tax subsidy should be limited to encourage the purchase of catastrophic, no-frills health insurance, and higher credits (including refundable credits) should be established to make it easier for low-income families to acquire health insurance.

In a competitive insurance market, there may be economies of scale in the purchase of group health insurance negotiated by employers, trade associations, or other groups. The tax law should not ignore this possibility. But the law should also encourage personal and portable benefits, so that health insurance meets long-term individual needs. When policies are purchased by employers, the value of the premium payment should be part of the taxable wages of employees, who would be able to take a tax credit for health insurance on their personal income tax returns.

Income Tax Treatment of Self-Insurance by Individuals

The current federal income tax system encourages the use of wasteful third-party insurance, instead of self-insurance for small medical bills. Although it encourages employers to self-insure for medical expenses, employees are penalized if they do the same thing. To remedy this defect, it should be a matter of national policy to encourage individual self-insurance through Medisave accounts, with third-party insurance being used only for large medical bills. People should receive no tax encouragement for the purchase of low-deductible health insurance. They should receive tax credits (including refundable tax credits) for making deposits to Medisave accounts. The funds in their accounts would grow tax-free and would be restricted to the payment of medical expenses.

Income Tax Treatment of Employee Benefits

At one time, it was thought that the tax laws governing employee benefits would encourage employers to extend health insurance coverage to more employees. Today, such laws are having the reverse effect, as employees of large companies choose not to cover their own dependents and small firms end their health insurance programs altogether. The tax law is so constraining that no insurance is sometimes seen as the best alternative.

To remedy this defect, employee health insurance benefits must be individualized. Employees should be able to exercise the same choices as if they were self-employed. That means they should be able to choose between wages and tax-favored health insurance and among all of the available health insurance options.

Income Tax Treatment of Savings for Postretirement Health Care

As we move into the 21st century, the United States—along with other developed countries—will face a financial crisis of unimagined proportions. Millions of elderly people will continue to look to government for pension income and health insurance. Yet the tax burden required to pay those benefits will take more than half of the average worker's income. This financial crisis will arise because both public and private methods of paying for postretirement health care are based on pay-as-you-go finance.

To avert the financial crisis, the United States must move quickly to a system under which each generation pays its own way. Instead of subsidizing current consumption of medical care and penalizing savings for future health care, there should be a system that encourages savings. As people age, they typically experience more and more expensive medical episodes. Thus the federal government should encourage the use of medical IRAs (MIRAs) primarily designed to pay medical expenses during retirement. The funds in such accounts would grow tax-free and would gradually substitute for Medicare.

The Role of Public Subsidies

A hallmark of cost-plus health care is the elaborate system of price discrimination known as cost shifting. Historically, in the market for physicians' services, hospital services, and health insurance, some people paid more so that others could pay less. This practice was defended on the grounds that higher income people should subsidize the expenses of lower income people. However, there is no clear evidence that this system really serves the interests of low-income people—or any other well-defined social purpose.

The failure to have competitive prices in the health care sector produces many undesirable side effects. People who are overcharged for medical care may decide not to purchase the services they need. People who are overcharged for health insurance may decide not to buy the coverage they should. The lack of competitive prices also causes individuals and employers to make inefficient decisions with respect to the choice between self-insurance and third-party insurance.

To the degree that prices are competitive (and reflect real production costs), they signal producers and encourage them to innovate and find lower cost methods of supplying those services. If the price system is distorted or if real prices are virtually nonexistent, such important signals will not be present.

The goal of government should be to provide a legal framework that will encourage the development of competitive markets. To the degree that goal is achieved, the United States will enjoy the benefits that competitive markets produce in other sectors of the economy. But because competitive markets are inconsistent with price discrimination and cost shifting, their emergence will force Americans to rethink current public policies.

In a competitive market, if government underpays for services intended for Medicaid and Medicare patients, the services will not be provided. Hospitals will not be able to overcharge some patients to finance charity care for others, and health insurance companies will not be able to overcharge some policyholders to subsidize coverage for others.

If we adopt the policy of encouraging private health insurance, Medisave accounts, and medical IRAs, we may some day reach a point where there is no need for any further direct role for government. In the meantime, a responsible role for government would be to directly subsidize those needs that are clearly socially desirable. A system of income-related disability payments would help families with preexisting and expensive medical needs that cannot be covered by private health insurance. A system of income-related subsidies to help families purchase health insurance would help high-risk people obtain coverage they otherwise could not afford. Government efforts to assist low-income families should be direct and financed by general tax revenues. As market-based institutions arise to solve problems, the need for government intervention will diminish over time.

Eliminating Harmful Regulations

The medical marketplace is one of the most regulated sectors of the U.S. economy. These regulations are designed to serve as a replacement for the market. Yet all of the evidence points to the conclusion that a regulated, bureaucratic health care system is no substitute for informed consumers making decisions in a competitive marketplace.

Regulation of Physicians

Today's physicians are buried under a mountain of paperwork, red tape, and bureaucratic regulation. Partly as a result, applications to medical schools have declined almost steadily since the mid-1970s, and 40 percent of physicians doubt that they would go to medical school if they had to do it all over again. Increasingly, the practice of medicine is dictated by third-party payers to the detriment of good-quality medical care and the doctor-patient relationship. And success in medical practice is now determined by the ability to manipulate third-party reimbursement rules rather than by the ability to meet patient needs.

Almost all of the burdensome rules and regulations are related to the third-party payment of medical bills. Most of them would be unnecessary and irrelevant if patients were spending their own money. Thus an important benefit of the changes described above is that they would empower patients and diminish the role of third-party payers. Government should provide information and prevent criminal and civil fraud, but there is no need for government to dictate the price and quality of medical care.

Regulation of Hospitals

The hospital sector is the most regulated of all health care sectors. As a result, the hospital marketplace is a bureaucratic, institutionalized market in which prices do not allocate resources or reflect real costs. As in the case of the regulation of physicians, the vast majority of the hospital regulations are a result of third-party reimbursement. Some fear that future survival in the hospital market will depend more on skills at manipulating reimbursement formulas than on adopting efficient production techniques. Nowhere are the harmful results of the cost-plus system more evident than in the problems confronting patients, who ultimately make the purchasing decisions in the hospital sector. Patients rarely can find out the price of a procedure before "buying" it and usually receive line-item bills that neither they nor their physicians can understand.

Public policy should encourage a competitive market in which hospitals announce their prices up front for common procedures, so that patients can become informed shoppers in the hospital marketplace. The mere act of empowering patients will probably do more than anything else to cause change. As the market for cosmetic surgery shows, competitive pricing emerges quickly when third-party payers are not a factor.

Regulation of Health Insurance

Insurance for medical expenses does not function the way other insurance does. Whereas life insurance and casualty insurance protect consumers against the financial burdens of risky events, health insurance is largely prepayment for the consumption of medical care. Consumers are worse off as a result. Because health insurers are prevented from pricing risk accurately, individuals are making decisions with adverse social consequences. Healthy individuals who find they are being overcharged are declining to buy insurance, thereby adding to the ranks of the uninsured. State legislatures are pricing millions of people out of the market through mandated health insurance benefits, premium taxes, and risk pool assessments. Perhaps as many as one out of every four people who lack health insurance has been priced out of the market by these cost-increasing regulations.

When markets were more competitive and health insurance more closely resembled real insurance, a strong market for individual policies existed. Health insurers often sought out people in risky industries, and policies were usually guaranteed renewable. Today, an increasing number of large health insurers refuse to sell individual policies, and the small group market is in danger of collapsing. Although prepayment for the consumption of medical care is at least a possibility for large corporations, it is virtually an impossibility for individuals and small groups.

The most common proposals for health insurance reform promise more of the same. They would move the country in the direction of a one-price-fits-all approach, in which price and risk would be completely divorced. Legislators would dictate health insurance benefits based on special-interest pressures from providers, rather than on consumer preferences revealed in the marketplace. The urgent need is to move in the opposite direction. People should be free to purchase no-frills catastrophic health insurance, making selections among policies based on individual and family needs. Insurers should be able to offer real insurance and specialize in the traditional insurance function of accurately pricing risk.

Empowering People Covered by Government Health Care Programs

Government, both directly and indirectly, is responsible for more than half of the nation's health care spending. Moreover, the government sector is the fastest growing component of the health care system. It is also the source of some of the most critical health policy problems.

Because the supply of health care services is relatively inelastic, when government programs expand, each additional dollar of spending buys only 35 cents of real services. The remainder is consumed by inflation. When government expands benefits but refuses to pay for them, the result is cost shifting to the private sector, in addition to accelerating medical inflation. As government imposes more and more cost controls, the result is health care rationing for those that government programs were supposed to serve.

Medicare and Medicaid

Medicare and Medicaid are not just two more buyers in the medical marketplace. Through them government uses its monopsonistic power to dictate price and (indirectly) to dictate quality. Physicians and patients are virtually powerless to change the terms of the arrangement even if patients would clearly benefit. As a result, these programs are increasingly causing medical care to be rationed.

A major step toward empowering patients and freeing the marketplace would be to restrict Medicare and Medicaid to the original goal of providing funds for the purchase of medical care. Accordingly, these programs should limit the amount that government will pay for medical services, but leave patients completely free to negotiate the total price for the services they receive. An equally important step would be to reduce the role of government as a health insurer. Government can provide funds for the purchase of health insurance without providing health insurance itself. Accordingly, private insurers should be able to offer Medicare and Medicaid patients alternatives to the current one-size-fits-all programs. Government can empower people in the market for health insurance without regulating and controlling that market.

Over the long run, Medicare can and should be replaced with individual savings through medical IRAs (MIRAs). Medicaid can be greatly diminished in size through refundable tax credits for the purchase of health insurance and the establishment of medical savings accounts for low-income individuals.

Reestablishing the Safety Net

Other changes in the public sector are also needed, and the most important changes do not require more government spending. Medical Enterprise Zones (MEZs) and Medical Enterprise Programs (MEPs) would remove bureaucratic obstacles and allow rural residents and the urban poor access to the benefits of a competitive medical marketplace. In most cases, turning control of public health care dollars over to local communities would ensure that the same money would go further in meeting real needs.

At the same time, we need a national commitment to a fair and equitable method of paying for indigent health care. If every nonelderly family in America had the opportunity to receive a tax benefit for the purchase of health insurance, people would be free to make rational choices. Those who chose not to purchase health insurance would pay higher taxes. But those tax dollars should then be returned to local communities to pay for what is now uncompensated care for the uninsured.

Planning for the Future

If the recommendations above are adopted as national policies, virtually all the legal protections presently accorded to the system of cost-plus health care finance will have been removed. In response to these policy changes, market-based institutions will replace cost-plus institutions very quickly. What we have called an ideal health care system will rapidly emerge, and the market for health care will resemble other markets.

What will the new health care system look like? Although no one can be sure of the details, such a system is likely to solve the problems of ordinary people as well as major social problems in the health care sector. In the new medical marketplace, power will be transferred from huge bureaucracies to individuals acting on their own behalf. Patients rather than third-party payers will be the principal buyers of health care. Physicians will be the agents of patients. Hospitals will be businesses selling services to patients and physicians. Insurance companies will be insurance specialists only. Government will be simply a mechanism by which individuals become informed consumers in the medical marketplace.

No one can predict the changes that will take place in medicine in the 21st century. Fifty years ago, the most creative science fiction writers did not even come close to imagining what the practice of medicine would be like in the 1990s. Over the next 50 years, the changes almost certainly will be even more dramatic.

Our generation has the opportunity to build a framework that will enable future generations to cope with the advances of medical science, whatever they may be. That is the legacy we can leave to our children, to our grandchildren, and to all others who follow.

Index

Advertising, competitive, 171, 174
American Enterprise Institute plan, 68
American Hospital Association (AHA), 7
American Medical Association (AMA): Council on Medical Education, 143–44; establishment and fiat of, 139; fee-setting code of, 141; influence on medical insurance, 153–55, 158–61; as part of organized medicine, 137; position on HMOs, 153–54. *See also* Organized medicine

Benefits: exemption for, 342; to Medicare recipients, 423–27; recommendation for personal, portable, 280, 650; state laws capping annual, 353. *See also* Employee benefits; Fringe benefits; Health insurance benefit laws; Income tax system; Mandated benefits; Retirement benefits; Subsidies; Tax benefits
Blood and blood products laws (in MEZs), 637
Blood collection and distribution centers, 637
Blue Cross: charity reimbursement, 172; cost-plus reimbursement methods, 21, 164–66
Blue Cross and Blue Shield: AMA influence on development of, 153–55; effect of regulation on, 159–60; favored by organized medicine, 159; market dominance of, 160–61, 173, 188; relationship to medical community, 161. *See also* Medigap insurance
Blue Shield, 159
Bureaucratic organization: decisionmaking under Medicare Part B, 572–73; differences between market and nonmarket, 32–35; in health care sector, 20–23; in ideal health care system, 29; of Medicaid

program, 59; perception of individual in, 37; of tort system, 64
Bush administration health care plan, 222–27

Canada: access to medical technology in, 491–92, 493, 495, 496; administrative costs in, 527–28; comparison to U.S. health care system, 253–55, 479–83; cost using Medisave accounts, 254, 256–57; health care for elderly in, 530; health care needs in, 481–82; health care spending in, 523–24; inequality of health care in, 508–12, 513–14; nonprice rationing in, 499–505; preventive care in, 526; private health insurance in, 513, 590, 592; quality of health care in, 514–21; racial discrimination in, 532–33; rural health care in, 537–42; uninsured people in, 500–501
Capital reserves, 198
Capital spending, Great Britain, 559–61
Carnegie Foundation for the Advancement of Teaching, 143
Casualty insurance, 180, 183–84
Catastrophic health insurance: cost of, 233; demand for, 458; lack of tailored, 346–47; Medicare policy for, 582–84; Medigap insurance limits, 456; with Medisave account, 250–51; proposals for elderly, 58–59
Central Provident Fund (CPF), Singapore, 598–605, 606
Certificate-of-need (CON) regulations, 305
Charitable immunity doctrine, 619
Charity care: hospital tort liability for, 619; under proposed Kennedy plan, 375; reimbursement for, 172. *See also* Indigent people; Low-income people; Medicaid program; Uncompensated care

659

Chile: private pension funds and insurance policies in, 593–96; privatized health care program in, 421, 567, 588–89; social security system of, 593

Claims: employer audits of, 207; experience of large groups, 241

CMPs. *See* Competitive medical plans (CMPs)

Commercial paper (in MEZs), 637

Common-law doctrine, 619

Community-Centered Welfare (CCW), 614–16

Community mental health centers, 581

Community rating: favored by cost-plus system, 125–26; implementation of and proposals for, 223; in premium setting, 188, 271; state regulation for, 352

Competition: American Hospital Association effect on, 7; among physicians, 151–53, 158; in economics and politics, 551–52; effectiveness in health care system of, 652–53; in medical marketplace, 80, 125, 171, 173, 193–97; in Medisave concept, 250; methods to avoid, 125, 219–22; proposal to encourage, 641

Competitive medical plans (CMPs), 459

Consumer sovereignty, 32–35

Conventional insurance: conditions for benefits, 181–82; determination of premiums and payments under, 182–83; differences from health insurance, 178–90. *See also* Casualty insurance; Life insurance

Cosmetic surgery market, 28–29, 56, 297, 654

Cost-benefit analysis: applied to medical practice, 299–301; as new form of medical ethics, 121–22

Cost-control measures: by employer, 207–8, 217; penalized by tax law, 277; proposed legislation to stop or curb, 229

Cost-management techniques: employed by self-insured firms, 341; by employers, 197, 199–208, 210

Cost-plus system: consumer choices in, 299–300; cost-control phase of, 137–38, 300–301; cost shifting in, 172, 310–11; cross-subsidies in, 172;

determination of premiums under, 182–83; dominance in medical marketplace, 173; evolution of, 125; evolution of and requirements for, 137; hospital prices in, 54; impact of government policy on, 173; impact on patients of, 654; limitations for, 23; price discrimination in, 652; requirement for survival of, 192–93; requires prepayment for medical care consumption, 215–19. *See also* Blue Cross and Blue Shield; Medicaid program; Medicare program

Cost shifting: conditions for, 655; in cost-plus system, 172–73, 310–11; as effect of state mandated benefit laws, 326–29; of employer-provided health insurance, 463; under employer self-insurance, 214–15; Medicare methods for, 404–5; with premium increases, 221–22; as price discrimination, 652. *See also* Cross-subsidies

Cross-subsidies: in cost-plus system, 172; in hospital sector, 192–93

Debit cards, 252–53

Defensive medicine: costs of, 63; reasons for, 619. *See also* Malpractice insurance; Tort liability system

Defined-benefit plan: as pension plan, 417–18; postretirement health care benefits as, 418–20

Defined-contribution plan, 417

Diagnosis-related groups (DRGs): adoption by private insurers, 306; effect of system, 303–6; federal and state government payment for, 55, 302; as health care rationing device, 62, 308–11, 568; under Medicare, 60; reimbursement rates for, 568

Discrimination: Canadian and New Zealand racial, 532–33; in medical school enrollment, 147; by Medicare and Social Security, 428; against people in rural areas, 628; against small firms, 268–70; in U.S. health care system, 611–12. *See also* Price system

Diseases, childhood, 89–90

DRGs. *See* Diagnosis-related groups (DRGs)

substance abuse and mental health, 103–5; development of, 189–90; differences from conventional insurance, 178–90; employeee choice of policy for, 205; employer-provided spending for, 81–83; for expensive technologies, 109–11; incentives to purchase private, 69, 616–17, 641; inequality in tax-deductible, 264; laws in Medical Enterprise Zone for, 637; low-deductible, 233–40; market for individual, 217–18; pay-as-you-go basis for, 182; per condition deductible, 243; play-or-pay plans for, 68–69, 230, 376–82, 616, 641; as prepayment for health care consumption, 124–25, 189, 215–19; problems of mandated, 68–69; proposal for free choice of, 46–49; proposals for employer-mandated, 368; proposals to force people to have, 355, 364–73; proposed universal, 641; reasons for purchase of, 361–62; recommended personal, portable benefits, 229, 280, 650; recommended tax credits for, 650; requires prepayment for consumption, 654; as substitute for wages, 39, 49–50, 69, 83, 276; tailored to individual needs, 98–99; tax credit for, 39–41; when not personal and portable, 126–29, 228–29. *See also* Private health insurance

Health Insurance Association of America (HIAA), 173

Health insurance benefit laws: avoidance of, 340–41; consequences of, 340; mandated, 47–49; rationale for, 346; state-level, 323–25. *See also* Mandated benefits

Health insurance costs: burden of regulated mandated benefits, 341; effect of mandated benefits on, 47–49; factors contributing to higher, 342–47; Medisave accounts to lower, 249

Health insurance marketplace: differences from insurance market, 25–26; dominance by Blue Cross and Blue Shield, 160–61; effect of cost-plus system on, 125–26; impact of government policy on, 173; impact

of state legislation on, 353; pricing of risk in competitive, 227; risk pools in, 339

Health maintenance organizations (HMOs): contracts with Medicare, 459; growth of, 194; in Hawaii, 364; incentives for low-cost consumption, 206; negotiation with health care providers by, 202; restricted choices under, 153; rules and restrictions of, 296–97; state prohibition or restriction of, 154–55. *See also* Competitive medical plans (CMPs)

Heritage Foundation health insurance plan, 68, 187 n. 32

High-risk individuals, 347

Hill-Burton Hospital Construction Act (1946), 157

Hospital chains, 158

Hospital costs: comparison of, 173–76; in cost-plus system, 22; effect of payer reduction in, 172–73; for elderly, 401; hidden, 177; lack of information affects, 52–56; payment guaranteed for, 169–70; when DRG payments are below, 308–11. *See also* Hospital prices; Hospital revenues

Hospital marketplace: cost-plus system drives, 168–69; with fixed-price system, 60–62; proposal for freedom of information in, 52–56; regulation of, 654; rural, 628

Hospital prices: in cost-plus system, 176–78; incentive to manipulate of, 167; regulation of, 301–11

Hospital revenues: government control of, 293–94; percent from Medicaid and Medicare, 306; as reimbursement for costs, 302; sources of, 167–68

Hospitals: in competitive environment, 30; discouragement of competition among, 171; government payment in Britain and New Zealand to, 590; incentives to maximize revenues, 167; in Medical Enterprise Zones, 638; Medicare reimbursement to rural and urban, 572; nonprofit, 157–58; proprietary or for-profit, 156–58, 193; public, 580; reimbursement in cost-plus system, 163–67; requirements to serve LHCA card-holders, 642. *See also* Hospital chains

under state law, 47–49, 197–98, 323–25, 326–39; state role in reform of, 350–53; variation in state-level, 348

Market system: cost-plus system as opposite to, 168; perception of individual in, 37; relationship of buyer and seller in, 26–29; self-interest in, 37, 300. *See also* Health care marketplace; Hospital marketplace; Medical marketplace; Price system

Massachusetts health care plan, 355, 364–67

Medicaid patients: accessibility of health care to, 511; in LHCAs, 643; rationed care to, 574–75, 578–79

Medicaid program: adoption of DRG system by state, 306; cost-plus reimbursement methods of, 166–67; effect of payment reduction, 172–73; effect of spending by, 231, 288–90; experimental alternative reimbursement under, 191; policy changes needed for, 319–20; proposal to dismantle bureaucracy of, 60; quality of service for patients under, 59, 67; recommendation to decentralize, 614; recommendation to restrict or replace, 656; representation of minorities in, 429; spending for elderly, 67

Medical care: emergence of free market in, 138–39; factors in consumption, 231–32; for indigents, 360–61; for infants and children, 84–87, 89–92; legal right to, 360–61; unnecessary, 114–20

Medical costs: hospital role in lowering, 158; inflation in, 286–87; for terminally ill, 105–9, 439. *See also* Hospital costs

Medical education. *See* Medical schools

Medical Enterprise Programs (MEPs), 66; effect of proposed, 656; for underserved population, 613–14

Medical Enterprise Zones (MEZs), 65–66; conditions for areas qualified as, 635–36; effect of proposed, 656; elements to create, 633–41; to meet needs of underserved population, 612–13, 633–41

Medical ethics, 120–23; AMA code in nineteenth century, 141–42; fee-setting as requirement for, 141, 151

Medical examining boards, 142–43, 144

Medical insurance plans: AMA influence on, 153–55; created by local medical societies, 159; development of prepaid, 159; indemnity and nonindemnity, 153; prepaid with restricted choices, 153

Medical IRAs (MIRAs): benefits of proposed, 449–50; concept behind, 440–41, 452; defect of, 416; NCPA proposal for, 441–45; for postretirement medical expenses, 652; as postretirement saving device, 415–16; proposed tax credits for, 441–49; proposed tax incentives for contribution to, 57; as replacement for Medicare, 656; Slaughter proposal for, 445–49. *See also* Super IRAs

Medical laboratories (in MEZs), 636

Medical marketplace: with competition, 80, 129–31, 192; for cosmetic surgery, 28–29; in cost-plus system environment, 22; differences from other markets, 20–21; effect on rural health care services, 626–27; emergence of competitive market for, 173; HMOs in, 194; information availability in, 27–28; as it should be, 14–17; market forces in, 649; Medisave idea in competitive, 250; NCPA report perspective of, 19; package price system in, 55–56, 297; private nature of U.S., 558; proposed transformation, 657; regulation of, 290–98; trend toward competition in, 208–9; where patients use own funds, 28–29. *See also* Health care marketplace; Hospital marketplace

Medical practice: direct and indirect government controls over, 315–16; federal cost-benefit analysis of, 301, 315; Medicare role in, 312–15. *See also* Licensing laws; Medical schools; Physicians; Tort liability

Medical rationing. *See* health care rationing

Medical records (on credit cards), 252

Medical savings accounts: advantages of, 249–51; effect on administrative costs of, 528; lifetime use of, 416; postretirement, 57; proposed, 46, 244; proposed for public programs,

248; proposed Medisave, 46; questions and answers about, 257–61; recommended for large medical bills, 651; in Singapore, 31, 248; using deductibles with, 244–47. *See also* Debit cards

Medical Savings Accounts (Medisave accounts): combined with MIRAs, 450–51; proposals for, 57, 326, 618

Medical schools: AMA-appproved, 139–40; decline in applications to, 294, 653; factors influencing student reduction in, 155; foreign, 155; goals of nonprofit, 158; government control of, 632; impact of Flexner report on, 144–47; in Medical Enterprise Zone, 635. *See also* Flexner report

Medical societies, 137, 158, 159. *See also* Organized medicine

Medical spending accounts, 617–18

Medical standards, 139–43. *See also* Licensing laws; Medical schools; Physicians' standards review boards (PSROs)

Medical students: conditions for priority status, 635

Medical technology: acccess in Great Britain to, 493; access in cost-control cost-plus system, 498; comparison of U.S. and Canadian, 491–92; rationing under Medicare DRG system, 62, 308–11, 568–70

Medical waste laws (in MEZs), 637

Medicare: policy changes needed for, 319–20

Medicare Catastrophic Coverage Act (1988), 456–59, 583–84. *See also* Catastrophic health insurance

Medicare insurance: privatized, 458–59; proposed private market in, 451

Medicare insured groups (MIGs), 597

Medicare Part B, 572–73

Medicare patients: insured expenses of, 454–55; rural, 572

Medicare program: catastrophic illness policy, 582; cost-plus reimbursement methods of, 166–67; determination of procedures under, 27; diagnosis-related groups (DRGs) under, 60–62; effect of payment reduction, 172–73; effect of spending by, 231, 288–90; eligibility for, 430–36; fixed price

project of, 55; information shortage in, 28; long-term funding for, 436–37; projections for future expenses of, 56; proposals to privatize, 416, 421; proposal to opt out of, 440; proposed MIRAs to privatize, 57, 416; rationing of health care under, 568–69; recommendation to restrict or replace, 656; regulation by, 312–15, 630–31; reimbursement system, 191–92, 302, 304–5; repackaging as alternative to, 58–59; representation of minorities in, 429; taxpayer funding for, 428–30; value and benefits of, 423–36; wealth redistribution under, 428–30. *See also* Diagnosis-related groups (DRGs); Medicaid program; Medigap insurance

Medigap insurance, 337, 406–7; limited coverage under, 582; restrictions on payments by, 455–56, 571

Medisave accounts. *See* Medical Savings Accounts (Medisave accounts)

Mental health coverage, 103–5

MIRAs. *See* Medical IRAs (MIRAs)

Montserrat, 598

Mortality rates: comparison of U.S. and developed country infant, 485, 487–89; correlation with hospital charge regulation, 305; infant, 84–86, 543; with infrequent use of surgical procedures, 170–71; in nursing homes, 306. *See also* Low-weight babies

National Center for Policy Analysis (NCPA): MIRA proposal by, 441; report of, 19

National health insurance system, hypothetical: additional taxes to fund, 465–69; arguments to justify, 553–54, 55; bias against rural communities, 571–72; Canadian system for, 253; costs of, 464–65; gains and losses under a, 470–75; government role in, 24; perverse incentives in, 24; preferences for, 547–48; requirements for and consequences of, 463–64

National health insurance systems, existing: administrative costs in, 526–28; benefit to elderly, 528–31;

benefit to organized labor, 544; costs in other countries, 502–5; effect of health care rationing in, 512–14; effect on international competitiveness, 544–46; equality of access, 505–12; minorities in, 532–33; New Zealand's privatization plan for, 608–9; nonprice rationing in, 499–500; popularity of, 548–49; preferred by people in developed countries, 547–48; preventive services in, 524–26; quality of care in, 514–17; reforms for use in United States, 546–47; service to rural residents, 533–44; spending priorities in, 522–24; unnecessary medical care in, 517–21. *See also* Canada; Great Britain; New Zealand

National Health Service (NHS), Great Britain: market-based reform in, 587; reform proposals in, 607–8; support for, 565–67

National Organ Transplant Act (1984), 132–33

Nepal, 598

Netherlands, the, 587

New Zealand: incentives for private insurance, 587–88; inequality in health care in, 507–8; market for private health insurance, 513; nonprice rationing in, 499–500, 503–5; privatization in, 608–9; racial discrimination in, 533

Nonphysician medical personnel: effect of medical licensing laws on, 150–51; licensing and regulation in MEZs, 634; regulation of, 631–32; regulations restricting treatment by, 65–66

Nonprice rationing: in British health insurance system, 559; impact of, 554–55; in national health insurance systems, 499–500, 533

Nonprofit institutions: in health care sector, 12–13, 129–31; role of organized medicine in creation, 137

Norway, 533

Nursing homes: long-term care in, 107–9; in Medical Enterprise Zones, 638; Medicare payments for, 394

Old elderly people: growth in number of, 408; health care use by and costs of, 401; out-of-pocket health care spending by, 407–8

Organization for Economic Cooperation and Development (OECD) countries, 484–85, 488, 504, 531

Organized medicine: activities in nineteenth century of, 139; control of medical education and practice by, 144–49, 155; definition and goals of, 137; influence on medical insurance plans, 159; role in decline of proprietary hospitals, 157–58; role in preventing competing medical insurance plans, 159–61

Outpatient care: state law–mandated benefits for, 333

Outpatient surgery units, or surgi-centers, 130, 192, 211

Package pricing, 28–29, 55–56, 130, 297, 654

Patients: as buyers of health care, 29, 30, 657; contract with doctor, 65; in cost-plus system, 24–25; effect of cost-plus system on, 22, 24; effect of empowering, 654; as informed consumers, 32–35; proposal to empower Medicaid, 60; recommended step to empower, 656; risks under cost-plus system to, 170–71. *See also* Medicaid patients

Pay-as-you-go systems: health insurance as, 182; incentives for employers to adopt, 57; for elderly people, 412; Social Security and Medicare as, 56

Payroll taxes, 56

Peer review organizations (PROs), 318

Pension plans, overfunded, 414

Perverse incentives: conditions for creation of, 60, 65; in cost-plus insurance system, 168–73, 232; proposals to eliminate, 244–51; in U.S. tort system, 64–65

Pharmaceuticals (in MEZs), 639–40

Philippines, the, 590

Physician Payment Review Commission, 574

Physicians; acceptance of medical ethics concept, 120–23; contract with patients, 65; in cost-plus system, 22; dependence on medical societes, 158; discouragement of competition

667

Public choice theory: analysis of unequal spending, 555–56; chances of winning using, 552; to explain national health insurance, 553–55; to explain political phenomena, 551; explanation of capital spending choices, 560–61; prediction of administrative inefficiencies, 562–64

Public policy: health care proposals of, 649–50; recommended reform for employee benefit, 278–81

Pulse Card, 252

Quality of care: in cost-plus system, 24–25; in health care system, 303–5; information about, 34–35; under Medicaid, 59, 67; Medicare control of, 318; in a national health insurance system, 514–17

Reagan administration Medicare reform proposals, 582–83

Regulation: avoidance by employer self-insurance, 197–99, 340–42; for Blue Cross and Blue Shield, 188; cross-subsidies in regulated markets, 172–73, 192; of drug therapy, 131–32; effect on medical insurance plans, 159–60; for hospitals, 630–31; of medical marketplace, 290–98, 312–18; of organ transplants, 131; of physicians' fees, 312–15; of premium prices, 337–38; in proposed Medical Enterprise Zones (MEZs), 636; for rural hospitals, 65–66; state-level, 47

Reimbursement: in cost-plus system, 21, 163–67; in delivery of preventive medical care, 88; by DRGs, 568; to hospitals under Blue Cross, 161, 163; Medicare rules for, 27; for patients in Medical Enterprise Zones, 640

Reimbursement rates: effect of limited Medicare, 568–69; under Medicaid, 166–67, 191–92, 302, 304–5, 574–75, 578; Medicare rural compared to urban, 572

Resource-based relative value scale (RBRVS), 314

Retirement benefits, 403–4. See also Postretirement health care

Risk: accurate pricing of, 219, 221, 226–27; assessment in insurance market, 25; in competitive markets, 163; in conventional insurance

market, 178–90, 232–33; in cost-plus system, 188–90; in early health insurance schemes, 187–88. See also High-risk individuals

Risk pools: covering losses of, 339; exemption of self-insured from taxes on, 198; legislated state-level, 339; under Massachusetts insurance law, 186–87; proposed for uninsurable people, 228; of self-insured employers, 217; to subsidize uninsured, 98

St. Louis Area Business Coalition on Health, 54

Savings. See Medical savings accounts; Medical Savings Accounts (Medisave accounts)

Security Plus, 252

Self-employed people, 247, 264

Self-insurance: as alternative to third-party insurance, 232–33; creating individual accounts for, 44–46; proposal for individual, 44–46; Singapore's individual, 598–605; taxation of individual, 39–41. See also Employer self-insurance; Medical savings accounts; Medisave

Self-interest: differences in market and bureaucratic systems, 37; effect on cost-plus system, 193–97; in health care sector, 13–14, 20–21

Senate Democrats' health care plan, 376–82

Singapore: Medisave accounts in, 248, 598; private system of forced savings, 421–22; privatized health care system of, 31–32, 567, 589; provident funds in, 598–605

Slaughter MIRA proposal, 445–49

Small firms: disadvantages for health insurance in, 268–70; effect of proposed Kennedy plan on, 375; response to tax law by, 277; state laws impacting, 350–53; state-level regulation of insurance for, 350–52; tax subsidies for employees in, 268. See also Self-employed people

Social Security Administration: forecasts of, 56, 387–94, 402–3; proposal to privatize, 421; surpluses of, 405–6, 407

South Korea, 590

Special interest groups, 229; allied
medical practioners as, 329–30; in
Great Britain, 553–67; in ideal health
care system, 30; mandated benefit
laws from, 325; in a national health
insurance system, 24; under
proposed Kennedy plan, 375–76;
specific diseases or disabilities as,
331–33
Subsidies: amounts for health care
expenditures, 412; government-
provided for current medical needs,
57; inequality in employee benefits,
263–64, 268; inequality of health
insurance tax, 41–43, 69; for
postretirement medical needs, 57; as
proposed alternative to mandated
benefits, 325–26; provided by tax
law, 276; recommendation for equal,
279; recommended limits to tax, 280.
See also Cross-subsidies; Tax subsidy
Substance abuse coverage, 103–5
Super IRAs, 421
Surgi-centers. *See* Outpatient surgical
units
Sweden, 587

Tax benefits: under Bush proposed
health care plan, 222; for employer
self-insurance, 247; for self-
employed health insurance, 247
Tax credits: for health insurance
purchase, 650; proposed, 641; for
proposed MIRAs, 441–49
Tax law: controls deductions for
employee benefits, 263–64;
distortion of health insurance
pricing, 270–78; effect on large firms'
premium pricing, 270–75; impact on
employers' health insurance plans,
263; incentives for employee benefits
in, 41–44, 265–67; incentives for
large firm employer, 41–44, 49–51,
275–77; influence on postretirement
medical needs, 278; philosophy
related to employee benefits, 269;
recommended reform for employee
benefit, 278–81
Tax subsidy: for health insurance, 616;
recommendation for universal,
616–17. *See also* Subsidies
Tax system: funding for a national
health insurance plan, 465–69; policy
for nonprofit medical insurers,

159–60; proposal for equity in,
39–41; proposed incentive for
uninsured, 248; proposed incentives
to purchase health insurance, 641;
rate for self-insured or uninsured
people, 69; risk pool taxation under,
198; rules for paying for health care,
650; for Social Security, 390, 392;
treatment of self-employed
insurance, 247, 264. *See also* Income
tax system; Payroll taxes
Third-party payers: consequence of,
77; in controlled cost-plus system,
23; in cost-plus system, 22–23;
dictates of, 653–54; increase in, 231;
as major source of hospital income,
167; under a national health
insurance system, 24; payment for
uncompensated care, 102; payment
reduction by, 172–73; rules imposed
by, 26–27; spending for substance
abuse and mental health, 103–4. *See
also* Bureaucratic organization
Tort liability system: effect on
Medicaid patients, 578–79; impact
on health care costs, 62–65; role of,
619. *See also* Defensive medicine;
Malpractice insurance

Uncompensated care: in Canada, 501;
incidence of and payment for,
101–3; under proposed Kennedy
plan, 375
Underserved population: areas of, 633;
MEPs and MEZs to serve, 612–14,
633–41
Unemployed people, 250
Uninsurable people, 95–99, 228
Uninsured people: access to health
care, 361–62; are not free riders, 69;
under Bush proposed health care
plan, 223–24; in Canada, 500–501;
characteristics of, 357–60, 362;
choices of, 99–101; decision to be,
346, 353; dependents of insured as,
51–52, 278; factors influencing
decisions of, 347–48; health status
of, 228; higher insurance prices for,
362–63; incidence of, 99–100;
number of, 46–47; pool of, 356–57;
proposed tax incentive for, 69, 248;
state laws requiring medical care for,
360–61; tax law contribution to

increase in, 277–78; without
  insurance tax subsidy, 40–41, 616
U.S. Administrators, Inc., 200–201

Veterans Administration hospitals,
  638–39
Voluntary employee beneficiary
  associations (VEBAs), 414

Voucher system: patient choice under
  proposed, 620; proposal for health
  insurance, 618–19

Wages, 39, 49–50, 69, 83, 276
War on Poverty, 425
West Germany, 587
Wisconsin health care plan, 368

Zambia, 598

About the Authors

John C. Goodman is president of the National Center for Policy Analysis. Goodman earned his Ph.D. in economics at Columbia University and has engaged in teaching and research at six colleges and universities, including Columbia University, Stanford University, Dartmouth College, and Southern Methodist University. Goodman has written widely on health care, Social Security, privatization, the welfare state, and other public policy issues. He is the author of six books and numerous scholarly articles. His published works include *National Health Care in Great Britain, The Regulation of Medical Care: Is the Price Too High? The Economics of Public Policy,* and *Social Security in the United Kingdom.* In 1988 Goodman won the prestigious Duncan Black award for the best scholarly article on public choice economics.

Gerald Musgrave is president of Economics America, Inc., in Ann Arbor, Michigan. He has engaged in teaching and research at California State University, Michigan State University, the U.S. Naval Postgraduate School, Stanford University, and the University of Michigan. Musgrave has written widely on health care and other issues. He is the author or coauthor of over 60 publications. He is the chairman of the Health Economics Roundtable of the National Association of Business Economists and is a Fellow of the NABE, the organization's highest honor. He served as a presidential appointee to the National Institutes of Health Recombinant DNA Advisory Committee.

Cato Institute

Founded in 1977, the Cato Institute is a public policy research foundation dedicated to broadening the parameters of policy debate to allow consideration of more options that are consistent with the traditional American principles of limited government, individual liberty, and peace. To that end, the Institute strives to achieve greater involvement of the intelligent, concerned lay public in questions of policy and the proper role of government.

The Institute is named for *Cato's Letters*, libertarian pamphlets that were widely read in the American Colonies in the early 18th century and played a major role in laying the philosophical foundation for the American Revolution.

Despite the achievement of the nation's Founders, today virtually no aspect of life is free from government encroachment. A pervasive intolerance for individual rights is shown by government's arbitrary intrusions into private economic transactions and its disregard for civil liberties.

To counter that trend, the Cato Institute undertakes an extensive publications program that addresses the complete spectrum of policy issues. Books, monographs, and shorter studies are commissioned to examine the federal budget, Social Security, regulation, military spending, international trade, and myriad other issues. Major policy conferences are held throughout the year, from which papers are published thrice yearly in the *Cato Journal*. The Institute also publishes the quarterly magazine *Regulation* and produces a monthly audiotape series, "Perspectives on Policy."

In order to maintain its independence, the Cato Institute accepts no government funding. Contributions are received from foundations, corporations, and individuals, and other revenue is generated from the sale of publications. The Institute is a nonprofit, tax-exempt, educational foundation under Section 501(c)3 of the Internal Revenue Code.

CATO INSTITUTE
1000 Massachusetts Ave., N.W.
Washington, D.C. 20001